Software-Defined Vehicles

From Silicon Architecture to Platform Monetization

Sankalp Agarwal

Apress®

Software-Defined Vehicles: From Silicon Architecture to Platform Monetization

Sankalp Agarwal
Munich, Germany

ISBN-13 (pbk): 979-8-8688-2717-4 ISBN-13 (electronic): 979-8-8688-2718-1
https://doi.org/10.1007/979-8-8688-2718-1

Managing Director, Apress Media LLC: Welmoed Spahr
Acquisitions Editor: Aditee Mirashi
Editorial Assistant: Rachel Zhang

Cover designed by eStudioCalamar

Cover image designed by Magnific

Distributed to the book trade worldwide by Springer Science+Business Media New York, 1 New York Plaza, New York, NY 10004. Phone 1-800-SPRINGER, fax (201) 348-4505, e-mail orders-ny@springer-sbm.com, or visit www.springeronline.com. Apress Media, LLC is a Delaware LLC and the sole member (owner) is Springer Science + Business Media Finance Inc (SSBM Finance Inc). SSBM Finance Inc is a **Delaware** corporation.

For information on translations, please e-mail booktranslations@springernature.com; for reprint, paperback, or audio rights, please e-mail bookpermissions@springernature.com.

Apress titles may be purchased in bulk for academic, corporate, or promotional use. eBook versions and licenses are also available for most titles. For more information, reference our Print and eBook Bulk Sales web page at http://www.apress.com/bulk-sales.

Any source code or other supplementary material referenced by the author in this book is available to readers on GitHub. For more detailed information, please visit https://www.apress.com/gp/services/source-code.

If disposing of this product, please recycle the paper

Dedicated to my late grandmother (Amma) and late grandfather, whose loving memories continue to guide me.

To my parents, distinguished scholars, educators, academic leaders, and authors, whose lifelong commitment to academic excellence remains a lasting source of inspiration.

To my dear wife and beloved daughter, whose love, encouragement, and unwavering support have carried me through this journey.

And to my dear sisters and extended family, with love and gratitude.

Table of Contents

About the Author

Sankalp Agarwal is a Product Marketing and Strategy leader with over a decade of experience across microcontrollers, SoCs, safety-critical software, and automotive system architecture. At Infineon Technologies, he worked on automotive microcontroller and SoC platforms, including Aurix, Traveo T2G, and Auto PSoC, focusing on product definition, technical enablement, and ecosystem development. Earlier, he spent eight years at Arm Holdings as a senior applications engineer, delivering technical training, toolchain integration support, and ecosystem onboarding for partners in automotive, industrial, and IoT markets. His background spans functional safety (ISO 26262), embedded security, RTOS integration, vehicle E/E architectures and in-vehicle compute platforms, zonal architectures, and SDV software stacks. In addition to his technical experience, he brings a strong commercial understanding of market needs, product positioning, and lifecycle planning gained from cross-functional engagements with engineering, sales, and partner networks. He holds an MTech in Embedded Systems from École centrale d'électronique, Paris, and has published research at international conferences.

About the Technical Reviewer

Rafiuddin Syed is a Director of Engineering with 20 years of experience in the embedded systems domain. He works on next-generation software-defined vehicle (SDV) automotive platforms, focusing on system-level architecture and real-time computing systems. His expertise includes operating systems, hypervisors, Linux kernel development, USB architectures, and device driver programming. Over the years, he has worked on complex embedded platforms involving low-level system software and hardware integration. He has also collaborated with major semiconductor companies such as NVIDIA and Intel on advanced platform technologies. He has contributed to open source Linux kernel development and actively participates in technical research, publications, and technical reviews in the systems and embedded computing community.

Acknowledgments

This book reflects a long journey of study, professional development, and engagement with individuals and institutions whose guidance and support have shaped my thinking over many years. I would like to express my sincere gratitude to those who have contributed to that journey.

I am especially grateful to Dr. Anand Lakshmanan from the Centre of Excellence in Advanced Automotive Research (CAAR) at IIT Madras for writing the foreword to this book. His academic leadership, perspective on the evolving automotive landscape, and commitment to strengthening the connection between academia and industry are deeply appreciated.

I would also like to acknowledge those who played an important role in my academic development. From my early years in Pilani, I would like to thank Mr. Solanki for his guidance and encouragement. During my time in Paris, I am grateful to Monsieur Hua and Monsieur Baujault for their support and for helping shape my technical foundation in embedded systems and engineering practice. I also value the broader perspective gained through my training in innovation management at the London School of Economics, which strengthened my understanding of the relationship between technology, strategy, and value creation.

My years in Munich marked an important stage in my professional development. During my time at Arm, I would like to thank Hans for his support, encouragement, and professional guidance. I also acknowledge the valuable experience gained during my time at Infineon Technologies, which contributed significantly to my understanding of automotive semiconductors, embedded computing, and platform technologies.

I am also grateful to colleagues, experts, and professionals across the broader automotive semiconductor, platform, and software ecosystem whose perspectives, feedback, and professional exchanges helped sharpen the ideas presented in this book.

If this work contributes to a clearer understanding of software-defined vehicles and the broader ecosystem surrounding them, it will have served its purpose.

Sankalp Agarwal

Foreword

A few decades ago, the automobile was largely characterized as a mechanically engineered system powered by fossil fuels. By the late twentieth century, the fundamental principles of vehicle dynamics, powertrain engineering, and mechanical design had reached a high degree of maturity. Incremental refinements continued, but a steep change in capability required a technological disruption rather than iterative optimization.

That disruption emerged through electronics. The rapid evolution of electronics—from bulky, valve-based systems to highly miniaturized integrated circuits—reshaped multiple industries, including automotive engineering. Vehicles transitioned from purely mechanical systems to electromechanical systems, with electronic control units (ECUs) progressively embedded to manage discrete functions. Early implementations were largely standalone modules controlling specific subsystems such as infotainment, climate control, and engine management. This marked the inception of software as a functional layer within the vehicle architecture.

Over the past two decades, automotive electronics has expanded both in scale and in functional criticality. What began as feature-specific electronic augmentation has evolved toward deeply integrated digital control. The industry is now undergoing a structural transition from hardware-defined functionality to software-defined capability—culminating in the paradigm of the software-defined vehicle (SDV).

The SDV concept has gained significant momentum, further accelerated by the rise of battery electric vehicles (EVs), whose architectures are inherently more amenable to centralized computing and over-the-air (OTA) software updates. In the SDV model, hardware increasingly serves as a programmable platform, while features, performance characteristics, and user experiences are determined—and continuously enhanced—through software. This transformation positions the vehicle closer to a computing device on wheels, analogous in certain respects to the evolution of the smartphone.

An SDV is not a single technology but a convergence of multiple domains. At its foundation lie high-performance processors, controllers, and semiconductor platforms. Above this hardware layer sits the electrical and electronic (E/E) architecture, which governs how subsystems interconnect and communicate. Robust in-vehicle networking and external connectivity are essential, particularly as vehicles interface with cloud infrastructures for data exchange, remote diagnostics, and OTA updates.

Connectivity, however, introduces expanded threat surfaces. As vehicles evolve from isolated systems to networked nodes within a digital ecosystem, cybersecurity and functional safety assume central importance. Ensuring resilience against cyberattacks while maintaining compliance with safety standards becomes a foundational design requirement rather than an afterthought.

The integration of high-performance computing (HPC) platforms within vehicles further enables advanced artificial intelligence (AI) workloads. AI applications—ranging from perception and driver assistance to predictive maintenance and adaptive user interfaces—can operate both at the edge (within the vehicle) and in the cloud. This necessitates architectural decisions regarding workload partitioning, latency management, data governance, and model lifecycle management. Over time, it is plausible that the SDV will evolve toward an AI-driven vehicle paradigm, where intelligent decision-making becomes intrinsic to the vehicle's operational identity.

Despite the breadth of this transformation, much of the existing literature approaches SDV from narrow disciplinary perspectives—focusing exclusively on E/E architecture, connectivity, advanced driver assistance systems (ADAS), or regulatory frameworks. Comprehensive treatments that integrate silicon architecture, system design, software platforms, cybersecurity, safety, cloud integration, and monetization strategies remain limited.

In this context, the book *Software-Defined Vehicles: From Silicon Architecture to Platform Monetization* by Sankalp Agarwal represents a timely and substantive contribution. The author begins by establishing a clear and rigorous definition of SDV, providing conceptual boundaries that frame the subsequent discussion. This definitional clarity is particularly valuable in a domain where terminology is often inconsistently applied.

The narrative appropriately commences at the hardware layer—examining semiconductor platforms, system-on-chip (SoC) design, and computing architectures—before progressing to software, security, and safety considerations. This bottom-up structuring reflects the technical reality that SDV capabilities are ultimately constrained and enabled by silicon architecture.

The book also addresses the architectural evolution from traditional distributed ECU-based systems to zonal and centralized computing models. Historically, automotive E/E architectures were highly distributed, with individual ECUs operating in relative isolation. While effective for function-specific control, this model exhibits scalability limitations in a software-centric paradigm. Aggregated zonal architectures and centralized compute platforms offer improved scalability, enhanced cybersecurity management, and more efficient feature deployment. The author provides a structured exploration of these architectural trajectories.

Connectivity to the cloud introduces further dimensions. Vehicle-generated data can be transmitted to cloud platforms for analytics, fleet management, AI training, and service optimization. Conversely, actionable insights, software updates, and configuration changes can be deployed back to the vehicle. At the same time, latency-sensitive workloads—particularly those associated with safety-critical systems—must remain at the edge. The trade-off between edge and cloud processing is therefore a strategic architectural decision, and the book contextualizes this balance within the broader SDV ecosystem.

Although SDV adoption remains in a formative phase, with substantial unrealized potential, the author extends the discussion toward platform monetization models and evolving career pathways. By connecting technological evolution with business strategy and workforce implications, the book broadens its relevance beyond pure engineering audiences.

In summary, this work offers an integrated view of the SDV stack—from silicon architecture through software platforms to monetization strategies. It addresses a notable gap in the current body of literature and has the potential to serve both as a professional reference and as a structured academic text for courses dedicated to software-defined vehicles.

Dr. Anand Lakshmanan
CoE in Advanced Automotive Research,
IIT Madras, Chennai

Preface

The automotive industry is undergoing one of the most significant technological transitions in its history. For more than a century, vehicles were defined primarily by mechanical engineering and incremental improvements in electronics. That paradigm is now changing. Vehicles are increasingly evolving into programmable platforms whose capabilities can be continuously enhanced through software, connectivity, and data. This transformation is captured in the concept of the software-defined vehicle (SDV).

Over the past decade, advances in semiconductor technology, high-performance computing, cloud infrastructure, artificial intelligence, and wireless connectivity have accelerated this shift. Modern vehicles increasingly resemble distributed computing systems that interact with cloud platforms, data services, and digital ecosystems far beyond the vehicle itself. The boundaries between automotive engineering, computing systems, and digital platforms are rapidly dissolving.

During my professional journey in the semiconductor and automotive technology ecosystem in Europe, I had the opportunity to work across several layers of this evolving stack. These experiences spanned embedded systems, automotive silicon, system architecture, and connected mobility platforms. Through this work, one observation became increasingly clear. The transition to software-defined vehicles is not merely the introduction of new technologies. It is a system-level transformation that changes how vehicles are designed, developed, validated, deployed, and ultimately monetized.

Yet understanding this transformation is often difficult because knowledge about SDVs is distributed across many disciplines. Semiconductor engineers focus on processor architectures and system-on-chip design. Software engineers concentrate on operating systems (OSs) and middleware. Cloud specialists address large-scale infrastructure and analytics platforms. Automotive engineers must integrate all these technologies while satisfying demanding safety requirements, regulatory frameworks, and real-time constraints.

Each of these perspectives is valid, but none of them alone explains the complete system.

This book was written to address that challenge.

The goal of this work is to present the software-defined vehicle as a layered technological platform that spans semiconductor architectures, vehicle electronics, embedded software, networking, cloud infrastructure, artificial intelligence, cybersecurity, safety engineering, and digital services. Understanding how these layers interact is essential for anyone seeking to understand how modern vehicles are evolving.

At the same time, the emergence of software-defined vehicles is reshaping the economic structure of the automotive industry. Vehicles are no longer static products delivered once at the factory gate. They are becoming continuously evolving platforms whose functionality can expand throughout their lifecycle. Connected services, software features, digital upgrades, and data-driven services are opening new opportunities for innovation and value creation across the mobility ecosystem.

Education is another motivation behind this book.

In discussions with students, researchers, and early-career engineers, it became clear that many people encounter SDV technologies in isolation. Courses may focus on embedded systems, machine learning (ML), cloud computing, or networking, but rarely present these topics as parts of an integrated automotive platform. One objective of this book is therefore to help connect academic knowledge with the realities of modern automotive systems.

For this reason, the material has been structured to support multiple audiences. Engineers and architects working in the automotive industry may find a system-level perspective that connects decisions across hardware, software, and cloud platforms. Product leaders and technology strategists may gain insight into how SDV architectures influence platform strategies and digital services. Students and researchers can use the book as a structured entry point into a rapidly evolving field that sits at the intersection of automotive engineering, computer science, and digital infrastructure.

The transition to software-defined vehicles is still in its early stages. Architectures will continue to evolve, computing capabilities will expand, and new applications will emerge as artificial intelligence, connectivity, and cloud ecosystems mature. The coming decade will likely redefine not only how vehicles are built but also how mobility itself is experienced.

If this book helps readers understand that transformation and equips them to participate in the next generation of vehicle platforms, it will have fulfilled its purpose.

Sankalp Agarwal

CHAPTER 1

Foundations of Software-Defined Vehicles

1.1 Chapter Goals

After this chapter, you will be able to

- Define the concept of a software-defined vehicle (SDV) and contrast it with legacy electrical/electronic (E/E) architectures.
- Understand the #DigitalFirst approach to vehicle design and validation.
- Describe the layered SDV stack—hardware, middleware, applications, cloud—and the role of each layer.
- Identify key industry drivers for SDVs: electrification, connectivity, regulation, and monetization.
- Connect academic and professional programs (e.g., TH Deggendorf—M.Eng. in Automotive Software Engineering (ASE) [1], IIT Madras—Accenture SDV Academy [2], BITS Pilani WILP—M.Tech. in Automotive Engineering [3]) to SDV-related competencies.

Critic's Note Foundations are often treated as "introductory fluff." Resist this temptation. Weak foundations in defining SDVs lead to misaligned architectures and billion-dollar recalls.

S. Agarwal, *Software-Defined Vehicles*, https://doi.org/10.1007/979-8-8688-2718-1_1

1.2 Introduction

The automotive industry is undergoing its most profound transformation since the assembly line. Where vehicles were once defined by their mechanical systems and fixed electronic functions, the software-defined vehicle represents a fundamental inversion: hardware becomes a flexible platform, and software becomes the primary source of features, value, and differentiation. This shift affects not only how vehicles are engineered, but how they are sold, maintained, and improved throughout their operational lifetime.

This chapter establishes the conceptual foundation for understanding software-defined vehicles. We begin by defining what distinguishes an SDV from traditional automotive architectures, examining the key characteristics that enable continuous evolution through software.

The chapter then introduces the layered SDV stack—from silicon and sensors through middleware and applications to cloud services—showing how each layer contributes to the whole.

We also examine the industry drivers accelerating SDV adoption: electrification simplifies powertrains while demanding sophisticated battery management; connectivity enables over-the-air updates and new services; regulations like UNECE (United Nations Economic Commission for Europe) R155/R156 mandate cybersecurity and update management capabilities; and new business models promise recurring revenue beyond the initial vehicle sale. Understanding these foundations is essential before diving into the architectural, silicon, and software details that follow in subsequent chapters.

1.3 Defining the Software-Defined Vehicle

A software-defined vehicle (SDV) is a vehicle in which a significant share of functionality, differentiation, and lifecycle improvement is delivered through software rather than being fixed entirely by hardware at launch. The hardware remains safety-critical, but it is designed as a reusable compute, sensing, and I/O platform so that many functions can be updated, calibrated, or extended after start of production, including through OTA updates where appropriate.

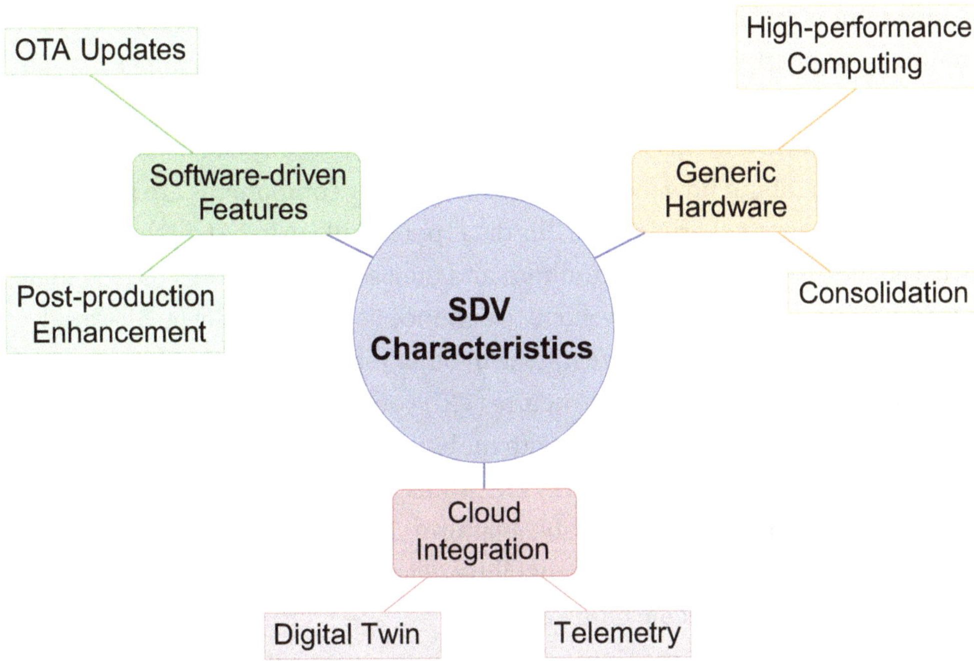

Figure 1-1. *Key characteristics of software-defined vehicles*

1.3.1 Key Characteristics of SDV

Software-driven features and updates: Vehicle functions (from infotainment to safety systems) are primarily implemented in software and can evolve post-production. New features, performance tweaks, and safety improvements can be sent to the car via over-the-air updates, often remotely [4]. For example, an SDV might receive an update that enhances its battery management for better range or adds an advanced driver assistance systems (ADAS) feature, without any mechanical change. This software-centric model allows an SDV to continuously provide new value to users through code changes over its lifespan [5].

Consolidated high-performance compute: Instead of relying on around 100 dedicated ECUs, SDVs consolidate many functions onto a smaller number of domain or zonal controllers, often supported by one or more central vehicle computers. These platforms provide greater compute headroom and can host multiple software functions with appropriate isolation mechanisms such as virtualization. The degree of consolidation varies by OEM, but the overall trend is toward fewer controllers, higher compute density, and a simpler wiring harness [6].

Continuous cloud integration: SDVs are connected vehicles by default—they communicate regularly with cloud servers and services. This enables things like cloud-based *digital twins* of the vehicle, continuous telemetry upload, and data analytics that inform product improvements [4, 5]. In an SDV, there is typically a constant feedback loop: in-field data (about how the vehicle is used or how components are performing) is sent to the cloud; automakers analyze this data (potentially using AI on the digital twin of the car) to detect issues or opportunities; and then software updates (OTA updates) are prepared and sent back to the vehicle to enhance its functionality [4, 5]. Cloud connectivity also allows SDVs to integrate with other digital ecosystems—e.g., vehicle-to-vehicle (V2V) or vehicle-to-infrastructure (V2I) communication for cooperative safety and traffic management or integration with mobile apps and smart home systems [4, 7].

In essence, an SDV treats software as the primary source of innovation and value, with hardware providing a reconfigurable platform. This is a paradigm shift from the legacy approach, where the car's capabilities were mostly fixed at the time of manufacture and tied to specific hardware.

1.4 SDV vs. Legacy Architectures

To appreciate the SDV concept, it is important to contrast it with legacy automotive E/E architectures (the traditional electrical/electronic design of cars).

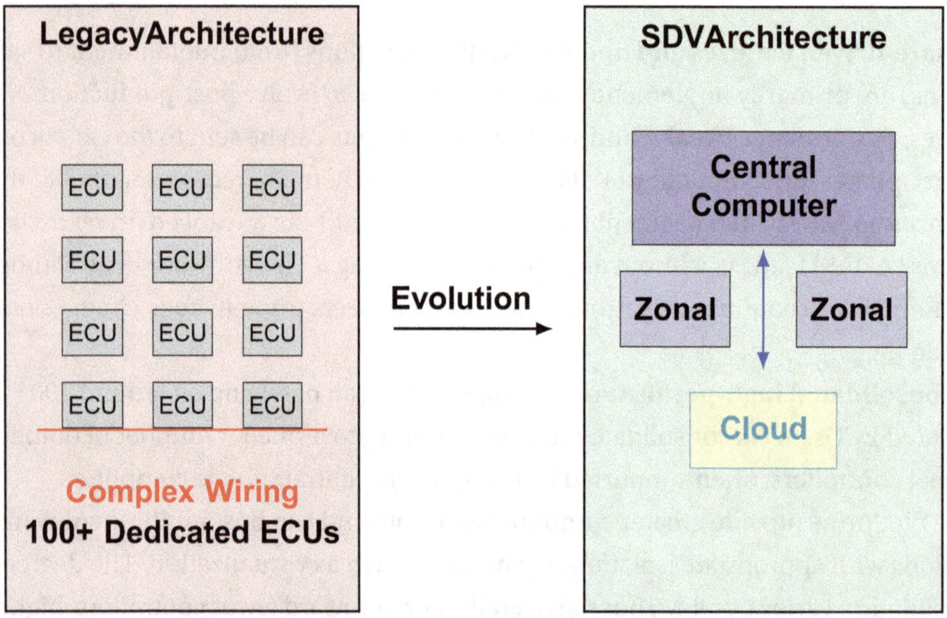

Figure 1-2. *Evolution from legacy to SDV architecture*

1.4.1 Legacy Vehicle Characteristics

Distributed ECU architecture: Legacy vehicles (pre-SDV) typically have a large number of fixed-function ECUs distributed around the car. Each ECU is a small computer dedicated to one feature or subsystem—e.g., an ECU for the engine, one for the transmission, one for power windows, and others for Anti-lock Braking System (ABS) brakes, airbags, steering, etc. High-end cars today might contain *over 100 ECUs*, each with its own software and often supplied by different Tier-1 vendors [6, 8]. These ECUs communicate over buses like Controller Area Network (CAN), Local Interconnect Network (LIN), or FlexRay in a distributed architecture. The result is a complex network of devices, miles of wiring, and significant integration effort to make them all work together [4].

Limited software updates: Software updates in legacy architecture are very limited. Most ECU software is not designed to be updated frequently—updates might only happen at the dealer during a recall or maintenance, if at all. New features generally cannot be added to legacy ECUs after production because of limited memory, strict homologation tied to hardware, and lack of secure update mechanisms. The functionality is essentially frozen at SOP. This static nature is why traditional cars do not improve much over time—a five-year-old car has essentially the same capabilities it had when sold (barring minor dealer-installed updates for bug fixes).

AUTOSAR Classic and static software: Many legacy ECUs run on AUTOSAR (AUTomotive Open System ARchitecture) Classic Platform (CP) (an automotive standard for ECU software) or other real-time operating systems (RTOSs). These systems are often *monolithic*—tightly integrated software with fixed schedules and no room for dynamic changes. Adding new software components or updating them can be extremely costly and risky without extensive retesting, so it's rarely done post-production.

Integration challenges: Because each ECU in a legacy car might come from a different supplier (each with its own development process), the OEM acts as a system integrator bringing together dozens of black boxes. The supply chain is fragmented: one supplier provides the engine control module, another the airbag module, another the infotainment head unit, etc. Integration and testing of the whole vehicle become a huge effort, and introducing changes or updates is difficult—often requiring coordination across multiple suppliers. This fragmentation also leads to inconsistencies and slow progress; it's been noted that legacy OEMs, reliant on suppliers, face structural hurdles in delivering a cohesive, updatable software experience [8, 9].

Hardware-defined limitations: In legacy designs, if a new feature wasn't anticipated when the car was built, it's usually impossible to implement later. For instance, if a car didn't ship with a certain sensor or a capable ECU, you cannot simply add that feature via software—the hardware isn't there for it. In SDVs, by contrast, the hardware (sensors, computing units) is often designed with *headroom* and flexibility, so that new software features can leverage existing generic hardware resources.

1.4.2 SDV Architecture Paradigm

Now, SDV architectures change this paradigm fundamentally:

Centralized or zonal computing: SDVs use a centralized or zonal computing architecture. Rather than dozens of independent ECUs, an SDV might have a handful of powerful computers: e.g., one or two central "vehicle computers" and several *zonal controllers* that gather inputs from sensors/actuators in each zone of the car (front, rear, cabin, etc.) [10, 11].

These controllers run many software tasks in parallel (using multi-core processors, virtualization, etc.), effectively replacing many separate ECUs. This shift greatly reduces the count of physical ECUs. (Some modern electric vehicles (EVs) have reduced the ECU count by over 20–30% via consolidation.) The wiring harness becomes simpler because devices in each area connect to a nearby zonal hub instead of each running a long wire across the car to a dedicated ECU [6, 12].

Centralization does not mean that essential vehicle functions are allowed to depend on an uncontrolled single point of failure. In production SDV architectures, resilience is achieved through safety partitioning, watchdog supervision, safe-state strategies, and, where required, redundant compute, communication, and power paths [10, 11]. Depending on function criticality, the system may either fail safe or continue operating in a limited degraded mode until the vehicle can be brought to a safe condition [12].

In practice, redundancy is applied selectively rather than uniformly across the vehicle. Safety-critical functions such as braking, steering, and power management may use independent monitoring paths, fallback controllers, duplicated communication channels, or power-domain separation. Centralized compute should therefore be understood as architectural consolidation with managed resilience, not as a monolithic replacement of all safety paths [10–12].

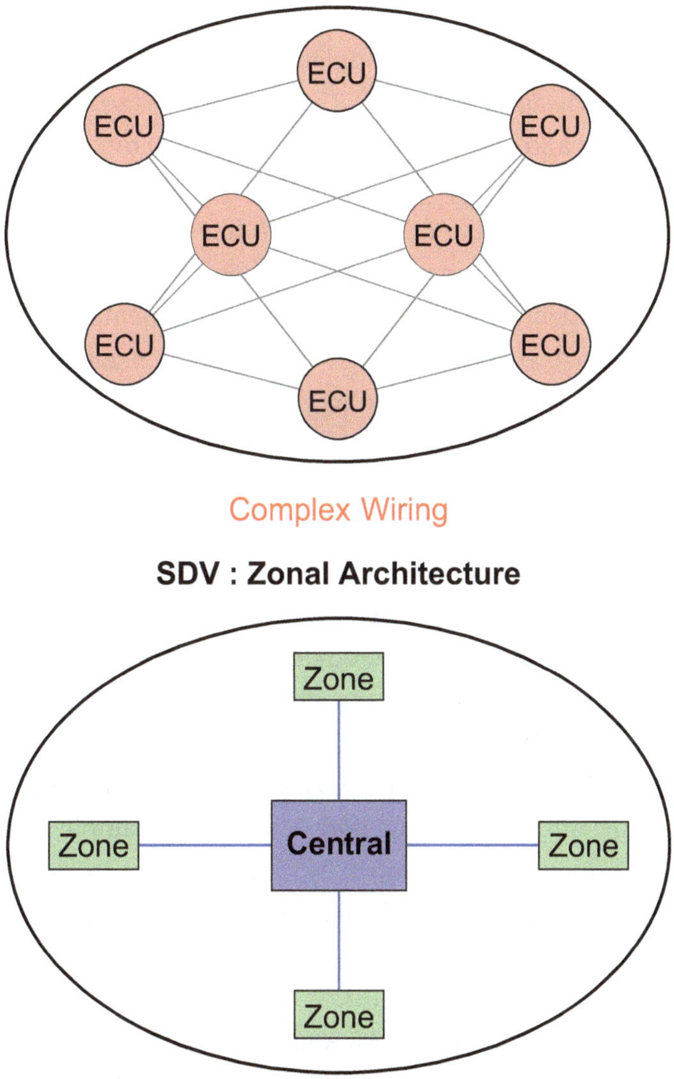

Figure 1-3. *Comparison of legacy distributed ECU architecture vs. SDV zonal architecture*

This simplifies the wiring harness—a major source of mass and integration effort. In traditional designs, harnesses can weigh approximately 50–60 kg and extend several kilometers. Zonal architectures shorten runs to local hubs and reduce cross-car wiring, which cuts weight, cost, and failure points without relying on OEM-specific claims.

Legacy vehicles contain a sprawling wiring harness (illustrated in red) connecting dozens of ECUs—often more than 100 modules with dedicated wires—leading to heavy, complex, and inflexible designs [6, 10]. SDVs streamline this by using a few high-performance computers and networked zones, dramatically reducing wiring.

Reduced bill of materials: With fewer ECUs, the bill of materials (BOM) and parts complexity go down. There are fewer electronic modules to source and assemble. This not only saves cost but can also improve reliability (fewer connectors and points of failure) and makes manufacturing easier (wiring harness assembly is one of the few processes still often done by hand because of its complexity in legacy designs [11]).

However, *each* of the remaining controllers in an SDV tends to be much more powerful (and expensive) than a single legacy ECU. They often use high-end automotive system-on-chips (SoCs) fabricated at advanced semiconductor nodes (7 nm, 16 nm, etc.) to pack enough compute power [10]. This introduces a dependency on high-performance silicon availability and the need for the OEM to invest in software competence to fully utilize these chips. In other words, the vehicle becomes more like a high-end computer on wheels, and the automaker needs to manage software versions, chip shortages, and cybersecurity patches much like a tech company would.

Dynamic software platform: SDVs run a modern software stack that can be updated OTA. Instead of static, fixed-function code, SDV software is often designed as a set of microservices or applications running on middleware. For example, an SDV might have containerized services for navigation, voice assistant, adaptive cruise control, battery management, etc., all managed by a sophisticated operating system (OS)/hypervisor. This allows new software components to be deployed or existing ones to be upgraded with much less effort than in legacy systems.

We see automakers adopting AUTOSAR Adaptive (the newer adaptive platform supporting C++ and POSIX operating systems like Linux/QNX) for their high-performance controllers, precisely to enable more flexible and modular software that can be updated over time [4, 12]. Legacy AUTOSAR Classic remains for time-critical tiny microcontrollers, but the trend is toward more adaptive, update-friendly environments for most of the car's functionality.

Improved integration and cross-domain functions: By consolidating computing, SDVs can break down the silos of legacy ECUs. In a traditional car, each ECU might operate fairly independently, and coordinating a feature that spans multiple ECUs (say a safety feature that involves powertrain + braking + sensor data) is complicated. In an SDV, having a central computing platform means different functions can share data more readily and be orchestrated by central logic. This is essential for advanced features like autonomous driving, which require fusing inputs from many sensors and controlling multiple actuators together. Indeed, industry analysis notes that the move to domain/zonal architectures is necessary to handle the complexity of features like ADAS and autonomy that legacy distributed setups struggle with [9, 10].

In summary, legacy architecture means many little computers with fixed functions and wires everywhere, whereas SDV architecture means fewer big computers with lots of software and continuous connectivity. The SDV is often described as a "computer on wheels" or "smartphone on wheels," emphasizing that most innovations will come from software updates and data, not from new mechanical components [4, 13].

Business Note It's worth noting the business implications of this shift. Legacy OEMs managing approximately 100 ECUs per vehicle deal with highly fragmented supply chains and integration overhead. The SDV approach of consolidating into zonal controllers reduces the number of components, wiring, and suppliers, which can lower manufacturing costs and vehicle weight [6, 10]. However, it also means carmakers must take on greater responsibility for software development and rely on a few critical semiconductor providers for advanced chips. The competency focus shifts from managing suppliers to building software platforms. Companies that successfully make this transition can unlock faster development cycles and potentially avoid issues (like complex recalls) by updating software quickly. Those that fail to adapt might face software bottlenecks and even larger recalls—e.g., if a core software platform has a flaw, it could affect many vehicles. This is why getting the foundation definition of an SDV right is critical—it drives both the technical architecture and the business model.

1.5 The #DigitalFirst Approach

Transitioning to software-defined vehicles requires not just new hardware and software, but a new development philosophy. This is where the "#DigitalFirst" approach comes in. *Digital-first* means that software and virtual testing take precedence early in the vehicle development process, rather than the traditional hardware-centric approach. In essence, it advocates that we design, prototype, and validate in the digital realm (in simulations, models, virtual ECUs) before physical prototypes are built.

1.5.1 Principles of Digital-First Development

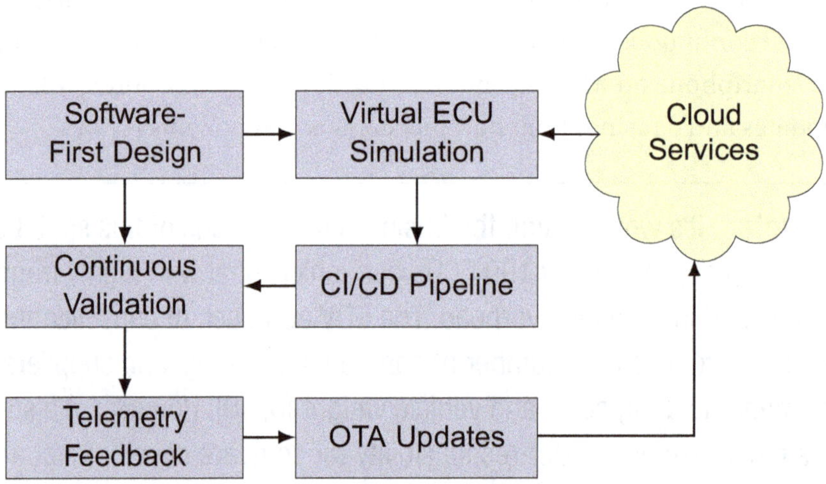

Figure 1-4. *Digital-first development cycle for SDVs*

Software-first design: In a digital-first methodology, you start by designing the vehicle's features and behavior in software *before* finalizing the hardware. Instead of hardware dictating what software can do (the old way), engineers define what the software needs to achieve and then ensure the hardware platform will support it [9, 12]. This flips the mindset to "What hardware does our software require?" rather than "Here's hardware; what can we run on it?"

For example, if you plan a sophisticated driver assistance algorithm, you would simulate it, determine computing requirements, and choose a processor that can run it, rather than being stuck with an underpowered ECU that was selected too early. This principle also involves treating the software architecture (the network of services and communications in the car) as a first-class design artifact, on par with the mechanical chassis design.

Virtual ECUs and simulation: A cornerstone of digital-first is using *virtual ECUs* (vECUs)—essentially software-emulated versions of the car's electronic control units—to integrate and test software long before any actual hardware is available [9, 14].

Engineers can take the code that would run on a physical ECU and run it on a PC or cloud-based simulator that mimics the ECU's behavior. This is often done using virtualization tools or simulation environments that replicate the microcontroller instruction set and peripherals. By doing so, you can perform integration testing of the automotive software in a complete vehicle simulation (including virtual sensors, actuators, etc.) months or even years before the real car electronics are ready[9, 14].

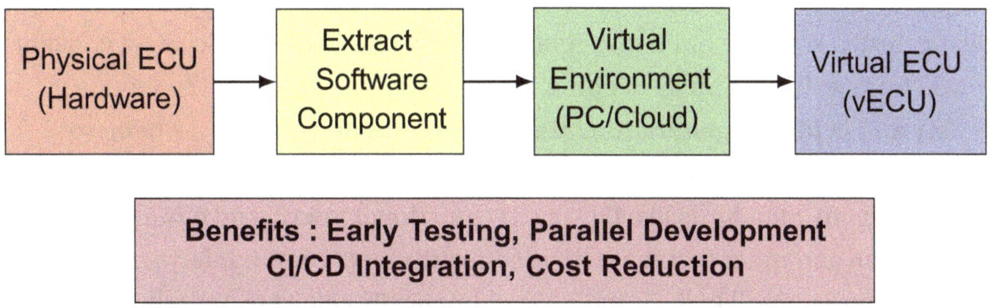

Figure 1-5. *Migration path from physical ECU to virtual ECU*

For instance, instead of waiting for an actual prototype of the braking ECU to test your new ABS algorithm, you run that algorithm on a virtual model of the ECU and see how it interacts with a physics simulation of the car braking. This front-loads the validation effort—problems in software can be found and fixed early, rather than discovered late on physical prototypes [14]. It also allows development of software and hardware in parallel; since automotive hardware lead times are long, vECUs ensure software teams aren't idle waiting for chips—they can keep building and testing against the virtual model [14].

Continuous integration and continuous deployment (CI/CD): The digital-first approach brings modern software development best practices into the automotive realm. This means establishing *continuous integration/continuous deployment* (CI/CD) pipelines for automotive software—where code changes are regularly built, tested (in simulation or on Hardware-in-the-Loop (HIL) rigs), and integrated, rather than big infrequent drops. Every time a developer updates a piece of code (say for the adaptive cruise control), an automated pipeline might build the new software, run a battery of regression tests (including simulation scenarios), and report if anything broke.

Ultimately, this can extend to continuous deployment of updates to test fleets or even customer vehicles over-the-air, once proper validation is done. Embracing CI/CD is crucial for SDVs because software updates are much more frequent (frequent OTA updates). This necessitates a development culture where integrating changes and testing is a nonstop process, with a high degree of automation to ensure safety and reliability each time [15, 16].

Along with CI/CD, practices like *continuous validation* come into play, meaning you don't wait until a vehicle is almost finished to do big validation campaigns—you validate continuously as features are developed. Techniques like impact analysis (to smartly retest only affected components) help manage the enormous testing burden that continuous updates imply [14, 17]. The end goal is that at any given time, you have a working, tested software build that could be safely released to vehicles—a concept borrowed from web and app development but now applied to cars.

Safety and evidence generation: Automotive is a safety-critical domain, so digital-first also means building processes to generate safety evidence in tandem with development. Standards like ISO 26262 (functional safety) and others require documentation and proof that the vehicle software meets certain safety goals. A digital-first approach will include tools to automatically collect test results, coverage metrics, formal verification results, etc., as part of the CI pipeline, so that when a new software release is being readied, engineers can quickly assemble the *safety case* for it—demonstrating that it's as safe as the previous version, that all requirements are traced and tested, and so on [14, 17]. In a way, the development pipeline also becomes a compliance pipeline.

Closed-loop feedback via telemetry: Unlike in the old model where after a car was sold, engineering had little data until a failure was reported or a car came in for service, SDVs enable a continuous feedback loop. Vehicles can stream telemetry data (with appropriate privacy safeguards) about how systems are performing, how drivers are using features, and any error codes or anomalies encountered. This data can feed into a *digital twin* of the vehicle—a virtual representation living in the cloud that mirrors the state of the real car [5].

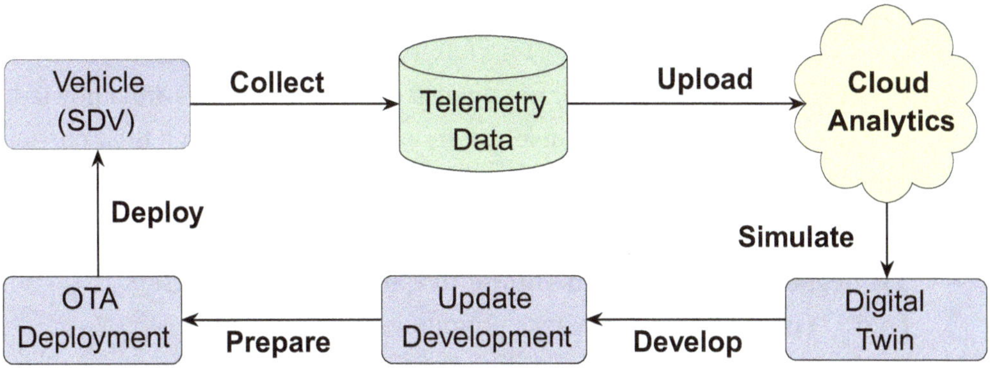

Figure 1-6. *Continuous improvement loop via OTA updates and cloud analytics*

Engineers use digital twins to reproduce issues (e.g., if a car in the field had a sensor glitch under certain conditions, the digital twin can simulate that scenario with a new software fix to see if it resolves it). The feedback loop is in-field data ➤ analysis ➤ update development ➤ OTA update back to vehicles [5].

This is essentially applying agile improvement cycles *after* the car is on the road. For example, a manufacturer might notice from telemetry that a particular driver assist feature is not being used by many customers; this might prompt them to redesign the feature or improve its user interface in the next software update. Or if data shows an ADAS camera occasionally misidentifies an object in a specific lighting condition, engineers can retrain the detection algorithm and deploy an update to fix it. This continuous improvement would be impossible without a digital-first, connected strategy.

Critic's Note Digital-first is no longer a buzzword; it is a competitive filter. OEMs that cling to hardware-first, multiyear waterfall cycles and treat software as a late integration activity will not be able to support frequent, safe OTA changes. EV-first players already operate with software release cadences measured in weeks or months. Traditional OEMs do not need to copy consumer app practices, but they do need CI/CD, virtual integration, and safety-aware automation just to remain viable. Without that, every software change becomes a mini-program, and the SDV promise collapses under its own process weight.

1.5.2 Curriculum Tie-In

The shift to SDVs and digital-first development also impacts what skills and knowledge are needed from engineers. Academic institutions are beginning to align their curricula to produce graduates ready for this new automotive paradigm. Let's see how some specific programs map to SDV competencies:

TH Deggendorf—M.Eng. in Automotive Software Engineering (ASE) [1]: This German master's program explicitly covers modern automotive software architectures, embedded systems, and even cloud computing aspects. Students learn about both low-level embedded programming and higher-level software engineering, which is a natural fit for SDVs. Key topics include AUTOSAR Adaptive, real-time systems, vehicle networking (CAN, Ethernet), and even some Internet of Things (IoT)/cloud integration. By covering embedded-to-cloud knowledge, the program ensures that graduates can develop on-vehicle software and also understand back-end services—exactly the combination needed for features like OTA update systems or connected vehicle services. In an SDV, the car is not an isolated unit; it continuously interacts with cloud services. A curriculum that spans embedded systems and cloud computing (as TH Deggendorf's ASE does) produces engineers who can build end-to-end solutions for SDVs (e.g., a student project might involve creating a vehicle software component and a cloud application that communicates with it).

IIT Madras—Accenture SDV Skilling Programs [2]: The IIT Madras Centre of Excellence in Advanced Automotive Research (CAAR) and Accenture jointly offer SDV skilling for OEMs and global capability centers, blending embedded, cloud, cybersecurity, functional safety, and DevOps for OTA. This is representative of the industry-aligned, hands-on programs now emerging to close SDV skills gaps. Consider also vendor-neutral offerings (e.g., NXP's SDV Academy, UL's SDV training) that span standards (AUTOSAR, SOAFEE, COVESA/Eclipse SDV) and toolchains. Overall, these curricula indicate academia's recognition that future automotive engineers need software, systems, and IT skills in addition to classical mechanical/electrical know-how. Courses on automotive networking, cybersecurity, functional safety, DevOps, and cloud back-ends are increasingly part of the mix—reflecting the industry's needs for SDV development and maintenance.

BITS Pilani WILP—M.Tech. in Automotive Engineering [3]: Designed for working professionals, this program emphasizes system-level automotive engineering, blending fundamentals of vehicle dynamics, electronics, and software. Such a holistic systems perspective is ideal for SDV development, where one needs to understand how software, electronics, and mechanical systems integrate. The curriculum's focus on automotive systems design, control systems, and integration testing directly supports SDV concepts like integrating virtual ECUs into a full vehicle model. BITS Pilani's approach of mixing theory with industry projects means graduates are prepared to handle SDV integration challenges—e.g., they learn how an electric powertrain, an autonomous driving algorithm, and a networking stack all come together in a vehicle. This system-level thinking is crucial for orchestrating the complex software of SDVs.

1.6 SDV Layered Stack

One useful mental model for understanding an SDV is as a layered stack of technologies, very much like a computer system. We can broadly think of four layers in the SDV stack, each building on the one below it.

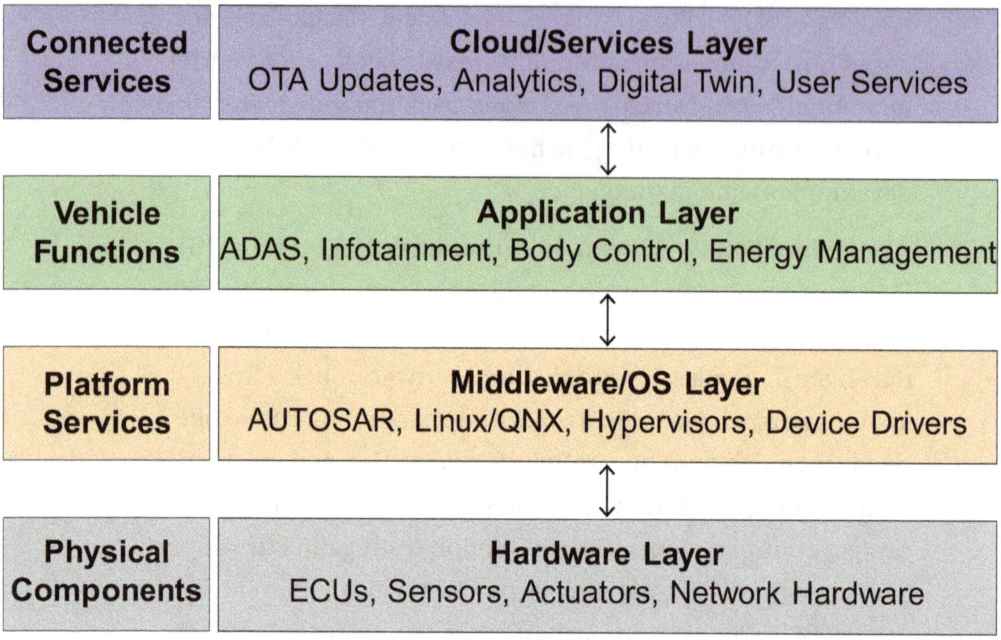

Figure 1-7. *The Four-layer SDV stack architecture*

1.6.1 Layer 1: Hardware

This bottom layer includes all the physical components—the vehicle's electronic hardware and electromechanical parts that interface with software. Key elements are the silicon chips (microcontrollers, microprocessors, system-on-chips) that run the software, as well as sensors and actuators. For example, the hardware layer has the various ECUs or domain controllers (with their Central Processing Units (CPUs), memory, etc.), the sensor suite (cameras, radars, Light Detection and Ranging (LiDARs), ultrasonic sensors, Global Positioning System (GPS), inertial sensors), and output devices/actuators (motors, brakes, steering actuators, displays). It also includes the networking hardware (buses like CAN and LIN and especially Ethernet Physical Layer (PHY) chips, network switches, and wireless modems for connectivity). Essentially, this is the "body" of the SDV—all the devices that the software will control or read from.

A trend in the SDV hardware layer is the use of high-performance, often centralized computing units. Recent central compute examples include NVIDIA DRIVE Orin/Thor [18], Qualcomm Snapdragon Ride Flex for High-Performance Computing (HPC) [19], and Renesas R-Car S4 [20]—all targeting centralized/zonal E/E designs. Another aspect is the inclusion of connectivity hardware by default—e.g., 4G/5G telematics control units and V2X radio modules—making sure the car can communicate externally (a prerequisite for OTA updates and connected services).

In short, the hardware layer provides a flexible, powerful platform ("vehicle computer") and a suite of sensors/actuators, on top of which the rest of the stack operates.

1.6.2 Layer 2: Middleware/Operating System

Above the raw hardware, an SDV relies on a software platform that manages hardware resources, provides common services, and enables the higher-level applications to run. This includes operating systems (OSs) and middleware frameworks. In SDVs, you might have a mix of OSs: an AUTOSAR Classic OS or a real-time OS for time-critical microcontroller tasks and a more powerful OS (like a specialized Linux/QNX or AUTOSAR Adaptive) for application processors [4]. The middleware encompasses things like device drivers, communication stacks, and basic services that all applications use. For instance, a middleware might provide a *publish/subscribe bus* for different software components to exchange messages (some SDV platforms use Data Distribution Service (DDS) or a similar middleware for inter-module communication).

This layer also can include hypervisors or container runtimes. Hypervisors (e.g., QNX Hypervisor for Safety) allow multiple OS instances to run on one SoC with isolation; QNX OS and Hypervisor for Safety [21, 22] are assessed for ISO 26262 ASIL D (Automotive Safety Integrity Level D) and IEC 61508 SIL 3 (Safety Integrity Level 3), which is relevant when consolidating mixed-criticality workloads on central controllers. Container runtimes (like Docker or custom lightweight alternatives in automotive) allow packaging applications in containers for easier deployment and update.

Essentially, the middleware/OS layer is the "software platform" of the vehicle—analogous to an operating system on a computer or phone that provides a standardized environment. A concrete example: Many SDVs will have an ADAS middleware that handles sensor input management, time synchronization between sensors, safety monitoring, etc., so that application developers can just use those services instead of writing low-level code. Similarly, this layer handles the complexities of OTA update application—ensuring that new software can be downloaded and installed safely (often an A/B partition update system to allow rollback if something fails).

Standards and technologies often seen here include ROS 2 (Robot Operating System 2) for prototyping; Adaptive AUTOSAR for POSIX systems; Classic AUTOSAR for microcontrollers; various RTOSs (real-time operating systems) like FreeRTOS, QNX, or VxWorks; and AUTOSAR ara::com or SOME/IP (Scalable service-Oriented MiddlewarE over IP) for communication. The goal of this layer is to decouple the hardware from the applications—providing hardware abstraction (so apps don't care what exact sensor or chip is used) and common services like network communication, file systems, graphics, etc. Importantly, a well-designed middleware can allow software reuse across different car models and even different OEMs (if standardized), accelerating development [4].

1.6.3 Layer 3: Applications

This is the layer of vehicle functions and features—essentially the software applications that implement the end user functionality. In an SDV, applications can be numerous and are often modular. They include traditional automotive functions (implemented in software) such as

1. ADAS algorithms (e.g., lane keeping, adaptive cruise control, automatic emergency braking)
2. Infotainment apps (navigation, media streaming, voice assistant)
3. Body control functions (door lock control, lighting, climate control logic)
4. Powertrain control (especially in EVs, software managing battery and motor for efficiency)
5. Energy management (smart charging software, range predictions)
6. Many new possibilities like personalization settings, digital assistants, etc.

What distinguishes SDV applications is that they might be updatable and possibly even addable after production. For example, an automaker might offer a "feature store" where a user can download a new application that adds, say, a teen driver monitoring mode or a new sound theme for the electric motor. The application layer can also include things like machine learning models that run in the car (e.g., a computer vision model for pedestrian detection is essentially part of the ADAS application layer).

These applications rely on the middleware/OS beneath to get sensor data and to issue commands to actuators. They can be written by the OEM's internal software teams, by suppliers, or even by third parties if the platform is open enough. A critical point is that in SDVs, many applications can run concurrently and share the hardware. The design of this layer often uses a *service-oriented architecture (SOA)*—instead of monolithic code, you have services (applications) that could be independently developed and updated[4, 12].

For instance, the "parking assist" service could be one container and the "blind spot detection" another, each updatable on its own schedule. Some OEMs are moving toward publishing Application Programming Interfaces (APIs) for vehicle data so that external developers can create apps—analogous to smartphone app ecosystems. While not widespread yet, this is a logical extension of the SDV concept (treating the car as a platform).

1.6.4 Layer 4: Cloud/Services

At the top, we consider the external systems that interact with the vehicle—essentially the cloud services and back-end infrastructure that complement the in-vehicle software. This layer includes

1. OTA update servers that manage software update campaigns, distribute patches, and ensure security and regulatory compliance of updates [23]

2. Data analytics platforms that aggregate data from many vehicles to find insights (e.g., identifying a pattern of battery overheating in hot climates)

3. Digital twin simulations running in the cloud to test new software against real-world data

4. User-facing services like mobile apps to control the car or integration with voice assistants (Alexa and others)

5. Subscription platforms where users can purchase upgrades/ features on demand

For example, an OEM might have a cloud-based user account system that knows which features a user has subscribed to—when the user buys a "heated seats" subscription, the cloud sends a command to the car to enable that feature in the software [4]. Other cloud services include navigation and live traffic services, vehicle-to-infrastructure communication systems (sometimes infrastructure info is relayed via cloud), and fleet management platforms (important for robo-taxi or fleet scenarios, where a central system dispatches vehicles or manages software rollout across thousands of cars).

Essentially, the cloud layer turns the vehicle from a standalone product into part of an ecosystem. Many OEMs are investing in building their own cloud platforms (e.g., Volkswagen's "Automotive Cloud" or GM's OnStar/Ultifi platform) to have control over data and create new revenue streams.

One big aspect here is data. Data volumes vary widely: development/validation fleets can log 10–30+ TB per vehicle per day [24] when recording raw sensor streams, whereas production vehicles typically transmit selective [25, 26], rules-based telemetry to limit cost and protect privacy (e.g., using intelligent collection with AWS IoT FleetWise). Cloud analytics might enable predictive maintenance (e.g., analyzing vibration data from motors to predict bearing wear and alert the driver or schedule service proactively). They also enable AI training: data from the fleet can be used to train better machine learning models, which are then deployed back to the cars in a continual improvement loop.

Finally, the cloud is integral to vehicle personalization: a user's profile (seat settings, favorite music, etc.) might be saved in the cloud so that it can follow the user from one car to another or be restored after a software update.

1.6.5 Stack Integration

These four layers—hardware, middleware/OS, applications, and cloud services—together form the complete SDV stack [4, 9]. Each layer is critical and interfaces with the adjacent layers via well-defined APIs or protocols (e.g., apps talk to middleware via API calls, the car talks to the cloud via web APIs or Message Queuing Telemetry Transport (MQTT), etc.).

An advantage of conceptualizing this layered stack is that it helps teams specialize (you might have a team focusing on middleware, another on developing new applications, another on cloud analytics) and it underscores the importance of standard interfaces. Standardization (like AUTOSAR or vehicle API standards) at the interfaces can allow different parties (suppliers or partners) to work on different layers. It can also future-proof parts of the design—e.g., if the hardware changes (say a new chip vendor is used), in theory the middleware abstracts it so applications don't all have to be rewritten. Or if a new service is added in the cloud, as long as it communicates through the standard data pipeline, the car can make use of it without needing a redesign.

Understanding this stack is essential for SDV architects: It helps to pinpoint where a certain functionality should reside. For instance, should a particular piece of data processing be done on-vehicle (application layer) or in the cloud? If connectivity is fast and the data are not safety-critical, maybe the cloud is fine (like heavy AI training). But for real-time control, it must be in the vehicle. These decisions define the software-defined vehicle's partitioning of intelligence between car and cloud.

1.7 Industry Drivers

Several key industry forces are driving the adoption of software-defined vehicles. They come from both technological advancements and business motivations.

1.7.1 Electrification

The rise of electric vehicles (EVs) is a major enabler and driver for SDVs. EVs, by their nature, have simpler mechanical architectures than combustion engine cars—there's no complex transmission

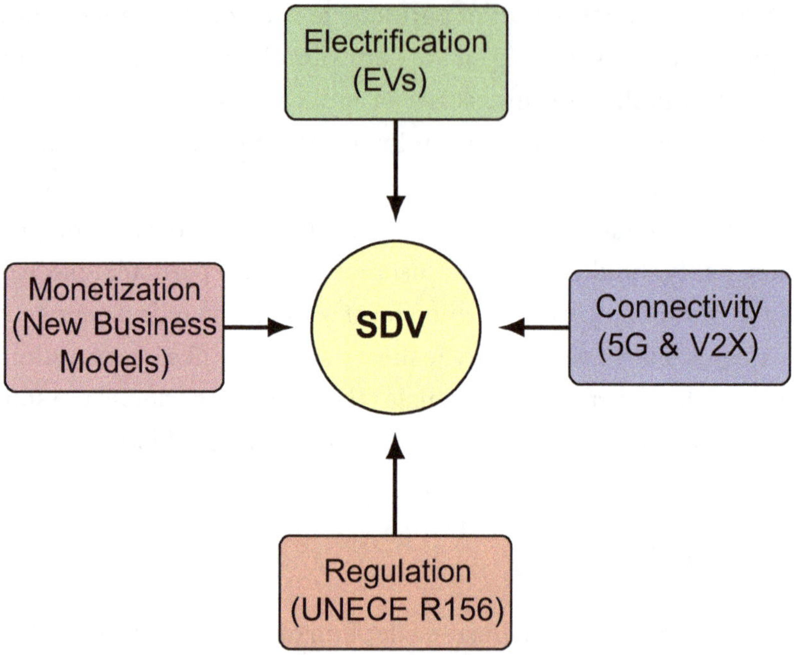

Figure 1-8. *Four key industry drivers accelerating SDV adoption*

or multi-thousand-part engine to dominate the engineering. This means a greater portion of an EV's value is in its software and electronics (battery management systems (BMSs), motor control algorithms, range optimization, etc.). New EV-focused OEMs (like Tesla, Rivian, NIO, etc.) had the opportunity to build their vehicle architectures almost from scratch in a very software-centric way. In many cases, they adopted centralized computing and strong connectivity from the get-go. This has set a precedent that modern vehicles, especially EVs, are high-tech gadgets on wheels.

From an engineering perspective, EVs accelerate SDV adoption because the electrical architecture is more straightforward (fewer legacy ECUs for engine and gearbox), leaving room to implement fresh zonal architectures and to allocate more computing power to user-facing features. Additionally, EV customers often expect technology-rich experiences (as many EV buyers are early adopters), further pushing OEMs toward SDV features. As IBM notes, SDVs complement EVs since both emphasize efficiency, connectivity, and reduced environmental impact—e.g., software can optimize efficiency and coordinate charging to reduce strain on the grid [4].

Another angle: Regulatory pressure for low-emission vehicles means automakers must invest in EVs, and to differentiate their EV models (since many electric powertrains offer similar performance), manufacturers compete on software features and driving experience. This naturally leads to SDV concepts (like unique software driving modes, advanced infotainment in EVs, etc.).

1.7.2 Connectivity (5G and V2X)

High-reliability cellular links underpin OTA updates and data services. In the United States, the Federal Communications Commission (FCC) finalized rules in November 2024 transitioning the 5.9 GHz Intelligent Transportation Systems (ITS) band to Cellular Vehicle-to-Everything (C-V2X) and codifying technical parameters. In Europe, industry roadmaps expect New Radio V2X (NR-V2X) (sidelink) mass deployment around 2026–2029, complementing network-based services. Together these steps normalize an always-connected car that can receive updates, share safety messages, and integrate with cloud services [7, 27–30].

Continuous connectivity enables cloud services and data-driven features in SDVs. Modern vehicles communicate with cloud platforms in real time, unlocking live navigation, remote diagnostics, V2X safety alerts, and over-the-air updates that deliver new capabilities [4, 7,]. This always-on data connection transforms the car ownership experience from a one-time product to an ongoing service.

1.7.3 Regulation

The United Nations Economic Commission for Europe (UNECE) regulations UN R156 (Software Updates/Software Update Management System (SUMS)) and UN R155 (Cybersecurity/Cybersecurity Management System (CSMS)) [31] apply to new vehicle types from July 2022 and became mandatory for all new vehicles produced from July 2024 in contracting markets (e.g., the EU (European Union), Japan, Korea). These rules require demonstrable update processes, version traceability, and cybersecurity management across the lifecycle—making robust OTA pipelines and secure boot nonoptional.

In the EU, the Data Act becomes applicable on September 12, 2025 [32, 33], with product design obligations for connected products (including vehicles) kicking in from September 12, 2026, shaping how in-vehicle data is accessed and shared. Standards such as ISO/SAE 21434 (cybersecurity) and ISO 21448 (Safety of the Intended Functionality (SOTIF)) complement functional safety ISO 26262 to provide a safety and security basis for continuous software change.

1.7.4 Monetization and New Business Models

One of the strongest business drivers for SDVs is the prospect of new revenue streams beyond the initial sale of the car. Historically, an automaker sold a car once, and that was largely the end of revenue except parts and service. SDVs open the door to the "software monetization" model. This includes *features on demand*—selling optional features that can be activated via software update.

For example, BMW ended its heated seats subscription in 2023 after customer backlash [34, 35]—illustrating that monetization models continue to evolve (see Chapter 10 for comprehensive coverage). Another model is *tiered performance*—some EVs can be sold with a certain range or horsepower, and the user can pay later to unlock more (since it's just software limits being lifted).

Beyond features, *usage-based services* like usage-based insurance are enabled by SDVs. If the vehicle's software can report data on how and how much it's driven (telematics), insurance companies can charge premiums based on actual usage or driving behavior (already happening via third-party dongles; integrating it into the car software is the next step). Automakers themselves might want a slice of this by partnering with insurers or offering their own insurance products leveraging vehicle data.

Data services form another pillar: Anonymized data from vehicles can be extremely valuable—for urban planners (traffic patterns), for map providers (road condition updates), for advertisers (understanding mobility patterns), etc. Some companies are looking at selling aggregated sensor data from cars to weather agencies (for hyper-local weather info from windshield wipers, ABS activity for road ice detection, etc.). SDVs are a prerequisite to these models because only with a connected, software-centric car can you flexibly gather data or change what the product offers after sale.

According to industry projections, digital and software-enabled services could grow to account for half of automotive industry revenue by 2035 (up from approximately 15% today) [4]. This dramatic potential is pushing automakers to invest in SDV capabilities now. The notion of the vehicle as a platform also means others can build on it—e.g., an "app store" for cars could allow third-party developers to sell apps/features to owners, with the OEM taking a cut (similar to smartphone app stores). Though in early stages, companies like Tesla have an "entertainment" platform, and others are eyeing in-car gaming or productivity apps for when autonomous driving frees up driver time. All these monetization ideas require the vehicle to be software-configurable and updateable—hence directly driving the SDV transformation. It's a chance for automakers to have recurring revenue (subscriptions, upgrades) and stronger customer engagement (if a customer regularly interacts with the brand for software updates or new services, that's better loyalty than just selling a car every five to seven years).

While SDV capabilities enable new business models, not every technically feasible monetization scheme is commercially or regulatorily viable. Customers react strongly to perceived double-charging for hardware they already own, regulators are scrutinizing data usage and tying core safety features to subscriptions, and right-to-repair debates influence how much capability can be locked behind software. Product managers must therefore balance technical feasibility, willingness to pay, long-term brand trust, and legal constraints. A mature SDV strategy optimizes lifetime relationship value, not just short-term feature-unlock revenue.

1.7.5 Customer Experience and Expectations

Lastly, an overarching driver is customer experience (CX) and expectations. Consumers are increasingly tech-savvy and expect their car's software to be as seamless as their smartphone's. If their phone can get monthly updates improving battery life or adding a new emoji, they start to expect their EV to get updates improving range or adding a new driving sound. Automakers that deliver delightful digital experiences—such as a car that personalizes itself to each driver or adds fun features (like Tesla's "caraoke" or light shows via updates)—can stand out and build brand loyalty.

On the flip side, a failure in software (bugs, poor user experience (UX)) can quickly sour customers and even lead to recalls that are incredibly costly. A famous example: An automaker had to recall vehicles due to software glitches in their infotainment or ADAS; with a solid SDV approach, that could have been an OTA fix with far less expense and hassle. Thus, the push for SDVs is as much about staying competitive and relevant to customers as it is about tech. As one study found, 75% of auto executives believe the software-defined user experience will be the primary driver of brand value by 2035 [4]. In other words, companies see that in the future, consumers might choose a car for its software features and user experience more than for traditional metrics like horsepower. This realization is incentivizing OEMs to invest in SDV platforms to deliver those experiences.

Flagship experience tie-in: The convergence of artificial intelligence (AI) and SDV technologies allows automakers to redefine the customer experience in a vehicle. Instead of a static set of features, the car becomes a dynamic, personalized environment.

For instance, AI algorithms can learn a driver's preferences—adjusting seat, music, and climate automatically— creating a personalized cockpit experience. The SDV platform might offer on-demand upgrades: imagine a rental car that can have features enabled or disabled depending on what the customer pays for or a family sedan that can download a "sport mode" for a weekend trip to a track.

Predictive safety is another experience enhancer: using AI, the vehicle can anticipate hazards (by analyzing driver behavior, road conditions, vehicle telemetry) and warn or adjust systems preemptively—essentially the car gets "smarter" and more protective over time. All these capabilities are only possible when the vehicle is seen as a software-first product. OEMs that treat customer experience as a core deliverable (not just meeting minimum regulatory requirements) are likely to gain lasting loyalty.

For example, Tesla's habit of surprising customers with Easter eggs or new features via updates (like new arcade games or improved acceleration) keeps owners engaged and delighted—they feel their car is always getting better and more fun. Traditional OEMs are starting to emulate this, with some announcing they will provide regular enhancement updates, not just fixes. The key is that an SDV can be a platform for continuous innovation in the user experience realm. Those companies that leverage that—turning the car into a service platform that adapts to user needs—can differentiate themselves strongly. Conversely, companies that only do the bare minimum (like only issuing software updates when something breaks or when forced by regulation) risk being seen as stagnant. In the age of SDVs, innovation is a continuous process, and the customer increasingly expects a relationship with the automaker that extends throughout the vehicle's life. Building that relationship through software (features, services, and improvements) will be a hallmark of the winners in the SDV era.

1.8 Key Takeaways

- **SDV paradigm shift**: A software-defined vehicle is a vehicle whose features and value are largely defined by software, not just hardware. Unlike legacy cars with static functions and dozens of fixed ECUs, an SDV has generic hardware and can evolve through software updates. Features can be added or improved after the car is produced[5, 13]. This flexibility is a game-changer for the industry, enabling continuous improvement and new business models.

- **Digital-first development**: To build SDVs safely and efficiently, automakers must adopt a digital-first approach. This means designing software before hardware is finalized, using virtual ECUs and simulations to test early and often, and establishing CI/CD pipelines for automotive software. Digital-first methodologies (including vECUs, continuous validation, and telemetry feedback loops) ensure that frequent OTA updates can be delivered without compromising quality or safety [14, 17]. Essentially, it's bringing the speed of software industry practices into the automotive world, which is necessary for SDVs.
- **Engineering foundations remain central**: SDV development builds on embedded software, real-time systems, vehicle networking, systems integration, cybersecurity, and functional safety. What changes in the SDV era is the need to connect these disciplines across the full vehicle lifecycle, including cloud services, continuous validation, and software updates [1–3].
- **Industry drivers (tech and business)**: The move to SDVs is propelled by both technology trends and market forces. Electrification is making cars more software-centric, connectivity (5G, V2X) enables continuous engagement with vehicles, and regulations (like UNECE R156 for software updates and ISO 21434 for cybersecurity) are mandating new processes [23]. On the business side, companies see huge revenue potential in selling software-enabled services and features (subscriptions, upgrades) and improving customer experience through software. Those drivers together create a sense of urgency: to stay competitive (and compliant), OEMs must develop software-defined vehicle capabilities.

CHAPTER 2

E/E Architectures: Domain ➤ Zonal ➤ Central Compute

2.1 Chapter Goals

After this chapter, you will be able to

- Trace the evolution of in-vehicle E/E (electrical/electronic) architectures from traditional domain-based ECUs to zonal controllers and finally to centralized compute units.
- Explain the trade-offs in wiring harness complexity, weight reduction, and network latency/determinism across these architectural paradigms.
- Map automotive functions to network and middleware choices, understanding when CAN/LIN vs. Ethernet TSN (Time-Sensitive Networking) or service-oriented middleware (SOME/IP, DDS, etc.) are appropriate.
- Plan a migration strategy from a legacy architecture to a zonal/centralized one, considering functional safety, cybersecurity, and over-the-air update requirements.

S. Agarwal, *Software-Defined Vehicles*, https://doi.org/10.1007/979-8-8688-2718-1_2

Critic's Note Architecture is not a beauty contest. SDV success depends on how well your electrical/electronic (E/E) architecture supports updatability, observability, and compliance evidence.

2.2 Introduction

The electrical and electronic (E/E) architecture of a vehicle is its central nervous system—the foundation upon which all software-defined capabilities are built. While the previous chapter introduced the concept of software-defined vehicles and their key characteristics, this chapter examines the physical and logical infrastructure that makes such vehicles possible. Without the right E/E architecture, even the most sophisticated software cannot be deployed, updated, or maintained effectively.

For decades, automotive E/E design followed a simple pattern: add a new feature, and then add a new electronic control unit (ECU). This approach worked when vehicles had a handful of electronic functions, but modern vehicles now contain 100+ ECUs, kilometers of wiring, and software complexity rivaling that of fighter jets. The resulting "spaghetti" of hardware and networks has become a bottleneck—limiting the speed of innovation, increasing manufacturing costs, and making over-the-air updates nearly impossible to execute reliably.

The industry's response has been a fundamental rethinking of vehicle architecture, moving from function-based organization (domains) to location-based organization (zones) and ultimately toward centralized high-performance computing. This chapter traces that architectural evolution—examining the trade-offs in wiring complexity, network determinism, service placement, middleware selection, safety, security, and updatability that shape modern E/E design.

2.3 From Domain to Zonal to Central

Modern vehicles have undergone a significant shift in how their electronic control units (ECUs) and networks are organized [36]. Historically, the domain-based architecture grouped ECUs by function (powertrain, chassis, body, infotainment, etc.). Newer designs introduce zonal architectures, where ECUs are grouped by physical location (zones) rather than function [37].

In parallel, many OEMs are moving toward *central compute*—high-performance computers that consolidate many functions in one place [38]. Each OEM follows its own path: some evolve from domain ➤ zonal ➤ central, and others go from domains directly to domain controllers + a central high-performance computer (HPC) or introduce partial zonalization around an existing domain backbone. Each step, in whatever order, addresses specific pain points of the previous generation but also introduces new challenges.

2.3.1 Legacy Domain Architecture

In a domain architecture, dozens of function-specific ECUs are spread around the vehicle but are logically clustered by domain [11]. For example, all engine-related controls might report to a powertrain domain controller, while separate controllers handle chassis functions (ABS, stability), body electronics (doors, climate), and infotainment. These domain controllers communicate over legacy automotive networks like CAN, LIN, and FlexRay within and sometimes across domains.

Benefits of Domain Architectures

This approach served well for a time: it encapsulated complexity within functional "islands" and allowed each domain to be developed somewhat independently. Critical real-time loops (like engine timing or airbag deployment) stayed within a single domain, which helped maintain deterministic timing in those silos.

It also gave OEMs clear subsystem boundaries (e.g., a supplier might deliver the powertrain domain as a package). In short, domain architectures provided clear ownership and contained, deterministic islands of control [36].

Drawbacks and Limitations

However, the domain approach has serious drawbacks as electronics content grows: the wiring harness became extraordinarily complex and heavy due to numerous point-to-point connections.

High-end vehicles can have hundreds of meters to several kilometers of wiring (often >**1.5 km**; some luxury SUVs exceed ~60 kg of harness mass) and scores to over 100 ECUs—hence the push to zonalization.

Each new feature often meant a new ECU with its own wiring, leading to *redundant sensors and cables crisscrossing the vehicle*. This "copper spaghetti" not only adds weight (reducing fuel efficiency or EV range) but also cost and reliability risks (many connectors and longer signal paths). Additionally, updatability suffers: pushing an over-the-air (OTA) software update to dozens of separate ECUs (from different suppliers, with different software) is complex and fraught with compatibility issues.

In summary, the domain architecture was an improvement over earlier flat architectures (where everything was independent), but it merely grouped functions and did not solve the wiring explosion [11]. Deterministic real-time behavior was ensured within domains, but cross-domain communication was limited and often had to hop through gateways, adding latency. The approach was reaching its limit as software-defined vehicle demands outpaced the manageable complexity.

2.3.2 Zonal Architecture

In response to wiring and integration complexity, automakers and suppliers have increasingly adopted zonal architectures [37, 39]. In a zonal E/E architecture, the vehicle is divided into physical zones such as front, rear, left, right, or cabin, each managed by a zonal controller. Local sensors and actuators connect first to the nearest zonal controller through short local wiring or subordinate buses. The zonal controllers are then linked through an Ethernet backbone or switch fabric to other zones and, where applicable, to one or more central compute platforms. In this context, Ethernet is the communication backbone, not a controller or functional node.

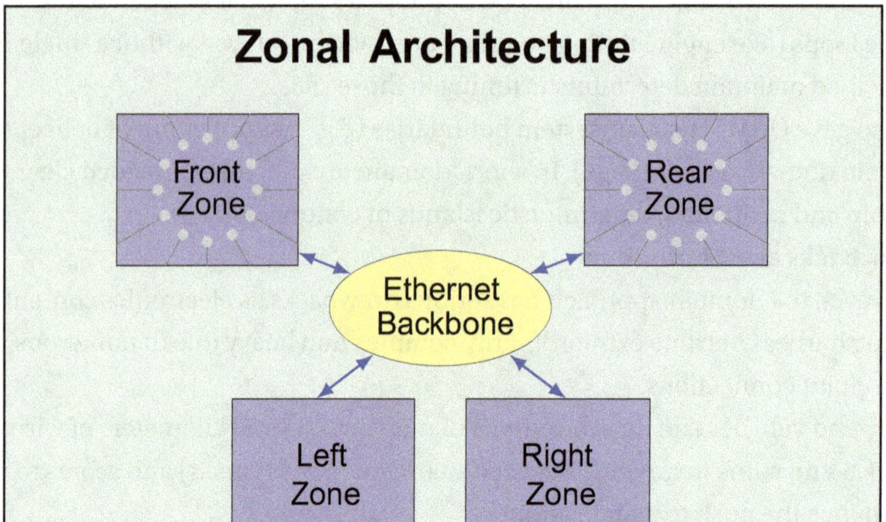

Figure 2-1. *Conceptual zonal E/E architecture with local I/O aggregation in zone controllers connected through an Ethernet backbone or switch fabric*

What Is a Zonal Controller?

In production designs, zonal controllers typically use ASIL-capable MCUs, such as Renesas RH850/U2x, Infineon AURIX TC3xx/TC4xx, or NXP S32Z, to support deterministic local fallback behavior in case of backbone or central compute issues. Some architectures use S32G-class devices for non-ASIL-D zones.

In practice, a zonal controller is a regional gateway and I/O hub: it aggregates all sensors and actuators in its physical vicinity (via short local wires or sub-buses like CAN FD, LIN, or 10BASE-T1S) and translates these to Ethernet flows for the central network. As a result, physical grouping is by location, while functional grouping is increasingly done in software or at the central computer.

For example, a front-left zone module might handle the left headlight, left suspension actuator, and left radar sensor, even though those belong to different traditional domains (lighting, chassis, ADAS). The zonal module would send its data over Ethernet to whichever unit needs it (central computer or another zone).

Key Benefits

The benefits of zonal architecture are significant:

1. **Reduction in harness length and weight:**

   By aggregating connections locally and then using a few high-speed data links, the long runs of copper are minimized [40]. Public examples and studies show that harnesses in the three-mile (≈5 km) range for legacy/domain designs can shrink toward ~1.5–3 km in zonal layouts, with weight savings often reported in the 20–50% range depending on vehicle segment and scope of consolidation. The exact figures are highly program-specific; what matters is the clear trend toward less copper and simpler routing.

   - **Tesla Model 3:** Reorganized body electronics and reduced wiring from ~3 km (Model S) to ~1.5 km, roughly halving length; larger "85–95%" reductions often quoted refer to future patent targets rather than Model 3 production. The key trend—more centralized body controllers and zonalization—is real and now industry-wide [41].

   - **Rivian's platform:** A recent platform with three zone controllers removed almost 20 kg of wiring compared with its earlier design [42, 43]. Lighter harnesses not only improve vehicle efficiency but also simplify manufacturing—fewer unique harness variants and simpler installation.

- **BMW Neue Klasse:** BMW states its Neue Klasse zonal wiring harness is ~30% lighter with ~600 m less wiring, and corporate materials add an ~×3,000 reduction in harness variants—key to automation and cost [44].

2. **Easier scalability and variants:**

   Zonal systems make it easier to add or remove features by zone [38]. Need to offer a new sensor in the next model? You can often plug it into the nearest zone controller and update software, rather than running new wires to a distant ECU. The architecture becomes more modular—add or upgrade a zone controller for a higher-end variant, or remove one for a base model, without redesigning the whole network.

3. **Flexibility for high-speed data:**

   With an Ethernet backbone, the vehicle begins to resemble a routed data network rather than a collection of isolated field buses. This is particularly valuable for cross-domain communication, diagnostics, OTA distribution, and service-oriented data exchange. High-bandwidth sensors such as cameras still typically connect to local processing units through dedicated interfaces such as MIPI CSI, GMSL, or FPD-Link, while Ethernet carries processed data, metadata, and inter-controller traffic across zones and central compute platforms. The key benefit is therefore not that Ethernet replaces every sensor interface, but that it provides a scalable backbone for inter-zone and central communication [45].

4. **Simplified power distribution options:**

   Many zonal controllers also handle local power distribution (sometimes replacing traditional fuse boxes with solid-state switches in each zone) [40]. This shortens the power cabling as well and can improve electrical efficiency and safety (e.g., easier to shut off power to a zone in case of a fault). (We will revisit power distribution in a later chapter.)

New Challenges

However, zonal architectures bring new challenges. They essentially shift complexity from hardware to software: since physical proximity, not function, dictates wiring, the software and networking have to ensure that the right data gets where it needs to go. The central backbone must carry a diverse mix of traffic (video streams, real-time control signals, diagnostics, etc.), so achieving network determinism and security on that single network becomes critical (addressed later in this chapter).

The zonal controller itself is a more powerful and complex device than most legacy ECUs, since it must handle multi-domain I/O and act as a router/gateway. This increases the software complexity and integration effort—the zonal controller's software has to interface with many components and protocols [45]. It also means a failure of a zonal controller can affect multiple functions in that area, so redundancy and fault containment strategies are needed (sometimes a neighboring zone can take over in limp mode and so on).

It is important to note that zonal architectures do not eliminate traditional field buses overnight. In most production programs, local devices still generate CAN, CAN FD, or LIN traffic, and zonal controllers continue to host these interfaces for legacy and cost-optimized endpoints. The zonal controller then acts as a protocol gateway: it receives local messages, extracts or aggregates the relevant signals, and repackages them into Ethernet/IP traffic for transmission across the backbone to other zones or to central compute platforms. Ethernet therefore becomes the inter-zone and central backbone, while CAN and LIN remain important local networks for many body, comfort, and cost-sensitive functions.

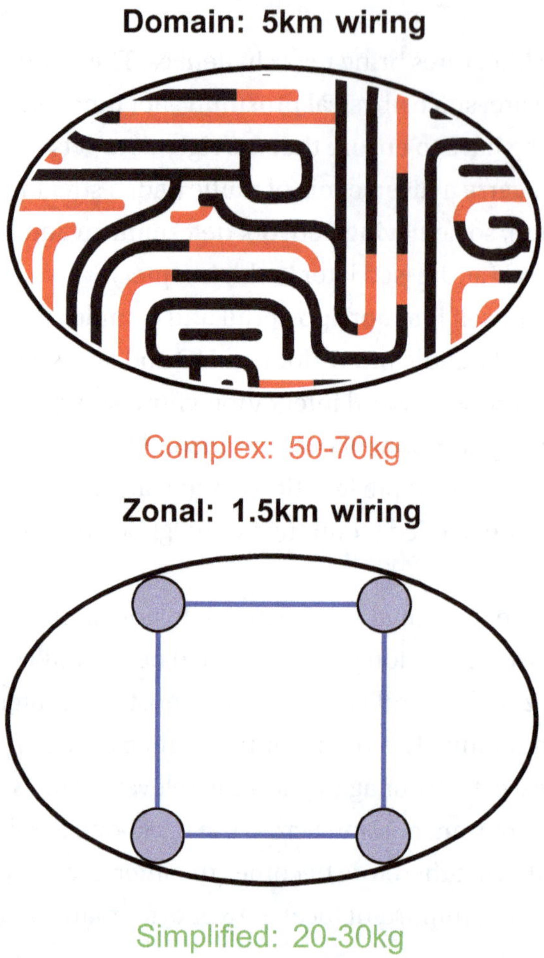

Figure 2-2. *Wiring harness complexity: domain vs. zonal architecture*

Overall, the industry consensus is that zonal E/E architecture is a necessary stepping stone to manage vehicle complexity and enable the software-defined vehicle (SDV) future [37]. In fact, phased adoption is common: manufacturers introduce zonal concepts gradually, perhaps first consolidating a few ECUs into a "mini-zonal" module in one area (while the rest of the car remains domain-based) and then expanding in subsequent models. This hybrid approach can yield immediate weight and cost savings while smoothing the migration path for legacy platforms.

2.3.3 Central Compute

Zonal architecture deals with wiring and physical distribution, but another orthogonal trend is the rise of **centralized compute** [46]. This refers to having one or a few HPCs in the vehicle that host the software for many functions that used to live on separate ECUs. In other words, instead of dozens of microcontrollers each running a specific application, you have server-like nodes (often multi-core SoCs or even automotive-grade GPUs) that run a hypervisor or OS and multiple software services together. Central compute nodes go hand in hand with zonal layouts: the zones provide the "spokes" collecting I/O, and one or more central processors act as the "hub" doing the heavy lifting.

Most OEM roadmaps show partial zonalization coexisting with early central compute integration for at least one full model cycle.

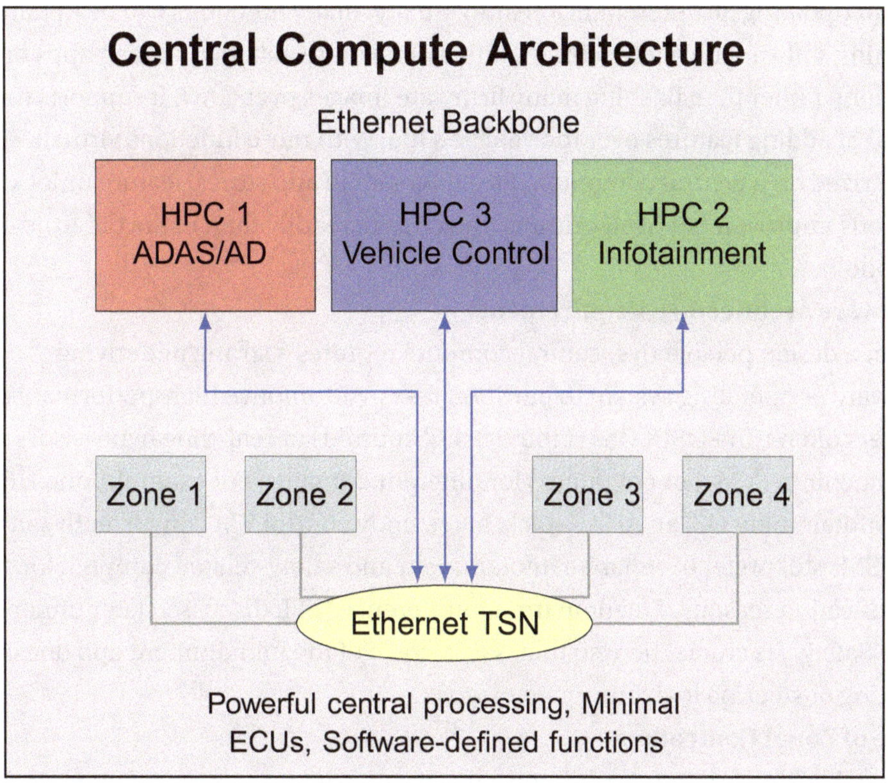

Figure 2-3. *Central compute architecture in which zone controllers and high-performance computers communicate over an Ethernet backbone with TSN features*

Here, Ethernet TSN refers to the communication backbone and timing profile that connect the architectural nodes; it is not itself a controller or compute element.

First and foremost, raw computing power. Advanced driver assistance systems (ADAS) and autonomous driving require AI algorithms, sensor fusion of camera/LiDAR/radar data, path planning, etc., which in sum demand tens to hundreds of trillions of operations per second—far beyond what a traditional ECU can handle. By concentrating compute in a few capable processors (with proper cooling and power), automakers can implement these cutting-edge features.

For instance, Tesla famously centralized its Autopilot computer (two redundant AI chips) to handle all vision processing for self-driving; similarly, many OEMs are now planning domain "supercomputers" for automated driving, cockpit/infotainment, etc., often supplied by companies like NVIDIA, Qualcomm, or Intel/Mobileye.

Central compute also facilitates software updatability and deployment [38]. Instead of updating 50 different ECUs individually, many functions can be updated by patching software on a few central units. This is more akin to updating apps on a smartphone rather than flashing many firmware images over CAN. It supports the SDV goal of adding features over the vehicle's life. With more functions virtualized or containerized on a central computer, one can imagine app stores, feature unlocks, and continuous improvement of algorithms much more readily than in the old fixed-function ECU model.

Software Architecture Requirements

From a design perspective, central compute requires a strong underlying middleware or operating system to partition tasks. Automotive high-performance computers often run POSIX OSs (Linux/QNX/Android) or real-time hypervisors, hosting virtual machines (VMs) or containers for different domains. For example, one HPC *could* run an infotainment OS, an ADAS stack, and a body control VM concurrently, although many OEMs still prefer to separate infotainment and safety-related compute for security and certification reasons. Freedom from interference (FFI; discussed later under the section "Safety") is crucial here so that, say, a crash of the infotainment app doesn't affect the braking or steering logic running next to it.

Role of Zonal Controllers

Even with a beefy central computer, you cannot wire every sensor and motor directly to it—that would reintroduce the wiring mess we're trying to avoid. Instead, zonal controllers act as intelligent I/O concentrators. They typically handle raw I/O, signal conditioning, and simple local control loops that need immediate response (e.g., debouncing inputs, basic actuator supervision, or fallback behaviors), while most complex perception (radar, camera, LiDAR) still runs on dedicated sensor ECUs or the central HPC. They also receive high-level commands (e.g., "set steering angle to *X*") from the central unit and directly drive the actuators or local ECUs to achieve them. In essence, zonal controllers become the interface between the raw physical world and the high-level software. They're sometimes called "smart gateways" or "edge processors."

A practical example is an autonomous driving system: The central computer might determine a desired trajectory and send steering and acceleration commands. The front-left and front-right zone controllers could each control a portion of the chassis—reading wheel speeds, accelerating a specific wheel (torque vectoring), applying brake pressure, etc., under coordination of the central command. If the central brain fails, the zonal units may have limited fail-safe routines to bring the vehicle to a stop using redundant paths.

Network Topology

Centralized architectures also simplify vehicle network topology. Instead of many inter-ECU CAN buses, there's typically an Ethernet backbone (often with Time-Sensitive Networking features; see section "Determinism with Ethernet TSN") linking zones and central nodes in a star or ring. Some OEMs have introduced two or three main computers—e.g., one for autonomous driving, one for infotainment, and one for body/chassis—connected via Ethernet. For instance, Audi's latest E/E architecture has a "central driver assistance controller" and a separate "infotainment central" plus zone gateways. Over time, these may merge further as processing power increases.

Advantages and Disadvantages

Pros: The benefits of central compute include easier updates, as mentioned, and the potential to rationalize hardware (fewer distinct ECU types, leveraging high-volume powerful SoCs instead of many bespoke microcontrollers). It can also reduce duplication: instead of each ECU having its own processor, memory, and power supply, a central processor can be shared by multiple functions. In some programs this leads to cost benefits; in others the HPC itself is more expensive than the ECUs it replaces, but the OEM accepts that in exchange for software velocity and feature flexibility. Critically, only a central architecture can realistically handle the data throughput of future vehicles (imagine dozens of high-resolution sensors producing gigabits of data—feeding that through daisy-chained ECUs would be untenable; a network feeding a central "data center on wheels" is the feasible approach).

Cons: The downsides revolve around risk concentration and complexity. If one central computer fails or needs a reboot, it could knock out numerous vehicle functions at once, whereas in a federated domain architecture a single ECU failure was more isolated. This necessitates robust redundancy (we'll discuss later how redundancy and fail-operational designs mitigate this). Also, consolidating software from different domains onto one platform means integration challenges—e.g., mixing a safety-critical real-time control task with a Linux-based infotainment system on one chip is nontrivial. You often need hypervisors, redundant MCUs, or lockstep cores to ensure critical tasks get the resources and isolation they need.

In short, central compute architectures, enabled by zonal networks, represent the computing backbone of the software-defined vehicle. Many new EV startups and tech-forward automakers embraced this from scratch (having no legacy baggage)—e.g., Tesla's vehicles drastically reduced the ECU count by combining functionality, and Rivian's Gen2 architecture went from 23 ECUs to just 3 zone controllers + 4 other units [42, 47]. Traditional OEMs are also moving this way but often in stages: first domains → then a few domain consolidation (like "domain control units" for powertrain, chassis, etc.) → then eventually full central computer. We are currently in a transition period industry-wide, exploring the best partitioning between edge and center, as subsequent sections will explore in detail.

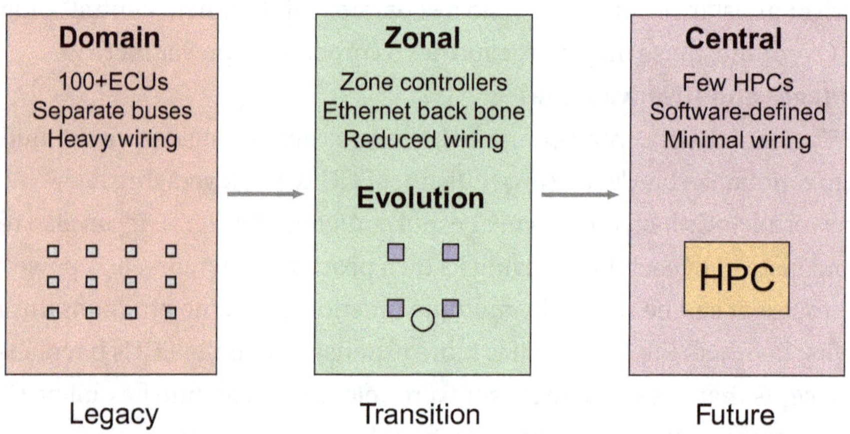

***Figure 2-4.** Evolution of E/E architectures: from domain to zonal to central*

2.4 Harness Weight and Network Determinism

A key motivation to adopt zonal and centralized architectures has been to reduce the physical complexity of the wiring and to modernize the in-vehicle networking for better performance. In this section, we quantify the wiring improvements and discuss how new Ethernet-based networks can still meet the real-time determinism requirements historically handled by field buses.

2.4.1 Wiring Reduction

Reducing harness complexity is one practical advantage of zonal architectures, but it should be treated here as one architectural consequence rather than the sole motivation. By aggregating local sensors and actuators within each zone and replacing many long point-to-point runs with shorter local connections plus a smaller number of backbone links, zonal layouts can reduce copper mass, simplify routing, and ease assembly. The exact benefit is highly vehicle-specific, but the broader trend toward less wiring and fewer harness variants is well established [40, 42, 44].

Local Aggregation

In a domain architecture, if the rear left door has a window motor ECU that is controlled by the body domain controller in the front dash, you'd have a dedicated pair of wires running all the way from the dash to that door (plus maybe a LIN bus in the door). Multiply such runs by hundreds of sensors/actuators scattered around, and you see why the harness is so extensive.

In a zonal architecture, that door's ECU could be integrated into a zone controller in the left side of the car, just a short cable away. That zone controller connects to the central network with maybe one or two high-speed cables, which now carry data for many devices. Net effect: Point-to-point cable runs shrink dramatically, replaced by a few backbone links.

Studies and OEM reports have quantified this benefit:

- Tier-1s and reviews report ~15–30% wiring harness mass reduction from zonalization [40]. For a harness mass of ~80 kg in a high-end vehicle, that's on the order of 24 kg saved—a very significant figure.
- Park et al. (researchers) projected that using a six-zone architecture could cut communication harness length by ~50% compared with a domain-based layout.

- One OEM example: Rivian said their second-gen architecture (with three zone controllers) allowed a weight reduction of ~20 kg of wiring [42]. BMW indicated that its upcoming Neue Klasse platform's zonal harness will be 30% lighter than the previous design (and far simpler in variant count) [44].
- Tesla's Model 3 redesign is often cited: it reportedly dropped from ~3 km of wiring in Model S to ~1.5 km in Model 3, largely by using body controllers and more centralized wiring [41]. (Tesla also innovated by using aluminum wires and multi-core cables for further weight savings.)

Reducing, say, 20 kg of copper may improve an EV's range by a few percent or allow designers to add other features with that weight budget. It also makes assembly easier: imagine trying to route a 5 km spaghetti of wires vs. a more modular harness by zones. In fact, harness manufacturing historically required significant manual labor (it's one of the few parts often hand-assembled, due to complexity); simplifying it opens the path for more automation.

Another benefit: Shorter wiring runs mean lower voltage drop and often faster signal response. Long cables introduce resistance and capacitance that can slow down edges and require thicker gauges for power delivery. By localizing connections, the electrical performance improves (e.g., sensors can use lower power signals over short runs reliably).

Optimized Power Distribution

As mentioned, zonal architectures usually come with decentralized power management. Instead of routing heavy 12 V lines from a central fuse box to every corner, you might route a higher voltage feed (like 48 V or 12 V main lines) to each zone and then locally distribute/regulate it.

A higher voltage like 48 V significantly reduces current for the same power, allowing much thinner and lighter wires for power distribution [48, 49]. For example, delivering 2 kW at 12 V requires ~167 A, which demands very thick cables; at 48 V it's ~42 A, enabling far thinner wires. Modern designs increasingly use 48 V zonal power for high-load devices (fans, pumps, heating elements) to cut copper weight. Moving high-load circuits to 48 V cuts current by ~4× for the same power, enabling much smaller cross-sections and significant copper mass savings on those runs (actual savings depend on load mix and routing) [50]. This also reduces resistive losses (heat), improving overall energy efficiency [49].

Industry Insight A typical conventional car might have to shed loads when too many systems draw power (e.g., temporarily disable rear defrosters when the power steering is at max draw) due to the 12 V system limits. With a robust 48 V supply in zones, these power management trade-offs are reduced. Vehicles can simultaneously run more features (ADAS, climate, chassis control) without brownouts, thanks to higher capacity and better distributed power.

In summary, wiring reduction is one of the clearest wins of moving to zonal/centralized E/E architectures [40, 43]. It's common to achieve double-digit kilogram weight savings and to eliminate kilometers of wiring. The car essentially becomes closer to a computer network and power bus on wheels, rather than a bundle of dedicated circuits. This sets the stage for easier manufacture and improved performance, but it does mean that more data is funneling through fewer channels—which raises the question: can those channels handle the real-time needs of the vehicle? That leads us to Time-Sensitive Networking.

2.4.2 Determinism with Ethernet TSN

Moving from domain-specific buses (CAN, FlexRay) to unified Ethernet raises timing concerns. Automotive control systems require bounded latency and minimal jitter for safety-critical messages [51].

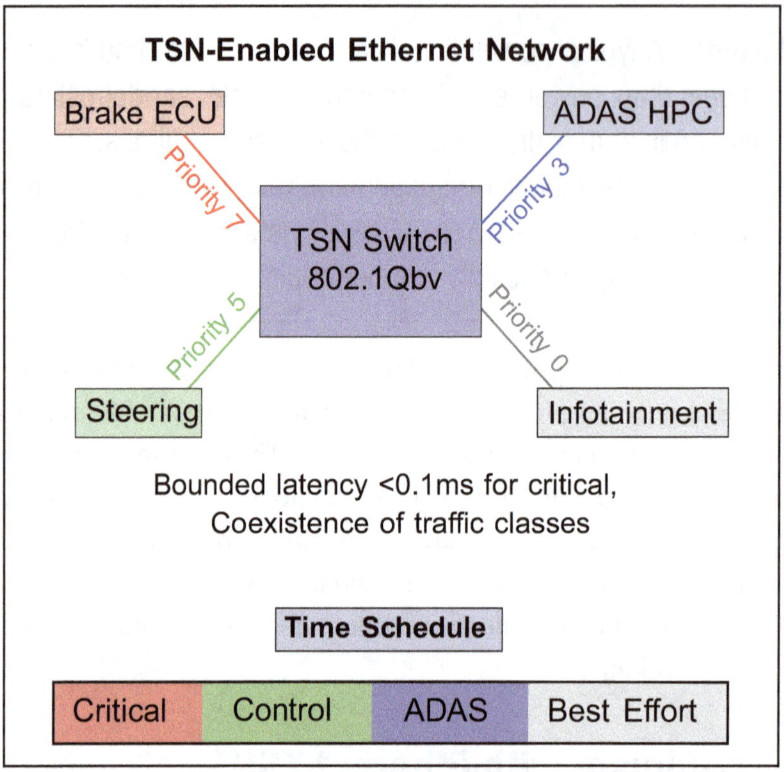

Figure 2-5. *TSN-enabled Ethernet network with time-aware shaping*

Time-Sensitive Networking (TSN) is a set of IEEE 802.1 standards that make Ethernet deterministic while allowing noncritical traffic to coexist [52]. Key mechanisms include

- **Time synchronization (802.1AS):** Sub-microsecond clock alignment across all nodes.
- **Scheduled traffic (802.1Qbv):** Time-aware shaping with protected transmission windows.
- **Frame preemption (802.1Qbu/802.3br):** Critical frames can interrupt lower-priority transmissions.
- **Stream reservation (802.1Qcc):** Centralized or distributed bandwidth allocation.

For automotive applications, the IEEE 802.1DG profile specifies how these mechanisms combine to achieve sub-millisecond bounded latency for safety-critical traffic alongside best-effort data streams.

Key Point For comprehensive TSN coverage including protocol details, configuration examples, automotive profiles, and performance benchmarks, see **Chapter 5**.

2.5 Service Placement and Middleware

We've discussed how the hardware architecture is changing (from many ECUs to zones to central compute). Equally important is how software is structured and communicates in these new designs. As functions migrate into consolidated controllers, designers must decide where to execute each service (at the edge vs. centrally) and how they will talk to each other over the network. This section explores the service placement considerations and the role of different middleware/communication frameworks (like SOME/IP, DDS, etc.) in an automotive context.

2.5.1 Edge vs. Central Placement

One of the first design decisions is what logic to keep at the edge (zonal controllers) vs. what to move to the central HPC. Essentially, we are dividing the vehicle's features into two buckets: those that run in zones (or dedicated small ECUs) and those that run on the big computer.

Generally, tasks that are I/O-heavy, time-critical, or safety-critical tend to remain at the edge (in zones), whereas tasks that are compute-heavy or system-wide integrate well centrally. Let's break that down.

Edge/Zonal Tasks

These include direct hardware control loops and any functionality requiring very low latency to physical signals. For example:

- Brake and restraint functions are usually kept in dedicated safety controllers primarily because of functional safety, independence, and fault containment requirements rather than simply because of network latency. ABS, ESC, and airbag deployment must continue to operate within tightly controlled safety architectures even if higher-level software or centralized compute platforms fail. Latency and jitter still matter, but they are secondary to the need for certified safety paths, deterministic local execution, and clear fault boundaries. In zonal concepts, OEMs may move selected monitoring or preprocessing functions closer to the zone while retaining the core safety logic in specialized, highly independent controllers.

- Similarly, an airbag sensor typically is wired to a small local controller that can fire the airbag within microseconds of *detecting* a crash, rather than relying on a potentially busy central computer. In short, safety-critical feedback loops (especially those with ASIL-D criticality) are often kept in dedicated microcontrollers or in the zone computers with high priority.
- Another edge function: Power and body control, such as turning on headlights, controlling door locks, and adjusting mirrors—these involve local actuators and often need to work even if central units reboot (for safety or convenience). Zonal controllers can handle these with simple logic or fallback default behaviors.
- Additionally, edge units handle all the raw I/O: analog–digital conversions, local sensor signal conditioning, and bridging old-school buses (LIN and others) to the Ethernet world.

Central Tasks

These are the big brains—sensor fusion, path planning, complex diagnostics, user interfaces, etc. They typically require gathering data from multiple zones, doing heavy computation (like running neural networks on camera feeds), or coordinating high-level decisions. For example:

- An autonomous driving function will pull data from cameras (front zone), radars (front/rear zones), and ultrasonics (all around), then run a perception algorithm to identify objects, then decide on a trajectory, and finally send a throttle/brake command. That's naturally suited to a central processor because of the computing load and the need to combine info globally.

- Similarly, an infotainment system that integrates navigation, audio, connectivity, etc. or a vehicle data logger sending info to the cloud—those live centrally.
- User experience and connectivity functions are also central (they often run on higher-level OS platforms like Android Automotive or QNX that wouldn't make sense to have multiple instances of in every zone).

Design Principles

A useful concept is to think in terms of **data locality and bandwidth:** Edge controllers should handle things that produce or consume a high volume of data locally (like a high-frequency sensor) to avoid saturating the network and to act quickly on it. The central computer should handle things where data from various places must come together or where outcomes affect the whole vehicle.

Determinism and fail-operational considerations also play a role. Some functions (like Level 3 autonomous driving) require fail-operational design—meaning if one computer fails, another can take over without losing control. Often, this is done by having redundant computers rather than trusting the network to reroute on the fly. For example, one OEM might have dual central ADAS ECUs both processing sensor data simultaneously, ready to take over if the other fails. In such cases, zones just duplicate the sensor data to both.

Another aspect is **serviceability and updatability.** Edge units (zonal controllers) might be running AUTOSAR Classic Platform for stability and certified safety, which isn't updated frequently OTA except for minor calibrations. The central unit might run AUTOSAR Adaptive or a Linux-based system where new features can be downloaded regularly. So splitting some functions centrally can allow more frequent updates, which is desirable for user-facing features, whereas the edge might remain static to minimize regression risk in safety code.

Increasingly, automakers talk about the vehicle in terms of domains or functions running on a virtual platform rather than tied to a physical ECU. For instance, "chassis domain" software might run partly on zones (edge) and partly on central. A practical approach is virtual ECUs: e.g., you simulate a "virtual powertrain ECU" on the central compute that handles non-time-critical engine management, but leave the hard real-time ignition timing on an actual microcontroller on the engine. Over time, as confidence in central computing grows, more of these could be pulled into the center.

In summary, there's a continuum:

- Real-time critical, high-rate control → keep at the edge (zones or dedicated microcontrollers).
- Coordinated, global or heavy processing → move to the central HPC.

You might see this reflected in car E/E block diagrams: often two or three "domain controllers" remain for powertrain/chassis (for fast control) and the rest—ADAS, infotainment, and body—on a central or a few central units. The exact split is OEM-specific and also evolves with technology improvements. Our Worked Example later will demonstrate mapping a few functions to either zones or central for clarity.

2.5.2 Middleware Overview

When various software components are distributed across zones and central computers, they need a way to communicate. The choice of middleware has implications for latency, throughput, CPU load, and certification.

Key Point **SOME/IP** (Scalable service-Oriented MiddlewarE over IP) has become a de facto standard in many production cars, particularly as part of AUTOSAR Adaptive Platform (AP) [53, 54]. It provides remote procedure calls (RPC) and message passing over Ethernet with service discovery (SD).

DDS (Data Distribution Service) is a middleware from the industrial and defense world implementing a data-centric publish–subscribe model [55]. It has built-in Quality of Service (QoS) settings and automatic discovery and is used in ROS 2 and available in AUTOSAR Adaptive [56, 57].

For detailed comparison of middleware technologies, performance benchmarks, safety certification considerations, and selection guidelines, see **Chapter 4**.

The key trade-off: SOME/IP is simpler and proven in production with smaller footprint; DDS is more powerful for streaming data to multiple consumers but more complex. Many architectures use both, sometimes bridged through AUTOSAR Adaptive's `ara::com` abstraction layer [58].

2.6 Safety, Security, and Updatability

As we centralize and modernize the E/E architecture, it is paramount not to regress on functional safety (the vehicle must remain safe even with faults), cybersecurity, and the ability to update software reliably. In fact, these areas often drive requirements that significantly shape the architecture. This section discusses how safety and security are maintained in zonal/central architectures and how OTA updates are managed.

2.6.1 Safety

Functional safety per ISO 26262 [59] ensures that hardware or software faults do not lead to unacceptable risks. The core challenge in centralized architectures is **freedom from interference (FFI)**: ensuring non-safety code cannot hinder safety functions through timing interference, memory corruption, or unintended communication [60].

High-Performance SoC

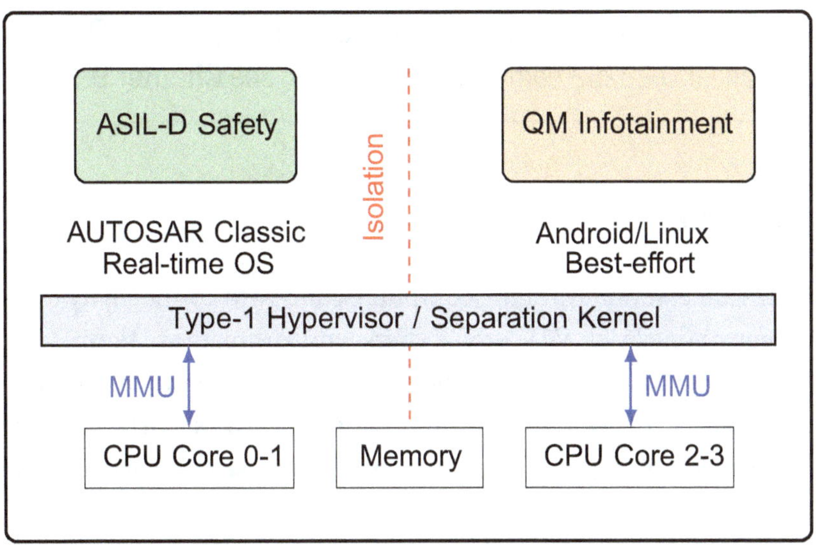

Figure 2-6. *Example of safety partitioning in a centralized SoC, where hypervisor-controlled MMU-based isolation separates mixed-criticality workloads*

Figure 2-6 is intended to illustrate isolation, not communication flow. In practice, the hypervisor runs on the CPU cores and configures the MMU or IOMMU to enforce memory separation between partitions. The MMU should therefore be understood as a hardware protection mechanism used to support isolation between ASIL and QM (Quality-Managed) workloads, not as a communication path between the hypervisor and the processor cores.

Key strategies for mixed-criticality systems include

- **Hypervisor partitioning:** Spatial and temporal isolation between ASIL-rated and QM workloads [22]
- **Lockstep cores:** Dual-core execution with cycle-by-cycle comparison for fault detection
- **Redundant compute paths:** Independent processors for fail-operational requirements [61]

Key Point For comprehensive coverage of ASIL decomposition, FFI techniques, safety cases, and ISO 26262 compliance strategies, see **Chapter 9**.

2.6.2 Security

Modern vehicles are essentially rolling computers, and with connectivity features (telematics, smartphone links, V2X, etc.), cybersecurity threats are significant [62]. An architecture with a central Ethernet backbone and powerful central nodes opens new attack surfaces and also provides opportunities for improved security measures. We need a "defense in depth" approach, as the chapter quote says—belt-and-suspenders at multiple layers.

Key Security Measures

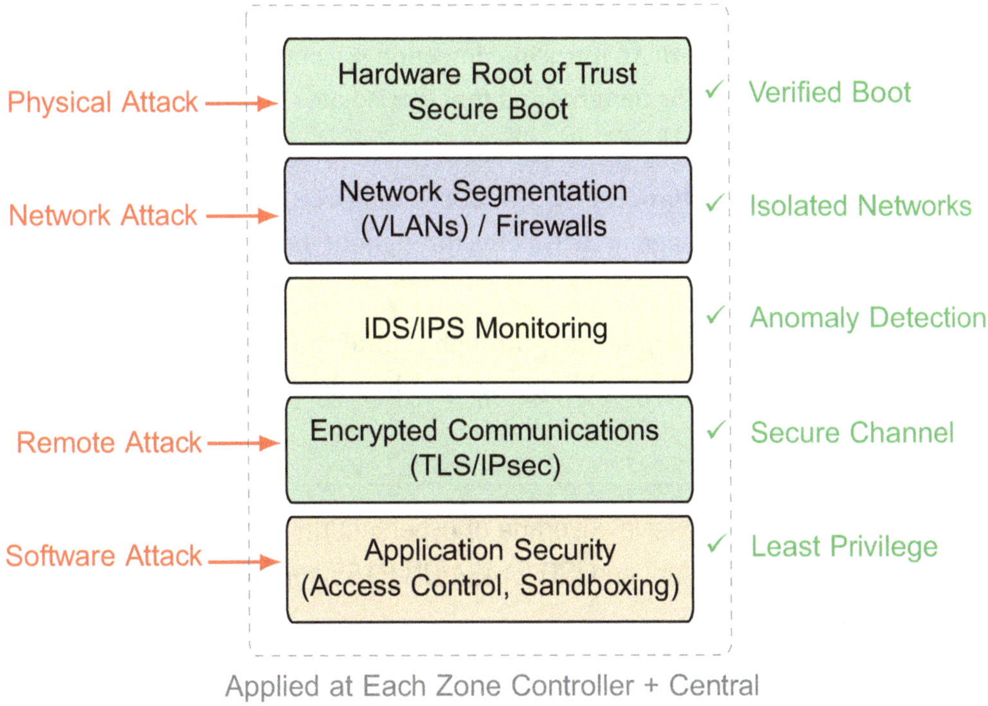

Figure 2-7. *Multi-layer security architecture in zonal/central design*

Key security measures in zonal/central architectures include

- **Secure boot:** Every controller verifies firmware signatures before execution, with immutable root of trust in hardware [63, 64].
- **Network segmentation:** VLANs and firewalls isolate safety-critical traffic from infotainment; zonal gateways validate messages before forwarding [39].
- **Authenticated communications:** SecOC for CAN messages, TLS/IPsec for Ethernet links, DDS Security for topic-level protection [65, 66].

- **Access control:** OS-level hardening (SELinux), role-based network access, certificate-based ECU authentication.
- **Intrusion detection:** An intrusion detection system (IDS) monitors for anomalous traffic patterns and that can isolate compromised nodes [67].
- **Regulatory compliance:** ISO/SAE 21434 and UN R155 require Cybersecurity Management Systems throughout the vehicle lifecycle [68, 69].

Zonal architectures can help security through centralized oversight, but also concentrate risk—a "defense in depth" approach with multiple overlapping layers is essential.

Key Point For comprehensive coverage of cybersecurity architecture, threat modeling, penetration testing, and ISO 21434/UN R155 compliance strategies, see **Chapter 9**.

2.6.3 Updatability

One of the driving forces of SDV (software-defined vehicle) is the ability to update and upgrade the car's software after production [38]. We have moved from a world where maybe a dealer would apply an update once in a recall to now vehicles receiving over-the-air (OTA) updates multiple times a year or even monthly. Designing the architecture for safe, efficient, and reliable updates is critical.

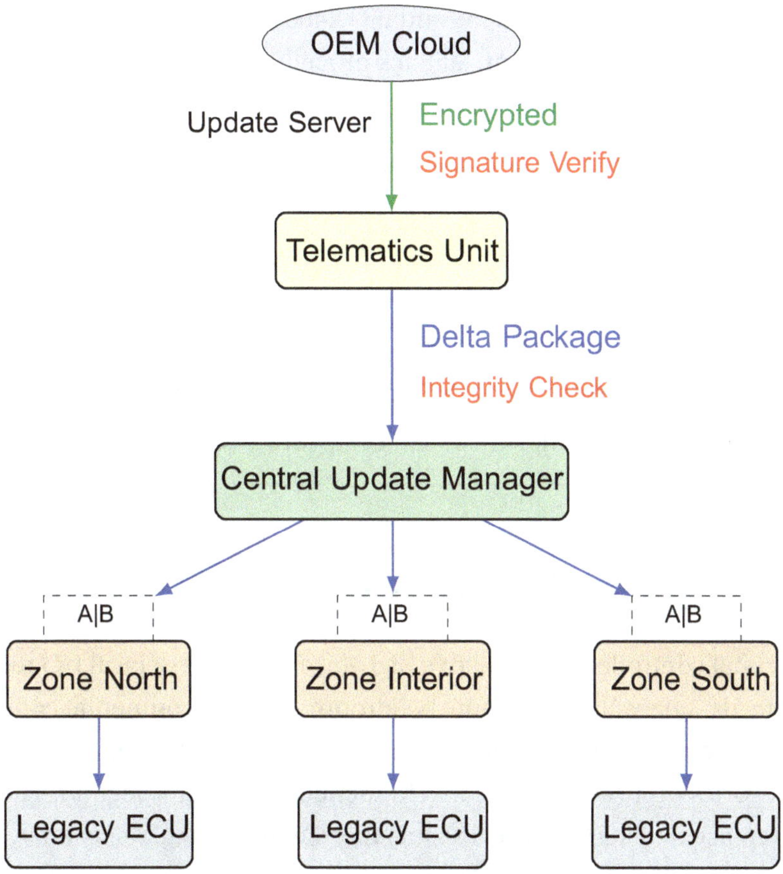

Figure 2-8. *OTA update architecture in zonal/central design*

Key Updatability Aspects

Modern OTA systems address several challenges:

- **Efficient updates:** Delta compression transmits only differences, reducing download size by 70–90%.
- **Atomicity and rollback:** A/B partition schemes enable safe recovery from failed updates; power loss during update must not brick devices [70, 71].
- **Update orchestration:** A central OTA manager coordinates multi-ECU updates with dependency management; zonal controllers can act as distribution hubs for their region.

- **SUMS compliance:** UN R156 and ISO 24089 require documented processes, risk assessment, fallback procedures, and evidence generation [72, 73].

Centralized E/E architectures simplify OTA—there are fewer boxes to update, and a central unit acts as the single point of distribution. However, robust rollback and fail-safes are essential since failure in an integrated system has wider impact.

Key Point For comprehensive coverage of OTA architecture patterns, delta mechanisms, rollback strategies, update orchestration, campaign management, and UN R156/ISO 24089 compliance, see **Chapters 7** and **11**.

2.7 Sizing Zonal Controllers

Designing a zonal controller begins with a high-level estimate of local I/O requirements, networking needs, safety class, compute headroom, and environmental constraints. The examples in this section are intentionally simplified and are included only to illustrate the main categories of considerations that influence controller selection. They are not intended to replace detailed electrical sizing, thermal modeling, safety analysis, or implementation-level design studies.

2.7.1 Compute and/or I/O Budgeting

A zonal controller can be thought of as a mini central for its area. To size it, an engineer lists all the endpoints in that zone:

- **Number of sensors** (digital inputs, analog inputs, camera links, radar links, etc.): For each, consider what interface it needs (GPIO, ADC, SPI, Ethernet, CAN, LIN, PSI5, etc.) and how many of each type.
- **Number of actuators or outputs** (PWM outputs for motors/valves, digital outputs for lamps or relays, etc.).
- **Network interfaces needed:** Typically at least one Ethernet port (often 100 Mb [74] or 1 Gb [75]; maybe two for redundancy or ring topology), plus possibly a few CAN FD controllers to talk to legacy devices in its zone and LIN controllers if needed for local LIN sub-buses (doors, seats, etc.).

For example, a door zone might need four LIN masters (one for each door's window/lock cluster). Some zones may also use 10BASE-T1S [76, 77] for lower-speed sensor networks.

- **Internal resources:** How much CPU performance to handle worst-case load? If the zone controller must, for instance, read 50 sensors at 1 kHz and execute a control algorithm for some (like suspension dampers control loop) and pack messages to send to central, we calculate the needed MIPS. We also consider that it might host some AUTOSAR applications or diagnostics [78, 79] tasks concurrently.
- **Safety margin:** We usually add some headroom (such as the zone CPU should not exceed ~70% usage in the worst case, leaving margin for future OTA updates that add functionality).

Inventory Approach

A concrete approach is to create an inventory listing each function assigned to the zone:

Item	Front Radar Sensor
Interface	Ethernet 100 Mb (BroadR-Reach)
Data rate	20 Mbps; forward raw point cloud to central at 10 Hz
Processing	Minimal in zone (just routing)
Safety	ASIL-B (robust data path required)

Item	Left Headlight
Interface	PWM driver or CAN
Data rate	Local control for adaptive lighting at 200 Hz
Processing	Zone must run headlight leveling algorithm
Safety	ASIL-B (algorithm needs reliability)

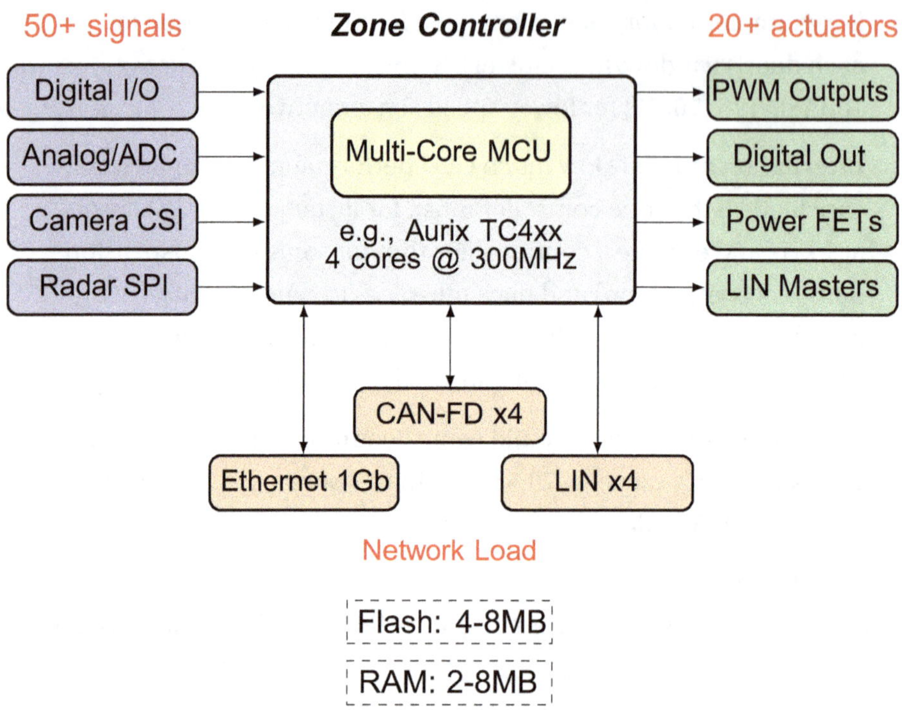

Figure 2-9. *Zone controller sizing considerations*

Hardware Selection

Often, zonal controllers use automotive microcontrollers or SoCs with multiple cores, some lockstep for safety, and some normal for generic tasks.

For example, the Renesas RH850/U2A/U2B series [80–82] or Infineon AURIX TC4xx series [83] are targeted at zone control: they offer several cores at a few hundred MHz, possibly split into lockstep pairs, with plenty of CAN/LIN interfaces and some Ethernet MACs.

For higher-end zones (like those handling cameras), a more powerful SoC (e.g., an NXP S32Z [84] or S32G [85] with 1 GHz+ Cortex cores) might be used to have on-chip acceleration or more RAM for buffering sensor data.

Memory budgeting: The zone needs enough flash to hold its software (and an update slot) and enough RAM for runtime (including buffers for Ethernet frames and so on). If it is running AUTOSAR Adaptive, memory requirements go up (tens of Mb). If only Classic, perhaps a few Mb suffice. But with consolidation, zone controllers tend to be beefier than old single-function ECUs, so maybe you look at something with, e.g., 8 Mb RAM and 4 Mb flash as a baseline, scaling up as needed.

Future-Proofing

We also consider **future expansion:** maybe today that zone has no LiDAR, but in a year a higher trim will add one—better to include an extra Ethernet port or spare high-speed interface now than to redesign later. This is where a lot of negotiation happens: over-provisioning vs. cost. OEMs might choose a more capable chip to be future-proof.

Headroom for OTA-era features: Because software can now change, we anticipate zones might get new tasks over time. So leaving CPU headroom (and even API hooks or spare I/O) is wise.

For example, an OEM might ship a car with basic Level 2 ADAS and two years later push an update enabling something more advanced that requires more local sensor fusion in zones—if the hardware cannot handle it, you are stuck. Tesla notably included a lot of spare compute in their Autopilot hardware for future self-driving upgrades. Traditional OEMs historically trimmed hardware to just meet current spec (to save cost), but the mindset is shifting to put a bit extra in anticipation of OTA upgrades.

2.7.2 Thermal/Power

With greater processing and networking in zone controllers, power consumption and heat dissipation must be managed carefully.

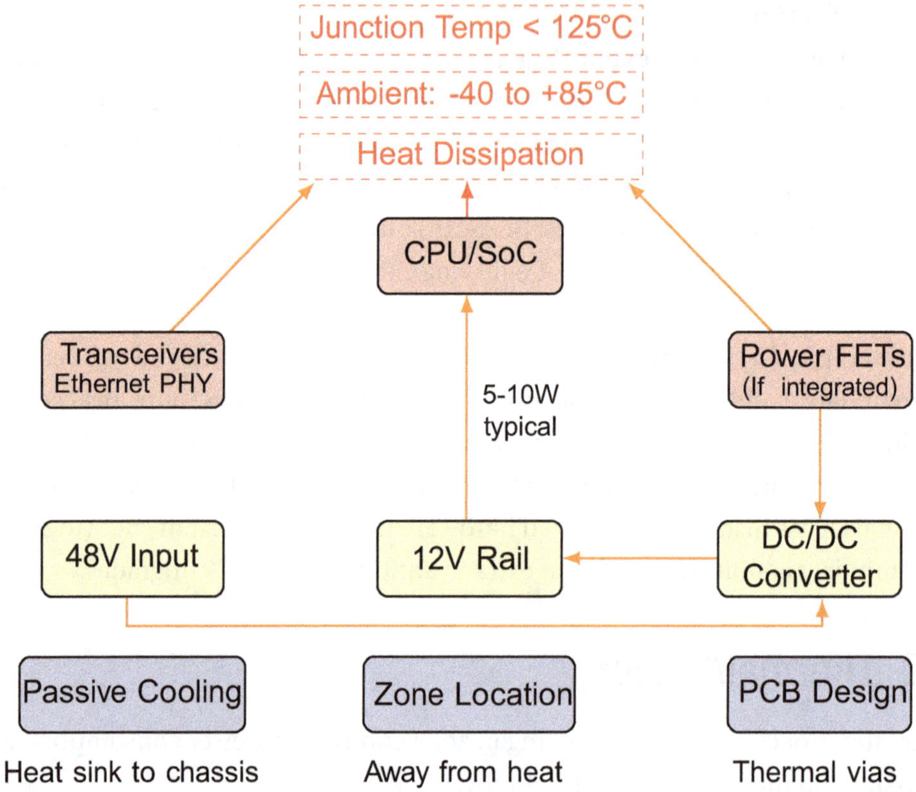

***Figure 2-10.** Thermal and power design considerations for zone controllers*

Power Budgeting

The worst-case power draw of the zone ECU must be estimated, and the vehicle power system must be sized to support it. In aggregate, zone controllers might draw more than old distributed ECUs because each now does more work and has high-speed transceivers.

If each zone controller consumes, say, 10 W, and you have five of them, that is 50 W, which might be fine. But if some zones double as power distribution units (with smart FETs for loads), they might handle tens of amps for motors/lights in their area—that has to be fed via sufficiently sized power wiring and local DC-DC conversion.

For example, a zone controller might be directly on 48 V [48, 49] and then internally convert to 12 V or 5 V for sensors; its power design must handle peak currents (like window motor stall current). The architecture team ensures that power and ground wiring to zones is adequate and perhaps redundant (some vehicles have dual 12 V feeds to critical modules for reliability).

Thermal Management

Zone controllers can reside in places such as the engine bay or pillar, where the ambient temperature can be high (85 °C or more in the summer sun in a pillar or very cold in winter). If the controller is doing a lot (multiple 400 MHz cores at high utilization, plus transceivers), it can generate heat.

Usually, these controllers are passively cooled (no fans in a car's body electronics typically), relying on the casing and maybe vehicle metal for heat sinking. We must check that at the worst case (e.g., 50 °C ambient, sun load), the chip junction stays in allowed range. This might limit how hard we drive the CPU or require thermal throttling strategies.

If a zone controller is also routing significant current (like for motors), the MOSFETs for that can heat it up too. So design might separate the power switching from the sensitive CPU (or ensure the board can dissipate it).

A strategy to reduce thermal issues is to use **48 V for high-power zones** (such as front zones that power the headlights, fans, etc.) [49, 50]. As noted in the MobilityTech article, the move to 48 V greatly reduces currents and heat losses on the wires. But each zone would then need a DC/DC converter to supply legacy 12 V components in that zone. That DC/DC itself generates heat. Often, it is efficient (such as 95%), but if a zone supplies 500 W of loads, 5% loss is 25 W heat to deal with. Some OEMs centralize the conversion to 48–12 V or have a couple of converters instead of one per zone to optimize cost and cooling (there is an ongoing debate on this).

Given that EVs and high-end cars have more electronics, it is not uncommon to see **liquid cooling or active cooling** for central computers (Tesla's Full Self-Driving (FSD) computer is liquid cooled). Zonal controllers, being more distributed and lower power, ideally remain passively cooled—but if one were in an exceptionally hot spot, maybe it would mount to a cooled chassis part.

Peak vs. Average Loads

We also consider **peak loads vs. average**. A zone may normally use 5 W, but during a certain event (say, seat heaters on, mirror adjusting, window rolling, all at once), it might spike to 50 W for a short time. The design should handle that without blowing fuses (hence, electronic fuses often with slow blow characteristics can allow short surges).

Another dimension is **EMC (Electromagnetic Compatibility)**. Higher-speed electronics and switching (Ethernet PHYs and microprocessors) can emit more electromagnetic noise. So zones need proper shielding or to be placed such that they do not interfere with radio antennas and others. In addition, more distributed power electronics (smart fuses in zones) can generate switching noise. This is not power/thermal per se but related in design considerations.

Vehicle Voltage Architecture

Finally, **vehicle voltage architecture:** Many new vehicles use dual voltage (48 V and 12 V) or even more (the main traction battery at 400 V or 800 V for EV drive, plus 48, plus 12). Zone controllers could integrate DC/DC converters to tap the high voltage and produce 48 or 12 locally. Or they might get 48 and 12 supplied.

If each zone has a DC/DC from the EV battery, that's a distributed conversion, which can reduce heavy 12 V cabling runs. But it adds cost and complexity at each zone. Some are doing it because it also localizes the effect of a failure (one zone's DC/DC failure only kills that zone's 12 V, not the whole car).

In terms of sizing, we ensure the zone's power electronics (voltage regulators and others) are rated above the max current of loads plus some margin. For example, if the rear zone has two fuel pumps at 15 A each, the zone's 12 V supply must handle 30 A plus any other minor loads, maybe design for 40 A to be safe, and ensure the thermal can dissipate that at duty cycle. At high currents, one considers using the car's body/chassis as a heat spreader or a heat sink.

In an **48 V zone example** [48–50] (like an EV's front zone powering the compressor, coolant pump, etc.), the zone might just pass 48 V through to those loads (with local fusing), rather than convert to 12 V and then up again at the load. But actuators for steering and so on might remain 12 V in many cases, though trends show e-turbos and others using 48 V.

Checklist Summary

To recap, for each zone we do: list loads with currents, list compute tasks with cycles, ensure hardware meets some of those with margins, check environment constraints (temperature), and verify fail-safe behavior (if overheated, does it shut down noncritical functions first? If undervoltage, does it reset gracefully?).

One more note: **Brown-out tolerance** [71, 86]—zone controllers might be expected to survive initiation (when the battery voltage dips to ~6–7 V for a moment). They should at least be reset safely or have hold-up capacitors. In addition, they may need to operate down to –30°C, where batteries are weak, so proper design of the power regulators is needed.

All of this goes into a zone sizing document. The result might be, e.g., choosing Infineon AURIX TC397 [83] for zone *X* due to the needed CAN interfaces and lockstep core, but choosing NXP i.MX [84, 85] for an infotainment-heavy zone that requires more multimedia.

2.8 Migration Patterns

Most car manufacturers cannot jump directly from dozens of legacy ECUs to a full zonal central architecture in one step, especially for vehicles already in production or in development. Thus, they adopt migration strategies that gradually evolve the E/E architecture. We'll consider two general patterns.

2.8.1 Brownfield (Legacy ➤ Zonal)

Definition : **Brownfield** refers to an existing platform (or any design that has legacy constraints) transitioning incrementally to the new architecture [36, 37]. The goal is to reap some benefits of zonal/centralized architecture without completely redesigning everything at once, thereby reducing risk and capitalizing on proven components.

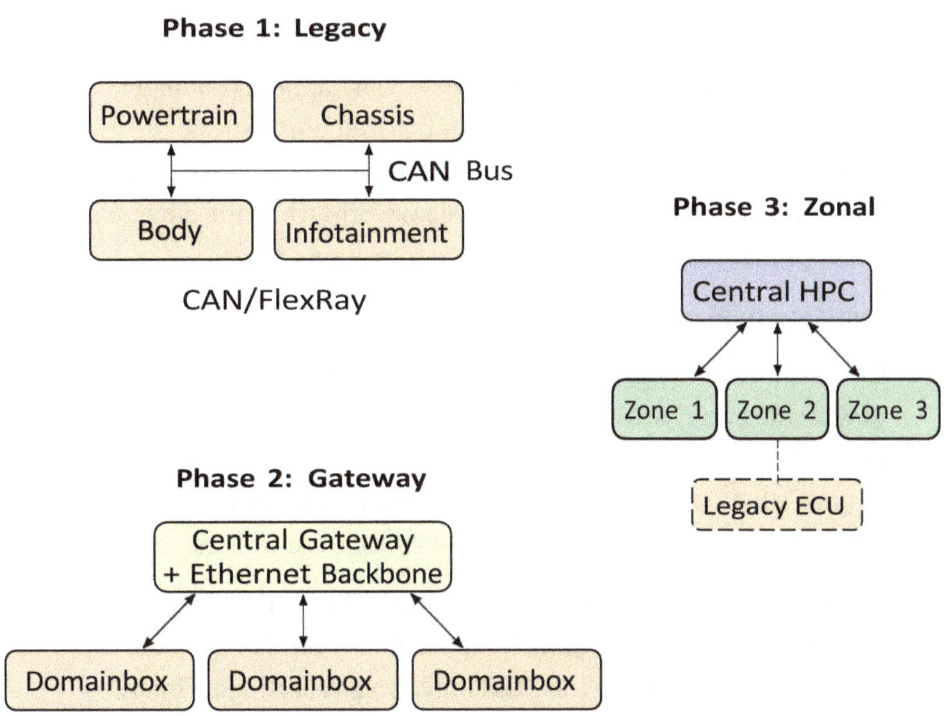

Figure 2-11. *Phased brownfield migration from domain to zonal architecture*

A typical brownfield migration might involve phased introduction of elements:

1. **Gateway integration phase:**

   Introduce a central gateway or domain consolidator that links the multiple CAN/FlexRay networks and maybe adds an Ethernet backbone [11]. For instance, the first step could be adding an Ethernet gateway ECU that connects all domain controllers. This by itself can enable faster data logging, OTA update distribution, and maybe some new features that use data from multiple domains.

2. **Zonal aggregators as add-ons:**

   Instead of a full zonal architecture, an OEM might start by adding "smart junction boxes" in zones [38]. For example, replace the traditional fuse box in the front with a smarter zonal module that aggregates some sensors in that area. But it might still output to the old domain ECUs to maintain functionality. Essentially it acts as a translator or concentrator.

   During this stage, **mirroring of services** can happen: you might have a new zone ECU running a copy of a function also still running in the old ECU, for testing and redundancy. This is like a shadow mode to prove the new system works while the old one still is primary (common in aerospace transitions as well).

3. **Function relocation and cut-over:**

   Once a particular domain's functions have been validated on the new architecture, you can remove the old ECU or turn it into a simpler I/O device. For example, suppose you have a body control module (BCM) that handles door locks, lights, and wipers. In a zonal concept, those are now handled by zone controllers.

   In migration, you might initially keep the BCM but feed it from zone controllers. Then gradually shift actual control logic to the zone controllers and use the BCM only as a passthrough. Finally, eliminate the separate BCM and let the zones and maybe central HPC fully handle body functions.

Managing Legacy Protocols and Messages

An important aspect of brownfield is dealing with **legacy protocols and messages**. New architecture often means moving to Ethernet and new software, but you can't change everything at once. So gateways are set up to do signal translation: converting old CAN messages to new service-oriented messages or vice versa [57, 58].

Key Point **Signal-to-Service Translation** allows a new HPC to request data that's originally on a CAN bus by asking a gateway, which then fetches it and returns it as a service, and similarly to send commands. Juggling these translations is complex but manageable with a well-planned gateway strategy (often the gateway knows the CAN database and can populate values into service fields).

Brownfield migrations also need careful **safety and reliability management**. You wouldn't immediately trust a new central computer to steer the car if the old power steering ECU is there. Instead, you might have the new computer issue a steering request in parallel with the driver input and so on and compare outcomes. Only once it's validated (and maybe gets regulatory approval) do you enable it fully.

Hybrid Architecture Considerations

During the interim, the vehicle is a **hybrid architecture**: part domain, part zonal [45]. This spreads out risk and development effort, though full wiring reduction isn't achieved until legacy ECUs are removed. Key challenges include ensuring backward compatibility (abstraction layers let older ECUs see expected interfaces) and increased testing cost during transition.

2.8.2 Greenfield (New EV Platform)

Definition **Greenfield** means starting from scratch (or nearly so) with no legacy constraints [41]. This is often the case for a brand-new EV platform or a new company's vehicle, where they have a clean sheet to implement a zonal, central architecture from day one. The advantage here is you can design everything holistically for the new approach; the challenge is you must get it right with less real-world iteration.

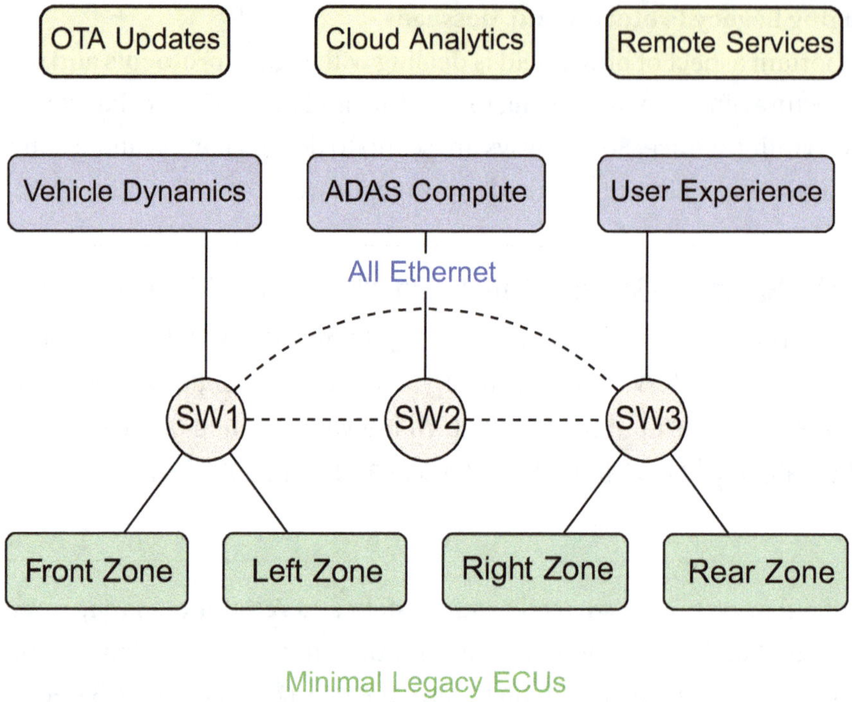

Figure 2-12. *Greenfield architecture: starting fresh with centralized design*

Greenfield Design Principles

In a greenfield scenario, one would typically

- **Adopt central compute from day 0:**

  For example, decide that you will have three central computers—one for autonomous driving, one for vehicle dynamics, and one for user experience—and minimal other ECUs. The entire network from the get-go is Ethernet-centric with zone controllers for I/O [38]. This is what many startups did—e.g., Byton (defunct now, but had announced a three-computer + zone architecture) or modern Chinese EV startups.

- **Simplify and dedicate safety islands:**

  Knowing that you don't have to accommodate old ECUs, you can plan redundancy in a clean way [61]. For instance, include two independent motor controllers for drive-by-wire right away, or design a power architecture with dual-battery feeds to each critical controller out of the box. Safety is designed in, not patched on.

- **Decide up front on middleware and OS:**

  A new platform can choose, say, "We use Linux with Adaptive AUTOSAR and DDS for all software components" [56, 57]. There's no need to support older AUTOSAR Classic (unless reusing components). This can greatly accelerate development if you have the talent for modern software. Tesla did similar—they avoided AUTOSAR entirely and developed in-house software on Linux and other OSs, which gave them agility (but also meant inventing a lot from scratch).

- **Adopt a service-oriented architecture:**

  You can structure all software as services from the beginning [53, 55], which aligns well with the zonal approach. This means defining clear interfaces and networks of communication (like a tech company might), rather than the older signal-based approach.

- **Fully integrate OTA and data collection:**

  New platforms often build in robust telemetry and update capabilities from scratch—no bolt-on modules needed [70, 73]. For example, an EV startup might design that every ECU can update via a central server, and every drive logs data to the cloud. This can inform continuous improvement.

Example One is Rivian's R1 platform [42, 43, 47]. It was mentioned that Gen2 E/E had only four ECUs beyond the three zone controllers—likely those four include the central computer(s) and maybe a couple of specialized units. That's a radical reduction achieved by designing fresh. Another is Lucid Motors's EV, which uses Ethernet and has a central computing module and then satellites for lights and others.

Greenfield Networking and Compute Strategy

Greenfield designs often use **high-speed networking extensively** [74-77]—possibly multi-gig Ethernet, CAN mainly for backup or low-speed nodes. They may incorporate unique ideas like putting compute close to sensors (some put AI chips right with cameras, though that's more a distributed approach).

However, going greenfield doesn't mean ignoring all legacy—they still have to interface with standard components (like maybe a bought-in ABS unit or airbag system that is a black box from a supplier using CAN). But a new player can push even suppliers to provide more modern interfaces or integrate them differently.

Mixed-Criticality Policy

In a fresh design, one might from the start decide a separation strategy [22, 60, 87]. For example, "All ASIL-D controls run on a QNX-based safety partition on the central computer, whereas infotainment runs on Android on a separate chip"—that's an architectural safety policy. With no legacy ECU boundaries, you enforce these through software and hardware partitioning. This was likely done by newer EV makers to satisfy safety in a one-box solution.

Supplier Ecosystem Considerations

One more point is **supplier ecosystem**: A greenfield OEM might have to work closely with suppliers to develop such architecture because not all Tier-1s were ready to supply a "zone controller" off the shelf until recently. We see collaborations (e.g., VW partnering with Bosch and others for software, GM working with NXP for their new VIP architecture hardware, etc.) [84, 85]. They sometimes source chips and develop a lot in-house.

Key Point From a learning perspective, the greenfield approach highlights the end goal—a fully software-defined vehicle where the distinction between ECUs is abstract; it's more about software deployment. It's akin to moving from physical servers to cloud computing in enterprise—now you have a few big "servers" in the car, and everything else is software on them.

2.9 Worked Example: Mapping Functions

Let's apply these concepts to a simple hypothetical example of mapping vehicle functions to a zonal + central architecture.

2.9.1 Scenario Setup

Scenario: We have three zones (front of car "Zone North," rear "Zone South," plus maybe an interior/cabin zone) and one central HPC. We have a set of legacy functions (around 20 as per lab, but we'll outline a few key ones), and we want to allocate them.

Suppose our vehicle functions include

- Front lighting (headlamps, turn signals)
- Rear lighting (tail lamps, brake lights)
- ABS (wheel speed sensors and brake actuators)
- Battery management system (BMS) for an EV battery (sensors in rear)
- Radar sensor at the front for adaptive cruise
- Rear camera for backup view
- Infotainment/navigation application
- Autopilot/path planning software (for ADAS)
- Instrument cluster display (in front of the driver)
- Climate control actuators (mix of front zone—blower motor—and maybe rear zone actuators)

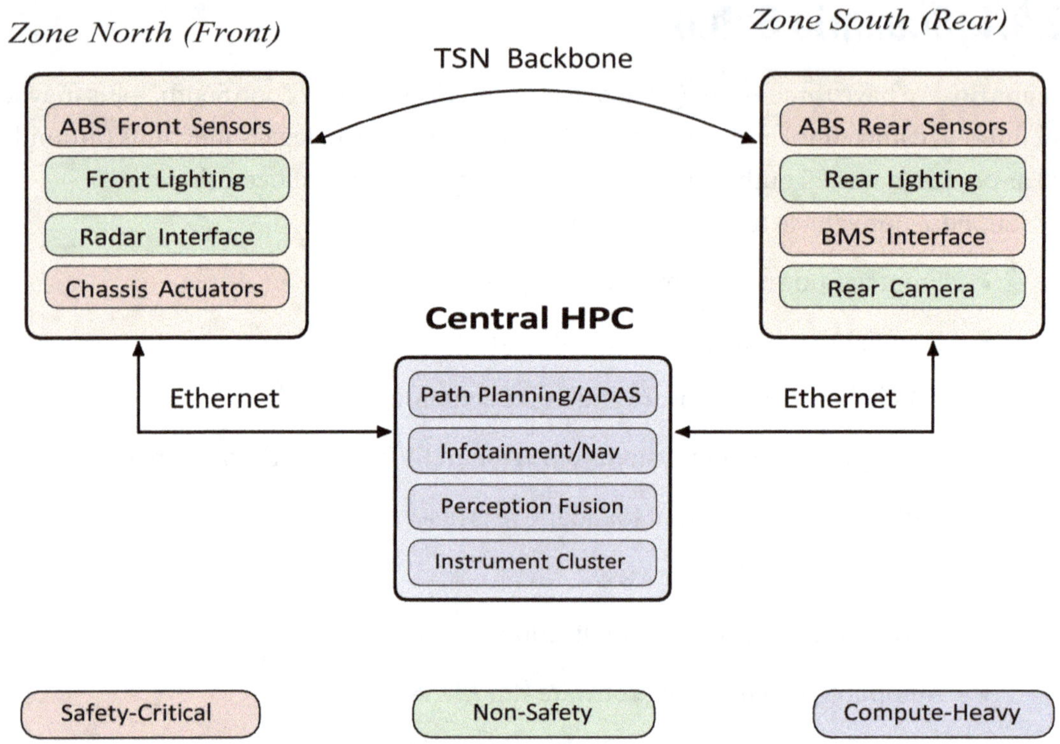

Figure 2-13. *Function allocation to zones and central HPC*

2.9.2 Function Mapping Strategy

Now, how to map.

Zone North (Front)

It's physically in the front, so it will handle front lighting (the headlights and front turn signals wiring all go to the front zone controller) [40]. It will handle ABS sensors for front wheels (since those sensors are located in the front wheels) and likely the front radar (since that radar is mounted in the front bumper and can connect to the front zone via a short Ethernet or SPI link).

So Zone North needs the I/O for those: outputs to headlight modules (maybe via LIN or direct PWM), inputs from wheel speed sensors (digital or maybe via a local CAN from an ABS pump), an Ethernet interface to the radar or CSI interface, etc. Zone North might also handle front chassis actuators like adaptive suspension if present. Essentially, anything at the front half of the car plugs in here.

Technical Detail For critical systems like ABS, the Zone North typically forwards wheel speed data to a dedicated ASIL-D brake/ESP controller rather than hosting the ABS logic itself. Only non-time-critical supervisory logic or monitoring may be co-located in a zone controller. Even in modern zonal architectures, ABS/ESC remains a standalone safety ECU or runs on a dedicated ASIL-D microcontroller with strict independence; integrating full ABS control into a zonal controller is not common in production programs.

Zone South (Rear)

Similarly, it will handle rear lighting (tail lamps, brake lamps), rear wheel speed sensors (for ABS/ESP), and the BMS interfaces because the battery pack is usually under the floor or rear, so temperature/voltage sensors from battery, contactors control, etc. would logically route to a controller near the battery.

BMS is typically implemented as a dedicated ASIL-C battery management unit (BMU), with cell supervision circuits at ASIL-B/QM depending on architecture. Because of stringent safety, thermal, and cell monitoring requirements—and supplier compliance constraints—production vehicles almost always retain a dedicated BMS ECU rather than integrating BMS logic into a zonal controller. While some research architectures explore co-housing supervisory BMS functions with rear zonal controllers, this is not common in series production. No known OEM production program has merged BMS control with zonal controllers due to ISO 26262 independence requirements and supplier homologation constraints.

Zone South also typically handles the rear camera feed (via SerDes from a trunk-mounted camera), rear radar or ultrasonics (if present), and rear HVAC actuators for vehicles with independent rear climate systems.

So Zone South's workload: Manage battery (monitor cells and others), control rear motors (if this is a dual-motor EV, perhaps rear inverter control loops could be here—or in central?), and general rear body functions like trunk lock, rear wiper, etc.

Central HPC

This will host heavy software services. For example, the route planning and infotainment algorithms (navigation map, voice assistant) clearly go central. Perception fusion and path planning for ADAS/autonomy—those take the radar data (from Zone North), camera feed (from Zone South for the rear camera and maybe from the front if a front camera exists), etc. and run on central because they might require an AI chip or at least a powerful CPU [46].

The infotainment head unit (what you see on the touchscreen) is also in central, possibly as a separate VM or process. The instrument cluster might either be another display driven by central or a semi-smart display—many modern clusters are computer-driven, so likely the central HPC is rendering cluster graphics too.

Key Point Essentially, any function that either needs data from multiple zones or requires significant processing ends up in central.

2.9.3 Edge vs. Central Trade-Offs

Trade Check: Where Should Functions Live?

Notice ABS could have been fully central (read all four wheel speeds and modulate brakes from central). But typically braking is so time-sensitive (milliseconds) that many would prefer it be edge (like a local zone takes care of ABS autonomously to ensure rapid response even if network is congested) [51, 52].

The central might send a desired brake force, but the zone ensures no wheel lock by local control. This is a decomposed function: central does high-level brake demand (like from adaptive cruise or stability control combining data), and zone executes low-level ABS loop.

Example **Adaptive front lighting** might use central to decide headlamp beam leveling based on speed/steering (global data), but the zone actually actuates the motors and ensures they don't overshoot and so on with a local control loop.

2.9.4 Detailed Mapping Summary

We can draft a mapping list like given:

Zone North (front):

- Handles front lighting (headlights, turn indicators)
- Front ABS sensors and maybe brake actuators

- Front radar sensor processing (or forwarding raw data to central)
- Possibly a front camera if it existed
- Some chassis actuators (active suspension) [80, 81]

This zone will likely host some safety-critical software (ABS control) and some best-effort (lighting control, which is not time-critical). It communicates with central via Ethernet, sending up sensor data (radar objects, wheel speeds) and receiving commands (e.g., central says "apply X% braking to front left"). It may have its own CAN sub-network for, say, connecting to the brake actuator module or headlamp modules, which it then abstracts to the Ethernet world.

Zone South (rear):

- Handles rear lights, rear ABS
- Battery management
- Might interface with the electric drive (if the rear motor/inverter is physically close)
- Sends battery status to central
- Receives torque commands for the motor
- Rear camera feed goes to central HPC (likely directly as video)
- Possibly manages the fuel system if it were an ICE (fuel pump and others, usually at rear)

Central HPC:

- Runs route planning (which might use cloud data, heavy compute)
- Perception fusion (combining front radar, camera, and other available sensors to identify vehicles—heavy compute)

- User interface logic (which takes input from various sensors, like climate knobs maybe read by zones, and decides what to display or do)
- Runs the supervisory control for advanced driver assist (taking inputs from all zones and issuing vehicle motion commands)
- Handles telematics (sending data to cloud, receiving OTA updates) [63, 72]

In some designs, telematics is separate for security, but let's assume central covers it.

2.9.5 System Integration Example

This example also highlights interplay: For example, radar data flows from Zone North to the central HPC; HPC's ADAS algorithm decides to brake for an obstacle; HPC sends a brake request to both Zones North and South (for front and rear brakes); the zones then actuate brakes and possibly engage ABS if slip is detected locally. Meanwhile, HPC might also flash a warning on the dashboard (instrument cluster)—since HPC runs the cluster, it does that directly.

Architecture Reasoning: Why not do everything centrally? Because in a braking scenario, if the network or HPC is slow for 50 ms, ABS can intervene faster at zone. This is that edge vs. central balance.

Why not do everything at edge? Because an automated emergency brake decision should be based on fused info (radar + camera + maybe LiDAR), which no single zone has in isolation. So central is needed to make the decision to brake.

Thus, the architecture splits responsibilities in a cooperative way.

2.10 Design Checklist

When designing or evaluating a modern E/E architecture, engineers should verify the following:

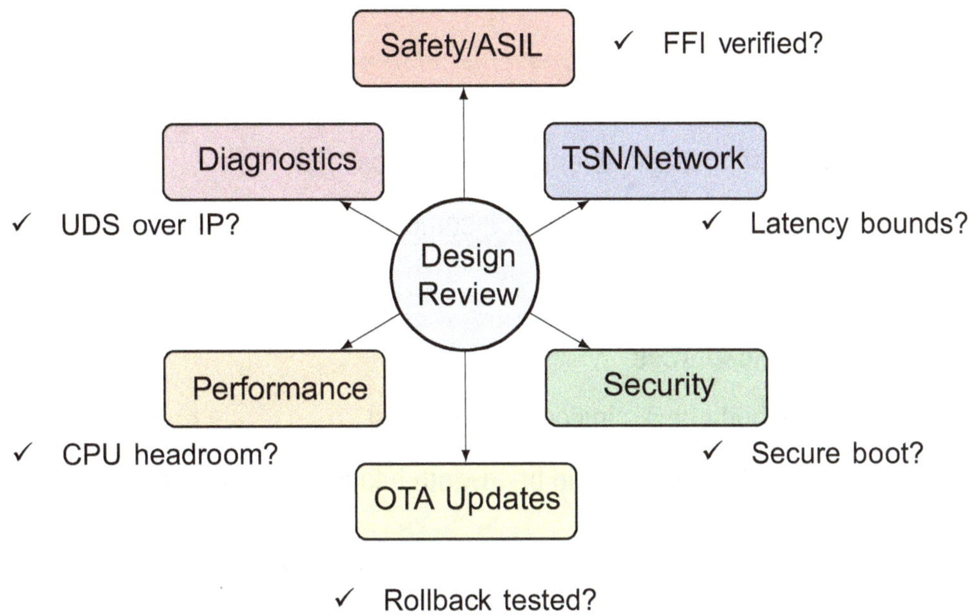

Figure 2-14. *E/E architecture design checklist categories*

Safety and ASIL Compliance

- All safety-critical functions assigned appropriate ASIL levels with FFI between mixed-criticality components [59, 60]
- Redundant paths for steer-by-wire or brake-by-wire [61]

TSN Network Validation

- Time-sensitive schedules configured and tested for worst-case load [88, 89]
- Switch configurations locked down against unauthorized high-priority traffic

Security

- All controllers employ secure boot [64, 68]
- Intrusion detection and network authentication (SecOC or equivalent) [65, 67]

OTA Robustness

- Fail-safe with rollback, tolerant to power loss [70, 73]
- Updates cryptographically signed; sufficient storage for A/B slots [63]

Performance and Resources

- No latency bottlenecks in control loops [58]
- Sufficient CPU, memory, and bandwidth headroom for future enhancements

Compliance and Diagnostics

- Evidence recorded for ISO 26262 [59], ISO 21434 [68], UN R155 [69], and UN R156 [72]
- Standardized diagnostic paths (UDS over IP) [78, 79, 90]
- Legacy gateways handle message translations with fail-safe behaviors
- Time sync (IEEE 802.1AS) verified across all nodes [91]

2.11 Key Takeaways

- **Architecture evolution and SDV foundation:** Modern vehicles are shifting from domain-based designs to zonal architectures and onward to centralized compute. These choices form the foundation of a software-defined vehicle (SDV), and decisions across topology, compute placement, and middleware determine how well a vehicle can evolve via software over its lifetime [11, 36, 38].

- **Zonal architecture benefits (physical simplification):** Moving from dozens of domain ECUs to a zonal structure localizes connections and can drastically reduce wiring harness length and weight (often 20–30% less mass) [40, 43, 44]. This simplifies the physical network, lowers cost, and improves manufacturability—but increases the burden on the network to remain deterministic for real-time control.
- **Determinism and TSN (network modernization):** Ethernet with Time-Sensitive Networking (TSN) extensions provides bounded latency and jitter akin to traditional automotive networks through time-triggered scheduling and per-stream QoS, enabling a single backbone to carry both critical and best-effort traffic [51, 52, 82, 88, 92].
- **Central compute—pros and cons (compute consolidation):** Consolidating compute in high-performance computers enables advanced features and easier updates while reducing ECU count. It also concentrates risk and requires robust partitioning to maintain safety (freedom from interference) and security when many functions share hardware [42, 46, 60, 87, 93].
- **Software abstraction and middleware choices:** The communication framework (SOME/IP vs. DDS and others) materially affects latency, scalability, certification effort, and developer ergonomics. SOME/IP (the AUTOSAR default) offers straightforward service-oriented RPC; DDS provides rich pub-sub with powerful QoS at higher complexity. Many architectures use both, sometimes bridged [53–58, 66].
- **Migration strategy (legacy ➤ zonal/central):** Most OEMs transition in phases—introducing Ethernet backbones, gateways, and zone controllers while legacy ECUs remain in place—so features and safety cases can be proven without big-bang risk [36, 37, 45].
- **Safety and security must evolve too:** Consolidation increases the blast radius of faults and attacks. Strong isolation (hypervisors/separation kernels, lockstep cores, safety islands), redundancy/fail-

operational design, secure boot, network segmentation, authenticated communications, and IDSs are essential to maintain ISO 26262 and ISO/SAE 21434/UN R155 compliance [22, 39, 59, 61, 62, 64, 68, 69, 94].

- **Updatability and compliance (SUMS):** Architectures should be OTA-first—using deltas to minimize download size and dual-bank/rollback for safety—while generating the evidence demanded by UN R156/ISO 24089-style processes [63, 70, 72].
- **Sizing zone controllers (now and later):** Right-size I/O, compute, memory, and networking per zone (with headroom for future OTA features) and engineer power/thermal budgets for mixed-criticality workloads using automotive MCUs/SoCs designed for zonal roles [80, 83, 85].

CHAPTER 3

Silicon for Software-Defined Vehicles

3.1 Chapter Goals

After this chapter, you will be able to

- **Differentiate a microcontroller, microprocessor, and system-on-chip in SDV**: Understand the hierarchy of compute units in a software-defined vehicle, from microcontrollers to microprocessors to high-performance system-on-chips (SoCs), and what roles they play.
- **Compare Arm, AURIX, RISC-V, and hybrid silicon ecosystems**: Recognize the major processor architectures and ecosystems used in automotive (Arm Cortex families, Infineon AURIX TriCore, emerging RISC-V designs, etc.) and their trade-offs.
- **Map AI/ML workloads to GPUs, NPUs, and DSPs**: Learn how different accelerator types (graphics processing units (GPUs), neural processing units (NPUs), digital signal processors (DSPs)) handle AI/ML tasks in vehicles.
- **Understand silicon-level safety and security features**: Grasp key hardware mechanisms that ensure functional safety (meeting ASIL levels) and cybersecurity in automotive chips, such as lockstep cores, safety islands, error-correcting memory, trusted execution environments, and hardware security modules (HSMs).

S. Agarwal, *Software-Defined Vehicles*, https://doi.org/10.1007/979-8-8688-2718-1_3

- **Relate silicon choices to OTA reliability and modulation resilience**: See how the choice of underlying silicon can affect over-the-air update reliability, including the ability to handle adaptive communication strategies and avoid bricking devices during updates.

Critic's Note Do not treat automotive silicon as "just hardware." Its ecosystem support, safety maturity, and update/communication capabilities often define whether an SDV program scales or collapses. Hardware specs alone (CPU speed or TOPS (Tera Operations Per Second)) are not the full story—the surrounding software and safety infrastructure are equally critical.

3.2 Introduction

The silicon powering a software-defined vehicle is far more than a commodity component—it defines what features are possible, how reliably they can operate, and whether the vehicle can evolve through software updates over its lifetime. This chapter surveys the landscape of automotive compute hardware, from simple edge microcontrollers to powerful central SoCs running AI workloads.

We begin by examining the compute hierarchy in modern vehicles: MCUs at the edge, real-time processors for safety-critical domains, and high-performance SoCs for ADAS and infotainment. We then explore the major silicon ecosystems—Arm's dominant portfolio, Infineon's safety-focused AURIX, NXP's scalable S32 platform, and offerings from NVIDIA, Qualcomm, and Renesas—before considering the emerging role of RISC-V.

The chapter also covers AI accelerators (GPUs, NPUs, DSPs, DLAs (deep learning accelerators)), the hardware mechanisms that enable functional safety and cybersecurity, and how silicon choices affect OTA update reliability. Throughout, we emphasize that ecosystem maturity, safety certification, and long-term supply considerations often outweigh raw performance specifications when selecting automotive silicon.

3.3 Classes of Compute in SDV

Modern software-defined vehicles use a hierarchy of compute classes distributed throughout the car [95].

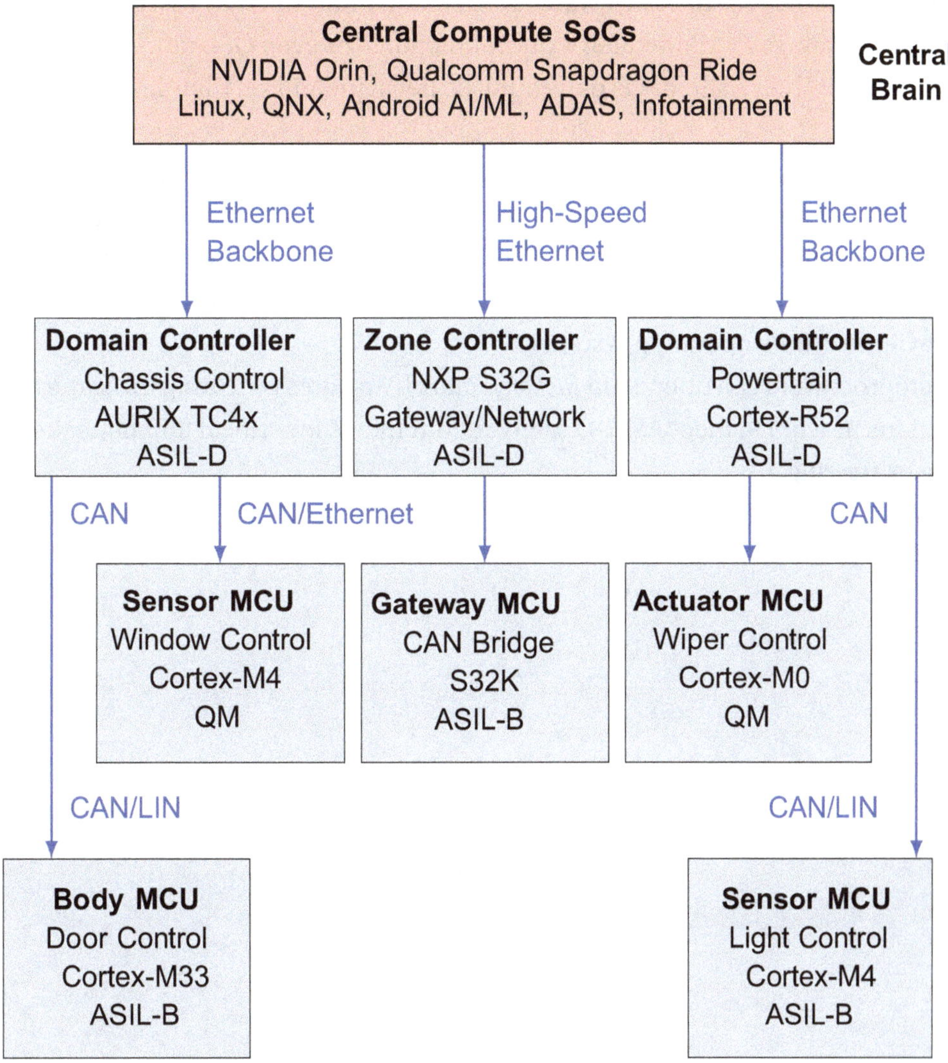

Figure 3-1. *SDV compute hierarchy showing the three-tier architecture from edge MCUs to central SoCs*

At the lowest level, numerous **microcontrollers** (MCUs) handle specific sensor/actuator tasks (e.g., window lifters, light controls, wiper motors). These 32-bit MCUs (often Arm Cortex-M based or similar) are low-power and cost-effective, interfacing directly with sensors and actuators via CAN, LIN, or other vehicle networks. They typically run simple real-time firmware for fixed functions and may carry ASIL-B or ASIL-C safety ratings for moderately critical functions (or even QM/non-ASIL for non-safety features). Their hallmark is deterministic behavior and very low latency in simple control loops.

In the middle of the hierarchy are **microprocessors** or domain controllers, which are more powerful real-time processors overseeing entire domains like chassis control, powertrain, or battery management [96]. These often use Arm Cortex-R series cores or high-end MCUs (e.g., Infineon AURIX, Texas Instruments Jacinto, Renesas RH850) and run heavier real-time operating systems.

Microprocessors can operate in *lockstep pairs* (two cores executing the same instructions in sync) to meet ASIL-D safety requirements for critical functions such as braking or steering.

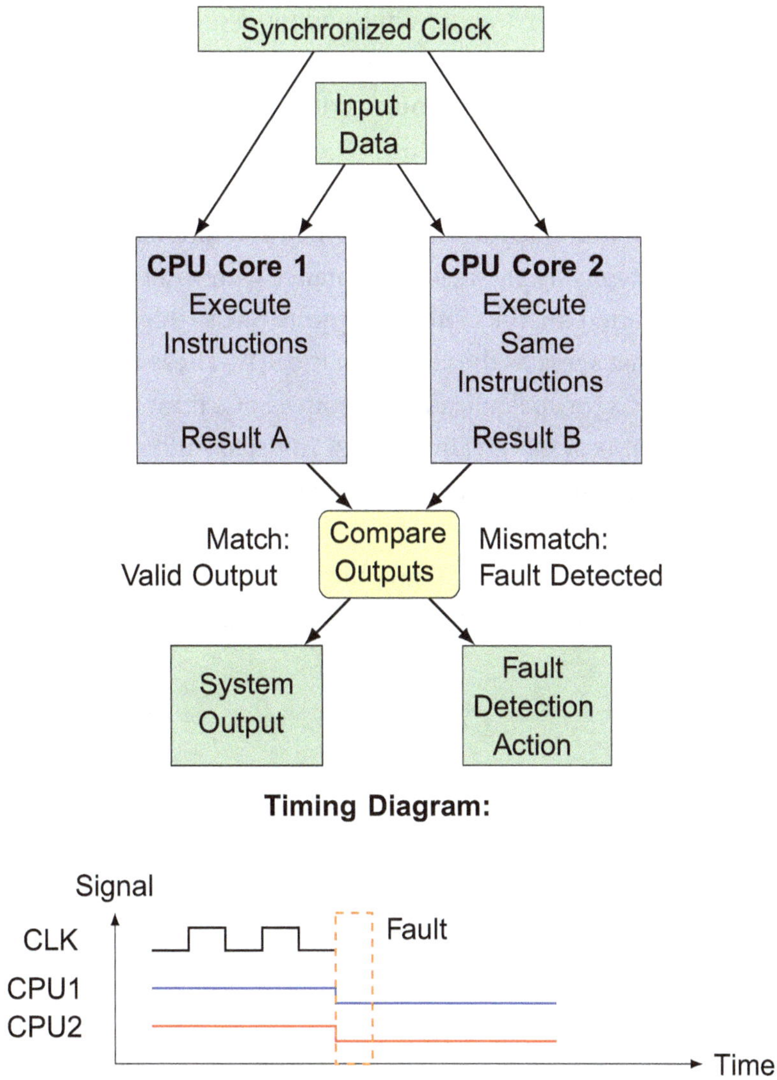

Figure 3-2. *Lockstep core architecture showing dual cores running identical instructions with comparison logic*

They tend to have faster interrupt handling and more on-chip peripherals for real-time tasks than general CPUs. The NXP S32Z/E series, e.g., features Arm Cortex-R52 cores that can run in split-lock mode for mixed criticality and also includes lockstep Cortex-M33 cores for supervisory tasks [84].

These mid-level processors often act as zone controllers or domain controllers—consolidating input from multiple MCUs in their area and interfacing upward to the central computer. They typically balance performance with strict timing guarantees.

At the top of the pyramid are the **central compute SoCs**—high-performance, multi-core processors that serve as the "brain" of the SDV. These are often multi-core Arm Cortex-A–based SoCs (or specialized automotive SoCs from NVIDIA, Qualcomm, etc.) that run rich operating systems (Linux, QNX, Android Automotive) and handle demanding workloads like ADAS perception, sensor fusion, and user infotainment [97, 98].

They integrate accelerators (GPUs for graphics/AI, NPUs, image signal processors (ISPs)) and can host virtual machines or containers for different vehicle functions.

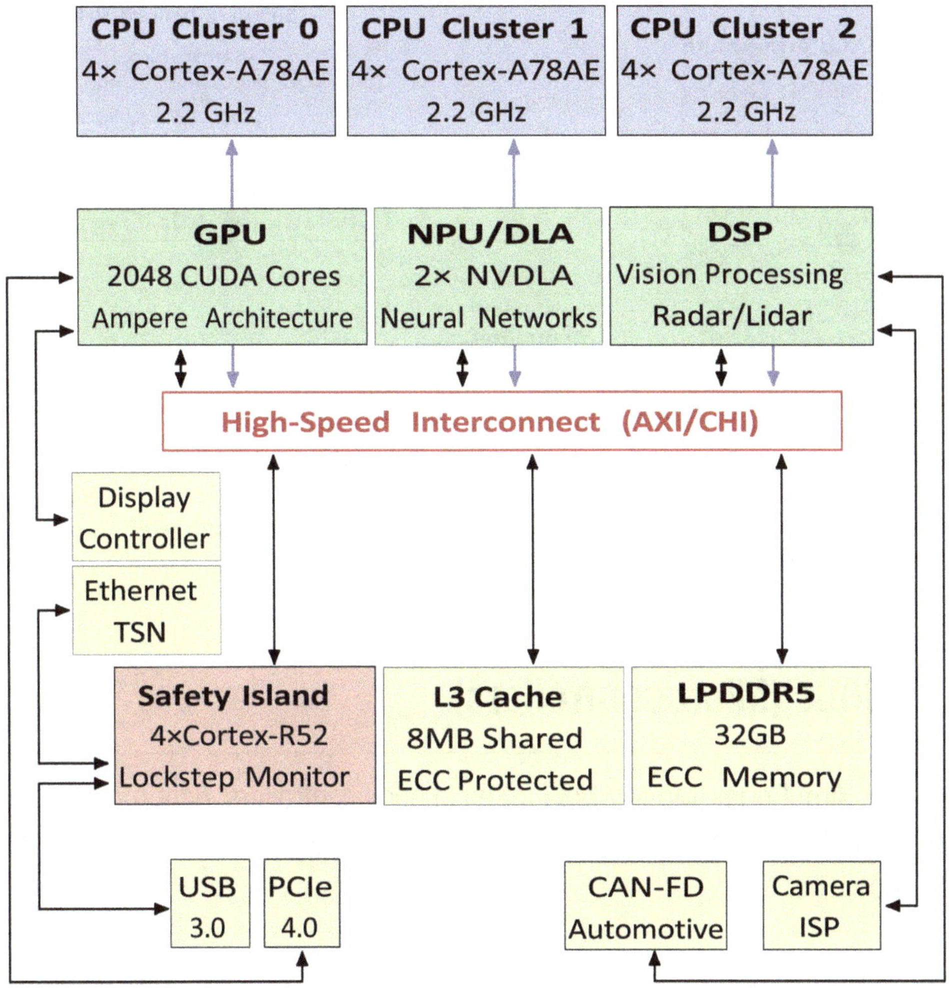

***Figure 3-3.** High-performance automotive SoC architecture showing CPU clusters, accelerators, and safety islands*

The central SoCs communicate with the rest of the vehicle over a high-speed Ethernet backbone, linking to the zonal/domain controllers, which in turn talk to edge MCUs. This SDV compute pyramid means fewer, more powerful central units orchestrating many simpler remote units.

Over time, some functionality that used to live in many separate ECUs is migrating upward—from edge MCUs into zone controllers and from zones into the central compute—as architectures consolidate for easier software updates.

Nevertheless, for fault tolerance and practical wiring considerations, a distributed hierarchy remains, with each class of compute playing distinct roles.

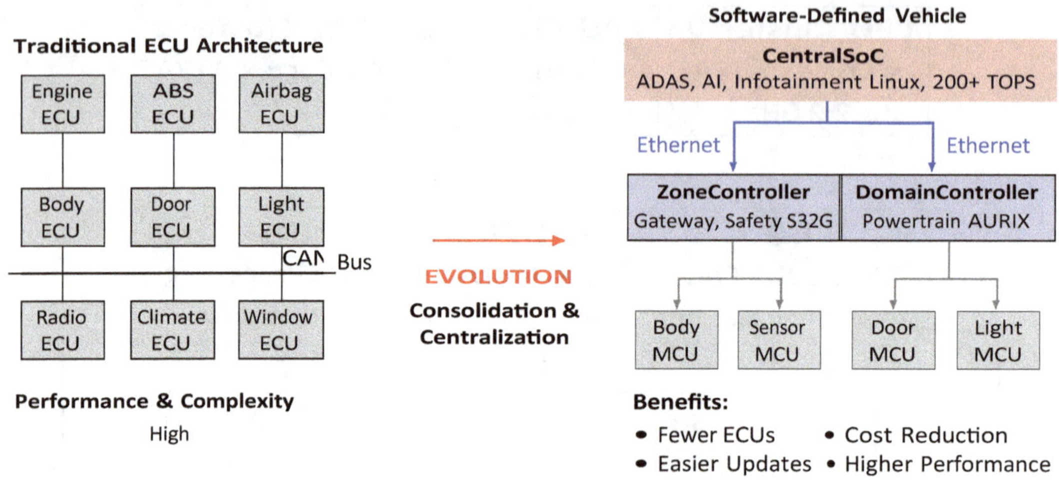

Figure 3-4. *Evolution of automotive compute architecture from distributed ECUs to centralized SDV architecture*

3.3.1 MCUs (Microcontrollers)

Example Arm Cortex-M0/M4/M33 (often in body controllers, door modules, sensor nodes) or higher-end MCUs like Infineon TriCore TC2xx for more demanding control domains.

Features: Very low power (typically in the 50–200 MHz range for body/comfort MCUs, with newer designs going higher), highly deterministic, and often include on-chip flash memory. Many are designed up to ASIL-B or ASIL-C for safety of auxiliary functions; some newer ones (like Cortex-M33-based designs) include security features like TrustZone-M for memory isolation [99, 100].

Key Point NXP S32K family MCUs (Cortex-M4/M7) managing window lifts or a gateway's CAN message routing [85] exemplify the role of MCUs at the edge of the automotive network.

3.3.2 Safety-Critical Real-Time Controllers (High-End MCUs and Control SoCs)

Example Arm Cortex-R5/R52–based controllers, Infineon AURIX TC3xx/TC4xx, and high-end Renesas RH850 variants. In automotive practice, these are better understood as high-end safety-oriented MCUs or real-time control platforms rather than as general-purpose microprocessors. They are used in domains requiring deterministic response and high safety integrity, such as braking, steering, powertrain control, battery management, airbags, and certain zonal or gateway functions [101, 102].

These devices typically run at 200-400 MHz or higher, feature dual-core or triple-core lockstep configurations for error detection, and use tightly coupled memory (TCM) for deterministic access speeds. They are designed for ASIL-D compliance and prioritize robust fault detection mechanisms including redundant monitoring units, self-checking ADCs, and hardware watchdogs.

For instance, the Infineon AURIX TC3xx has multiple TriCore CPUs, some of which run in lockstep, plus redundant internal monitoring units to achieve ASIL-D for engine or chassis domain control [103, 104]. Arm's Cortex-R52, similarly, was built for functional safety, supporting a split-lock mode where cores can either run independently or be paired in lockstep depending on the safety needs [101]. These processors typically run an RTOS like AUTOSAR Classic or bare-metal control loops.

3.3.3 SoCs (High-Performance System-on-Chips)

Example Qualcomm Snapdragon Ride, NVIDIA DRIVE Orin, NXP S32G or S32V, Tesla's FSD computer, etc., often built around Arm Cortex-A72/A78AE or newer cores (and in the future even Arm Neoverse cores) [85, 97, 98]. These are used for ADAS (advanced driver assistance systems), automated driving, central infotainment/cockpit computers, and vehicle "brain" duties.

Features: Multi-core 64-bit CPUs (often 4–16 cores), running at 1–2.5 GHz range, with large RAM and advanced accelerators (GPUs for running neural networks and rendering interfaces, NPUs/DLAs for dedicated AI inference, DSPs for radar/LiDAR processing). They support virtualization and separation of software domains.

For example, NVIDIA's Orin SoC includes 12 Cortex-A78AE cores and an Ampere GPU, achieving up to 200+ TOPS (Tera Operations Per Second) of AI performance [97, 105].

These chips often have *safety islands*—a small built-in MCU or R5 core that supervises the main processors—and hardware support for functional safety (lockstep, ECC (error- correcting code) memory, built-in self-test, etc.), but achieving ASIL-D on such complex SoCs is challenging.

Usually, only certain aspects of their operation are rated ASIL-D (e.g., a portion of the chip handling a critical function), while other parts might be ASIL-B or QM. A central ADAS SoC runs millions of lines of code (Linux, deep learning frameworks, etc.), so robust isolation and monitoring is essential.

In production, single-SoC modules like Jetson AGX Orin are configurable around 15–60 W, while multi-Orin boards used for higher-end AD/ADAS can exceed 100 W, which imposes stricter thermal design [105, 106]. Despite that, the performance per watt is unprecedented, allowing features like autonomous driving algorithms, high-definition 3D visualization, and sensor fusion that were impossible on older electronics.

> **Quote** In summary, an SDV's electronic architecture is layered: numerous simple MCUs at the edge, intermediate controllers for domains/zones, and one or a few centralized compute units. This hierarchy (sometimes called the *SDV compute pyramid*) provides both the fine-grained control needed for real-time vehicle functions and the centralized muscle needed for advanced software features.

As an order-of-magnitude guide, edge MCUs typically live in the sub-watt to ~1 W range, domain or zonal controllers in the few-watt to ~15 W range, and central ADAS/infotainment SoCs in the tens of watts (30–150 W depending on configuration and whether multiple chips are used). Exact numbers vary by vendor and SKU, but these bands are useful for thinking about thermal design and power budgeting in an SDV.

The trend in the industry is toward more consolidation (fewer, more powerful chips running many functions), but practical safety and bandwidth needs ensure that MCUs and real-time controllers will not disappear entirely. The challenge for engineers is managing this distributed computing stack with a coherent software platform, which is why choosing the right silicon for each layer—and leveraging its ecosystem (compilers, OS support, middleware)—is crucial for a successful SDV program.

3.4 Arm Architectures in Automotive

Arm-based processors dominate automotive computing, thanks to Arm's long-term focus on embedded and automotive use cases and the rich ecosystem of tools and software available [107]. Arm offers several lines of CPU cores, each targeting different needs.

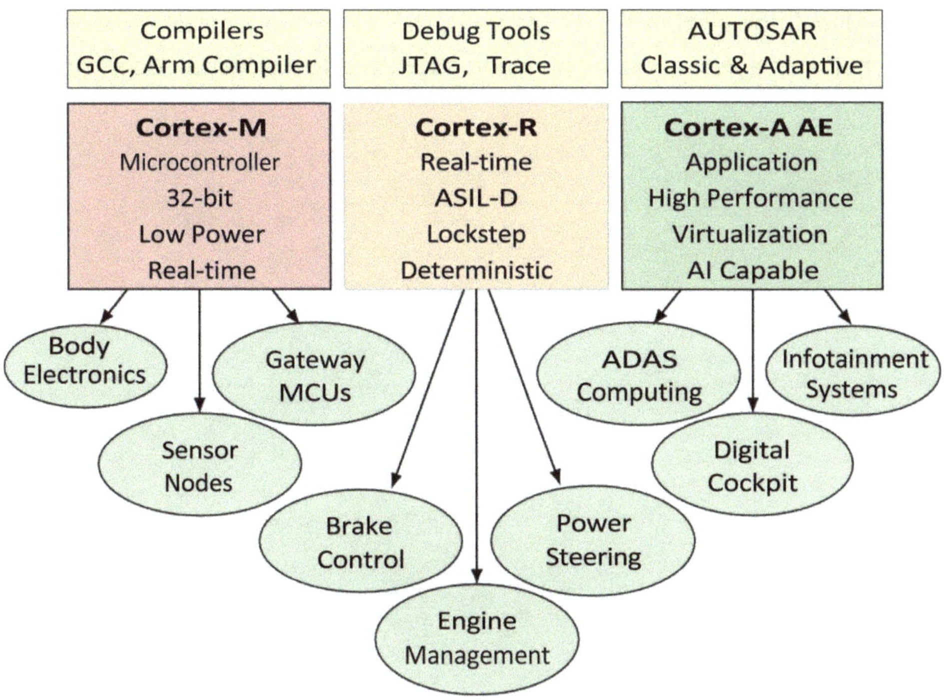

Figure 3-5. *Arm automotive ecosystem showing Cortex-M, Cortex-R, and Cortex-A families with their applications*

Cortex-M series cores are 32-bit microcontroller CPUs widely used in body electronics, comfort modules, sensor interfaces, and gateways in vehicles. They are highly efficient and intended for simple control tasks.

For example, the Arm Cortex-M4/M7 cores appear in many car MCUs (NXP KV series, STMicro STM32 family in some noncritical logging units, etc.), providing a good blend of performance and low power for tasks like reading sensor inputs, controlling motors, or bridging CAN messages.

The Cortex-M family is known for deterministic interrupt latency and real-time capability (no complex out-of-order execution or virtual memory). They typically run bare-metal or with a lightweight RTOS.

TrustZone-M security: One modern Cortex-M variant particularly relevant to SDVs is the Cortex-M33, which is Armv8-M based. Notably, the Cortex-M33 introduces TrustZone-M technology [99]. TrustZone on Cortex-M creates a hardware-enforced separation between a *secure world* and a *non-secure world* on the microcontroller.

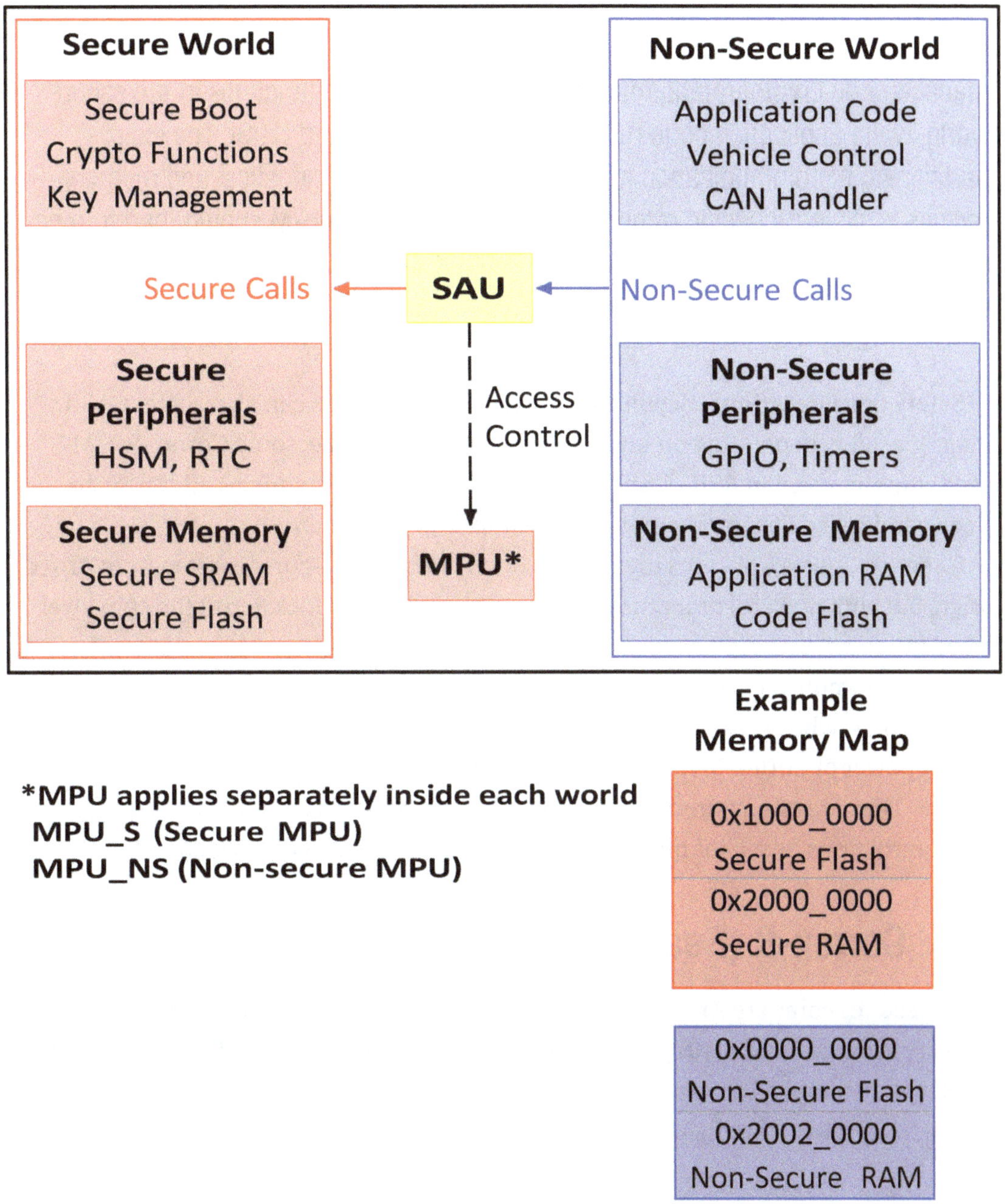

Figure 3-6. *TrustZone-M architecture showing secure and non-secure worlds on Cortex-M33*

This allows automotive developers to isolate critical code (e.g., cryptographic routines, secure boot loaders, or OTA update handlers) from the rest of the application.

Key Point In practice, a Cortex-M33–based design may place secure boot, key management, cryptographic routines, or selected update functions in the secure world, while application code runs in the non-secure world [100]. The exact partitioning of communication handlers, control logic, diagnostics, and memory regions is system-specific rather than universal. TrustZone-M should therefore be understood as a hardware-enforced partitioning mechanism whose final software allocation depends on platform and safety requirements.

Safety considerations: Beyond security, Cortex-M MCUs can also achieve ASIL ratings for safety depending on implementation. For instance, some Cortex-M4/M7-based chips are used in ASIL-B applications (with safety mechanisms added by the silicon vendor like ECC on memories, fault injection tests, etc.).

Generally, Cortex-M cores themselves don't feature dual-core lockstep from Arm's design, but chip makers sometimes put two M-core CPUs in lockstep at the chip level if needed.

More commonly, critical ASIL-D tasks are offloaded to the Cortex-R or custom lockstep cores, while Cortex-M handles less critical tasks. Nonetheless, the simplicity and low power of Cortex-M make it indispensable for the edge of the automotive network. They are often found in "end nodes" of the vehicle's compute hierarchy, such as door control units or sensor modules, where their job is focused and well-defined.

3.4.1 Cortex-R (Real-Time Series)

Cortex-R series cores are Arm's real-time processors, used where strict timing and reliability are paramount [101]. In automotive, Cortex-R processors (like Cortex-R5/R5F/R52/R52+) are employed for powertrain control, braking systems (ABS, ESC), airbag controllers, chassis domain, battery management systems, and other safety-critical tasks.

These cores are optimized for predictable low-latency response and include features that make them amenable to high-ASIL certifications:

- **Lockstep support**: Cortex-R cores can be configured in dual or even triple modular redundancy setups. For example, a chip may include two Cortex-R52 CPUs running in lockstep, comparing results cycle by cycle to detect any divergence caused by faults. This is a common approach to achieve ASIL-D compliance—if one core has a transient fault (e.g., a bit flip due to radiation), the discrepancy is caught immediately by the lockstep mechanism and the system can fault safely.
- **Split-lock mode**: Uniquely, the Cortex-R52 introduced a split-lock mode [101]. This allows the system to run cores in lockstep for the highest safety or run them independently for higher performance when full redundancy isn't required.

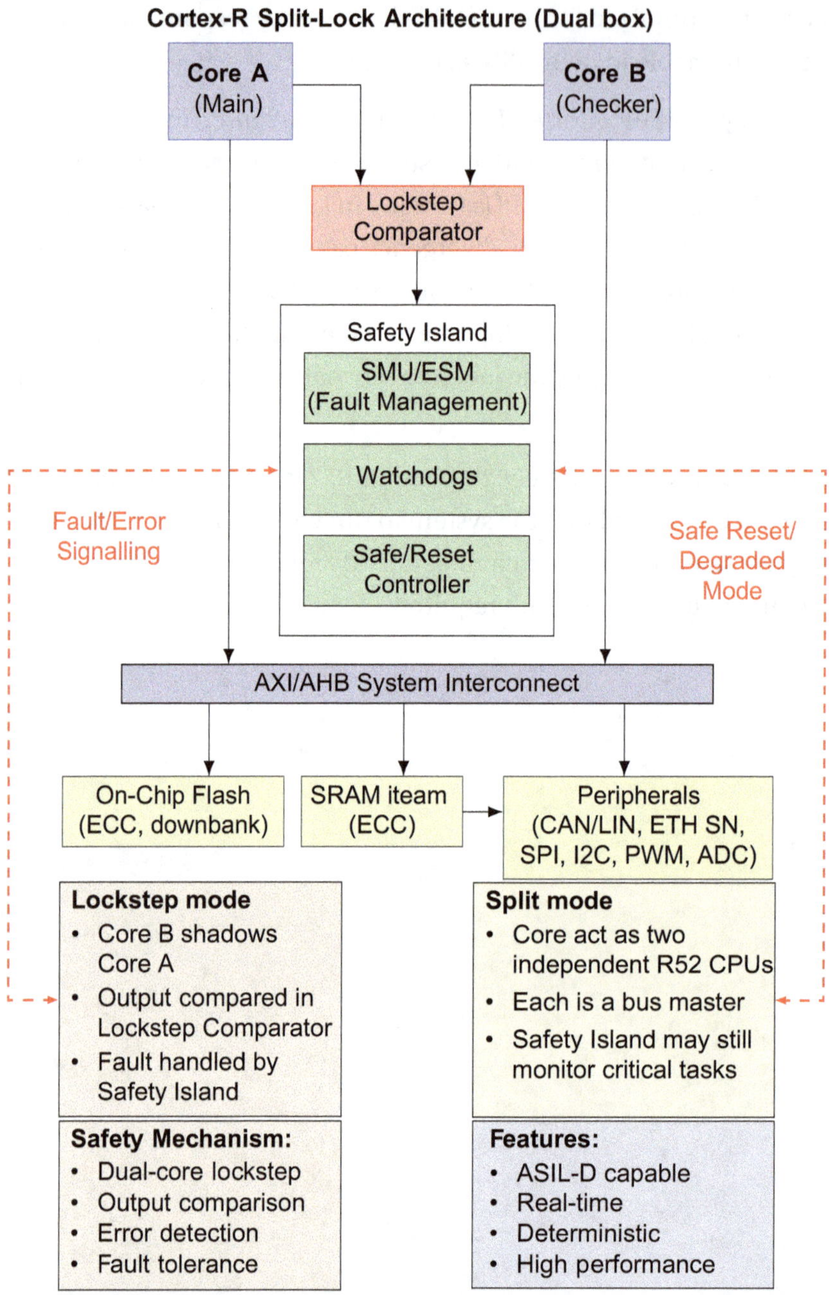

Figure 3-7. *Cortex-R52 split-lock mode showing configurable lockstep and independent operation*

NXP's implementations of Cortex-R52 (e.g., in the S32Z/E processors) take advantage of this: developers can decide to run two out of four cores in lockstep (for an ASIL-D control task) while using the remaining cores for less critical tasks in parallel [84].

- **Fast context switching and interrupts**: Cortex-R prioritizes real-time determinism. Interrupt latency is minimized and features like low-latency memory/tightly coupled memories avoid unpredictability from caches. This is crucial for systems like engine knock control or crash airbag deployment where microseconds matter.
- **Enhanced safety features**: Many Cortex-R designs include redundancy in internal buses, ECC on memories, and even CPU self-test capabilities. For instance, Arm announced Cortex-R52+ as an enhanced version with more built-in safety diagnostics [101].

Example A concrete real-world automotive example is Infineon's AURIX TC4x family, which remains TriCore-based; safety is achieved with lockstep TriCore CPUs, a Safety Management Unit (SMU), an HSM, and a Parallel Processing Unit (PPU) (Synopsys ARC EV) for vector workloads [103, 104]. TC4x also adds modern networking like CAN XL and 10BASE-T1S to support zonal architectures.

Another example Many modern SoCs (like NVIDIA Orin or some Renesas and Texas Instruments systems) include small Cortex-R5 or Cortex-R7 cores as part of a safety island to oversee the big application cores [97]. These R5 cores run a tiny safety monitor or RTOS that can take over if the main domain fails.

In summary, Cortex-R cores provide the backbone for ASIL-D real-time control in many designs. They often run an AUTOSAR Classic OS or bare-metal control loop and sometimes a thin hypervisor for isolation of tasks. Cortex-R's ability to handle "hard" real-time deadlines with certified determinism makes it ideal for steering control units, brake controllers, and other systems where missing a timing deadline is unacceptable.

3.4.2 Cortex-A (High-Performance Application Cores, Automotive Enhanced)

The Cortex-A series cores are high-performance application processors [107]. In consumer electronics, Cortex-A powers smartphones and tablets; in automotive, special *Automotive Enhanced* (AE) variants of these cores are used in the central compute and heavy-domain SoCs—e.g., digital cockpits, infotainment systems, advanced ADAS controllers, and autonomous driving computers.

Automotive Cortex-A cores include Arm's standard features for performance (pipelining, caches, out-of-order execution) but add modifications for safety and reliability:

Automotive Enhanced (AE) features: Arm's AE cores like Cortex-A76AE, Cortex-A78AE, and the latest Cortex-A720AE incorporate design changes for safety [107, 108].

One key feature is support for split-lock operation at the cluster level similar to Cortex-R. For instance, Cortex-A78AE can run pairs of CPU cores in lockstep mode within a cluster, comparing results for error detection.

A typical usage is to run two out of four cores in lockstep for an ASIL-D critical thread (like running a Level 3 ADS perception stack), while other cores handle non-safety tasks. The AE cores also often have redundant components in the memory system (the DynamIQ Shared Unit in A76AE/A78AE is made fault-tolerant when in lockstep mode).

Armv8.3+ and Armv9 security enhancements: Automotive Cortex-A cores have been quick to adopt Arm's latest architecture features that improve safety and security.

For example, *Pointer Authentication Code* (PAC) was introduced in Armv8.3 and was supported in Cortex-A76AE onward. PAC appends a cryptographic signature to return addresses and pointers, so that if a pointer is corrupted or an attacker attempts a ROP (return-oriented programming) exploit, the signature check will fail. This significantly raises the bar against software attacks, which is important in connected vehicles.

Memory Tagging Extension (MTE), an Armv8.5/Armv9 feature, provides hardware checks for memory safety (tagging allocations to detect out-of-bounds or use-after-free errors). In an automotive context, memory tagging can help catch software bugs that might otherwise lead to random failures. New AE cores based on Armv9 (like Cortex-A720AE) inherently include these features [107].

Hardware virtualization and isolation: Cortex-A cores support full virtualization (a hypervisor mode), allowing multiple operating systems or virtual machines to run on the same processor with isolation.

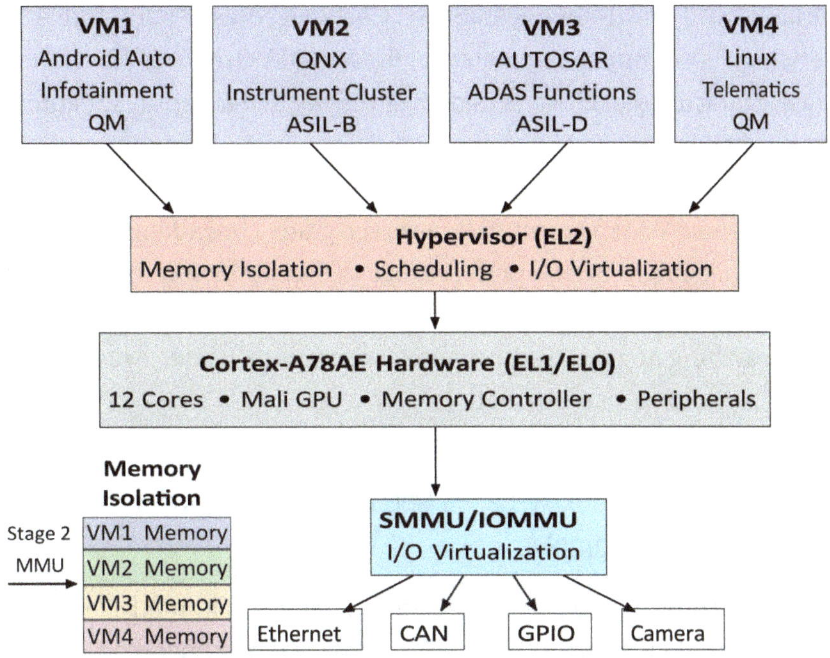

Figure 3-8. *Cortex-A virtualization architecture showing multiple VMs running different automotive OS*

Automotive systems use virtualization to host different software environments in isolated guest domains, e.g., Android Automotive in one VM and a QNX- or Linux-based cluster or control environment in another. AUTOSAR Adaptive would normally execute within a POSIX-based guest operating system rather than existing as a standalone virtual machine.

Isolation is achieved through the hypervisor together with stage-2 address translation and device virtualization for DMA-capable peripherals such as Ethernet, storage, or GPU-class devices. Not every peripheral participates in SMMU/IOMMU-based translation; simpler devices such as GPIO are typically handled differently. The architectural point is that virtualization enables mixed-criticality consolidation, while the exact memory and device model remains platform-specific.

Even GPUs like Arm's Mali-G78AE support partitioning of resources into independent contexts with up to four hardware-isolated execution partitions, enabling safe consolidation of cluster and IVI (in-vehicle infotainment) graphics on one GPU. These partitioning and VM features are pivotal for "mixed-criticality" systems—allowing QM (Quality-Managed; no safety requirement) and ASIL-rated software to coexist on one silicon without interference.

Performance and multi-core scalability: Cortex-A cores in automotive SoCs are scaled to very high core counts. For instance, the NVIDIA Orin uses 12× Cortex-A78AE cores at 2.2 GHz, arranged in clusters to deliver the needed compute for autonomous driving software [97].

Arm's next-gen automotive CPUs (like Arm Neoverse V3AE introduced in 2024) push this further—Neoverse V3AE is essentially a server-grade core adapted for automotive, allowing even higher single-thread performance and up to 14 cores per cluster with the new DSU-120AE coherence unit [109]. This shows the trend: automotive central processors are catching up with data center class compute, because tasks like AI perception and sensor fusion demand it.

Example In practice, Cortex-A–based SoCs dominate the infotainment and ADAS domain. Here are a few examples:

- The Qualcomm Snapdragon SA8155P chip (used in many infotainment systems) has 8× Kryo cores (Kryo is based on Cortex-A architecture) along with an Adreno GPU—essentially a customized Cortex-A app processor for automotive IVI [110].
- The Tesla FSD computer uses custom 64-bit cores (not exactly Cortex-A, but comparable class) along with neural accelerators—illustrating the heavy-duty compute at the center.
- Arm Cortex-A78AE cores are at the heart of NXP's latest BlueBox central computer and also in some of NVIDIA's DRIVE Orin configurations [97, 108]. They bring features like Temporal Fault Detection (via dual-core lockstep) and architectural resiliency while still offering significant uplift vs. A76AE/A77AE.
- The new Arm Cortex-A720AE (Armv9) provides an ~30% performance uplift over A78AE on automotive workloads and is designed with enhanced split-lock and fault detection features for safety [107]. It's targeted at central ADAS and "digital cockpit" convergence—meaning one core type could potentially run both your cluster and your autonomy algorithms with proper isolation.

In summary, Arm Cortex-A (AE) cores bring high performance with added safety mechanisms to automotive SoCs. They excel in the central compute role, running complex software while meeting (or approaching) safety standards. Combined with Cortex-R and Cortex-M in a heterogeneous design, they allow a single chip to handle diverse workloads—from a Linux-based UI to hard-real-time motor control—which is exactly what a software-defined vehicle needs.

Critic's Note Arm's near-monopoly in automotive CPUs stems from its mature ecosystem (software stacks, compilers, AUTOSAR support) and proven IP. However, beware of licensing and lock-in risks. Automakers and Tier-1s have voiced concerns about relying solely on Arm's proprietary IP and licensing model—this has fueled interest in open ISA alternatives like RISC-V (discussed later).

Also, while Arm cores are excellent, automotive programs must consider long-term availability and the cost structure of scaling with Arm's licensing. It's a classic debate of ecosystem maturity vs. potential vendor lock-in.

3.5 Infineon AURIX (TriCore) Microcontrollers

While Arm dominates, Infineon's AURIX family (based on the proprietary TriCore architecture) is a cornerstone of automotive microcontrollers for high-safety applications [102]. AURIX (which stands for *AUtomotive Real-time Integrated neXt-generation architecture*) combines three aspects—a RISC processor core, a microcontroller (with on-chip flash, peripherals), and a DSP—into one architecture (hence TriCore).

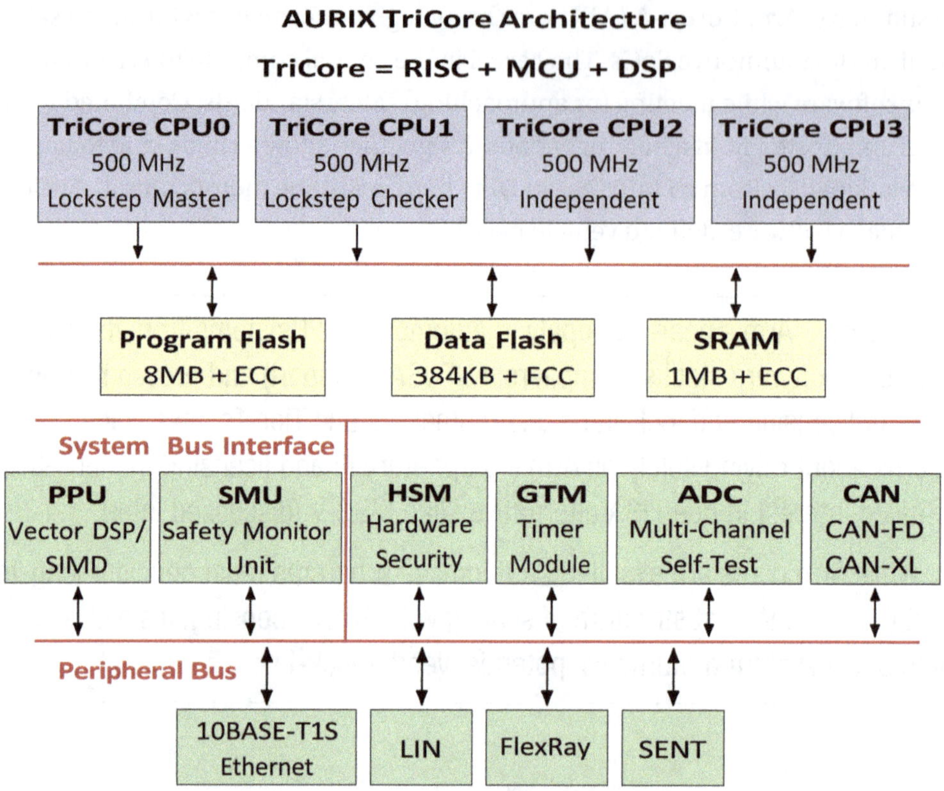

Figure 3-9. *AURIX TriCore architecture (example configuration) showing RISC, MCU, and DSP components integrated on a single chip*

The latest-generation AURIX TC4xx offers a robust solution for powertrain, chassis, and safety domains [103, 104].

AURIX TC4x can have up to six TriCore 1.8 CPUs, with top SKUs reaching 500 MHz [103]. These cores are optimized for real time; they offer predictable execution and low-latency response, crucial for engine control or braking systems.

Infineon often implements a mix of lockstep and standalone cores. For example, some cores might run in lockstep pairs (to achieve ASIL-D for critical tasks), while others run independently to handle less critical tasks or provide redundancy.

The architecture is designed to meet ISO 26262 ASIL-D across the chip's functionality—functional safety is ingrained in the design pedigree (Infineon has decades of safety MCU experience since the Lockstep C166 and TriCore 1.0 days).

3.5.1 Safety and Monitoring Features

AURIX is known for a comprehensive safety concept [104]. It includes things like

- Redundant cross-checking CPU units
- A Safety Management Unit (SMU) that collects safety error signals from all blocks
- Memory ECC on all RAM/flash
- Built-in self-test capabilities
- Analog monitors

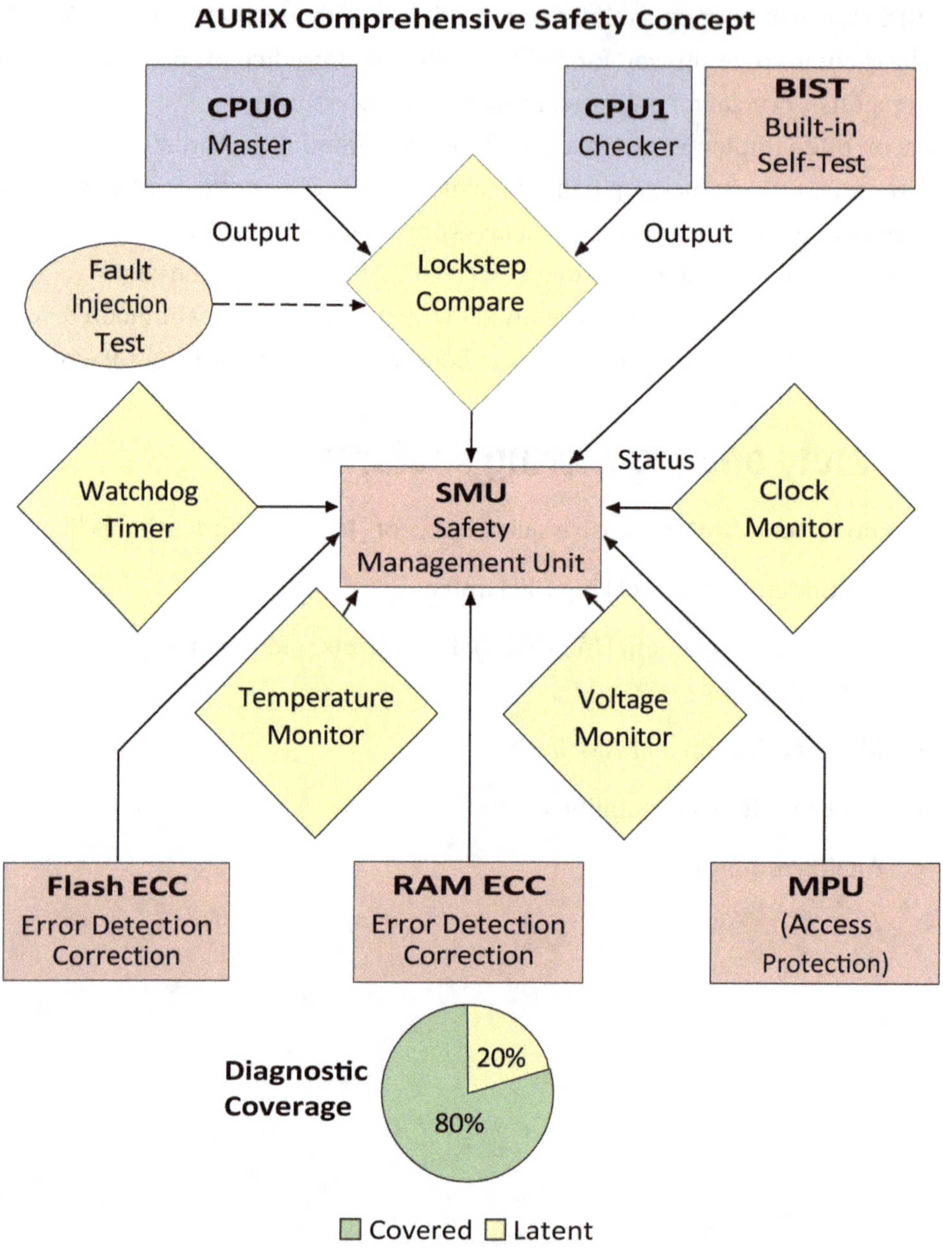

Figure 3-10. *AURIX comprehensive safety concept showing SMU, lockstep cores, and safety monitoring*

Key Point A "safety island" concept is often implemented—a small portion of the chip that runs independently to supervise the rest (similar in concept to what Arm calls a safety island with an R52, but here it's all TriCore).

For instance, the TC4xx has redundant safety alarm handlers and a dedicated safety firmware library, so that if any core or peripheral goes astray, the system can take corrective action or reset. This is one reason AURIX MCUs have a strong track record in applications like electronic steering or braking—they are built to detect faults at every turn.

3.5.2 Security and HSM

Beyond functional safety, modern cars demand security. AURIX MCUs include a *hardware security module* (HSM)—essentially a dedicated crypto engine and secure storage area on-chip [111]. Infineon's latest TC4x MCUs have an upgraded HSM (sometimes called the Safe Secure Module), which serves as the root of trust. It can

- Securely store cryptographic keys
- Perform encryption/decryption
- Execute sensitive code (like challenge-response for immobilizers or secure boot verification) in isolation

The cybersecurity architecture in AURIX TC4x is compliant with ISO 21434 (the automotive cybersecurity standard). Infineon even mentions support for secure over-the-air (SOTA) updates with zero downtime—meaning the MCU can update its firmware in the background and switch over safely, thanks to dual-bank flash and robust verification [111]. These features are critical as vehicles become connected and subject to potential cyberattacks.

3.5.3 Accelerators and Peripherals for Automotive

The TriCore architecture isn't aimed at high-end infotainment or AI, but Infineon has added some acceleration to TC4xx to handle signal processing tasks [103]. Notably, there is a *Parallel Processing Unit* (PPU) in TC4x—a vector DSP accelerator (Infineon collaborated with Synopsys, using an ARC EV processor as the PPU). The PPU can perform SIMD vector operations ideal for things like radar signal processing or even rudimentary neural network inference.

While it's not a GPU or large NPU, it gives the AURIX an ability to offload math-heavy computations from the main cores, which is helpful for emerging needs like sensor fusion or on-chip diagnostics.

Additionally, AURIX MCUs come with rich automotive peripherals:

- CAN FD
- The newer CAN XL and 10BASE-T1S Ethernet support on TC4x for faster in-vehicle networking
- Lots of ADC channels
- Timer/PWM units for motor control

This makes them system-on-chip controllers that can directly interface with the vehicle's electrical components.

3.5.4 Use Cases

AURIX is heavily used in electric vehicle (EV) powertrain and hybrid drivetrain management [102]. For example, an AURIX might

- Control the motor inverter (with its PWM timers and fast ADC reading currents)
- Implement the high-voltage battery management (monitor cell voltages and temperatures with redundant checking)
- Coordinate regenerative braking—all under ASIL-D requirements

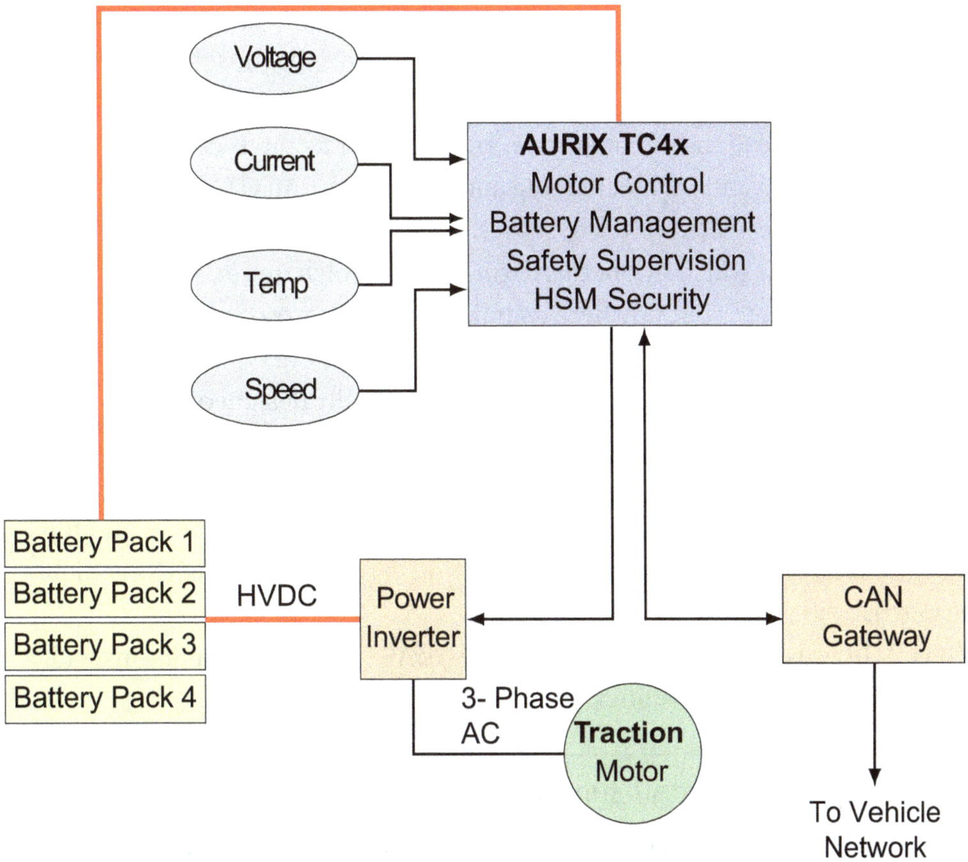

Figure 3-11. *AURIX in EV powertrain application showing motor control, battery management, and safety supervision*

The EV domain values AURIX for its safety and Infineon's long experience in power electronics. Additionally, AURIX MCUs appear in gateway modules, steering (EPS), and domain controllers for chassis and even as companions to larger SoCs.

Example For instance, some autonomous driving stacks use an AURIX as a fail-safe supervisor: the AURIX monitors the high-level system (perhaps running on an NVIDIA or Mobileye chip) and will enact a safe stop maneuver if it detects a failure.

Strengths: AURIX's strengths lie in its deterministic real-time performance and safety pedigree. Infineon as a vendor provides extensive safety documentation, FMEDA (Failure Modes, Effects, and Diagnostics Analysis) data, and even software libraries to help customers reach compliance. This ecosystem maturity in safety is why many OEMs trust AURIX for airbag or powertrain—components that absolutely cannot fail uncontrolled. Also, the integration of security (HSM) means it can do secure boot and encrypted communications out of the box, an important factor as cars implement features like theft prevention, EV charging authentication, and OTA updates.

Weaknesses: The AURIX/TriCore ecosystem is smaller than Arm's. Developers are generally less familiar with TriCore than Arm Cortex; toolchains exist (like Infineon's tools, HighTec GCC, etc.) but nowhere near the breadth of Arm compiler support. This can mean a higher learning curve or porting effort for software.

Additionally, AURIX, being an MCU, was not originally designed for heavy AI or graphics workloads—so it lacks the kind of neural accelerators or GPUs that newer automotive SoCs have. Infineon has partially addressed this by the PPU vector unit, but it's still modest (e.g., it could accelerate a small neural network for an on-chip diagnostics or sensor processing, but it's not going to run big vision CNNs at high frame rates).

Thus, AURIX usually isn't used for primary ADAS vision processing—instead, it might play a supporting role alongside an AI SoC.

Quote In the era of the SDV, AURIX chips often serve as the "safety backbone": they ensure that regardless of what the high-level software is doing, the vehicle can always revert to a safe state. For example, if an autonomous driving computer misbehaves, an AURIX could detect this and trigger braking or provide a wake-up signal to the driver.

Infineon continues to evolve AURIX (with TC4xx focusing on e-mobility and even having some audio processing capabilities for engine sound management). They are a prime example of evolutionary automotive silicon that has added features to keep up with software-defined needs (like more connectivity and security) while preserving the ultra-reliable core needed for vehicle control.

3.6 NXP S32 Automotive Platform

Where AURIX illustrates a safety-first MCU family for high-integrity control, NXP's S32 platform shows how a vendor can span from simple MCUs to full SDV-class domain and central controllers under one unified ecosystem.

NXP Semiconductors is another key player in automotive silicon, and their S32 platform illustrates a comprehensive approach to SDV computing [85, 112]. NXP's S32 line is designed as a coherent family from low-end MCUs to high-end SoCs, all with a unified software ecosystem. The platform includes several product series.

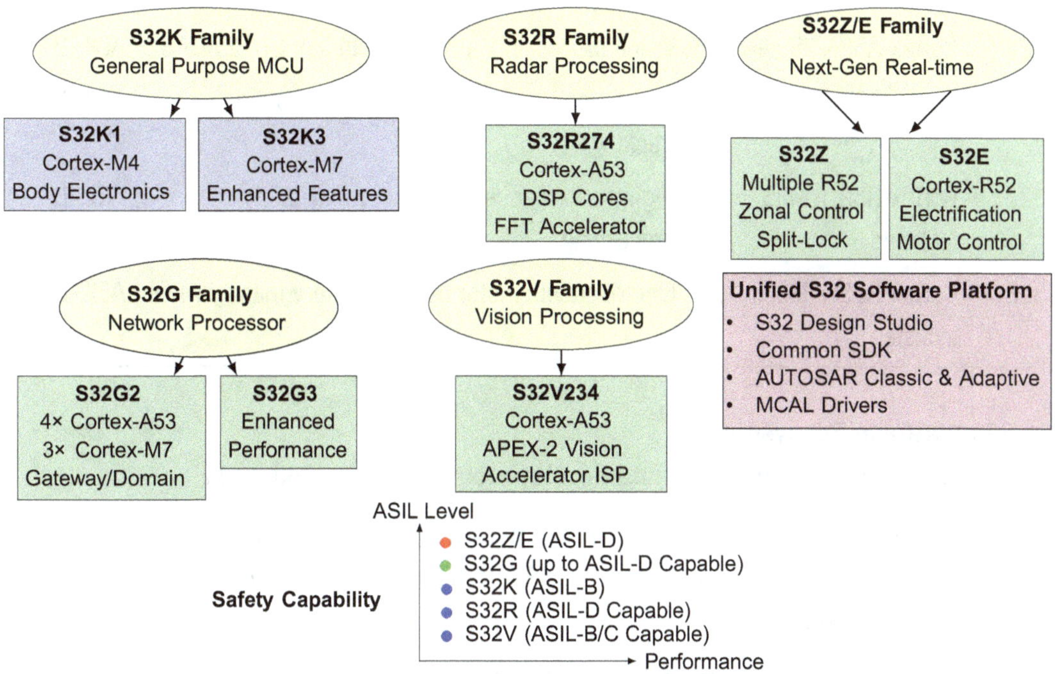

Figure 3-12. *NXP S32 platform overview showing the complete family from MCUs to high-end SoCs*

The S32G series exemplifies NXP's SDV approach [85, 112]: it combines four Cortex-A53 application cores with triple-lockstep Cortex-M7 real-time cores, a Packet Forwarding Engine for high-throughput routing, and up to 20 CAN FD interfaces alongside multiple-gigabit Ethernet ports. This makes S32G well-suited for central gateways and zonal controllers that must bridge legacy networks to Ethernet backbones while maintaining ASIL-D safety ratings.

Table 3-1. *NXP S32 Platform: Device Families and Target Applications*

Family	Core(s)	Target Application	Safety
S32K	Cortex-M4/M7	Body electronics, simple powertrain, general ECU	ASIL-B/C
S32G	Cortex-A53 + lockstep M7	Vehicle gateway, zonal controller, service-oriented architecture	ASIL-D
S32V	Cortex-A53 + ISP + APEX	Vision processing, driver monitoring, L1/L2 ADAS	ASIL-B
S32R	Arm + DSP	Radar signal processing, FFT acceleration, tracking	ASIL-B
S32Z	Cortex-R52 + M33 lockstep	High-performance real-time, zonal safety processing	ASIL-D
S32E	Cortex-R52 + M33 lockstep	Electrification: motor control, battery management	ASIL-D

S32 Platform Ecosystem

The S32 family provides a unified development ecosystem [85, 113]:

- **Software portability:** Common SDK and MCAL (Microcontroller Abstraction Layer) drivers across S32K, S32G, and S32Z enable code reuse.
- **Virtualization support:** S32G and S32Z support multiple OS domains via certified hypervisors (Green Hills Integrity, OpenSynergy COQOS) with hardware-enforced I/O partitioning.
- **Integrated security:** Hardware Security Engine (HSE) provides secure boot, crypto acceleration, and OTA update verification.
- **Safety certification:** ISO 26262 support up to ASIL-D with lockstep cores, safety monitors, and SafeAssure documentation packages.
- **Companion ecosystem:** Matched PMICs, CAN/LIN transceivers, and TSN-enabled Ethernet switches (SJA1110) simplify board design.

Key Point NXP's Vehicle Integration Platform (VIP) provides reference designs and cloud-connected frameworks for OTA systems, demonstrating that S32 is a platform—not just chips—aligned with SDV continuous-update requirements.

3.6.1 Practical Use Case

Example A practical use case scenario highlighting the S32 platform could be a service-oriented gateway in a modern car: An S32G processor is at the center, linking the vehicle to cloud services and also shuttling data internally between domains (powertrain, ADAS, infotainment). It ensures messages are secure and prioritized (using built-in network acceleration and filtering).

If an OEM wants to add a new feature via software update (say improved adaptive cruise control algorithms running on an ADAS computer), the S32G can update the relevant firmware securely and manage the data flowing from sensors to that ADAS module.

Meanwhile, S32K MCUs scattered in the car handle local duties like window motors or seat heaters, and they can be updated over-the-air as well through the gateway. Because all these are S32, NXP's unified tools can theoretically manage the entire deployment.

Ecosystem: NXP has a broad partner network. They provide AUTOSAR stacks (Classic and Adaptive), have reference integrations with middleware like Elektrobit and QNX, and support functional safety software frameworks [113]. Their SafeAssure program provides documentation and support for ISO 26262 compliance.

Furthermore, NXP produces companion chips (power management ICs, CAN transceivers, Ethernet switches like the TSN-enabled SJA1110) designed to seamlessly work with S32 processors, making them a one-stop shop for car computing needs.

Quote In practice, the PMIC often constrains thermal envelopes, supply sequencing, and startup behavior; choosing a CPU without a mature PMIC and companion chip story can delay SOP or force painful late-stage redesigns.

In short, NXP's S32 platform exemplifies scalability and integration: you can build a low-end ECU or a high-end autonomous vehicle domain controller using S32 components and have them interoperate. This approach is quite aligned with SDV principles—it eases software reuse and system integration.

Strengths: Comprehensive safety/security, strong networking capabilities, and a family concept that eases integration. Also, long product support (NXP typically guarantees automotive products for 15+ years).

Weaknesses: While NXP covers many bases, for bleeding-edge AI performance, they still rely on partners; e.g., the S32V was not as competitive in vision processing as NVIDIA or Mobileye offerings for higher levels of autonomy.

Thus, OEMs might use NXP for gateways and safety controllers but opt for a more powerful dedicated AI chip for front-line ADAS. NXP is addressing some of this by working on next-gen vision processors and by emphasizing that multiple S32 chips can work in concert (e.g., an S32G + external accelerator).

But the competitive landscape for central ADAS SoCs often tilts toward NVIDIA, Qualcomm, Tesla's in-house silicon, etc., which offer massive TOPS. NXP's stance is often that deterministic performance and safety are more important than raw TOPS—a fair point in automotive.

3.7 Silicon from Qualcomm, NVIDIA, and Renesas

As vehicles become more software-driven, tech companies and traditional silicon vendors alike have introduced automotive platforms. We'll look at three notable players: Qualcomm (a newcomer from the mobile SoC world), NVIDIA (leveraging GPU prowess in automotive), and Renesas (a Japanese leader blending traditional automotive with newer AI capabilities).

3.7.1 Qualcomm Snapdragon Ride Platform

Qualcomm is well-known for smartphone chips, but it has leveraged that expertise to create the Snapdragon Ride platform for automotive ADAS and autonomy [98, 110]. Snapdragon Ride SoCs typically combine

- **Multi-core application CPUs**: Custom Qualcomm Kryo cores or standard Cortex-A cores (often Arm Cortex-A78 or similar) for the main compute. These run the OS and ADAS software.
- **Adreno GPU**: A powerful graphics processor (inherited from mobile), which can be used not only for visualization (instrument clusters, AR heads-up displays, etc.) but also for parallel compute like running neural networks (GPUs excel at CNNs and image processing).
- **Hexagon DSP/AI Engine**: Qualcomm includes its Hexagon DSP, which over generations has evolved to accelerate AI. The Hexagon can handle fixed-point arithmetic very efficiently, and Qualcomm often brands the AI acceleration portion as the "Hexagon AI Engine." This can offload things like object detection networks at lower power than running them on the GPU.
- **Dedicated ISPs and other accelerators**: For camera-heavy applications, Qualcomm SoCs integrate image signal processors (ISPs) to ingest and preprocess camera feeds, important for autonomous driving perception.

One of Qualcomm's automotive strengths is its Android Automotive and infotainment ecosystem [110, 114]. They have a dominant position in in-vehicle infotainment (IVI)—many cars' infotainment systems (digital dashboards, head units) are built on Snapdragon chipsets running Android or QNX.

This means Snapdragon Ride platforms come with mature support for Android Automotive OS (AAOS), multimedia, connectivity (Bluetooth, 4G/5G), etc. For OEMs looking to have an integrated cockpit domain (infotainment + cluster) and an ADAS domain, Qualcomm's strategy is to offer both or even a combined solution.

In 2023, Qualcomm announced the Snapdragon Ride Flex SoC, which explicitly allows mixed-criticality workloads—running Android-based infotainment and ASIL-D-rated ADAS tasks on one chip, with hardware isolation in between—and is intended to enter volume production in mid-2020s vehicles such as Cadillac models using Ultra Cruise [110, 115].

This is achieved through hypervisor partitions and a concept of a safety island on the SoC (an internal core or subsystem that monitors the rest for safe operation).

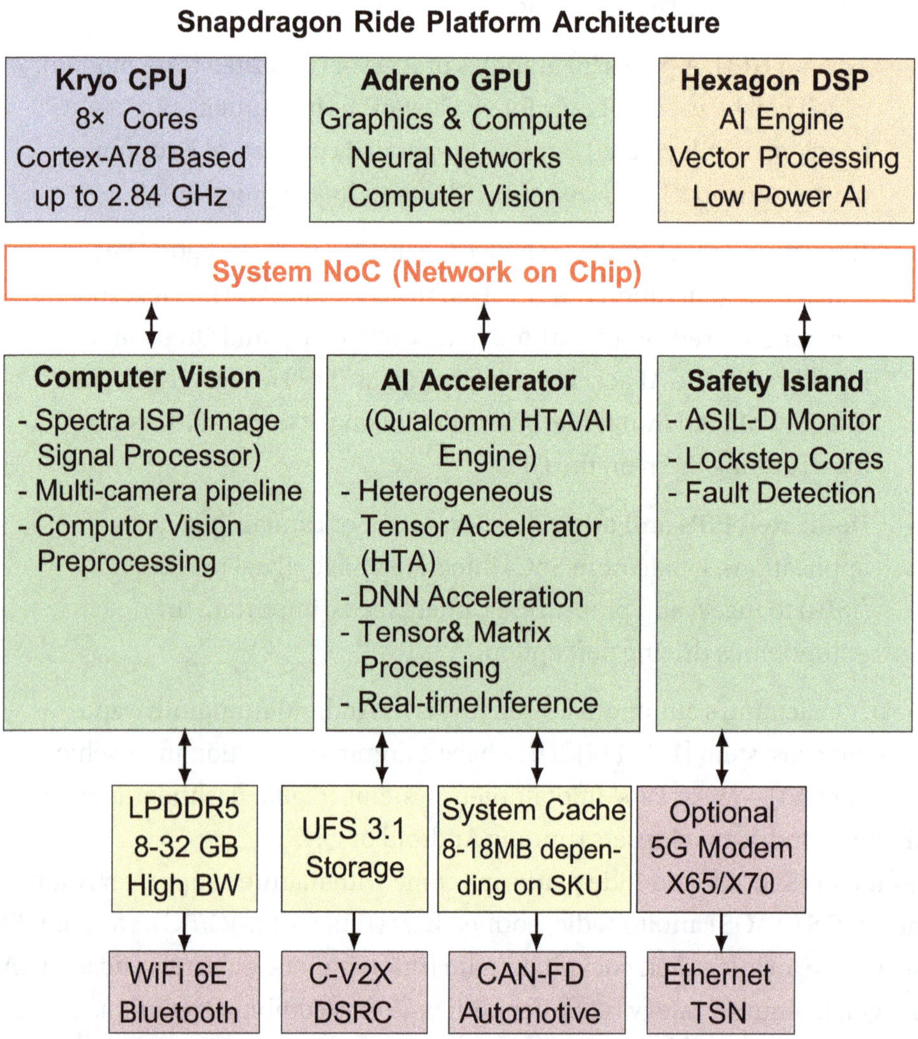

Figure 3-13. *Snapdragon Ride platform architecture showing CPU, GPU, Hexagon DSP, and automotive-specific accelerators*

The Snapdragon Ride family's initial offerings (like SDM855-based Ride or later variants) were aimed at L1–L2 ADAS. They now scale up to higher performance for L2+ and L3. For instance, the Snapdragon Ride "Vision" SoC can process dozens of camera, radar, and LiDAR streams in real time, supporting over 40 sensors. Qualcomm also offers a complete Ride SDK and middleware for perception and drive policy, trying to give carmakers a one-stop solution similar to NVIDIA's DriveWorks [98].

Key Point

Safety certification: Earlier Qualcomm automotive SoCs (like those for infotainment) didn't need ASIL-D. But for ADAS, Qualcomm had to meet automotive safety standards. This has been a learning curve.

The Snapdragon Ride platform system (multiple chips and software) is being engineered to achieve ASIL-D for functions like highway pilot. The newer Ride Flex includes an ASIL-D safety island and meets ASIL-B/D for different domains on-chip.

The weakness historically was that Qualcomm was a bit behind rivals in having top safety credentials—e.g., NVIDIA Xavier and Orin were designed from the ground up with ASIL-D in mind, whereas Qualcomm had to evolve its approach.

That said, by 2025 Qualcomm has made big strides: the Snapdragon Ride Flex (on 4 nm process) is slated to appear in production vehicles around 2024–2025 (Cadillac was an early announced customer for Ultra Cruise L3 driving with Qualcomm chips) and is the first to combine ADAS and cockpit on one SoC at mixed ASIL levels [115, 116].

- **Performance and power**: Qualcomm's chips, leveraging advanced mobile silicon techniques, are quite power-efficient for the compute they provide. For example, they emphasize performance-per-watt, crucial in passively cooled ECUs. The exact TOPS numbers vary by product, but they are in the order of 10s to low 100s of TOPS (not as high as NVIDIA Thor's promises, but enough for current L2/L3 needs).

- **Connectivity and ADAS data**: Qualcomm also integrates car-to-cloud connectivity solutions. A software-defined vehicle might rely on 5G connectivity for certain features (map updates, V2X communication). Qualcomm's strength in 4G/5G modems could synergize such that a Snapdragon automotive platform might include on-die or companion modem chips that ensure the ADAS system stays updated and connected.

In summary, Qualcomm's Snapdragon Ride targets the convergence of ADAS and infotainment, leveraging its consumer electronics ecosystem. It has a strong cockpit/IVI background (Android ecosystem, multimedia), and it's expanding that into full self-driving compute.

Automakers like GM have partnered with Qualcomm—for instance, GM's Ultra Cruise L3 system for Cadillac was announced to use Snapdragon Ride SoCs—highlighting industry confidence [115]. The Ride Flex SoC in 2025 being able to run instrument cluster (ASIL-B) and autonomous driving (ASIL-D) side by side on a single chip with hypervisor separation is a notable achievement.

One must note that Qualcomm provides not just chips but a lot of software—including AI algorithms, perception stacks, and an SDK for customers to develop their own ADAS features on top of Qualcomm's frameworks. This is again akin to NVIDIA's approach, and it shows how the line between a silicon company and a software provider is blurred in the SDV era.

3.7.2 NVIDIA DRIVE (Orin and Thor)

NVIDIA is a pioneer in pushing high-performance computing into cars [97, 117]. It started by leveraging its GPU technology for infotainment graphics and then quickly moved into using GPUs for AI processing in autonomous driving. NVIDIA's automotive lineup (branded NVIDIA DRIVE) has seen generations like Tegra, Parker, Xavier, Orin, and upcoming Thor.

NVIDIA Orin (DRIVE AGX Orin)

Architecture: The Orin SoC features 12× Arm Cortex-A78AE CPU cores for general computation and two major accelerators: an NVIDIA Ampere family GPU (with 2048 CUDA cores and 64 Tensor Cores for AI matrix ops) and two NVIDIA Deep Learning Accelerators (NVDLAs), which are fixed-function neural network inference engines [97, 105].

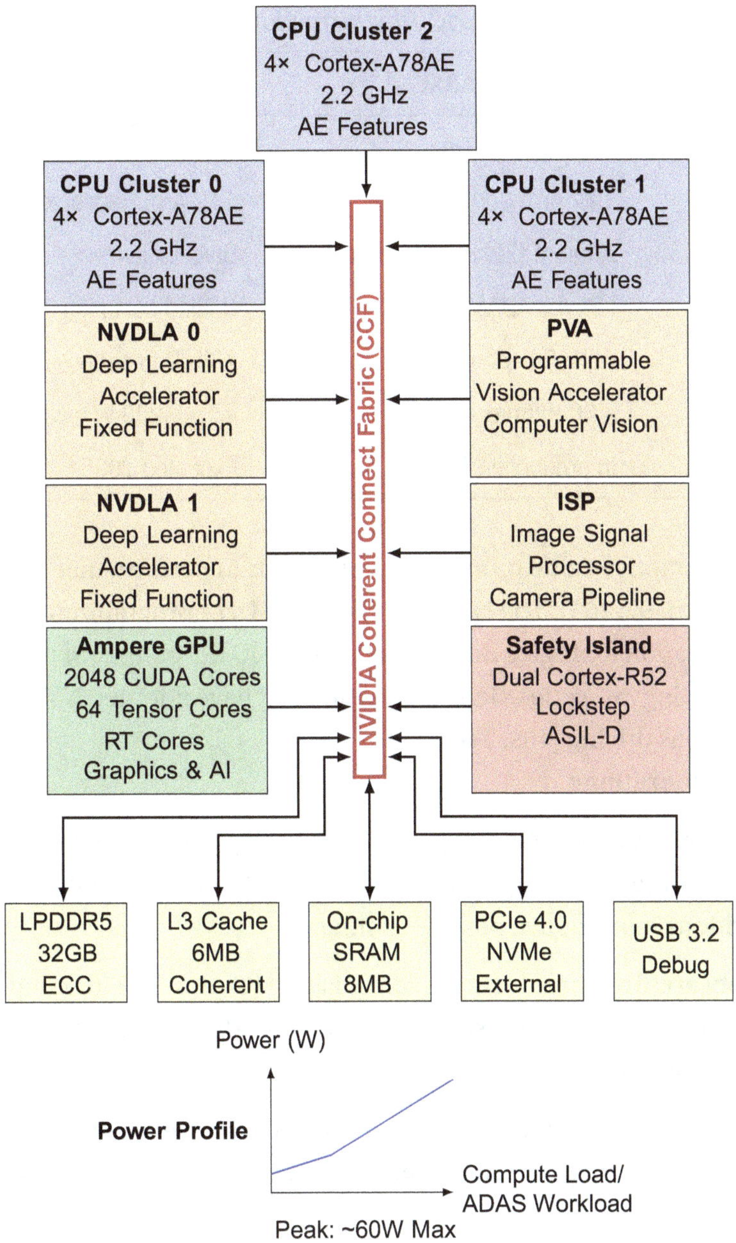

***Figure 3-14.** NVIDIA Orin architecture showing CPU clusters, Ampere GPU, NVDLA engines, and safety island*

Additionally, Orin has image signal processors and video codecs to handle camera inputs.

Table 3-2. *NVIDIA Automotive SoC Platform Comparison*

Attribute	Orin (DRIVE AGX)	Thor (DRIVE Thor)
AI performance	254 TOPS (INT8)	~1,000 TOPS (INT8)
CPU cores	12× Arm Cortex-A78AE	14× Arm Neoverse V3AE
GPU architecture	Ampere (2048 CUDA cores)	Blackwell
Target use case	L2+/L3 ADAS, robotaxi	Unified cockpit + L4/L5 AD
Safety rating	ASIL-D capable	ASIL-D capable
Typical power	~60 W (max load)	~150–200 W (estimated)
Production timeline	In production (2022+)	Expected 2025+

NVIDIA's automotive value proposition centers on AI performance with a mature software ecosystem [97, 105]. The DriveWorks SDK, CUDA programming model, and TensorRT optimization tools give developers familiar AI development workflows. Companies including Mercedes-Benz, Volvo, and JLR have adopted NVIDIA platforms for L3+ autonomous driving [109, 118].

Design Considerations

- **Thermal management:** High power consumption (60–200 W) requires liquid cooling or large heatsinks—a departure from traditional automotive passive cooling.
- **Safety architecture:** Includes safety island (Cortex-R52 lockstep), GPU compute determinism modes, and ISO 26262 certification for safety domains.
- **Consolidation vision:** Thor aims to unify cockpit, infotainment, driver monitoring, and ADAS on one platform, reducing ECU count.

3.7.3 Renesas R-Car SoCs

Renesas is a top automotive semiconductor company (formed from Hitachi, Mitsubishi, NEC's semiconductor units) [119]. Aside from their MCU lines (like RH850 MCUs that compete with Infineon AURIX), Renesas has the R-Car family of automotive SoCs aimed at both infotainment and ADAS.

R-Car Gen 3 and Gen 4 have been used in a range of applications, especially by Japanese OEMs and their suppliers.

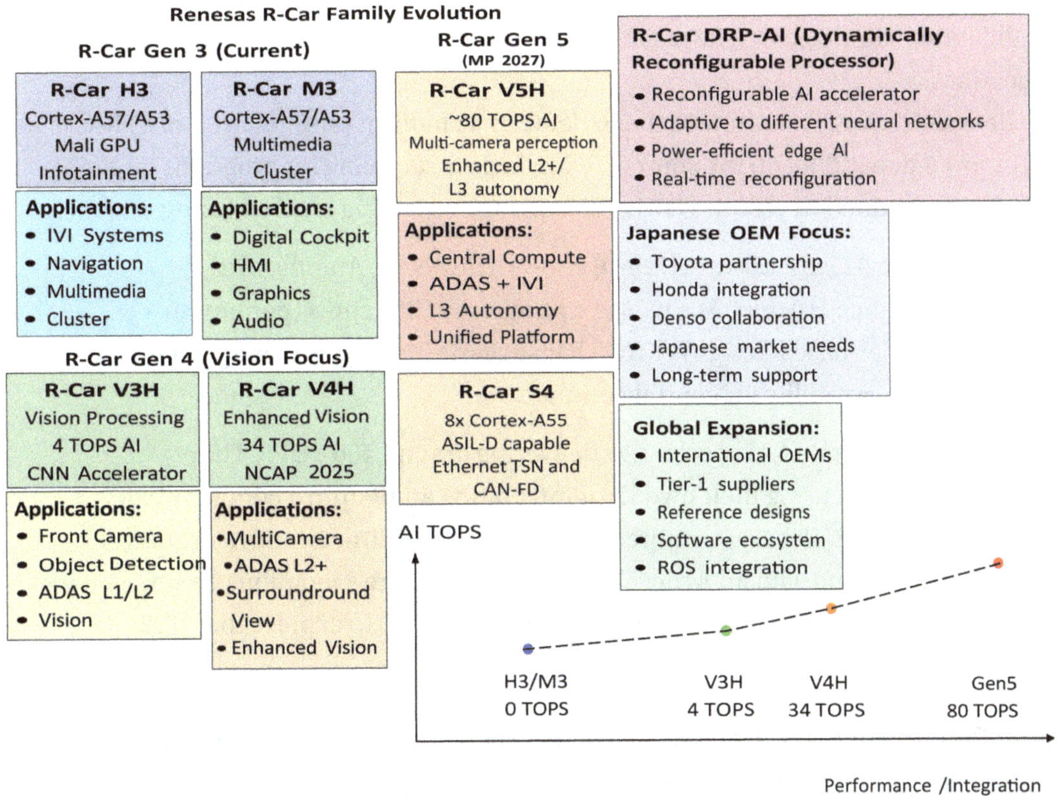

Figure 3-15. *Renesas R-Car family showing different variants for infotainment, vision processing, and integrated applications*

Table 3-3. *Renesas R-Car Family: Variants and Applications*

Series	Generation	Target Application	AI Performance
R-Car H3/M3	Gen 3	Cockpit, IVI, digital cluster, AGL/Android	GPU only
R-Car V3M/V3H	Gen 3	Camera-based ADAS (L1/L2), surround view	~4 TOPS
R-Car V4H	Gen 4	NCAP 2025 L2+, multi-camera fusion	~34 TOPS
R-Car S4	Gen 4	Gateway, communication, zonal controller	–

Renesas differentiates through integrated heterogeneous processing [119]: R-Car devices combine Arm CPU cores, GPU, ISP, DSP, and the proprietary DRP-AI (Dynamically Reconfigurable Processor for AI) [120]. The DRP-AI can be reconfigured for different neural network layers at runtime, balancing performance and power for edge AI tasks.

Renesas recently announced the R-Car Gen 5 platform (also referred to as R-Car S5 or R-Car X5 depending on the source), with devices sampling for programs targeting mid-2020s production vehicles [121, 122]. The Gen 5 is a big leap, featuring

- Up to 32 Arm Cortex-A720AE cores (Armv9; AE, Automotive Enhanced), which is a massive number of CPU cores (perhaps in a chiplet-based design) [121]. That suggests Renesas is scaling out in CPU capability for central compute.
- An integrated AI accelerator delivering around 400 TOPS. They might be using their own IP or integrating an IP from a company like aiMotive (Renesas acquired the Hungarian AI firm aiMotive in 2022) or working with an AI accelerator partner. There's mention of using chiplets and possibly external AI accelerator IP to achieve that [122].

Key Point For SDVs, a chiplet-based approach makes it easier to scale CPU and AI accelerator resources independently, mix different process nodes (e.g., leading-edge logic with mature-node I/O and analog), and potentially service or respin only part of the silicon stack as workload patterns evolve.

These Gen 5 SoCs are intended to be multi-domain: meaning one SoC could potentially handle infotainment, cockpit, and ADAS together (similar goal as NVIDIA Thor and Qualcomm's offerings) [121].

Renesas is also fostering an ecosystem—they developed reference software for surround view systems, automated parking, etc., around their R-Car chips. They have a program called R-Car Consortium with software vendors in Japan and abroad to support things like ROS-based AD kits, perception libraries, etc.

Strength in the Japanese OEM ecosystem: Renesas R-Car is often the default choice for Japanese carmakers (Toyota, Honda, etc.) for certain domains, because of trust and long-term support. Renesas tailors solutions to their needs (e.g., providing tools in Japanese, working closely with Tier-1s like Denso). That close relationship is a strength—

it ensures that R-Car SoCs are designed with the exact requirements of those OEMs in mind (be it fast boot times for IVI, compliance with Japan's security regulations, etc.).

Renesas also has a broad portfolio beyond the SoC—they make analog, power management, and MCUs. Often, an R-Car SoC will be complemented by Renesas PMICs, power supply chips, and maybe an RH850 safety MCU as a companion. They often market combined solutions (e.g., a camera system reference design including both an R-Car SoC and an RH850 doing low-level supervision).

Weaknesses: In the international market, Renesas's profile is a bit lower. They face tough competition from NVIDIA and Qualcomm for the very high-end ADAS SoC slots. Their AI accelerators historically lagged a bit in absolute performance and developer familiarity.

For example, programming their DRP or IMP-X5 (Image Recognition Processor in earlier R-Cars) is not as straightforward as using CUDA on NVIDIA or open tools for something like a Google Edge TPU. Renesas has been improving this, providing more standard toolflows (like supporting ONNX for their AI translator and so on), but it's an evolving area.

Another challenge is that as systems consolidate, some OEMs that use Renesas MCUs might look at centralized computing with other chips, which could erode some of Renesas's socket share if they don't capture those central compute slots. The R-Car Gen 5 seems to be Renesas's answer to that, ensuring they have an offering for centralized SDV computers.

Quote In summary, Renesas R-Car SoCs serve as the "brains" in many infotainment and mid-range ADAS systems, especially in Asia. They come with specialized accelerators (like the DRP-AI engine for efficient on-chip AI inference) and are often packaged in solutions that emphasize reliability and ease of integration with existing vehicle electronics.

They might not always grab headlines for highest TOPS, but they are designed to meet OEM requirements thoroughly (e.g., the R-Car V4H hitting the sweet spot for 8 MP camera processing at 36 TOPS within a power envelope suited for an engine control box is a targeted solution). Renesas's approach underlines that not all SDV computing is about brute force—sometimes it's about a balanced SoC that meets just the needed performance at low power and cost, integrated into a bigger safety concept with companion chips.

Selection Criteria for Automotive Silicon

When choosing silicon for an SDV program, architects and product managers should weigh

- **Cost vs. safety capability**: Look beyond raw $/TOPS and consider a $/ASIL-D-capable control channel. A "cheap" device that cannot carry safety-critical loads may force extra companion MCUs and inflate total BOM.
- **Tooling and engineering cost**: Factor in ecosystem maturity (compilers, AUTOSAR stacks, hypervisors, debug tools). A slightly more expensive chip with a strong ecosystem can cut months from schedule and reduce lifetime engineering effort.
- **SKU layering and reuse**: Ensure the portfolio supports clear trim steps (low-end MCU, mid-range domain controller, high-end central SoC) so you can reuse software across segments instead of maintaining unrelated platforms.
- **Long-term support and supply**: Confirm roadmap, longevity (10–15+ years), and multi-source options, especially after the 2020s shortages; silicon that cannot be procured in volume will kill even the best SDV architecture.

3.8 RISC-V in Automotive

The rise of RISC-V, an open standard Instruction Set Architecture (ISA), is a notable development across computing, and it has not left automotive untouched [123, 124]. Why does RISC-V matter for cars? Because carmakers and suppliers are increasingly interested in open, customizable, and license-free alternatives to traditional CPU IP, to reduce costs and avoid single-vendor dependence (like on Arm), echoing the licensing and lock-in concerns discussed earlier in this chapter.

3.8.1 Open ISA: Flexibility and No Royalties

RISC-V is an open ISA, meaning anyone can design a processor core that executes RISC-V instructions without paying royalties. For silicon vendors and OEMs, this promises more control and potentially lower costs.

They can customize the processor to their needs, adding extensions for specific computations (e.g., a special instruction for cryptography or sensor processing). In the automotive context, one can imagine customizing a RISC-V core to optimize certain automotive math or to integrate safety checks at the ISA level. Companies like Andes, SiFive, etc. offer RISC-V IP cores that can be tailored in ways Arm cores cannot (since Arm's design is fixed) [125, 126].

3.8.2 Adoption Status

As of 2024/2025, RISC-V in production automotive roles is still emerging, but momentum is building [123]:

- Big names are getting involved. For example, Renesas has embraced RISC-V and announced it will develop RISC-V–based automotive chips [127, 128]. Renesas has announced automotive- oriented RISC-V MCU families alongside its existing RL78 and RH850 lines, positioning RISC-V as a complementary option rather than a replacement overnight. Also, European projects like the European Processor Initiative (EPI) are looking at RISC-V for automotive and HPC to reduce dependence on foreign technology.
- Companies like Bosch, Infineon, NXP, and Qualcomm joined the RISC-V consortium or are exploring RISC-V in some capacity [123, 124]. Qualcomm, for instance, has used RISC-V cores as DSP replacements or management cores in some SoCs.
- Some ADAS vendors are exploring RISC-V as auxiliary or management cores in their SoCs, but most public production deployments still center on proprietary or Arm-based CPU clusters.
- We also see RISC-V being used in peripheral controllers: e.g., some car Wi-Fi or modem chips use a RISC-V core inside to run firmware.

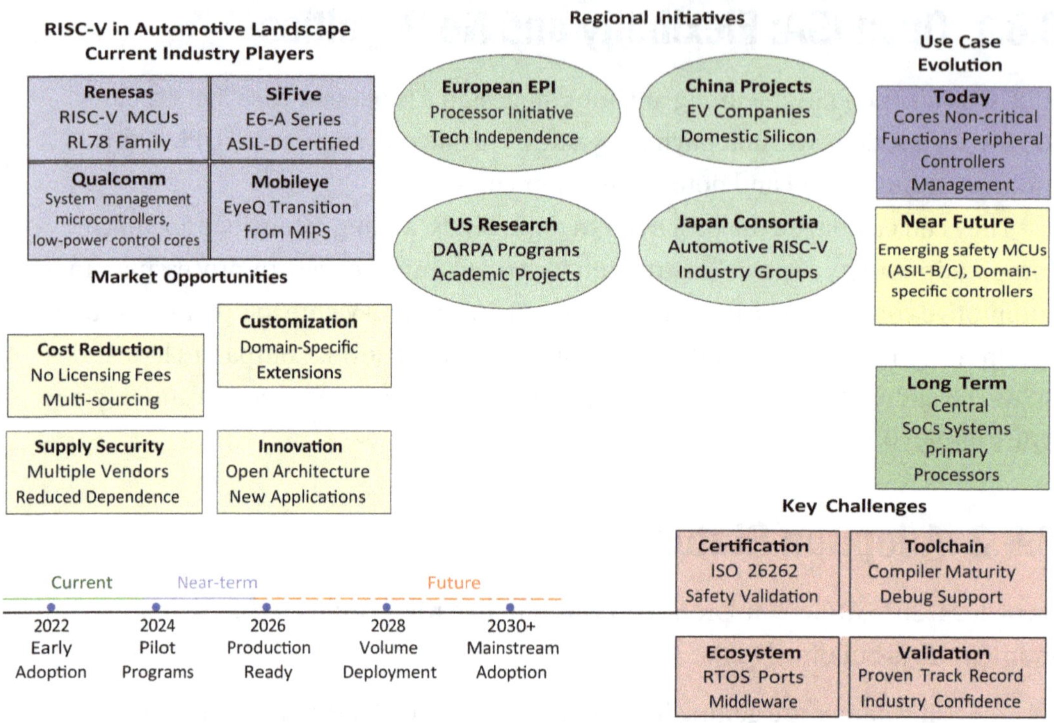

Figure 3-16. *RISC-V automotive landscape showing current adoption status and future potential*

3.8.3 Challenges: ISO 26262 Certification and Ecosystem

The biggest hurdle for RISC-V in automotive is achieving the required functional safety and having a strong development ecosystem:

- **ISO 26262 certification**: Any processor core intended for ASIL-D systems must have a safety case (prove via analysis that it can meet fault metrics and so on). Arm cores come with long track records and safety packages (Arm offers certified versions of Cortex-R and some Cortex-A). For RISC-V, each new core design has to undergo this process from scratch or via new methodologies. There is progress: for instance, SiFive has obtained ISO 26262 ASIL-B and ASIL-D certification for several of its RISC-V cores, such as the SiFive E6-A series [125, 129, 130]. SiFive's E6-AD and others are explicitly targeting automotive safety MCUs, with split-lock support and safety mechanisms built in. Also, Codasip and other IP vendors have announced certification of their development processes [131]. This shows RISC-V IP can indeed be made safe—but it's still relatively new, so customers will scrutinize it heavily.

- **Toolchain fragmentation**: With Arm, you have well-established compiler support (GCC, Arm Compiler, IAR, etc.), debuggers, trace tools, and AUTOSAR OS ports that everyone has been using for years. RISC-V, being open, has many toolchains, but they might not all be as mature or optimized (especially for performance).

  However, this is improving: major tool vendors like Green Hills and IAR have added RISC-V support with functional safety in mind [132]. The LLVM project and GCC both have solid RISC-V back-ends now, and there are specialized AUTOSAR offerings for RISC-V (ETAS and others have done some).

- **Software ecosystem**: Arm's ecosystem advantages (middleware, RTOS, AUTOSAR stacks pre-ported) need to be replicated. We're seeing it happen slowly: e.g., Zephyr RTOS and AUTOSAR Adaptive both run on RISC-V already in demos. But an OEM might worry about integration effort if they move away from known quantity cores.

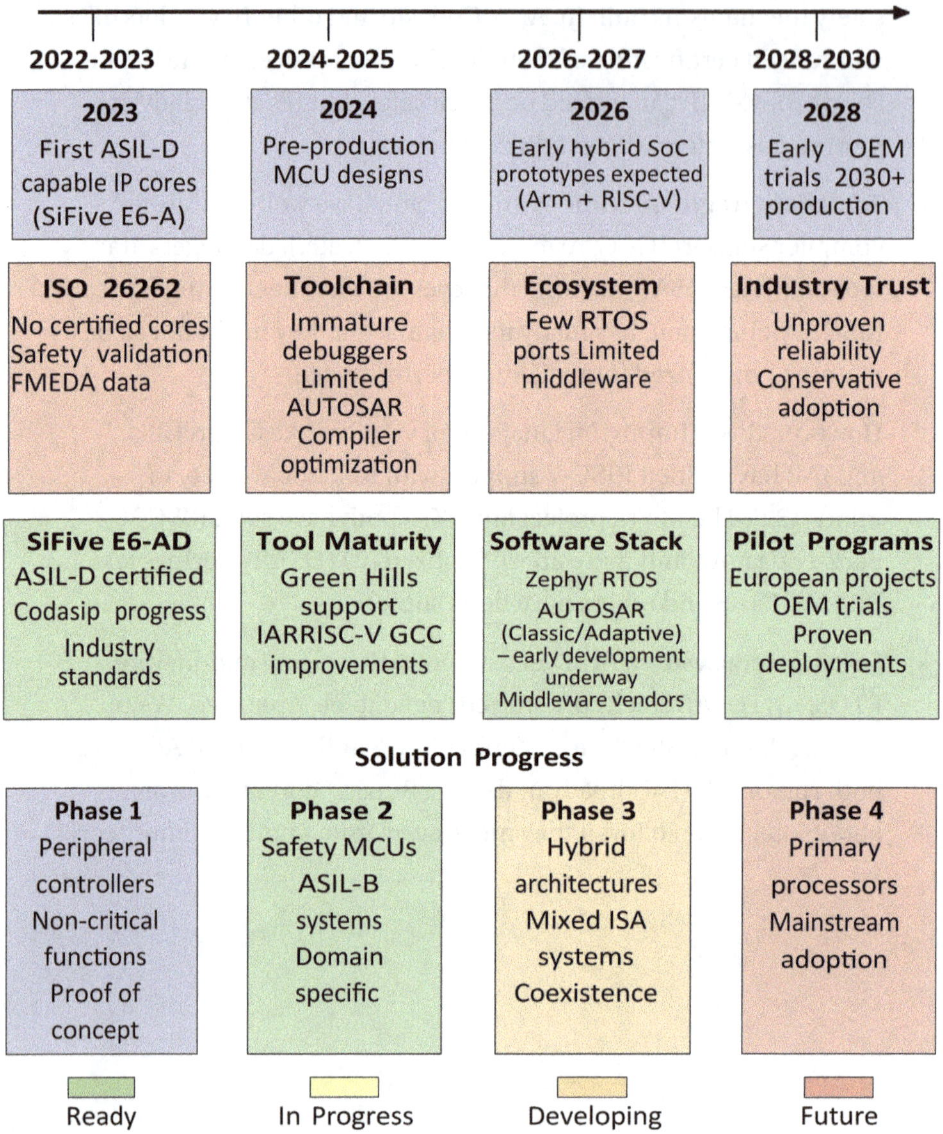

Figure 3-17. *RISC-V adoption timeline showing current challenges and projected milestones for automotive readiness*

3.8.4 Current RISC-V Automotive Use Cases

The likely near-term use of RISC-V in cars is in a coexistence model—i.e., hybrid SoCs with both Arm and RISC-V. For example, an SoC might use Arm Cortex-A for heavy lifting but include a RISC-V core as a safety monitor or for some peripheral control. This gives developers a chance to work with RISC-V in a limited capacity.

Key Point RISC-V can be used to implement custom accelerators (like a reconfigurable vector processor for AI) that sits alongside standard cores. Because it's modular, one can use the standard RISC-V vector extension to get a ready-made AI accelerator ISA rather than inventing one from scratch.

China has been quite aggressive in exploring RISC-V for automotive, driven by a desire for tech independence. There are reports of Chinese EV companies planning domain controllers on RISC-V or AI chips using RISC-V for ADAS (e.g., Huami and Horizon Robotics have discussed RISC-V for some cores).

3.8.5 Hype vs. Reality

The hype is that RISC-V will free the automotive industry from the shackles of proprietary IP and spur innovation. The reality is that it's going to be a gradual integration, not an overnight replacement.

Mission-critical, ultra-validated systems (like airbag controllers or powertrain MCUs) will be conservative in switching to new CPU architectures. They will require proof over many years that RISC-V can be just as reliable. We are likely to see coexistence—Arm and RISC-V together—with early ASIL-B/C pilot deployments entering production around 2024–2025 and broader ramp-up through 2025–2030.

Example A future car's central computer might run an Arm-based SoC for infotainment and ADAS, but use RISC-V–based controllers for some auxiliary systems or as a fallback redundant core that can take over in a limp-home mode if the main chip fails. In fact, one of Arm's own presentations acknowledged the likelihood of heterogeneous ISAs in future vehicles (since even Arm has to prepare for competition).

The multi-sourcing advantage of RISC-V is very attractive: OEMs could potentially have multiple suppliers offering compatible RISC-V chips, increasing competition and supply security. This is something the industry has learned to value after chip shortages and such. It's telling that Europe's automotive industry is investing in RISC-V (via projects and consortia) as a strategic move [123].

In summary, RISC-V in automotive is on the horizon—starting to appear in niche roles, with pilot programs in Europe and China, and likely ramping up by 2025–2030. It won't outright replace Arm in the short term, especially not in high-performance domains where Arm still has a large lead in available IP and proven designs.

Instead, expect RISC-V and Arm to coexist in many designs, each used where it makes sense: RISC-V for highly customizable, perhaps cost-sensitive or specialized parts of the system and Arm where ecosystem and performance are paramount. Over time, if the RISC-V ecosystem matures robustly, we could see full-fledged automotive SoCs (even for ADAS or infotainment) built on RISC-V; a few startups are certainly aiming for that. The automotive industry is naturally cautious, but it definitely has its eye on RISC-V as a key enabler for the next generation of silicon innovation.

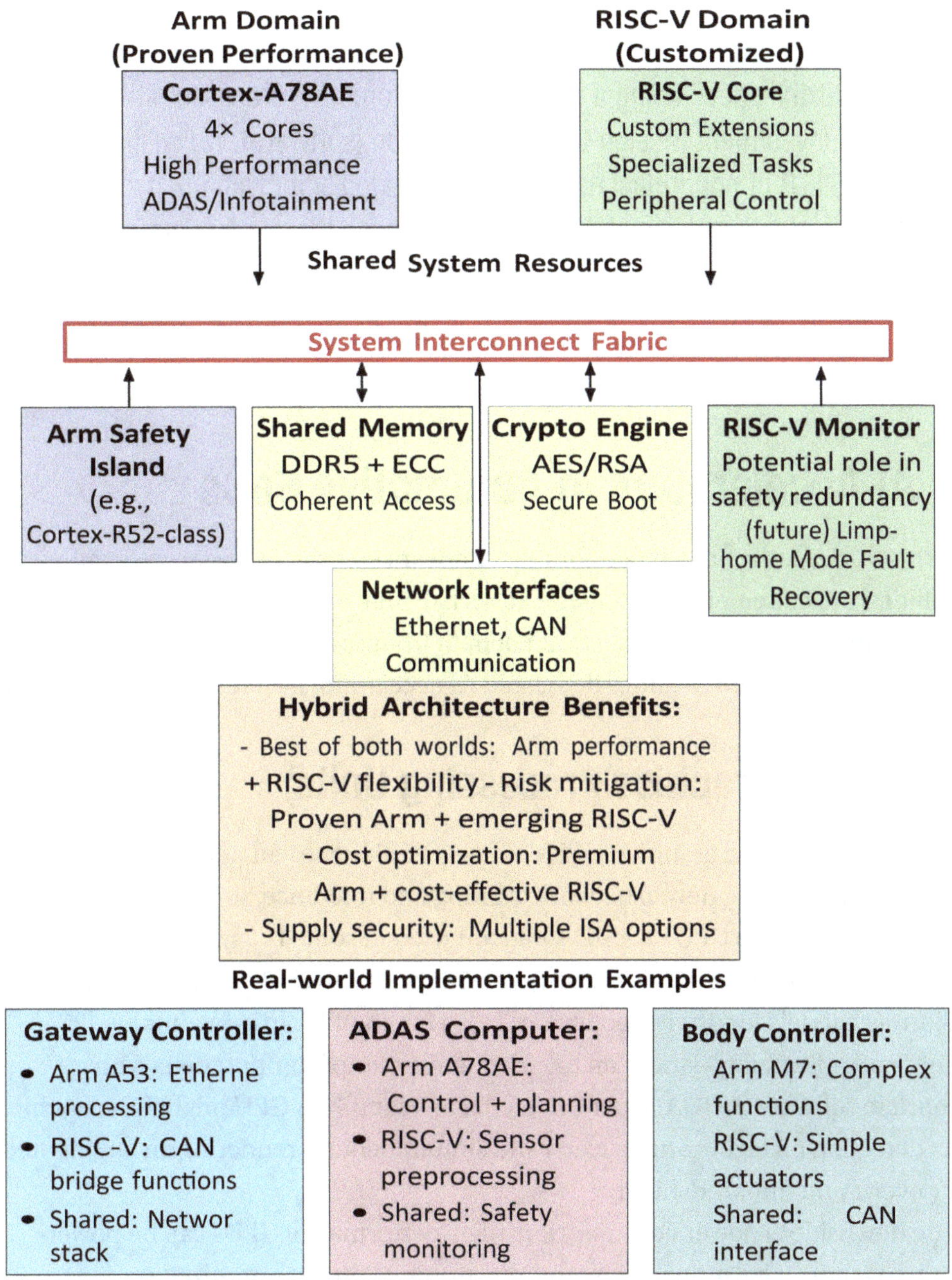

Figure 3-18. *Hybrid Arm–RISC-V architecture showing a coexistence model for automotive applications*

Critic's Note RISC-V hype is real, but so are the challenges. While it's touted as "free" and flexible, developing a safe RISC-V automotive processor still requires tremendous investment (design talent, verification, software). We will likely see RISC-V in ASIL-B or noncritical roles first and gradually moving up. It's not a magic bullet—more of a long-term strategic shift. For now, the prudent outlook is hybrid: leverage RISC-V where it adds value, but keep Arm where it's already solving the problem efficiently.

3.9 AI Accelerators in Automotive SoCs

Modern vehicles, especially those aiming for advanced driver assistance or autonomous capabilities, are extremely AI-intensive. Tasks like image recognition, sensor fusion, path planning, voice recognition, etc. all benefit from specialized processing. Thus, automotive silicon often includes dedicated AI accelerators. Here are the main classes.

3.9.1 GPUs (Graphics Processing Units)

Originally for rendering graphics, GPUs are now workhorses for general parallel computation, including neural network training and inference. In automotive, GPUs (like NVIDIA's Ampere GPU or AMD's Radeon used in some IVI systems) are used for deep learning (e.g., running convolutional neural networks on camera images or transformer models for driving policy) and also for graphics in infotainment [97].

GPUs offer flexibility—they can handle many types of computations with appropriate software (CUDA, OpenCL, etc.). For example, a GPU might be crunching object detection on eight camera feeds and simultaneously rendering an augmented reality overlay on the windshield.

The downside is power consumption: high-performance GPUs can be power-hungry, so automotive usage often requires running them at optimized settings. Nonetheless, GPUs are ubiquitous in high-end ADAS computers—e.g., Tesla's Hardware 3 has a tiny GPU for certain tasks [133], NVIDIA's DRIVE series centers around a GPU, and even some cockpit chips now include GPUs to support fancy UIs. When an automaker quotes "TOPS," often a large chunk comes from the GPU.

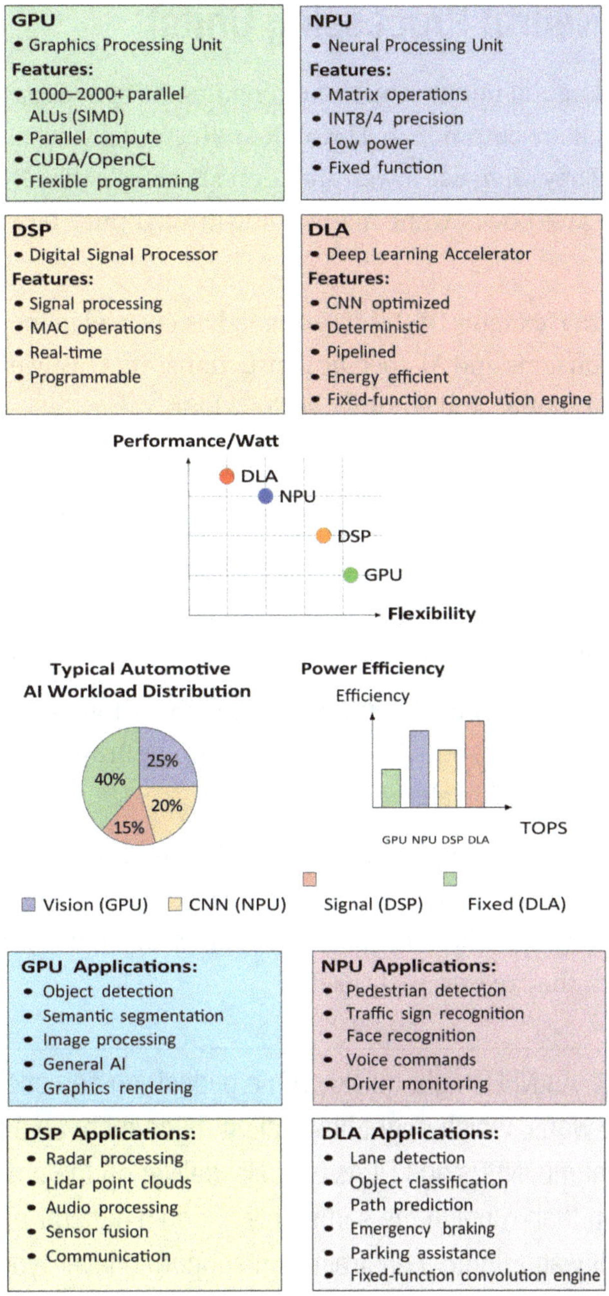

Figure 3-19. *Types of AI accelerators in automotive SoCs: GPUs, NPUs, DSPs, and DLAs*

3.9.2 NPUs (Neural Processing Units)

These are dedicated neural network inference engines, designed to execute matrix and vector operations that are common in AI workloads (especially deep neural nets) with extreme efficiency. They often use lower-precision arithmetic (like INT8, or even 4-bit, or sparsity tricks) to save power while maintaining throughput. Here are examples in automotive:

- **Qualcomm Hexagon DSP/AI**: Hexagon has evolved to include vector extensions and AI-specific instructions, effectively making it an NPU for mobile and automotive SoCs [98].
- **Arm Ethos**: Arm offers Ethos cores (like Ethos-U and Ethos-N series), which some automotive vendors might integrate for AI acceleration.
- **Tesla's Neural Processing Unit**: Tesla's FSD computer has dual NPUs, each delivering 36 TOPS, purely dedicated to neural network inferencing (these handle the bulk of the camera perception tasks).
- **Mobileye's EyeQ chips**: They are loaded with custom AI cores (not exactly called NPUs, but they have matrix multiplication engines for their computer vision algorithms).

NPUs are typically more energy-efficient for AI inference than GPUs, because they are optimized for the specific data flows of neural nets. They can lack some flexibility (they might need the network layers to fit certain patterns), but for production deployable networks, they're extremely useful.

Technical Detail An NPU might quickly run a pedestrian detection network at 30 FPS with a few watts, which might have taken much more on a CPU or general DSP. As a rule of thumb, NPUs and DLAs typically deliver on the order of 2–5× better inferences per watt than running the same network on a general-purpose GPU, at the cost of less flexibility and tighter constraints on supported layer types and data flows.

Modern NPUs increasingly exploit structured sparsity (skipping zero weights or activations) to effectively double or even triple useful TOPS at the same power, but only when networks are pruned and quantized appropriately to match the accelerator's sparsity scheme.

3.9.3 DSPs (Digital Signal Processors)

DSPs are processors optimized for signal processing tasks—fast multiply-accumulates, data moves, etc. They've been around for decades and were originally used for things like audio processing or modem algorithms. In automotive, DSPs play a key role in radar and LiDAR processing and sometimes for multi-sensor fusion.

Texas Instruments's Jacinto (TDA) processors are a good example: they incorporate TI C66x/C7x DSP cores, which handle pre-processing of radar returns, doing FFTs, filtering, etc. extremely fast. A DSP is also good for LiDAR—handling the accumulation and basic object clustering from the point cloud data. Additionally, DSPs might run things like engine sound synthesis, active noise cancellation, or other real-time math-heavy tasks in a car.

Many automotive SoCs (even those primarily CPU/GPU based) include a DSP: e.g., NVIDIA's DRIVE chips include a PVA (Programmable Vision Accelerator), which is like a small DSP for image processing; Qualcomm's chips as mentioned have Hexagon (a hybrid DSP/NPU) [97, 98].

Compared with NPUs, DSPs are more programmable/flexible, but typically a bit less efficient on strictly AI tasks. However, they can be repurposed—e.g., the same DSP core might do radar processing one moment and run a small neural network for radar target classification the next.

Legacy uses: Prior to the current AI wave, DSPs in cars handled things like video compression (H.264 encode/decode for parking cameras), and some still do, although dedicated video units often take that role now.

3.9.4 Dedicated DLAs (Deep Learning Accelerators)

These are fixed-function or semi-fixed accelerators specifically for neural networks, often provided as licensable IP or built in-house. NVIDIA's NVDLA is a prime example: an open source deep learning accelerator design that NVIDIA also integrates into chips like Orin (two NVDLA engines on-chip) [97].

These are not programmable like a DSP; instead, they are fed a neural network (which is compiled to their supported operations), and they execute it with minimal overhead, often in a pipelined fashion that guarantees a certain throughput.

Because they are fixed-function, they can be made very power-efficient and deterministic—a quality valued for safety (you can calculate exact latency for a given network). Many automotive vendors use DLAs for tasks like pedestrian detection or lane detection where the network architecture is known and not going to change drastically. They free up GPU/CPU resources for other tasks.

- Tesla's NPUs could be considered a type of DLA since they are fairly fixed-function for NN workloads.
- Some Infineon AURIX TC4x MCUs even have a tiny DLA for things like basic AI, given the mention of Parallel Processing Unit—though that's more of a vector DSP, but it plays a similar role for small networks [103].
- Renesas's R-Car H3 had IMP-X accelerators, which were somewhat like a DLA for certain vision algorithms (though not as general as modern DLA) [120].

The presence of these accelerators leads to a heterogeneous computing environment on automotive chips. Software has to distribute workloads: e.g., run camera neural nets on the NPU, do occupancy grid on the GPU, run a vehicle dynamics model on the CPU, etc. and all concurrently. This is orchestrated by runtime frameworks (like ROS 2, AUTOSAR Adaptive, or custom frameworks by NVIDIA/Qualcomm).

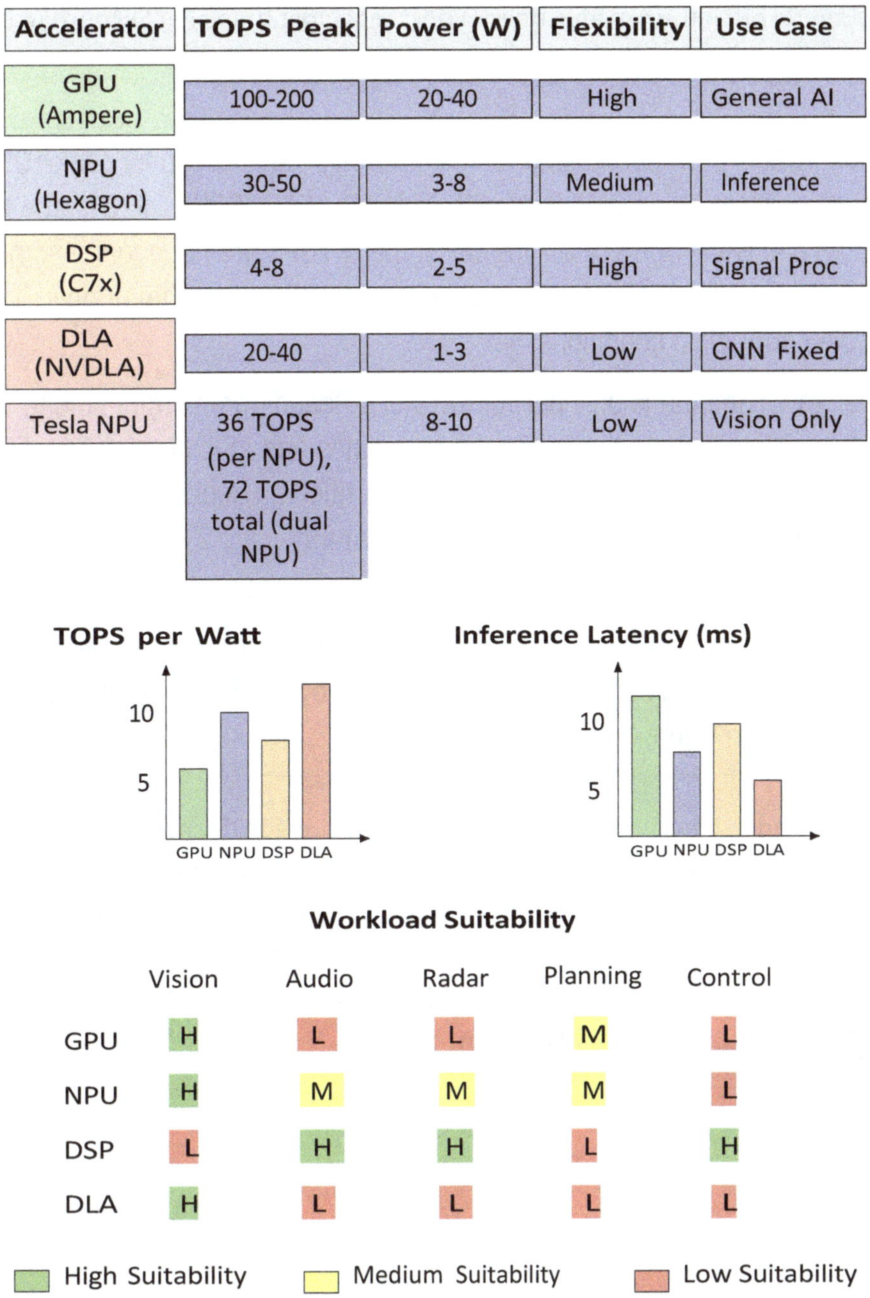

***Figure 3-20.** Comparison of AI accelerators showing performance vs. flexibility trade-offs*

A key metric often thrown around is TOPS (Tera Operations Per Second) to indicate AI capability. However, as a business note, one should be cautious:

Business Note OEM purchasing teams often mis-rank silicon by peak TOPS number. It's easy to be dazzled by a chip claiming "500 TOPS" and assume it's better than one with "300 TOPS." In reality, many TOPS are not equal—some might be at low precision or not usable by your specific algorithm or only achievable under ideal conditions.

Moreover, raw compute is only part of the story. Real differentiators among automotive silicon include things like safety islands and ASIL certification, ECC memory protection, strong virtualization and partitioning support, robust and well-supported toolchains, and overall ecosystem maturity.

A device with slightly lower TOPS might outperform a "paper tiger" if it can sustain performance in real workloads (thermal design) and if it integrates easily into your software environment. In short, don't judge a chip by TOPS alone—look at the complete platform value.

This note underscores that while AI accelerators provide the needed muscle, what makes them truly valuable is how they are integrated and supported. For example, NVIDIA's advantage is not just GPU/DLA hardware, but that developers have CUDA, TensorRT, tons of pre-trained DNN examples, etc. Similarly, Qualcomm's advantage is that their AI engine comes with an Android Neural Networks API support and many optimizations pre-tuned for their Hexagon.

From an SDV perspective, having the right balance of GPU, NPU, and DSP is important. If an automaker focuses mainly on vision, heavy NPUs/GPUs make sense. If they also want to consolidate something like in-cabin occupant monitoring and digital cockpit on the same SoC, they need GPUs for rendering and maybe multiple accelerators to handle different AI tasks concurrently (face recognition, speech recognition, etc.).

Automotive chip designers thus often include a mix: e.g., one high-power GPU for flexibility + one NPU for efficient CNN inference + one or two DSPs for signal processing and backup.

Example The Tesla FSD computer (Hardware 3) doesn't use a big GPU, but instead has 2× 36-TOPS NPUs, some GPUs for minor tasks, and CPUs for control. Tesla optimized for pure inference efficiency for their known workload (camera nets), whereas Audi's zFAS (older-gen central controller) had an NVIDIA GPU and Mobileye EyeQ working together—GPU for some nets, EyeQ (which is like a DLA) for others.

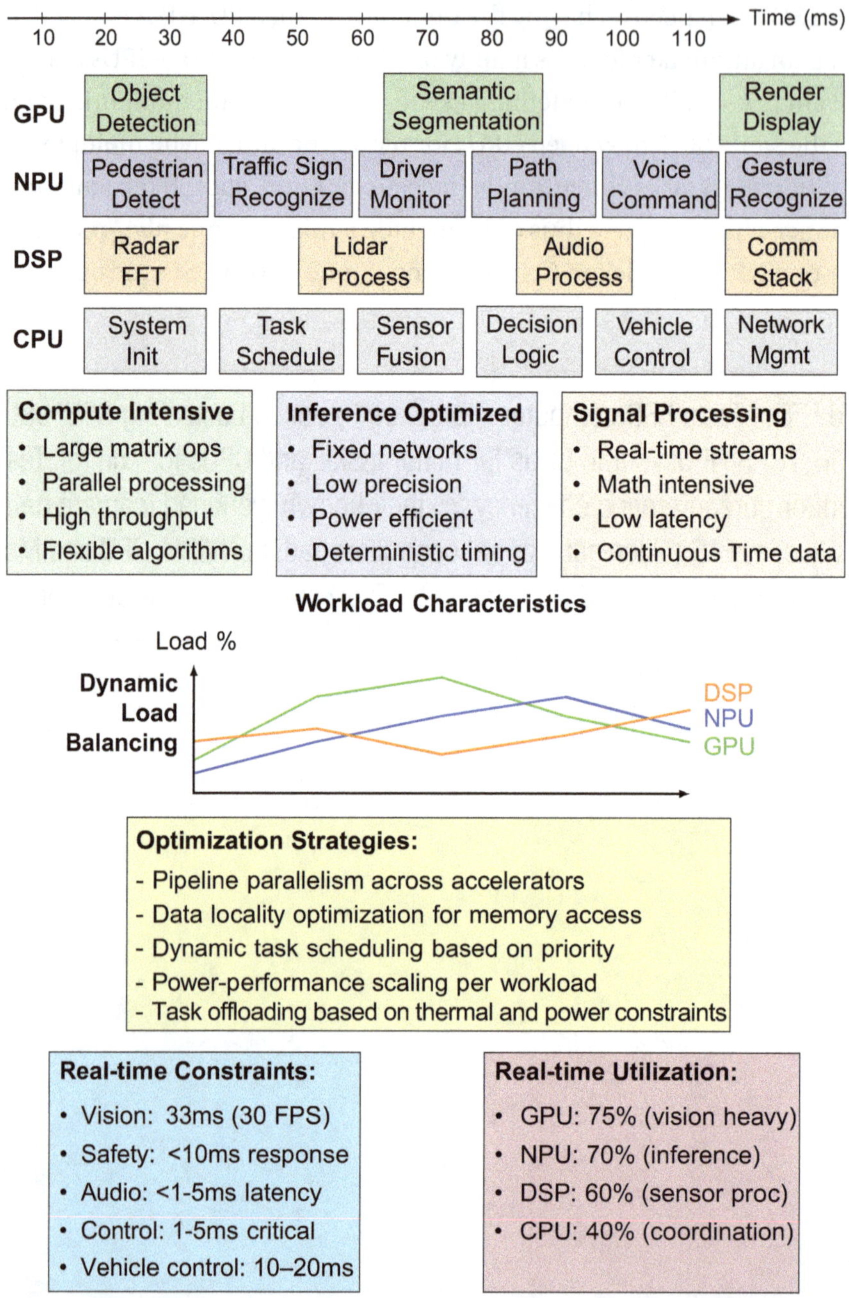

Figure 3-21. *Heterogeneous AI workload distribution across different accelerators in automotive SoC*

In summary, AI accelerators in automotive are the enabling force behind the software-defined vehicle's advanced features. They turn the massive amounts of sensor data into meaningful decisions in real time. Without them, a car would need a data center's worth of CPUs to do what a single SoC can do with accelerators.

Selecting which accelerators to use (and programming them effectively) is a critical part of SDV development. It's a quickly evolving field—every generation brings new types (like "NPUs with sparse compute" or "graph neural net accelerators" perhaps in future). Automotive engineers need to not only look at the current needs but also anticipate where AI algorithms are heading (e.g., the rise of transformer models for perception) and ensure the silicon will support those or can be updated.

3.10 Safety and Security Mechanisms in Silicon

Automotive electronics must meet stringent safety requirements (ISO 26262, derived from the more general IEC 61508 functional safety standard) and withstand cyber threats [96]. Silicon vendors include a suite of hardware mechanisms to support these needs.

The convergence of safety and security in automotive silicon represents one of the most significant shifts in chip design philosophy over the past decade. Traditionally, safety mechanisms focused on detecting and mitigating random hardware failures—bit flips from cosmic rays, transistor aging, or thermal stress. Security mechanisms, by contrast, addressed intentional attacks—malicious code injection, key extraction, or unauthorized access. Today's software-defined vehicles require both simultaneously, and modern automotive SoCs must provide robust defenses against failures that are both accidental and adversarial.

This dual mandate creates interesting design trade-offs. Safety mechanisms like lockstep cores add redundancy that increases power consumption and die area. Security features like hardware security modules (HSMs) require dedicated silicon real estate and careful isolation from the rest of the chip. Yet skimping on either is not an option: a vehicle that passes ISO 26262 certification but can be remotely hacked is no safer than one that resists hackers but suffers from undetected memory corruption. The best automotive silicon integrates both concerns from the ground up, treating safety and security as complementary rather than competing requirements.

Definition **Defense in depth:** A security and safety architecture principle where multiple independent protective mechanisms are layered such that the failure or bypass of one layer does not compromise the entire system. In automotive silicon, this manifests as hardware watchdogs backing up software monitors, ECC memory protecting against corruption even when lockstep cores detect CPU faults, and HSMs securing keys even if TrustZone is somehow breached.

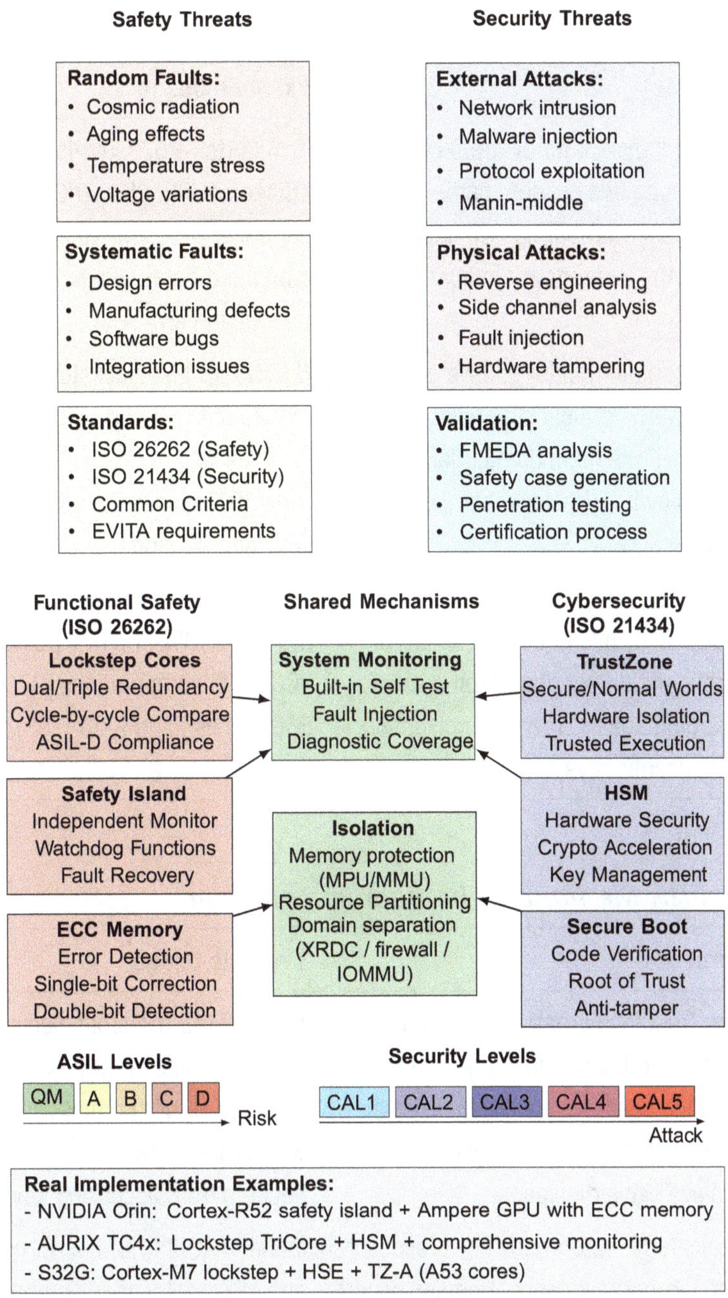

***Figure 3-22.** Overview of safety and security mechanisms implemented in automotive silicon*

Table 3-4. *Safety Mechanisms in Automotive Silicon*

Mechanism	Purpose	Example Usage
Lockstep cores	Detect transient hardware faults by running two or more cores in synchrony, comparing outputs cycle by cycle. Any discrepancy indicates a fault.	Arm Cortex-R52 (split-lock mode) [101], Infineon AURIX (dual TriCore) [103]. A brake controller MCU with dual lockstep ensures a bit flip triggers a safe fault rather than an undetected error.
Safety island	Independent monitor subsystem that runs safety- critical supervision and can act if the main domain fails. Often has its own CPU, clock, and power domain.	NXP S32G has a lockstep Cortex-M7 island monitoring A53 cores [85]. NVIDIA Orin includes 4× Cortex-R52 cores for safety tasks [97]. Can reset frozen CPUs or trigger limp-home mode.
ECC memory	Error-correcting code stores redundancy bits to correct single-bit errors and detect double-bit errors, guarding against memory corruption from cosmic rays and others.	All ASIL-D SoCs use ECC on SRAMs and DRAM. NVIDIA Orin's LPDDR interface uses ECC for AI computations [97]. AURIX has ECC on flash and RAM [103].

Table 3-5. *Security Mechanisms in Automotive Silicon*

Mechanism	Purpose	Example Usage
TrustZone	Arm TrustZone creates secure and normal worlds on the same CPU, isolating sensitive code/data from the main system [99]. Security enclaves achieve similar isolation.	Cortex-M33 TrustZone secures firmware update routines [100]. Cortex-A78AE runs a secure OS for crypto, while the normal world runs Linux. Prevents infotainment hackers from accessing keys.
HSM	Dedicated cryptography co- processor with tamper resistance. Handles secure boot, authentication, and encryption and stores keys in hardware fuses or protected memory.	Infineon AURIX HSM performs secure boot and AES/CAN authentication [111]. NXP HSE on S32G handles similar tasks [85]. Keys remain inaccessible even if main code is compromised.

In an ISO 26262 context, these mechanisms are not ends in themselves but inputs into quantitative analyses such as FMEDA (Failure Modes, Effects, and Diagnostics Analysis). FMEDA connects concrete hardware features (e.g., lockstep coverage of CPU faults, ECC coverage of memory faults) to architectural metrics like single-point fault metric (SPFM) and latent fault metric (LFM) for a given ASIL target.

These mechanisms form a layered defense and robustness strategy [96]. The silicon-level features are ultimately consumed by system-level safety processes (ISO 26262 V-model development, ASIL decomposition, and safety case construction).

Key Point For comprehensive coverage of ISO 26262 ASIL levels, diagnostic coverage requirements, FMEDA methodology, safety case construction, and ASIL decomposition strategies, see **Chapter 9**.

Here are a few additional notes on these mechanisms:

- **Lockstep is fundamental** for meeting low failure rates required by ASIL-D. Typically, two cores in lockstep will detect a single fault in either within a few cycles, allowing the system to initiate fail-safe. As an example, many powertrain MCUs have two lockstep cores running the same engine control algorithm—if a cosmic ray flips a register in one core, their outputs diverge and the discrepancy is caught, triggering a controlled engine shutdown instead of potentially wrong actuation.

- **Safety islands implement concepts** like redundant "heartbeat" monitoring (the island expects periodic alive signals from the main CPU; if missed, it assumes the main CPU failed and resets or informs other ECUs). They often also handle watchdog timers and can run simplified control tasks to bring the vehicle to a safe stop if needed.

  For instance, in an ADAS SoC, the safety island might monitor that the object detection tasks are running within frame deadlines—if not, it might alert the system or take over with a minimal safety algorithm (like triggering brakes based on last known data). Safety islands are often designed to ASIL-D even if the rest of chip is ASIL-B/QM, to serve as a reliable caretaker.

- **ECC memory everywhere**: Automotive memories (SRAM, DRAM, flash) often use ECC or at least parity. For example, an SRAM might use Single Error Correction, Double Error Detection (SEC-DED) codes. This is crucial because vehicles can face many environmental stresses (heat, radiation at high altitudes, etc.).

  A single bit error in the wrong place, say in the program counter or in a critical sensor reading, could cause serious malfunction. ECC ensures most such errors don't even propagate. In software, developers also adhere to safe patterns (such as initializing variables and using safety compiler checks), but hardware ECC is the bedrock for preventing random hardware faults from becoming system faults.

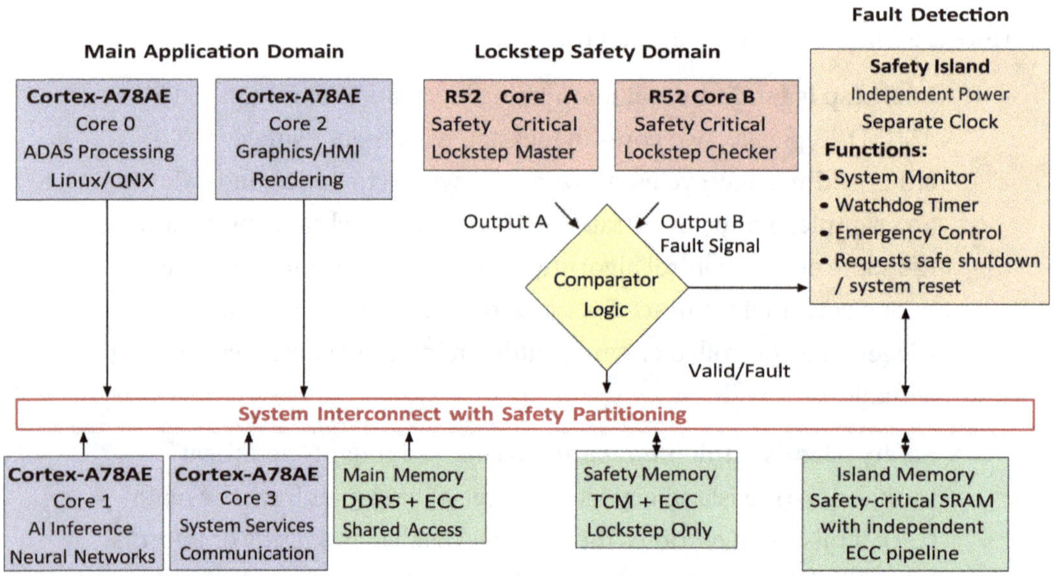

***Figure 3-23.** Safety architecture showing lockstep cores and safety island implementation*

- **TrustZone and HSM (security features)**: With cars being connected, hacks are a real threat (there have been cases of cars being hacked remotely via their infotainment). Therefore, modern automotive MCUs and SoCs implement secure boot—using an HSM or secure ROM to verify signatures of software at boot time, ensuring only OEM-approved code runs [85, 111]. TrustZone allows creating a "trusted execution environment" to, e.g., perform an OTA update decryption and signature check in the secure world, without exposing the private decryption keys to the rest of the system [99]. This means even if an attacker gets control of the Linux infotainment stack, they cannot easily alter the secure bootloader or read out the keys—the hardware will not allow the normal world to access secure memory.

  Some systems also use things like authenticated debugging (requiring special tokens to use JTAG) to prevent thieves from extracting code or secrets from ECUs.

- **HSM implementations** in automotive often follow standards such as EVITA (a European project defining secure automotive hardware requirements) and ISO 21434 (cybersecurity). They handle things like accelerating cryptographic algorithms (AES, SHA, RSA/ECC), since automotive CPUs may be too slow in software for heavy crypto.

  They also often support Secure Hardware Extension (SHE)—a simpler set of crypto services many MCUs provide (NXP and Infineon both had SHE implementations). The presence of an HSM is what enables features like an immobilizer with challenge-response, secure onboard communication (e.g., encrypting CAN messages to prevent tampering), and vehicle-to-infrastructure authentication (like verifying that a firmware update server is legitimate).

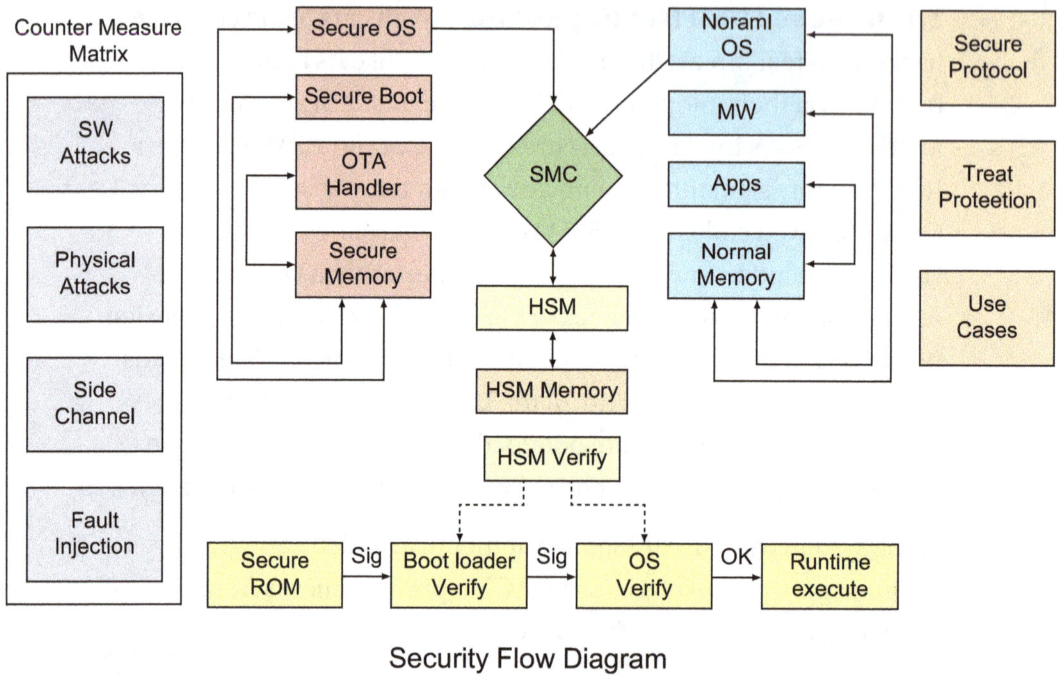

***Figure 3-24.** Security architecture showing TrustZone and HSM implementation for secure boot and crypto operations*

In conclusion, the safety/security mechanisms at silicon level are what allow automakers to build trusted, reliable SDV platforms. The car's critical functions are protected against random failures by lockstep, safety monitors, ECC, etc. and protected against intentional malicious interference by secure boot, TrustZone, HSM, etc.

A software-defined vehicle, which heavily relies on software updates and connectivity, would simply not be feasible without these hardware supports—the risk of bricking a car or getting it hacked would be too high. That's why when evaluating automotive chips, one must look closely at these features (often more so than raw CPU speed). It's also why sometimes automotive chips lag a gen behind consumer chips in process tech—they need time to integrate these safety features and certify them.

Key Point These mechanisms are the unsung heroes behind the scenes. For example, earlier we discussed OTA updates and reliability—ECC and safety islands directly play into that (ensuring memory errors during an update don't corrupt it and a safety core can recover a failed update). Or when comparing architectures (Arm vs. AURIX vs. RISC-V), a key differentiator is how robustly each implements these safety/security features (Arm's TrustZone, Infineon's redundant safeguards, etc.).

3.11 OTA Reliability and Adaptive Modulation

Over-the-air (OTA) update reliability is critical for SDVs—a failed update could leave a vehicle inoperable [72, 73]. While detailed OTA transport and modulation mechanisms are covered in Chapters 5 and 7, silicon choices directly impact update robustness:

- **Dual-bank flash with hardware-assisted swap:** Enables atomic A/B partition switching and rollback.
- **Crypto accelerators:** Speed signature verification to minimize programming-mode exposure.
- **Hardware watchdogs:** Recover stuck update procedures automatically.
- **ECC-protected storage:** Prevent bit flip corruption during update transfers.
- **Hypervisor isolation:** Run update processes in protected partitions.

Quote Prioritize A/B image layout, secure boot with HSM or TrustZone, rollback, ECC-protected storage, and resume-capable transport, aligned with ISO 24089 and UNECE R156 software update standards [72, 73, 134].

From a safety standpoint, OTA must be fail-safe [134]. If an update fails midway, the system should revert to old software automatically—this is why A/B partitions are essential. The communication stack must not hang or misbehave in edge cases, requiring thorough testing on bare-metal or an RTOS. Ideally, updates for safety-critical ECUs occur only when the vehicle is parked; central compute updates for autonomous driving modules might happen overnight while connected to home Wi-Fi.

When evaluating an automotive chip for OTA capability, key questions include: Does it support dual-bank firmware with hardware-assisted swap? Does it have sufficient non-volatile memory for a full backup image? Can it perform secure verification quickly using crypto accelerators to minimize programming-mode exposure? Does it allow flexible interfacing with different communication modules (Ethernet, Wi-Fi, 5G)? These questions address features deep in the silicon that directly determine whether your OTA strategy will succeed or fail at fleet scale.

Critic's Note Always tie silicon capabilities to OTA reliability in system design. A flashy SoC with great AI but lacking a safety island or dual-image update support could put your entire OTA strategy at risk. When planning a software-defined vehicle, scrutinize how the hardware will handle the update cycle—it is just as important as how it handles the normal drive cycle.

Key Point For detailed coverage of OTA transport protocols, adaptive modulation techniques, and network resilience strategies, see **Chapters 5** and **7**.

3.12 Key Takeaways

- **Compute hierarchy in SDVs**: Software-defined vehicles deploy a range of compute units: MCUs at the edge for simple real-time control, microprocessors/microcontrollers for safety-critical domains such as chassis and powertrain (often in lockstep for ASIL-D), and powerful SoCs at the center for ADAS, autonomy, and high-level infotainment. Each class has different performance and safety characteristics.
- **Dominance of Arm and rise of others**: Arm architectures (Cortex-M/R/A AE) currently dominate automotive due to their proven ecosystem and IP portfolio [107]. However, Infineon's AURIX (TriCore) remains a popular choice for ultra-reliable control [102], Renesas R-Car and RH850 serve many OEMs [119], Qualcomm and

NVIDIA have stormed into the high-end space with SoCs [98, 97], and RISC-V is emerging as a flexible alternative for future designs [123, 125].

Each comes with an ecosystem, e.g., Arm with broad tool support, AURIX with deep safety documentation, and NVIDIA with CUDA and AI tools. From a practical standpoint, this ecosystem translates into more toolchains, AUTOSAR stacks, safety libraries, and trained engineers per dollar of silicon cost than most competing architectures today.

- **Supply chain and node risk**: The post-2020 semiconductor shortages exposed how fragile reliance on a single process node, foundry, or vendor can be. Silicon selection is no longer just about features and benchmarks, but also multi-sourcing options, long-term capacity commitments, and geographic risk diversification.
- **Safety and security outweigh raw specs**: In automotive, a chip's safety integrity (ASIL capability), fault tolerance mechanisms (lockstep, ECC), and security features (secure boot, HSM) often matter more than who has the fastest CPU or highest TOPS [96].

  For instance, an ASIL-D braking controller will choose a slightly lower-performance MCU if it has proven diagnostics and certification, over a faster one without that pedigree. Similarly, an SDV platform values chips that can be securely updated and partitioned (to avoid one domain's failure or hack affecting others).
- **AI acceleration and heterogeneity**: Automotive SoCs now pack various accelerators—GPUs for heavy lifting in AI and graphics, NPUs for efficient neural net inference, DSPs for signal processing, and so on. Each type of workload (vision CNN vs. radar FFT vs. voice recognition) maps to a different accelerator for optimal performance.

  The ability to orchestrate these (with good software support) is a key advantage for platforms like NVIDIA DRIVE or Qualcomm Snapdragon Ride [97, 98].

- **OTA and comms considerations**: As vehicles rely on OTA updates, the resilience of communication and update mechanisms is tied to hardware capabilities [72, 73, 134]. Chips that support error correction, dual firmware banking, and even adaptive communication strategies (such as modulations or robust protocols) provide a safety net for the OTA.

  An SDV's silicon should ideally facilitate fail-safe updates, meaning that no single update issue can render the vehicle inoperative. This is a new requirement that legacy ECUs did not care about, but now it is vital for customer trust in continuously updating cars.

CHAPTER 4

Operating Systems and Middleware

4.1 Chapter Goals

After completing this chapter, you will be able to

- Explain the role of operating systems and middleware in software-defined vehicles (SDVs).
- Compare AUTOSAR Classic, AUTOSAR Adaptive, and real-time operating system (RTOS) solutions.
- Understand the role of Linux, Android Automotive, and containerization in modern vehicle software stacks.
- Assess Software Update Management Systems (SUMSs) and digital-first CI/CD tie-ins for automotive software.
- Build and deploy a minimal AUTOSAR Adaptive service on a virtual ECU (vECU) platform.

Critic's Note Many SDV failures stem not from bad silicon, but from brittle middleware. OS and middleware choices shape updatability, security, and total cost of ownership (TCO) over a vehicle's lifespan. A robust middleware foundation is essential for long-term success.

S. Agarwal, *Software-Defined Vehicles*, https://doi.org/10.1007/979-8-8688-2718-1_4

4.2 Introduction

The software stack between vehicle hardware and applications—collectively called middleware—has become the critical enabler of software-defined vehicles. This chapter examines the operating systems and middleware frameworks that make SDVs possible, from traditional AUTOSAR Classic for deeply embedded ECUs to modern AUTOSAR Adaptive for high-performance computing and from certified real-time operating systems to consumer-grade platforms like Linux and Android Automotive.

We explore how these technologies coexist through virtualization and containerization, enabling mixed-criticality systems where safety-critical functions run alongside feature-rich applications. The chapter also addresses the regulatory landscape—particularly UNECE R156 and ISO 24089—that now mandates robust Software Update Management Systems (SUMSs) and examines how digital-first development practices enable continuous improvement of vehicle software throughout its lifecycle.

Understanding these middleware choices is essential because they directly determine a vehicle program's ability to deliver OTA updates, achieve safety certification, and maintain developer velocity at scale.

4.3 The Middleware Landscape

Modern vehicles run on layered software stacks between hardware and end user functions. At the top sit applications such as ADAS, infotainment, telematics, and HMI logic. Beneath them are middleware and platform services, which provide communication, service discovery, diagnostics, execution support, and hardware abstraction. Beneath that sits the operating system layer, while vehicle networks such as CAN, LIN, and Ethernet provide the communication fabric rather than constituting middleware themselves.

In a software-defined vehicle, middleware is crucial for abstracting hardware differences and enabling new software features via updates [135]. Without middleware acting as a bridge, pushing over-the-air (OTA) updates or integrating new functions would be impractical in a car that may contain over 100 electronic control units (ECUs) from different suppliers [9].

Middleware provides a service-oriented architecture that decouples application software from the underlying hardware specifics, allowing developers to focus on functionality rather than low-level device details [136, 137]. For example, an infotainment app can send a climate control command without knowing which microcontroller controls the AC—the middleware translates the high-level request into hardware-specific signals behind the scenes [138].

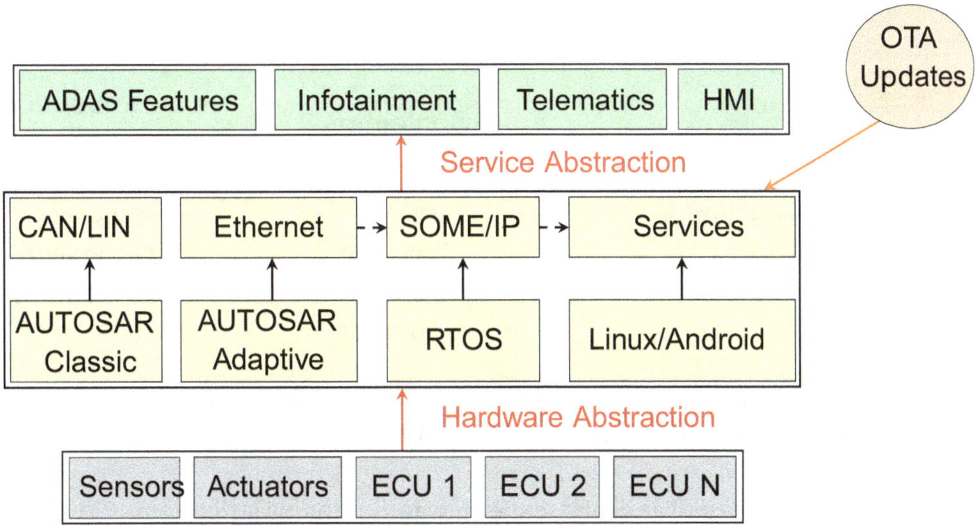

***Figure 4-1.** Conceptual layering of applications, middleware/platform services, operating systems, and vehicle communication technologies in SDVs*

In the automotive domain, several middleware standards and platforms have emerged. **AUTOSAR** (AUTomotive Open System ARchitecture) is a key family of standards that define both Classic Platform (for traditional ECU software) and Adaptive Platform (for new, high-performance applications) [136]. Additionally, vehicles make use of real-time operating systems (RTOSs) for safety-critical tasks, as well as general-purpose OSs like Linux and Android for non-safety domains. We also see virtualization layers and containers being adopted to partition software and manage updates more flexibly. Each of these components plays a distinct role.

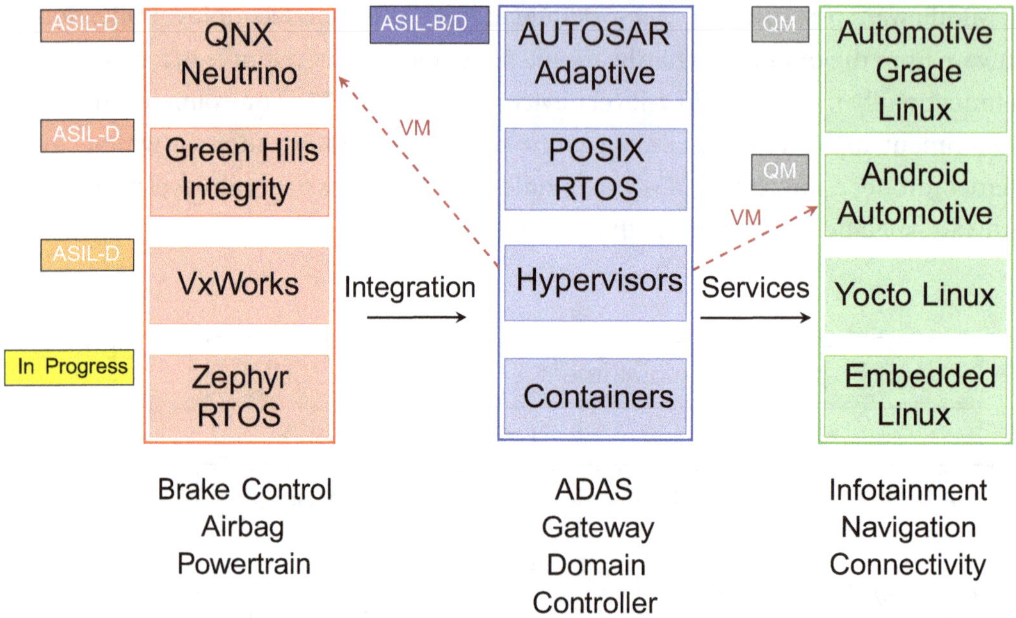

Figure 4-2. *Automotive software platform landscape, showing operating systems, middleware platforms, and isolation mechanisms as distinct categories*

Figure 4-2 should be read as a landscape view rather than a strict stack. RTOSs, Linux, and Android Automotive are operating system choices; AUTOSAR Classic and Adaptive are software platforms or middleware environments built partly above those operating system assumptions; and hypervisors or containers are isolation and deployment mechanisms that may sit alongside or underneath those environments depending on the architecture.

4.4 AUTOSAR Classic

AUTOSAR Classic is the traditional automotive middleware/OS stack designed for the deeply embedded ECUs that handle static functions (think body control modules, engine management, braking, etc.). Introduced in the 2000s, Classic Platform was built around a static architecture in which all software components, scheduling, and memory allocations were defined at design time. It typically runs on an OSEK/VDX-based real-time OS (OSEK is a precursor standard for automotive RTOS).

The key characteristics of AUTOSAR Classic include the following:

Static configuration and real-time determinism:
The software components (runnables) and their scheduling are defined in advance via the configuration files (ARXML). Tasks are executed in a predetermined schedule, producing highly deterministic timing behavior necessary for hard real-time control (e.g., airbag deployment and brake control loops operating within tightly bounded millisecond deadlines) [139]. Because everything is fixed at compile time, the system is predictable and easier to validate for safety.

Signal-based communication:
AUTOSAR Classic favors signal-level I/O—e.g., periodic signals over the CAN bus or LIN carry sensor readings and actuator commands. This works well for the types of simpler data exchange in legacy ECUs. Classic Platform includes SOME/IP and service discovery (SD) via the SOME/IP Transformer and SoAd modules [54, 140], enabling service-style interactions over Ethernet. However, CP remains less dynamic than AP and still emphasizes statically configured communication [136].

Low resource footprint:
AUTOSAR Classic targets MCUs that often lack an MMU, but the AUTOSAR OS supports memory protection with MPUs between OS applications when configured. Whether protection is available depends on hardware and integrator choices. The upside is that it can run on cheap, small MCUs; the downside is less isolation—a faulty component can corrupt others (mitigated by thorough testing).

Maturity and safety certification:
AUTOSAR Classic has been used in production for more than a decade, and its components (OS, communication stack, etc.) are proven. Many Classic implementations have been certified up to the highest Automotive Safety Integrity Level, ASIL-D, for use in systems like braking or airbag control. The Classic development process (using tools to autogenerate code from models and configurations) is well-understood and supported by many vendors, which helps in meeting standards like ISO 26262.

Figure 4-3 intentionally compresses the Classic stack, but a fuller AUTOSAR Classic implementation typically distinguishes several additional layers inside Basic Software. These include the Microcontroller Abstraction Layer (MCAL), the ECU Abstraction Layer, complex device drivers where standardized abstraction is insufficient, and clearer separation around the AUTOSAR OS and service layers. For production-grade explanation, readers should therefore interpret the figure as a simplified conceptual view rather than a complete Classic Platform decomposition.

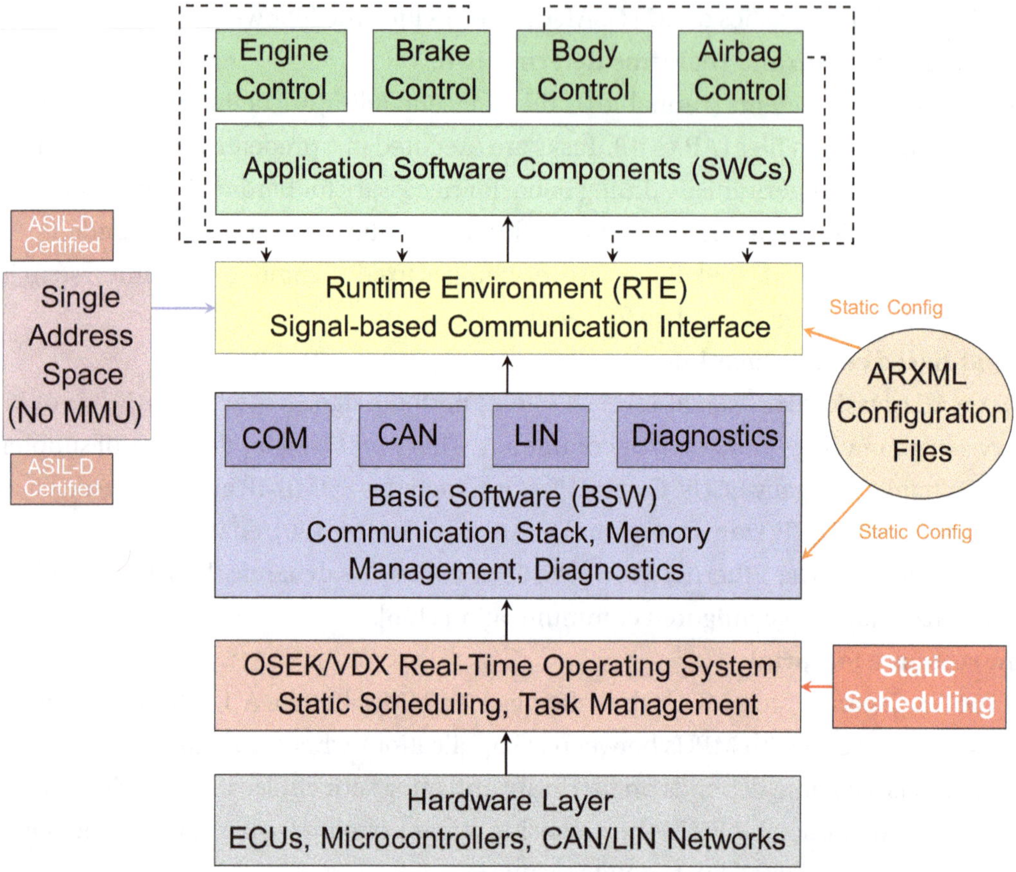

Figure 4-3. *Simplified AUTOSAR Classic Platform view. Core production implementations also distinguish MCAL, ECU Abstraction, complex drivers, and AUTOSAR OS layering*

In summary, AUTOSAR Classic's strength is its deterministic, safety-mature nature. It provides reliable real-time scheduling and has a track record in high-ASIL systems. However, a key weakness is that it is rigid—software on a Classic ECU cannot be easily updated or extended at runtime. There is no concept of dynamically installing applications at runtime. While partial flashing of SWCs is possible, updates are still managed as ECU-level or SWC-level reflashes rather than app store–style deployment. This rigidity and the focus on signals (not services) make it ill-suited for the "digital-first" model, where features are added or evolved over a vehicle's life. AUTOSAR Classic remains essential for certain low-level functions, but it alone is not sufficient to enable the concept of continuous software-defined vehicle upgrades.

4.5 AUTOSAR Adaptive

AUTOSAR Adaptive is a newer platform (first released in 2017) created to meet the needs of high-performance automotive computing—domains like automated driving, advanced infotainment, and vehicle gateways. Unlike Classic Platform, Adaptive is built on a dynamic OS (POSIX-compliant), meaning it assumes the presence of an underlying operating system (such as a Linux or a specialized POSIX RTOS) that supports processes, threads, and dynamic memory.

AUTOSAR AP requires a POSIX PSE51-compliant OS interface [141, 142], and its Update and Configuration Management (UCM) [143] and manifests formalize deployment, permissions, and OTA update flows at runtime.

4.5.1 Key Features of AUTOSAR Adaptive

Service-oriented architecture (SOA):
Adaptive systems communicate through service-oriented interfaces rather than only through statically configured signals. In production AUTOSAR Adaptive environments, SOME/IP and service discovery are the most common baseline communication model [54], while DDS may be integrated in some architectures as an optional data distribution technology rather than assumed as a native core building block. Applications therefore act as service providers or consumers, and the Adaptive runtime manages discovery, communication, execution, and lifecycle coordination across those services [144].
Dynamic application management:
On Adaptive, application executables (typically C++ programs) can be started and stopped during runtime. They are deployed in the ECU's filesystem and loaded into memory as needed [137]. This means an Adaptive ECU can potentially receive a new software package via OTA and launch it without rebooting the entire device—a big step toward continuous updates. The platform includes an Update and Configuration Management (UCM) service [143] to handle deploying new application versions in a controlled manner [145]. Each Adaptive app comes with an execution manifest (metadata describing its resource needs and permissions), which the system uses to allocate resources and ensure security for that app [146].
POSIX-based OS underpinnings:
Adaptive Platform requires a POSIX PSE51-compliant OS interface [141, 142] and uses execution manifests together with an Update and Configuration Management (UCM) [143] to control deployment, permissions, and in-field updates at runtime. In practice, this

means Adaptive can run on Linux, QNX, or a specialized POSIX RTOS. It also implies use of memory protection (MMU)—each Adaptive application can run in its own process address space, improving fault isolation compared with Classic where everything is in one address space [136]. The trade-off is higher overhead and hardware requirements (Adaptive is intended for powerful SoCs, not tiny microcontrollers).

High computing power, less stringent in real time:
Adaptive Platform is meant for high-performance ECUs (think multi-core 64-bit processors, possibly with accelerators). While it can be used for time-sensitive functions, its timing is less tightly deterministic than Classic's. It targets applications that may need to crunch a lot of data (like sensor fusion for ADAS) and can afford the slight nondeterminism of a multi-threaded POSIX environment. In terms of safety, Adaptive-based ECUs are being integrated into systems with ASIL-B–ASIL-D safety goals. Achieving ASIL-D compliance with an Adaptive stack is possible but vendor- and architecture-specific and requires careful safety partitioning. Achieving hard real-time behavior requires careful design since a general-purpose OS scheduler is in play. In practice, some safety-critical functions may still rely on a Classic or an RTOS, while Adaptive handles the higher-level decision-making.

Figure 4-4 should be interpreted as a simplified platform view. Core Adaptive concerns include execution management, communication management, state management, manifests, and the POSIX-based runtime environment. OTA back-ends and broader deployment infrastructure sit outside the in-vehicle runtime architecture, while DDS should be understood as an optional integration path rather than a mandatory native AUTOSAR Adaptive element.

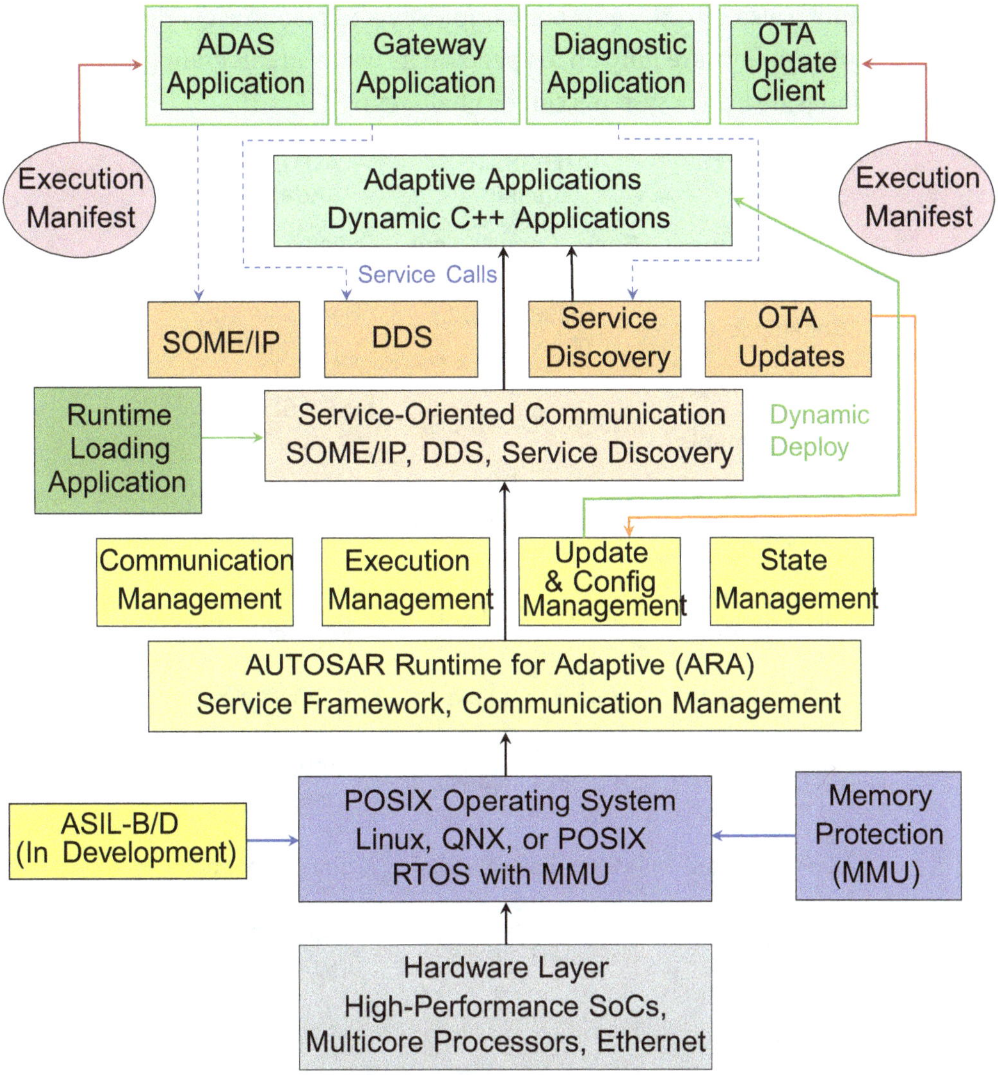

Figure 4-4. *Simplified AUTOSAR Adaptive runtime view. External OTA infrastructure and optional communication integrations should be distinguished from core platform services*

In short, AUTOSAR Adaptive's strength is that it brings flexibility and modern software paradigms (service-oriented communication, dynamic deployment) to the automotive world [146]. It is designed to support OTA updates and "apps" in the car, enabling features to be added or improved after vehicle manufacture. Its weaknesses include the fact that it is still an evolving standard—the tooling, developer familiarity, and overall maturity are lower than those of Classic Platform, which has 15+ years of history [9]. Adaptive also introduces more complexity and resource overhead; not all OEMs and Tier-1 suppliers are fully up to speed on its use, and integrating Adaptive components alongside legacy systems can be challenging.

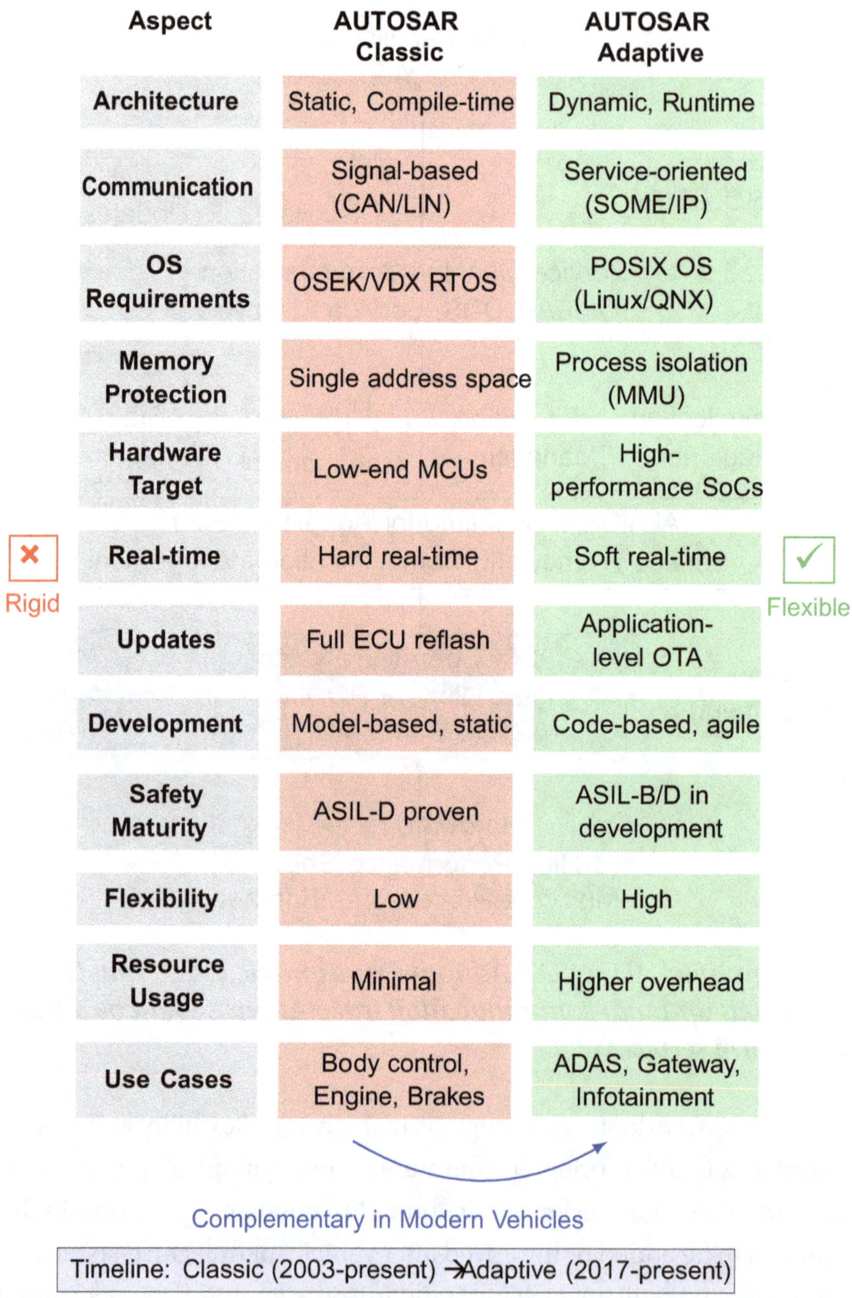

***Figure 4-5.** High-level comparison of AUTOSAR Classic and Adaptive tendencies. Real vehicle systems often combine multiple communication models*

Critic's Note AUTOSAR ≠ SDV: Embracing AUTOSAR (Classic or Adaptive) alone does not magically yield a software-defined vehicle. AUTOSAR provides important base functionality (especially for in-vehicle communication and basic services), but it is not sufficient for a "digital-first" vehicle development lifecycle. For example, AUTOSAR Adaptive enables service-oriented apps, yet it doesn't provide out-of-the-box solutions for cloud connectivity, large-scale container orchestration, or machine learning integration.

To truly operate like a smartphone on wheels, automakers must integrate additional cloud-native technologies—containerization, service meshes, DevOps toolchains, etc.—on top of AUTOSAR [147]. In other words, AUTOSAR is a necessary piece of the puzzle for automotive software architecture, but achieving rapid iteration and deployment at scale will also require adopting the practices and infrastructure seen in IT industries (e.g., running AUTOSAR Adaptive applications inside Docker containers for easier updates or using a service mesh for communications between in-car services and cloud services). SDVs will rely on AUTOSAR for core in-vehicle services and on modern software frameworks to extend those services into a fully connected, continuously evolving ecosystem.

4.5.2 Middleware Protocols: SOME/IP vs. DDS

The choice of communication middleware has significant implications for latency, throughput, CPU load, and certification effort. Two protocols dominate modern automotive service-oriented architectures:

SOME/IP (Scalable service-Oriented Middleware over IP):

SOME/IP has become the de facto standard in AUTOSAR Adaptive, providing remote procedure calls (RPC) and message passing over Ethernet (TCP/UDP) with a service discovery mechanism [54]. It uses a client-server model where services offer functions that applications call over the network. SOME/IP is relatively lightweight with a small footprint, making it suitable for resource-constrained zonal controllers. However, it has higher latency for some operations when using TCP for guaranteed delivery.

DDS (Data Distribution Service):
DDS is an OMG standard implementing a data-centric publish–subscribe model, where publishers write to "topics" and subscribers receive updates without explicit knowledge of each other. DDS has built-in QoS settings (reliability, durability, deadlines, liveliness) and automatic discovery, making it powerful for streaming data to multiple consumers. It is used in ROS 2 and available as an alternative binding in AUTOSAR Adaptive. DDS is more heavyweight than SOME/IP but scales better with many publishers/subscribers.

Selection guidelines: Use SOME/IP for request–response services in AUTOSAR environments where it is proven in production. Use DDS for real-time data streaming to multiple consumers with flexible QoS requirements. Many architectures use both, bridged through the AUTOSAR Adaptive ara::com abstraction layer. For safety certification, simpler protocols are easier to validate—SOME/IP's narrower scope may be easier to analyze than DDS's rich feature set.

4.6 RTOSs and Safety-Critical OSs

Not all vehicle software runs on AUTOSAR or heavy POSIX platforms. Many critical functions require a **real-time operating system (RTOS)**—a lightweight OS that provides highly predictable timing and safety isolation. RTOSs are used in cases where failing to meet a timing deadline or having the system crash could be catastrophic (e.g., an airbag controller, power steering controller, or braking system ECU). Unlike general-purpose OSs, RTOS kernels are designed to guarantee that high-priority tasks execute within strict time bounds, and they often undergo rigorous certification for safety standards.

Here we survey a few important RTOS and safety-focused OS choices in the automotive domain.

4.6.1 Commercial Real-Time Operating Systems

QNX
QNX (developed by BlackBerry) is one of the most widely used commercial RTOSs in automotive. It has a microkernel architecture, meaning the core kernel is minimal (handling only basic IPC, scheduling, and interrupts) and most drivers and services run in user space. This design boosts isolation—if a peripheral driver crashes, it doesn't necessarily take down the whole system. QNX is known for its reliable real-time

performance and has been deployed in everything from automotive infotainment systems to digital instrument clusters and ADAS domain controllers. It offers full POSIX compliance for portability of software [139].

Crucially, QNX has safety-certified versions (up to ISO 26262 ASIL-D, the highest level for automotive) and a long track record in safety-critical applications [148, 149]. As of mid-2024, QNX was reported to be embedded in over 255 million vehicles worldwide—a testament to its dominance as an automotive OS [148].

A key trade-off of QNX is that it is a commercial, closed-source platform with licensing cost and vendor-dependent customization paths [150]. In automotive practice, these are often accepted in exchange for certification pedigree, tooling maturity, and long-term support. Despite that, for any application that absolutely requires certification and proven reliability (say a Level 3 ADAS controller that cannot fail), QNX is often the go-to choice.

Green Hills Integrity

Integrity is another RTOS used in both aerospace and automotive. It is a separation kernel design, meaning it enforces strict memory and time partitioning between tasks. Integrity has heritage in avionics (where it complies with DO-178C Level A for flight software) and has been adapted to meet ISO 26262 ASIL-D in automotive as well [150]. Its architecture focuses on security and safety—every application or subsystem runs in its own hardware-enforced partition, which makes it almost impossible for a fault in one to affect another. This suits mixed-criticality scenarios (e.g., running a cluster and an infotainment system on one SoC).

Table 4-1. *Comparison of RTOS and OS Options for Safety-Critical Automotive Systems*

OS/RTOS	Strengths	Trade-Offs	Automotive Use Cases
QNX Neutrino	ASIL-D certified; microkernel isolation; real-time deterministic; mature ecosystem [148, 139]	Licensing cost; closed-source; less flexible to customize [150]	Digital instrument clusters, ADAS controllers, safety-critical gateways
GHS Integrity	Proven separation kernel with hard partitioning; certified to highest safety levels (ISO 26262 ASIL-D, DO-178C) [150]	Very expensive; proprietary tools; smaller community of developers	Powertrain and braking ECUs; domain controller requiring strong isolation (often used in aviation- derived platforms)
Wind River VxWorks	Hard real-time performance; supports modern features like containerized apps [151, 152]; long track record in critical systems	Proprietary; significant license cost; expertise needed to integrate containers with safety	Autonomous driving systems (sensor fusion, vision processing) where modular updates are needed; aerospace- influenced automotive projects
Zephyr RTOS	Open source (no royalties); highly modular and configurable; growing community support; memory footprint scalable down to very small MCUs [153]	Not yet ASIL-D (safety certification in progress) [153]; newer project (less proven in production); requires in-house integration effort	Prototyping of new ECUs; noncritical controllers (e.g., smart lighting, seat controllers); potential future use in cost-sensitive/open development vehicles

Green Hills also offers a product called Integrity Multivisor, which can act as a hypervisor to host other OSs alongside Integrity. The strengths of Integrity are its proven safety record and robust isolation; however, like QNX, it is proprietary and comes with a high price tag. It tends to be used in high-assurance use cases such as brake control systems, autonomous drive platforms that evolved from aerospace systems, or in-vehicles where the cost is justified by the need for maximum security (some military or specialized commercial vehicles). Developers also note that working with Integrity requires specific tools and training, which can increase development effort.

Wind River VxWorks

VxWorks is a veteran commercial RTOS from Wind River (now part of Aptiv). It has been used historically in aerospace and industrial systems and has made its way into automotive as well (e.g., some advanced driver assistance systems use VxWorks). VxWorks is designed for hard real-time performance and modularity.

Wind River has added OCI-compatible containers to VxWorks to modernize modular deployment. QNX has similarly introduced OCI/Podman-compatible containers in QNX SDP 8.0 [151, 152], so multiple safety-oriented RTOSs now offer container options. This is intended to allow dynamic updates of parts of an otherwise static RTOS image (helpful in, say, updating an AI module in an ADAS ECU without recertifying the entire software).

VxWorks has been certified for ISO 26262 at least up to ASIL-D in specific configurations. Its weakness, similar to other commercial RTOSs, is cost and vendor lock-in. However, since Aptiv's acquisition of Wind River, we may see tighter integration of VxWorks with automotive middleware and Aptiv's platform solutions [138].

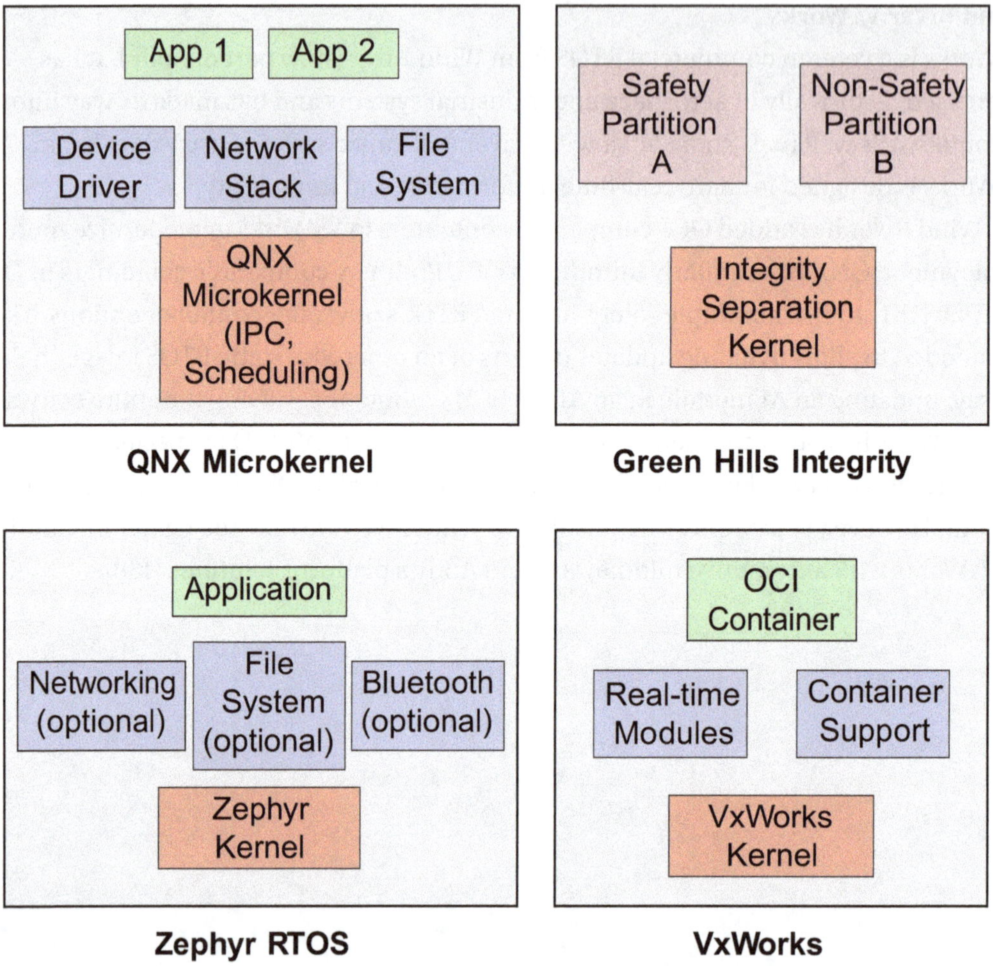

Figure 4-6. *Architecture comparison of different RTOS solutions*

4.6.2 Open Source Real-Time Operating Systems

Zephyr

Zephyr is a rising open source RTOS hosted by the Linux Foundation. It is a community-driven, modular RTOS aimed at small embedded devices (originally IoT sensors, but increasingly more). Zephyr is open source (Apache 2.0), which makes it attractive for companies wanting full control and no licensing fees [144]. It has a growing ecosystem of supported boards and features, and importantly, the Zephyr project has a Safety Committee that is actively working toward functional safety certifications.

The Zephyr project is advancing a functional safety program centered on IEC 61508, with public disclosures of safety process progress [153]. ISO 26262 certification has not been achieved as of 2025 [153]. But it's already used for prototyping and some secondary vehicle systems (e.g., some OEMs might use Zephyr on low-end microcontrollers inside smart sensors or simple ECUs, where open source flexibility is a bigger advantage than immediate certification) [153].

The strengths of Zephyr are its small footprint and flexibility—you can include only the components you need, making it extremely lightweight, and its open nature encourages rapid innovation (it even maintains an official software bill of materials for transparency) [144]. The weakness is the relative immaturity in automotive safety and the need for each integrator to do more validation (since you don't have a single vendor warranting its safety out of the box). Nevertheless, Zephyr is being evaluated in automotive for noncritical uses, and it may play a larger role as certification efforts progress [153].

4.6.3 Embedded Linux in Safety Applications

It's worth noting that embedded Linux (discussed more below) is also part of the picture for safety, though Linux by itself is not an RTOS. Some projects (like ELISA—Enabling Linux In Safety Applications) [154] are working to use Linux in safety-critical contexts, but usually this involves adding a thin hypervisor or isolation layer because the Linux kernel is large and was not designed for guaranteed real-time behavior [145, 155].

Thus, many production vehicles adopt a hybrid approach: they'll run an RTOS like QNX or Integrity on the same processor alongside a Linux-based system, isolating the safety-critical functions on the RTOS side and using Linux for high-level functions. Hypervisors (see below) make this possible by allowing multiple OSs on one SoC. For instance, an automotive cockpit controller might use QNX for the cluster graphics (to ensure the speedometer and telltales are updated reliably), while an Android or Linux runs the infotainment apps—both OSs operating concurrently on different virtual machines of one processor [146]. This combination leverages the strengths of each type of OS.

4.7 Linux and Android Automotive

Beyond the specialized AUTOSAR environments and RTOS kernels, automakers have increasingly turned to general-purpose operating systems for certain domains of the car—especially those interacting with the driver's infotainment, navigation, or connected services. The two major players here are Linux (often in the form of or custom embedded Linux builds) and Android Automotive OS. These platforms offer rich functionality and a vast developer ecosystem, but they come from the consumer electronics world, so integrating them into a car's safety-critical architecture requires careful handling.Automotive Grade Linux (AGL)

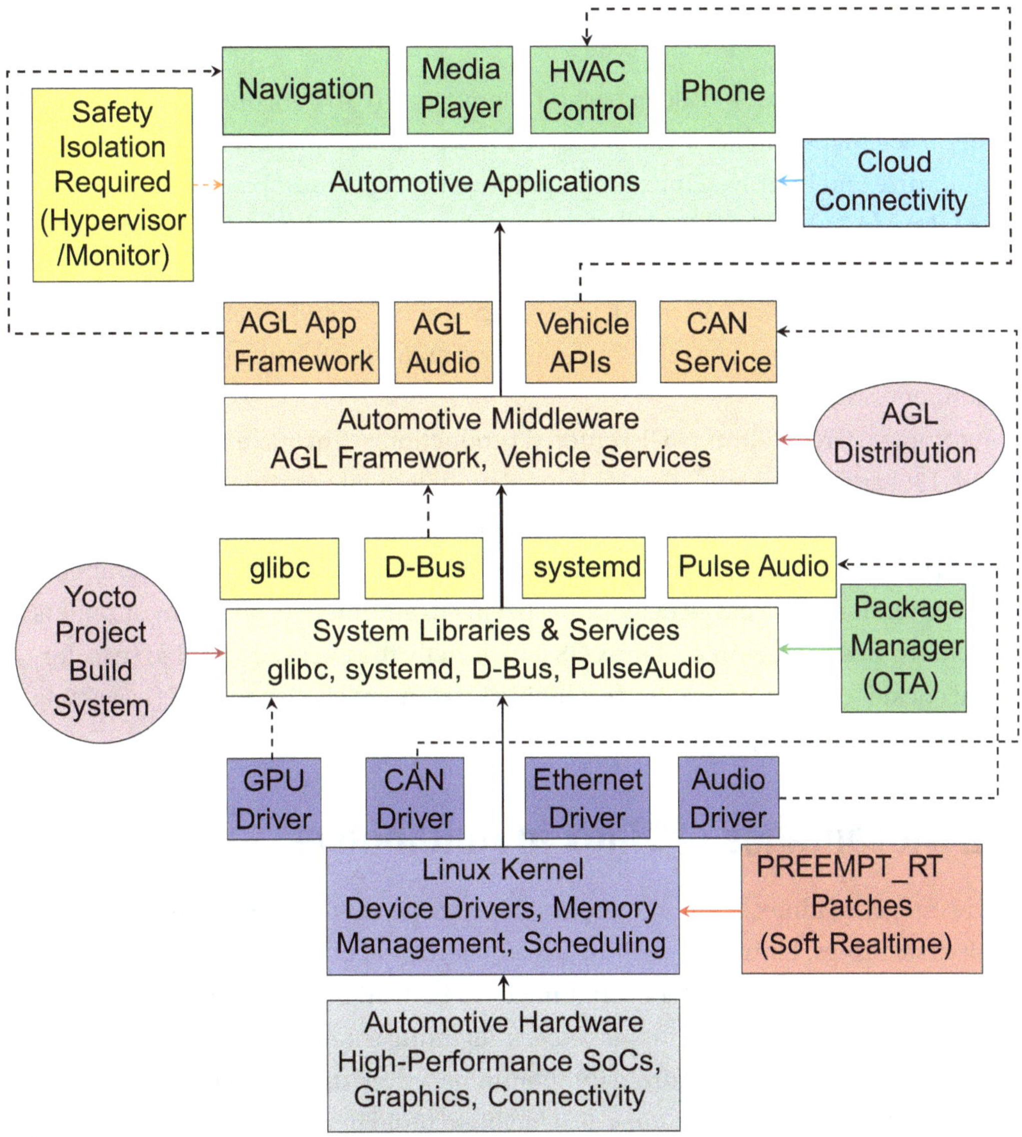

Figure 4-7. *Simplified Linux-based in-vehicle software stack. Development tooling and external cloud/update services should be treated as adjacent infrastructure rather than core runtime layers*

Figure 4-7 should be read as a simplified in-vehicle runtime view. The Linux kernel already contains the core driver framework, so individual driver blocks need not be shown as separate architectural layers. Likewise, Yocto belongs to build and image construction infrastructure, while cloud connectivity and OTA services belong to adjacent platform and back-end infrastructure rather than the core Linux runtime stack in the vehicle.

4.7.1 Automotive Grade Linux (AGL)

Embedded Linux has been used in cars for many years (early on, often for navigation systems or telematics units). What's changed is the formation of collaborative projects to standardize and improve Linux for automotive use. One example is **Automotive Grade Linux (AGL)**, a Linux Foundation project that provides a base Linux distro and middleware tailored for cars. AGL aims to create a de facto standard infotainment platform shared across OEMs. It provides components for audio management, GUI, CAN bus access, etc., so manufacturers don't reinvent the wheel for each new infotainment system.

Automotive Grade Linux (AGL) entered production at Toyota (e.g., the 2018 Camry) [156] and has expanded to additional models, while Android Automotive OS is deployed at Volvo [157, 158] and GM and across the Renault-Nissan-Mitsubishi Alliance [159]. Another approach is using the Yocto Project to build custom embedded Linux distributions for a car—Yocto is not specific to automotive, but many suppliers use Yocto recipes to assemble a Linux OS with exactly the packages needed (e.g., for a digital cockpit domain controller combining instrument cluster and IVI (in-vehicle infotainment) functions).

4.7.2 Advantages of Linux in Automotive

The advantages of Linux in automotive are the huge ecosystem of software and developers it brings. Linux supports an array of hardware out of the box, and one can tap into open source libraries for everything from networking to machine learning. This accelerates development: for instance, integrating a new streaming music service is much simpler on a Linux/Android infotainment system than it would be on a proprietary OS. Linux-based systems also facilitate rapid iteration—developers can use modern DevOps practices and even simulate or run the exact software stack on a PC for testing (something not possible with a custom RTOS without special tools). According to industry analyses, embedded Linux powers a significant share of infotainment and connectivity systems in production vehicles, with AGL and Android being prominent choices [9].

4.7.3 Safety Challenges with Linux

However, Linux is not designed for functional safety out of the box. The Linux kernel is large (millions of lines of code) and was built for throughput and features rather than guaranteed real-time performance. It can be tweaked for better real-time behavior (with the PREEMPT_RT patches [155], developers can achieve "soft" real-time scheduling on Linux) [145], but it still can't match a true RTOS for worst-case latency determinism.

Moreover, certifying Linux under ISO 26262 is extremely challenging—every part of the kernel and its toolchain would need qualification. Projects like ELISA [154] are investigating methodologies to use Linux in safety applications, possibly by proving certain parts of it or by containing its scope, but this is an ongoing effort [9, 146].

Therefore, when Linux is used in a car for anything impacting vehicle control, it is almost always paired with safety mechanisms: either run Linux in a sandbox (virtual machine) that is monitored by a safety supervisor, or use a separate safety MCU alongside the Linux processor to cross-check critical signals (sometimes called a safety island architecture).

4.7.4 Mixed-Criticality Domain Controllers

A classic example is a combined infotainment and instrument cluster domain controller. The instrument cluster (speedometer, warning lights) is safety-relevant (ASIL-B or higher), whereas the infotainment (navigation, media, apps) is QM (Quality-Managed; no safety requirement). If an automaker chooses Linux or Android for the infotainment portion, they will isolate the cluster portion by either running a small RTOS for the cluster on another core or using a hypervisor to give Linux one virtual machine and the cluster software another.

The cluster software might even run on QNX or Integrity in a VM, while Linux runs concurrently—thus, if the Linux side crashes or reboots, the cluster can continue to run. As an example, one integrated cockpit controller architecture uses a single high-performance SoC to run Android Automotive (as the IVI, classified QM) and a parallel instrument cluster application (classified ASIL-B) on the same chip, with both sharing a GPU for graphics—a hypervisor ensures time partitioning of the GPU and isolation of memory [9]. Industry case studies report material cost savings by consolidating ECUs into domain controllers (figures around 20% are cited in some public examples), though actual savings depend heavily on vehicle architecture and sourcing strategy [146].

In summary, Linux is embraced for feature-rich, consumer-facing functionality and fast development, but it "complicates the safety case"—extra work is needed to guarantee that any failure in the Linux domain can't propagate to critical vehicle controls [9].

4.7.5 Android Automotive OS (AAOS)

Android Automotive OS (AAOS) is essentially Google's Android OS adapted to run natively in a vehicle's infotainment system (as opposed to Android Auto, which runs on a smartphone). Android Automotive provides the same Android SDK for apps but includes vehicle-specific extensions (APIs for HVAC, radio, etc.) [160] and is intended to allow third-party apps (navigation, music, voice assistants) to run directly on the car's hardware.

Many OEMs (Volvo [157, 158], GM, Renault [159], etc.) have adopted Android Automotive for their latest infotainment platforms, often with Google Automotive Services (Play Store, Google Maps, etc.) included. The appeal is obvious: access to a massive developer community and existing apps, plus rapid update cycles that Google pushes for its OS.

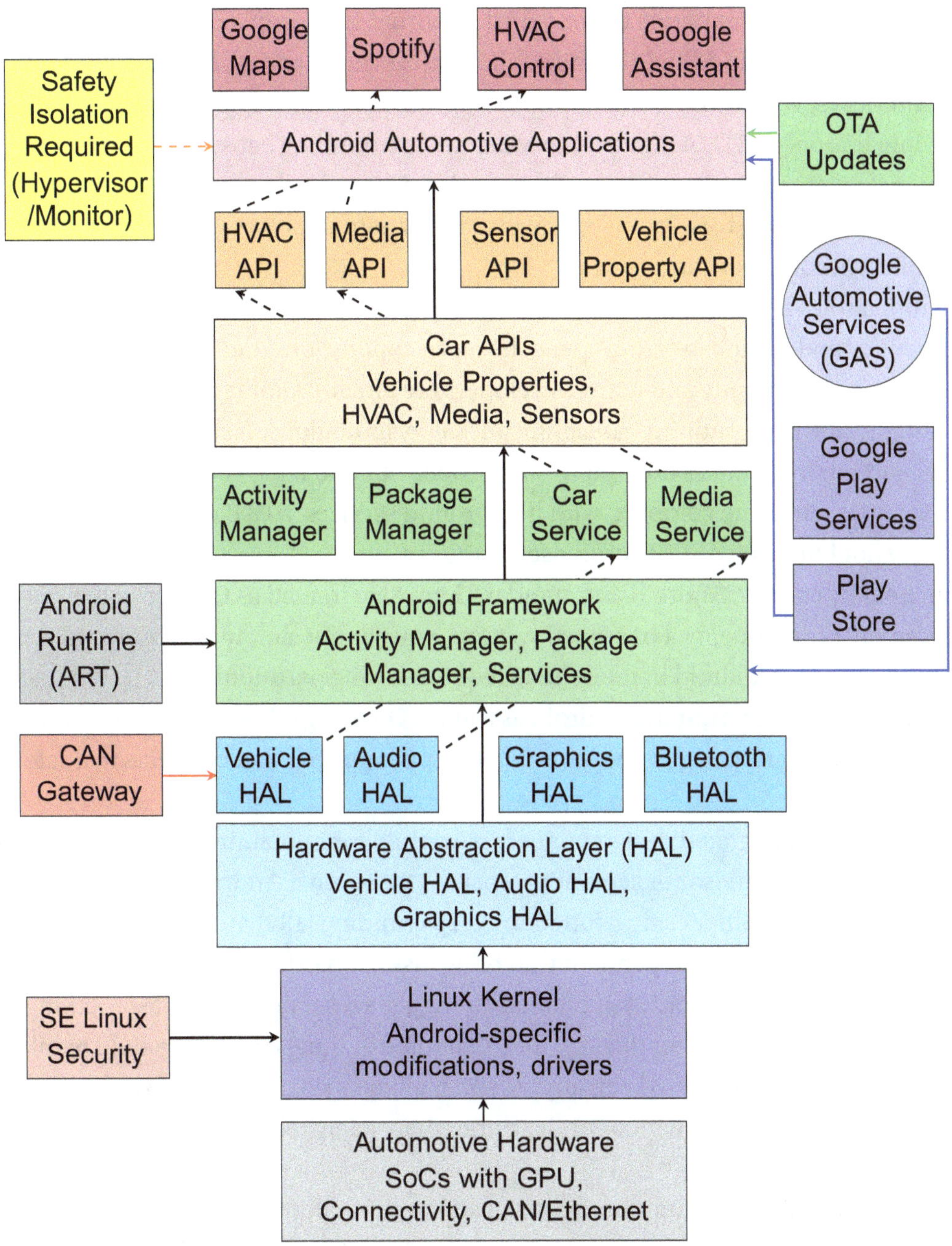

Figure 4-8. *Simplified Android Automotive software stack in the vehicle. External ecosystem and update services should be distinguished from the core in-vehicle OS architecture*

Figure 4-8 should separate the in-vehicle Android stack from ecosystem services surrounding it. Core in-vehicle elements include the Linux kernel, Android framework, HAL interfaces, vehicle APIs, and applications. By contrast, Google Play services, Play Store integration, and OTA platform services are surrounding ecosystem or deployment services rather than intrinsic layers of the local runtime architecture. Similarly, any hypervisor-based safety isolation operates at the system or hardware management level, not at the Android application layer.

From a software delivery standpoint, Android Automotive can improve developer productivity and feature iteration speed, because applications and services can be updated more frequently and many developers are already familiar with the Android ecosystem. However, Android has significant safety limitations. It sits on top of the Linux kernel and inherits Linux's nondeterministic behavior and large codebase. Android itself is even larger and more complex, with background services, a GUI stack, and so on—certainly not built with ASIL-D processes in mind.

In a safety context, Android and standard Linux are treated as QM (no safety requirement) components. For critical systems, you cannot simply trust Android. Thus, any deployment of Android in the vehicle requires strong partitioning [161]. This can be done via a hypervisor (running Android as a guest OS alongside a safety guest) or via a dedicated SoC (some designs put Android on a separate chip that connects to a safety microcontroller).

As noted, an integrated design might run Android for infotainment and an RTOS for the cluster—the hypervisor or separation ensures that even if Android hangs or reboots, the cluster (and any other critical function) keeps running [138]. Another measure is adding safety monitors: independent watchdog tasks or hardware that supervise the outputs of the Linux/Android system and can trigger a reset or fallback if something goes wrong (e.g., if the cluster display doesn't update in time, a monitor could blank it to a safe state). Automakers also keep any essential telltales (like an airbag warning light) under direct control of a microcontroller rather than solely relying on a fancy graphical display.

In summary, Android Automotive OS's weakness in safety domains is that it is not ASIL-certified or designed for deterministic behavior—it cannot be solely responsible for anything life-critical [9]. Its strength is the rich ecosystem and updatability, making it ideal for noncritical domains (navigation, entertainment, etc.). Many cars now effectively have a dual-OS strategy: a safety RTOS for critical tasks and Android/Linux for the rest.

Critic's Note Consumer-grade OSs like Linux and Android bring unmatched developer productivity and a vast feature set, but they inevitably complicate safety assurance. In an SDV, you cannot avoid using such OSs for cutting-edge features, yet you must encapsulate them carefully.

Partitioning via hypervisors, using dedicated safety processors, and implementing independent safety monitors are now mandatory practices when incorporating these OSs [138, 161]. Additionally, initiatives such as the Linux Foundation's ELISA project [154] are exploring how to adapt and certify Linux for safety to reduce this gap [9, 146].

Still, the rule of thumb is clear: use Linux/Android to accelerate innovation and leverage connectivity, but assume they will fail at some point and architect the system such that those failures don't compromise essential functions.

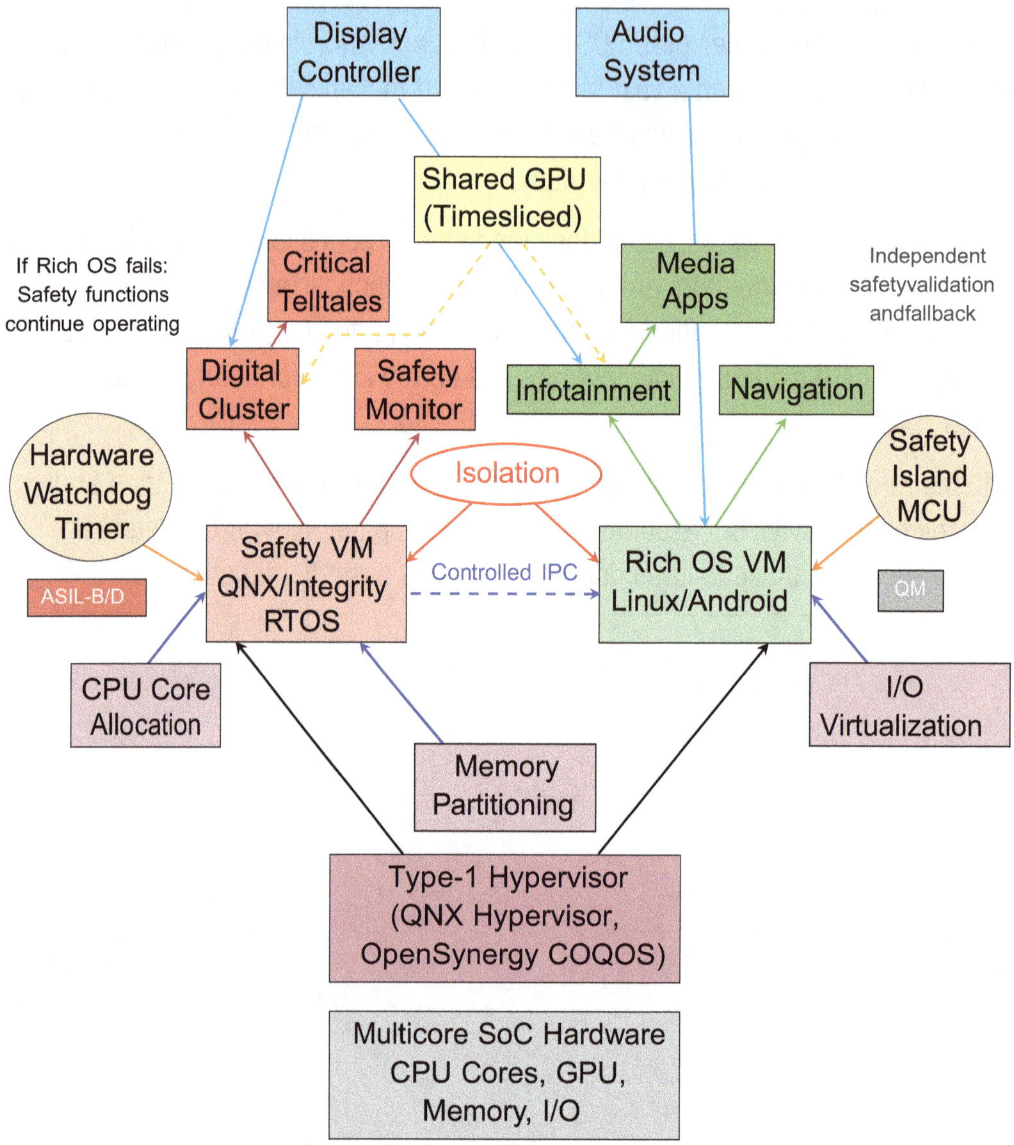

Figure 4-9. *Conceptual mixed-criticality dual-OS architecture. Hypervisor-managed partitioning applies across all guest domains*

In a production mixed-criticality design, the hypervisor is responsible for partitioning CPU time, memory regions, interrupt routing, and device access across all guest domains, not just the safety side. Inter-VM communication is normally bidirectional and governed through controlled communication channels. Similarly, watchdog supervision and safety monitoring functions typically observe the system more broadly than a single guest alone, and shared resources such as GPUs may rely on hardware-assisted virtualization or vendor-specific partitioning mechanisms rather than simple software time-slicing.

4.8 Containers and Virtualization

As software-defined vehicles adopt more complex software stacks, containers and virtualization have emerged as key technologies to manage that complexity. They offer ways to isolate applications, run multiple different systems on the same hardware, and deploy updates more seamlessly. These concepts are borrowed from enterprise IT and cloud computing, but they are increasingly tailored to automotive needs.

4.8.1 Containerization in Automotive

Containerization in a vehicle context means packaging selected applications into lightweight, isolated software units that run on top of a host operating system kernel—most commonly Linux or another environment that explicitly supports OCI-style runtime behavior. In automotive, containers are best understood as a deployment and modularization mechanism rather than as a replacement for AUTOSAR itself. They are particularly useful on high-performance compute platforms where selected applications, analytics functions, or AI services benefit from modular deployment and constrained update scope.

1. **Microservice architectures:** They allow microservice architectures inside the car. Rather than a monolithic program, functionality can be split into independent services (e.g., one container for the lane detection algorithm, another for driver monitoring). This aligns with AUTOSAR Adaptive's service-oriented approach, but using standard container tools gives more flexibility in deployment.

2. **Independent updates and constrained revalidation scope:** Containers enable OEMs to update individual software components without rebuilding the entire ECU image. For example, a speech recognition engine or driver monitoring algorithm can be packaged as a container and rolled out as a

new version while the rest of the system remains unchanged. Architecturally, this helps to constrain the impact of a change: regression testing and safety analysis can focus first on the updated unit and its interfaces, rather than on every binary on the ECU. However, this does not eliminate the need for system-level verification. For safety-related functions, ISO 26262 still requires that the overall safety case be revisited and that critical integration paths are retested after each change. Containers, therefore, are a powerful tool for modular deployment and operational agility, but they are not a shortcut around functional safety or homologation obligations.

3. **Cloud-to-vehicle consistency:** They promote consistency from cloud to vehicle. Developers can use the same container image in a cloud simulation (or digital twin) as they deploy to the car, ensuring that what was tested in the lab is exactly what runs in the vehicle [162]. This parity is valuable for continuous integration: companies like VW, Toyota, etc. are exploring CI pipelines where a car's software is first validated in cloud-based virtual ECUs (vECUs) using container orchestration and then pushed to the actual car if tests pass [147, 162]. The container serves as a consistent deployment unit across these environments.

4. **Secure update infrastructure:** Containers also typically come with infrastructure for image signing and verification, which can be integrated with the vehicle's secure boot and update management. Using Docker/OCI images means OEMs can leverage existing tools for managing software versions, scanning for vulnerabilities, and rolling out updates gradually (as is done in cloud deployments).

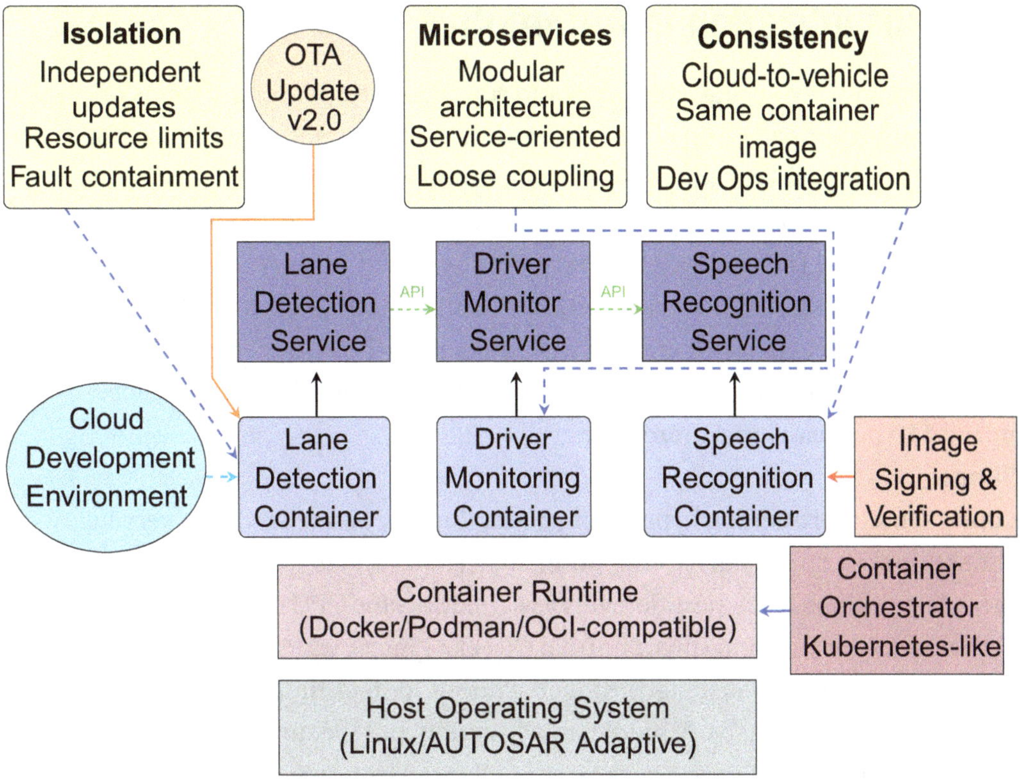

Figure 4-10. *Conceptual benefits of containerized deployment in automotive software. Cloud development infrastructure and in-vehicle runtime should be understood as related but distinct environments*

In practice, implementing containers in resource-constrained or safety-critical environments is nontrivial. Standard Docker, for instance, has a large footprint and daemon process that might not fit well on an AUTOSAR Adaptive ECU. Thus, more lightweight alternatives like Podman or other minimal OCI runtimes are often considered. Some automotive-specific middleware is also embracing container concepts—e.g., Adaptive AUTOSAR's Execution Management is conceptually similar to a container orchestrator for in-vehicle services, and Wind River's VxWorks now supports running OCI containers on an RTOS to get the benefits of microservices in a deterministic environment [138]. QNX has similarly introduced OCI/Podman-compatible containers in QNX SDP 8.0 [151, 152].

4.8.2 Virtualization in Automotive

Virtualization refers to using a hypervisor to run multiple operating systems or multiple instances of an OS on the same hardware. In automotive, virtualization is the cornerstone of mixed-criticality systems, where you want to consolidate what used to be separate ECUs onto a single powerful SoC but maintain isolation between their functions. A Type 1 (bare-metal) hypervisor is often used—this is a thin layer that sits directly on the hardware and creates virtual machines (VMs), each of which can run its own guest OS. The hypervisor ensures strong isolation (both in memory and CPU time) between the VMs and can allocate devices or I/O privileges selectively to each.

Common Hypervisors in Automotive

Jailhouse

An open source partitioning hypervisor (maintained by Siemens) that is very lightweight. Jailhouse doesn't do full device emulation; instead, it "carves" a multi-core processor into static partitions (each partition gets assigned specific CPU cores, memory regions, and devices). One partition runs a normal OS (like Linux), which then launches Jailhouse, and then Jailhouse starts other partitions for real-time tasks. The advantage is near-zero overhead and very predictable isolation, but the downside is less flexibility (partitions are fixed, and guest OS choices are limited by hardware partitioning). This is used in some prototypes where a simple separation between Linux and a critical task is needed.

Xen

An open source hypervisor originally from the IT world, which has also been adapted for automotive (Xen has even been used in some production IVI systems). Xen can run multiple Linux, Android, or RTOS guests. It provides more dynamic management than Jailhouse (e.g., you can schedule VMs). Some companies (like Elpis and others) have demonstrated Xen running an Android IVI and a Linux-based cluster on automotive-grade chips. However, Xen's complexity is higher, and shrinking it for automotive safety certification is challenging.

KVM (Kernel-based Virtual Machine)

This is Linux's built-in virtualization feature. Technically, KVM turns the Linux kernel into a hypervisor. In automotive HPC contexts, if you already run a Linux, you could use KVM to spin up additional VMs for, say, an Android instance or an RTOS instance. This approach is being explored because it leverages familiar Linux tooling (QEMU for device emulation and so on). There are efforts to optimize KVM for real time and safety, but like Xen, a full Linux + KVM stack is large for formal certification.

Automotive-Specific Hypervisors

Several commercial players offer hypervisors tuned for automotive: ETAS RTA-HVR (a micro-hypervisor for AUTOSAR systems), OpenSynergy COQOS (hypervisor with a focus on IVI and cluster consolidation, advertised as ISO 26262 ASIL-B compliant) [163], SYSGO PikeOS (a safety-certified hypervisor/RTOS combination often used in rail/aerospace and now in some car systems), and BlackBerry QNX Hypervisor (which is ISO 26262 ASIL-D certified and often used to run QNX + Android combos) [144, 164]. Green Hills Integrity, as mentioned, doubles as a hypervisor via its Multivisor technology. Wind River's Helix Virtualization Platform (coming from their acquisition by Aptiv) is another entrant, aiming to combine an RTOS and Linux on one SoC with safety isolation [137].

Feature	Jailhouse	Xen	KVM	QNX HV	Open Synergy
Type	Partitioning	Full	Hosted	Embedded	Embedded
Footprint	Very Small	Medium	Large	Small	Small
Real-time	Excellent	Good	Fair	Excellent	Excellent
Safety Cert	None	Custom	None	ASIL-D	ASIL-B
Flexibility	Low	High	High	Medium	Medium
Cost	Free	Free	Free	Expensive	Expensive
Guest OS	Limited	Multiple	Multiple	QNX+Linux	Android+RTOS
Automotive Use	Prototype	Some IVI	Research	Production	Production

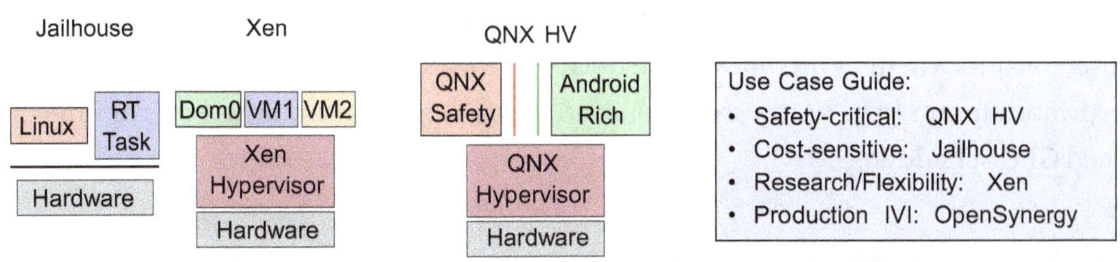

Figure 4-11. *Comparison of automotive hypervisor solutions*

4.8.3 Benefits and Challenges of Virtualization

Hypervisors as the backbone of mixed-criticality ECUs: In a zonal or domain controller, a hypervisor allows multiple operating systems with very different characteristics to share a single SoC without violating freedom from interference requirements. A safety RTOS hosting ASIL-B/D control functions can run alongside a Linux or Android guest providing user-facing features. The hypervisor enforces isolation in time and memory and, in safety-certified products such as QNX Hypervisor or PikeOS, becomes part of the safety architecture itself. If the consumer OS guest crashes, reboots, or misbehaves, it cannot overwrite the memory of the safety partition or starve it of CPU time. This consolidation reduces hardware BOM and wiring complexity, but moves significant responsibility into the hypervisor: its implementation, configuration, and safety argumentation must be treated as first-class elements of the overall safety case.

Virtualization is a key enabler of the domain controller and mixed-criticality trend because it allows multiple software environments to share one SoC while remaining partitioned in time, memory, and device access [137, 144]. Instead of assigning each major function to a separate ECU, OEMs can consolidate selected functions onto a smaller number of powerful controllers and use a hypervisor to maintain separation between guest environments. The architectural benefit is therefore not simply ECU reduction, but controlled consolidation with freedom from interference and clearer resource management.

Of course, virtualization comes with challenges: the hypervisor itself becomes a critical piece of software (it must be secure and reliably enforce separation), and there is overhead in sharing devices. Embedded hypervisors have to be real-time-friendly (some early attempts to use enterprise hypervisors resulted in poor, unpredictable interrupt latencies). Automotive hypervisors address this by offering features like virtual interrupts that are prioritized and giving RTOS guests direct access to interrupts or even whole cores. Additionally, when sharing devices like GPUs or networks, virtualization must either partition them or provide virtual devices—this is complex and sometimes requires hardware support (e.g., hardware virtualization features in automotive SoCs or time-sliced GPU scheduling).

4.8.4 Containers vs. Hypervisors

In summary, containers and hypervisors are complementary:

- **Containers** isolate applications from each other above the OS level, which is great for modular deployment, but all containers share the same OS kernel. So if the underlying OS crashes, all containers go down. This is why containers are typically used on top of a general-purpose OS (Linux) that itself might run in a protected VM if safety isolation is needed.

- **Hypervisors** isolate at the OS level, allowing different OS kernels to coexist. This addresses scenarios where you need different operating environments (e.g., an AUTOSAR Classic environment alongside Android). Hypervisors provide stronger isolation than containers (because even the OS is separate), which is needed for mixing safety-critical and noncritical systems.

Modern automotive architectures often use both: e.g., a hypervisor splits a chip into a Linux domain and an RTOS domain; within the Linux domain, the OEM might use containers to further compartmentalize applications for easier updates.

Figure 4-12 is intended to show that hypervisors and containers are complementary rather than interchangeable. In practice, the hypervisor and hardware virtualization features together provide memory isolation, CPU allocation, interrupt routing, and device assignment across domains. Inter-domain communication is normally bidirectional and governed through controlled IPC channels, while containers provide additional modularity within a guest operating system domain rather than replacing VM-level isolation.

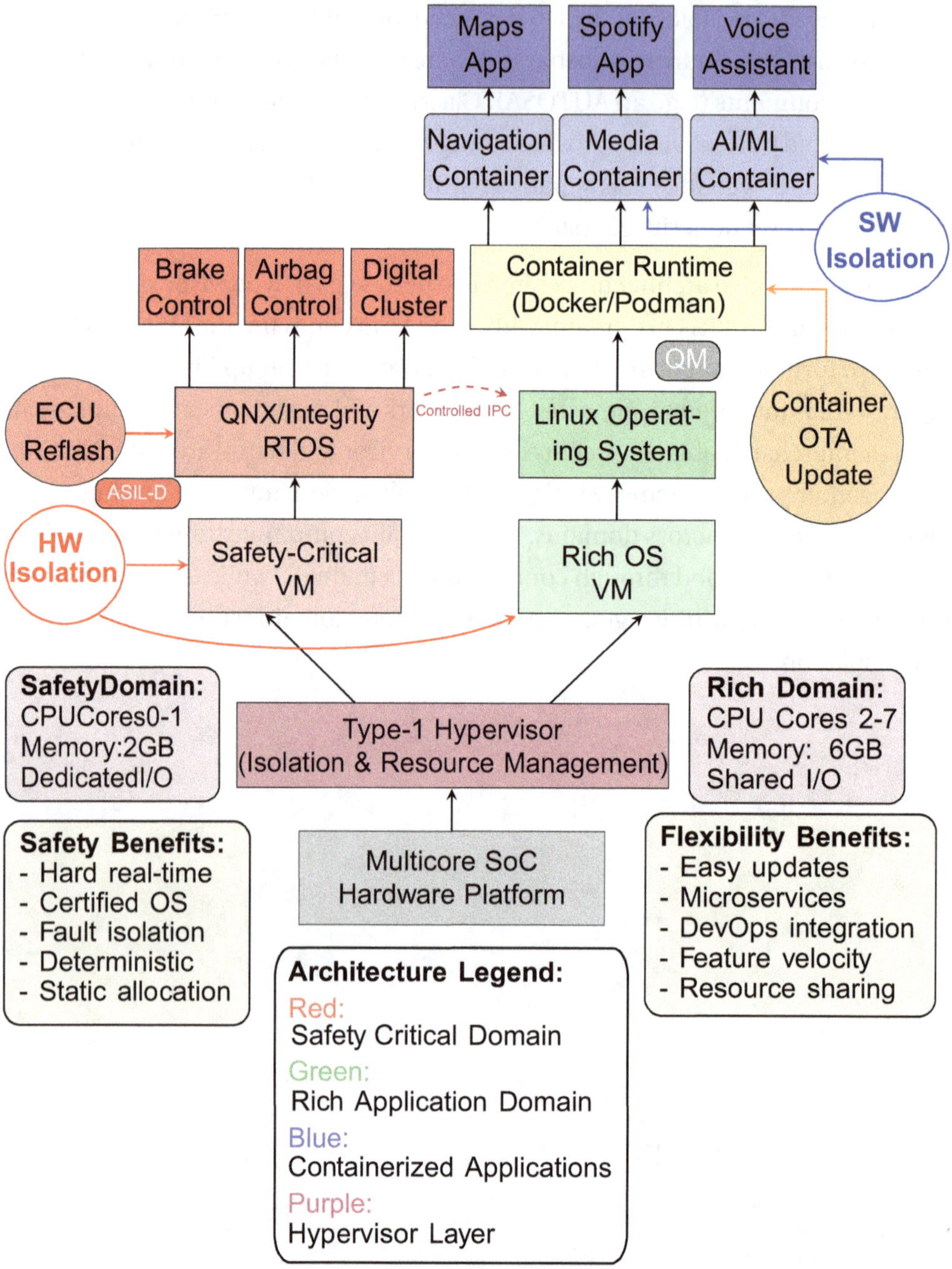

Figure 4-12. *Conceptual combination of hypervisor-based isolation and containerized application deployment in automotive systems*

Business Note SUMS and Regulation A major driver for adopting these middleware technologies (especially robust update mechanisms) is regulatory compliance. UNECE WP.29 regulations—specifically UN Regulation 156 [72]—now mandate that automakers have a Software Update Management System (SUMS) in place for any vehicle with OTA update capability [72, 145, 146]. This means you must be able to show regulators how you manage software updates throughout the vehicle's life: how you discover what software versions are in each vehicle, how you securely deliver updates, how you handle rollback if an update fails, and how you monitor cybersecurity issues in the field.

ISO 24089:2023 [73] is an engineering standard aligned with these requirements, detailing best practices for software update engineering [146]. For OEMs, failing to implement a proper SUMS can block vehicle type approval—in the EU you literally cannot sell the car [9].

This regulatory push means middleware that doesn't support robust update and version management hooks is a liability. In other words, if an OS or platform in the vehicle can't report its software version, accept signed update packages, support dual-bank updates (for safe fallback), or integrate with the OEM's back-end for update status reporting, then using it risks non-compliance. Automakers are now scrutinizing middleware choices through the lens of "Does this make OTA easy and safe, and can I provide evidence of the process?" The best-in-class middleware will have built-in support for update campaigns, cryptographic update validation, and telemetry for update results. Those that don't will require additional adaptation or might be phased out in favor of more update-friendly platforms [9, 138].

4.9 Digital-First and the Continuous Update Loop

One of the core promises of the software-defined vehicle is that cars can be continually improved and personalized through software updates—much like how our smartphones receive regular updates. Achieving this requires a **digital-first development approach**, meaning that software takes center stage in the vehicle lifecycle. The middleware and OS stack must enable a continuous update loop: develop → test (often in virtual environments) → deploy OTA → collect feedback/telemetry → repeat. Let's break down what this entails.

4.9.1 CI/CD Pipelines Extending into the Car

In modern software companies, continuous integration/continuous deployment (CI/CD) pipelines automate the building, testing, and deployment of code changes. Automakers are adopting the same for vehicle software [147]. This means whenever developers commit changes, those are integrated and tested (first in simulation or with virtual ECUs and then perhaps on hardware-in-the-loop rigs), and if all checks out, an update package can be generated for vehicles [147].

Some forward-thinking OEMs have set up the infrastructure such that they can push out minor software changes to a test fleet on a weekly or even daily basis, something unimaginable in the old automotive model where updates took months or years. The middleware needs to support this by providing automation hooks—e.g., a head unit OS might automatically fetch and apply updates in the background, or AUTOSAR Adaptive Platform might allow deploying a new service version without a full reflash.

A robust CI/CD for cars also involves gate checks for safety: e.g., ensuring that any update passes all unit tests, integration tests, and static analysis for safety rule violations before it can be signed and delivered to vehicles [9, 146]. This is where the concept of a digital factory for cars comes in—a combination of cloud services and in-car software that enable continual integration of improvements.

4.9.2 Vehicle Telemetry and Data Collection

A digital-first approach uses real-world data to guide development. Cars equipped with connectivity can stream telemetry data (with appropriate privacy and security measures) about how systems are performing. For example, an automated driving system might log how often a certain sensor goes offline or how the algorithm behaves in rare road conditions. This data is gold for developers—it allows creation of a digital twin of the vehicle in the cloud, where the exact scenarios can be reproduced.

The middleware plays a role by facilitating this data gathering: perhaps a logging service in the OS that can batch and upload logs or support for querying system health. Crucially, data from the fleet can highlight issues or opportunities that drive the next software update. For instance, if telemetry shows a feature is causing unexpected high CPU load in some conditions, engineers can fix it and then OTA an update.

We see this already with companies like Tesla, which heavily uses fleet data to refine their Autopilot features and push updates addressing observed weaknesses (Tesla's "shadow mode" is essentially collecting data from the fleet to validate new algorithms before activating them). Traditional automakers are now also building cloud data pipelines for their vehicles. The term **digital feedback loop** is often used: vehicles send data to the cloud; that data is used in simulations and development; improved software is sent back to vehicles [9].

4.9.3 Digital Twin and Simulation Before Deployment

Before an OTA update is rolled out fleet-wide, it is often tested on a digital replica. A **digital twin** is a virtual model of the vehicle (or a specific ECU) that runs the same software as the real thing. Automakers are increasingly running digital twins of their cars' electronic systems in cloud data centers or in labs, which allows testing how an update would behave without risking a customer vehicle[147, 162].

For example, if a new Adaptive AUTOSAR service is developed, it might first be deployed to a virtual ECU (vECU) that mimics the target hardware. With containerization and virtualization, this is easier—one can instantiate a VM or container that has the same environment as the car's ECU. Using these twins, the CI/CD pipeline can automatically run regression tests and even simulate thousands of miles of driving with the new software in a fraction of the time it would take physically. Only when the software passes these digital tests would it be packaged for OTA to real cars [9, 162].

This approach dramatically accelerates development: as noted in an EDN industry article, virtual testing can shrink perceived test cycles "from months to minutes" by catching issues early and often[9, 146].

4.9.4 Continuous Safety Assurance

One might wonder, with all these continuous updates, how do we ensure the vehicle remains safe and compliant? This is indeed one of the hardest aspects of the SDV paradigm. The goal is that safety evidence (the documentation and test results that show a system meets safety requirements) must be regenerated continuously as well, in lockstep with software changes. In practice, most OEM programs still apply ISO 26262 in a stage-gate fashion. Truly continuous safety assurance is an emerging practice rather than the norm and is currently more visible in research projects and pilot programs than in mainstream series production.

Practically, what this means is: whenever a safety-related component is updated, the safety case for that component (and any interactions) needs updating. Automation can help here— e.g., generating safety analyses from models or using formal verification for certain algorithms that are frequently tweaked. Some research is focusing on formal verification of containerized automotive services (to prove that a microservice update doesn't introduce hazards) and continuous homologation (where regulators might be provided with automated reports for each software version).

The middleware can assist by enforcing modularity—if the system is clearly partitioned, one can argue that an update in one partition doesn't affect another, reducing the scope of re-certification. Additionally, monitoring features can ensure that if an updated component misbehaves in the field, the system detects it and intervenes (e.g., rolling back the update or switching to a safe mode).

4.9.5 Over-the-Air (OTA) Update Loop

Once an update has been developed and tested, it is delivered OTA to vehicles. But the loop doesn't end there—after deployment, the OEM watches metrics: Are there crash reports or anomalies from the new software version? Are customers using the new features? If something goes wrong, a rollback might be issued (which means the middleware should support dual-bank firmware or container rollback to a previous version). Regulations like R156 [72] explicitly require that OEMs have the ability to roll back software if an update has issues [145].

In a digital-first paradigm, the expectation is that software updates will be much more frequent (perhaps quarterly or monthly feature drops, plus urgent hotfixes). For example, GM stated plans to issue regular updates for their vehicles' software platform. This cadence pushes OEMs toward an almost IT-like operations model, sometimes dubbed "DevOps for automotive" [9, 146]. There is even the inclusion of machine learning model updates (MLOPs) in this loop—many SDVs will have AI components that need periodic retraining on new data (for better object recognition and so on), and those models must be validated and OTA updated as well [9].

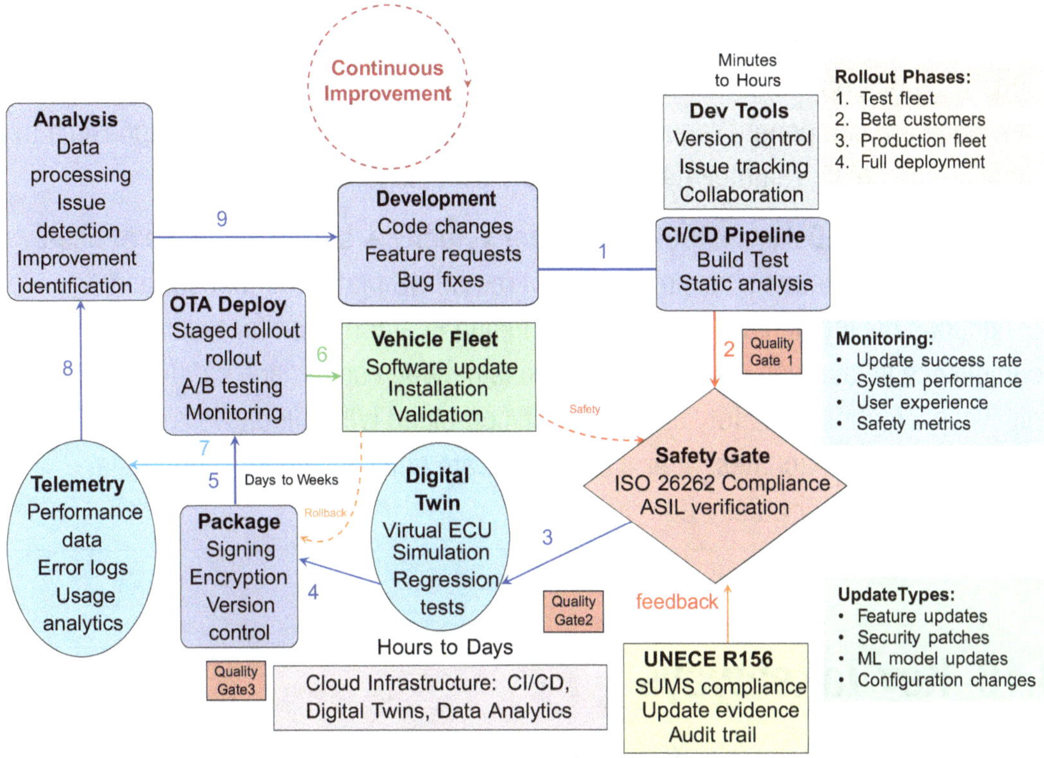

***Figure 4-13.** Digital-first continuous update loop in software-defined vehicles*

The bottom line is that a brittle or overly closed middleware stack would break this continuous update promise. If your OS/middleware requires a vehicle to come to a dealership for reflashing or can't accommodate partial updates, you're not truly leveraging SDV potential. By contrast, if your middleware is designed with remote updates, logging, and modular certification in mind, you can achieve "software agility" at scale. As an NXP automotive director put it, SDVs are designed for continuous improvement—manufacturers will push features and fixes throughout a car's life [137].

This calls for a much more agile, software-centric mindset where updates that used to take years now happen in weeks or days [9, 146]. The winners in the industry will be those who manage to combine developer velocity (fast, frequent updates) with safety assurance at scale (ensuring each update maintains or improves safety) [9]. Achieving that dual goal relies on everything we've discussed: robust middleware enabling modular updates, extensive virtualization and digital twins for testing, containers for isolating changes, and data-driven development to focus efforts.

Critic's Note A brittle middleware stack can break the digital-first promise. If the underlying platform is not built to handle frequent changes (e.g., if integrating one new software component requires rebuilding half the system or if it's impossible to monitor and debug remotely), then attempts at rapid iteration will falter.

Success in the SDV era equals developer velocity + safety evidence at scale. In practice, this means choosing middleware and OS platforms that support continuous deployment by design and investing in automation for testing and compliance so that you don't have to choose between speed and safety. CI/CD pipelines with built-in safety checks [146], combined with middleware that can compartmentalize updates, offer a path to iterate quickly without "hitting the brakes" on safety or quality [9].

4.10 Key Takeaways

- **OS and middleware define SDV agility:** The choice of underlying operating systems and middleware largely determines how quickly and safely a vehicle's software features can evolve. A well-designed middleware abstracts hardware differences and provides the mechanisms for OTA updates [135], enabling the concept of a software-defined vehicle. Conversely, poor middleware can bottleneck development and updates.
- **AUTOSAR Classic vs. Adaptive:** AUTOSAR Classic is suited for traditional ECUs with static functions—it offers real-time determinism and decades of proven reliability, but it's inflexible. AUTOSAR Adaptive is aimed at new high-performance domains—it introduces flexible service-oriented communication and dynamic apps on POSIX OSs [136, 139, 141, 142]. Rather than replacing Classic, Adaptive complements it: modern vehicles often use Classic for certain components (engine, body control) and Adaptive for others (ADAS, central gateway). Understanding which platform to use where is crucial.

- **Safety-critical RTOS vs. consumer OS:** Domains that involve safety (powertrain, chassis control, etc.) rely on RTOSs or specialized OSs (e.g., QNX, Integrity) with certification [148, 150, 153]. These ensure tasks run reliably on time. On the other hand, infotainment and connectivity features are implemented on consumer-grade OSs like Linux [154, 156] or Android [157, 159, 160], which provide rich functionality and faster development [9]. Because these OSs are not inherently safe, architects must bridge the two worlds—often by running them side by side with hypervisors or on separate hardware and by using monitors to ensure non-safety systems cannot compromise safety.
- **Containers and hypervisors for flexibility:** To achieve both safety and flexibility, cars are using virtualization (hypervisors) and containerization. Hypervisors allow running multiple OSs on one ECU (e.g., an RTOS for critical tasks and Linux for others) with strong isolation [144, 163]. Containers [151] allow microservices to run on top of an OS with isolation from each other, enabling easier updates of individual functions [138]. Together, these technologies let automakers consolidate hardware (reducing the number of ECUs) while still compartmentalizing risk and update software in a fine-grained way.
- **SUMS and continuous updates—the new normal:** Software Update Management Systems are now a must due to regulations like UNECE R156 [72] and ISO 24089 [73, 145, 146]. This pushes OEMs to adopt a "digital-first" mindset: vehicles need to be treated like software products with ongoing support and improvements. Continuous integration and deployment practices, cloud-based development, and in-car telemetry are becoming standard to support this lifecycle [9, 147]. Middleware that supports logging, OTA, rollback, and security checks is not just a technical choice but a compliance requirement. The ability to update software over the air, quickly and safely, will define competitiveness in the automotive industry going forward.

CHAPTER 5

Networking and V2X in Software-Defined Vehicles

5.1 Chapter Goals

After this chapter, you will be able to

- Explain the evolution of in-vehicle networking from CAN to Ethernet TSN and CAN XL.
- Understand deterministic communication requirements in SDVs and why they matter for safety.
- Compare the DSRC (Dedicated Short-Range Communications), C-V2X, and 5G NR-V2X communication stacks.
- Connect OTA update reliability with dynamic modulation techniques and error resilience measures.
- Evaluate business models around telecom–OEM cooperation in V2X services.

Critic's Note Networking is not just wires and protocols. It defines whether SDV functions are deterministic, updatable, and monetizable.

S. Agarwal, *Software-Defined Vehicles*, https://doi.org/10.1007/979-8-8688-2718-1_5

5.2 Introduction

Networking forms the nervous system of the software-defined vehicle, carrying everything from safety-critical brake commands to gigabytes of sensor data and over-the-air software updates. This chapter examines the evolution of in-vehicle networking from legacy CAN buses to high-speed Ethernet with Time-Sensitive Networking (TSN) and explores how Vehicle-to-Everything (V2X) communication extends the vehicle's perception and coordination capabilities beyond its physical sensors.

We begin with the transition from domain-specific buses (CAN, FlexRay, LIN) toward unified Ethernet backbones, examining why deterministic communication matters for safety-critical functions and how TSN achieves bounded latency on shared networks. The chapter then surveys V2X technologies—DSRC, C-V2X, and emerging 5G NR-V2X—comparing their technical characteristics and deployment status across regions.

The chapter also addresses OTA update reliability, explaining how adaptive modulation and robust protocols ensure software reaches vehicles intact even under poor network conditions.

Finally, we examine the business models emerging around connected vehicles and V2X services, recognizing that networking choices have commercial implications beyond their technical merits.

5.3 Legacy to Modern In-Vehicle Networks

Early vehicle networks were domain-specific and relatively low-bandwidth, but highly reliable for their purposes. Modern SDVs demand much more data throughput and deterministic behavior, prompting a shift in networking technologies.

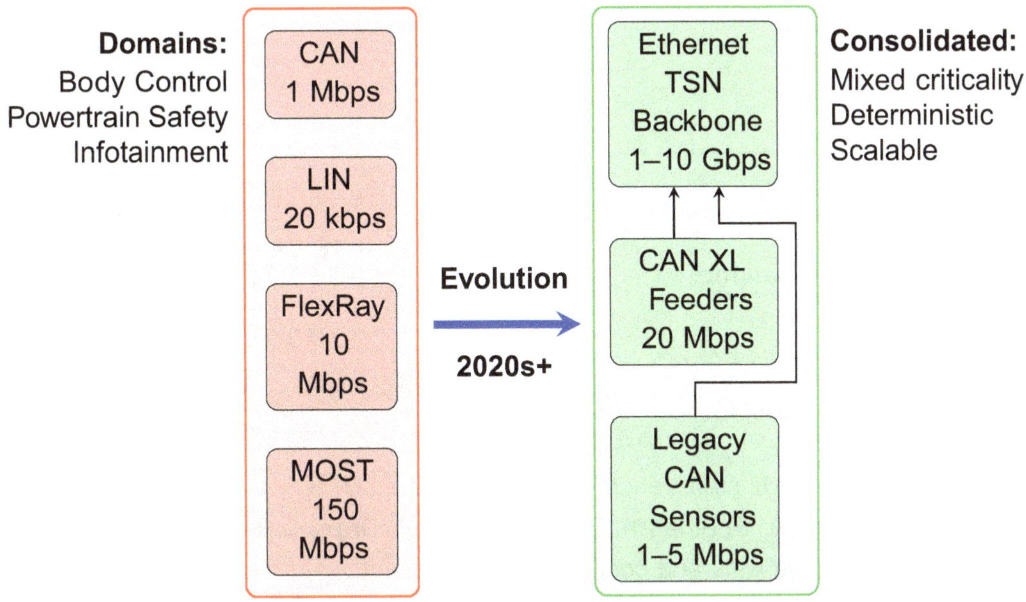

Figure 5-1. *Evolution from legacy buses to Ethernet TSN*

5.3.1 CAN and FlexRay

CAN (Controller Area Network): CAN is a robust, low-cost bus technology that remains widely used for body, powertrain, and control applications. Its key architectural strength is priority-based **non-destructive arbitration**: when multiple nodes start transmitting simultaneously, the frame with the numerically lower identifier continues, while the others stop transmitting and retry later. This allows urgent messages to gain bus access first without corrupting the winning frame. In practice, CAN's usefulness in modern SDVs comes less from protocol detail and more from its combination of simplicity, maturity, and predictable operation under bounded bus load. Its main limitation is bandwidth, which is why higher-speed technologies increasingly complement it rather than replace it outright.

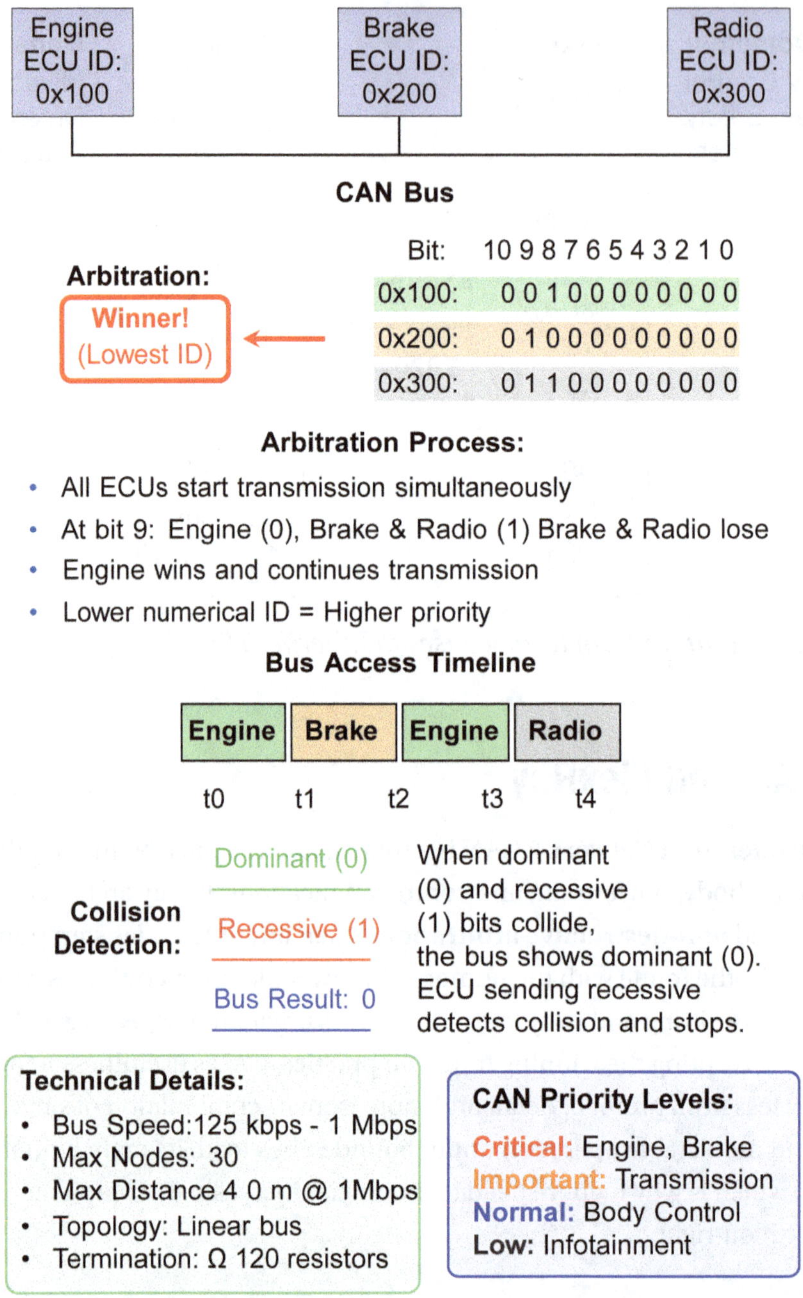

***Figure 5-2.** CAN bus priority arbitration mechanism*

FlexRay: A later (2000s) high-speed bus designed for safety-critical “x-by-wire” applications (steering, braking). It provides time-triggered messaging with dual channels for fault tolerance, at speeds up to 10 Mbps. FlexRay saw use in some luxury and high-end vehicles (notably by BMW, GM, etc.) for chassis control.

However, its complexity and cost, combined with emerging Ethernet-based solutions, have led to a decline in new implementations. In practice, FlexRay is fading for new architectures in favor of Ethernet Time-Sensitive Networking (TSN), which can offer similar determinism on a standard Ethernet network.

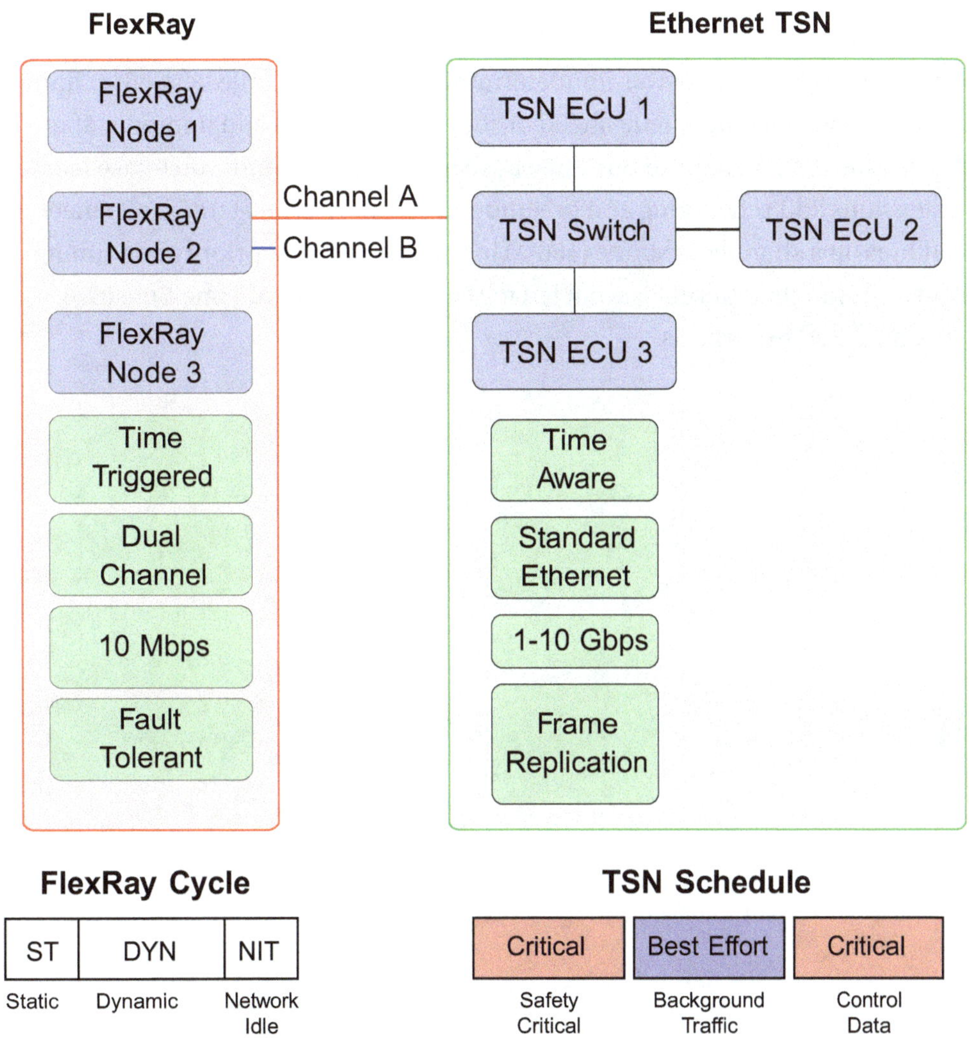

Figure 5-3. *FlexRay vs. Ethernet TSN comparison*

5.3.2 Automotive Ethernet and TSN

Automotive Ethernet: Standard Ethernet technology adapted for in-vehicle use (using lightweight cabling like 100BASE-T1 (IEEE 802.3bw) single-pair Ethernet). It offers high bandwidth (100 Mbps up to 10 Gbps) and supports IP networking, enabling a unified backbone for data-intensive domains like ADAS (advanced driver assistance systems) and infotainment [165].

The motivation for Ethernet was to reduce the "cacophony" of separate networks (CAN, LIN, FlexRay, MOST, etc.) and consolidate vehicle communications into one network, often structured as domains or zones [166].

Early in-vehicle Ethernet was nondeterministic: bursts of large best-effort frames (e.g., video streams) could queue ahead of control frames and add unpredictable delay. Without TSN, there is no built-in way to analytically bound worst-case latency; TSN extensions add scheduling and preemption so safety-critical traffic can meet its deadlines on a shared backbone [166]. This lack of inherent priority and timing guarantees in vanilla Ethernet is what led to the development of Time-Sensitive Networking (TSN) extensions.

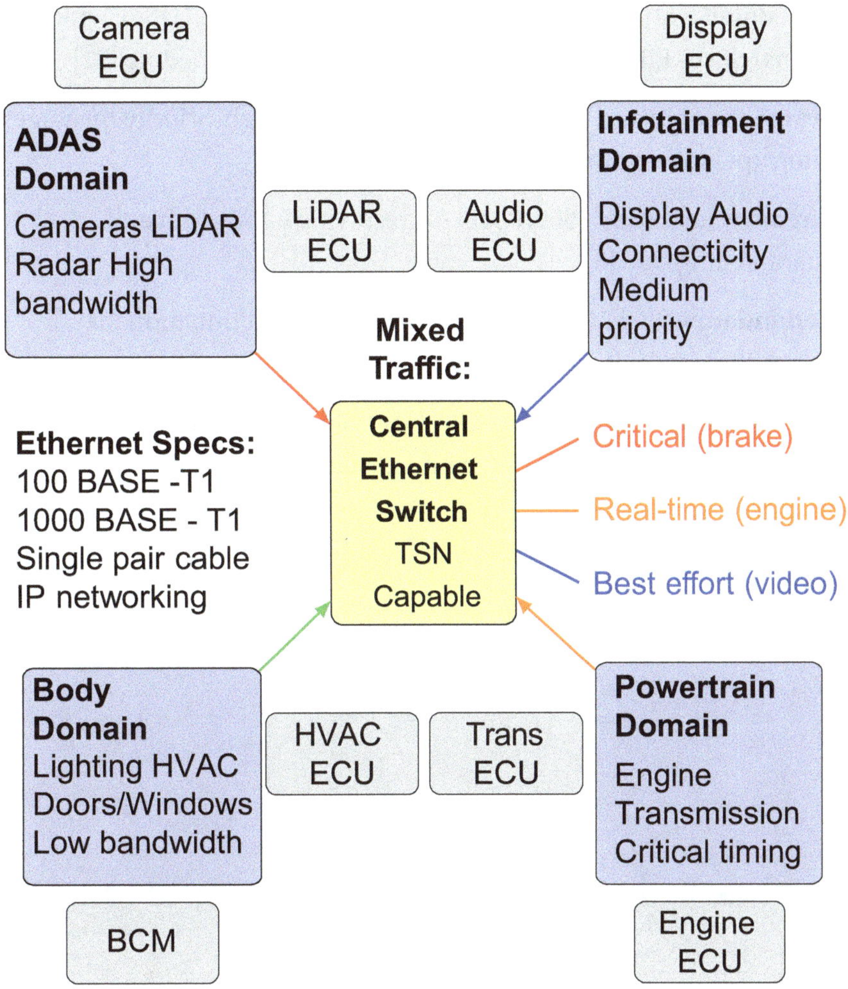

***Figure 5-4.** Conceptual illustration of Ethernet as a higher-bandwidth backbone in mixed automotive network architectures. Production systems typically use multiple switches, gateways, and cross-domain data paths.*

Time-Sensitive Networking (TSN): TSN is a suite of IEEE 802.1 standards that make Ethernet deterministic, providing bounded latency and delivery guarantees for critical traffic [51, 166].

Key TSN features include

- **Time synchronization** (IEEE 802.1AS gPTP provides sub-microsecond clock sync across devices) [52, 88, 166]

- **Scheduled traffic** via a time-aware shaper (IEEE 802.1Qbv), which opens/closes Ethernet gates according to a global schedule [51]
- **Frame preemption** (802.1Qbu/802.3br) to let high-priority messages interrupt lower-priority ones [51]
- **Stream reservation** (802.1Qcc) for reserving bandwidth and guaranteeing QoS [51]
- **Redundancy** (802.1CB Frame Replication and Elimination for Reliability) for fault-tolerant delivery [51]

Automotive profile: IEEE 802.1DG (2025) profiles TSN for automotive Ethernet [88] and is a key reference for in-vehicle deterministic networking [88].

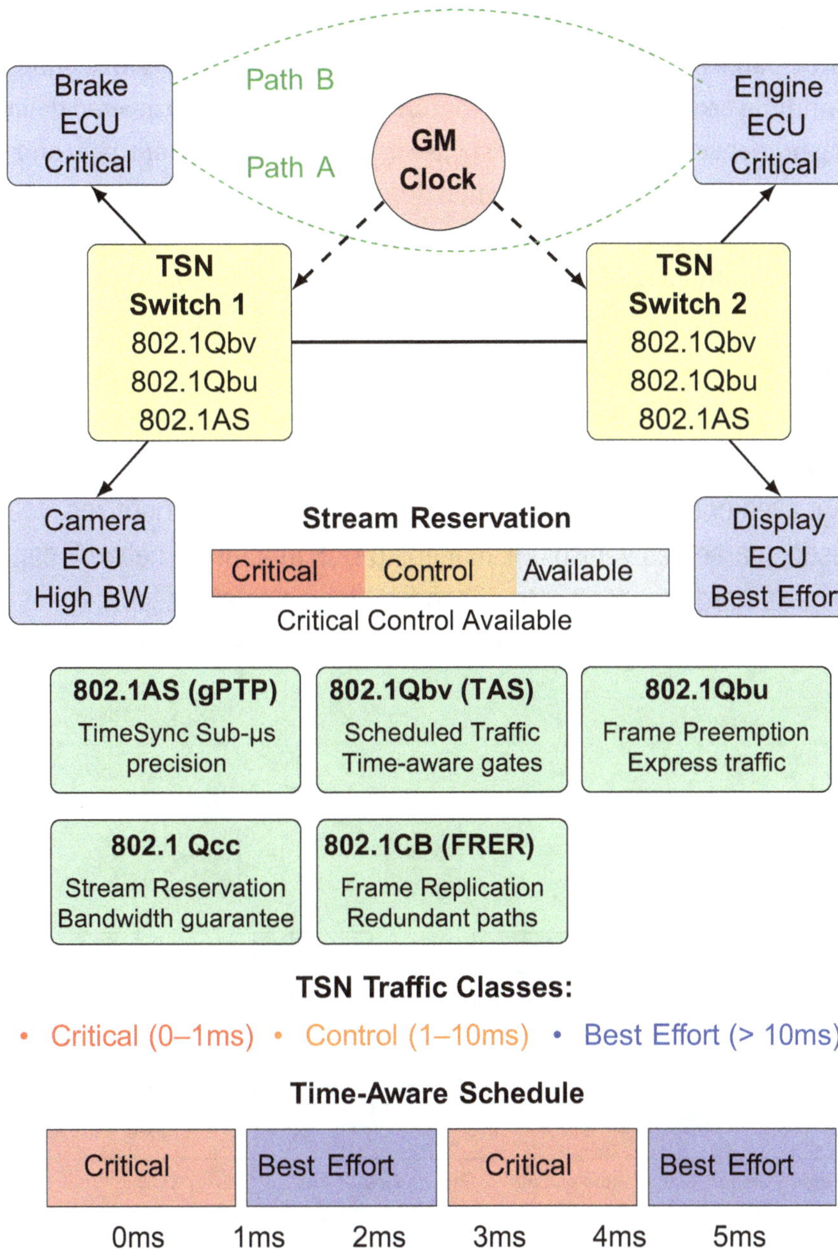

Figure 5-5. *TSN architecture with key IEEE 802.1 features*

In essence, TSN allows critical signals (like brake commands or sensor feeds) to be carried with analytically bounded latency on a shared Ethernet backbone—provided that all participants are correctly configured and the network operates within the assumed traffic and fault conditions. However, TSN's power comes with complexity: all network participants must be precisely configured and scheduled. A misconfigured TSN schedule or timing error can collapse determinism, leading to unexpected delays [166].

Deriving proper schedules and worst-case latency bounds is nontrivial and an active research area [51]. Despite this, when done correctly, TSN enables one Ethernet backbone to carry both high-bandwidth data (cameras, LiDAR, etc.) and real-time control messages without the latter being starved. Many modern cars now include Ethernet TSN for backbones (often 100BASE-T1 or 1000BASE-T1 links between domain controllers).

Engineering Insight Ethernet TSN is powerful but complex. In a time-triggered schedule, if even one device is out of sync or one queue mis-prioritized, your deterministic guarantees vanish. Mismanaging QoS in a mixed network can be as dangerous as a hardware fault—treat bandwidth as a safety resource.

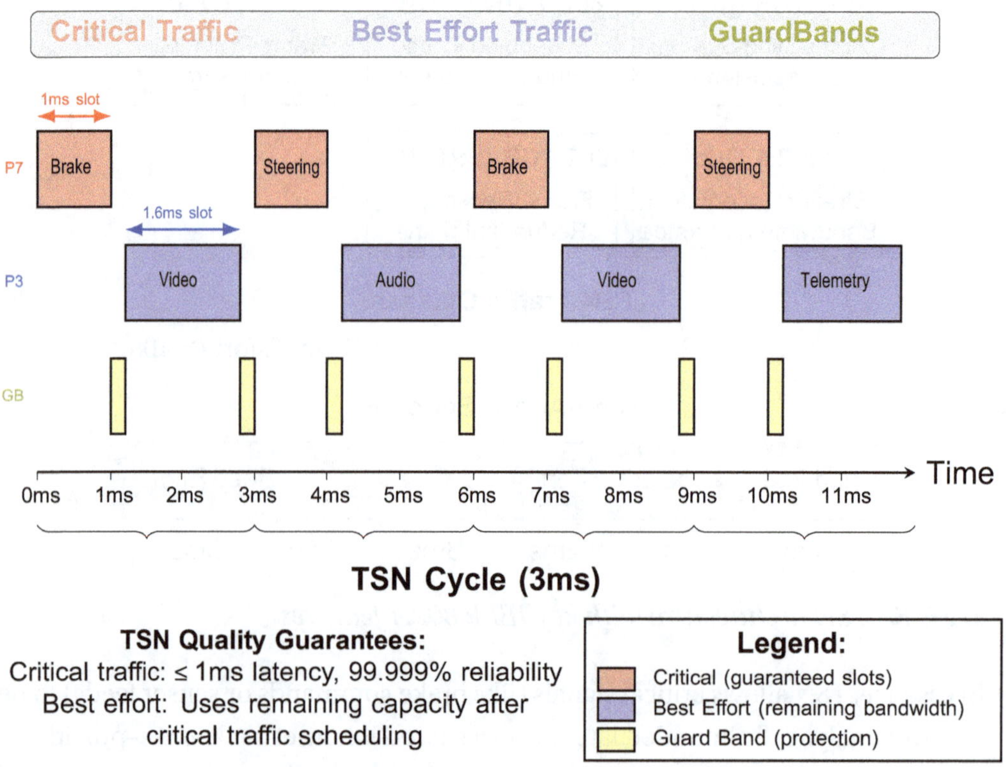

***Figure 5-6.** TSN time-aware scheduling example*

Figure 5-6 is intended to illustrate the core idea of time-aware scheduling. The network cycle is divided into windows in which critical traffic is guaranteed transmission opportunity, while best-effort traffic is sent only in the remaining capacity. Guard bands prevent large lower-priority frames from blocking the start of a scheduled critical window. The point is not that every automotive network uses the exact slots shown here, but that TSN can reserve deterministic transmission opportunities for safety-relevant traffic on a shared Ethernet backbone.

Cost Reality: TSN Is Not Free TSN is not a drop-in upgrade. It needs TSN-capable switches and PHYs, more expensive ECUs, specialized network design tools, and engineers who understand how to use them. Verification and regression testing of TSN schedules across multi-supplier programs is a major cost driver.

Many OEMs therefore keep CAN and LIN in low- to mid-bandwidth domains and only deploy Ethernet TSN where the additional bandwidth and flexibility clearly offset the cost (e.g., ADAS sensor networks or domain/zonal backbones).

In theory, using "standard Ethernet" should make interoperability easier. In practice, TSN profile fragmentation and OEM-specific network designs create new interoperability headaches: two OEMs can both use Ethernet TSN and still have completely different traffic classes, schedules, and configuration models.

Tier-1 suppliers therefore end up supporting multiple TSN profiles and configuration toolchains, increasing development and validation cost instead of reducing it.

5.3.3 CAN XL

CAN XL: The newest generation of CAN bus, designed to bridge the gap between legacy CAN and Ethernet. CAN XL builds on CAN FD and targets up to 20 Mbps (early silicon commonly around 10 Mbps) while allowing much larger payloads (up to 2,048 bytes per frame) [167].

It retains CAN's priority arbitration philosophy for reliability, but pushes that model into the 10–20 Mbps range—well above classic CAN and CAN FD, though still below 100BASE-T1 Ethernet. The core value proposition is to keep the familiar CAN arbitration and error-handling model while increasing payload and bit rate, not to compete with Ethernet on raw bandwidth.

A more useful architectural view is to treat **CAN XL as a higher-speed feeder network** rather than as a replacement for Ethernet. In practice, CAN XL can aggregate data from local devices or sub-networks and pass that traffic through a gateway into an Ethernet backbone. The gateway is responsible for translating or mapping the relevant payloads into the Ethernet/IP communication model used upstream. The important point for this chapter is therefore not the low-level encapsulation detail, but the role of CAN XL as an intermediate bus that extends familiar CAN concepts into the multi-megabit range while still fitting into a broader Ethernet-based vehicle architecture.

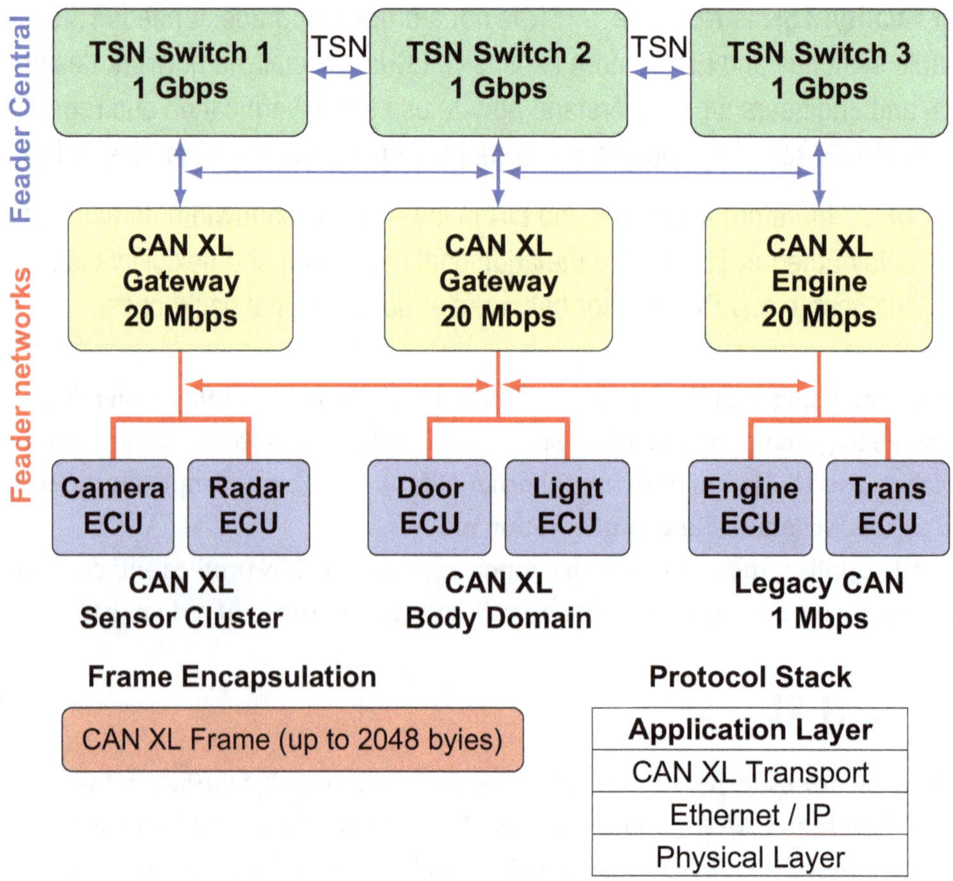

Figure 5-7. *CAN XL as feeder to TSN backbone*

Why CAN XL now? As vehicles became software-defined, even traditional CAN domains (body, powertrain) started needing more bandwidth (e.g., high-resolution sensor data or firmware updates to many ECUs). CAN XL offers an evolutionary step:

much faster than classic CAN/CAN FD while still using CAN controllers and wiring schemes familiar to OEMs [167].

Early CAN XL silicon and tools are appearing (Bosch, NXP, Vector, and others have prototypes in 2024–2025) [167], and standardization is in ISO 11898-1/2 [167].

We can expect CAN XL to augment Ethernet TSN networks, not completely replace lower-speed CAN—it will likely be used for mid-tier bandwidth needs or as a transition in parts of the car that don't justify full Ethernet. It shows the industry's recognition that not all corners of the vehicle need multi-gigabit Ethernet; sometimes a 10 Mbps robust bus is exactly the right fit.

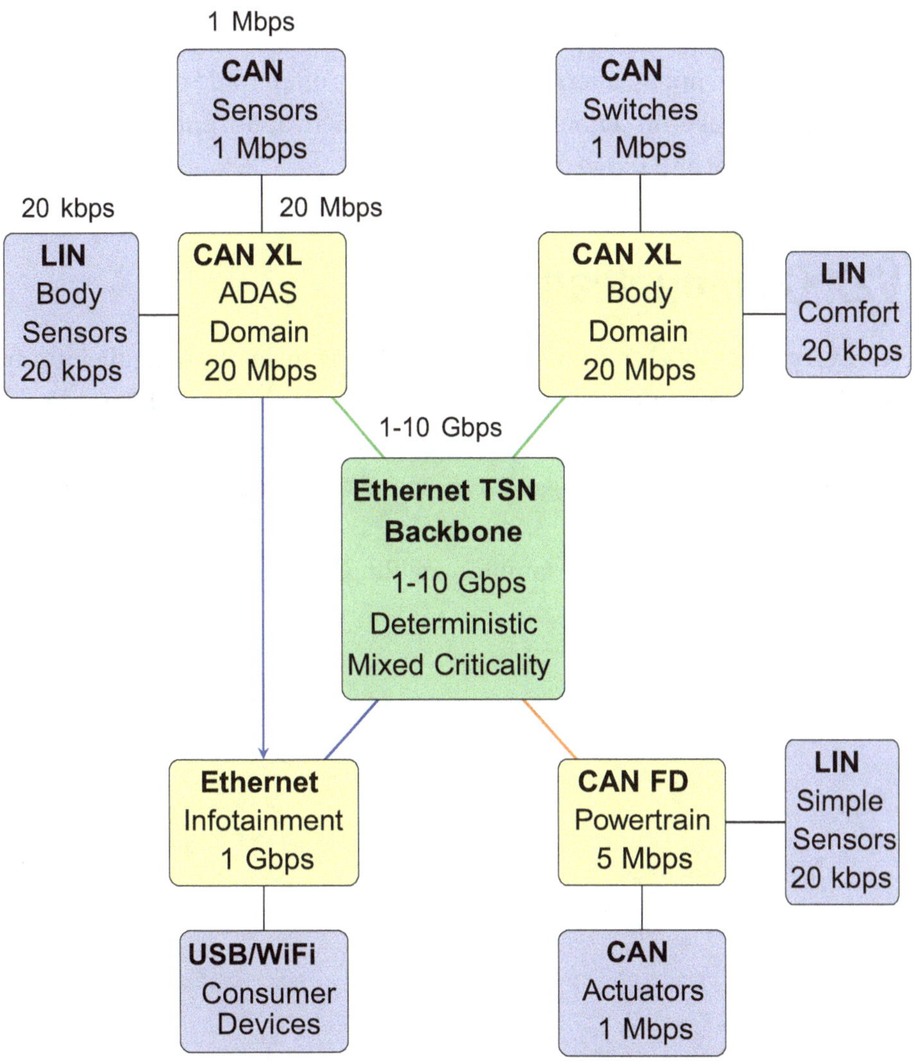

Figure 5-8. *Vehicle network hierarchy with CAN, CAN XL, and TSN*

5.3.4 Power and Thermal Considerations

Networking choices also affect the vehicle's power budget and thermal design. Single-pair Ethernet PHYs at 100 Mbps or 1 Gbps consume significantly more power than classic CAN or LIN transceivers, and TSN-capable switches add both idle and active power overhead.

Central compute nodes that terminate many Ethernet links further increase baseline consumption. In parallel, keeping multiple buses alive (e.g., CAN FD, Ethernet TSN, and LIN) adds quiescent current that matters for parked battery drain.

For an EV, a few watts of continuous networking overhead across dozens of ECUs translates directly into lost range; power budgeting for networking is therefore a first-class design constraint, not an afterthought. Architects often trade off "always-on" connectivity against wake-up schemes, selective link activation, and low-power islands to meet both functional and range targets.

5.4 V2X Communications

Vehicle-to-Everything (V2X) communication refers to vehicles exchanging information with other road users and infrastructure: V2V (vehicle-to-vehicle), V2I (vehicle-to-infrastructure; e.g., traffic signals), V2P (vehicle-to-pedestrian devices), V2N (vehicle-to-network/cloud), etc. SDVs leverage V2X to extend their perception and coordinate maneuvers.

There are two major technology families enabling V2X.

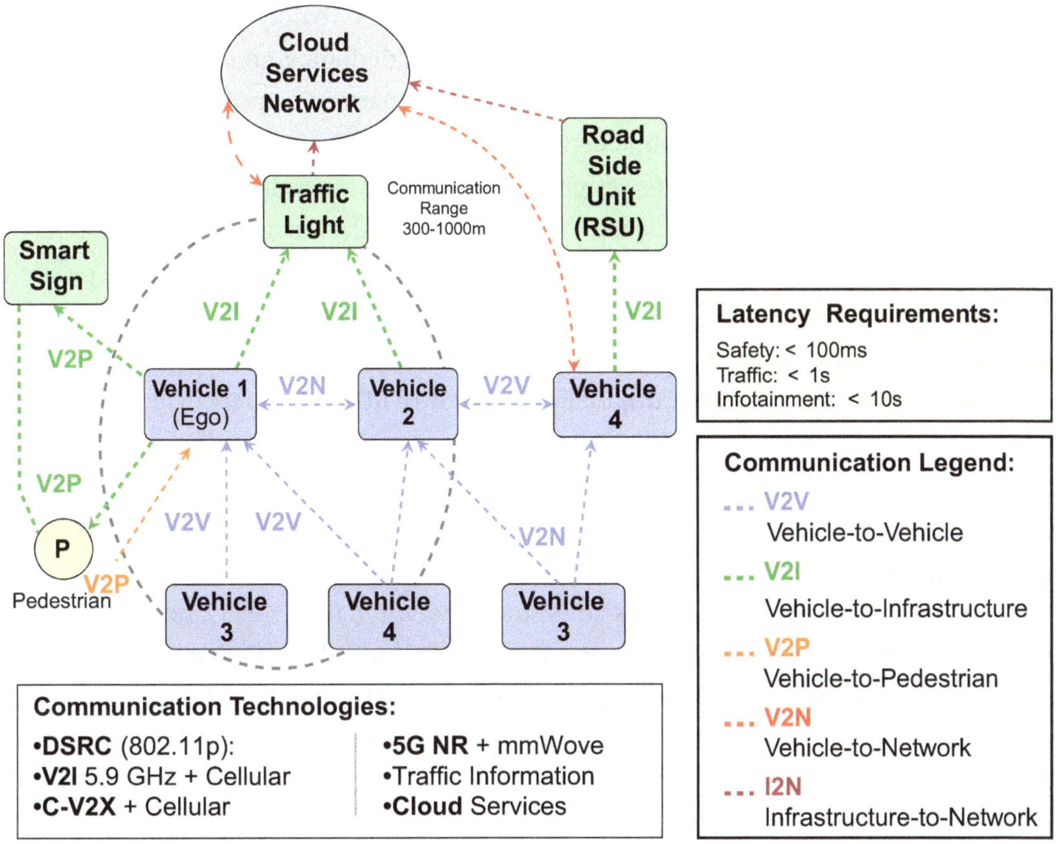

Figure 5-9. *V2X communication types and ecosystem*

5.4.1 DSRC vs. C-V2X

DSRC (Dedicated Short-Range Communications): Based on the IEEE 802.11p standard (also known in Europe as ITS-G5). It's essentially a Wi-Fi derivative tuned for vehicular use, operating in the 5.9 GHz band. DSRC was the first V2X technology, with standards finalized around 2010. It offers low latency (messages delivered in ~10 ms in practice) and works in ad hoc fashion—vehicles broadcast to each other directly without needing cellular networks [168].

This made DSRC appealing for safety applications (basic safety messages, collision warnings, etc.), and it has been proven in numerous pilot deployments. For example, Japan and parts of Europe deployed some DSRC/ITS-G5 roadside units, and in the United States, various pilot programs used DSRC for V2V safety messages.

Technically, DSRC achieved its design goals: it's low-latency and reliable for line-of-sight communications, and because it's decentralized, there's no subscription cost—vehicles communicate peer-to-peer. However, DSRC's downside has been more political and economic than technical: it requires dedicated spectrum, and after many years of delay, regulators and industry started pivoting to newer options.

In the United States, the FCC originally allocated 75 MHz of spectrum at 5.9 GHz for DSRC back in 1999, but by 2017–2020 they moved to repurpose the band and in 2024 finalized rules designating the upper 30 MHz (5.895–5.925 GHz) for C-V2X and sunsetting DSRC. This "spectrum challenge" left DSRC with only 30 MHz and effectively stalled large-scale adoption.

Europe, where early policy discussions strongly favored an ITS-G5-first approach, shifted to a technology-neutral stance in 2019 (a DSRC-only delegated act was rejected), allowing either ITS-G5 or cellular-based V2X. As a result, DSRC is now fading in favor—there are deployed cars (e.g., some Volkswagen models around 2019 had ITS-G5 units, and Toyota in the United States briefly offered DSRC in select models), but momentum has swung to C-V2X for future projects.

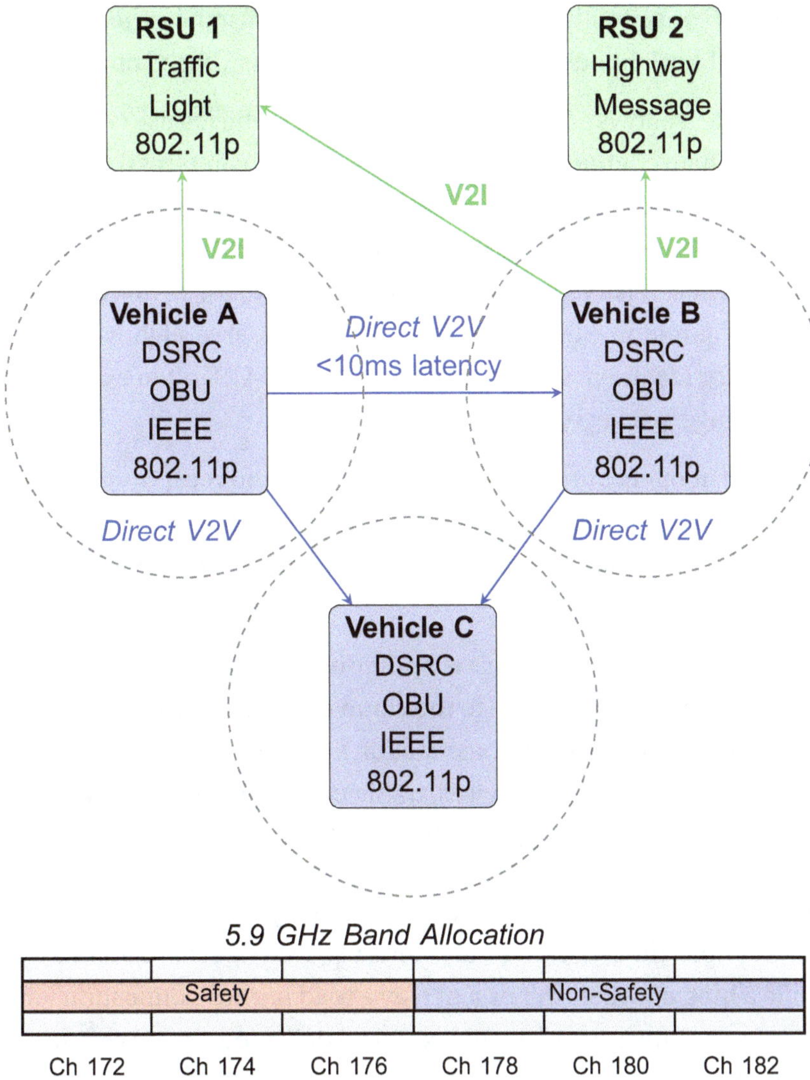

Figure 5-10. *DSRC 802.11p direct V2V and V2I communication*

C-V2X (Cellular V2X): An umbrella term for V2X communication using cellular radio technology, defined by 3GPP. It includes two modes:

- **Direct (PC5 sidelink):** Vehicles communicate directly with each other or road infrastructure using cellular radio interfaces but without going through the cellular network. This mode, defined in LTE Release 14/15 (often called LTE-V2X), operates in the same 5.9 GHz band as DSRC

[169]. It's conceptually similar to DSRC (broadcast messages, short range ~300 m–1 km), but uses a different physical layer (based on LTE).

PC5 mode 4 allows autonomous scheduling (vehicles use GPS timing to coordinate channel access), whereas mode 3 can be assisted by a cellular network if one is available. Measured one-way latencies for ITS-G5 and LTE-V2X PC5 are both typically in the low tens of milliseconds; relative performance varies with load, environment, and configuration. Several link-level studies observe slightly lower latency for ITS-G5 in some scenarios, with LTE-V2X often exhibiting better range/packet reliability [169].

However, it offers other benefits: better range and reception in non-line-of-sight situations due to LTE's forward error correction and receiver diversity and a clear evolution path as part of the cellular roadmap.

- **Network (Uu interface):** This is traditional cellular connectivity (4G/5G). Vehicles send data to the cloud or to each other via the mobile network (through a base station). This is useful for V2N applications (e.g., cloud services, traffic updates) but not for ultra-low-latency needs (since going through the network adds latency).

Still, having both direct and network options gives C-V2X flexibility. For example, time-critical safety alerts use PC5 direct broadcast, while a message that isn't urgent (say a road hazard notification far ahead or a software update file) could be delivered via the cellular network.

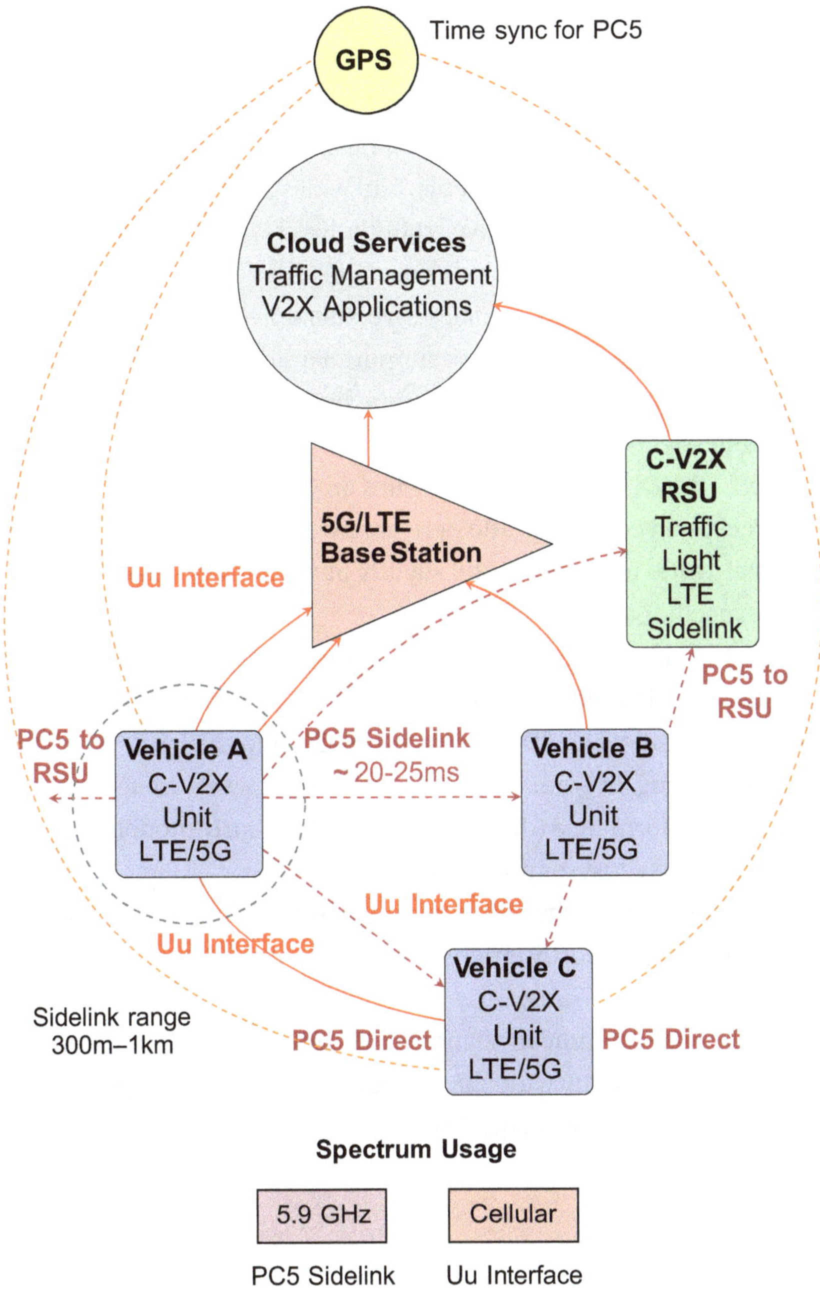

Figure 5-11. *C-V2X PC5 and Uu communication modes*

The strength of C-V2X is the backing of the cellular ecosystem. Silicon vendors like Qualcomm, Huawei, and others have heavily invested in C-V2X chipsets. Many automakers see the appeal of C-V2X because it aligns with 5G development and potentially allows leveraging mobile network infrastructure.

C-V2X has a roadmap into 5G (see the next section) and integration with future smartphones and smart city infrastructure. China in particular has prioritized C-V2X, with extensive pilots, roadside deployments, and widespread OEM support as part of national and provincial intelligent transport initiatives [170].

The weaknesses or challenges include coverage fragmentation and interoperability concerns. Unlike DSRC that works vehicle-to-vehicle universally, C-V2X in practice might depend on region-specific network support. For instance, if one country uses a certain band or requires network coordination, how do cars from another region interoperate seamlessly?

Additionally, LTE-V2X sidelink mode 4 relies on GNSS (GPS) for timing sync; loss of GPS or poor reception could degrade performance [169]. Some critiques point out that in certain real-world tests, DSRC still slightly outperforms LTE-V2X in latency and reliability under specific conditions [169].

That said, the overall industry trend is clearly toward C-V2X. By 2025, most new V2X efforts (especially in the United States, EU, and China) are based on C-V2X, not 802.11p. Europe's latest releases allow C-V2X alongside ITS-G5, and the US DOT is funding C-V2X pilots after the FCC ruling. In summary, DSRC/802.11p is a mature technology with proven low-latency performance (deployed in pilots and early models), but its future is limited by spectrum and ecosystem support.

C-V2X is a growing technology with a strong roadmap (into 5G), but still in early stages of large deployment (mostly emerging in China and pilot programs elsewhere).

A comparison is shown in Table 5-1.

These latency values are indicative and come from controlled trials; real-world performance varies significantly with channel load, interference, deployment configuration, and implementation quality.

Table 5-1. *Comparison of V2X Technologies: DSRC, LTE C-V2X, and 5G NR-V2X*

Technology	Typical One- Way Latency	Strengths	Weaknesses
DSRC (802.11p)	Low tens of ms (typ.)†	Proven in tests; low latency; infrastructure-light (no cellular needed)	Losing spectrum and regulatory support; limited future roadmap
C-V2X (LTE-V2X PC5)	Low tens of ms (typ.)†	Backed by the cellular industry; can leverage both direct and network links; evolution to 5G	Requires GPS/cellular for sync; fragmentation in adoption (different regions, modes)
5G NR-V2X	Single-digit ms (target)	Ultra-low latency and high throughput potential; supports advanced use cases (platooning, sensor sharing)	Immature—still in trials; no large-scale deployment yet; new hardware required

† In typical link-level tests, ITS-G5 often measures slightly lower one-way latency, while LTE-V2X often shows better range/packet reliability; absolute values depend on configuration and channel load [169].

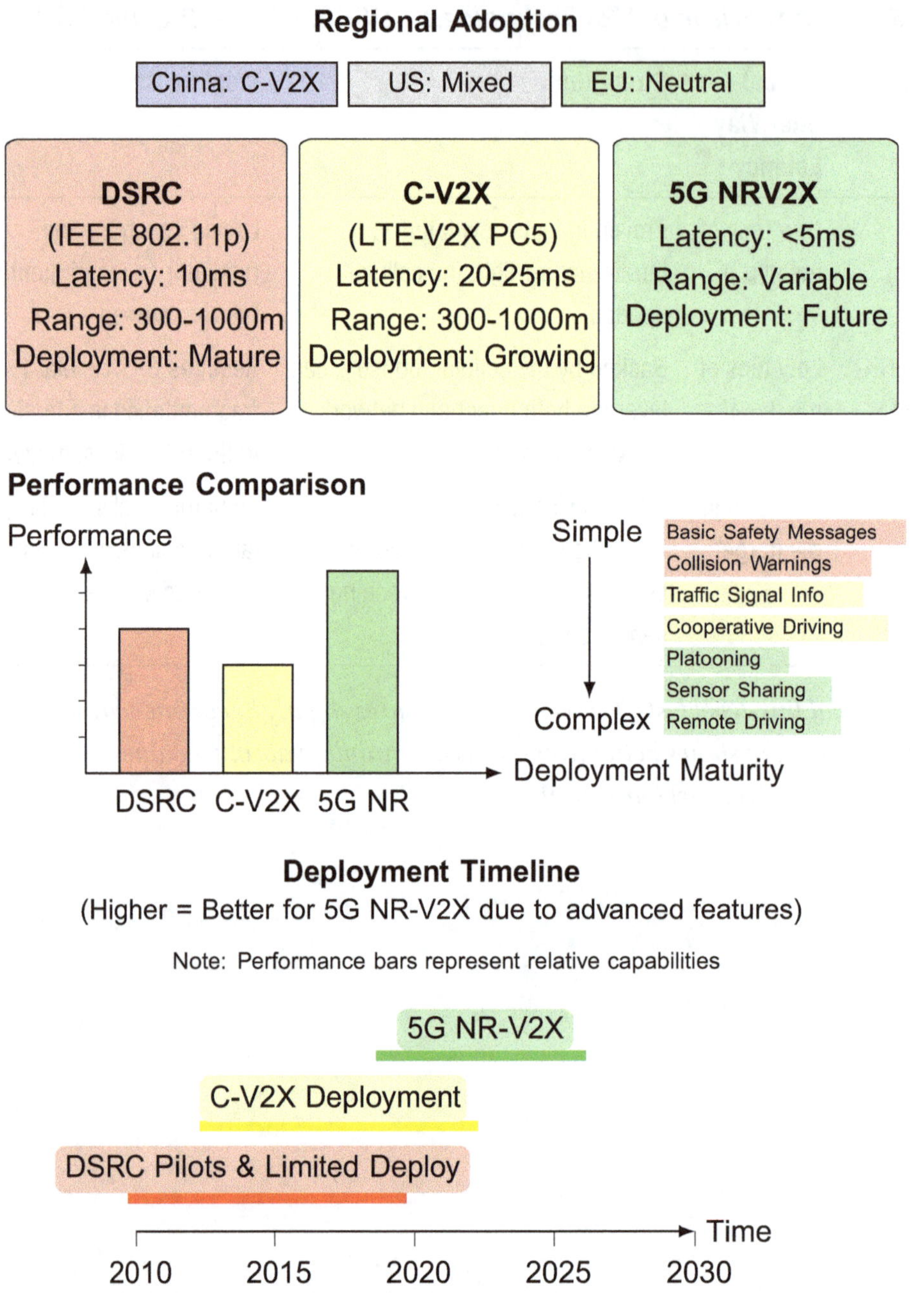

Figure 5-12. Comparison of V2X technologies and performance

5.4.2 5G NR-V2X

The arrival of 5G brings a new chapter for V2X, often termed NR-V2X (New Radio V2X). This is defined in 3GPP Releases 16 and 17, building upon the LTE-V2X foundation. The goal of 5G NR-V2X is to enable advanced cooperative maneuvers and higher levels of automation by providing URLLC (Ultra-Reliable Low-Latency Communications) in vehicular scenarios.

Key aspects include

- **Even lower latency and higher reliability:** 5G's physical layer targets ultra-low latency in the single-digit-millisecond range at the radio layer and very high reliability under URLLC profiles in ideal conditions; real-world fleet-scale data is still emerging.

  NR-V2X uses these enhancements to support scenarios like coordinated emergency braking, where cars must virtually instantaneously exchange sensor and intent data. Certain safety services that require <5 ms latency and >99% reliability are supported by NR-V2X [171].

- **New use case groups:** NR-V2X sidelink enables vehicle platooning, extended sensor sharing, advanced cooperative driving, and even remote driving use cases[171, 172].

  For example, platooning—a convoy of trucks driving with minimal gaps to reduce drag— demands sub-10 ms reaction times and high message reliability. NR-V2X can allow platooning vehicles to exchange acceleration/braking control messages in a few milliseconds, far faster than human reaction time, thereby maintaining tight synchronization.

  Extended sensors refer to one vehicle's ability to stream its sensor data (camera, radar, etc.) to another vehicle—5G's higher bandwidth supports sending high-resolution video or LiDAR point clouds between cars to "see through" other vehicles or around corners [171].

- **Technical features:** NR-V2X introduces new transmission modes (unicast and groupcast in addition to broadcast) for sidelink [171]. It also can operate on multiple carriers simultaneously (e.g., using wider bandwidth or multiple frequency bands for resiliency) [171].

While LTE-V2X and NR-V2X are not directly interoperable (they use different PHY/MAC), it's expected that vehicles will carry both for some time—with multi-mode chipsets—to ensure backward compatibility [171]. Initial NR-V2X sidelink operates in similar frequency ranges (5.9 GHz for direct, potentially mmWave in future for high-bandwidth needs) [171].

- **Deployment status:** As of 2025, NR-V2X remains immature in deployment. Prototype chipsets and test vehicles exist, and standardization is largely done, but wide-scale deployment awaits spectrum allocation and ecosystem readiness, with only pilot or very limited production deployments, if any, on the road.

  For instance, one challenge noted in the United States is that after allocating 30 MHz to LTE-V2X, only a very small band might remain for NR-V2X unless more spectrum is opened [172].

  Automakers are experimenting with NR-V2X in pilots and test fleets; limited production features on high-end models may appear in the latter half of the 2020s, but widespread deployment will depend on spectrum, infrastructure investment, and clear regulatory support.

  In regions such as the United States, recent spectrum reallocations have effectively reset parts of the V2X roadmap and added further delay. China's roadmap includes NR-V2X in the next wave of smart highway infrastructure. Europe's projects (like Horizon 2020 and beyond) have demos of NR-V2X for cross-border traffic and advanced driverless functions, but no production vehicles yet.

  In short, NR-V2X is promising but not yet pervasive: it's the enabler for the highest levels of cooperative automation, but for now, LTE-V2X (and even DSRC in some places) will coexist until 5G coverage and maturity reach critical mass.

Figure 5-13 is meant to show why NR-V2X is discussed as more than just a faster version of LTE sidelink. The main idea is that NR-V2X is designed for **more demanding cooperative scenarios**, such as platooning, sensor sharing, and other low-latency multi-vehicle coordination tasks. Network slicing and edge computing appear in the figure because these are often discussed as supporting infrastructure for such services, not because every NR-V2X deployment requires all of them simultaneously. The teaching point is that NR-V2X extends V2X from message exchange toward richer cooperative functions.

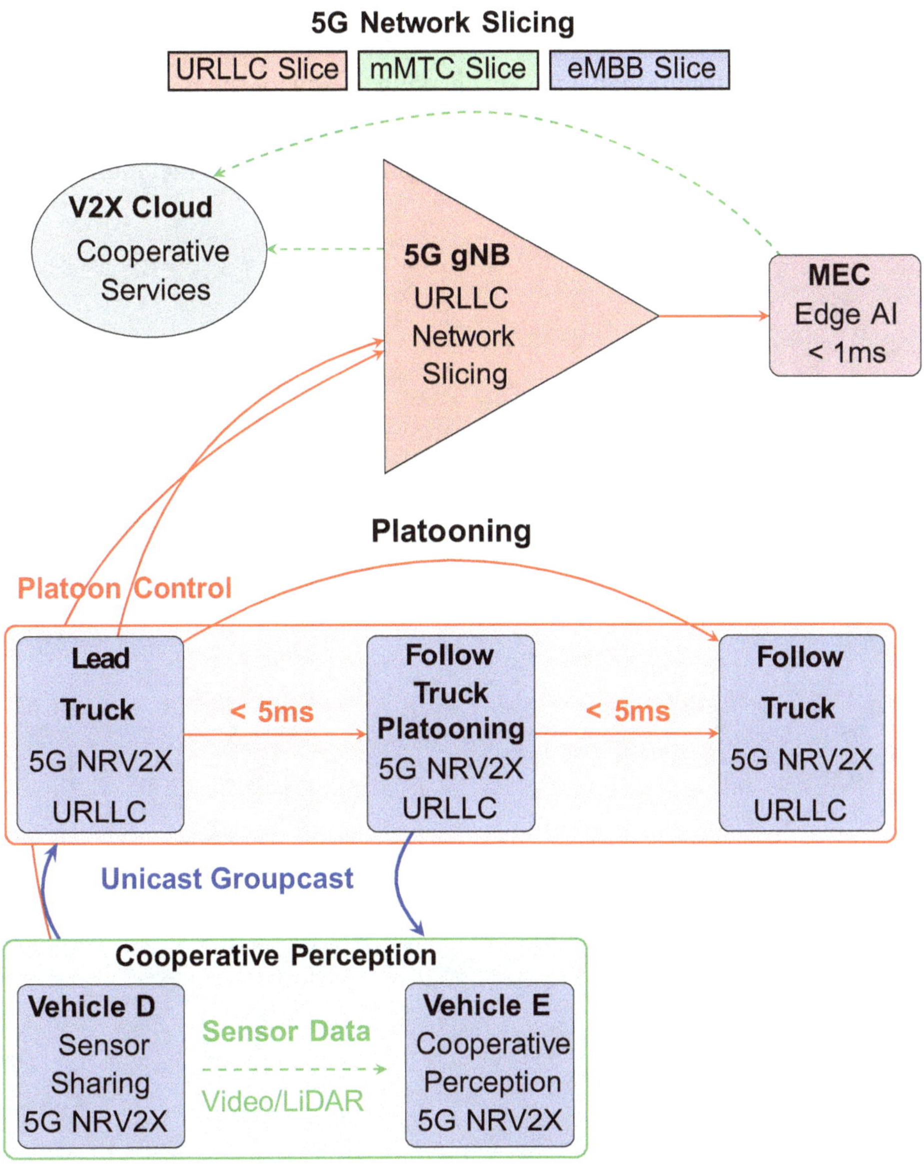

Figure 5-13. *5G NR-V2X advanced low-latency use cases*

5.5 Determinism and Real-Time Constraints

One of the most critical aspects of SDV networking is determinism—the ability to guarantee that certain messages (especially those related to safety) are delivered within strict deadlines. In a vehicle, not all data is equal. A packet telling a brake actuator to engage is vastly more urgent than a packet carrying a song for the music player.

Failing to deliver safety-critical data on time can have fatal consequences, so we manage this via both network design and QoS (Quality of Service) mechanisms.

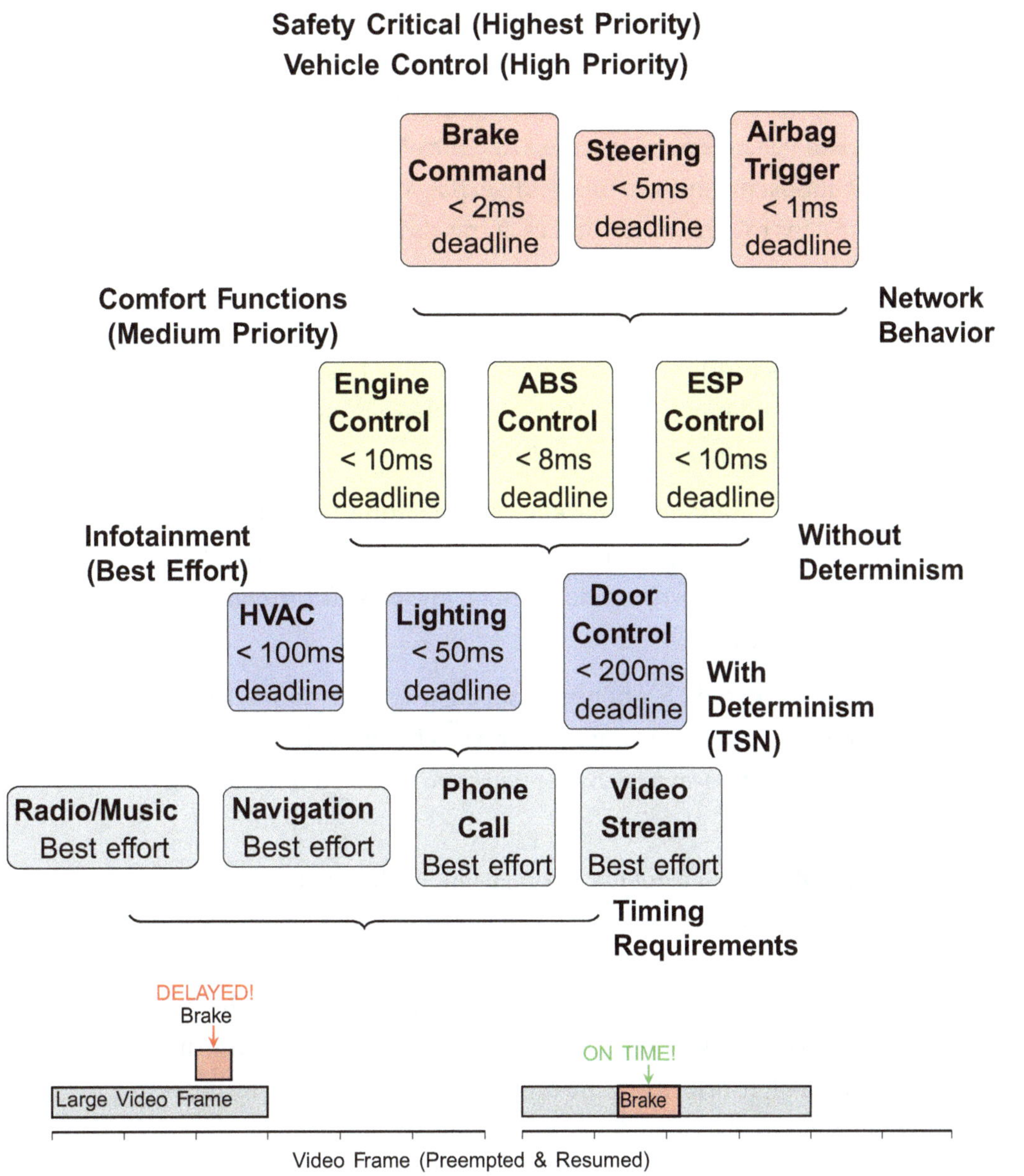

Figure 5-14. Deterministic communication with priority traffic

- **Latency requirements:** Many safety-critical control loops in vehicles require latency on the order of 10 ms or less. For example, an automated emergency braking system that shares sensor data between vehicles or between an AI controller and a brake ECU must react almost instantly to be effective. If a vehicle at 100 km/h waits even 50 ms extra to apply brakes, it travels about 1.4 m in that time.

  Thus, safety-critical control loops are often engineered with single-digit-millisecond end-to-end budgets (exact values vary by function and architecture) [166]. Ethernet frames on a busy network can experience queuing delays that exceed these budgets unless the network is engineered for real time.

  This is why Time-Sensitive Networking features (e.g., IEEE 802.1Qbv time-aware shaping) are employed—they allow the network to schedule high-priority traffic so that it always gets through within a bounded time.

  A well-configured TSN network can ensure, for instance, that an emergency braking message never waits behind a large video file transfer; the time-aware shaper will have reserved timeslots for critical traffic [173].

- **Bounded jitter:** It's not just average latency but worst-case latency (latency plus jitter) that matters. "Deterministic" communication means you can guarantee an upper bound. In a mixed network, without controls, worst-case delays can no longer be analytically bounded (e.g., if someone floods the network with low-priority frames, a high-priority frame might be delayed arbitrarily unless policing is in place).

  TSN's toolkit (priority-based scheduling, stream reservation, policing, etc.) is designed to give hard guarantees. For example, using TSN scheduling and preemption, one can ensure a high-priority signal experiences (hypothetically) no more than say 100 μs delay per switch hop [51]. It essentially creates a virtual circuit with guaranteed service.

TSN also supports Frame Replication and Elimination for Reliability (802.1CB) where duplicate copies of critical messages can be sent along diverse paths—so even if one path fails or is congested, the other gets through [51].

- **Mixed-criticality networks:** Modern vehicles carry a mix of traffic: some "safety-critical," some "infotainment or best-effort." A big challenge in SDVs is that these share network infrastructure. You could segregate completely (e.g., two separate physical networks), but that adds weight and cost. Instead, we logically segregate via VLANs or virtual networks and prioritize appropriately.

  The worst-case scenario to avoid is a lower-criticality function impacting a higher-criticality one. For instance, consider a 1 Gbps Ethernet backbone used by both an IP camera sending a video feed to the infotainment system and the drive-by-wire steering controller sending steering angle commands.

  If the network is not properly configured, a burst of video packets (huge in size and continuous) could delay a steering command frame, introducing lag in steering response— clearly unacceptable.

  By using TSN, we can assign the steering traffic to a high-priority class that always preempts the video traffic. IEEE 802.1Qbu frame preemption allows a large video frame to be interrupted mid-transmission to let an urgent frame through [51], and the video frame resumes after—meaning the steering command gets through with minimal delay.

  Meanwhile, bandwidth management (802.1Qav/Qcc) ensures the video still gets a fair share of bandwidth when available, but never at the expense of critical control data.

  The take-home message: In a mixed network, mismanaging QoS is as dangerous as a hardware fault. Engineers must treat network scheduling and bandwidth as safety resources, subject to verification and validation just like brakes or airbags [166].

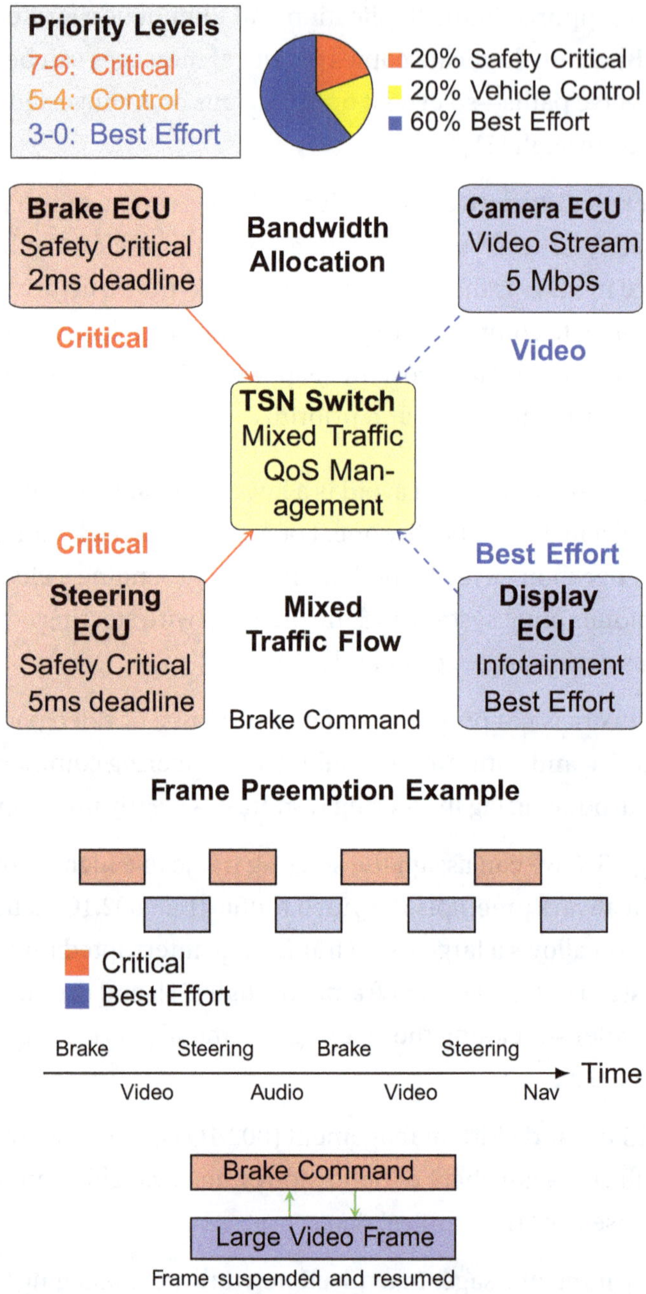

Figure 5-15. *Mixed-criticality networking with TSN guarantees*

- **Time synchronization:** Determinism often relies on all devices having a common sense of time (global clock). Protocols like IEEE 802.1AS (gPTP) are used to synchronize ECUs to sub-microsecond precision [51]. This is essential for features like 802.1Qbv scheduling—all nodes need to switch queues at the same instants [51].

  Automotive networks now typically include a grandmaster clock (could be in an automotive Ethernet switch or a central ECU) that syncs the others. A synchronized network also enables coordinated actions—e.g., triggering multiple actuators at the exact same time or timestamping sensor data for sensor fusion.

Figure 5-16 has two purposes: to show the **clock hierarchy** used in IEEE 802.1AS and to illustrate the **message flow** by which synchronization is maintained. The first explains who provides time; the second explains how that time is distributed and preserved across the network.

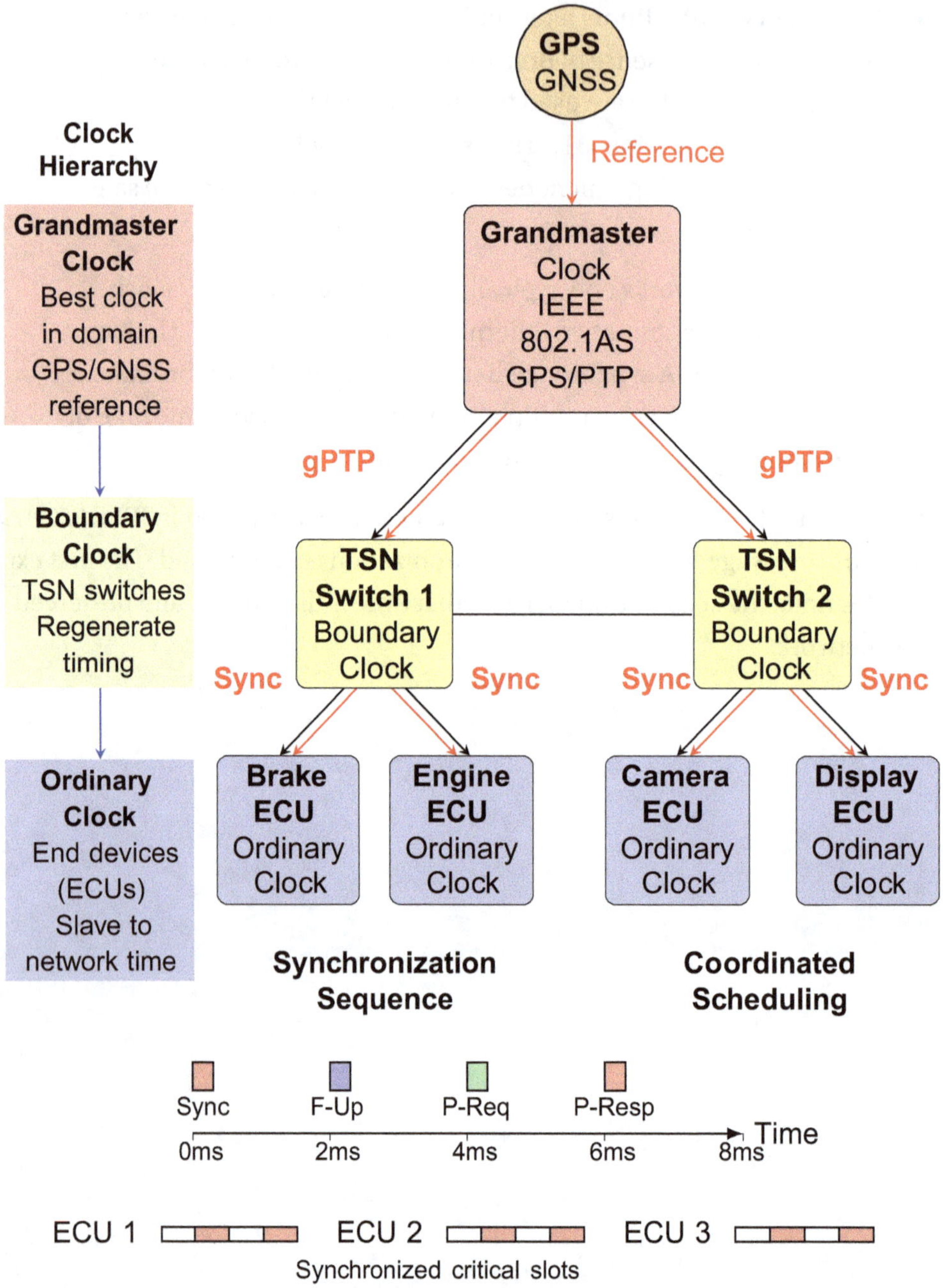

Figure 5-16. *TSN time synchronization using IEEE 802.1AS*

In summary, determinism in automotive networking means more than just "fast" communication. It means being able to prove that every safety-relevant message will meet its end-to-end deadline, including worst-case queuing and jitter, under defined assumptions about load and faults.

Technologies like CAN and FlexRay achieved this with dedicated buses and conservative utilization. Ethernet TSN brings similar guarantees to shared Ethernet backbones by combining precise time synchronization, time-aware shaping, frame preemption, bandwidth reservation, and redundancy.

However, these mechanisms only deliver their promises if the network is engineered, configured, and verified as carefully as any other safety mechanism. From a safety engineer's perspective, bandwidth, schedules, and QoS policies become part of the safety argument: they are treated as safety-relevant resources alongside sensors and actuators, even though deterministic networking alone does not make a system functionally safe.

In practice, ISO 26262 safety goals are achieved by combining deterministic communication with diagnostics (timeouts, sequence checks, plausibility checks), redundancy, and defined safe states. You can have a highly deterministic network that still fails a safety audit, and you can have safety-certified systems that tolerate some nondeterminism by design.

5.5.1 Security Considerations in Networking

Each in-vehicle and V2X network technology brings its own security profile and attack surface. Classic CAN is a broadcast bus with no built-in authentication or encryption; once an attacker breaches the perimeter (e.g., through a compromised gateway), spoofed messages can affect any ECU on that segment.

Ethernet and IP-based networking introduce much richer security tools (firewalls, TLS, segmentation), but also add complexity and more code that can contain vulnerabilities in stacks, service discovery, and diagnostics.

V2X technologies (DSRC, C-V2X, NR-V2X) expose the vehicle directly to external radio traffic. This requires robust public key infrastructure (PKI), misbehavior detection, and privacy- preserving credential management so that safety messages can be authenticated without turning vehicles into tracking beacons.

For an SDV architect, security posture is inseparable from the networking choice: each bus and link type changes who can attack you, from where, and how quickly.

5.6 OTA and Modulation Reliability

Over-the-air (OTA) updates are a cornerstone of the software-defined vehicle. They allow automakers to fix bugs, add features, or patch security issues without a service visit. However, performing OTA software updates to a vehicle presents unique reliability challenges: a failure or corruption in an update can potentially "brick" an ECU or even disable a car, which is unacceptable from both a safety and a customer trust perspective.

Networking plays a key role in OTA robustness, particularly through error resilience and dynamic adaptation to link conditions.

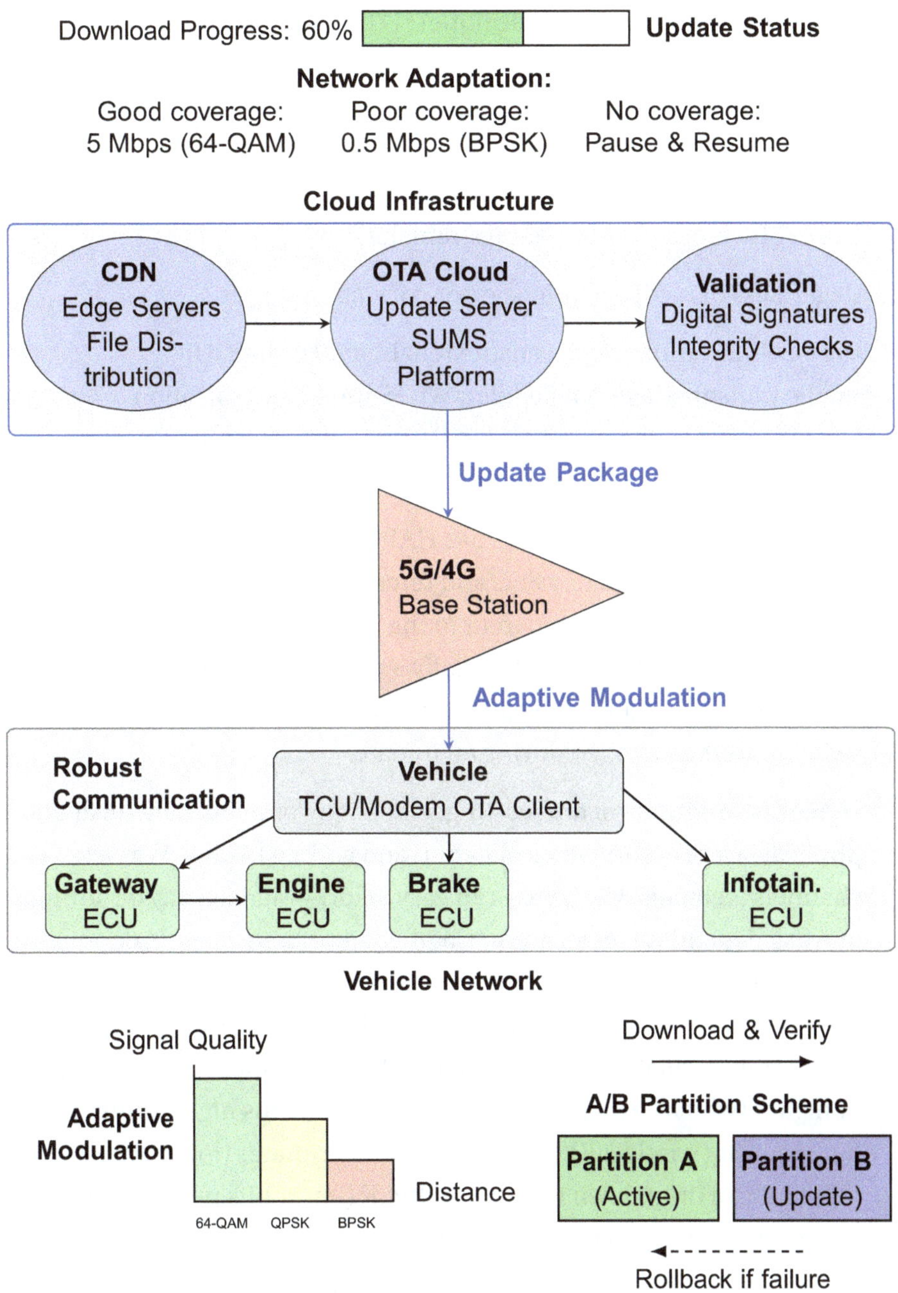

Figure 5-17. End-to-end OTA update architecture

- **Robust communication techniques:** OTA updates typically involve transferring large files (tens of Mb or even several Gb for full vehicle updates) to the car. In production today, these transfers typically use cellular networks (and sometimes Wi-Fi in garages); V2X links are being explored for smaller updates or map data, but are not used for large software packages in series vehicles.

  Regardless of medium, robust error correction is used.

  Protocols at various layers ensure reliability: TCP or QUIC on the transport layer for cellular/Wi-Fi updates, application layer resumable download protocols, and underlying link layer retransmissions and forward error correction (FEC) at the radio level.

  For instance, cellular networks use HARQ (hybrid automatic repeat request), which combines FEC and retransmission to dynamically cope with errors—all transparent to the higher layers. The car's TCU (telematics control unit) is essentially a modem that continuously monitors signal quality and can request retransmission of lost data or switch towers as needed during an update.

- **Dynamic modulation and coding:** One important mechanism at the physical layer is adaptive modulation and coding (AMC). Wireless channels (cellular, Wi-Fi, etc.) can vary wildly—signals may be strong or weak depending on location, weather, interference, etc. Adaptive modulation means the transmitter (e.g., a cellular base station or the car's TCU in a client role) adjusts the modulation scheme on the fly to maintain a reliable link. In good conditions, it might use 64-QAM or higher (which carries many bits per symbol, thus high throughput but requiring good SNR). If the channel deteriorates (low signal, high noise), it can drop down to QPSK or BPSK (fewer bits per symbol, lower throughput but more robust to noise).

  In practical terms, your car might download at, say, 5 Mbps with 64-QAM when coverage is great, but fall back to 0.5 Mbps with QPSK when signal is weak—ensuring the data still gets through correctly, just more slowly.

Without this, the update might keep failing or timing out in poor coverage. Modern cellular systems handle this automatically via their link adaptation algorithms [174].

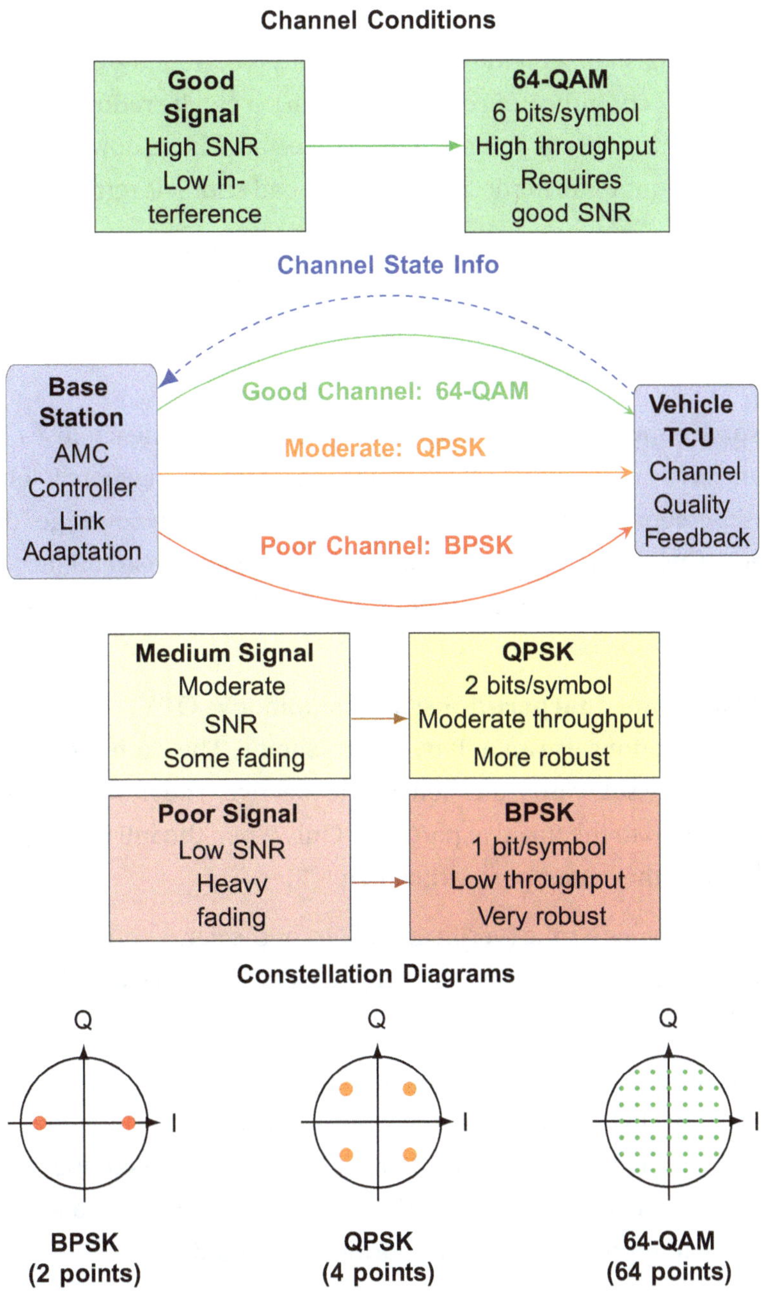

***Figure 5-18.** Adaptive modulation and coding for OTA reliability*

- **Error resilience and integrity checks:** Beyond the physical layer, OTA systems incorporate higher-level error checking and fallbacks:
- **Packets and chunks:** The update file is usually broken into chunks, each cryptographically hashed. The vehicle will verify each chunk (using the hash or a digital signature) as it's received. If a chunk doesn't match (indicating data corruption), it can be redownloaded. This chunking means you don't have to restart a huge download from scratch if a minor error occurs—only the bad chunk is retried.
- **Redundancy:** Some OTA systems send critical pieces of data twice via independent paths or times. For example, important metadata or manifest files (which tell the car how to apply the update) might be sent early and then repeated.
- **Resume capability:** If the download is interrupted (the car loses connectivity or is turned off), it can resume later from where it left off. This is essential because vehicles often move through coverage "dead zones." Customers might not even notice—the download might pause when you go into an underground parking garage and resume when you come out.
- **Rollbacks and dual partitions:** Most automotive OTA implementations use an A/B partition scheme. The car has two copies of the software—one active, one inactive. The new software is downloaded to the inactive partition. Only when the full package is verified do they attempt to switch to it.

  If anything goes wrong (verification fails, or the car reboots into the new software and it doesn't run properly), the system can fall back to the old partition.

  This ensures that a failed update does not brick the vehicle. Regulation UNECE WP.29 now actually requires that "the vehicle can be placed into a safe state after a failed or interrupted update"—meaning rollback is mandatory [72]. The OTA system must also record and report failures to authorities as needed.

- **Silicon and SUMS integration:** Modern vehicle connectivity chipsets (whether dedicated TCUs or integrated SoCs) often have DSPs and logic to support these robust communication features. Additionally, vehicle Software Update Management Systems (SUMSs) are designed per standards like ISO 24089/UNECE R156. They ensure end-to-end security (updates are signed/encrypted) and safety.

  Part of compliance is showing that you have a secure and robust update delivery process. That includes demonstrating that you adapt to adverse conditions (so, e.g., using store-and-forward via edge servers if a direct push fails or, as mentioned, the ability to switch modulation/coding to maintain data flow).

  In other words, OTA reliability isn't just a nice-to-have—it's becoming a regulated requirement. OEMs must prove that their OTA pipeline is resilient—this includes network adaptation, error handling, and customer communication [72].

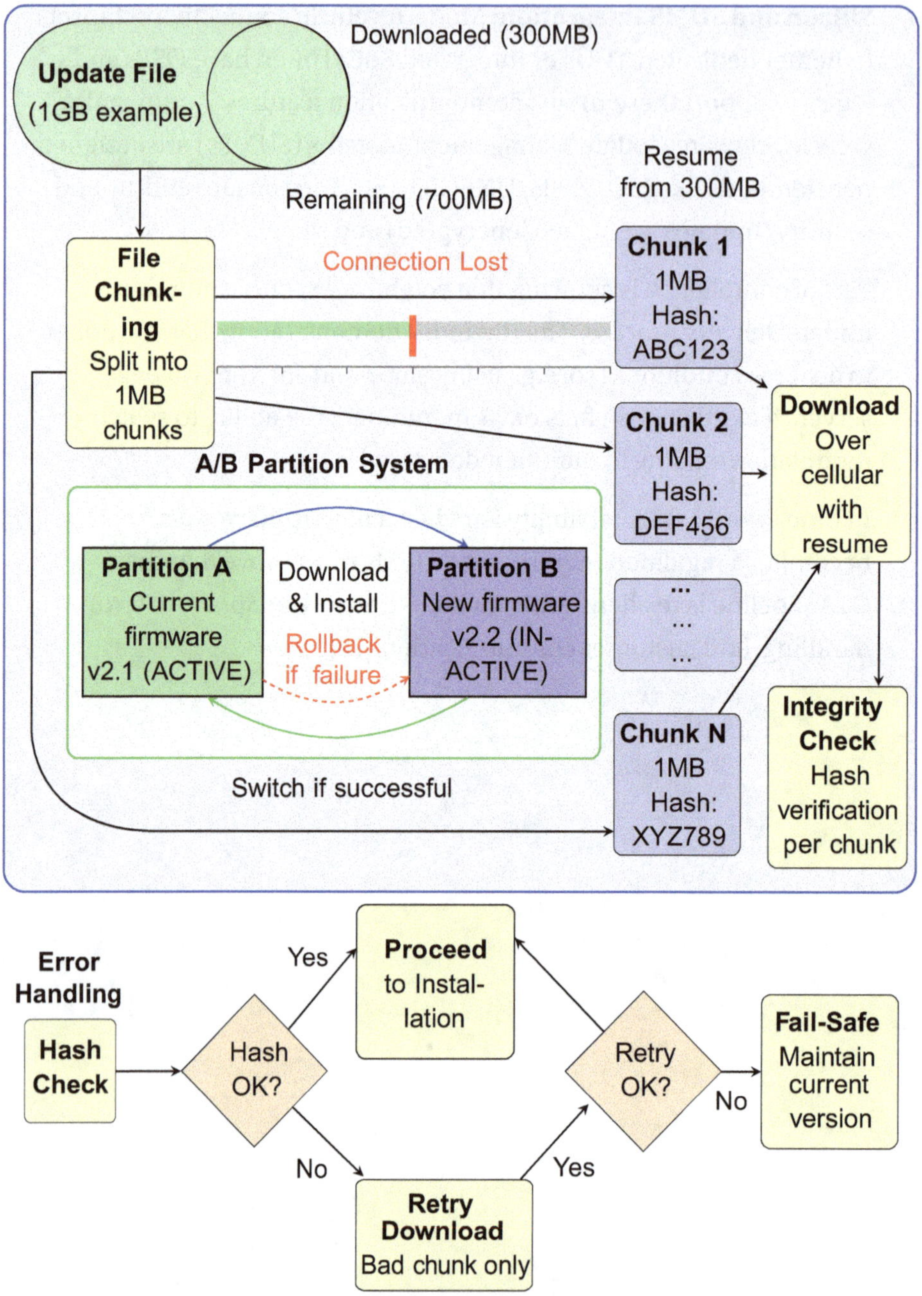

***Figure 5-19.** OTA resilience with chunking, A/B, and resume*

Example—dynamic modulation in action: Imagine an OTA update broadcasting over a cellular network to many vehicles (say, a recall fix). Cars in cities with good 5G coverage might use high modulation, efficiently downloading the update in minutes.

Cars out on rural roads with spotty 3G/4G will automatically fall back to lower modulation and stronger error correction. They might take an hour to get the file, but they will get it intact.

If a car goes through a tunnel—no signal—the download halts, but because of forward error correction and buffering, often no data is lost; when the car exits the tunnel, it picks up again. Throughout, if any data chunk can't be verified, the system requests a repeat.

From the user's perspective, it may simply show a progress bar that goes slower or faster depending on coverage, with perhaps a note "Download paused, awaiting connectivity" in dead zones.

The bottom line: OTA updates tie together many networking concepts—from physical layer modulation up through cloud services—all focused on reliability. OEMs treat OTA failures very seriously, as they directly impact customer trust.

A high-profile failure (e.g., an update that disables vehicles on a mass scale) can cause massive brand damage. This is why companies invest in robust OTA protocols, extensive testing (including pushing updates under various network conditions), and graceful recovery strategies. OTA also raises nontechnical questions. If an update changes the behavior of a safety function (braking, steering, ADAS) and contributes to an accident, courts and regulators must decide who is liable—the OEM, Tier-1 supplier, or even software vendor. Right-to-repair debates, customer consent to updates, and the ability (or not) to roll back to previous versions are all active legal and policy topics that SDV architects cannot ignore.

Business Note OTA failures = brand damage. OEMs must demonstrate that their OTA stack has error-resilient communication (adaptive modulation, strong error correction), fail-safes like rollback partitions, and customer transparency.

For instance, if an update cannot complete after several attempts, the system should notify the user in clear terms and defer the update—not leave the vehicle in limbo. Earning customer trust in OTA is essential for the SDV future; it's not just a tech issue, but a business reputation issue.

5.7 Connected Cars: Foundation of SDVs

The software-defined vehicle is an evolution that is based on the connected car revolution of the past two decades. Long before cars had centralized high-performance computers or "app stores," they started getting embedded connectivity for telematics services.

Understanding the connected car is crucial, as it established the core paradigms (and even infrastructure) that SDVs now use for software updates, data collection, and cloud integration.

In the early 2000s, automakers began adding telematics control units (TCUs) to vehicles—dedicated modules with cellular modems, GPS receivers, and some processing capability. General Motors was a pioneer with its OnStar system: first introduced around 1996–1997 on Cadillac models [175], OnStar combined cellular connectivity (initially using analog mobile networks, later CDMA digital networks) [175] with GPS and a call center service.

Its primary function was safety: automatic crash notification (when airbags deploy, the car calls an operator), emergency assist, stolen vehicle tracking, etc. [175]. Over time it expanded to remote diagnostics, turn-by-turn navigation, and concierge services.

OnStar demonstrated that there was real value in connecting vehicles: by the mid-2010s, GM noted they had fielded over one billion customer requests through OnStar, from emergency calls to remote door unlocks [176].

Other manufacturers followed with their own telematics: Ford's early "RESCU" system, Mercedes's TeleAid, BMW's Assist/ConnectedDrive, etc., throughout the late 1990s and 2000s.

Let us break down the connected car stack and its implications.

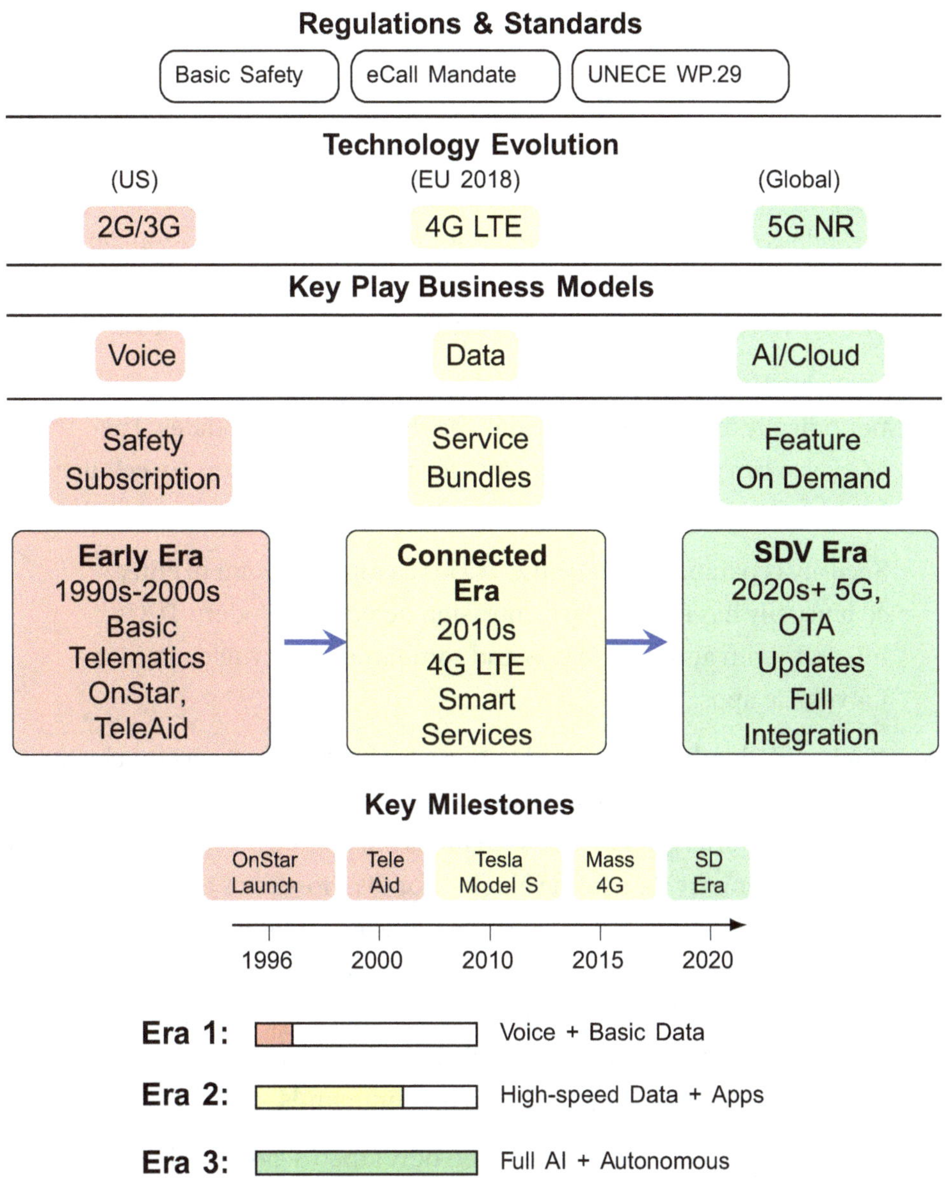

Figure 5-20. *Evolution of connected car platforms*

5.7.1 Telematics Architecture

A typical connected car architecture includes the following:

- **Telematics control unit (TCU):** This is the in-vehicle gateway to the outside world. It contains a cellular modem (with its own SIM or nowadays eSIM), a GNSS receiver (for GPS/GLONASS location data), and interfaces to in-vehicle networks (CAN, LIN, Ethernet). The TCU often runs an embedded OS and manages communication sessions.

  For example, it might connect to the OEM's cloud platform periodically to upload vehicle data or check for OTA updates. The TCU also can act as a Wi-Fi hotspot for passengers (using the cellular backhaul).

  Security is paramount here: the TCU is a common point of entry, so it usually has firewalls and intrusion detection. Modern TCUs integrate with automotive OSs and sometimes even run containers for vehicle apps.

- **Back-end cloud:** The automaker operates back-end servers (or cloud services) that communicate with the vehicle fleet. This back-end performs a variety of functions—it hosts the update files for OTA, collects telemetry data from vehicles (for diagnostics or aggregate analytics), and provides services like traffic information, weather data for vehicles, or even ecommerce. Companies often partner with cloud providers (AWS, Azure, etc.) to build these systems at scale. For instance, the Tesla fleet is managed via Tesla's cloud servers—every car regularly uploads logs and receives commands.

  Another example: Toyota Connected developed a global "Mobility Services Platform (MSPF)," which acts as a data hub and API platform for their connected vehicles [177]. This back-end also ties into third parties (e.g., usage-based insurance via Connected Analytics Services) [178].

To visualize, Figure 5-21 illustrates a connected car reference architecture. The TCU acts as the bridge: vehicle ↔ TCU (via CAN/Ethernet) ↔ cellular network ↔ OEM cloud ↔ service providers. The data paths are bidirectional, enabling both teleoperation (commands from cloud to car) and telemetry (data from car to cloud).

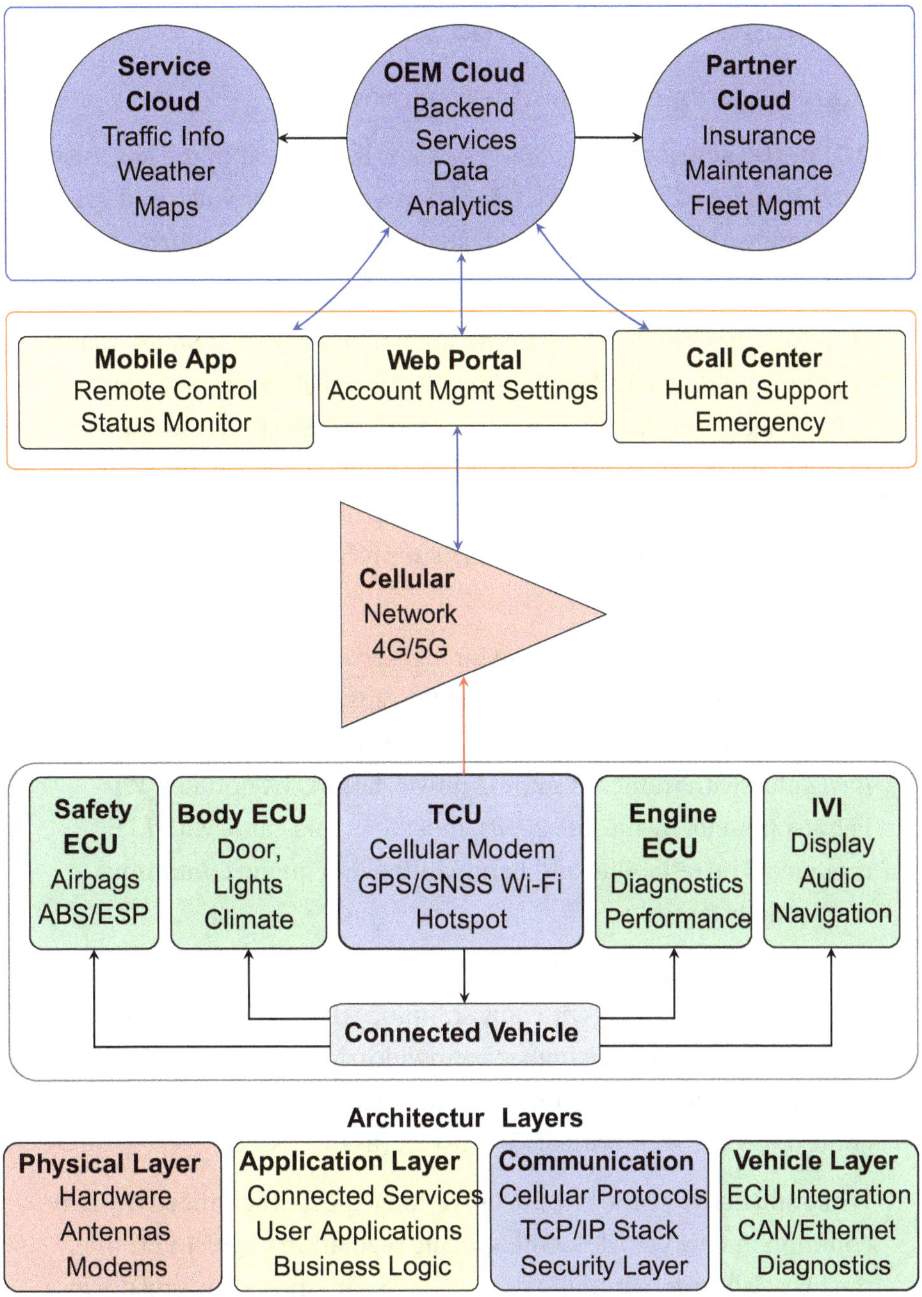

Figure 5-21. *Connected car reference data flow architecture*

5.7.2 Connectivity Standards Evolution

Connected cars ride on the evolution of cellular networks:

- **2G/3G (legacy networks):** Early systems like OnStar in the late 1990s used analog and 2G (GSM/CDMA) networks just for voice and very low-bandwidth data. 3G allowed faster data and more capacity. Many first-gen telematics ran on 2G/3G.

  However, these networks are now sunset: in the United States, major carriers shut down 3G by 2022 (e.g., AT&T in February 2022), and 2G has been phased out by many carriers as well [179]. This forced automakers to upgrade older cars (if possible) or see features die. Some OEMs offered retrofits or software patches to connect via 4G instead, but many 2010-era cars simply lost some connected capabilities because of this sunset.

- **4G LTE:** The current workhorse for connected vehicles. LTE networks, widely deployed from ~2010 onward, offered high-speed IP data. This enabled mainstream connected services: real-time navigation with traffic, streaming music, large OTA updates, Wi-Fi hotspots, etc. By the late 2010s, most new cars came with LTE modems. The reliability and bandwidth of LTE made continuous connectivity feasible.

- **5G NR (New Radio):** Starting around 2020, 5G networks rolled out. Some premium vehicles are now shipping with 5G-capable modems. 5G's advantages include higher bandwidth, lower latency (useful for edge computing), and network slicing for dedicated QoS. In the context of V2X, 5G is critical for NR-V2X (as discussed).

  While still early, by the late 2020s we can expect 5G connectivity to be common in new vehicles. One specific regulation angle: In Europe, the EU eCall system initially used 2G/3G; with those shutting down, they migrate to 4G/5G [179].

- **DSRC vs. C-V2X:** These were covered earlier, but in the connected car context, they are complementary to cellular. DSRC and C-V2X are usually not used for general internet connectivity, but for direct local communications. A connected car might use cellular for cloud services but DSRC/C-V2X for safety messages with other cars nearby or with smart traffic lights.

Many automakers have tested combinations (hybrid V2X networks). NXP, 5GAA, and others have tracked global status and regulatory progress [170, 180].

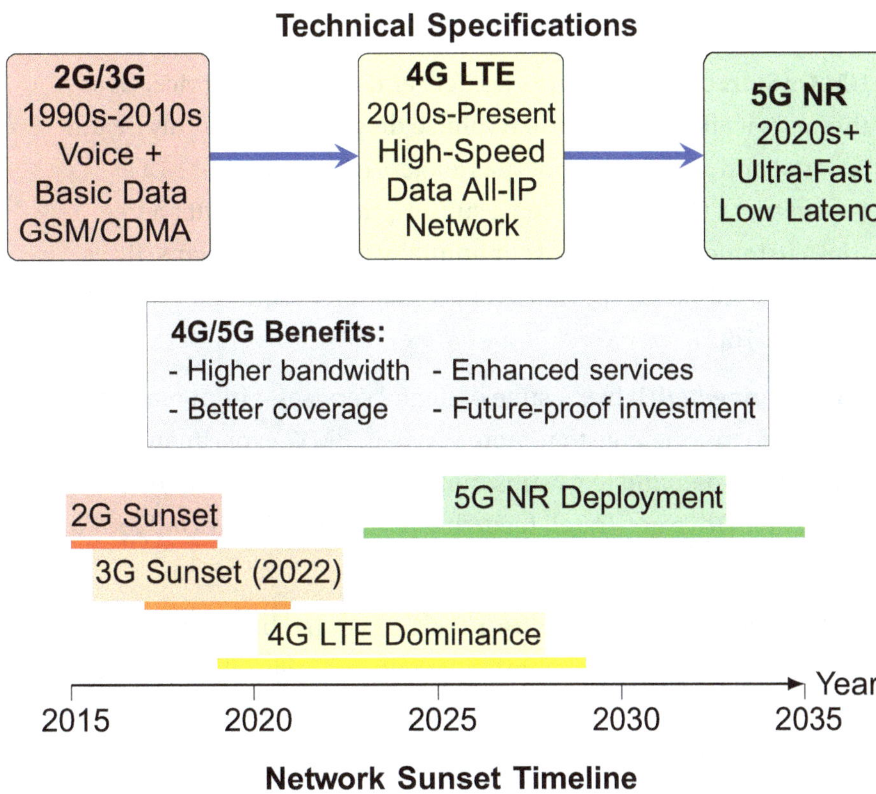

Figure 5-22. *Evolution from 2G and 3G to 5G NR*

Critic's Insight Connected cars demonstrated that connectivity is not optional for future vehicles. An SDV that cannot communicate is isolated—it can't get software improvements, it can't leverage cloud AI updates, and it can't participate in cooperative functions.

Thus, regulations now treat some connectivity (like eCall, cybersecurity updates) as mandatory features, not add-ons. And business models increasingly assume every car is online at all times.

5.7.3 Industry Case Studies

Here are a few examples of connected car platforms and their business implications:

- **GM OnStar:** OnStar began as a safety and concierge service. Over the years it added features like vehicle diagnostics (monthly health reports) and a Wi-Fi hotspot (passengers can use the car's LTE for internet). OnStar has been a subscription service; after a free trial, customers pay monthly or annually for different plans. By the mid-2010s, GM reported over 1B customer requests served via OnStar [176].
- **BMW ConnectedDrive:** A suite of digital services—from real-time traffic info to concierge to remote services. BMW experimented with features-on-demand (e.g., subscriptions for infotainment functions). ConnectedDrive generated recurring revenue for BMW (millions of subscribers by 2018).
- **Tesla "Premium Connectivity":** Tesla separated basic connectivity from premium, charging monthly for live traffic visualization, video/music streaming, etc. [181]. This created a recurring revenue stream years after vehicle sale.
- **Toyota Connected/Lexus Enform:** Toyota Connected's MSPF provides data services, proactive maintenance, and insurance data partnerships [177, 178].

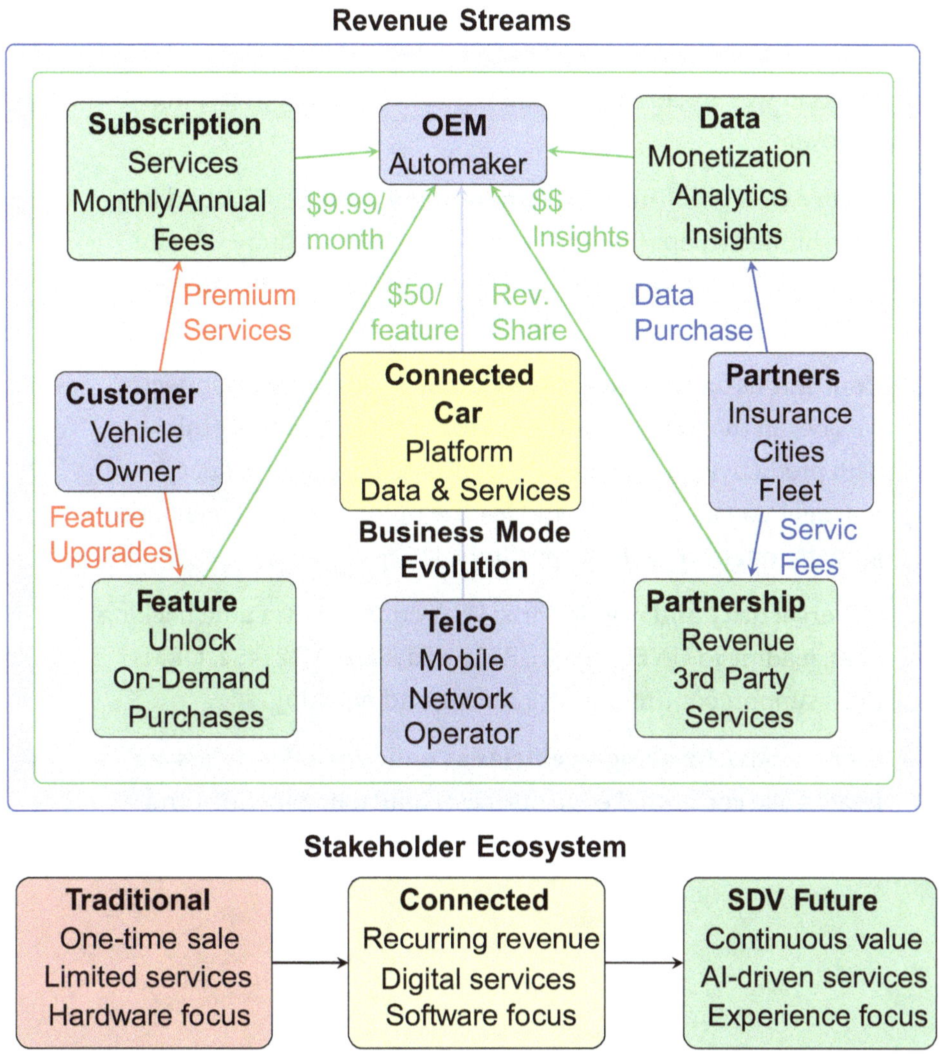

Figure 5-23. *Connected car business model overview*

5.7.4 Connected Car ➤ SDV Evolution

The connected car was version 1.0; the SDV is version 2.0. Key learnings and transitions include as follows:

1. **Secure OTA pipelines are foundational:** Initially, OTA updates were limited (maps/infotainment). Now SDVs assume OTA for any ECU. Regulations like UNECE WP.29 R156 require certified Software Update Management Systems [72].

2. **Continuous data monetization enables new value:** Connected cars began the trend of post-sale revenue. SDVs amplify this with predictive maintenance, usage-based insurance, fleet management as a service, and feature unlocks. Global telematics growth underscores the opportunity [182].

3. **Cybersecurity and regulations:** With connectivity came hacking risks, leading to UNECE R155/R156 and ISO/SAE 21434. OEMs must support continuous monitoring and patching.

4. **Cloud-native thinking—vehicles as nodes in a fleet:** Cars are treated like connected edge devices; cloud data pipelines and digital twins support continuous improvement.

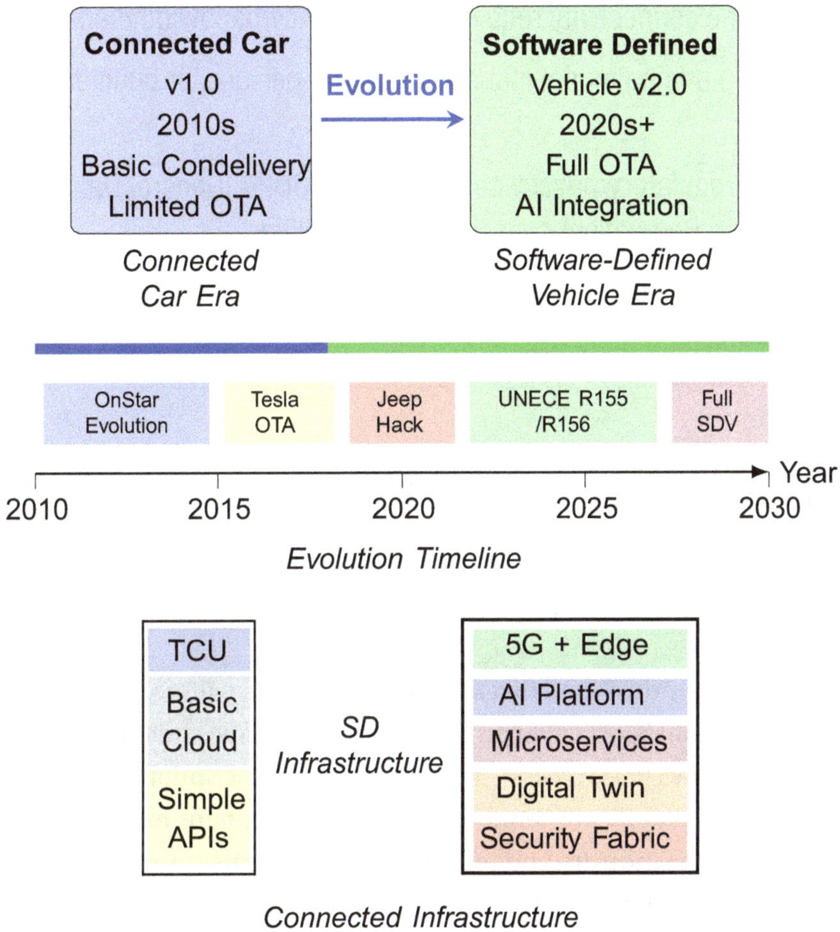

Figure 5-24. *Transition from connected cars to SDVs*

Lab Design a connected car monetization plan.

Objective Create a basic business model for a new connected car service.

Steps:

1. Select a potential feature that leverages connectivity—e.g., predictive maintenance, insurance risk scoring, or remote cabin pre-conditioning as a paid convenience service.

2. Define the connectivity requirements (latency/bandwidth/sensors).
3. Choose a pricing model (subscription, pay-per-use, or bundled) and justify it.
4. Identify regulatory/privacy concerns (e.g., GDPR (General Data Protection Regulation) consent, safety liabilities).

Deliverable A two- to three-page business case (service, target customers, revenue projection, and a pitch slide).

5.7.5 Review: Connected Cars' Legacy

Connected cars are, indeed, the bridge from traditional vehicles to SDVs. They established the technical infrastructure (TCUs, cloud platforms, OTA processes) that SDVs now build upon.

Connected cars demonstrated that some customers are willing to pay for digital services and that automakers can, in principle, create revenue streams beyond the initial sale, even though many OEMs have struggled with low subscription renewal rates once free trials end and profitability of connectivity programs remains mixed.

They also forced the industry and regulators to address new areas—data privacy, security, and software updates—which are now non-negotiable aspects of any future SDV platform.

5.8 Business Models in V2X

As vehicles become connected not only to the cloud but to each other and infrastructure (V2X), an important question arises: Who owns/profits from the data pipe and services?

There is an ongoing tussle (and likely regional variation) in the V2X business models, mainly between these stakeholders:

- **OEM-centric model:** The automaker treats V2X data as part of their product value. For example, an OEM might enable cooperative safety or perception features and charge customers (or fleets) for them as a subscription.

In this model, the OEM sets up the data infrastructure (likely cloud-based) and possibly even their own roadside units or partnerships to get the data, monetizing it. OEMs could also sell "swarm data" subscriptions to cities.

- **Telco (MNO)-centric model:** Mobile network operators (MNOs) see V2X as a new vertical. Network slicing (5G) for automotive could be sold to OEMs with guaranteed QoS [180]. Operators might aggregate cross-brand data and build services (e.g., V2I via cellular). 5GAA highlights MEC-based V2X platforms.
- **Shared ecosystem/neutral host model:** Consortium or public entities operate neutral V2X platforms. EU CCAM-style approaches or Chinese city platforms (e.g., Wuxi pilots) share safety data across brands [170]. Funding can be public or fee-based; ensures interoperability [183].

Model	Primary Control Point	Main Value Proposition	Typical Weakness
OEM-centric	Vehicle brand/ platform	Direct customer relationship, branded features	High platform cost, limited interoperability
Telco-centric	Mobile network/edge provider	QoS, slicing, regional edge services	Risk of OEM disintermediation concerns
Neutral/ shared	Public or consortium platform	Interoperability, public safety alignment	Harder monetization, governance complexity

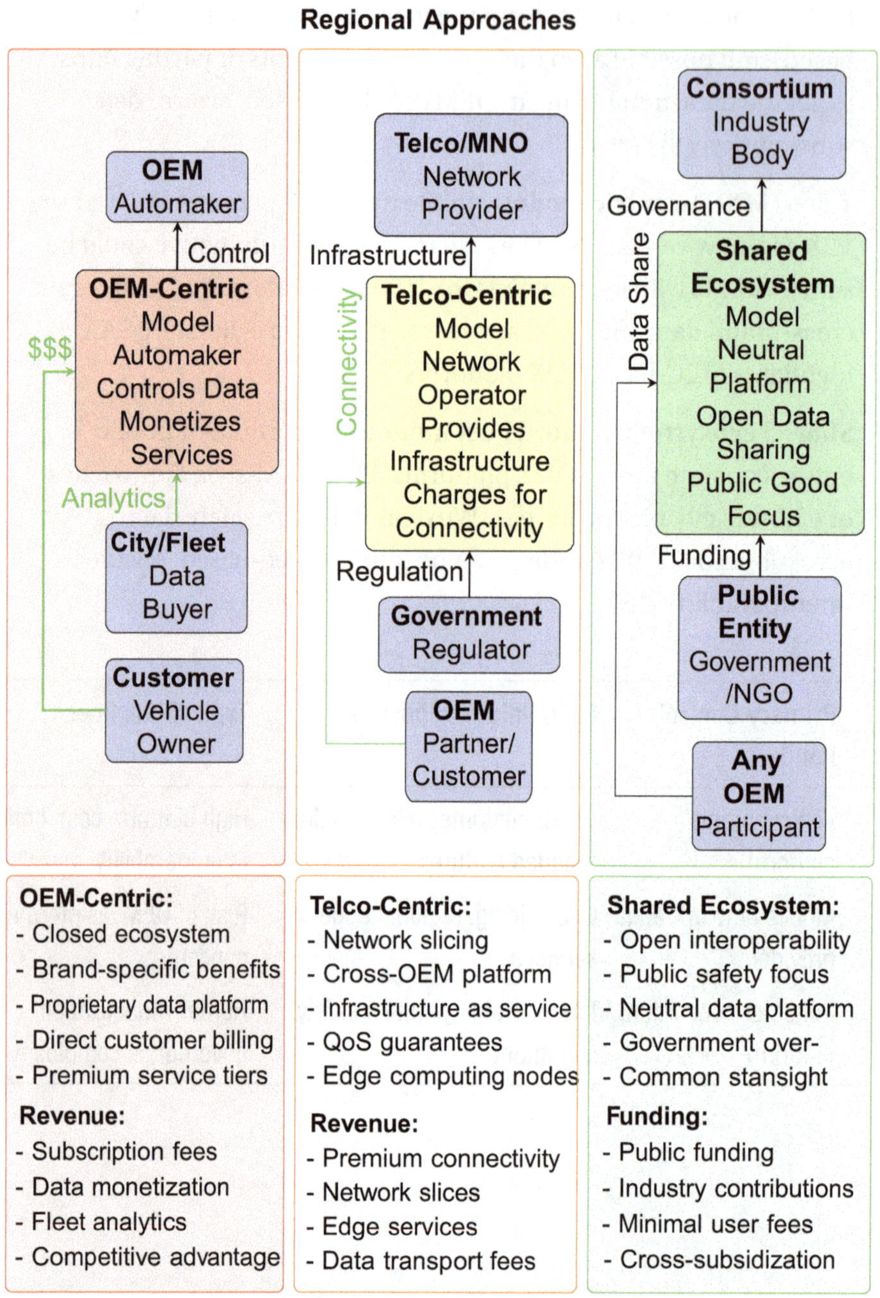

Figure 5-25. *V2X business model comparison*

A shared approach is likely to coexist with OEM and MNO models, with regional differences. Revenue will likely be shared (e.g., OEM pays carrier for QoS slices; carrier monetizes V2X-as-a-service; public mandates basic safety data free access).

After more than two decades of V2X standardization and pilots, there are still very few examples of sustainable, large-scale V2X-specific revenue streams. Most deployments to date are justified on safety and regulatory grounds rather than direct monetization.

The OEM-centric, MNO-centric, and neutral host models discussed here should therefore be read as emerging patterns and negotiation positions, not as proven business templates.

Critic's Note The fight over "who owns the pipe (and the data)" in V2X echoes smartphone-era tensions. With public safety at stake, expect regional splits: more cooperative models in Europe, more commercial tilt in the United States, and state-orchestrated models in China [170].

Key Point For comprehensive coverage of SDV monetization strategies, subscription models, and ecosystem partnerships including telecom cooperation, see **Chapter 10**.

5.9 Case Study: Platooning

To tie many of these networking and business concepts together, let us examine a concrete case of V2X application: truck platooning.

Case Study: Truck Platooning **Context:** Truck platooning is when two or more trucks drive in tight formation on the highway, electronically linked. The lead truck is driven (human or eventually AI), and the following trucks automatically follow at a very close distance.

The rationale is reduced aerodynamic drag: the lead truck cuts the air, and the followers in its slipstream save fuel (and even the lead truck sees a bit less drag at its tail).

Reported trial results under controlled highway conditions (favorable traffic, weather, and road profile) often show fuel-saving magnitudes on the order of ∼4% for the lead truck and up to ∼10% for the follower in two-truck platoons [184].

Real-world savings vary significantly with route, load, wind, traffic density, and driver behavior and can be lower—or even negative for the lead truck in some conditions. For fleets, even a few percent average saving is significant for cost and also cuts emissions [185].

Networking To safely equip the platoon, especially with short gaps of 15 m or even as low as 5–10 m at highway speeds, communication must be ultra-reliable and low-latency. The following truck needs to know the lead truck's actions immediately to brake or accelerate in unison.

Human reaction time (∼1 s) is far too slow; therefore, V2V communication is used.

Platooning systems typically require end-to-end latencies below 10 ms and in practice aim for ∼5 ms or less for the control messages [171].

Technologies used include DSRC and now C-V2X/NR-V2X. In Europe, the 2016 European Truck Platooning Challenge used DSRC to connect trucks of different brands and demonstrated safe operation at gaps as small as 15 m with coordinated braking [184].

Networking challenges include maintaining communication in tunnels or around interference and ensuring security (you don't want a malicious actor sending false brake commands). 5G NR-V2X is expected to improve platooning by allowing larger convoys (more trucks) with even tighter control, perhaps <5 ms latency with 99.999% reliability [171].

Business Who benefits and who pays? The value proposition is clear for fleet operators (fuel savings and possibly higher throughput if regulations allow tighter following) [186]. Models tested include platooning-as-a-service, in which fleets subscribe to a service that matches and manages platoons on corridors. Fees can be a fraction of fuel savings. Regulators and highway operators may incentivize or invest in roadside units to assist.

Cross-border/cross-operator roaming, liability, and standards alignment remain practical hurdles. Fleet operators therefore treat the headline fuel-saving figures as upside scenarios, not guaranteed outcomes.

5.10 Key Takeaways

- **Evolution of in-vehicle networks:** Legacy field buses like CAN (and LIN, MOST, FlexRay) are giving way to an Ethernet TSN backbone. CAN is still used for low-level, cost-sensitive domains, and CAN FD/XL extend its life with higher speeds [167].

  FlexRay is no longer chosen for new architectures; Ethernet TSN backbones now provide comparable determinism on standard Ethernet, while existing FlexRay deployments continue in legacy platforms. CAN XL fills a niche between CAN and Ethernet, offering up to 20 Mbps and large payloads with CAN's simplicity [167].

- **V2X technologies:** DSRC (802.11p) was first out of the gate and is technically mature, but due to regulatory changes and limited deployment, it's waning. C-V2X (LTE sidelink) is the current focus—slightly higher latency than DSRC in many tests [169], but with strong industry support and a path to 5G.

  5G NR-V2X is on the horizon, promising <5 ms latency for new cooperative use cases [171, 172].

- **Deterministic communication for safety:** Deterministic communication is a prerequisite for many safety goals in SDVs, but must be combined with diagnostics, redundancy, and safe-state concepts from ISO 26262. TSN brings determinism to Ethernet through time-triggered schedules, preemption, and redundancy [51, 166].

  Misconfigurations can be catastrophic; treat bandwidth and scheduling as safety resources.

- **OTA and modulation adaptation:** Reliable OTA updates combine robust protocol design (resume, integrity check, rollback) and communication robustness (adaptive modulation/coding) [72]. A/B partitions and secure validation ensure updates don't brick vehicles.
- **V2X business landscape:** Expect a mix of OEM-centric, Telco-centric, and neutral/shared models [170, 180]. Public interest safety data may be mandated to be open, while premium services (e.g., HD maps) remain monetized.

  Global OEMs must also navigate highly fragmented regional regulations (United States, EU, China, and many smaller markets), which makes any "unified" V2X or networking architecture more of a long-term aspiration than a short-term reality.

CHAPTER 6

Zonal and Centralized Architectures

6.1 Chapter Goals

After this chapter, you will be able to

- Explain the shift from domain to zonal to centralized SDV architectures.
- Identify benefits and risks of consolidation in automotive E/E design.
- Analyze wiring, cost, and performance trade-offs between architectures.
- Understand Tesla's central compute vs. VW's zonal approach through case studies.
- Design a basic zonal map for a mid-size electric vehicle.

Critic's Note Architecture is destiny. The wrong partitioning (too fragmented or too centralized) locks an OEM into decades of technical debt. The real danger is rushing into aggressive centralization before your organization, tooling, and safety case are ready and then being trapped by sunk cost in a fragile design.

S. Agarwal, *Software-Defined Vehicles*, https://doi.org/10.1007/979-8-8688-2718-1_6

6.2 Introduction

The electrical and electronic (E/E) architecture of a vehicle fundamentally shapes its capabilities, cost structure, and ability to evolve through software. This chapter examines the ongoing transformation from traditional domain-based architectures—where dozens of specialized ECUs handle individual functions—toward zonal and centralized designs that consolidate computing power into fewer, more capable units.

We begin by tracing the evolution from domain to zonal to central compute architectures, explaining the motivations behind each transition and the trade-offs involved. The chapter then presents detailed case studies of Tesla's central compute approach and Volkswagen's zonal strategy, illustrating how different organizational starting points lead to different implementation paths and challenges.

The chapter also addresses the critical insight that hardware consolidation alone delivers only partial benefits. Without adopting digital-first development practices—continuous integration, virtual ECUs, OTA update pipelines, and telemetry-driven improvement—a zonal architecture becomes merely "domain with fewer wires." Understanding both the hardware topology and the software lifecycle is essential for architects designing next-generation vehicle platforms.

6.3 From Domain to Zonal

The evolution of in-vehicle electronics has moved from a domain-based architecture (many function-specific control units) toward zonal architectures and now even centralized computing. Each stage aims to reduce complexity and improve software-defined capabilities.

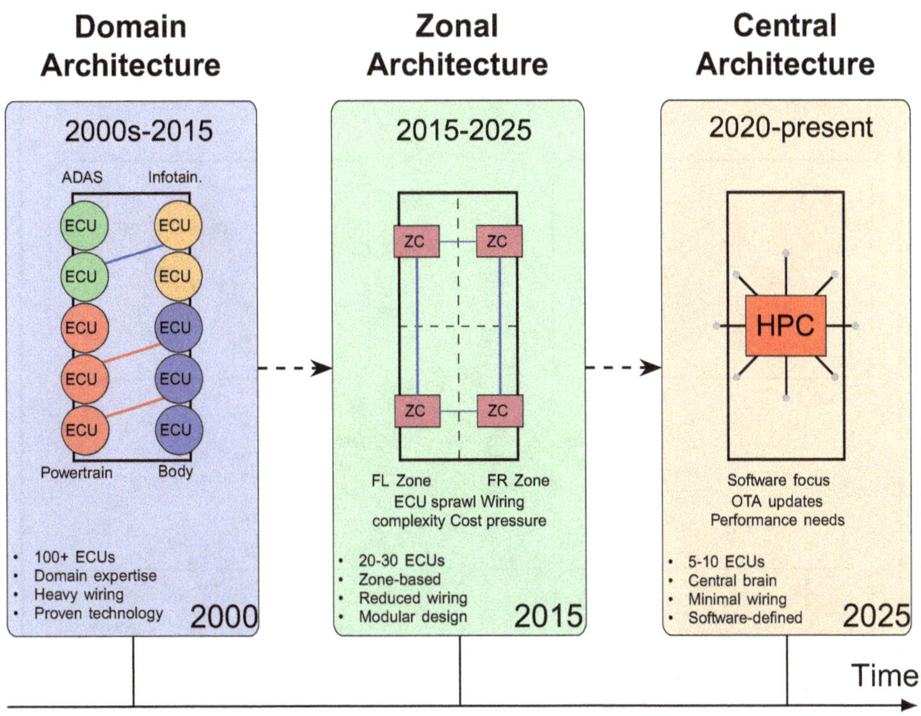

Figure 6-1. *Evolution of automotive E/E architectures*

6.3.1 Domain Architecture

In a traditional domain architecture, electronic control units (ECUs) are grouped by function (or "domain") across the vehicle. Typical domains include powertrain, chassis, body (comfort), infotainment, and ADAS (advanced driver assistance systems). Each domain has its own set of controllers and network buses. This approach was a natural progression from very distributed designs, attempting to bring some order by clustering related functions together.

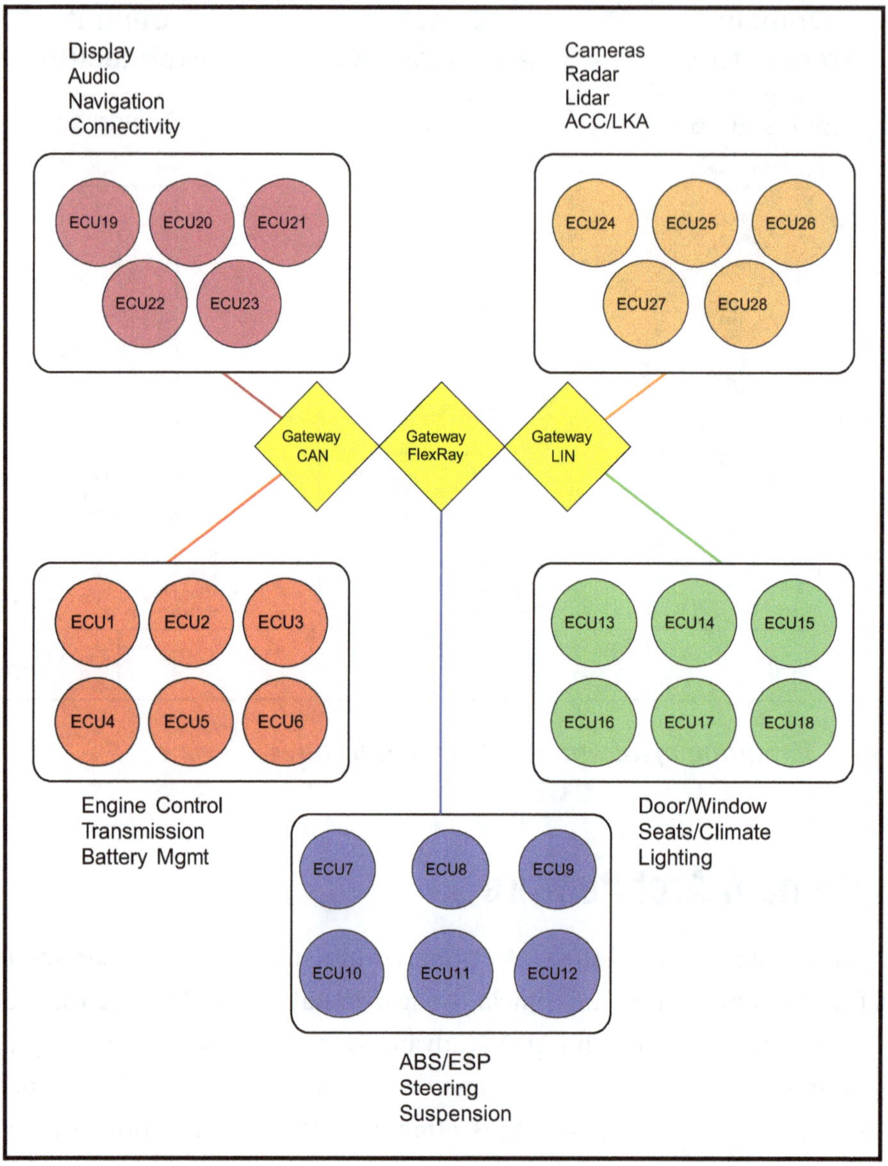

Figure 6-2. *Illustrative domain-oriented E/E architecture showing functional grouping of controllers and representative network segmentation*

Figure 6-2 is intended as a schematic illustration of domain-oriented partitioning rather than a literal production network. In real vehicles, each domain usually spans multiple bus segments, gateways, and bandwidth classes. Low-speed body functions may remain on CAN or LIN, while high-bandwidth sensors such as cameras are typically connected through dedicated high-speed links or Ethernet-based interfaces. The key architectural idea is functional grouping by domain, not the exact number of gateways or the precise network technologies shown in the illustration.

Benefits: Domain architectures are mature and proven. OEMs and suppliers have decades of experience with these systems, and each domain's ECU could be optimized for its specific tasks. The specialization meant that, e.g., powertrain ECUs were rugged and real time, while infotainment ECUs could be more computing-heavy, without one interfering with the other. This separation also allowed different Tier-1 suppliers to handle different domains, leveraging their expertise.

Weaknesses: Over time, the number of ECUs in high-end vehicles exploded into the dozens. Modern luxury cars often contain 100–150 ECUs scattered throughout the vehicle [11]. Each ECU typically required dedicated wiring for power and data. The result was a wiring harness that became one of the major sources of mass, cost, and assembly complexity in the vehicle, with the exact harness weight varying significantly by program, segment, and feature content [49].

This "ECU sprawl" and wiring bulk drives up cost and weight, and it also makes integration difficult—each time a new feature was added, engineers had to add or update an ECU and run more wires. By the late 2010s, some vehicles had over 1,000 wire circuits running several kilometers of total length [38]. Beyond weight and cost, this complexity became a limiting factor for innovation: integrating features that span multiple domains (e.g., an ADAS feature that needs powertrain and braking data) meant many ECUs communicating over gateways with latency and compatibility issues.

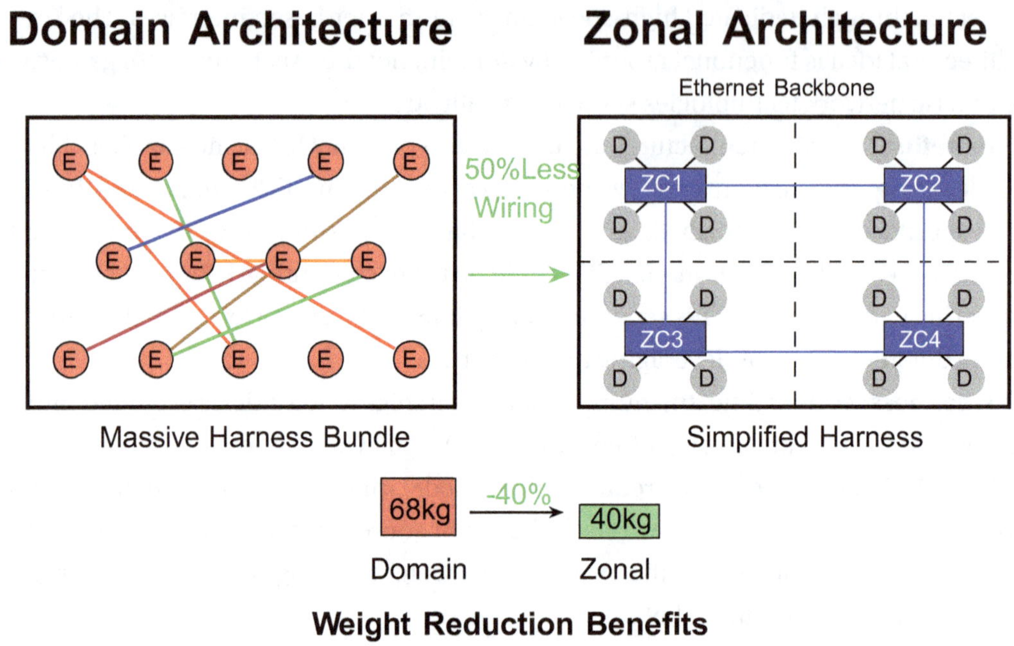

Figure 6-3. *Conceptual comparison of wiring harness complexity in domain and zonal architectures. The magnitude of mass, length, and cost reduction is vehicle-dependent*

In short, domain architecture served well for a time but began hitting a scalability wall in terms of weight, cost, and complexity. OEMs started looking for a new approach to handle increasing software content in vehicles.

6.3.2 Zonal Architecture

Zonal architecture is a newer approach that reorganizes the vehicle's electronics by physical location (zones) instead of function. The vehicle is divided into zones (e.g., front-left, front-right, rear-left, rear-right, or other logical physical groupings). Each zone has a zonal controller (a high-performance gateway ECU) that connects to all devices (sensors, actuators, etc.) in that physical area, regardless of their function. In other words, a single zonal controller might manage power seats, door locks, speakers, sensors, and lighting in its area. In more advanced designs, it can also host safety-related control logic, but typically with strict safety partitioning and, for ASIL-C/D goals, dedicated safety microcontrollers or safety islands rather than a single shared general-purpose OS.

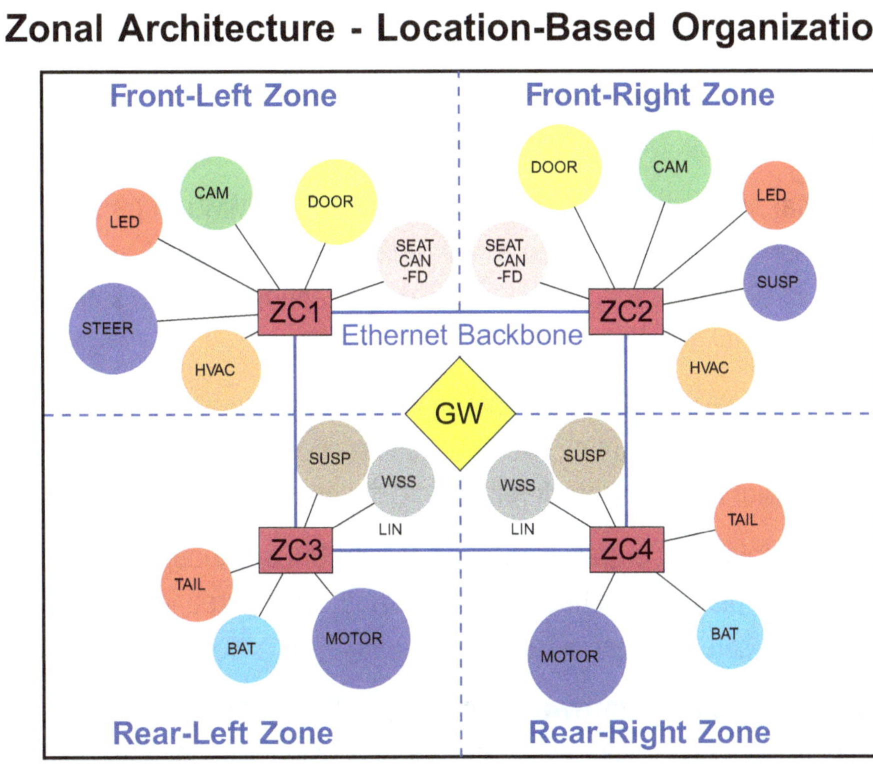

Figure 6-4. *Zonal architecture with location-based organization*

How it works: Rather than every device having a long dedicated wire back to its domain ECU, devices connect to the nearest zonal controller. The zonal controller aggregates data and power for that area and bridges local legacy buses (CAN, LIN) to a higher-speed backbone, typically automotive Ethernet. Zonal controllers then connect upstream to central backbones or high-performance computers that share data between zones.

In safety-relevant designs, the zonal controller is not a single monolithic box that casually mixes everything. Safety-critical loads (e.g., brakes, steering actuators) are often driven via dedicated safety microcontrollers or safety islands within the zone, separated—either physically or by a certified hypervisor—from non-safety functions like window lift or ambient lighting. ISO 26262 "freedom from interference" requirements mean that a fault in a noncritical app must not compromise ASIL-C/D control software, even if both reside in the same physical enclosure.

Safety Partitioning on Shared Controllers When a zonal controller hosts both safety-critical and non-safety functions, the safety case hinges on robust partitioning. In practice, OEMs typically combine several mechanisms:

- **Spatial separation:** Memory protection via MPU/MMU, separate address spaces, and protected I/O regions for ASIL-rated software so that faults in QM applications cannot overwrite safety data or code
- **Temporal separation:** Time-partitioned scheduling on the safety RTOS or hypervisor (e.g., fixed time slices reserved for ASIL-D tasks, with bounded interference from lower-criticality workloads)
- **Communication supervision:** End-to-end CRCs, sequence counters, plausibility checks, and watchdog-monitored interfaces between safety and non-safety partitions
- **Dedicated safety hardware:** Lockstep safety cores or separate safety microcontrollers within the same housing, running only high-criticality software and supervising the more complex general-purpose OS

These patterns allow ASIL-C/D safety goals to be realized on platforms that also host non-safety software, but they substantially increase the design and verification effort. Details of these mechanisms and their ISO 26262 implications are discussed in Chapter 9.

This decentralized, modular structure shortens cable runs dramatically while still allowing OEMs to respect safety partitions. For example, Tesla's harness design for Model 3 (often cited as an early quasi-zonal approach) reduced cable length from about 3 km to 1.5 km by reorganizing the wiring and using local controllers rather than routing every wire back to a central point [187]. Zonal designs also simplify manufacturing: instead of one gigantic, highly vehicle-specific wire harness, each zone's wiring can be built as a smaller sub-harness and plugged into the car during assembly [188].

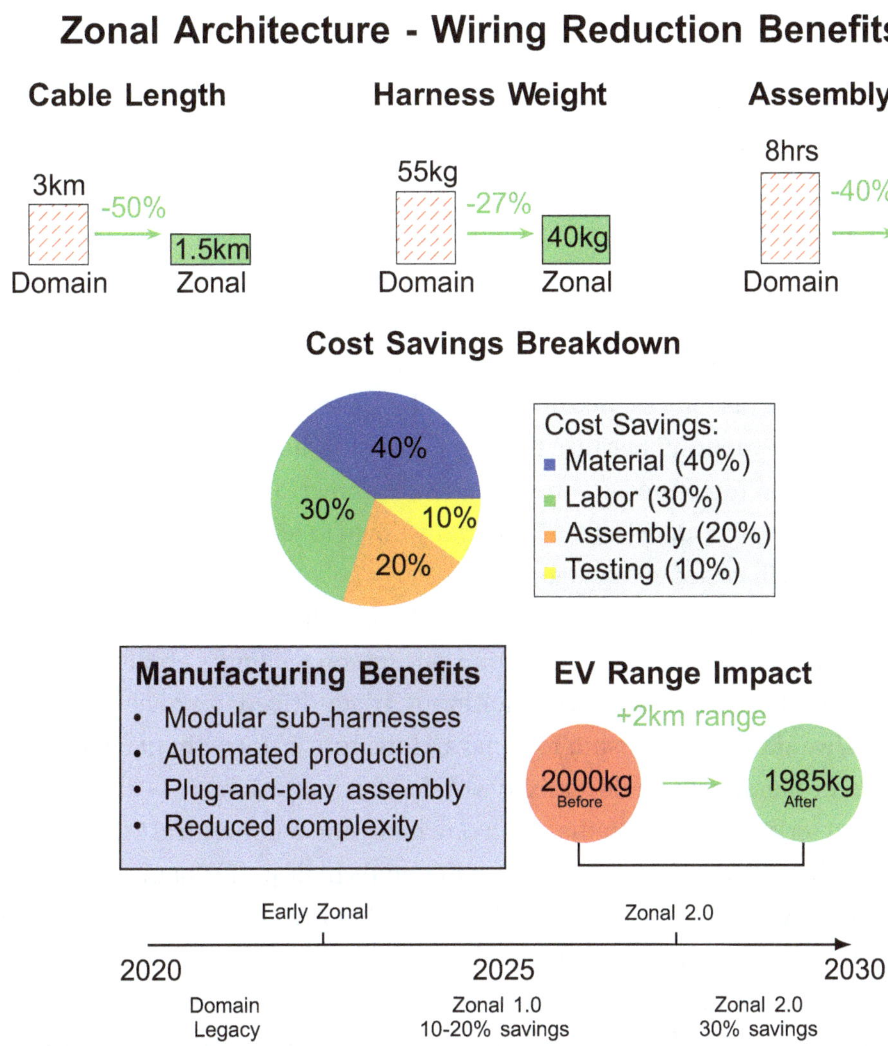

Figure 6-5. *Wiring length and weight reduction benefits of zonal architecture*

Benefits: The deeper architectural value of zonal design lies in software scalability, compute consolidation, and a cleaner path toward lifecycle updates. By aggregating local I/O into zonal controllers and linking those controllers to higher-performance backbones, OEMs gain a platform that is easier to evolve, easier to update, and better aligned with centralized software services. Harness simplification is a meaningful secondary benefit, because shorter local cable runs can reduce material usage, assembly effort, and vehicle mass, but the broader motivation is to create a vehicle architecture that supports shared compute resources, cross-domain data exchange, and faster feature deployment [188].

Zonal architecture also tends to reduce the number of ECUs because one powerful zonal controller can host functions that previously required multiple separate domain ECUs—while still allowing safety-critical functions to remain on dedicated safety microcontrollers or safety islands where required. Traditional OEMs aim to shrink from ~100 ECUs down to on the order of 30 or even fewer consolidated units by using zones and central computing [189].

Another benefit is that it creates a more modular and OTA-friendly platform. Since functions are now mostly software running on a few powerful controllers, features can be updated or added via software downloads, with less concern about the exact hardware variant in each vehicle (as long as the zonal controller has enough capacity). This consolidation is "OTA-friendly" because there are fewer modules to update and a more centralized software architecture—for instance, Tesla's move to a centralized electronics design cut the number of update targets from many down to just a handful, making software updates much easier to manage [190].

Additionally, having zonal data concentrators aligns well with advanced data analytics and connected car services: each zone can stream telemetry about its components to the cloud, enabling a feedback loop of data-driven improvements.

Challenges/weaknesses: The shift to zonal architecture is not without challenges. First, a zonal controller must handle a mixed workload of many domains—it might need to control a safety-critical braking actuator on one hand and a noncritical infotainment speaker on the other, all on one processor. This demands high-performance controllers (often multi-core SoCs rather than simple microcontrollers) and sophisticated software to ensure real-time deadlines and safety isolation are met.

In practice, new middleware and virtualization technologies are required to partition software on these controllers [191]. For example, a single zonal controller might run a real-time operating system for critical control tasks alongside a general-purpose OS (Linux, QNX, etc.) for infotainment tasks, possibly using hypervisors or multi-kernel RTOS setups to ensure freedom from interference between functions. Developing and validating this software stack is a nontrivial task for automakers traditionally used to one-function-per-ECU setups.

Additionally, moving to zones means a radical change in the E/E network topology of the car. Legacy buses (CAN, LIN, FlexRay) are usually retained for local loops, while the higher-level topology shifts toward an Ethernet-based backbone (often with TSN for time-critical traffic). The transition is additive—Ethernet is layered on and gateways are re-architected—rather than a simple "rip-and-replace" of all CAN/LIN networks [192].

Designing this mixed network is nontrivial. Time-Sensitive Networking requires carefully engineered schedules, priorities, and traffic shaping to guarantee deterministic behavior across multiple zones, and every gateway between CAN, LIN, FlexRay, and Ethernet becomes a potential bottleneck and failure point. In practice, a significant share of E/E architecture effort is spent on Ethernet/TSN configuration, gateway behavior, and verifying that real traffic patterns still meet latency and jitter requirements once the vehicle is fully optioned.

Finally, supplier ecosystems are disrupted: instead of each Tier-1 delivering a self-contained subsystem (engine ECU, airbag ECU, etc.), the OEM now needs to orchestrate software from multiple suppliers on a shared zone computer or develop more in-house software. This can increase the complexity of integration (who is responsible for a bug in a zonal controller that runs code from five different suppliers?). We will see in case studies how these challenges have caused some pain for incumbent OEMs.

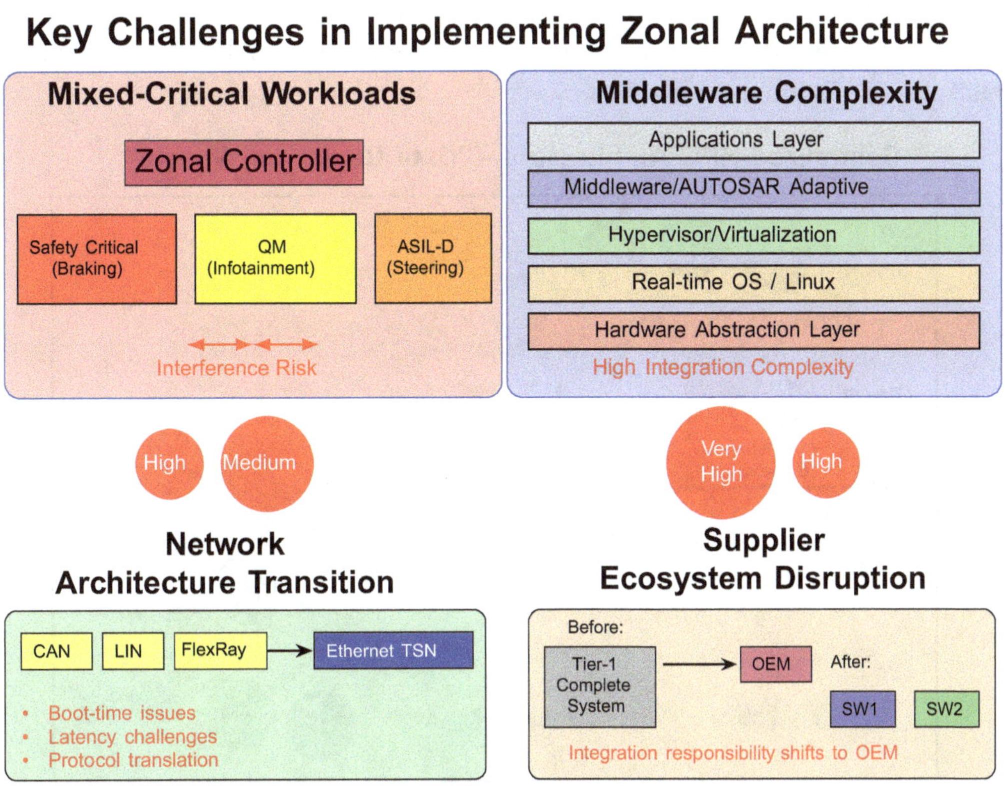

Figure 6-6. *Illustrative challenge areas in zonal architectures: mixed-criticality hosting, network transition, and supplier integration*

Figure 6-6 should not be read as a strict software stack. Instead, it highlights several challenge categories that often appear together in zonal programs: hosting mixed-criticality workloads on shared controllers, transitioning from legacy in-vehicle networks to Ethernet-based backbones, and shifting more integration responsibility toward the OEM. In implementation terms, an operating system or hypervisor provides execution and isolation, while middleware frameworks such as AUTOSAR Adaptive provide communication and service abstractions above that execution layer.

6.3.3 Centralized HPC (Central Compute)

Pushing consolidation to its extreme, some modern designs use centralized high-performance computers (HPCs) to handle the majority of vehicle functions. In a central compute architecture, the car might have one or a few "vehicle supercomputers" that all sensors and actuators ultimately connect to (often via intermediary zone controllers or gateways). Instead of dozens of distributed brains, there is essentially a central brain (or a small cluster of brains) in the vehicle.

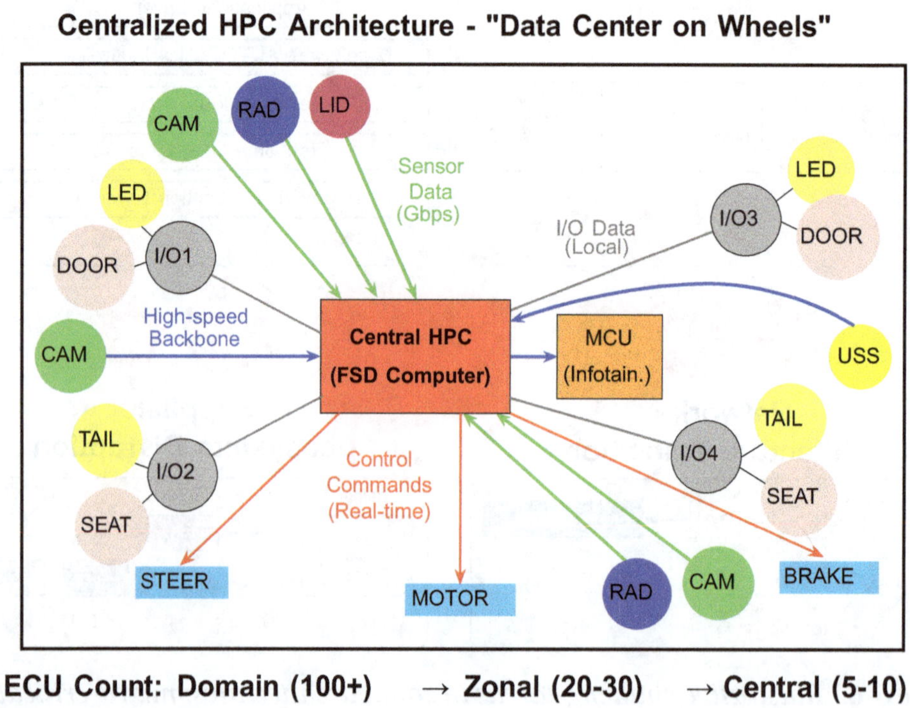

Figure 6-7. *Centralized HPC architecture with the central brain concept*

Concept: Central compute architectures push function consolidation further by concentrating major data processing and coordination on one or a few high-performance computers, typically supported by zonal controllers or I/O concentrators at the vehicle edge. In this arrangement, perception, sensor fusion, user interface logic, and cross-domain orchestration can be hosted on shared compute platforms, while some local control and safety functions remain distributed where needed. Depending on the OEM and platform, infotainment may either be integrated into the main central compute platform or handled by a separate cockpit-oriented computer. The architectural point is not that every function runs on one processor, but that the vehicle's main software platform becomes far more centralized than in traditional domain architectures [189].

Benefits: Central compute architectures simplify the software landscape by reducing the number of major execution targets and enabling broader reuse of shared compute resources. They can also make cross-domain data sharing easier, since perception, cockpit, connectivity, and vehicle control services exchange data over a smaller number of well-defined interfaces. In practice, this can support more coordinated OTA campaigns, greater software reuse across programs, and improved integration of compute-intensive functions such as ADAS and digital cockpit services. The precise compute, cost, and update-time benefits, however, depend heavily on the platform design and should not be treated as universal numeric outcomes.

However, this is not "free reliability." While component count drops, the criticality of each central computer increases. The architecture must therefore be explicitly designed for redundancy (e.g., dual SoCs, independent power domains, diversified software) and for fail-operational behavior where required by safety goals, rather than assuming that fewer boxes automatically mean fewer problems.

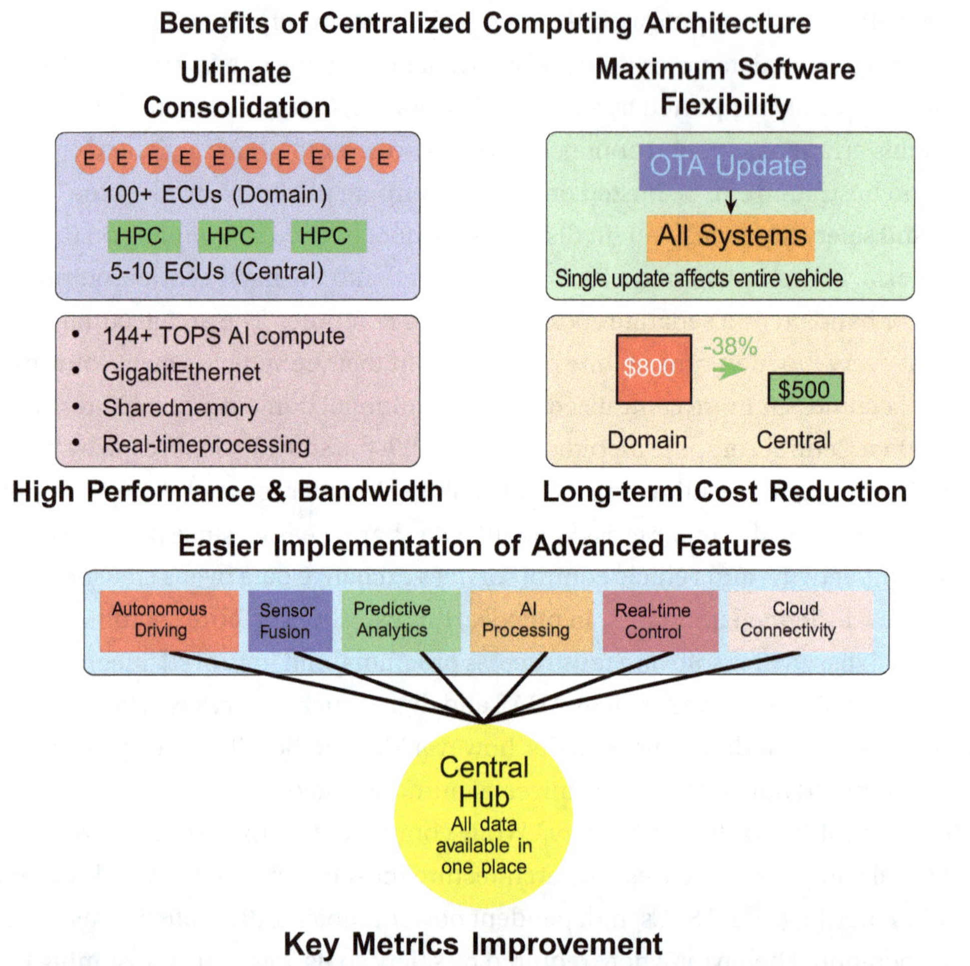

Metric	Domain	Central	Improvement
Update Time	Days-Weeks	Hours	10-50x faster

Figure 6-8. *Conceptual benefits of centralized computing architecture, including software consolidation, shared data access, and coordinated OTA management*

Weaknesses: The trade-offs of central computing are significant. A primary concern is the risk of concentrated failure: if a central computer that hosts many functions fails—whether due to hardware fault or software crash—the impact can be much broader than in a domain architecture where infotainment, powertrain, and chassis live on separate ECUs. To mitigate this, central architectures must be designed for redundancy and fail-operational behavior, e.g., through dual SoCs, independent power domains, and carefully partitioned safety channels [191]. Even then, certain safety functions (such as airbag deployment or some powertrain monitoring) are often kept on dedicated, simpler controllers to avoid dependence on a complex, general-purpose platform.

Central computing also concentrates thermal and power management demands. High-performance automotive compute platforms may consume substantially more power than traditional low-end ECUs, and they must be cooled and packaged within automotive reliability constraints. The exact power budget depends strongly on workload, silicon generation, safety architecture, and how much functionality remains distributed, so broad headline numbers should be treated cautiously.

Centralization also changes the software engineering problem. More functions now share common compute platforms, which raises the importance of modular software architecture, ownership boundaries, regression testing, controlled release processes, and resilience mechanisms. The challenge is not that the entire vehicle suddenly becomes one undifferentiated codebase, but that integration discipline becomes much more critical when shared platforms host many interdependent functions.

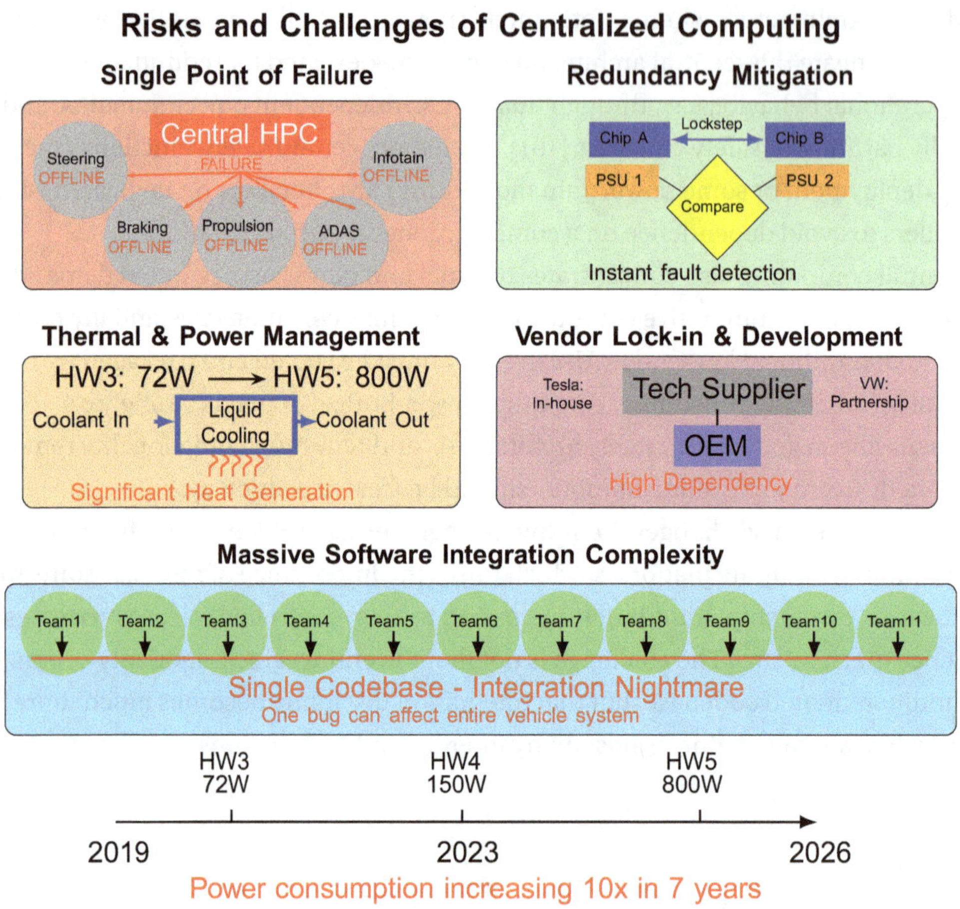

Figure 6-9. *Key engineering challenges in centralized compute architectures, including resilience, thermal management, software integration, and platform dependency*

In practice, many OEMs are converging toward a hybrid of zonal and central architectures—using a few central HPCs for the most computational tasks (ADAS, infotainment, etc.) and zonal controllers to handle I/O and real-time control in each physical area of the car [14]. This hybrid can achieve much of the wiring reduction and software flexibility goals while still isolating some functionality per zone (and providing fail-safes if one zone goes down). The next sections will examine trade-offs and real-world examples of these approaches.

6.4 Architecture Trade-Offs

Every approach—domain, zonal, and central—comes with its own pros and cons.

Table 6-1. *Architecture Trade-Offs*

Architecture	Pros	Cons	Notes
Domain (distributed)	Well-understood; specialized ECUs per function; established supplier base	Wiring bulk: long, duplicated cabling; ECU sprawl (100+ modules); high integration complexity	
Zonal (modular)	Reduced wiring: shorter harness ➤ weight/cost savings; modular sub-harnesses (automation potential); consolidation: fewer ECUs (simpler updates)	Requires TSN/modern Ethernet; new integration patterns and maturity	
Central compute	Fleet features via software; better resource utilization; OTA-friendly	Single point of failure risk; thermal/power concentration; R&D cost and supply risk	

In choosing an architecture, automakers must balance flexibility, integration burden, safety strategy, software maturity, and migration practicality rather than assuming a single universal end state. Many production vehicles will continue to combine domain, zonal, and centralized elements for years, so the most useful comparison is qualitative rather than a rigid scorecard [193].

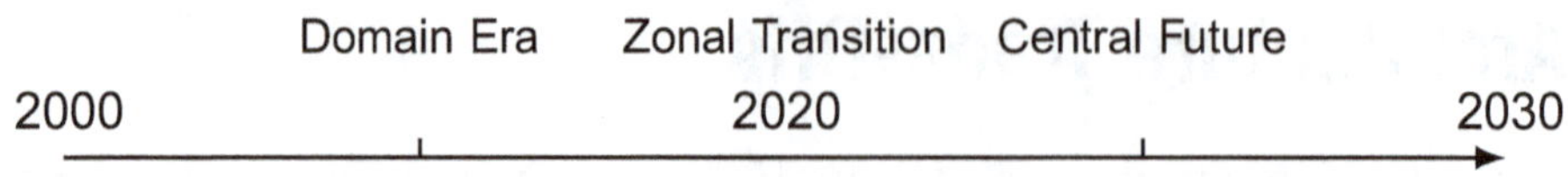

Comprehensive Architecture Comparison

Metric	Domain	Zonal	Central
ECU Count	100-150	20-30	5-10
Wiring Length	3+ km	1.5 km	0.8 km
Harness Weight	55-68 kg	35-45 kg	25-35 kg
Development Cost	Low	Medium	Very High
Integration Effort	Very High	High	Extreme
OTA Capability	Limited	Good	Excellent
Feature Flexibility	Very Low	High	Maximum
Software Complexity	Low	Medium	Very High
Failure Risk	Distributed	Zone-level	Single Point
Supplier Dependence	High	Medium	Low/High*
Time to Market	Fast	Medium	Very Long
Maintenance Cost	High	Medium	Low
Scalability	Poor	Good	Excellent
Performance	Moderate	High	Maximum
Power Consumption	Distributed	Moderate	High
Regulatory Compliance	Moderate	Good	Excellent
Market Readiness	High	Medium	Low
Overall Risk	Low	Medium	High

Advantage Neutral Disadvantage

Figure 6-10. *Qualitative comparison of domain, zonal, and centralized architectural tendencies. Many production programs combine elements of more than one approach*

Business Note Zonal and centralized architectures can shift cost rather than simply reduce it. Simplified harnesses and fewer discrete controllers may lower some material and assembly costs, but these gains are often offset by higher spending on high-performance silicon, middleware, virtualization, validation, cybersecurity, OTA infrastructure, and integration engineering [188, 193]. The economic case therefore depends less on harness savings alone and more on platform reuse, software reuse, lifecycle update efficiency, and whether the OEM can recover the higher upfront investment through scale, reduced complexity over time, or post-sale software revenue. From a business perspective, the strongest architectural value comes when hardware consolidation is matched by software platform discipline and lifecycle operating capability.

6.4.1 Pragmatic Migration Paths

Most OEMs will not jump directly from a traditional domain architecture to a fully centralized zonal design. Instead, they follow staged migration paths that align with platform lifecycles and organizational readiness. A typical sequence might look like this:

1. **Domain consolidation:** Multiple small ECUs within a domain are first consolidated into a domain controller (e.g., powertrain or ADAS "servers"), while the overall topology remains domain-based.

2. **Domain-plus-zone hybrids:** Next, a few physical zones are introduced (front, rear, cabin), sometimes with local I/O concentrators, while legacy domain controllers continue to exist. Zones may initially behave mostly as "smart gateways" rather than full compute nodes.

3. **Zonal with central HPC:** As software and networking maturity grows, more logic moves into zonal controllers and one or more central HPCs. Domains become primarily logical groupings, and the hardware topology is mostly zonal plus central.

Different brands and programs will occupy different points along this spectrum for many years. The important architectural decision is not only the "end state" but also the migration path: which domains to consolidate first, when to introduce Ethernet backbones, when the organization is ready to host mixed-criticality workloads on shared compute, and how to keep legacy and new architectures interoperable during the transition.

6.5 Case Studies

To illustrate these concepts, this chapter uses two public, high-level examples that are frequently discussed in industry analyses: a centralized-first approach associated with newer EV-native programs and a more gradual transition strategy associated with established multi-brand OEM groups. The examples that follow should be read as illustrative summaries based on public reporting and disclosed platform directions, not as complete or authoritative disclosures of proprietary vehicle architectures.

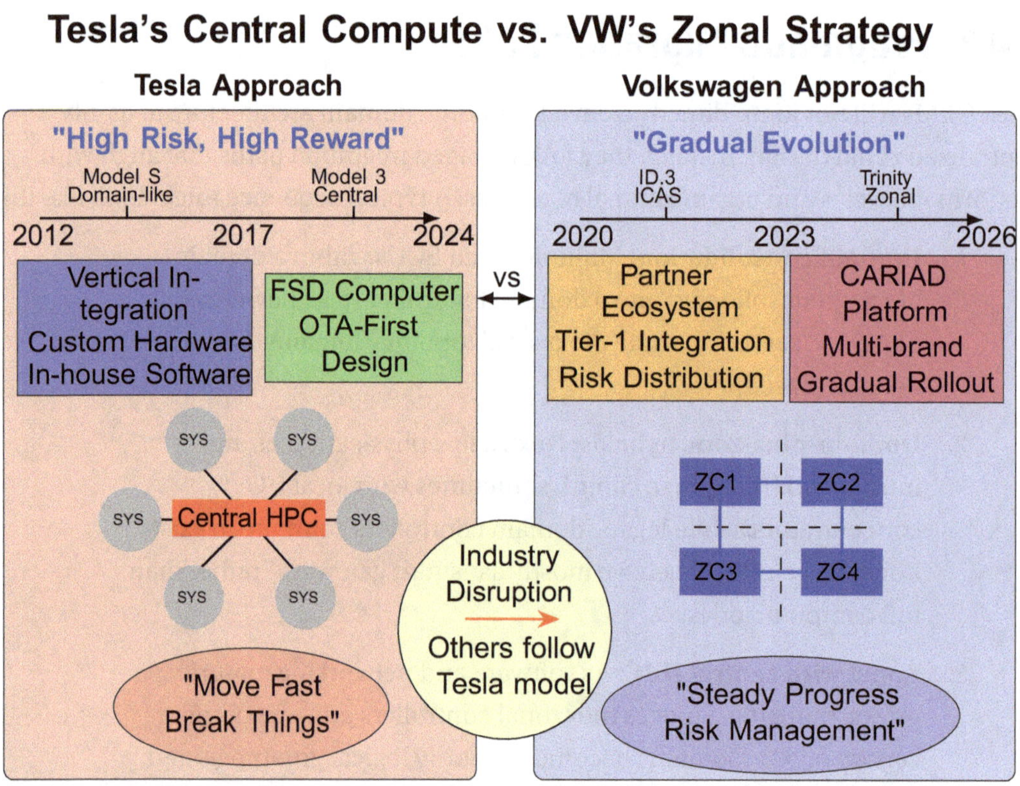

Figure 6-11. *Illustrative comparison between a centralized-first approach and a staged zonal transition approach, using public industry examples*

6.5.1 Tesla: Central Compute Pioneer

Tesla is often cited as a trailblazer in modern E/E architecture, effectively using a centralized computing approach. In Tesla's newer models (since the Model 3 launch in 2017–2018), the electronics architecture was designed almost from scratch to prioritize software and OTA updates.

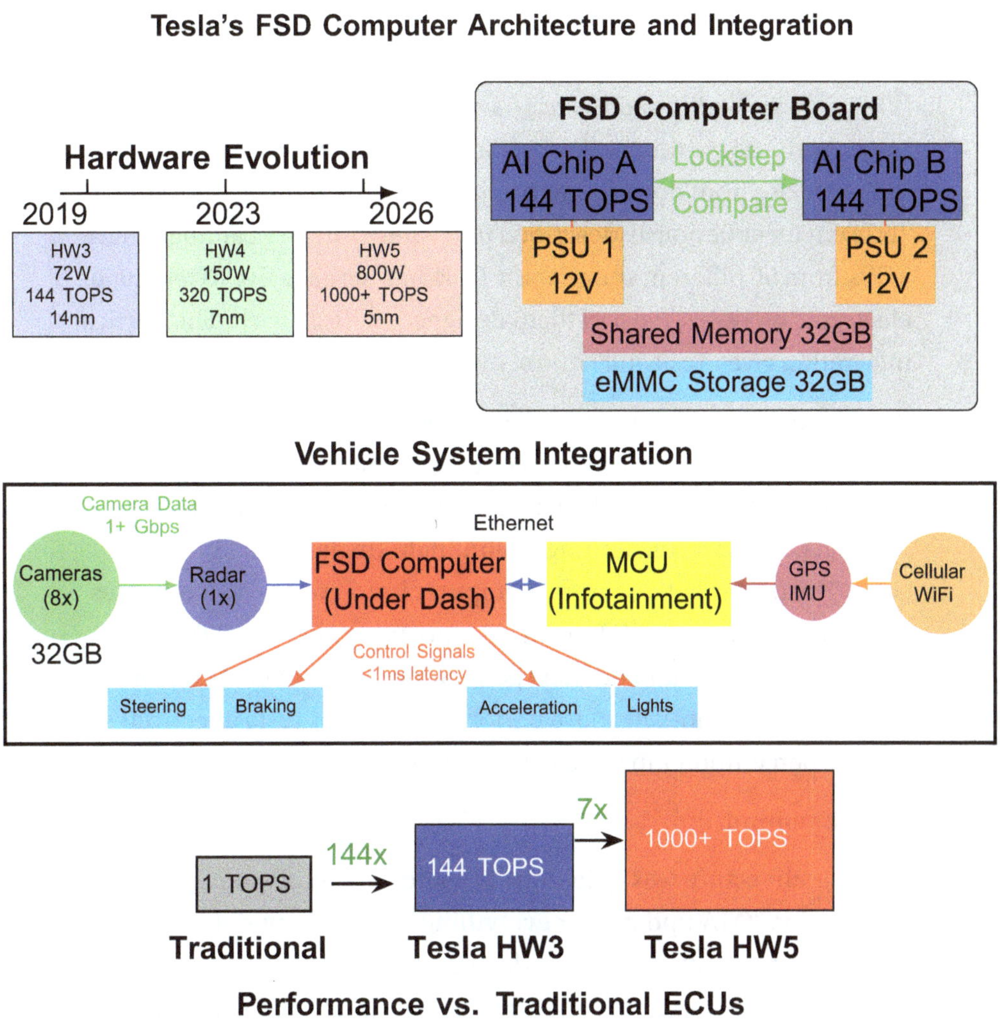

***Figure 6-12.** Tesla's FSD computer architecture and integration*

- **Custom central hardware:**

  Tesla developed an integrated central control unit called the Full Self-Driving (FSD) computer, which comprises two custom-designed AI chips on one board for redundancy [189, 191]. This computer (also known as Hardware 3, with Hardware 4 introduced in 2023) is responsible for running the Autopilot neural networks and many other vehicle functions.

In addition, Tesla has a high-end infotainment system (MCU) but even that is tightly integrated, and many previously separate functions (like gateway, body control, etc.) have been absorbed into a few modules. By doing this, Tesla slashed the total number of ECUs in their vehicles from dozens down to just a few main processors [189]. A Tesla engineer famously described that where a luxury car might have ECUs from 50 different suppliers, a Tesla has perhaps five to ten major electronic modules, most of them designed by Tesla itself. This vertical integration gives Tesla full control over hardware and software design.

It's also worth noting that the FSD computer is designed with safety in mind: the dual chips run the same calculations in parallel and compare results to instantly detect failures, and the board has dual power feeds and so on, aiming to eliminate single-point failures [191]. The power of this central computer is noteworthy—it operates at ~72 W for dual chips (Hardware 3) providing about 144 TOPS of NN compute [189], and the next generation is expected to consume ~200 W for substantially more performance [191]. Tesla effectively put a supercomputer in the car, behind the glovebox.

- **OTA-first mindset:**

  Tesla's architecture was built hand in hand with a software philosophy: "OTA updates for everything." All Tesla models can receive over-the-air software updates routinely, which can range from UI improvements to significant performance updates or new features (Tesla has even added range and power enhancements via software, as well as safety updates).

  Because the electronics are centralized, Tesla can update multiple systems in the car with a single coordinated software push. For example, an Autopilot update might involve motor control, braking, and steering—functions that in other cars span different ECUs—but in a Tesla, these subsystems are all supervised by the central computer or tightly networked, so an OTA package can update the necessary components together.

Tesla typically rolls out updates incrementally (to a small percentage of vehicles and then expanding) to catch any issues early, reflecting how critical software reliability is when a change affects the whole fleet. The result is a rapid innovation cycle: owners come to expect that their car will improve over time. This OTA-centric approach was enabled by the centralized E/E design and has set Tesla apart from traditional automakers. It also aligns with a Silicon Valley–style development cadence rather than the slower automotive recall/service bulletin model. Essentially, Tesla treats the car like a smartphone in terms of updates.

The smartphone analogy, however, has limits: vehicles have 10–15-year lifespans, strict safety obligations, and regulatory constraints that consumer electronics do not. OTA agility in automotive must therefore be balanced with disciplined safety analysis, traceability, and long-term maintainability.

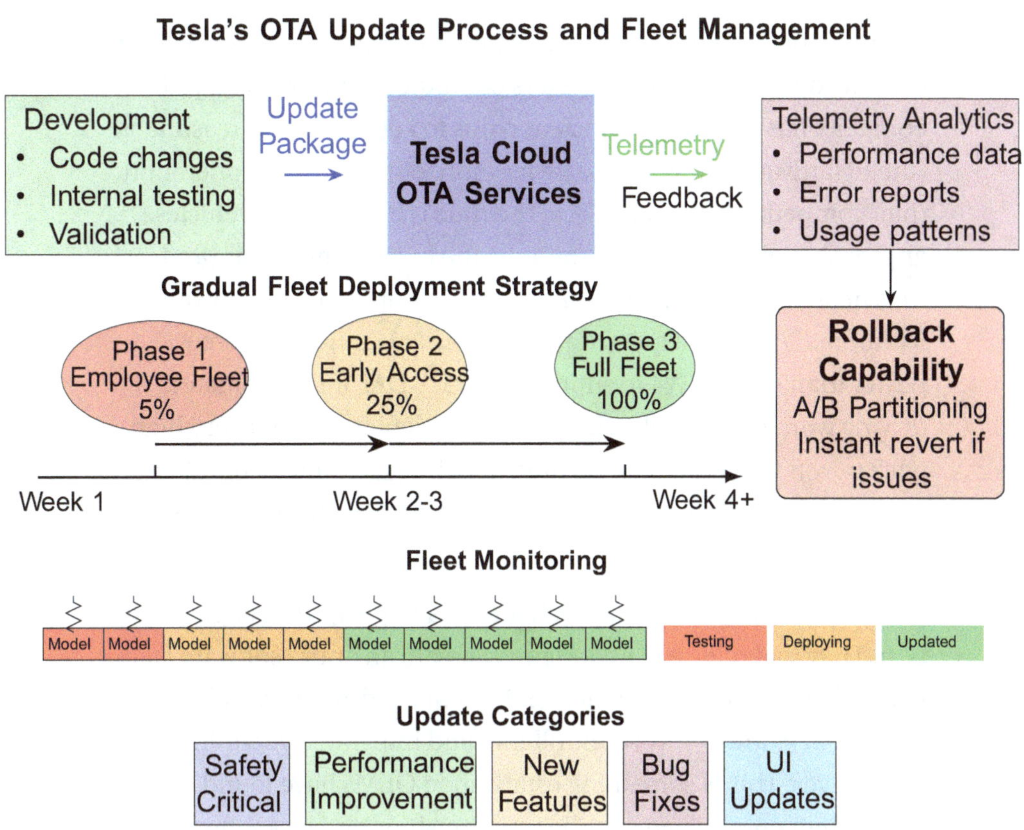

Figure 6-13. *Tesla's OTA update process and fleet management*

- **Risks and challenges:**

  The flip side of Tesla's strategy is that it comes with bold risks. Because so many vehicles run essentially identical software on identical hardware, any systemic flaw can have wide impact. There have been instances where a Tesla software update had unintended effects—e.g., in late 2020 a firmware update led to some cars losing heating functionality in extreme cold, requiring a quick fix via software rollback.

  Tesla's "fleet-wide" outages are rare, but the possibility is a specter that haunts any centrally designed system. A bug in code that manages multiple systems could, in theory, knock out critical functions across thousands of cars at once. Tesla mitigates this by extensive internal testing and gradual rollouts, but it's a known trade-off.

  Another challenge is thermal management and power draw of their central computer. As noted, Tesla's compute is power-hungry; the company has invested in efficient chips to keep the draw reasonable (their Hardware 3 was said to be far more efficient per AI operation than competitors like NVIDIA at the time) [194]. Still, as vehicles approach higher levels of autonomy, the computing needs (and thus heat dissipation needs) climb—Tesla's upcoming Hardware 5 (dubbed "AI 5") is expected to consume substantially more power than HW3/HW4 to support higher ADAS and automated driving workloads. Public rumors have speculated about very high peak power figures, but at the time of writing, no official numbers were disclosed; designers should therefore treat such figures as speculative, not as design facts [191].

  Lastly, Tesla's in-house approach meant a huge upfront engineering cost. They had to hire chip designers, create an entire software stack nearly from scratch (much of it on Linux-based systems and some AUTOSAR in lower-level controllers), and integrate everything themselves. This is something established OEMs have found difficult due to their entrenched supplier relationships and less software-centric culture [195]. Tesla essentially bet the company on this vertical integration, and so far it has paid off, but not without some very public learning curves (e.g., earlier Model S/X had slower MCUs that Tesla had to upgrade later, and some owners experienced touchscreen failures, which led to recalls).

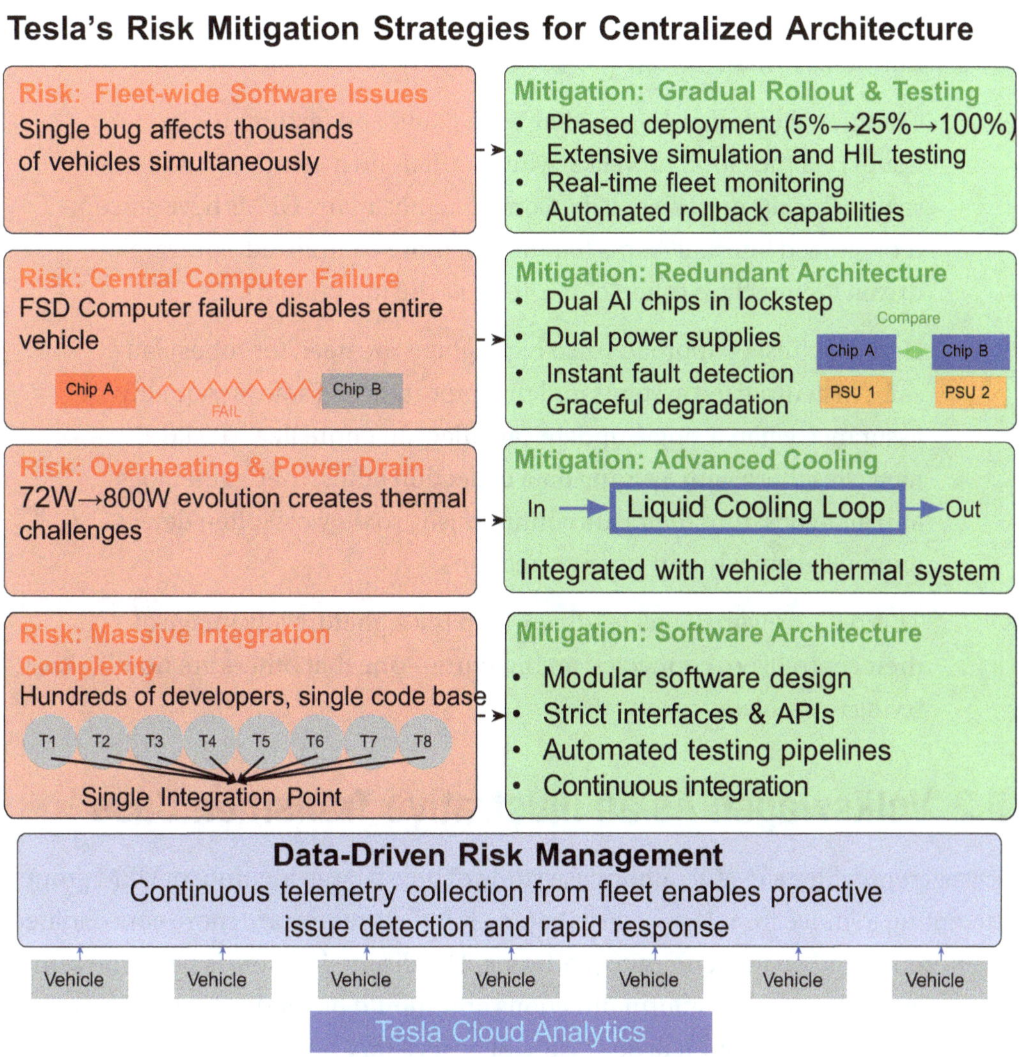

Figure 6-14. *Tesla's risk mitigation strategies for centralized architecture*

- **Outcome:**

  Tesla's central compute architecture has proven successful in enabling fast software updates and features like Full Self-Driving beta releases fleet-wide. It gave Tesla a perceived lead in the software-defined vehicle race, to the point that engineering tear-downs by other OEMs resulted in comments like "this will not be available to us until 2025" [188].

  Traditional automakers saw that Tesla could add features (or fix issues) via the cloud in weeks, whereas their own vehicles would require recalls or dealer visits. Consequently, many OEMs have since reorganized internal teams to pursue a more centralized, software-driven architecture (often citing Tesla as the inspiration).

  However, Tesla's approach also highlighted the need for robust fail-safes in centralized systems and the importance of software quality assurance when a single update can affect an entire fleet. Tesla navigates these with a strong data collection ethos: they gather logs and analytics from their cars continuously, so they can often detect anomalies quickly and issue corrections.

  This data-driven, digital feedback loop is a signature advantage of their centralized, connected architecture—one that others are now trying to emulate.

6.5.2 Volkswagen As an Illustrative Transition Case

Volkswagen provides a useful public case study of how a large incumbent OEM group is attempting to move from legacy distributed architectures toward more consolidated domain, zonal, and central compute platforms. The discussion here is based on public reporting and announced platform directions and should be read as an illustrative summary rather than a complete disclosure of proprietary production architectures. VW's journey shows the challenges of evolving an existing product lineup and the importance of software middleware in that process.

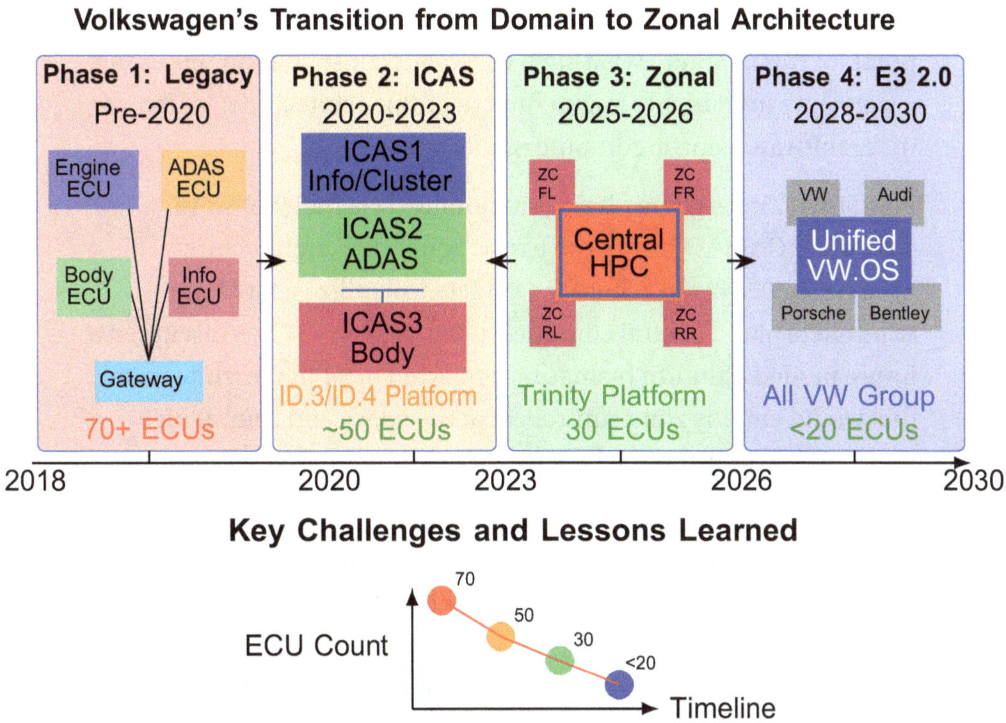

Figure 6-15. *Illustrative public view of transition from domain-oriented architectures toward more consolidated controller topologies*

- **Incremental shift from domains:**

  Volkswagen's recent vehicles (e.g., the electric ID.3, ID.4 series on the MEB platform) started to move away from the fully distributed domain approach. VW introduced a concept of domain "servers" or centralized domain controllers in these models—for instance, a high-performance module called ICAS (In-Car Application Server) is used in the ID series.

  Public reporting on transition platforms such as the ID.3 has described a consolidation step in which several higher-level controllers handle groups of functions that were previously distributed across many ECUs. This should be understood as an intermediate architectural direction rather than as a complete or authoritative disclosure of the production network. The important point for this chapter is that such controller consolidation represents a step away from highly fragmented domain architectures and toward more software-centric compute platforms.

From there, VW's game plan (as announced via their software subsidiary CARIAD) is to evolve to a "zonal" E/E architecture by around 2025–2026, where the vehicle will utilize a few zone controllers plus a central computer [195]. In fact, VW has discussed a future unified platform (sometimes referred to as "E3" architecture) that would employ zone controllers at the edges and central high-performance units for the heavy lifting.

They have partnered with tech companies for this purpose: e.g., using NVIDIA's Orin chips for ADAS domain compute in upcoming models and co-developing their own SoCs with STMicroelectronics for general zone controllers [192]. The idea is that different VW Group brands and models will all use a common hardware and software platform, greatly simplifying complexity across the portfolio (in theory).

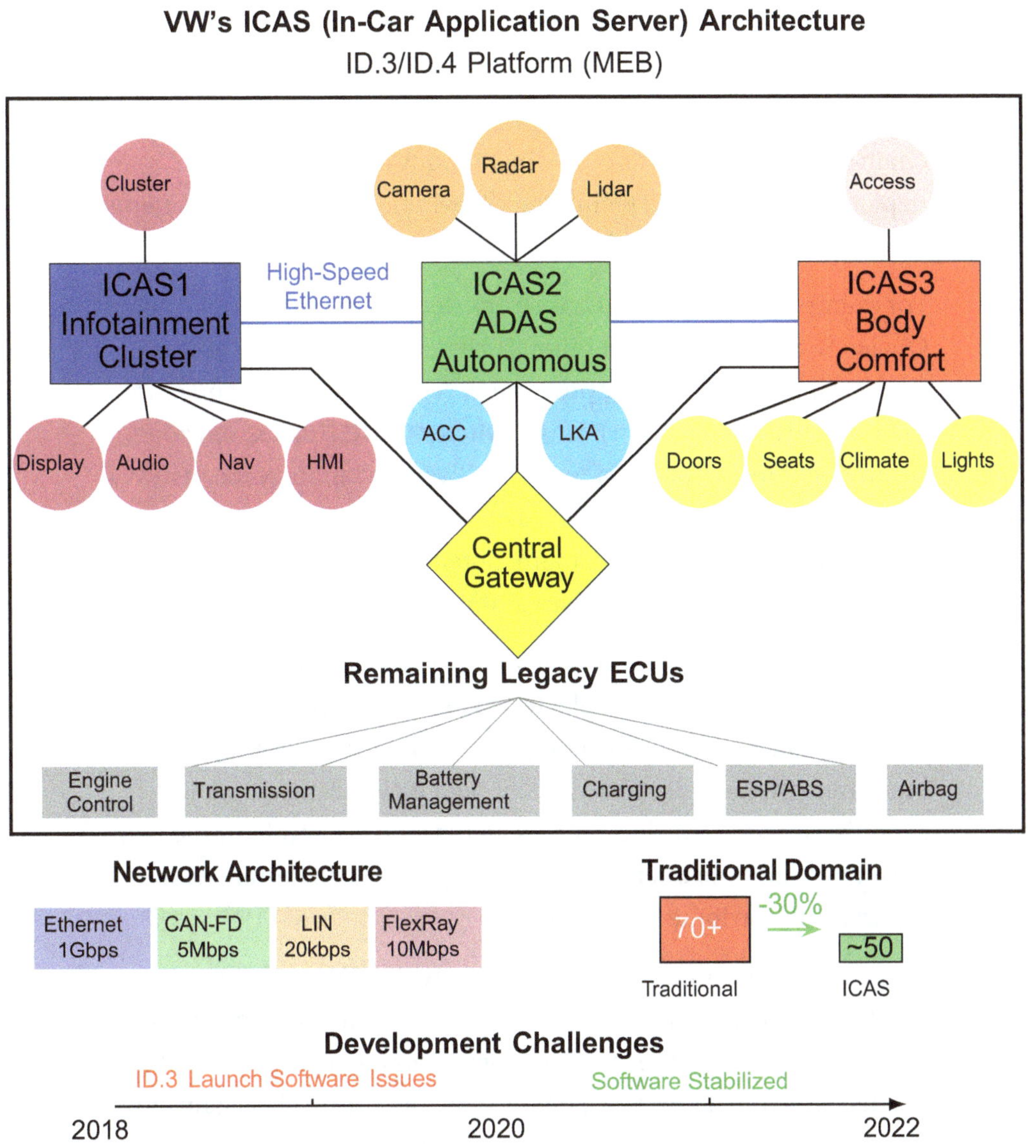

***Figure 6-16.** Simplified public illustration of domain controller consolidation on a transition platform using an ICAS-style approach*

- **Supplier diversity and ecosystem:**

  Unlike Tesla, which built almost everything in-house, VW leverages a vast network of suppliers and is trying to manage a diverse supply chain during this transition. On one hand, VW wants to avoid dependence on a single technology provider for critical components (to prevent vendor lock-in).

  For example, VW's CARIAD has struck deals with multiple partners: Qualcomm (for some autonomous driving chips), Intel/Mobileye (for certain ADAS in earlier programs), NVIDIA (for high-end chips in the Audi/Porsche realm), and STMicro/TSMC (for custom zone/controller chips) [192]. This "supplier diversity" strategy means VW isn't putting all its eggs in one basket—it can source different pieces from those who specialize in them, potentially getting the best each has to offer and maintaining bargaining power.

  It also means VW can continue working with traditional Tier-1 suppliers (Bosch, Continental, etc.) to develop software for those zone controllers and central computers, rather than writing everything from scratch. The benefit here is risk mitigation and expertise sharing: VW doesn't have to develop every microprocessor or software module internally as Tesla did; they collaborate with experts and distribute the workload.

  Additionally, by co-developing chips (as with STMicro's Stellar family), VW aims to ensure the silicon perfectly fits their needs and that supply is secured years in advance (a lesson learned from chip shortages). From a business perspective, this approach sustains the supplier ecosystem that VW has long relied on, albeit with updated roles—but it also introduces new questions around IP ownership and liability when multiple suppliers share a common zonal controller or HPC. Contract models and responsibility boundaries must evolve in parallel with the architecture so that it is clear who owns which software assets and who is accountable when integrated software fails.

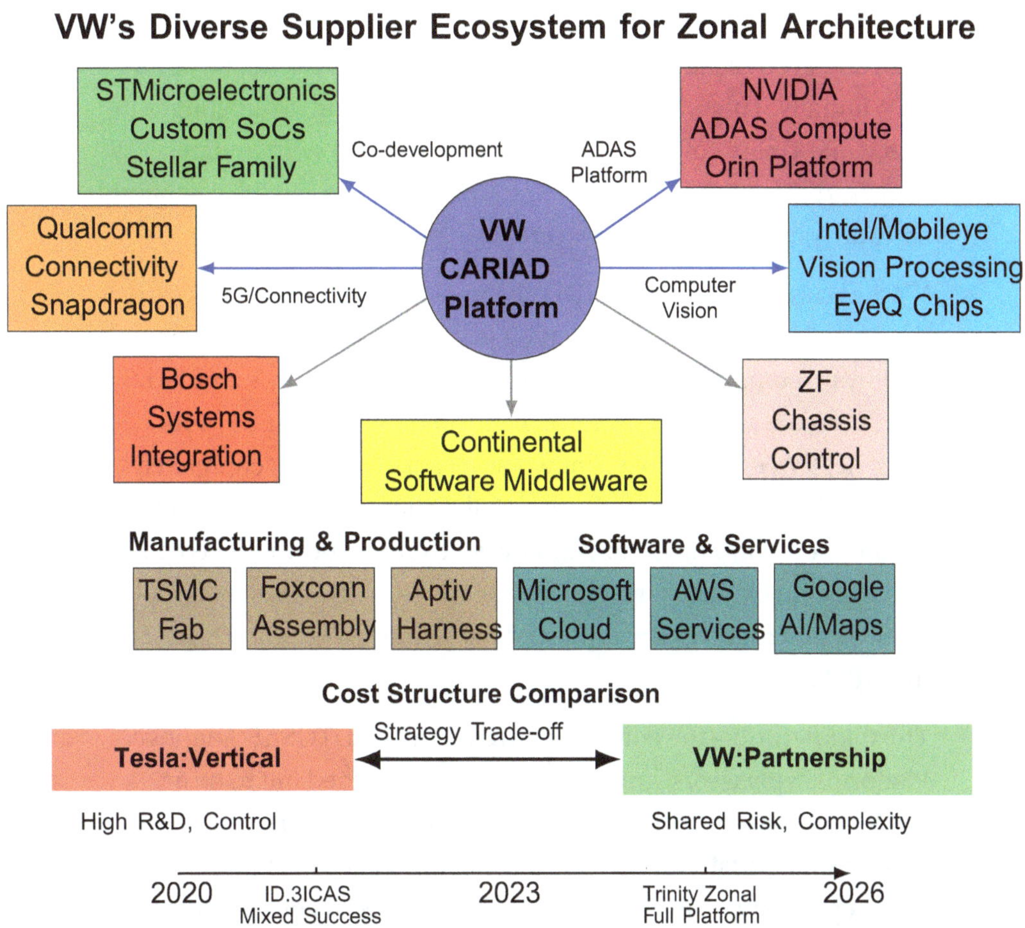

Figure 6-17. *VW's diverse supplier ecosystem for zonal architecture*

- **Middleware complexity—lessons learned:**

  The downside of VW's multi-supplier, multi-component approach is integration complexity, especially on the software side. Indeed, VW encountered major challenges in the software of its first ID.3 electric cars around 2020. Early ID.3 vehicles were delayed and delivered with incomplete software; customers and press reported glitches in the infotainment and driver assists.

  The root cause was attributed to CARIAD's struggle to integrate a new software stack that spanned the vehicle—essentially the car was architected with a new centralized logic, but the software wasn't ready or mature [195]. Volkswagen had to issue numerous software fixes and even recall some cars for updates that could not be done OTA initially. This was somewhat embarrassing for VW, highlighting that while Tesla's software-centric design enabled swift updates, VW's initially did not—they had the centralized hardware in the car, but the software pipeline and architecture were playing catch-up.

VW has since improved the ID software with OTA capabilities, but the episode exposed how difficult it is for a legacy OEM to become a software company overnight. Moreover, the company's ambitious plan to create a unified software platform for all its brands (Audi, Porsche, VW, etc.) by 2026, known as E3 2.0, had to be "completely reworked" after internal setbacks [195]. Different brands had different requirements and timelines, and the software platform proved harder to build than expected, resulting in delays (e.g., the launch of Audi/Porsche's next-gen EVs was pushed back, and VW shuffled leadership in CARIAD).

The middleware—the core operating systems, AUTOSAR Adaptive Platform, hypervisors, and vehicle services—turned out to be a bottleneck. Mixed-criticality scheduling on shared cores, certifying hypervisors for safety-related workloads, and getting multiple suppliers' Adaptive AUTOSAR and non-AUTOSAR components to coexist without breaking timing budgets are a very different problem from integrating separate classic ECUs. VW's case shows that middleware complexity is a real "con" of the zonal/central approach: without a robust software base, the fancy new hardware can become a headache instead of an advantage. Indeed, VW's CEO was quoted saying "software is where the future will be decided," and they learned it the hard way when initial software issues hurt the ID.3's launch reputation.

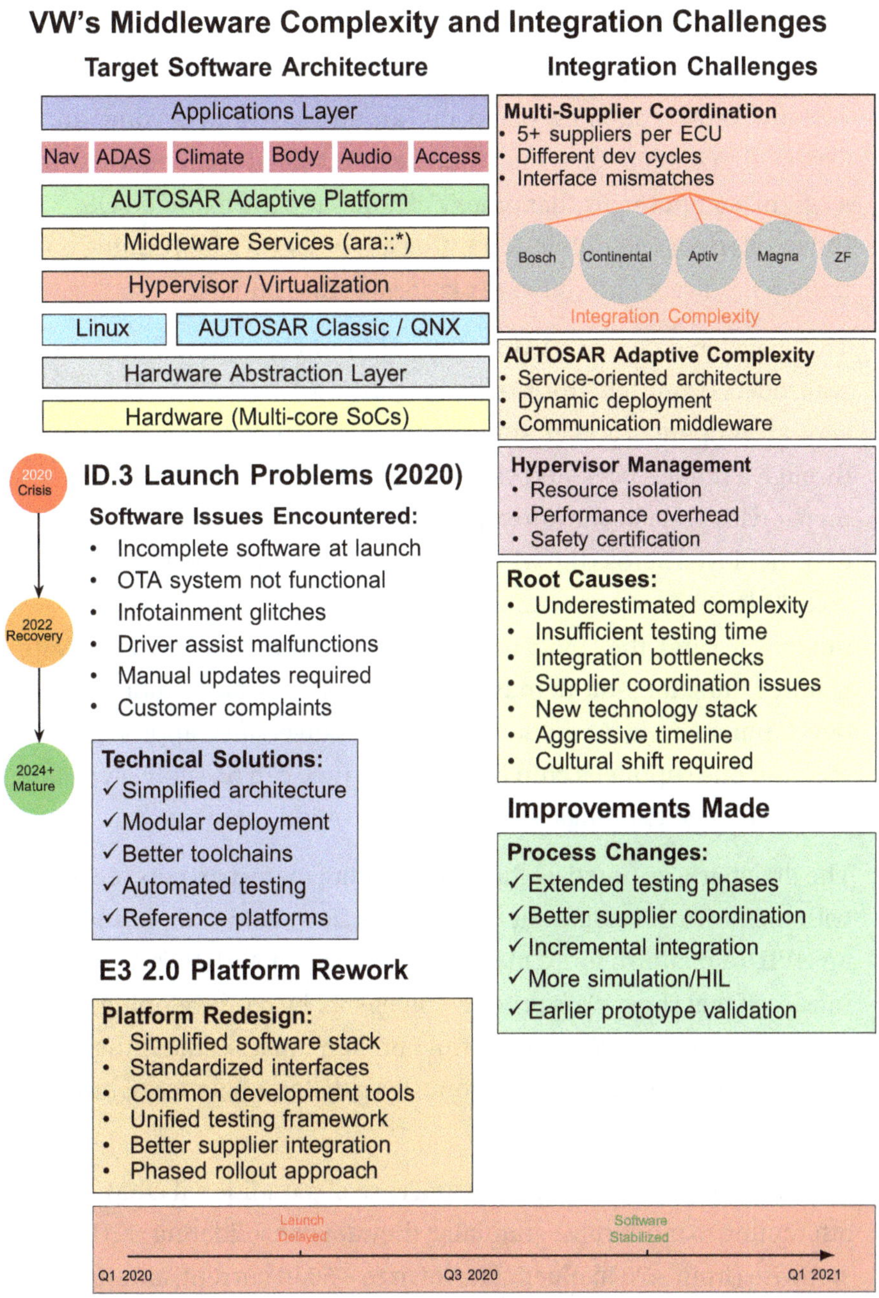

Figure 6-18. *Illustrative sources of software integration complexity during a transition from distributed ECUs to shared compute platforms*

- **Current status:**

  Volkswagen is still committed to the transition. The upcoming "Trinity" project and new platforms (around 2026 and beyond) are expected to implement a more fully realized zonal architecture with a central computer. By that time, VW hopes to have a unified OS (often referred to in public communications as VW.OS) running on a unified hardware and software platform across brands.

  The goal would be that a VW Group car would have, say, four zone controllers (front-left, front-right, rear, central) plus one to two central computers, and all software updates can be delivered OTA through a unified back-end cloud platform. This would put them on par with Tesla in software update capability and allow features to be deployed across the whole group. The benefits VW is chasing include lower hardware variant costs (common modules across millions of cars), the ability to introduce revenue-generating software features (functions-on-demand (FoD) and so on), and a more agile development cycle. At the same time, VW's diversified approach means if one supplier's chip has an issue, they can possibly pivot, and they aren't tied to a single source for innovation.

  The drawback, as noted, is that coordinating many partners (each with their own development timelines) is slow. For example, using an NVIDIA platform for ADAS means waiting for NVIDIA's next chip release; if that slips, VW's product might slip. By co-developing their own chip with ST, VW gains control but then must shoulder the software development largely alone. It's a delicate balance of buy vs. build.

  In summary, VW's zonal strategy is a case of a traditional OEM attempting to modernize gradually: they are consolidating ECUs stepwise (from ~70 in older cars down to ~50 in current, aiming for ~30 or fewer in future) [190] and learning to become system integrators of software. The middleware complexity remains the critical challenge—a lesson for any OEM making this transition. As one industry observer put it, "Volkswagen's CARIAD needed to not only build the car software but also transform the company's culture," which is a monumental task. The ongoing effort underscores that technology change must be met with organizational change.

In comparing Tesla and VW: Tesla took a "high risk, high reward" path by leaping to central compute with in-house development, whereas VW is taking a more incremental and partnership-based path to zonal architectures. Both ultimately aim for a similar endpoint (software-defined, updatable cars), but their journeys reflect their starting points—a tech disruptor vs. an established giant.

6.6 Digital-First Modularity

One recurring theme in modern E/E architecture is that hardware changes alone won't yield full benefits without a "digital-first" approach to the vehicle's lifecycle. Whether an OEM chooses zonal or central architectures, they need to pair it with software development practices and business models that take advantage of the new flexibility. This section discusses how digital-first thinking and modular software go hand in hand with zonal/central designs:

- **Virtual ECUs and containerized services:**

  In a software-defined vehicle, the idea is that many functions of the car are essentially apps or services running on common compute resources. Zonal controllers and HPCs provide a natural host for these virtual ECUs (vECUs)—software equivalents of what used to be standalone ECUs. During development, engineers can simulate vECUs on a computer (using virtual machines or Docker-style containers) to test functionality long before actual hardware is available [196].

  In a vehicle with a powerful zonal controller, one might literally run multiple vECUs as separate processes or virtual machines on that single controller. For example, instead of a physical ECU for seat heating and a separate one for window lift and another for mirror control (each with its own microcontroller), a zonal computer can run a seat heating service, a window control service, and a mirror control service, all in software, isolated but sharing the same CPU. These could even be developed by different teams or suppliers and then deployed together.

Using technologies like containers or hypervisors, the software can be sandboxed so that an update to the mirror control service doesn't break the seat heater and others, similar to how apps on your phone are separated. This modularity in software allows faster updates and upgrades. For instance, if an AI-based climate control algorithm is developed, it could be rolled out as a software update to the zone controller managing the HVAC without changing any hardware. The zonal architecture thus blurs the line between an ECU and an application—what was once fixed in firmware on a dedicated ECU can become just one of many apps on a zone computer.

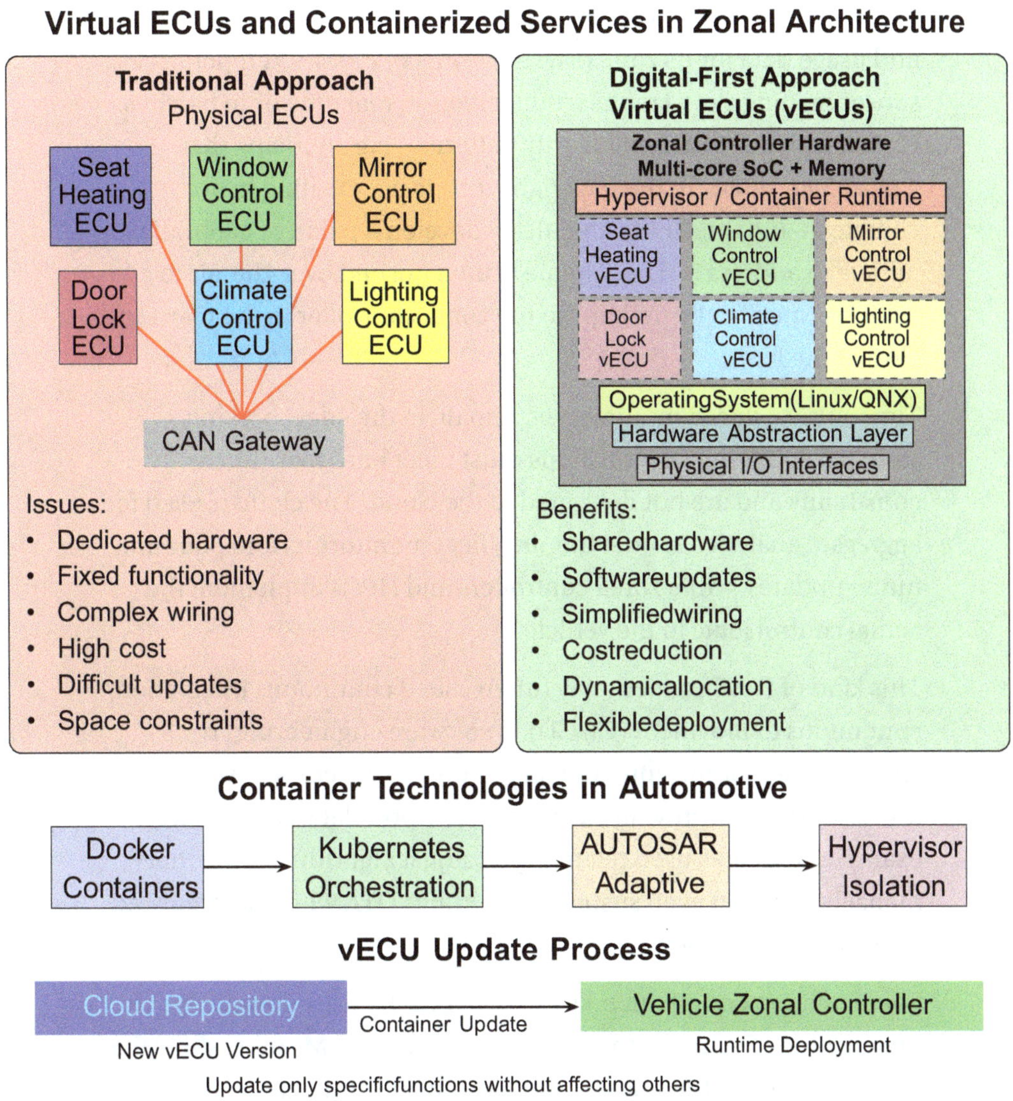

***Figure 6-19.** Virtual ECUs and containerized services in zonal architecture*

- **Continuous feedback loop (telemetry ➤ cloud ➤ OTA):**

  A hallmark of digital-first vehicles is that they continuously collect data (telemetry) from onboard systems, upload it to cloud servers for analysis, and then use the insights to provide OTA updates that improve the product. Zonal and central architectures greatly facilitate this because they concentrate data streams.

Each zonal controller can act as a data hub, sending diagnostics and usage data for its zone (say, the status of motors, temperatures, sensor readings, etc.) to the cloud, either in real time or in batches. Cloud analytics can then identify patterns—e.g., noticing that a particular motor in the rear-right zone is overheating in hot climates—and the OEM can quickly develop a patch or calibration update to address it. That update is then pushed over-the-air to all vehicles, specifically perhaps to the zonal controller in the rear-right, closing the loop.

Time-critical decisions, however, remain at the edge: braking, steering, and other control loops must meet hard real-time constraints and are not delegated to the cloud. The cloud is used for aggregate analytics, model training, fleet monitoring, and planning future updates, while zonal controllers and HPCs implement the actual control logic in the vehicle.

This kind of DevOps mentality (often called continuous integration/continuous deployment (CI/CD) in software engineering) is revolutionary for the auto industry. It means the car is never static; it's continually improving based on real-world data. As a concrete example, Tesla has used telemetry to adjust algorithms for battery management and even suspension settings OTA when data showed room for improvement.

For regulatory compliance, such as UNECE R156 (Software Update Management Systems), this loop is essential—OEMs must show they can safely and systematically update software and handle any issues. A vehicle that can report its software versions and health status zone-by-zone can help an OEM remain compliant with R156 by having a clear inventory and control of software in the fleet [196]. In summary, the zonal architecture provides an efficient pipeline for data to go up and software to come down.

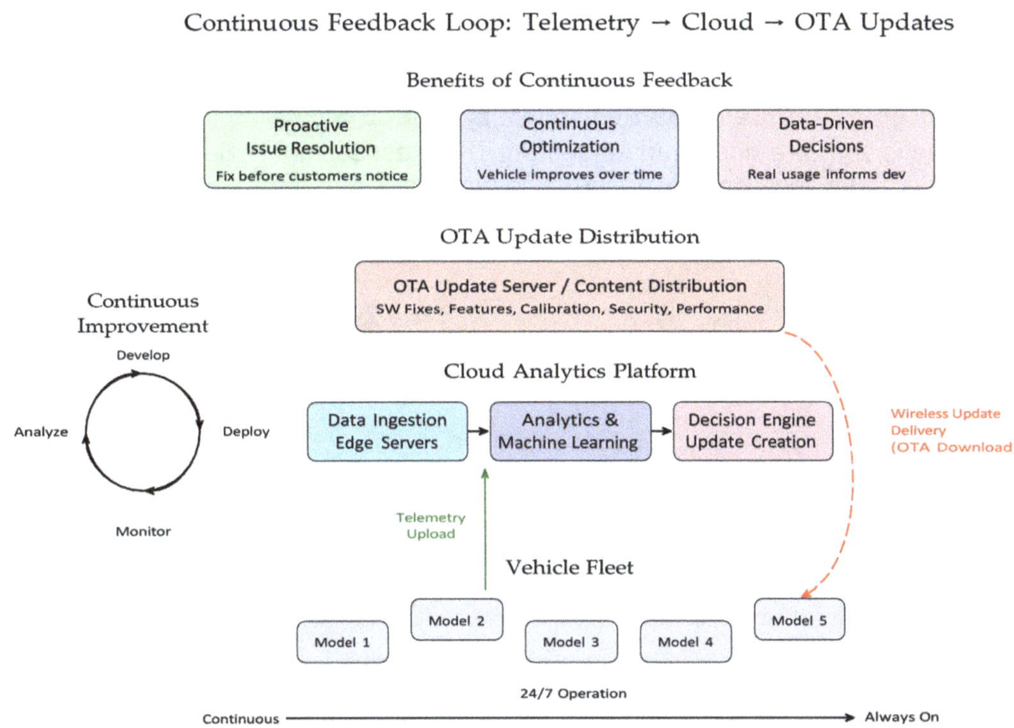

***Figure 6-20.** Continuous feedback loop: telemetry to cloud to OTA updates*

- **SUMS compliance:**

  UNECE R156 defines a software update management process, not a preferred hardware topology. SUMS compliance depends on having controlled processes for risk assessment, validation, secure distribution, installation control, logging, rollback or recovery, and evidence generation regardless of whether the vehicle uses domain, zonal, hybrid, or centralized electronics.

  Consolidated architectures can still be advantageous in practice because they may reduce the number of major execution targets and make coordinated updates easier to orchestrate. But that is an implementation convenience, not the definition of SUMS itself. The compliance requirement remains process-driven: the OEM must be able to show that updates are managed systematically, securely, and recoverably across the lifecycle.

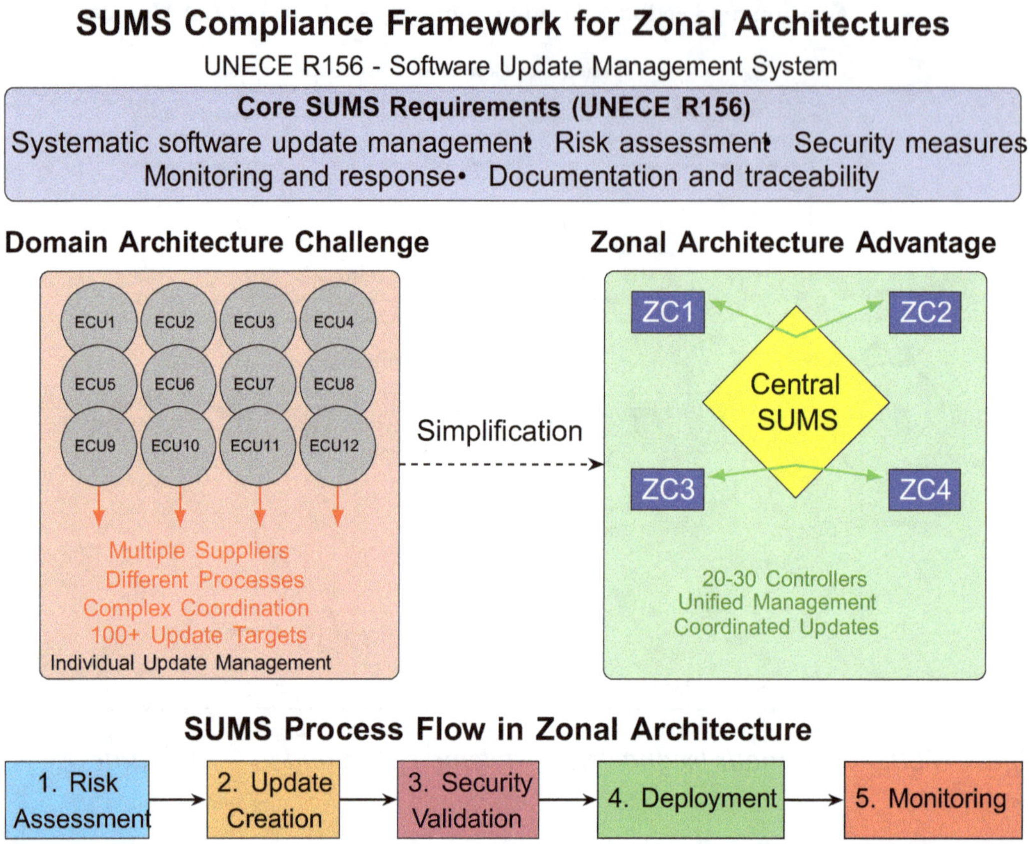

Figure 6-21. *Relationship between SUMS process requirements and update orchestration in consolidated architectures*

- **Security implications of consolidation:**

  Centralized and zonal architectures increase the impact of any security breach: compromising one zonal controller or central HPC can affect many functions at once. To manage this, modern designs rely on secure boot chains (from hardware root of trust up through bootloaders and OS), hardware security modules (HSMs) in zonal controllers and HPCs, strong isolation between security domains (e.g., separating externally connected services from safety-critical control loops), and authenticated, encrypted OTA mechanisms. Regulations such as UNECE R155 and ISO/SAE 21434 formalize these expectations; security architecture must therefore be considered alongside safety and performance from the earliest E/E design stages.

- **Lifecycle and CI/CD:** A key lesson from recent programs is that changing hardware topology without changing software processes yields only partial gains. Moving from 100 ECUs to a handful of zonal controllers does reduce harness weight and assembly complexity, but if software is still developed in long waterfall cycles with minimal post-SOP updates, the OEM captures only the "cost" side of the SDV equation and very little of the "value" side.

  A digital-first approach treats the car as a continuously evolving software product, but within automotive-specific constraints. That means investing in virtual ECUs, SIL/HIL validation, safety and cybersecurity evidence generation, controlled OTA pipelines, and telemetry-driven analytics rather than simply copying consumer-internet DevOps practices. New features and calibrations may still be delivered incrementally, but only within a framework of regression testing, release governance, homologation awareness, and rollback readiness. Regulations such as UNECE R156 and R155 reinforce this discipline by requiring systematic update and cybersecurity control across the lifecycle.

  In consolidated architectures, validation complexity grows sharply: a single zonal controller or HPC may host dozens of functions from multiple suppliers, so any change can interact with many others. Large-scale SIL/HIL farms, scenario-based testing, and automated regression suites are needed to exercise the most important combinations before every OTA release. Virtual ECUs are valuable here, but at some point behavior must be confirmed on real hardware under realistic loads to catch integration and performance issues.

  Zonal and central architectures are powerful enablers for this lifecycle because they centralize update points and data flows. But they are enablers, not guarantees: without CI/CD and strong software governance, a zonal architecture risks delivering mainly wiring and assembly savings—cheaper to build, but still slow to evolve and fragile in the field.

Beyond individual OEM efforts, several industry initiatives are attempting to standardize elements of this software stack. Frameworks such as SOAFEE (Scalable Open Architecture for Embedded Edge) and projects under the Eclipse SDV umbrella aim to bring cloud-native development patterns, containerization, and common middleware abstractions into the automotive world. While still evolving, these efforts are an important signal that zonal and central architectures are not being tackled in isolation by each OEM, but increasingly in a shared ecosystem.

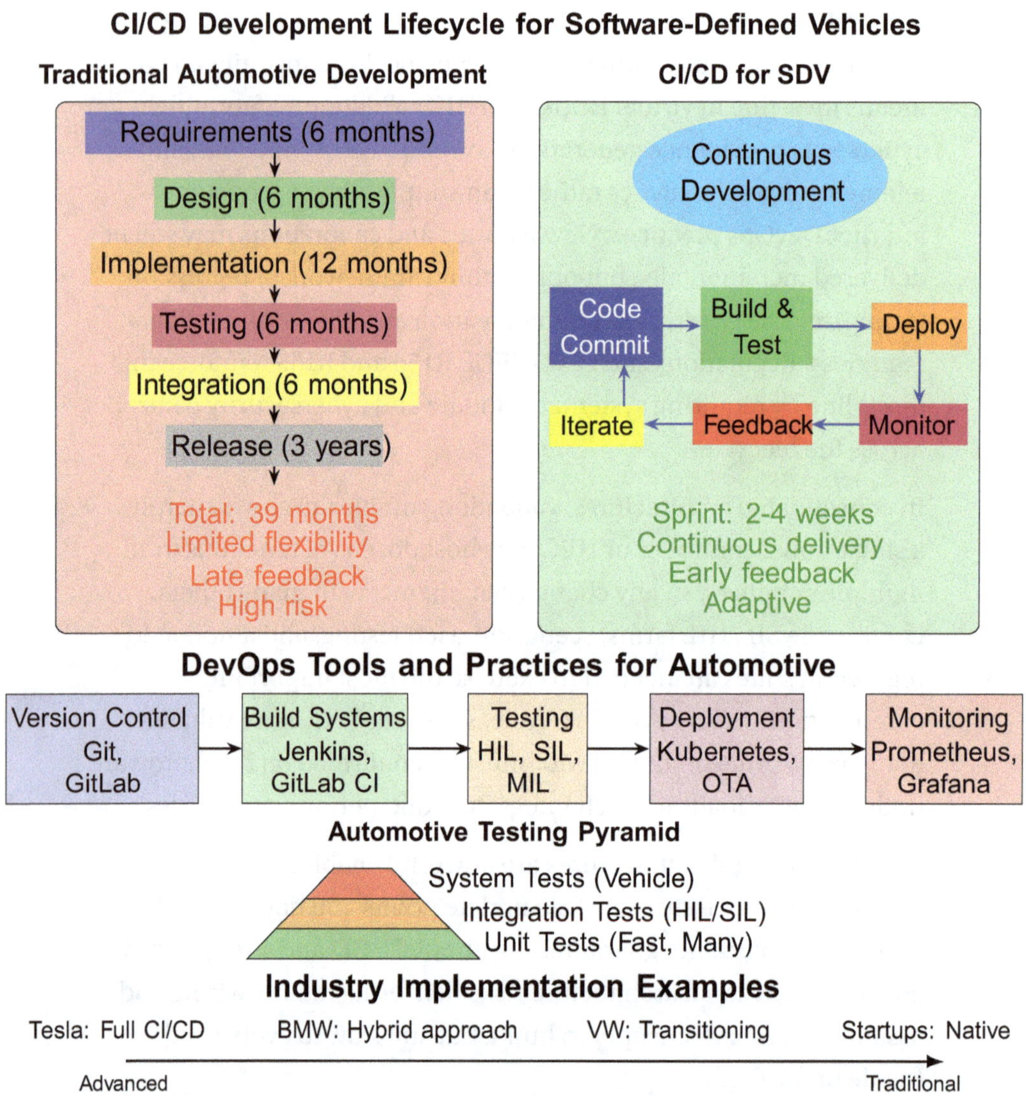

Figure 6-22. *CI/CD lifecycle for SDVs, emphasizing automotive-specific validation, safety, cybersecurity, and release constraints*

Critic's Note Zonal is only valuable if paired with digital-first lifecycles. Without CI/CD, zonal is just "domain with fewer wires."

In summary, digital-first modularity means designing the vehicle so that it can evolve. Zonal and centralized architectures provide the canvas for that evolution by simplifying the hardware layout and concentrating compute resources. On that canvas, automakers must paint an evolving picture—continuous updates, data-driven improvements, and a software ecosystem that can grow over time. Those that master this will deliver vehicles that actually improve with age, a concept that flips the traditional depreciation model on its head.

6.7 Key Takeaways

- **E/E architecture evolution—domain ➤ zonal ➤ central:**

  Each step in this evolution generally increases consolidation of functions, although many production programs land on hybrids rather than a pure "end state." Domain architectures had 100+ separate ECUs for specific tasks. Zonal architectures group those tasks into maybe a dozen powerful zone controllers. Centralized architectures go further, potentially using only a few supercomputers for the whole car. The trend is toward fewer, more powerful computing units running more software [190]. This consolidation is driven by the need to reduce complexity and enable the vehicle to be software-defined (updated and repurposed via code) [190]. However, higher consolidation also means new challenges in ensuring reliability and safety.

- **Architectural and cost implications:**

  Zonal and centralized architectures are attractive primarily because they support software scalability, compute consolidation, and faster lifecycle updates. Harness simplification is a real secondary benefit, since local I/O aggregation can reduce some wiring mass, material cost, and assembly effort [193], but the stronger motivation is to create a platform that can support shared compute resources, coordinated OTA updates, and cross-domain feature deployment. The cost trade-off is therefore not simply "less wiring equals cheaper vehicle"; rather, cost shifts from distributed hardware and harness complexity toward higher-performance silicon, middleware, validation, cybersecurity, and lifecycle software operations.

- **Performance and feature trade-offs:**

  Zonal and central architectures enable high-bandwidth data sharing (e.g., a central computer can instantly use camera data from anywhere on the car, since it's all networked). This is great for performance of features like ADAS—sensor fusion is easier when data is centralized. Also, OTA updates are most effective in a centralized architecture, where the OEM can update many features at once across the fleet [191].

  As an order-of-magnitude guide, modern ADAS/automated driving stacks may consume tens to hundreds of Tera Operations Per Second (TOPS) on the central compute, aggregate multi-gigabit per second camera and radar bandwidth across the vehicle, and rely on backbone latencies in the sub-millisecond range for time-critical traffic. These figures are highly program-dependent, but they illustrate why centralized, high-bandwidth architectures are attractive for advanced features.

  However, the risks include that if something fails, it can take down multiple features at once. For example, in a domain architecture, an infotainment crash doesn't affect engine control; but in a centralized system, a software fault might affect several functions unless properly isolated. Thus, safety considerations like redundant processing, fail-safe modes, and strict software isolation are critical in consolidated architectures.

- **Real-world approaches—Tesla vs. VW:**

  Tesla adopted a central compute, OTA-first strategy. They designed custom hardware and wrote most software in-house, resulting in a very integrated system that allowed them to push updates continuously and add capabilities (the quintessential SDV approach). The reward was a tech advantage and simplified electronics (only a few ECUs) [189], but the risk was high (they assumed full responsibility for any failures and had to build up software competency from scratch).

Volkswagen, by contrast, is moving more incrementally via zonal architecture. They started by consolidating ECUs into a few domain controllers and are progressing toward zones with a central brain. VW leverages traditional suppliers and new partners to get there, which spreads risk and cost, but it also led to coordination problems and software delays (as seen with ID.3's software issues) [195]. Their approach shows the challenge of integrating new architectures in a legacy company—it's as much about changing processes as it is about changing hardware. There's no one-size-fits-all; each OEM must navigate its own legacy and strengths.

- **"Digital-first" is essential:**

  Simply redesigning the E/E architecture isn't enough. To truly benefit from zonal or central hardware, an OEM must adopt a digital-first lifecycle—meaning agile development, continuous integration, strong DevOps pipeline, and treating the car's software like a constantly improving product. Without these, a zonal architecture might just end up being "a domain architecture with fewer wires" as the critic quip says—you'd get some cost savings, but not the full value of faster feature velocity and post-sale revenue opportunities.

  In essence, the organizational and process change must accompany the technical change. OEMs need to invest in software platforms (middleware, OTA infrastructure, cybersecurity) and in teams that can rapidly develop and validate updates. Those that do will unlock the true promise of the software-defined vehicle—a car that can evolve and adapt long after it leaves the factory.

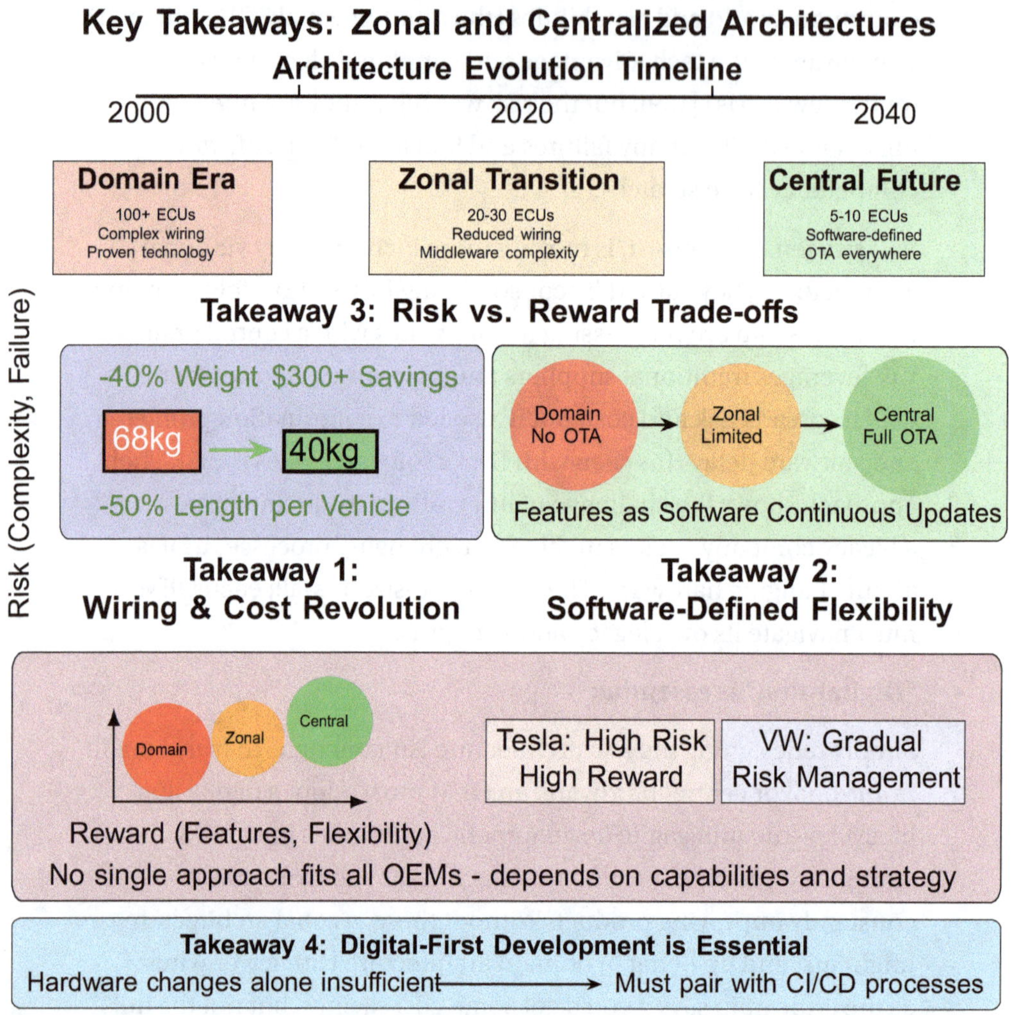

Figure 6-23. *Summary of key takeaways from zonal and centralized architectures*

CHAPTER 7

Cloud and Edge in Software-Defined Vehicles

7.1 Chapter Goals

After this chapter, you will be able to

- Explain the role of cloud, edge, and onboard compute in SDVs.
- Differentiate between OEM cloud platforms and hyperscaler partnerships.
- Understand Gaia-X and data sovereignty in Europe.
- Describe telco multi-access edge computing (MEC) for V2X and OTA.
- Evaluate OTA rollback, fleet management, and service monetization.

Critic's Note Cloud is not a dumping ground for "car data." It is the orchestrator of the SDV lifecycle: development, deployment, update, and monetization.

7.2 Introduction

The software-defined vehicle extends far beyond the metal and silicon within the car itself—it encompasses a distributed computing architecture spanning onboard processors, network edge infrastructure, and hyperscale cloud platforms. This chapter examines how cloud and edge computing enable the continuous evolution of vehicle capabilities through over-the-air updates, fleet-wide learning, and new service-based business models.

S. Agarwal, *Software-Defined Vehicles*, https://doi.org/10.1007/979-8-8688-2718-1_7

We begin by exploring the distinct roles that cloud infrastructure plays in SDV ecosystems: telemetry ingestion, digital twins, OTA orchestration, and AI training pipelines. The chapter then examines strategic choices OEMs face between building proprietary cloud platforms vs. partnering with hyperscalers and how European initiatives like Gaia-X and Catena-X address data sovereignty concerns.

Multi-access edge computing (MEC) receives detailed treatment as an enabler of low-latency V2X applications, bridging the gap between distant cloud data centers and real-time vehicle needs. The chapter also covers OTA update management with emphasis on reliability, rollback mechanisms, and regulatory compliance (UNECE R156, ISO 24089). Finally, we examine how connected car data pipelines create value and the emerging business models—from usage-based insurance to feature subscriptions—that cloud connectivity enables.

7.3 Cloud Roles in SDVs

Modern software-defined vehicles heavily leverage cloud infrastructure across their lifecycle. The cloud serves as the nerve center that connects vehicles, developers, and services in real time. Key roles of the cloud in SDVs include the following.

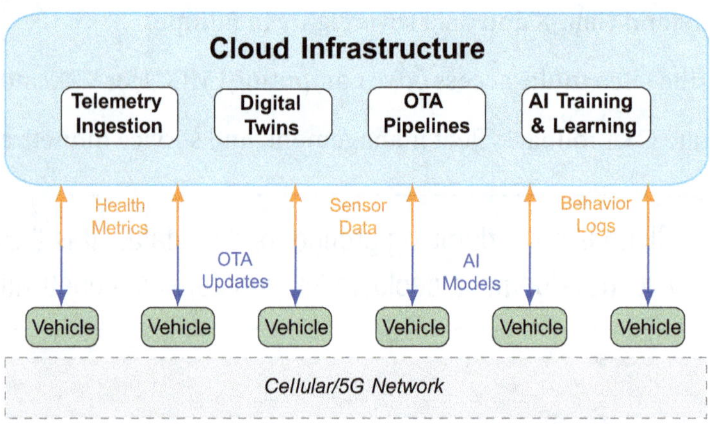

Figure 7-1. *Cloud roles in the software-defined vehicle ecosystem*

7.3.1 Telemetry Ingestion

Cloud back-ends aggregate streams of vehicle data—health metrics, sensor readings, and user behavior—from millions of cars in the field. For example, Toyota Connected uses AWS to power connected vehicle services and respond in seconds to driver emergencies, processing very large volumes of vehicle data across its fleet [197]. This massive telemetry ingestion allows continuous monitoring of vehicle fleets for anomalies, customer usage patterns, and preventative maintenance triggers.

7.3.2 Digital Twins

Cloud platforms maintain digital twins—virtual representations of vehicles or subsystems—to simulate and predict behavior. Engineers can evaluate software changes against these models before deploying them OTA to actual cars [198]. By mirroring a fleet's state in the cloud, OEMs can run large-scale what-if scenarios, safety validations, and performance optimizations without risking real vehicles.

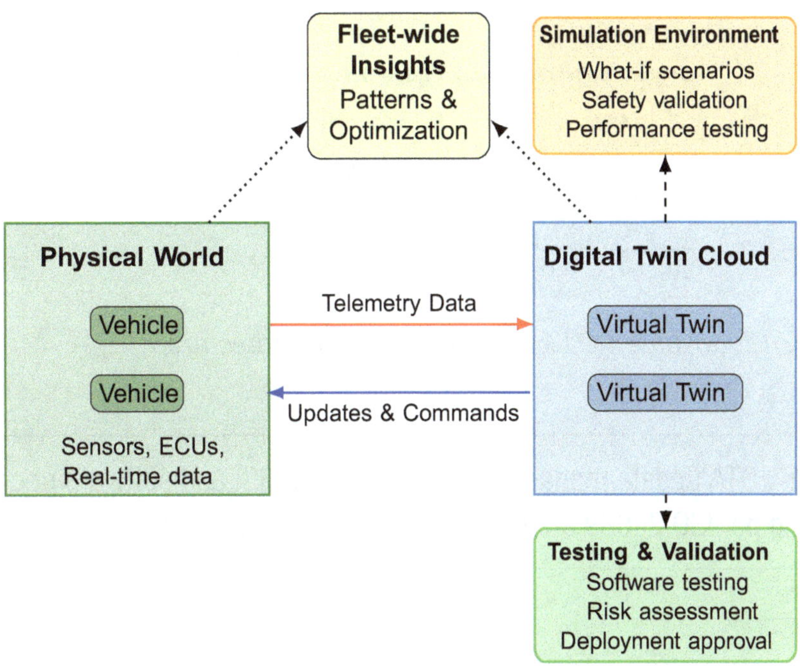

***Figure 7-2.** Digital twin architecture for vehicle fleet management*

7.3.3 OTA Pipelines

A core cloud role in SDVs is orchestration of over-the-air software updates. At a high level, the cloud manages update packaging, campaign scheduling, staged rollout, fleet status monitoring, and recovery actions such as campaign pause or rollback coordination. The detailed engineering of reliability, rollback, and compliance is discussed later in this chapter; the key point here is simply that OTA depends on a cloud back-end capable of securely coordinating updates across large fleets rather than treating each vehicle as an isolated endpoint [199].

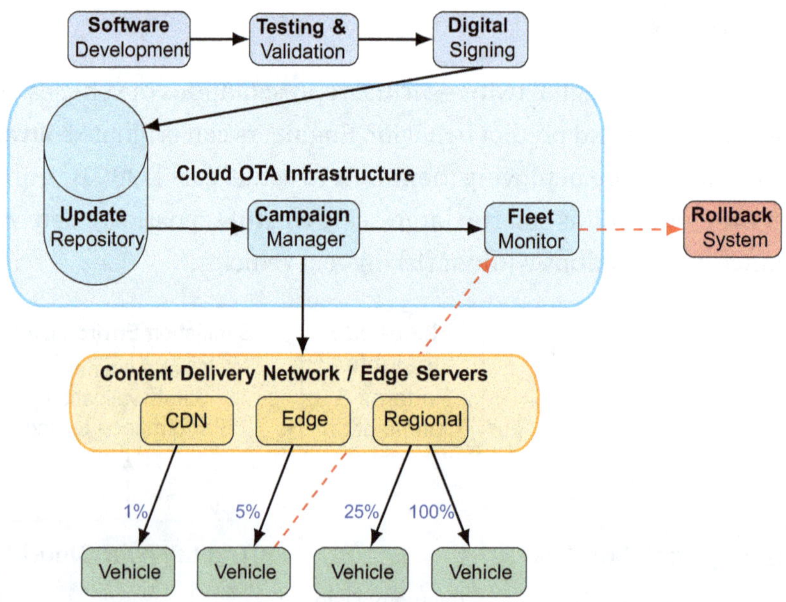

Figure 7-3. *Cloud-based OTA update pipeline architecture*

Key Point OTA update management systems (SUMS) and software update engineering per ISO 24089 are covered in detail in **Chapter 4**.

7.3.4 AI Training and Fleet Learning

The immense volume of data generated by vehicles (camera feeds, radar scans, driver behavior logs) cannot simply be streamed wholesale to the cloud in production—network cost, latency, and privacy constraints make that infeasible. Instead, OEMs define targeted collection policies so that only selected, often event-triggered slices of data are uploaded to cloud data lakes or training clusters.

For example, autonomous driving perception models or driver assistance algorithms are continuously improved by training on carefully curated real-world snippets in the cloud's GPU farms. When data sharing is enabled, Tesla states that certain vehicle data (including camera data) may be shared to improve features and describes learning from fleet data to enhance automated driving functions; other OEMs pursue similar fleet learning approaches. The cloud also enables federated learning (FL) concepts, where models are updated on-car and only aggregated parameter updates are collected centrally to balance privacy with improvement. In short, cloud AI farms turn a small but high-value fraction of fleet data into smarter software that is then sent back to cars as improved models.

Federated Learning for Privacy-Preserving Fleet Updates

Traditional fleet learning assumes that selected raw or preprocessed data is uploaded from vehicles to the cloud, where central training runs and updated models are pushed back OTA. Federated learning inverts part of this flow: model training steps run on the vehicle (or at the edge), and only model parameter updates or gradients are sent upstream. The cloud aggregates these updates from many vehicles to form an improved global model, without ever collecting the underlying raw data.

This approach can reduce backhaul bandwidth and mitigate some privacy concerns, because sensitive raw sensor data (e.g., in-cabin video or detailed location traces) never leaves the vehicle. However, it introduces its own challenges: heterogeneous hardware and connectivity, non-IID data distributions across the fleet, and the need to secure model updates themselves against poisoning attacks. As of today, automotive federated learning is mostly in pilot and research stages, but it is a promising technique to reconcile the desire for fleet-level learning with stricter data protection expectations.

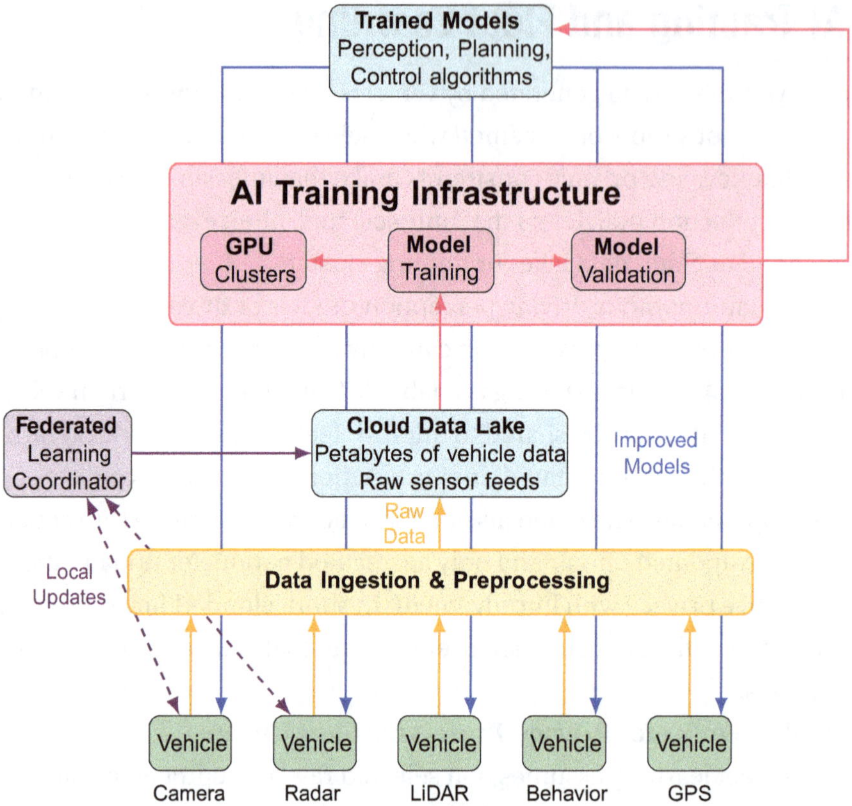

Figure 7-4. *Fleet learning and AI training pipeline*

These roles illustrate that the cloud is far more than storage; it acts as the coordination and orchestration hub for an SDV fleet at the back-end and fleet level, while real-time safety decisions remain on in-vehicle compute. Cloud systems oversee the entire software lifecycle—from development pipelines and simulation to live deployment, monitoring, and monetization of features.

Key Point For detailed coverage of federated learning architectures, privacy-preserving AI, and edge inference optimization, see **Chapter 8**.

7.4 OEM vs. Hyperscaler Cloud Strategies

Automakers face a strategic choice in how they implement cloud services for their connected vehicles. Some have built OEM-owned cloud platforms, while others partner with hyperscale cloud providers (or adopt a hybrid of both approaches).

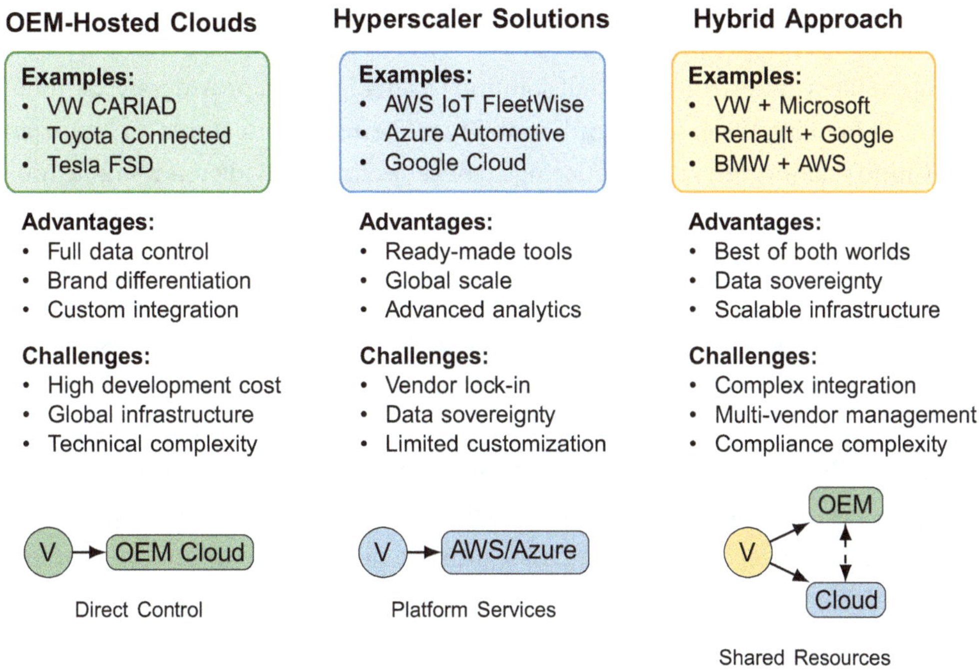

Figure 7-5. *Comparison of OEM vs. hyperscaler cloud strategies*

7.4.1 OEM-Hosted Clouds

In this model, the automaker develops and controls its own cloud platform (often still running on hyperscaler infrastructure under the hood, but fully branded and managed by the OEM). Examples include Volkswagen Group's CARIAD platform and Toyota's Toyota Connected services. These setups give the carmaker full control over data and direct customer relationships.

For instance, Volkswagen's CARIAD built a unified cloud for VW Group vehicles by collaborating with Microsoft Azure for underlying infrastructure [200]. Toyota Connected likewise leverages AWS for scalability but operates as Toyota's proprietary Mobility Services Platform [197]. The advantage of OEM clouds is data sovereignty and customization: OEMs decide how data is used and ensure deep integration with their vehicles' design. However, building a global cloud backbone is complex and costly, which is why OEMs often still enlist hyperscalers behind the scenes for reliability and scale.

7.4.2 Hyperscaler-Provided Automotive Cloud

Some automakers choose off-the-shelf solutions from big cloud providers. Examples include AWS IoT FleetWise, Microsoft's mobility reference architectures on Azure, and Google Cloud's connected vehicle offerings. These services provide ready-made tools for ingesting vehicle telemetry, updating software, managing digital twins, etc., with the hyperscaler handling the heavy lifting of infrastructure.

An automaker can accelerate their back-end development by building on these services, although significant OEM-specific integration, data modeling, and security engineering are still required. The trade-off is that much of the data and value creation might reside in the hyperscaler's domain. Hyperscalers tout their global compute elasticity and advanced analytics—e.g., AWS's automotive services can quickly scale to handle spikes in data and use AI/ML models that benefit from Amazon's expertise. This route can accelerate deployment, but OEMs must be mindful of potential vendor lock-in and loss of direct control over data.

7.4.3 Hybrid Approach

Increasingly common is a hybrid strategy where the OEM retains ownership of data and key platforms but uses hyperscaler infrastructure for scalability. In Europe especially, the EU Data Act and broader data residency expectations push OEMs to ensure data sovereignty (ownership and control of data) while still benefiting from cloud technology.

In a hybrid model, an OEM might keep encryption keys and dictate where data is stored (to comply with local laws), but rely on, say, Azure or AWS for global data centers and AI services. This offers a balance: the agility and innovation of hyperscalers with the oversight of the OEM. For example, an automaker might use AWS's global server network and IoT services, but design the system such that all sensitive personal data is stored in an OEM-controlled repository (or domestic cloud) to meet sovereignty requirements [201].

Business Note OEMs are weighing "build vs. buy" for cloud capabilities. Some, like Tesla, built an end-to-end stack in-house. Others partner deeply: Volkswagen and Microsoft, Renault and Google, Toyota and AWS, etc. A key concern is maintaining brand differentiation and data control. The trend is toward partnerships where automakers keep a hold on customer data and experience, while hyperscalers provide the under-the-hood muscle. This combination can yield the best of both worlds if managed correctly.

7.5 Gaia-X and Data Sovereignty

As vehicle data becomes strategically important, European OEMs are increasingly concerned not only with cloud capability but also with who controls the data, where it is stored, and how easily it can be moved between providers. Gaia-X is best understood as a **federation model** rather than a single cloud platform. It aims to define common governance, interoperability, transparency, and portability rules so that data and services can be exchanged across multiple providers without forcing participants into a single vendor-controlled ecosystem [202, 203]. In automotive terms, the value of Gaia-X lies less in raw compute and more in providing a framework for sovereign control of connected vehicle data.

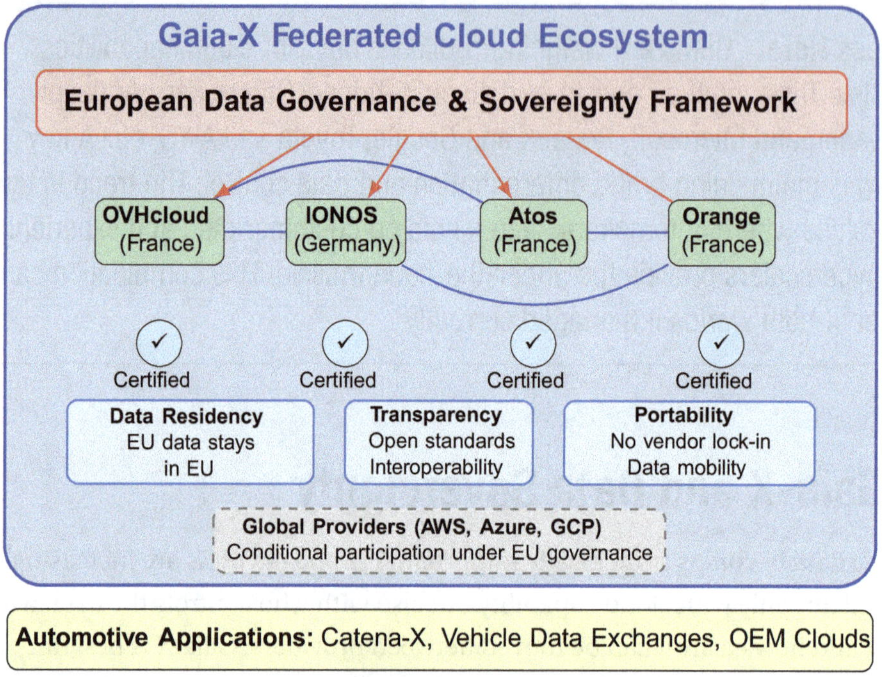

Figure 7-6. *Gaia-X as a federated governance framework for sovereign cloud and data exchange, rather than a single cloud provider*

In the automotive sector, Gaia-X has catalyzed projects like Catena-X, a collaborative data space for the European automotive industry [204]. Catena-X links OEMs, suppliers, and other stakeholders in a neutral platform where they can share data under agreed rules. For example, Catena-X includes major OEMs among its members; participants can contribute and consume manufacturing or vehicle data under sovereignty safeguards (each contributor controls access to its data) [205]. The goal is an interoperable network of automotive data and services that isn't entirely dependent on foreign cloud providers.

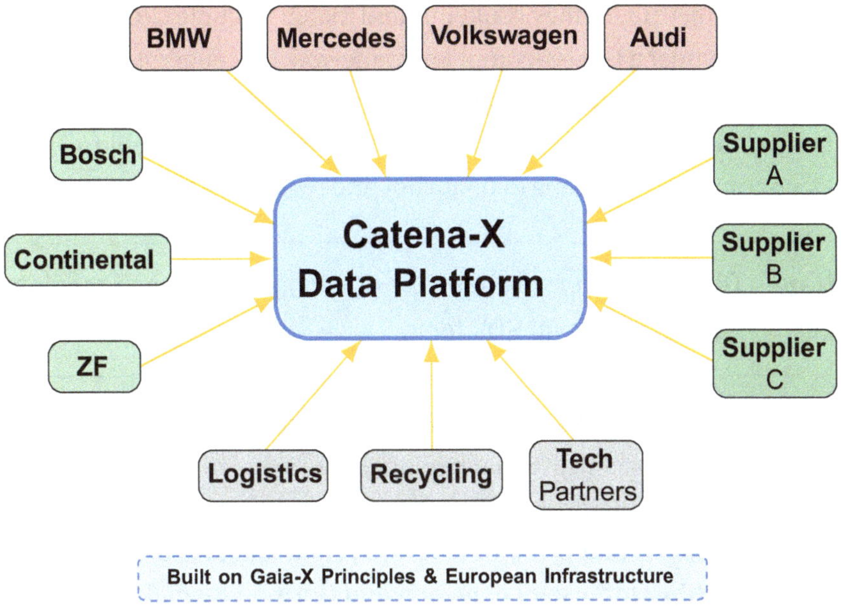

Figure 7-7. *Catena-X as a governed automotive data space in which participants contribute and consume specific datasets under controlled access rules.*

In practical terms, Catena-X is not just a list of participants connected to a shared platform. The intended flow is that each participant contributes selected datasets, e.g., manufacturing quality data, supply chain traceability records, battery information, or vehicle service data under controlled access policies. Other approved participants can then consume those datasets for defined use cases such as traceability, sustainability reporting, quality analysis, or cross-company process optimization. The architectural point is that the data remain governed by the contributor even while being made interoperable across the ecosystem [204, 205].

In practice, this might mean that data from vehicles sold in Europe is stored and processed on infrastructure operated under European governance, which can include Gaia-X-conformant services running on hyperscalers as long as they satisfy sovereignty and federation requirements, rather than defaulting to opaque, single-provider setups.

Gaia-X doesn't seek to replace hyperscalers on a technical level (it's not building physical data centers itself). Rather, it's creating an open architecture and set of rules so cloud services can be interconnected in a transparent way, with certifications for compliance to EU principles [203]. At the same time, analysts have criticized Gaia-X's governance and pace, even as sectoral projects like Catena-X show more tangible progress within the automotive domain.

For automakers, this means they could mix and match multiple cloud providers and on-premise systems, all under a Gaia-X-compliant framework that guarantees data sovereignty and portability. The initiative was spurred in part by concerns that without intervention, Europe's data (including car telemetry, user data from vehicles, etc.) would all funnel into a few foreign tech companies, creating dependency and regulatory risk [206].

Critic's Note OEMs ignoring sovereignty risk vendor lock-in and regulatory fines. Sovereignty is now a board-level SDV topic.

Indeed, new regulations (like the EU Data Act and GDPR) and industry pressure mean European OEMs must ensure that personal data from connected cars is handled according to EU laws and that they aren't completely beholden to outsiders for critical services. Gaia-X provides a blueprint for federated cloud collaboration. We see its influence in partnerships: for instance, French and German carmakers working with domestic IT providers (Orange, BMW's integration of SAP, etc.) under Gaia-X principles or efforts to define standard data schemas so that participants in the automotive value chain can exchange information seamlessly without ceding control [207].

In short, Gaia-X represents Europe's push to reclaim autonomy in the cloud. For SDVs, this means cloud and edge services that handle vehicle data will increasingly be expected to demonstrate data residency (e.g., EU car data stays in EU servers) and sovereign control (the automaker or user can dictate how and by whom data is used). Catena-X is a tangible example of this in automotive, creating a shared data infrastructure "by the industry, for the industry" under European governance [208]. Going forward, compliance with sovereignty requirements will be as important to SDV programs as technical performance or cost.

7.6 Edge and MEC (Multi-access Edge Computing)

While cloud data centers might be thousands of kilometers away, edge computing brings computation closer to the vehicle. Multi-access edge computing (MEC) refers to cloud-like resources hosted at the network's edge—e.g., in a cellular base station or regional data hub—to provide ultra-low latency and localized processing for connected devices (including cars). For software-defined vehicles, MEC can be a game-changer for certain time-critical and bandwidth-heavy applications.

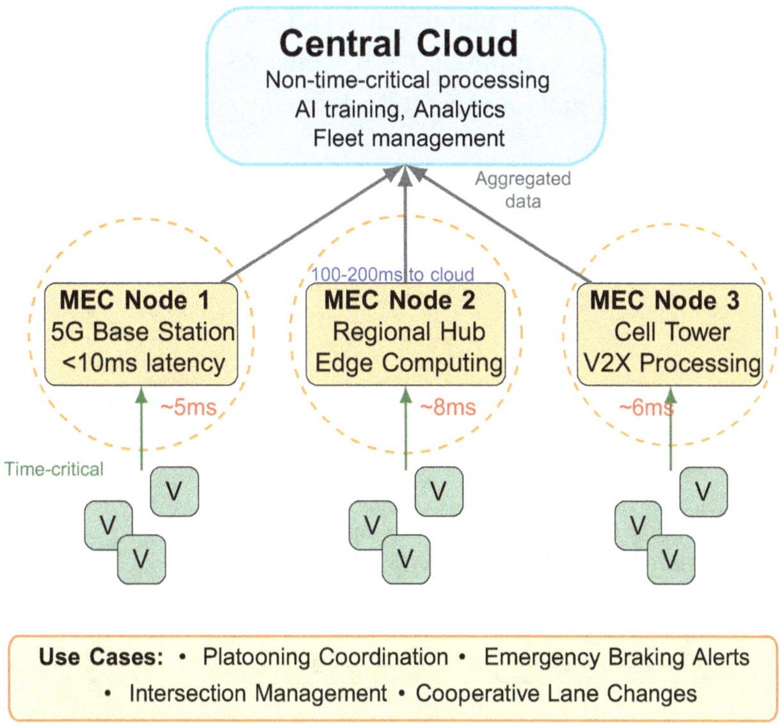

Figure 7-8. *MEC architecture for connected vehicles*

7.6.1 Latency Reduction

By processing data at an edge server just one or two network hops away from the vehicle, end-to-end latency can drop to single to low tens of milliseconds in well-engineered deployments [209]. This is crucial for V2X safety messages or cooperative driving.

For instance, if two cars are coordinating a platooning maneuver (tight formation driving), using a distant cloud 200 ms away might be too slow for real-time adjustments. An MEC node co-located with the 5G cell tower can assist with coordination within tight V2X latency budgets (single to low tens of milliseconds), *but safety-critical control loops must still be closed onboard so that the maneuver remains safe even if MEC connectivity is degraded or unavailable.*

Research in 5G automotive communications shows that edge servers can indeed cut latencies dramatically for vehicle communication, enabling scenarios like vehicles negotiating merges or hazard responses within a safer reaction time window [210]. It is important to note that such single- to low-tens-of-milliseconds figures are typically achieved in controlled lab or trial environments with good radio conditions and local break-out; real-world latency over public 4G/5G networks can be higher and more variable, so safety-critical functions must still tolerate degraded MEC performance.

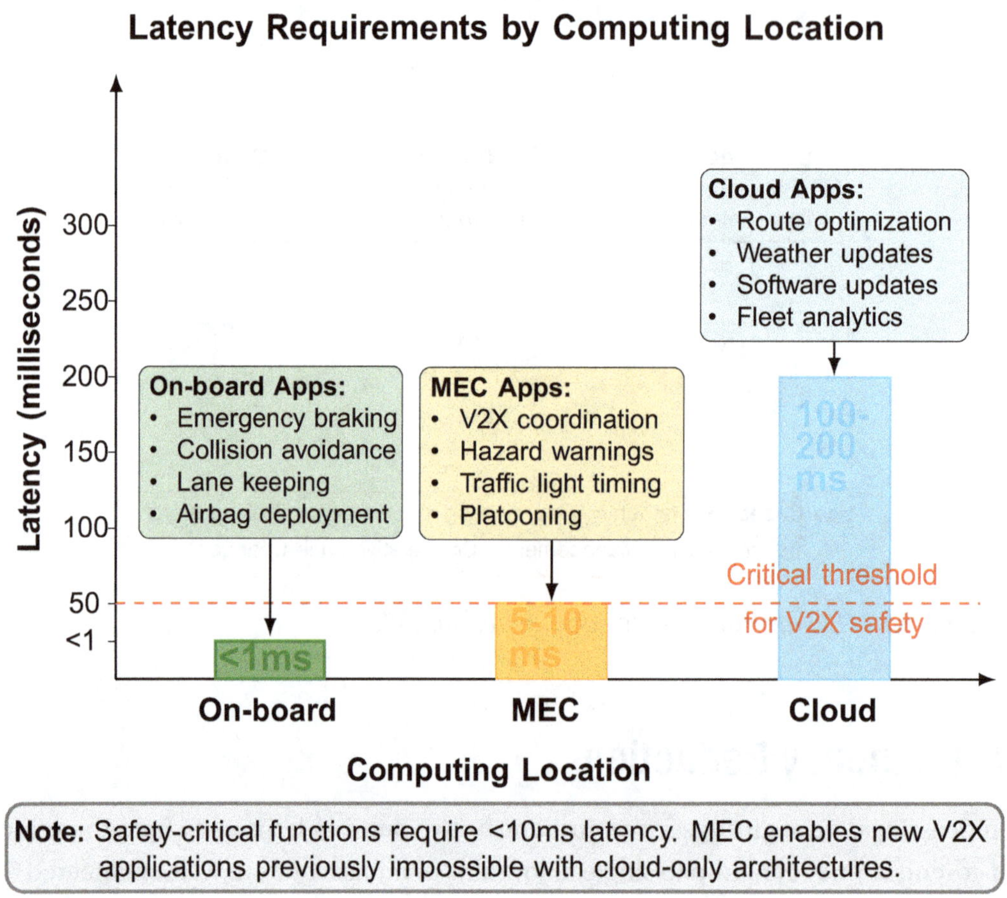

Figure 7-9. *Indicative latency ranges for onboard, MEC, and cloud processing. Actual performance depends strongly on deployment conditions and network design.*

7.6.2 Localized Data Processing

MEC is especially interesting for **localized cooperative perception**. Instead of each vehicle acting only on its own sensors, nearby vehicles can contribute selected observations to an edge node, which fuses them into a local situational view and redistributes relevant warnings or insights. For example, several cars approaching the same intersection may each contribute partial observations that, when combined at the edge, reveal a hazard not visible to any single vehicle alone. The practical value of MEC here is not replacing onboard perception, but extending local awareness for multi-vehicle scenarios where low-latency regional aggregation is useful.

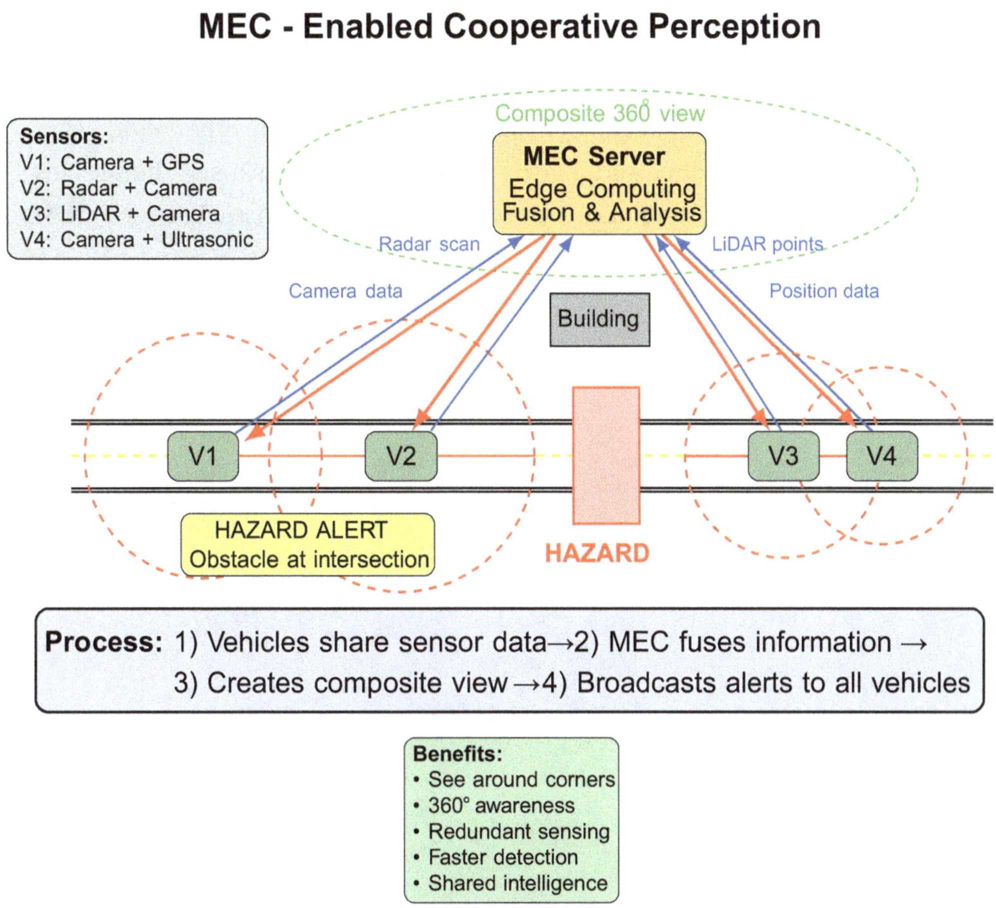

Figure 7-10. *MEC-enabled cooperative perception for connected vehicles*

7.6.3 Bandwidth Savings

Edge computing can drastically cut the bandwidth needed to send data to central cloud. As one telecom report put it, many automotive use cases involve large volumes of regional data that should be processed locally rather than "uploaded over the internet to cloud services"—otherwise, the network would be overwhelmed without added value [211]. MEC can preprocess or summarize data (e.g., performing AI inference on raw camera feeds to extract just the important events) and only send compact results to the cloud. This tiered approach relieves backhaul networks and cloud storage from the firehose of raw vehicle sensor data.

However, MEC also introduces a business question: who operates and monetizes these edge resources? Telecom providers (mobile network operators) see MEC as a way to add value and revenue beyond just selling SIM cards. They could offer "edge compute slots" or V2X services to automakers for a fee. Automakers, on the other hand, want to own the customer experience and may be hesitant to let telcos insert themselves between the car and the OEM's cloud. This has led to a bit of a tussle between OEMs and carriers over the control and billing of new edge-enabled services.

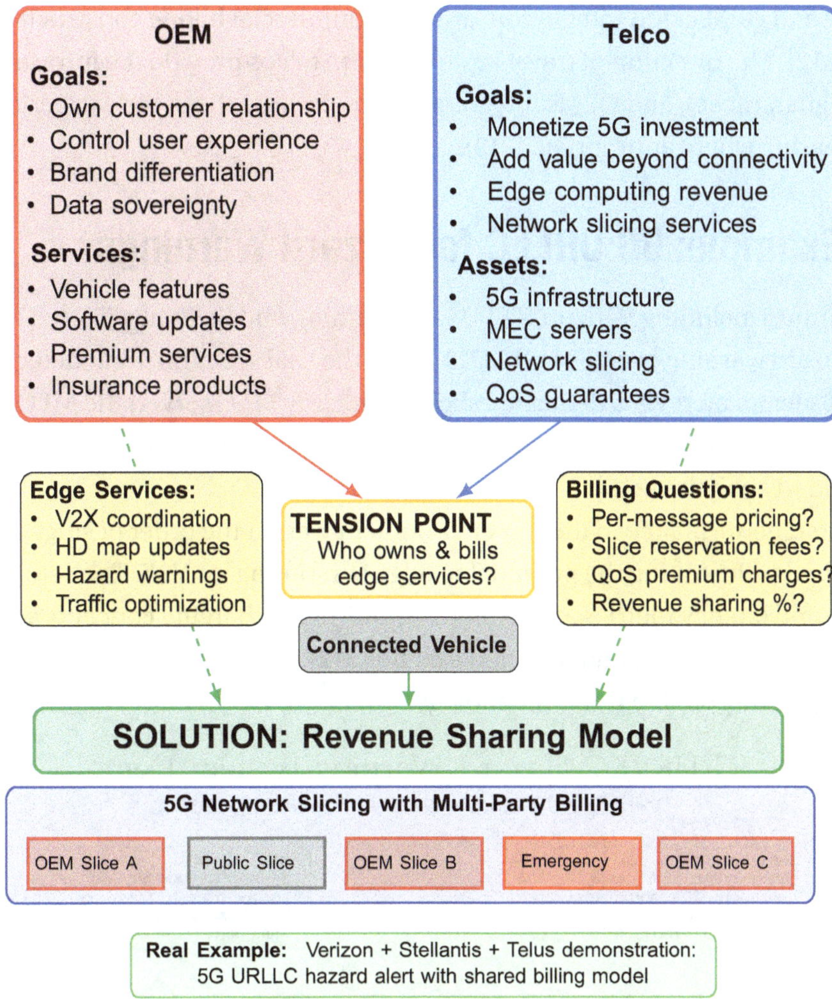

Figure 7-11. *Business model dynamics: OEM vs. telco at the edge*

7.6.4 Business Note: OEM vs. Telco at the Edge

OEMs want to retain customer ownership, while telcos want to monetize their network edge. The conflict comes down to who bills the fleet owner for low-latency, edge-enabled services (like collision warnings or HD map updates). A likely resolution is revenue sharing models. Standards and industry proposals describe slice resource isolation and multi-party charging, and operator trials (e.g., Verizon, TELUS, and Stellantis) have demonstrated feasibility for URLLC-class alerts with carrier MEC processing and OEM cloud integration; at-scale commercial billing constructs are still evolving [212]. The direction of travel is partnership: telcos provide the infrastructure (with QoS guarantees), and OEMs integrate the service into the vehicle experience—with revenue sharing where appropriate [213].

7.6.5 Example: 5G URLLC for Hazard Warnings

In 2021, a group including Verizon, TELUS, Capgemini, and Stellantis piloted MEC-assisted hazard warning over 5G URLLC [214]. In the trial scenario, a car detected road debris and sent an alert via a dedicated slice to a nearby MEC server; the MEC processed it in near real time and broadcast to other vehicles in the vicinity while also logging the event for cloud analytics [215].

Measured performance in the test environment was on the order of single to low tens of milliseconds, illustrating the potential of edge computing for V2X. The setup recorded slice usage and latency metrics and explored multi-party charging concepts across carriers, the MEC provider, and the OEM's cloud [212]. Such intricate models are new to automotive, made possible by 5G technology.

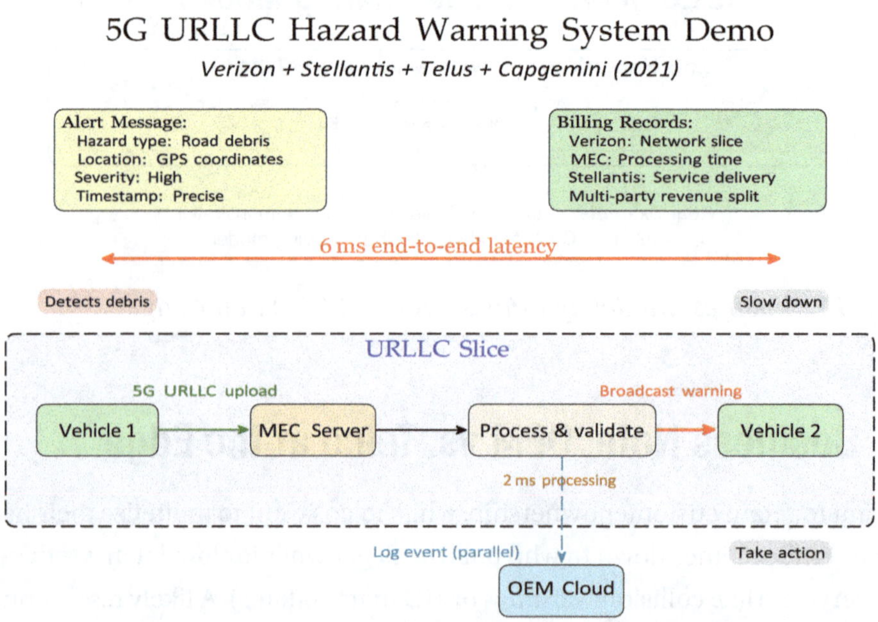

Figure 7-12. *5G URLLC hazard warning system: real-time MEC processing*

Key Point MEC brings cloud-like capabilities closer to the car and is a powerful *complement* to onboard compute, not a replacement. It is particularly well-suited for time-sensitive coordination across multiple vehicles (e.g., hazard aggregation, cooperative perception) and for offloading regional data processing to relieve backhaul networks.

As 5G coverage and MEC deployments expand, we can expect more production pilots around real-time HD map enrichment, intersection safety services, and fleet-oriented analytics, with more speculative AR/VR passenger experiences further out on the horizon. Technically, many of the building blocks (ETSI MEC standards, 5GAA trial architectures) are in place, but large-scale commercialization is still early: interoperability, roaming across operators, and viable revenue sharing models between automakers and telecom providers remain open issues.

As of the mid-2020s, most automotive MEC deployments remain trial- or pilot-scale rather than mass-market services, and many of the more ambitious visions from the 2018–2020 hype cycle have not yet materialized commercially. Distinguishing between proven patterns (e.g., limited hazard warning pilots, regional analytics) and more speculative use cases (e.g., fully MEC-orchestrated cooperative driving at scale) is essential when building realistic roadmaps.

The likely end state is a two-tier computing model in which onboard compute handles safety and core vehicle functions, MEC handles local multi-vehicle coordination and data reduction, and central cloud platforms take care of global analytics, AI training, and fleet-level orchestration.

7.7 OTA Update Management

One way to simplify OTA management is to view it as a five-stage lifecycle rather than as a stack of back-end modules. First, software is packaged, tested, and signed. Second, it is distributed through cloud and delivery infrastructure. Third, deployment is staged across the fleet in controlled waves. Fourth, telemetry is monitored to verify installation success and detect anomalies. Fifth, if health checks fail, the campaign is paused, and rollback or recovery logic is invoked. Security, compliance, and traceability matter throughout this lifecycle, but the core architectural idea is straightforward: safe OTA depends on controlled rollout plus reliable recovery, not just on moving files to vehicles.

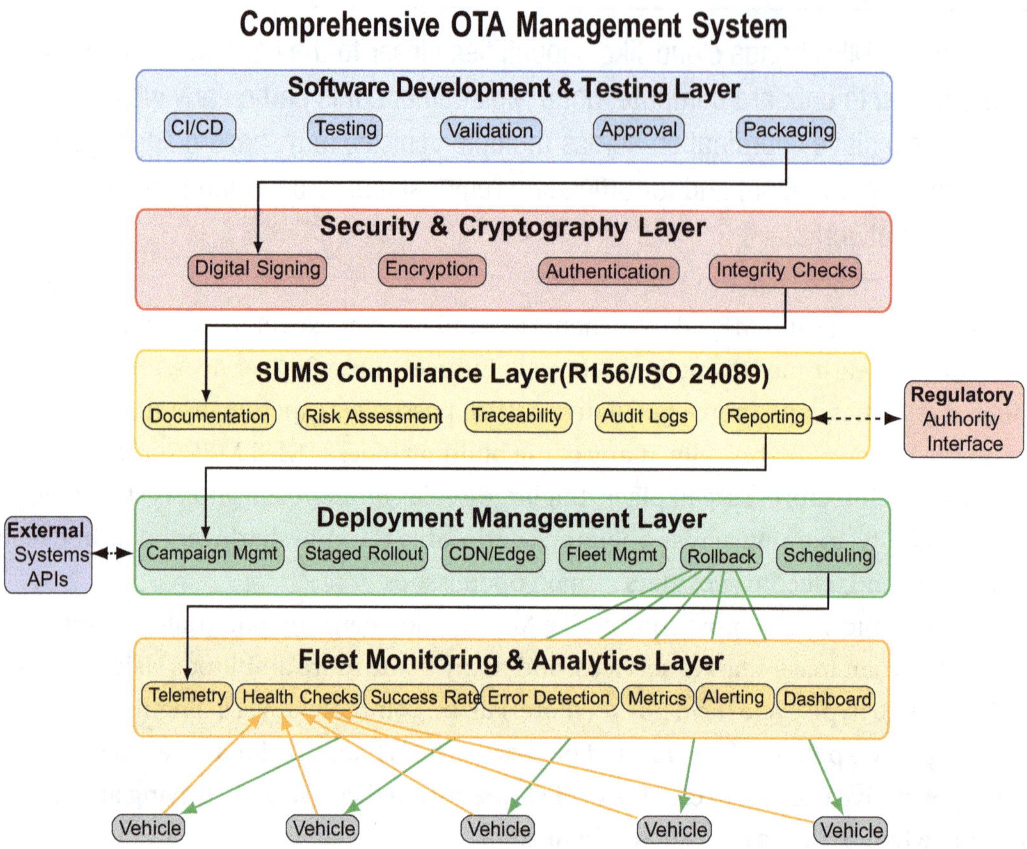

Figure 7-13. *Comprehensive OTA update management system architecture*

7.7.1 Reliability and Rollback

A robust OTA mechanism must ensure that vehicles are never bricked (left nonfunctional) by a bad update. Key practices to achieve reliability include

A/B partitions (dual-bank updates):

Modern vehicles (especially those running Linux-based OSs in the infotainment or central domain) often use dual-partition schemes for updates [216]. This means the system has two copies of the software: one active (current version) and one inactive. During an update, the new software is written to the inactive partition, while the car still runs on the active partition. Only after a successful download and verification does the vehicle switch to booting from the updated partition (now marked active).

If anything goes wrong—say a power loss during update or the new software fails a health check—the bootloader will revert to the old partition automatically [216]. This fail-safe boot design ensures there's always a known good software to fall back on. Automotive suppliers and open source projects (like Mender, Android's update system, etc.) strongly advocate A/B updates as a best practice for any mission-critical OTA [217]. While it requires more storage (essentially two copies of the software), this is considered a necessary trade-off for safety on rich compute nodes; smaller microcontrollers often rely on lighter-weight staged-update and rollback strategies because they cannot afford full A/B images.

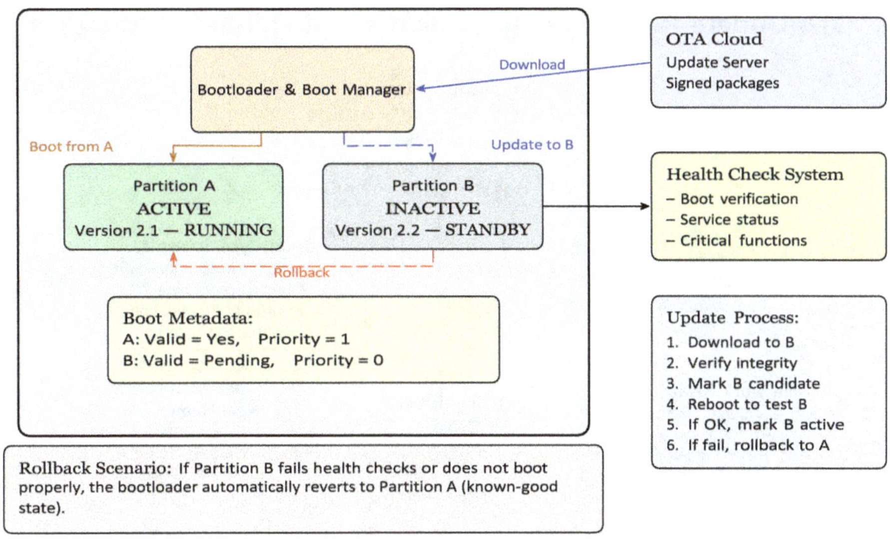

Figure 7-14. *A/B partition system for fail-safe OTA updates*

Incremental (delta) updates:

Pushing full software images to cars can mean gigabytes of data, which is inefficient and slow. Instead, OTA systems use binary diffs or incremental patches that only contain the changes from the previous version. This can reduce download size dramatically (sometimes by 90+%). Smaller updates not only save on bandwidth (a cost issue) but also lower the chance of failure (less data means a shorter update time and fewer opportunities for corruption). For example, Tesla's update packages for a given car model are often deltas from the last version, and Tier-1 software providers offer delta update tools as standard.

Resumption and robust delivery:

The system should handle interruptions gracefully. If connectivity is lost mid-update, the download should resume from the last verified chunk when reconnected (e.g., via HTTP range requests or equivalent), rather than restarting. Mature OTA systems also adapt transfer behavior to network conditions (e.g., pacing, compression, and prioritization) and pair this with delta payloads to keep downloads small. In practice, the cloud update service may start fast and then automatically throttle or retry with smaller chunks if packet loss is detected—ensuring the vehicle eventually obtains a complete, verified image without resorting to radio-layer modulation changes.

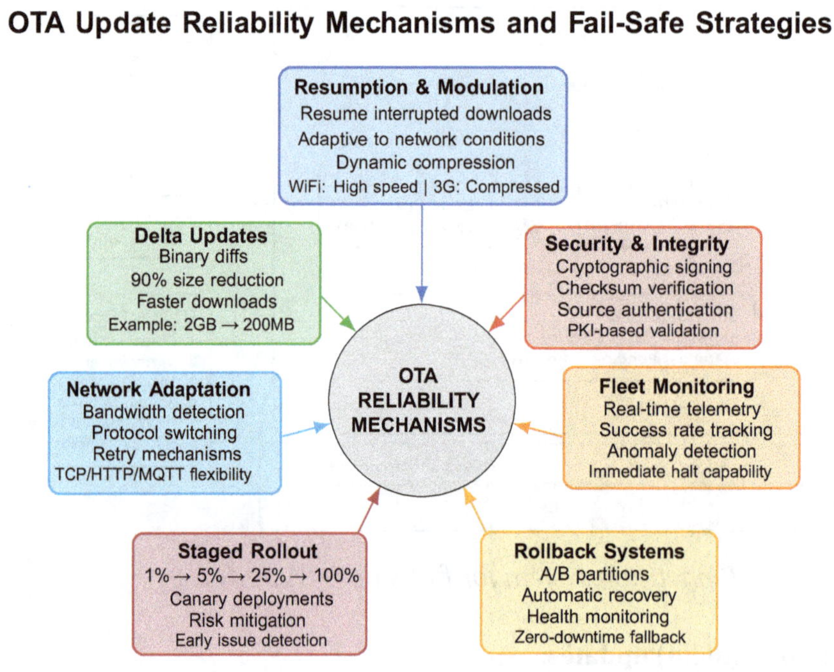

Figure 7-15. *OTA update reliability mechanisms and fail-safe strategies*

Integrity and security checks:

Reliability isn't just about successful delivery, but also making sure the update is correct and not tampered with. Each OTA package is typically signed with cryptographic keys. The vehicle verifies the signature before applying the update, ensuring it came from an authorized source (preventing malicious firmware). After installation, the system may do additional checks like verifying checksums of critical files, confirming that important services start correctly, etc., before marking the update as "successful." Only then does it delete the old software (if at all). If a critical check fails, the system rolls back. This process might be accompanied by a "safe mode" where a car with a failed update only starts minimal systems and signals the need for service or redownload.

Importantly, a robust OTA strategy also involves staged rollouts and monitoring. OEMs will often update a small percentage of the fleet (say 1% of vehicles of a given model) and then watch telemetry for any hiccups (crash reports, abnormal behavior). Only when an update is proven in the field do they ramp up to the rest of the fleet. If issues arise, an immediate rollback or fix can be issued before all cars are affected.

This prudent approach reflects the high stakes: among OTA practitioners it is widely accepted that operating without a robust rollback path is essentially malpractice, because brand damage from even a small bricked fraction of the fleet outweighs any gain in rollout speed. Staged rollouts let OEMs halt a campaign quickly if telemetry flags anomalies and roll back affected vehicles via the fail-safe path—limiting impact while an updated build is prepared.

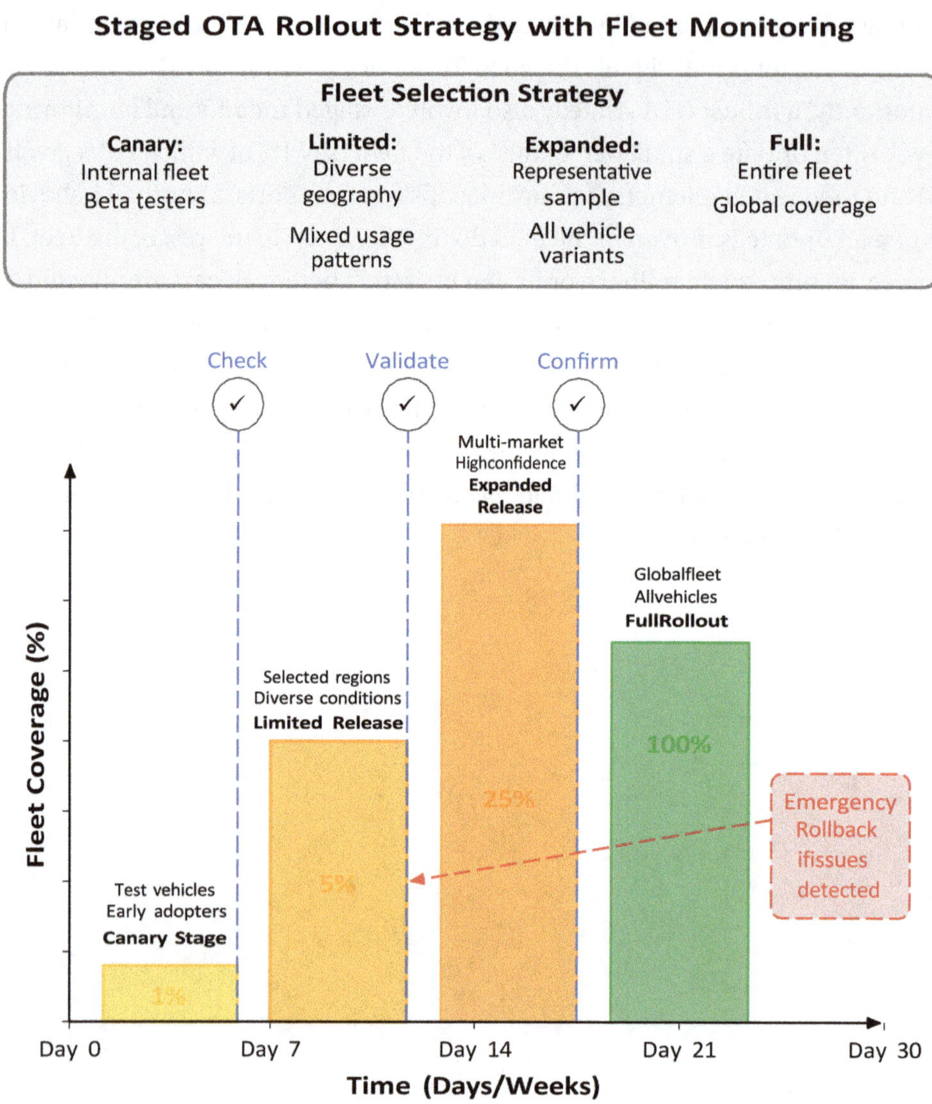

Figure 7-16. *Staged OTA rollout strategy with fleet monitoring*

7.7.2 SUMS Compliance

Beyond technical reliability, automakers must comply with new regulations governing software updates. UNECE WP.29 Regulation No. 156 (often shortened to R156) and the related ISO 24089 standard mandate that manufacturers implement a Software Update Management System (SUMS) for vehicles. In essence, this is a formalized process and set of requirements ensuring OTA updates are done safely and transparently.

Key aspects of SUMS compliance include [72]

Documentation and traceability:

R156 requires OEMs to have a documented process for every OTA update and to provide this documentation to regulatory authorities upon request [72]. This means an automaker must record each step of an update campaign—how the update was developed, tested, and validated, how it's delivered, and how issues are handled. Audit logs should show which vehicles received which software version, when, and with what result. Essentially, regulators want the ability to trace any safety or security issue post-update back through the pipeline to see how it was approved and rolled out.

Risk assessment and fallback planning:

The SUMS regulation expects manufacturers to assess the cybersecurity and safety risks of software updates in advance. For example, if an update affects braking software, the OEM must have conducted a safety analysis (in line with ISO 26262 perhaps) to ensure no unreasonable risk is introduced. They also need contingency plans—e.g., if an update is found to cause problems, how quickly can they inform drivers or roll it back? Regulators want proof that rollback mechanisms (like the A/B partition discussed) are in place and effective. Indeed, providing a robust fallback strategy (such as rollback or safe degradation) is effectively required; without evidence that the vehicle can recover from a failed update while remaining safe and compliant, an OEM would struggle to obtain or maintain type approval.

Security and access control:

Under R156 and its sister regulation R155 (cybersecurity management), the update process must be secure from end to end [69]. This includes authenticating update servers and vehicles, encrypting update files (or the channel) to prevent interception, and ensuring only authorized software (properly signed) can be installed. The cloud back-end should verify the identity of vehicles requesting updates, and vehicles should verify the source of updates—a mutual authentication.

Consumer transparency and consent:

Although not purely technical, compliance also involves informing vehicle owners about updates. Some regulations (and regional laws) require that for certain types of updates, the user must be notified or even give consent, especially if the update might change user experience or collect additional data. SUMS emphasizes that updates should not violate any regulatory provisions (e.g., an update cannot suddenly disable an emissions control system—that would be illegal tampering).

ISO 24089 (Road vehicles—Software update engineering) provides further guidance that aligns with R156, detailing recommended practices for designing the update system, verifying update integrity, and even post-update monitoring (to quickly detect anomalies introduced by new software). Adhering to these standards is now a prerequisite for selling vehicles in many jurisdictions. In UNECE-adopting markets (including the EU), UN R155 (CSMS) and UN R156 (SUMS) apply to new type approvals from 2022, with broader applicability phased in per local adoption—underscoring that "move fast and break things" does not apply to automotive.

To put it simply: A car company must treat software updates with the same rigor as a safety recall. The cloud systems play a big role here—they need to maintain logs, provide dashboards for authorities if needed, and enforce the rules (e.g., not updating a car that's in use in a way that could distract the driver). As a result, many OEMs are investing in integrated OTA management platforms (some partnering with specialized firms) that can provide all the needed evidence of control and quality for each update, satisfying regulators while delivering timely improvements to customers.

Critic's Note OTA without rollback is malpractice: brand damage from even a small bricked fraction of the fleet easily outweighs any benefit from marginally faster rollouts. This is why modern SDV programs invest heavily in fail-safe bootloaders, staged campaigns, and R156/ISO 24089–compliant evidence trails rather than cutting corners on update engineering.

7.8 Connected Car Data Pipelines

Before software-defined vehicles offered today's cloud-native functions, the earlier generation of connected cars laid the groundwork for how vehicle data flows to back-end systems. Understanding a generic connected car data pipeline provides insight into how modern SDV architectures extend and augment these fundamentals with edge computing and machine learning.

7.8.1 Pipeline Overview

At a high level, data from vehicles travels through a multi-stage pipeline to reach the cloud and be turned into valuable services. A typical pipeline consists of the following stages:

Stage 1—data generation: This starts at the vehicle's numerous electronic control units (ECUs) and sensors. In-car networks (CAN, LIN, FlexRay, Ethernet, etc.) carry signals ranging from engine temperature, wheel speed, GPS location, driver inputs, camera feeds, and so on. Highly instrumented AV/ADAS development vehicles can generate terabytes of data per day from high-bandwidth sensors like cameras and LiDAR, though production connected cars typically upload far less and rely on heavy on-vehicle filtering [24]. The generation stage is essentially the raw data being produced by the vehicle's operations and environment. For example, a braking ECU might generate a log of each ABS activation event; the infotainment system might generate usage data of an app.

Stage 2—data collection: A specialized onboard unit, often the telematics control unit (TCU), aggregates selected data from the various in-vehicle networks. The TCU serves as the gateway between the vehicle and external networks. It collects messages (according to rules set by the OEM: e.g., "report engine fault codes and fuel level every 1 hour, but report crash events immediately"), possibly buffers them, and prepares them for transmission. Crucially, the TCU also usually encrypts and signs the data packets for security before sending them out over the air. The TCU often includes a cellular modem (with its SIM or eSIM), GPS receiver, and sometimes Wi-Fi/Bluetooth for alternative connectivity. In early connected cars, this unit was essentially like a mobile phone embedded in the car, tasked primarily with emergency calls (e.g., eCall in Europe) and basic telemetry. Now, it's much more sophisticated, sometimes running a full Linux OS and capable of app-like logic. The TCU decides what data to send and when, based on OEM policies and network conditions.

Stage 3—transmission: Once data is packaged and possibly compressed, it is transmitted wirelessly to the back-end. Predominantly this is done via cellular networks (4G LTE and increasingly 5G). The car's SIM may connect to the automaker's contracted telematics service provider (e.g., AT&T or Vodafone automotive SIMs) to reach the internet. In some cases, Wi-Fi can be used (e.g., when the car is in the owner's garage on home Wi-Fi, large uploads or downloads might be deferred to that connection to save cost). Satellite communication is used in niche cases (like for remote area coverage or specific services such as SiriusXM radio data or Iridium for emergency messaging).

As data travels through the telecom network, it reaches the automaker's cloud endpoints via the internet or dedicated APN connections. Transmission is often using protocols like HTTPS or MQTT over cellular data. A key challenge here is ensuring reliable delivery over mobile networks—hence protocols that can handle dropouts and resume sending are important (TCP/IP itself, plus higher-level logic for retries). Many OEM back-ends use message broker systems (Kafka, MQTT brokers, etc.) to ingest these incoming streams efficiently.

Stage 4—edge processing: Prior to or during cloud ingestion, some edge computing may be applied to reduce and refine the data. "Edge" in this context can mean on the vehicle itself or a nearby edge server. On-vehicle preprocessing is increasingly common: the vehicle can run machine learning algorithms or filtering rules to decide which data is relevant to upload. For example, instead of uploading raw high-definition video from a camera, the car's computer might run an object detection algorithm and just send an event like "detected 3 pedestrians and 1 cyclist at 5:30 PM at GPS coordinates X" rather than the entire video. This dramatically cuts bandwidth while preserving the useful insight. Automakers are also exploring federated learning, where the car uses data to locally update a model and only uploads the model updates (which are much smaller than raw data). Additionally, if MEC servers are available (as discussed earlier), they can do near-real-time crunching of data from vehicles in their vicinity—for instance, aggregating traffic data from many cars or performing local map tile updates—and only send summarized results upstream.

The overall goal of edge processing: Alleviate the cloud and network load by handling as much as possible locally. Industry groups such as the Automotive Edge Computing Consortium (AECC) advocate processing the vast majority of data on-vehicle, a portion at the edge, and only a small fraction in the cloud [211]. Figure 7-17 illustrates a typical "90-9-1" rule-of-thumb distribution inspired by such AECC guidance, rather than a strict standard. Techniques like Opportunistic Data Transfer buffer noncritical data on the vehicle to send during off-peak network hours (e.g., late at night) [218], further easing real-time load. This edge-oriented approach prevents flooding of networks with unnecessary data and ensures that only high-value or urgent information travels to the central cloud.

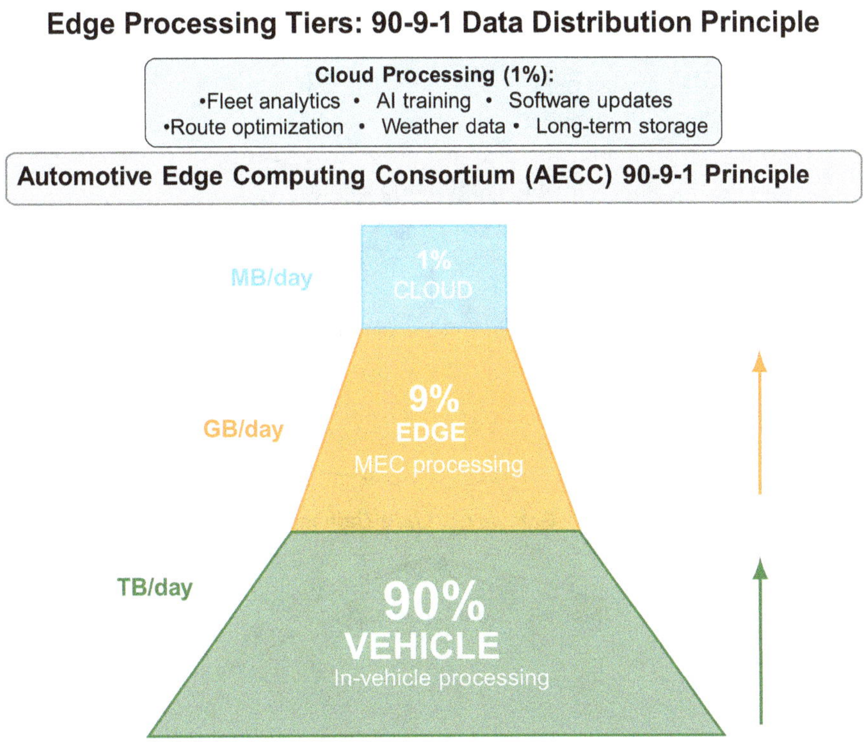

Figure 7-17. *Edge processing tiers: 90-9-1 data distribution principle*

Stage 5—cloud ingestion: When vehicle data reaches the cloud data center, it typically lands in an ingestion layer that handles the high throughput of messages coming from the fleet. Technologies here include message brokers or IoT hubs—e.g., AWS IoT Core, Azure IoT Hub, MQTT brokers like Mosquitto, or Kafka streams. The ingestion layer authenticates each message (checking that it's from a legitimate vehicle device using credentials) and then routes it to appropriate back-end services. Often data is tagged with metadata, vehicle ID, message type, timestamp, etc., at the ingestion point. Some OEMs use a RESTful API endpoint for ingestion (the TCU might call a REST API), but increasingly event-driven streaming (e.g., MQTT publish/subscribe) is favored for efficiency. In the cloud, a device management service keeps track of which vehicles are online and their software versions, to direct data and updates accordingly [219]. The incoming data might first hit a firewall/proxy and then a cluster of processing nodes that perform initial parsing. For example, JSON or Protocol Buffers messages from the car will be decoded into a standard data model used by the OEM's platform [220]. There might also be an enrichment step: augmenting the data with additional info—e.g., translate a GPS lat/long into a city name, or add a weather context for that location [221]. After this, the data is dispatched to various storage and processing engines.

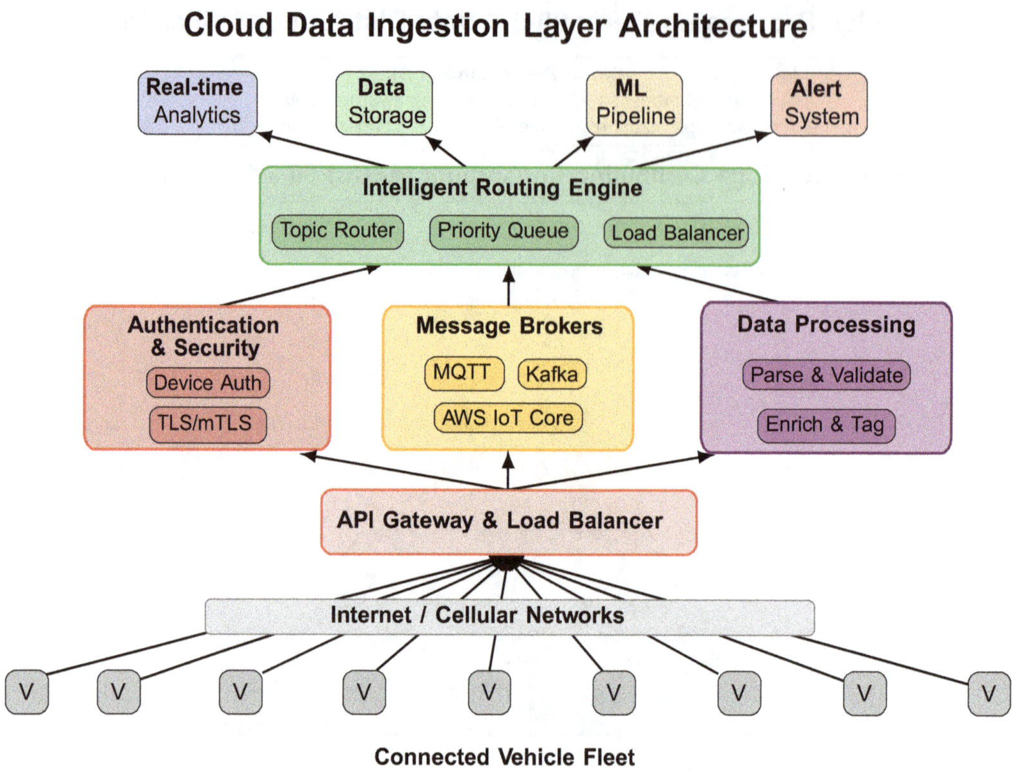

Figure 7-18. *Cloud data ingestion layer architecture*

Stage 6—storage and analytics: Processed vehicle data flows into storage systems appropriate for its form. Time-series sensor readings might go into a time-series database or cold storage if needed for compliance. Events like "airbag deployed" or "door unlocked" might be stored in a relational DB with vehicle history. Larger data, such as images from a drive event, could go into a data lake or blob storage. Cloud data warehouses might store aggregated data for enterprise analytics. On top of storage, stream processing frameworks (Apache Spark, AWS Kinesis, etc.) and analytics engines run continuous analysis. For example, a stream job might consume accelerometer data from all vehicles to detect driving behavior patterns or potholes on roads. Another might be correlating engine sensor data to predict failures. The cloud enables running complex queries and machine learning at scale across the entire fleet's data, something impossible to do on any single vehicle. Over time, the data can also be used to improve designs—feeding back into R&D. Automakers often pipe certain data to their enterprise IT systems or to partners. For instance, warranty and quality departments get defect-related data, and mapping partners might get anonymized GPS tracks to improve maps.

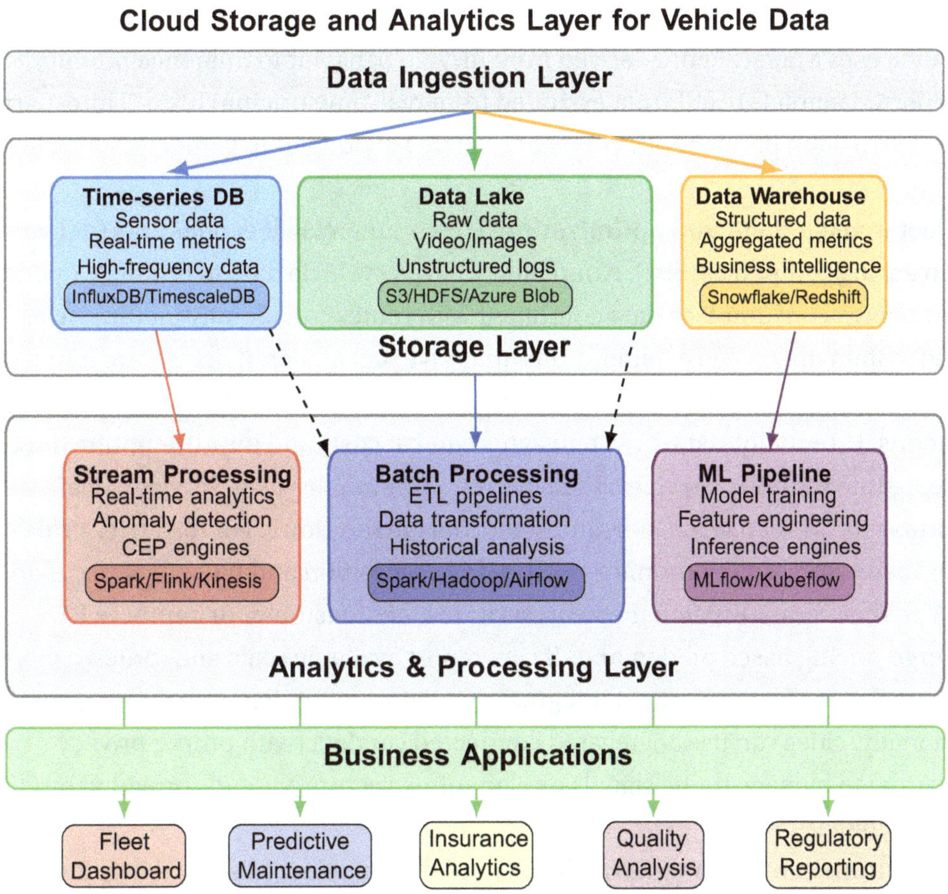

Figure 7-19. *Cloud storage and analytics layer for vehicle data*

Stage 7—applications and services: At the end of the pipeline, the data becomes actionable insights or user-facing services. Numerous applications leverage the ingested vehicle data:

Predictive maintenance: Cloud algorithms analyze engine and drivetrain data to predict component failures before they happen. If the data indicates an anomaly (say, a subtle increase in engine vibration frequency patterns), the system might flag that the engine mount or a bearing is likely to fail soon [222]. The cloud app then triggers a notification to the driver or dealer to schedule a preventive repair [222]. This turns raw sensor readings into a valuable service that reduces breakdowns.

Usage-based insurance (UBI): Driving data (speed, acceleration, braking habits, mileage, etc.) is aggregated to derive a driver risk score. Insurers use these scores to adjust premiums—safer drivers (calm driving style, less night driving, obeying speed limits) might get discounts, whereas frequent hard brakers or speeders pay more. Tesla's insurance uses a Safety Score derived from driving behavior to influence premiums in supported markets (California excluded from real-time pricing) [223]. Third-party insurers also often partner with OEMs or use OBD-II dongles to gather this data for UBI programs.

Fleet management and optimization: For commercial fleet operators (delivery vans, trucking companies, etc.), cloud platforms use vehicle data to optimize operations. Fuel or energy consumption data combined with routes can identify inefficiencies—e.g., a cloud system may suggest better routes that save fuel or alert if drivers are idling too long. Maintenance data across the fleet helps schedule service when it least disrupts operations. Essentially, data-driven insights can cut costs and improve uptime for fleets.

Real-time mobility services: Ridesharing and Mobility-as-a-Service (MaaS) platforms rely on vehicle location and status data in the cloud. For instance, a ride-hailing company's system monitors each vehicle's position and passenger occupancy live. With that, it can dispatch the nearest car to a new customer or compute ETA and surge pricing based on demand. If cars report available seats and routes, a city's public transit or MaaS app might integrate that data to offer dynamic shuttle services. Additionally, cities can use aggregated connected car data (with proper privacy safeguards) to manage traffic signals or plan infrastructure, via APIs provided by OEMs or data exchanges.

Infotainment and personalization: Cloud data pipelines also feed into the customer experience. A user's profile (saved in the cloud) might be sent to the car to personalize seat settings or music preferences. App ecosystems (like third-party apps in the car's infotainment) require cloud support—e.g., syncing the car's calendar app with cloud calendars, downloading content, etc.

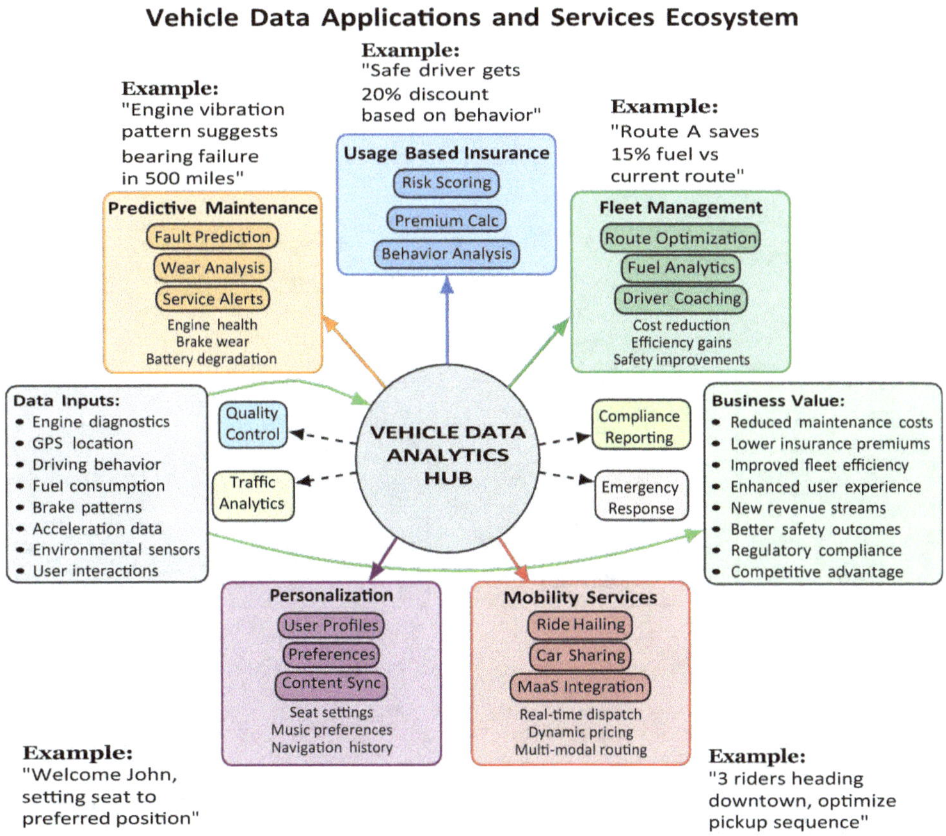

***Figure 7-20.** Vehicle data applications and services ecosystem*

A simplified illustration of the complete pipeline is shown in Figure 7-21, which depicts data flowing from in-vehicle sensors and ECUs through the TCU and wireless network, into cloud ingestion and analytics systems, and finally to business applications that close the loop by delivering value (alerts, services, dashboards). This backbone of vehicle-to-cloud connectivity is what enables an SDV to be more than just a standalone car; it becomes part of an integrated ecosystem of services.

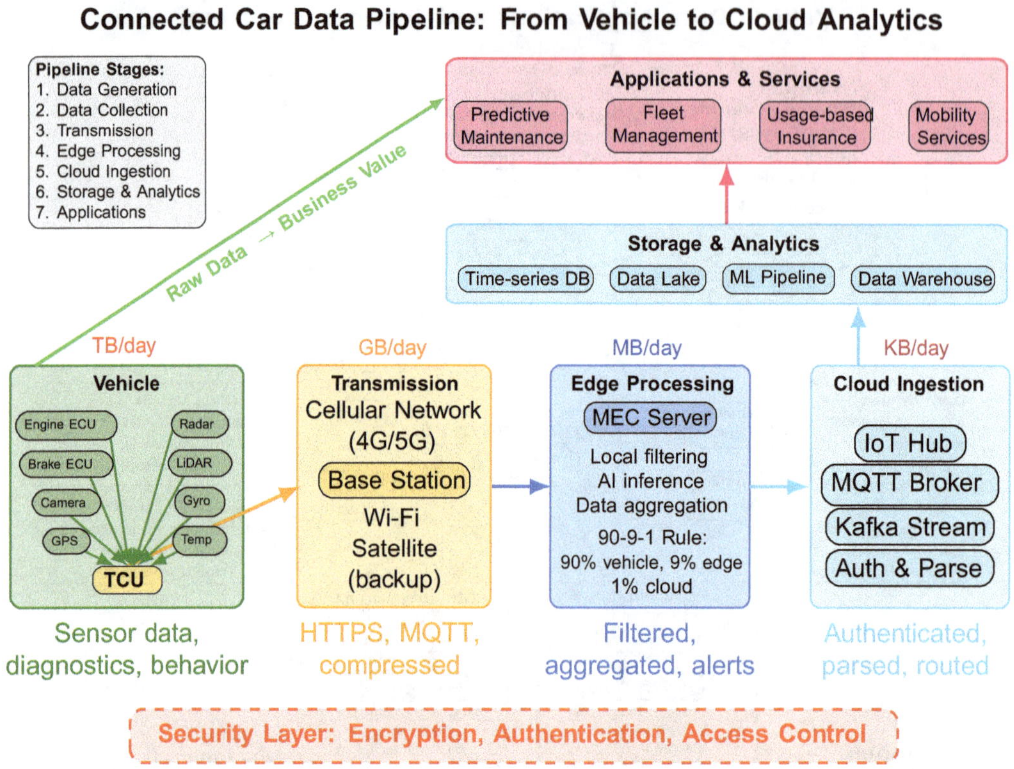

Figure 7-21. *Connected car data pipeline: from vehicle to cloud analytics*

7.8.2 Industry Example: Predictive Maintenance

To concretize the pipeline, consider a specific use case: predictive maintenance for an engine component.

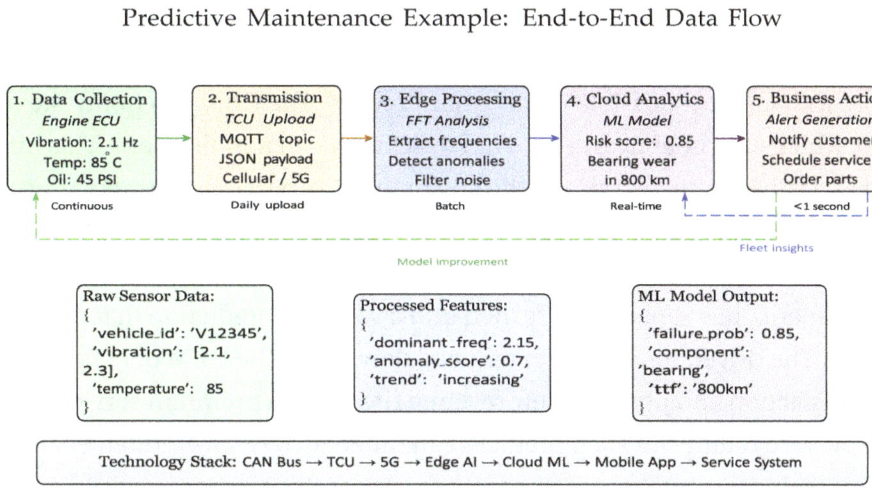

Figure 7-22. *Predictive maintenance example: end-to-end data flow*

Data collection: The engine's ECU continuously monitors parameters like vibration, temperature, and oil pressure. Normally, these fluctuate within a range, but a developing mechanical issue (e.g., bearing wear) might cause subtle changes in vibration frequency. The ECU can be configured to send a packet of summary statistics (or raw data if needed) to the cloud via the TCU every day or when an anomaly is detected.

Transmission: The TCU uses the cellular link to upload these packets. Let's say it sends a compressed JSON message via an MQTT topic called "/fleet/engine_health" for that vehicle. Included is the vehicle ID, timestamp, and the sensor readings or anomaly indicators.

Edge processing: Before sending, the car's firmware might perform an FFT (Fast Fourier Transform) on the vibration data to identify frequency spikes (a technique to spot imbalance or wear). Instead of raw time-series data, it sends the key frequencies and amplitudes. The TCU might only transmit when the values deviate beyond normal thresholds (outlier detection), thus filtering out routine data.

Cloud analytics: The message arrives in the cloud broker and is passed to a streaming analytics service. This service feeds the data into a machine learning model that has been trained to predict the probability of engine component failures. For example, a predictive model (perhaps a neural network or regression) takes in vibration frequencies, engine temperature trends, and maybe external factors (mileage, average RPMs) and outputs a risk score for, say, "turbocharger failure in next 1,000 km."

Business outcome: If the model's risk score exceeds a certain threshold, the system flags that vehicle. It can automatically generate a service alert to the owner: "Your vehicle may require a check-up—possible engine mount wear." The OEM can notify the nearest dealership, which can proactively reach out to schedule an appointment. This might be offered as a subscription service to the customer or as part of a warranty program. Additionally, the OEM aggregates these alerts across the fleet to see if a particular batch of engines has systemic issues—which feeds back to manufacturing quality control.

In this scenario, raw sensor data turned into a valuable prediction that prevents a breakdown. The driver benefits from reduced downtime; the OEM benefits from customer satisfaction and possibly new revenue (if sold as a premium service). Many car companies are rolling out such predictive maintenance services, often enabled by partnerships with cloud analytics providers or startups. It's a prime example of turning data into value through the connected car pipeline.

Critic's Note The biggest challenge is not collecting data but deciding what data to keep. Uploading terabytes of raw sensor data per vehicle is infeasible—hence the rise of in-vehicle AI preprocessing and federated learning. This highlights that more data isn't always better; smart data reduction and local AI are necessary parts of the pipeline to focus on quality over quantity of data.

7.9 Data Monetization Pathways

Connected car data opens up a variety of monetization avenues for OEMs and service providers. Some key pathways include the following.

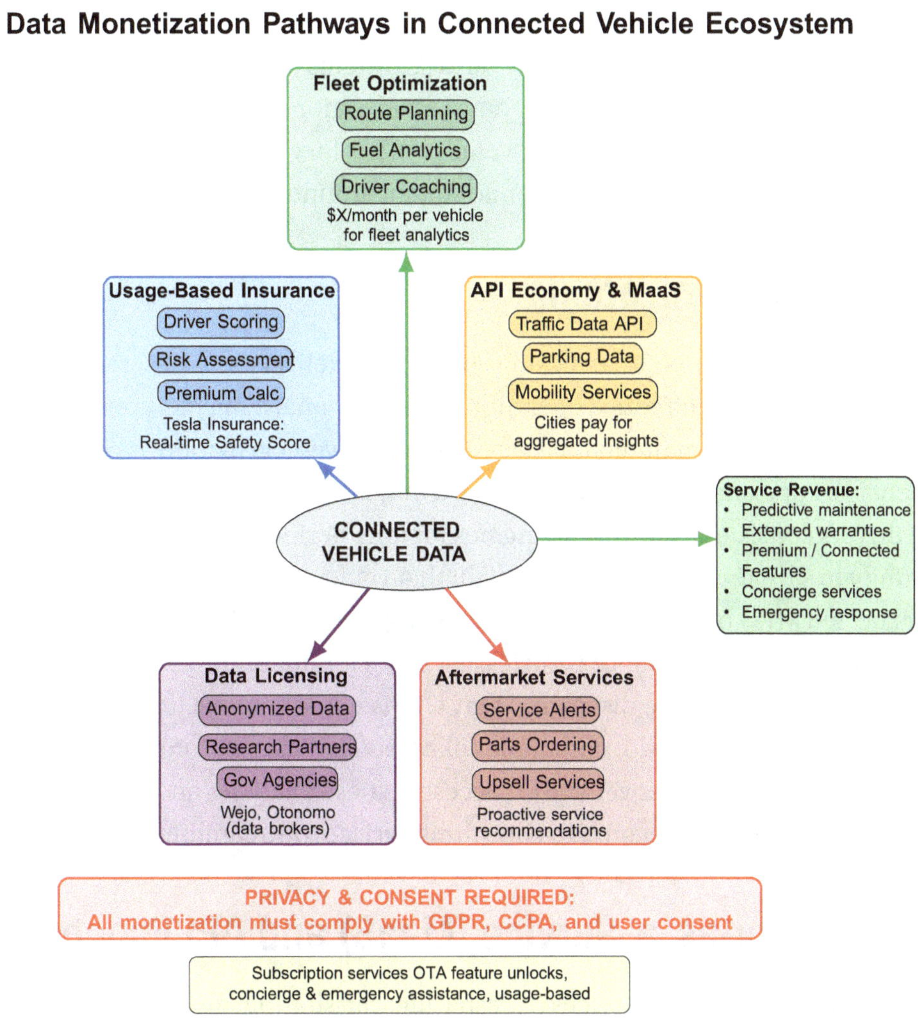

***Figure 7-23.** Data monetization pathways in the connected vehicle ecosystem*

7.9.1 Usage-Based Insurance (UBI)

Granular driving data enables insurance models where premiums are tailored to how and how much one drives, rather than traditional broad demographics. For instance, if telematics show that a driver never speeds, avoids hard braking, and drives only 5,000 km a year, they might pay a significantly lower premium than an aggressive driver with high mileage. Insurers either partner with OEMs to get this data (some OEMs provide driver score APIs) or issue OBD-II dongles/smartphone apps for data. Tesla took this in-house by launching Tesla Insurance, which uses real-time vehicle data and a proprietary Safety Score to set monthly rates [224]. This is a competitive advantage as Tesla has direct access to rich vehicle data (accelerations, Autopilot usage, etc.) that third-party insurers typically lack. The overall result is incentivizing safer driving (good drivers save money) and creating a revenue stream around data.

7.9.2 Fleet Optimization

Commercial fleet operators (like trucking companies, delivery services, rental car fleets) greatly value data that can reduce operational costs. By analyzing fuel consumption, idle times, routes taken, and maintenance logs, connected vehicle platforms can identify inefficiencies. For example, a cloud dashboard might show a logistics company that certain drivers consistently idle their engines for long periods—prompting a coaching opportunity to save fuel. Or it might highlight that vehicles of a certain model are getting below expected MPG on certain routes, suggesting an issue with those routes or vehicles. Fleet managers can also geofence vehicles, get alerts for unauthorized usage, and use real-time tracking to improve dispatch. Many OEMs now offer fleet telematics services (sometimes in partnership with companies like Geotab, Verizon Connect, etc.) where they charge a monthly fee per vehicle for access to these analytics and management tools. The data essentially becomes a consulting service to streamline fleet operations.

7.9.3 Mobility-as-a-Service (MaaS) and API Economy

As we move toward mobility services (ridesharing, car-sharing, multimodal transport apps), real-time data from vehicles can be monetized via developer APIs or platform integration. For example, an automaker could offer a Traffic Data API that cities pay for, providing aggregated speed and location data from all its connected cars to help in traffic management and urban planning. Another scenario: A parking app could integrate vehicle sensor data (like whether a car's parking sensors found open street parking spots) to crowdsource a parking availability service—the app might pay OEMs for that data feed. Occupancy data from rideshare vehicles can be used to inform public transit decisions. Even something like maps can benefit: companies like Waze or TomTom historically crowdsourced data from user devices; now connected cars can supply highly accurate, frequent data on traffic flow and road conditions (with OEMs potentially charging for access to that data).

This data marketplace idea led to startups like Otonomo and Wejo that attempted to broker car data to third parties [225]. In practice, these marketplace models have largely failed to achieve sustainable scale in automotive: Otonomo was acquired in a distressed reverse merger, and Wejo entered bankruptcy, highlighting both thin unit economics and the impact of privacy and consent constraints in real deployments. As of today, the most robust value capture tends to be OEM-internal (warranty, quality, in-house insurance, fleet optimization) rather than third-party resale of car data.

7.9.4 Aftermarket and Retail Services

Car data also feeds into services offered after the car sale. For instance, dealerships can get alerts when a customer's car throws certain trouble codes and then reach out to schedule service—driving more business to the service center (and convenience to the customer). Another example is personalized offers: if the telematics show a customer is nearing lease end and under-mileage, the OEM's sales team could proactively offer a new lease deal. Or if data shows frequent use of certain features, the OEM might try to upsell a related service (e.g., "I see you use navigation daily; consider our premium real-time traffic subscription"). Even third-party shops could, through user consent, get diagnostic data to provide quotes for maintenance. These are more indirect monetization routes but tie back to the data pipeline enabling them.

Overall, while selling cars was once a one-time transaction, connected data allows automakers to capture ongoing revenue. Subscriptions for features (we'll discuss below), insurance partnerships, data licensing, and value-added services mean the customer's vehicle usage generates continuous economic activity. One must note, though, that privacy and customer consent are critical—monetization can only be done if users (and regulators) trust how data is used, which is why clear opt-in mechanisms and anonymization strategies are essential.

7.9.5 Regulatory Considerations

The collection and monetization of connected car data doesn't happen in a lawless vacuum. Several major regulations around the world govern personal data and connected systems, which OEMs must navigate carefully:

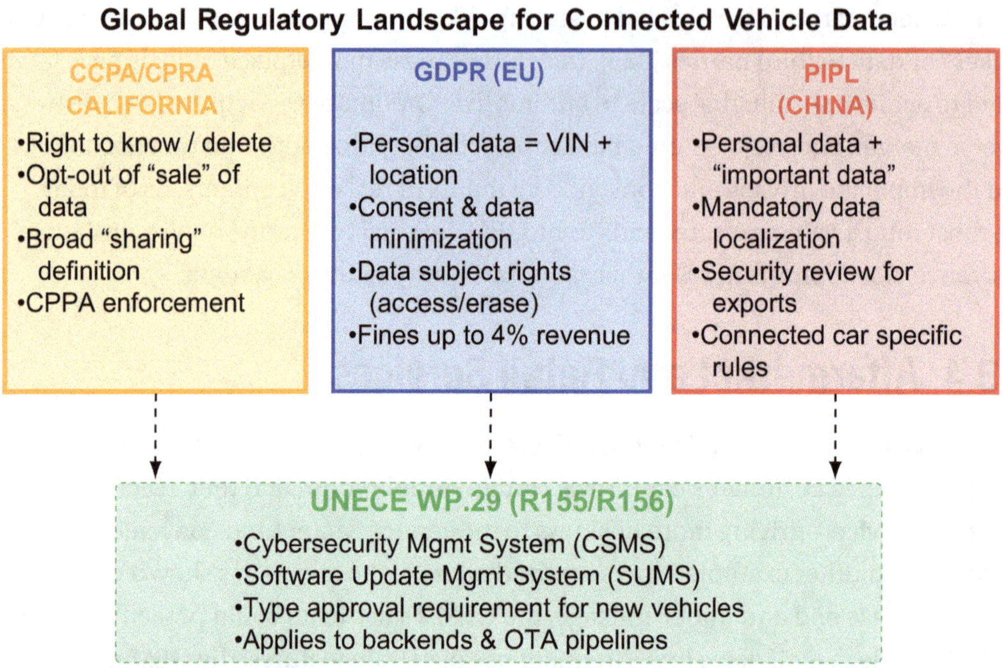

Figure 7-24. *Global regulatory landscape for connected vehicle data*

GDPR (EU):

The General Data Protection Regulation is perhaps the strictest framework. It treats much vehicle data (especially anything linked to a VIN and owner or precise location data) as personal data. This means car companies must obtain informed consent for processing such data for specific purposes [226]. For example, if an OEM wants to use a driver's location data to offer location-based services or share it with a third-party app, they likely need the driver to opt in. GDPR also gives consumers rights to access their data, correct it, and request deletion. In the connected car context, an EU user could request all telematics data collected on them or ask that it be erased (except for safety-critical or legal-required data). Also, GDPR's principle of data minimization pushes manufacturers to collect only what's needed for the service being provided [226]. The European Data Protection Board even issued specific guidelines on connected vehicles, emphasizing need for privacy-by-design in car systems [226]. Non-compliance can mean massive fines (up to 4% of global revenue), so automakers are very cautious in the EU: e.g., making sure the infotainment user settings include toggles for data sharing, anonymizing data for analysis whenever possible, and storing personal data on EU servers.

PIPL (China):

China's Personal Information Protection Law (2021) similarly regulates personal data. Additionally, China has data localization rules—important data (which likely includes detailed vehicle sensor data, especially if related to public security or infrastructure like HD maps) must be stored in China [227]. Automakers operating in China have to keep Chinese cars' data on local servers and go through security assessments if they need to transfer any of it abroad [227]. Moreover, China issued specific regulations for connected cars ("auto data regulation") requiring that in-cabin cameras, location data, etc. have user consent and that car owners have the ability to turn off data collection for certain types of data [228]. This is a fast-evolving area. Tesla stated in May 2021 that it established a data center in China to localize Chinese vehicle data. PIPL also mandates protections similar to GDPR (consent, purpose limitation, etc.) but with a state security overtone—companies might have to also share data with authorities upon request. The takeaway is that in China, data is considered a sovereign resource, and connected car platforms must be architected with local compliance from day one.

CCPA/CPRA (California, United States):

The California Consumer Privacy Act (and its amendment CPRA) gives Californians rights regarding their personal data. For connected cars, one implication is that owners can request to know what data is collected by their vehicle and request deletion of that data (excluding some necessary functional data). Also, if any vehicle data is sold or shared to third parties for business purposes, consumers have a right to opt out of that "sale." Recently, the California Privacy Protection Agency even announced it's reviewing connected vehicle data practices specifically [229]. While US federal law in this area is patchy, California's law effectively sets a bar that automakers apply across the United States (it's easier to have one standard). Thus, owners might find privacy settings in their car's mobile app where they can disable certain data collection and privacy policies explicitly stating what info the car collects (from geolocation to biometric data from driver monitoring cameras). The enforcement is ramping up: in 2023, some automakers faced inquiries in California about whether their data practices (like recording what the voice assistant hears or how camera images are used) comply with CCPA transparency requirements [229].

UNECE WP.29 cybersecurity and OTA regulations (R155 and R156):

We mentioned R156 for updates. Its sibling R155 requires a Cybersecurity Management System (CSMS) for vehicles, which touches data too—ensuring vehicles and their back-ends are secure against hacking, including the data in transit. Also, new standards like ISO/SAE 21434 require engineering processes to secure car data and communications. All these mean that data pipelines must implement state-of-the-art security (encryption, authentication) and be monitored for breaches. If a vulnerability is found, OEMs are expected to patch it (hence tying back to OTA).

These regulatory regimes directly shape the monetization pathways discussed earlier in this chapter: they constrain how driving and location data can be repurposed or exported, require explicit driver consent for many secondary uses, and in some cases mandate strict localization of sensitive vehicle data. In practice, viable SDV business models must be designed around these constraints from the outset rather than treating compliance as an afterthought.

In summary, data is power, and with power comes responsibility (and regulation). An SDV program has to build in compliance from the ground up: getting user consent during onboarding, allowing opt-outs, anonymizing or aggregating data whenever possible (e.g., using differential privacy techniques when analyzing driver data to monetize it without exposing personal details), and being prepared to service user requests around their data. Regulatory compliance isn't just a legal box-tick; it's crucial for customer trust. If consumers don't trust how their data is handled, they won't enable or use the connected features, defeating the purpose. Therefore, successful SDV data pipelines are those that can extract value from data while respecting privacy and legal boundaries—a delicate but achievable balance with modern tech.

Quote Review (connected car pipelines): Throughout this section, we saw how connected car pipelines turn raw vehicle data into business value in the cloud. Real-world deployments highlight that collecting data is only the first step—secure, scalable handling and smart analytics are essential to make it useful fleet-wide. Modern SDVs build on this backbone by adding more on-car intelligence (to manage the data deluge), leveraging edge computing for low-latency needs, and integrating stricter safety and privacy measures. The result is a more distributed computing system spanning car, edge, and cloud, all orchestrated to improve the vehicle experience continuously.

7.10 Business Models in Cloud/Edge for SDVs

Software-defined vehicles not only introduce new technologies but also enable new business models for automakers and mobility companies. Cloud and edge capabilities are the enablers for many of these monetization strategies.

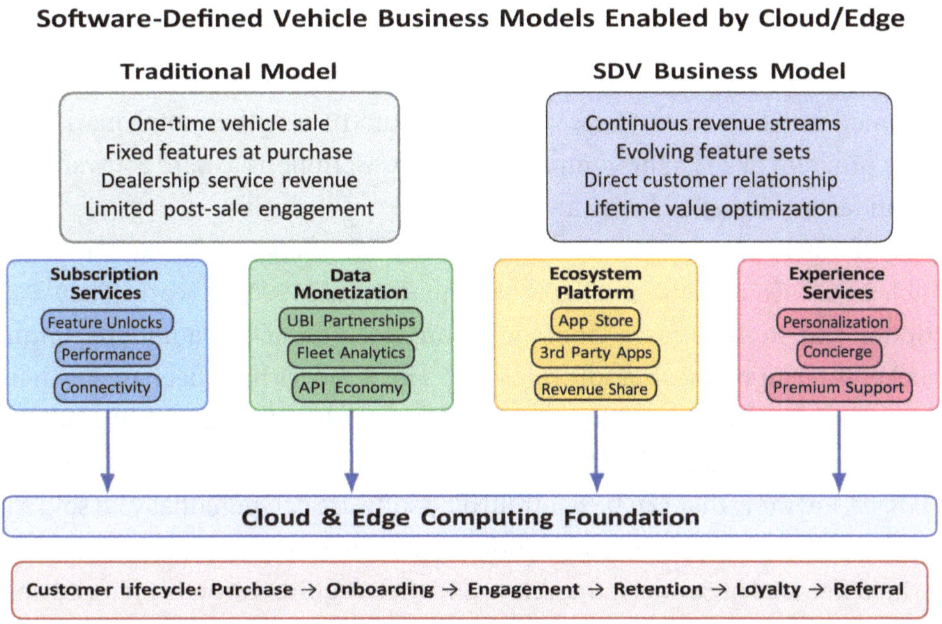

Figure 7-25. *Software-defined vehicle business models enabled by cloud/edge*

7.10.1 Data Monetization Services

As discussed, OEMs can monetize vehicle data itself (within privacy bounds). Insurance partnerships for UBI, selling aggregated traffic data, and offering analytics to fleet operators are ways to directly turn data into revenue. Some OEMs have even considered marketplaces where customers can opt in to share certain data in exchange for benefits (e.g., sharing anonymized driving data to help map providers, in return for a discounted navigation service subscription). This is an evolving area, balancing profit with privacy. Notably, several startups tried to broker connected car data, but the business is challenging [230]; still, the OEMs themselves possess a trove of information that, if leveraged carefully, can create new revenue streams beyond car sales.

7.10.2 Subscriptions and Feature Unlocks

As of the mid-2020s, one of the most visible new models is selling car features on a subscription basis or as on-demand upgrades. Traditionally, a car's features were fixed at purchase (based on trim level). Now, thanks to software controls and OTA, automakers can include hardware capabilities that are software-locked and later sell access. Examples include Tesla's "Full Self-Driving" software package, which can be bought outright or via monthly subscription to enable advanced driver assistance features. BMW experimented with heated seat subscriptions (about $18/month in some markets) but ended the program in 2023; the company shifted subscriptions toward software/services rather than factory-installed hardware [34].

In North America, as of 2024–2025, Mercedes-Benz offers Acceleration Increase on eligible EQE/EQS models—available as a monthly ($60–$90) or yearly ($600–$900) subscription and, in some cases, a one-time purchase—unlocking additional torque and quicker 0–60 mph times via software [231]. These moves have been met with mixed customer reactions (some see it as nickel-and-diming), but they represent a shift to viewing the car as a configurable digital platform. From premium sound systems to range boosts, anything that can be controlled by software can potentially be sold as an upgrade later. Subscriptions also include services like connectivity (e.g., many EVs come with a free trial of connected services and then require a monthly fee), advanced navigation or concierge services, etc.

The appeal to OEMs is clear: recurring revenue and a longer customer engagement post-sale. However, companies are learning to tread carefully to avoid backlash (offering clear value for the fee and not charging for things that customers feel should be standard). When done right, it can significantly boost lifetime revenue per vehicle. For instance, GM's OnStar started as a subscription safety service years ago; now GM is expanding into offering insurance, media streaming, and hands-free driving packages via subscription, aiming to double what they earn from a customer over the car's life.

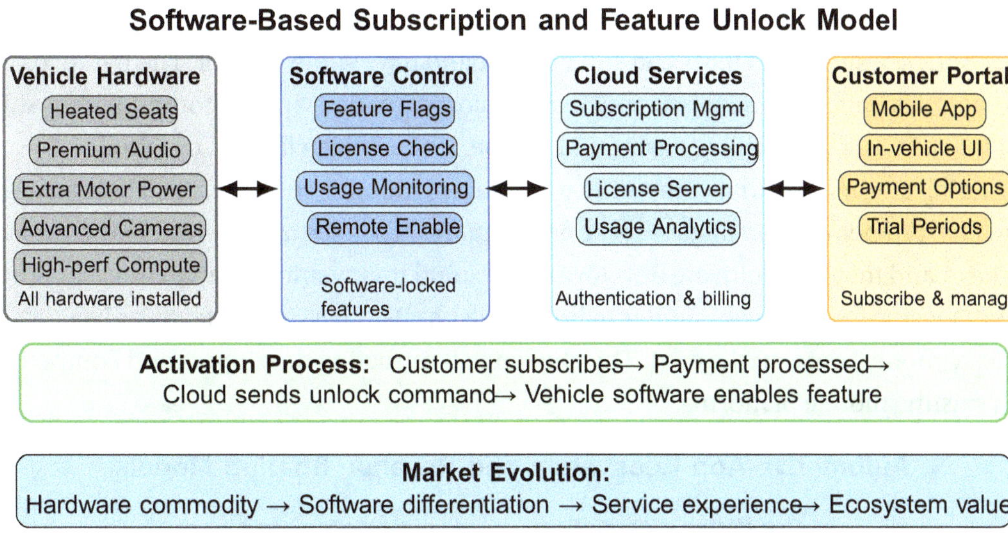

Figure 7-26. *Software-based subscription and the feature unlock model*

7.10.3 Ecosystem and App Store

Another model is creating an ecosystem of apps and services that run on or with the vehicle, akin to a smartphone app store. If an OEM controls the in-car platform (as with many moving to Android Automotive OS or similar), they can allow third-party developers to create applications (for infotainment, navigation, etc.) for the car. The OEM can take a revenue share from paid apps or services. This is similar to how Apple's App Store or Google Play operates, but in a car context.

However, a big tension exists: many consumers and developers just use Apple CarPlay or Android Auto, which bypasses the carmaker's own system. Some automakers are fighting back—e.g., GM announced it will begin phasing out CarPlay/Android Auto starting with select 2024+ EVs, in favor of its native Ultifi platform with Google-built-in services; as of late 2025 GM has reiterated the plan and signaled expansion beyond EVs, with rollout cadence varying by model [232]. Their goal is to own that digital real estate and the revenue that can come from it (like selling apps or collecting data). A thriving OEM-controlled ecosystem could mean, say, you have an app in your car to order Starbucks on the go and the OEM gets a cut of that transaction or a marketplace where you can buy OTA upgrades and third-party add-ons (like an advanced off-road gauge pack for a 4×4, developed by an aftermarket company but sold through the OEM store).

Android Automotive (with Google Play in the car) is an interesting middle-ground: it gives Google a slice, but OEMs can still brand it and have some control. The battle for the dashboard is ongoing, and it is as much about control of data and customer relationship as it is about user experience. Early OEM app stores have seen limited traction, reminding automakers that competing with mature mobile ecosystems will be a long-term effort rather than an instant revenue fountain. OEMs see a future where the car is a platform and they can cultivate developers to extend their vehicle's capabilities, building brand-specific experiences (similar to how Tesla has its ecosystem of features like Karaoke mode, Santa mode, etc.). The challenge is attracting developers and competing with existing mobile platforms.

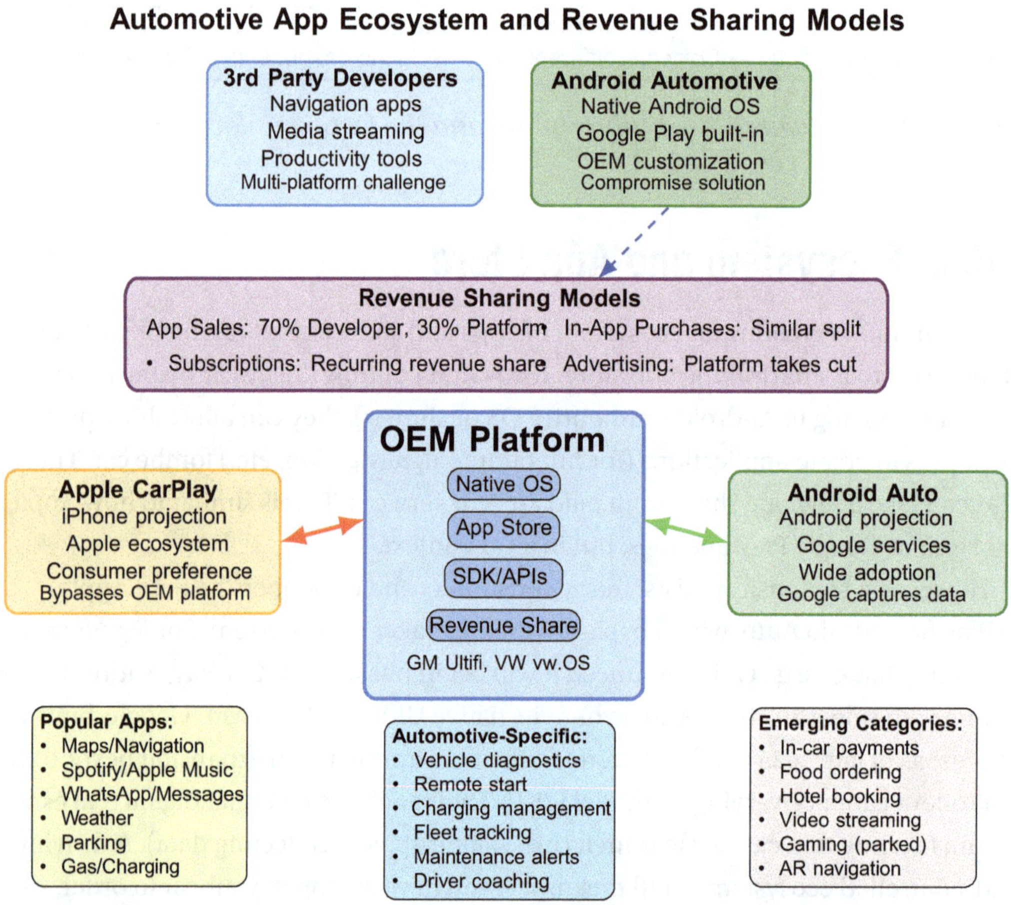

Figure 7-27. *Automotive app ecosystem and revenue sharing models*

In all these models, the cloud/edge is indispensable. You can't have dynamic subscriptions without a cloud back-end handling authentication and payment. You can't have an app store without cloud distribution and sandboxing. Data monetization obviously relies on cloud analytics.

Thus, the business side and technology side of SDVs are deeply intertwined. In economic terms, cloud-backed SDVs enable recurring, service-based revenue models that extend well beyond the one-time vehicle sale.

7.10.4 Flagship Customer Experience (CX) Tie-In

Cloud and edge capabilities also allow automakers to continuously evolve the customer experience, which itself becomes a selling point. For example, a car that gets better over time (through updates unlocking features or improving performance) can delight customers and justify premium pricing. Features like predictive maintenance or personalized AI assistants improve customer satisfaction and can be packaged as subscription services. Automakers now talk about "lifetime customer value"—using cloud connectivity to keep the customer engaged through the entire ownership lifecycle. A satisfied, engaged customer is more likely to stay with the brand (brand loyalty) and purchase services. Thus, cloud is not just technical but strategic: it's the channel through which customer relationships are managed post-sale.

In practice, many OEMs now treat customer experience as a direct driver of recurring revenue: if the experience is compelling (e.g., a subscription that genuinely makes driving easier or more enjoyable), customers are willing to pay continuously.

Cloud connectivity enables things like free trials (e.g., try enhanced autopilot for a month), feature on demand for when a customer actually needs it (e.g., subscribe to automated parking only during winter months), or family plans (multiple vehicles sharing data services). All these are levers to generate revenue while ideally providing value. The endgame many OEMs envision is a sort of ecosystem lock-in: if you love the software services and they integrate with your digital life, you'll be inclined to buy your next vehicle from the same brand to keep that experience.

In summary, the shift to SDVs turns automakers into service providers and platform operators, not just manufacturers. The cloud and edge are the backbone for this transformation, enabling new business models from subscriptions to data-driven services that were never before possible in the traditional auto industry.

7.10.5 Cost Realities and Unit Economics

Any cloud- and edge-enabled SDV business model also has to contend with ongoing operating costs. Telematics SIMs and data plans, back-end cloud infrastructure, storage for high-volume telemetry, and any MEC-based services all contribute to a cost-per-vehicle-per-month that can easily reach several euros or dollars for heavily connected offerings. If an OEM wants to bundle high-usage connectivity (e.g., frequent map updates, streaming services, rich telematics) into the vehicle price, those costs must be amortized over the vehicle lifetime or offset by subscription revenue. Conversely, if services are optional, pricing has to cover not only incremental cloud and connectivity charges but also platform development and support.

The result is that many SDV business cases are sensitive to assumptions about attach rates (what fraction of buyers activate a service), churn (how long they keep paying), and negotiated telecom and cloud pricing. A connectivity feature that looks attractive at "$1/vehicle/month" OPEX can become uneconomic if real usage drives that toward "$5/vehicle/month" without matching revenue. Grounding SDV roadmaps in realistic unit economics is therefore just as important as defining technically compelling features.

7.11 Case Study: GM Ultifi—A Software Platform Play

General Motors's Ultifi platform is a prime example of a legacy automaker embracing the SDV approach to combine cloud, edge, and onboard software into a unified business and technology strategy. Announced in 2021, Ultifi (a portmanteau of Ultimate + Wi-Fi/Connectivity, also tying into GM's Ultium battery brand) is an end-to-end vehicle software platform intended to roll out across many GM models starting 2023–2024 [233].

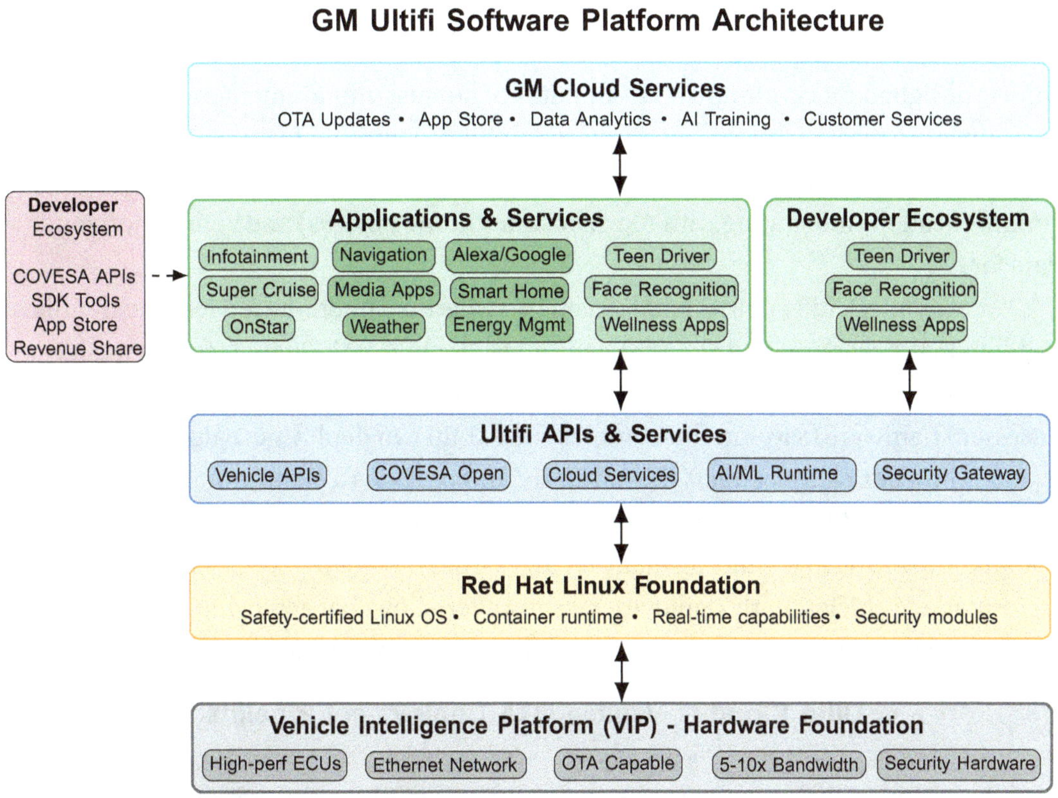

Figure 7-28. *GM Ultifi software platform architecture*

Some key aspects of Ultifi are as follows.

7.11.1 Linux-Based, Open Development

Ultifi is built on a Linux operating system foundation [234]. GM partnered with Red Hat to use a safety-certified Linux OS as the base for Ultifi in-vehicle software [235]. By using Linux, GM aims to leverage open source libraries and attract developers familiar with that environment. It also means a broad range of hardware can be supported. GM is making certain APIs available through the industry consortium COVESA (formerly GENIVI), essentially open-sourcing parts of its platform to encourage third-party development [236]. The idea is to create a developer ecosystem "like Apple or Google" but specific to GM vehicles[236]. Apps or software modules can be created by suppliers or indie developers (with GM as gatekeeper) to expand vehicle functionality.

7.11.2 Cloud Connectivity and OTA

Ultifi is designed for continuous OTA updates of not just infotainment, but potentially any software aspect of the car—even chassis or body controller features, provided safety is ensured [235]. Cloud connectivity underpins features like vehicle-to-home communication (integrating with Alexa or smart home devices) and vehicle-to-cloud data for AI.

For example, Ultifi could enable a scenario where a camera-based feature identifies children in the rear seat and automatically engages child lock—if that feature wasn't present at purchase, it could be added later via software update because the car has the necessary hardware (say, interior cameras) and Ultifi can deploy new algorithms to use it [233]. Ultifi basically abstracts the hardware and provides a cloud-managed software environment to add features over time. GM positions Ultifi as a way to reduce feature rollout time drastically—shifting many changes from model-year cycles to OTA updates on in-market vehicles. Early deployments, however, show that achieving smartphone-like cadence on safety-relevant systems is still a work in progress.

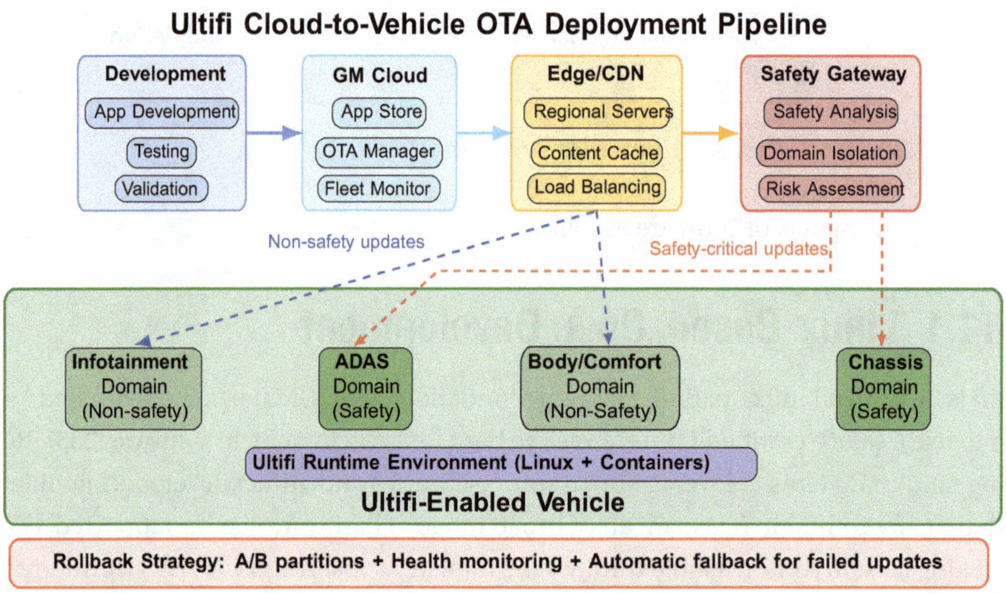

Figure 7-29. Ultifi cloud-to-vehicle OTA deployment pipeline

7.11.3 Features and Subscriptions

GM envisions multiple customer-facing features delivered via Ultifi. They've mentioned things like teen driver mode (which could impose speed alerts or curfews and report driving behavior to parents), energy management features for EVs (like smart charging schedules, integration with home solar, etc.), and concepts such as facial recognition-based access—presented as potential capabilities rather than confirmed feature commitments [237]. Many of these could be offered as subscription packages or one-time purchases. For instance, teen driver mode might be a monthly add-on parents activate during the months their teenager is learning to drive. GM's Super Cruise (hands-free driving) itself is a subscription after a trial period—Ultifi will handle those software activations and updates. The platform also supports third-party apps—think of apps for weather, gas payment, or streaming media running natively on the car—which GM can either include or sell through a marketplace.

7.11.4 Rivaling Big Tech

A major challenge and motivation for Ultifi is to compete with tech giants for the in-car digital space. GM has been vocal about not wanting to simply cede the dashboard to Apple and Google. By dropping CarPlay in future EVs and relying on Ultifi + Android Automotive (without phone projection), GM can try to own the customer interaction and data. It's a gamble because many consumers love CarPlay, but GM's bet is that they can offer an experience that's just as good and then monetize it. The CEO of GM, Mary Barra, has outlined plans for potentially billions in new revenue from software/services by later this decade—Ultifi is core to that plan. Essentially, GM wants to become a company that, in addition to making vehicles, operates a software platform (Ultifi) across millions of those vehicles, generating recurring revenue. It's analogous to how Tesla operates its fleet.

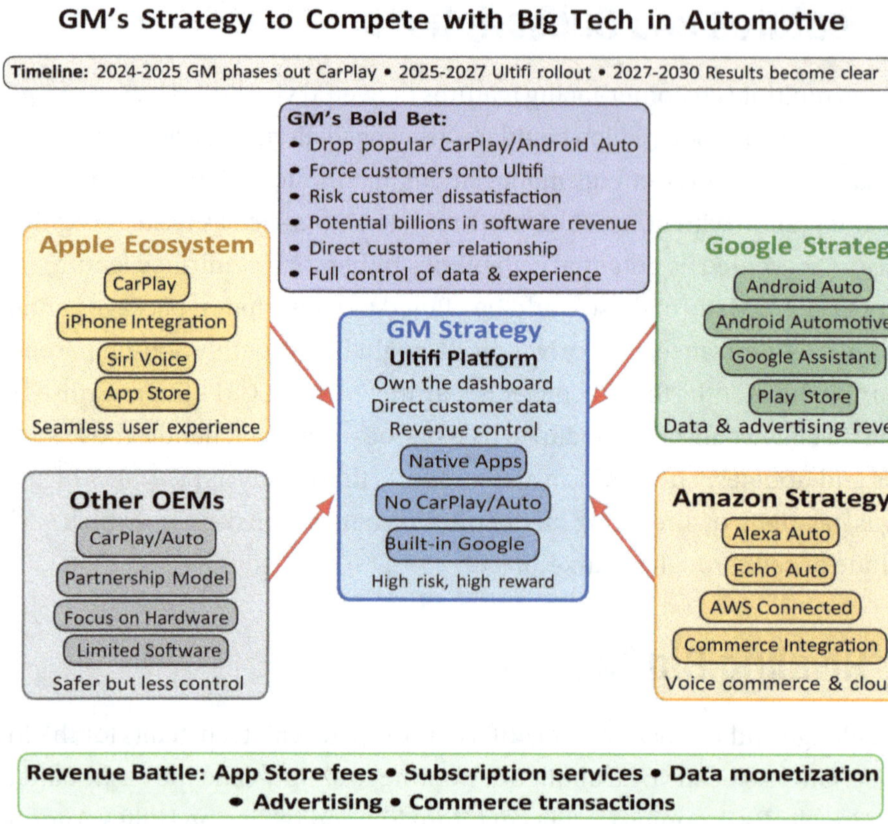

Figure 7-30. *GM's strategy to compete with big tech in automotive*

7.11.5 Technical Underpinnings

For Ultifi to work, GM had to upgrade the in-vehicle hardware and network architecture. They introduced the Vehicle Intelligence Platform (VIP) electrical architecture around 2019, which provides modern Ethernet networking, substantially higher data bandwidth than prior architectures, and built-in OTA capabilities [238]. Only cars with VIP will get Ultifi. This shows how the E/E architecture and software platform come together. VIP is like the "smartphone hardware," and Ultifi is the "operating system and app store." GM is also implementing strict cybersecurity; working with Red Hat suggests they want proven, updatable OS components to reduce vulnerabilities. Ultifi will interface with lower-level vehicle systems (some of which remain on AUTOSAR or other classic ECU platforms) through well-defined APIs—which is nontrivial in safety terms. GM likely separates non-safety (infotainment domain) and critical domains, but with communication via a gateway, so that apps can query vehicle data safely without risking interference.

7.11.6 Challenges

Building an ecosystem from scratch is hard. GM has to convince developers to build for Ultifi when the addressable market at first might be small (just new GM models). They also have to manage customer perception—there's skepticism after things like BMW's subscription backlash. GM has been careful to say features that have ongoing costs to maintain (like live services) are the ones likely to have fees, whereas pure one-time features might be one-time payments. They also have to execute on software—an area traditional OEMs have struggled with. There have been delays (Ultifi was expected in 2023 models like the Cadillac Lyriq, but full capabilities may roll out later). Meanwhile, competitors like Ford are opting to partner deeply with Google (Android) rather than do their own full stack. It's an open question which strategy pays off in the long run.

Business Note GM Ultifi illustrates an incumbent's attempt to transform its business via a cloud- and edge-enabled software platform. It's built on Linux + cloud APIs, aims to offer subscription features (from performance upgrades to new apps), and squarely targets the creation of an ecosystem that might one day rival what Apple/Google offers in automotive. If successful, GM could unlock significant new revenue and closer customer ties; if not, the risk is investing heavily in software for little return if customers instead stick their phones on the dash. Ultifi's progress in the next few years will be a bellwether for the broader industry's SDV ambitions.

7.12 Key Takeaways

- **Cloud as the orchestration backbone:** The cloud and edge form the orchestration backbone of SDVs, handling everything from data ingestion and digital twinning to OTA updates and AI model training. They enable the vehicle to be more than a standalone device—instead, it's part of a connected, updatable ecosystem.

- **Data sovereignty matters:** Gaia-X exemplifies the push for data sovereignty in Europe's automotive cloud. Initiatives like Catena-X under Gaia-X aim to ensure vehicle data and related services aren't solely under the control of foreign hyperscalers, aligning cloud infrastructure with European values and regulations [207].
- **MEC enables low-latency V2X:** MEC (multi-access edge computing) brings cloud capabilities closer to the vehicle, reducing latency for V2X and cooperative functions. This low latency is crucial for things like hazard warnings or platooning. However, MEC introduces new business dynamics, as OEMs and telecom providers negotiate who provides and profits from these edge services [213]. Revenue sharing models using mechanisms like 5G slicing are being explored and trialed, with broad commercialization still emerging.
- **OTA requires robust fail-safes:** OTA updates in vehicles must be engineered with robust fail-safes (e.g., A/B partitions, rollback) and formal Software Update Management Systems (R156/ISO 24089) to avoid bricking vehicles and to satisfy regulatory expectations around process, security, and traceability [72, 73].
- **Data pipelines create value:** Connected car data pipelines show how raw telemetry is turned into valuable services (e.g., predictive maintenance, fleet optimization). The biggest challenge is managing data volume intelligently—hence, on-car processing and selective cloud upload (only useful data) are key. New revenue in the SDV era comes from data-driven services and subscriptions.
- **New business models emerge:** Business models around SDVs include monetizing data (with user consent), selling features via subscriptions or on-demand unlocks, and building an app ecosystem. Continuous customer engagement through cloud services can provide recurring revenue far beyond the initial sale of the vehicle. For automakers, this is a major shift toward being software/platform companies in addition to manufacturers.

CHAPTER 8

AI and Data in Software-Defined Vehicles

8.1 Chapter Goals

After this chapter, you will be able to

- Explain how AI powers perception, decision-making, and personalization in SDVs. This includes understanding how modern vehicles use AI for interpreting sensor data (perception), planning maneuvers, controlling actuators, and tailoring the in-cabin experience to users.
- Understand supervised, unsupervised, and reinforcement learning (RL) in automotive contexts. You will grasp the differences between learning with labeled driving data, discovering patterns without labels, and learning by trial and error (and why real-car trial and error is impractical without simulation).
- Compare centralized vs. federated learning for fleet-wide AI. You should be able to discuss traditional cloud-centric model training vs. on-vehicle (federated) learning approaches that keep data on the car, as well as hybrid edge computing models.
- Assess explainability, ethics, and AI safety case requirements. You will learn about emerging standards and regulations (UNECE, ISO, IEEE) demanding safety evidence and fairness for automotive AI and techniques like explainable AI (XAI) to make "black-box" models more transparent.

S. Agarwal, *Software-Defined Vehicles*, https://doi.org/10.1007/979-8-8688-2718-1_8

- Identify monetization models built on vehicle and user data. This includes new business opportunities like usage-based insurance, data-driven fleet optimizations, personalized in-car services, and app ecosystems, along with the ethical implications of monetizing driver and vehicle data.

Critic's Note AI in SDVs is not "magic." Without robust data pipelines, explainability, and regulatory alignment, AI becomes a liability rather than an asset. In other words, merely adding a neural network to a car won't guarantee success—it requires reliable data feeds and careful validation. If an automaker cannot explain how an AI system makes decisions or ensure it behaves under all conditions, that "smart" system could introduce safety hazards instead of solving them.

8.2 Introduction

Artificial intelligence has become the defining technology of the software-defined vehicle, enabling capabilities from real-time perception and autonomous decision-making to personalized in-cabin experiences. This chapter examines how AI systems are designed, trained, deployed, and validated in the automotive context—where safety requirements and regulatory scrutiny far exceed those of typical consumer AI applications.

We begin by exploring the four key AI workload domains in SDVs: perception (understanding the environment through sensors), planning (deciding what maneuvers to execute), control (translating decisions into actuator commands), and personalization (tailoring the vehicle experience to individual users). The chapter then surveys machine learning approaches—supervised, unsupervised, and reinforcement learning—and their specific applications and limitations in automotive contexts.

Data infrastructure receives substantial attention, from on-vehicle buffering and edge processing to cloud-based training pipelines and digital twins. We examine federated learning as a privacy-preserving alternative to centralized data collection and address the critical challenges of AI safety and explainability that regulators and standards bodies are actively working to resolve. The chapter concludes with monetization pathways enabled by AI and data and a comparative case study of Tesla's and Waymo's contrasting approaches to autonomous driving.

8.3 AI Workloads in SDVs

AI in software-defined vehicles should not be understood as a single software block. In practice, AI is distributed across the vehicle architecture. Perception and prediction workloads typically run close to sensor-processing pipelines and central ADAS compute platforms; planning functions usually execute on centralized driving computers; control remains tightly coupled to deterministic vehicle control functions and safety controllers; and personalization spans cockpit software, user profile services, and cloud-connected applications. The four workload domains discussed in this chapter—perception, planning, control, and personalization—therefore correspond not only to functional tasks, but also to different architectural locations and safety expectations within the SDV stack.

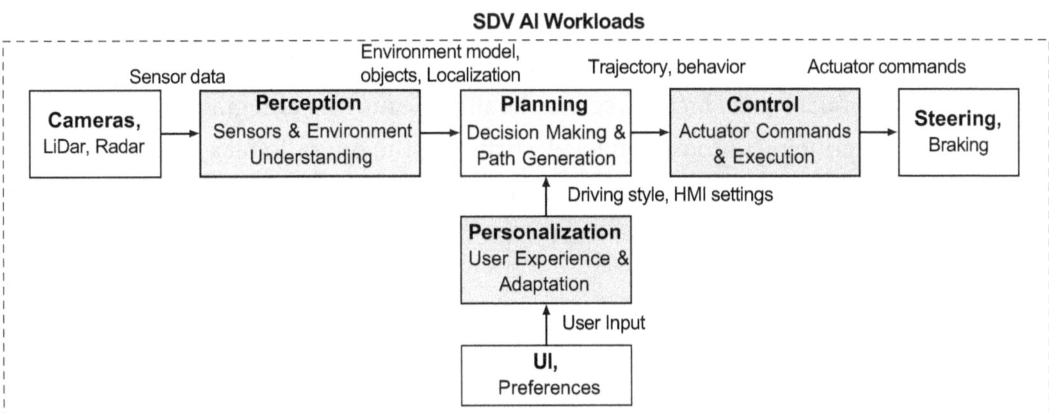

Figure 8-1. *Placement of AI workload domains across the SDV architecture, from sensing and perception to central planning, control execution, and user-facing personalization*

8.3.1 Perception

In an SDV, perception is the AI-driven ability for the car to "see" and interpret its environment. Using sensor data from cameras, LiDAR, radar, ultrasonic sensors, etc., the perception stack detects and classifies objects (vehicles, pedestrians, traffic signs, lane markings) and monitors the driver or occupants. For example, camera and radar inputs are fused to identify a pedestrian crossing the road or to gauge the distance and speed of the car ahead. Advanced driver monitoring AI can even track the driver's eye gaze or drowsiness level.

Perception provides the situational awareness on which all other decisions are based. It demands high accuracy and speed—a self-driving car must recognize objects and hazards instantly to react in time. This domain heavily leverages deep learning (e.g., convolutional neural networks for image recognition) to turn raw sensor signals into a structured representation of the world (often called an environment model). The output of perception is a list of "what's around me"—such as bounding boxes around pedestrians with predicted crossing paths, vehicles with their velocities, traffic light states, etc.

In the real world, perception also has to cope with sensor degradation: dirty or blinded cameras, LiDAR occlusion from snow or spray, radar interference, or partially failed sensors. Robust stacks include sensor health monitoring and graceful fallback strategies—e.g., reducing automation level, shrinking the operational speed envelope, or handing control back to the driver when enough sensors are degraded that the environment model can no longer be trusted for the current operational design domain (ODD).

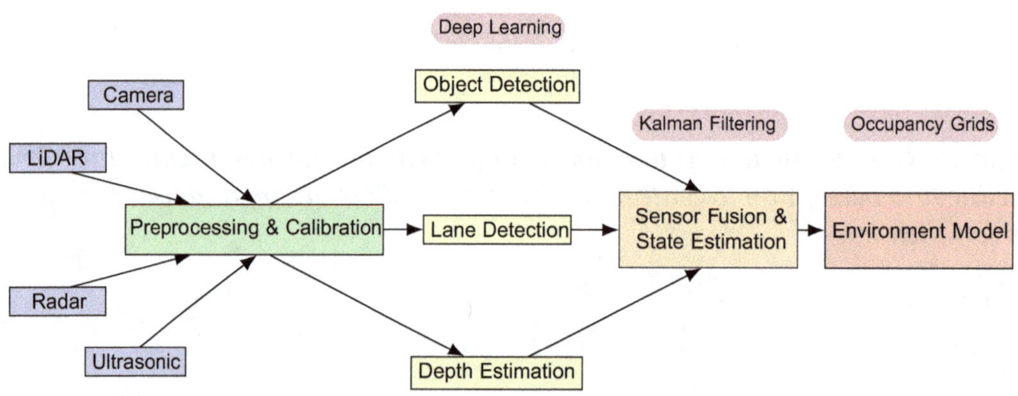

***Figure 8-2.** Perception system architecture with sensor fusion*

8.3.2 Planning

Planning is the AI task of deciding what the vehicle should do next, given the perceived environment. This covers both path planning—computing the trajectory the vehicle will follow—and behavior planning, determining high-level maneuvers (e.g., yield, overtake, stop, turn) and coordinating with other road users. In autonomous driving, planning might involve predicting the likely paths of nearby vehicles or pedestrians and then choosing a safe, comfortable trajectory for our car. For instance, if a bicycle is wobbling ahead, the plan may be to slow down and give a wider berth. If another car is merging, the plan could involve adjusting speed to let it in. In advanced scenarios like cooperative maneuvers, planning may include vehicle-to-vehicle communication—e.g., two autonomous cars negotiating lane merging order. Planning algorithms can be rule-based, but increasingly AI and ML are used to predict future world states (through trajectory prediction models) and evaluate many possible maneuvers efficiently. The output of planning is an intended path or action sequence for the next few seconds.

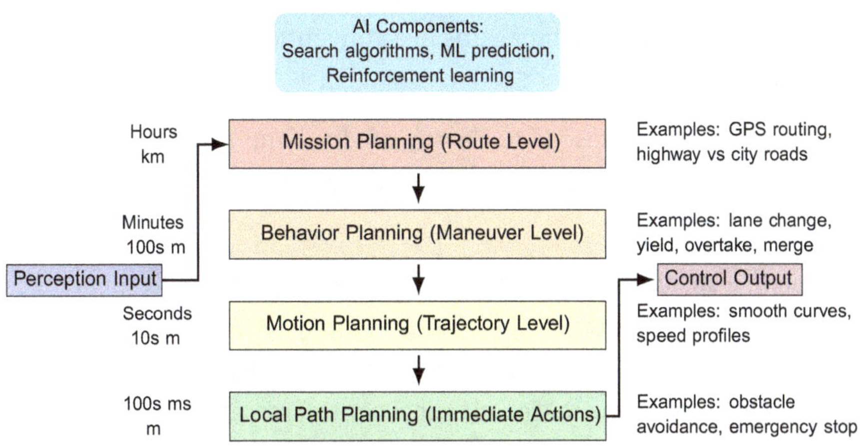

***Figure 8-3.** Hierarchical planning: from behavior to path planning*

In architectural terms, these planning layers do not usually execute in the same place. Mission planning is often associated with navigation and route services in the infotainment or connected services stack. Behavior and motion planning typically reside on centralized ADAS or automated driving compute platforms, where data from multiple sensors and zones can be fused. Immediate actuation and stabilization remain in lower-level control systems and safety controllers. This distinction matters because it separates compute-intensive decision logic from hard real-time vehicle control functions.

8.3.3 Control

Control is the real-time execution of the planned trajectory through low-level actuation—translating decisions into throttle, brake, and steering commands. Classic automotive control (cruise control, electronic stability programs, electric power steering) is built on control theory: feedback loops, observers, and often model-based or gain-scheduled controllers that can be rigorously analyzed, tested, and certified.

In today's SDVs, that foundation has not gone away. For safety-critical functions, especially those at ASIL-C/D, the inner control loops are still dominated by deterministic, well-understood algorithms. Where AI comes in is mostly *around* those loops, not inside them. For example:

- Perception networks identify obstacles and provide target time-to-collision to an AEB controller, but the braking profile itself is computed by a certified control function.
- A learned estimator infers tire–road friction or road surface type, which is then used to adapt gains in a conventional ESC or ABS controller.
- Supervisory logic uses ML to classify driving context (urban, highway, low grip) and select the most appropriate calibrated controller variant.

So when people speak about "AI-enhanced control," they usually mean AI-assisted control: machine learning improves the quality of inputs and tuning parameters, while the final torque and steering commands are still produced by controllers that can be audited against ISO 26262. One reason classical control remains dominant in ASIL-C/D loops is that it fits the safety toolchain: engineers can calculate worst-case execution times, analyze numerical stability, perform structural coverage on code, and argue traceability from requirements to implementation. For deep neural networks, all of these are still active research topics. You can test an NN extensively, but you cannot yet analyze it with the same formal rigor as a simple, well-understood controller, which is why most OEMs are cautious about letting ML anywhere near the final actuation chain. A sensible architectural pattern is to keep ML in an assisting channel monitored by a rule-based or model-based safety channel: if the ML output looks inconsistent or out of distribution, the system falls back to a conservative, purely classical controller.

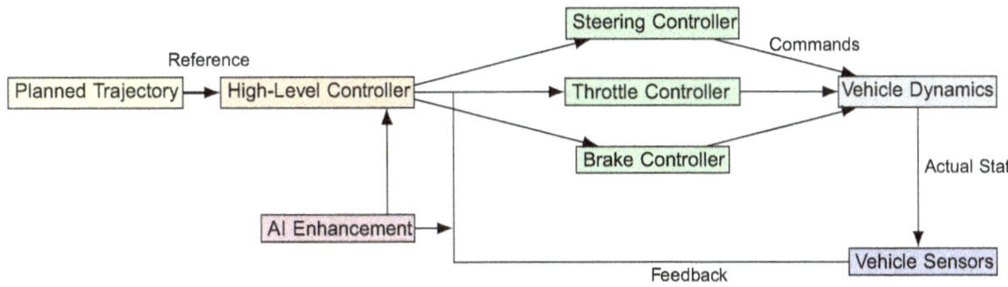

Figure 8-4. *AI-enhanced control system with classical and ML components*

8.3.4 Personalization

Beyond the driving functions, AI in an SDV also powers personalization in the cabin. Modern vehicles strive to create a "smartphone-like" user experience where the car learns the occupant's preferences and behaviors. Personalization workloads include user profiling (learning the driver's preferred seat position, mirror angles, favorite music, or climate settings) and infotainment recommendations (suggesting songs, destinations, or promotions tailored to the user). For example, an AI system might observe that a driver often goes to a certain coffee shop in the morning and proactively suggest a route there or display a coupon on the dashboard. Voice assistants in cars (like Alexa Auto or Siri in CarPlay) also use AI to understand natural language commands and personalize responses. Personalization extends to safety as well—e.g., adaptive driver assist systems that adjust their sensitivity based on whether the driver seems confident or timid. The goal is to make the vehicle feel like a "digital companion" that anticipates needs. However, these features raise privacy questions since they rely on collecting personal data—hence requiring transparent user consent and robust data security.

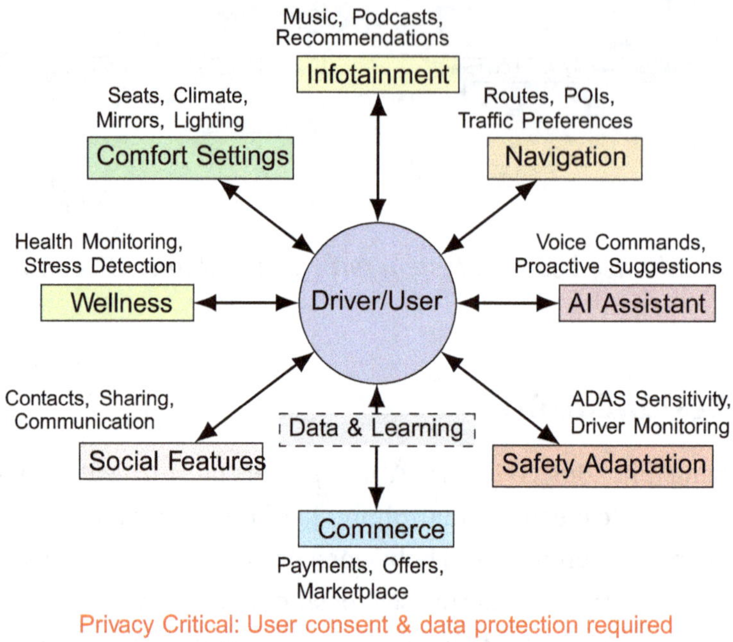

Figure 8-5. *AI-powered personalization ecosystem in SDVs*

These four AI workload domains often form a pipeline in autonomous driving: perception ➤ planning ➤ control, with personalization as an overlay improving user interaction. Figure 8-6 illustrates this pipeline, showing how raw sensor inputs get processed into decisions that move the car. A modular pipeline is commonly depicted in AV research: sensors feed into perception and localization modules, which feed into prediction and planning modules, culminating in control outputs. In this book we treat localization as part of perception and trajectory prediction as part of planning, so the four workload domains remain perception, planning, control, and personalization. While some companies (like Tesla) experiment with more end-to-end learned pipelines (blurring the line between perception and planning), the general structure remains: sense, think, and act—analogous to how a human driver sees, decides, and then steers/brakes.

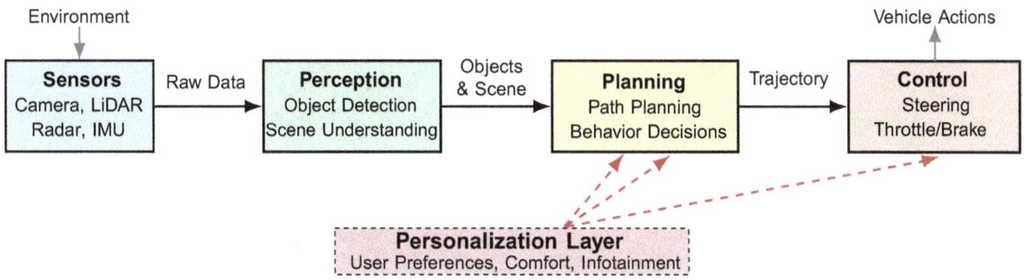

Figure 8-6. *Perception-to-control AI pipeline in SDVs*

8.4 Machine Learning Approaches

AI functionalities in SDVs are implemented using different machine learning (ML) approaches, each suited to different types of problems and data availability. The main categories are supervised learning, unsupervised (or self-supervised) learning, and reinforcement learning, all of which find unique applications in the automotive domain.

One practical constraint that shapes all of these AI choices is compute: in-vehicle ECUs have strict power, thermal, and cost budgets. A model that runs comfortably on a data center GPU may be impossible to deploy on an automotive SoC without heavy compression or distillation. This is one reason production stacks often lag behind the latest academic models (e.g., very large transformer architectures) and instead use carefully engineered networks that fit within tight latency and energy envelopes. Techniques such as knowledge distillation, pruning, and quantization are commonly used to compress large models into smaller, deployment-ready versions that still meet accuracy and latency targets on automotive hardware.

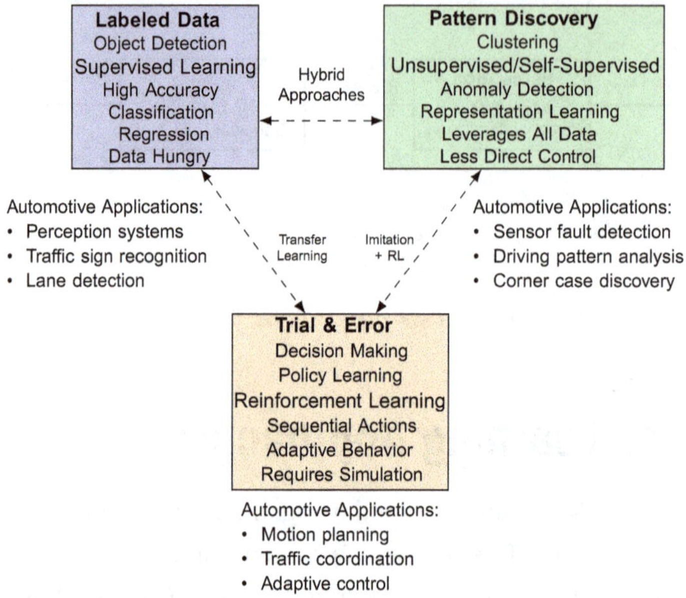

Figure 8-7. *Machine learning approaches in automotive AI*

8.4.1 Supervised Learning

Supervised learning is the dominant ML approach in current automotive AI. In supervised learning, models are trained on labeled datasets—meaning that each training example comes with a "ground truth" label or desired output that the model should learn to predict. In the context of SDVs, supervised learning powers tasks like object detection, lane marking segmentation, traffic sign recognition, pedestrian intention prediction, etc. For example, an automaker might train a neural network to detect pedestrians by feeding it thousands of images of street scenes with bounding boxes drawn around pedestrians as labels. Datasets such as Waymo Open Dataset, KITTI, and nuScenes provide large, richly annotated multi-sensor driving scenes (Waymo at a very large scale; KITTI and nuScenes smaller but influential), enabling supervised learning for perception tasks.

The strength of supervised learning is its high accuracy when a large, quality dataset is available. If you can collect and label enough examples of a scenario, a deep learning model can often learn to handle that scenario reliably. This has led to impressive perception systems—e.g., vision models that, on curated benchmark datasets and in clear conditions, can detect vehicles and pedestrians with superhuman accuracy—because they've seen virtually every common object from many angles during training. However, benchmark performance does not automatically translate to deployed performance: domain shift (different cameras, locations, weather, or signage) often degrades accuracy in the field, which is why calibration, robust validation, and monitoring are critical. Tesla, for instance, leverages fleet data from hundreds of thousands of customer cars to continuously train its vision models with human-reviewed labels (like "cut-in vehicle" or "pedestrian about to cross"), achieving rapid improvements via such supervision.

However, supervised learning in automotive faces significant challenges: chiefly, the expensive data labeling process and the difficulty of covering all possible cases. Hand-labeling driving data is labor-intensive and costly—think of drawing boxes around every pedestrian in thousands of ten-second video clips. Moreover, the "long tail" of rare events (a deer jumping out at night, an overturned truck on the highway, a pedestrian in an unusual costume) means that no matter how much data you label, something novel will appear on the road. Thus, supervised models can be brittle when they encounter situations that differ from their training data. Another issue is scalability: as SDVs operate in more locations, maintaining up-to-date labeled data for each city's unique environment (different signage, local anomalies) becomes onerous. Despite these issues, supervised learning remains the backbone for most deployed ADAS features because of its proven performance in well-defined tasks. Engineers mitigate its limits by constantly expanding datasets and using simulation to synthesize examples of rare events.

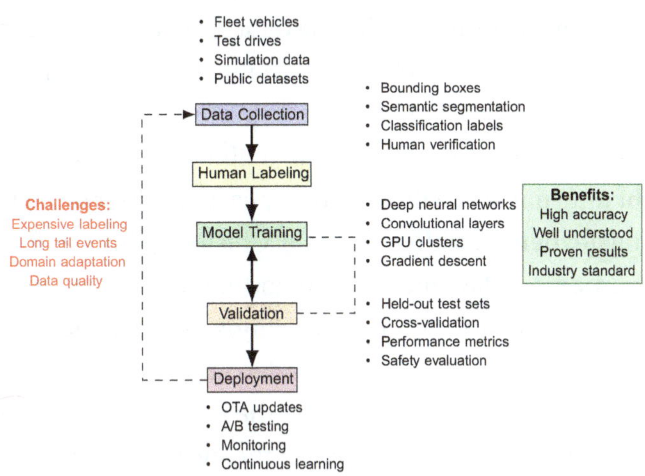

Figure 8-8. *Supervised learning workflow in automotive applications*

Critic's Note Looking ahead—foundation models and VLMs: While this chapter focuses on "classic" deep learning architectures (CNNs, RNNs, RL agents), automotive research is rapidly exploring large vision and vision–language models that can jointly reason about images, text, and map data. Today these models mostly live in the lab or in cloud-backed assistants, but over the next few years, we expect to see distilled or specialized variants used for richer scene understanding and natural human–vehicle interaction. The safety and compute challenges, however, remain the same or even more severe: bigger models are harder to verify and harder to run on constrained in-vehicle hardware.

8.4.2 Unsupervised and Self-Supervised Learning

Unsupervised learning refers to techniques that find patterns in data without explicit human-provided labels. In practice, completely unsupervised learning (with no guidance at all) is less common in automotive; more prevalent is self-supervised learning, where the data itself provides supervision in clever ways. The goal is to leverage the vast amounts of unlabeled data cars collect (which far outstrip what humans could ever label) to learn useful representations or detect patterns.

One example is using clustering on driving data. Imagine taking thousands of driving trajectories and having an algorithm cluster them into typical scenarios—it might naturally group data into clusters like "highway cruising," "stop-and-go city traffic," "sharp braking events," etc., without any human telling it what those clusters mean. This could highlight unusual anomalies or corner cases as their own clusters, guiding engineers to investigate them. Another example: Clustering images from forward cameras might separate clear daytime views, nighttime with glare, rain scenes, etc., effectively mapping out the distribution of conditions the fleet encounters. A major emerging trend is self-supervised learning for video and sensor data. In self-supervised approaches, the system creates proxy tasks from the raw data. For instance, a self-driving car's AI might take a video clip and try to predict the next few frames (a video prediction task)—not because we need the frames predicted per se, but because to do so the model must learn salient features of object motion. Or it might withhold one camera's view and have the model infer it from neighboring cameras (learning spatial consistency) or use a future segment of a trajectory as a "label" for the past (learning driving patterns).

These techniques let models learn from unlabeled dashcam footage or sensor logs. Recent research has shown the power of self-supervised sensor fusion embeddings, where, say, a network is trained to align LiDAR point clouds and camera images by learning a shared representation (the training signal being the consistency between the two sensor modalities). Such a model could then detect objects in LiDAR by leveraging camera texture, all without explicit labels.

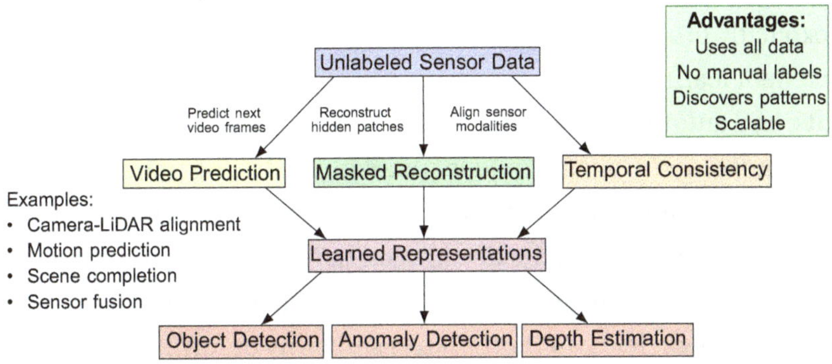

Figure 8-9. *Self-supervised learning techniques in automotive AI*

The advantage here is unlocking the "dark matter" of data—the 99% of data that isn't labeled due to cost. Unsupervised learning can surface new insights (like discovering that a certain sensor reading pattern precedes failures or grouping driving behaviors) that humans weren't explicitly looking for. Self-supervised pre-training can also initialize models that are later fine-tuned with smaller labeled datasets, improving performance (analogous to how large language models are pre-trained on raw text). For example, a network might learn general features of driving videos via self-supervision (e.g., understanding the concept of object permanence or typical motion flows) and then, with a relatively small labeled dataset, be fine-tuned to do lane detection much better than training from scratch.

Automotive applications of unsupervised ML are still nascent but growing. One practical use today is anomaly detection in sensors: an unsupervised model can learn the "normal" patterns of LiDAR scans on a clear day and then flag when current input looks out of distribution (like strange readings that could indicate sensor dirt or a truly novel obstacle). This is important for functional safety—alerting when AI might be in unfamiliar territory. In the future, as the amount of driving data explodes, unsupervised learning is expected to play a larger role because it's simply infeasible to label everything. Carmakers and tech firms are actively researching self-supervised methods (such as contrastive learning on video: e.g., "SimCLR" but for sequential frames) to create robust perception models that learn from the world itself.

8.4.3 Reinforcement Learning

Reinforcement learning (RL) is a third paradigm where an agent learns by interacting with an environment, receiving rewards or penalties for its actions, and improving its policy to maximize cumulative reward. In the context of SDVs, you can think of the "agent" as the car's driving policy and the environment as the road scenario. The promise of RL is to discover effective driving strategies through trial and error, rather than being explicitly programmed or directly trained on human examples.

Reinforcement learning has shown impressive results in games and simulated environments, and automotive researchers apply it to areas like decision-making and control. For instance, an RL agent could learn adaptive driving policies—maybe a policy for highway lane-changing that balances making progress with safety. The agent might get a positive reward for reaching the destination quickly or a negative reward for braking too hard (discomfort) or getting too close to other cars (risk). Over many simulated episodes, the agent might learn to merge lanes smoothly or form efficient platoons, discovering maneuvers that human drivers or basic algorithms might miss. RL has also been explored for complex control tasks, like learning how to handle a vehicle drifting on ice by repeated attempts (something hard to derive purely from first principles).

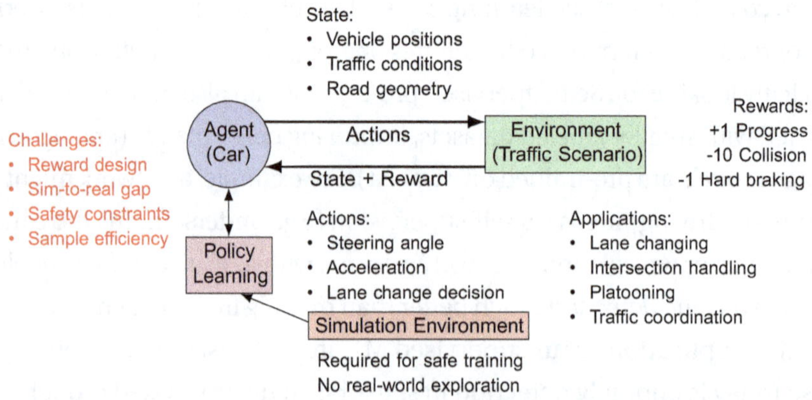

Figure 8-10. *Reinforcement learning framework for autonomous driving*

However, applying RL in real vehicles faces a fundamental hurdle: unsafe exploration. The classic RL process involves the agent taking random exploratory actions to see what happens—clearly, you cannot deploy an untrained RL agent in a real car and have it, say, randomly turn the wheel or ignore lanes to see if it yields higher reward! The risk of accidents is far too great. This necessitates the use of simulation environments for training RL agents. Fortunately, modern driving simulators (like CARLA [239], SVL Simulator [240] (formerly LGSVL), or proprietary ones by Waymo and others) have become quite realistic. Researchers can train an autonomous driving policy in simulation, letting it crash virtual cars thousands of times to learn what not to do, and then carefully transfer the learned policy to a real car (with lots of validation in between).

For example, an RL policy might learn how to handle an unmanned intersection by aggressive trial and error in a sim and then be fine-tuned and validated before being used in a physical vehicle.

Even with simulation, RL in driving is challenging. One major issue is defining the reward function properly—how do you mathematically specify "drive like a safe, courteous human"? A poorly designed reward can lead to undesirable behavior (the agent might game the metric—e.g., staying still to avoid any penalty for mistakes yields zero crashes but also zero progress!).

Another issue is the simulation-to-reality gap: policies might overfit to the simulator quirks and not generalize to real sensor noise or vehicle dynamics differences. Researchers address this with techniques like domain randomization (varying sim parameters) or combining RL with supervised learning (learning from human demonstrations first and then refining with RL—an approach called imitation learning + RL [241, 242], e.g., as Nuro has explored).

Despite the hurdles, RL is starting to see use in pilot projects and research deployments. One notable area is traffic management and coordination: e.g., research prototypes that control fleets of autonomous taxis or delivery bots to collectively minimize wait times or energy use—a problem well-suited to RL's strength in sequential decision optimization, but not yet deployed at large scale on public roads. Another is motion planning under uncertainty: researchers have trained RL agents that, for instance, learn to navigate crowded environments (like a game of *Frogger*) by inching forward when safe and holding back when uncertain, capturing a human-like defensive driving style that emerges from the reward structure. These successes underscore RL's ability to uncover novel solutions.

A practical compromise is using RL offline to test and validate scenarios. For example, an OEM might use RL to generate worst-case scenarios to challenge their rule-based system: essentially, an RL agent in simulation might control other vehicles or pedestrians with the objective to cause a collision, thereby identifying the weaknesses in the autonomous car's policy. This turns RL into a tool for safety validation.

A lot of recent work focuses on offline or "batch" reinforcement learning and conservative Q-learning, which try to learn policies from logged driving data without unsafe exploration. These techniques are promising for automotive because they respect the safety constraint of never letting an unproven policy explore freely on public roads, but as of 2025 they remain largely in the research and pilot deployment phase.

In summary, reinforcement learning holds a lot of promise for adaptive, self-improving driving strategies, but due to safety, its deployment in public road vehicles is cautious. As of 2025, you should treat RL in automotive as pre-production: highly promising, but not yet a mainstream choice for safety-critical control on public roads. It requires simulation (and often a human safety net even during on-road trials) because letting an AI "figure out driving" by trial and error in the real world is unacceptable. The current trajectory is to combine RL with other learning methods and extensive simulation, gradually increasing confidence until such policies can be entrusted with real vehicles. We can expect reinforcement learning's role to grow as simulation fidelity improves and as vehicles move toward fully autonomous operation in constrained domains (e.g., an RL agent might first be deployed to drive in a well-defined industrial park with geofencing before we ever see one in Manhattan traffic).

8.5 Federated and Edge Learning

Machine learning doesn't end once a model is deployed; automakers continually retrain and update AI models as they gather new data (e.g., to improve perception in new environments or update driving policies). Traditionally, this retraining has been centralized—all data is sent to a cloud server where a giant model update is computed. However, with the massive scale of connected cars, privacy regulations, and bandwidth costs, new paradigms like federated learning and edge learning are gaining traction in the automotive field.

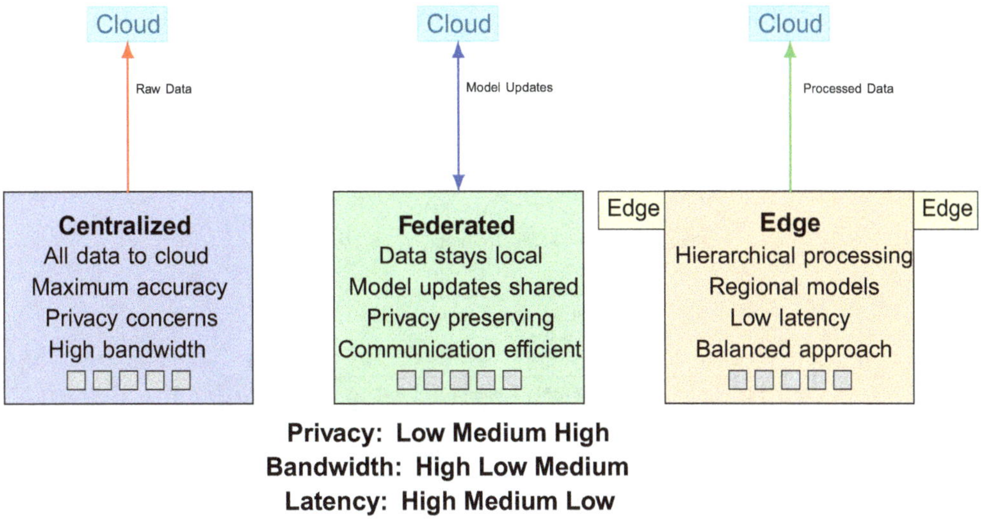

Figure 8-11. *Comparison of centralized, federated, and edge learning paradigms*

8.5.1 Centralized Learning

In the classic approach, raw data from vehicles (sensor logs, images, driver behavior data, etc.) is uploaded to a central cloud server. The OEM (or its cloud provider) maintains a centralized data lake and performs model training on this aggregated dataset. For example, 100,000 cars might each send video clips of rare pedestrian scenarios to the cloud, and the central system trains a better pedestrian detection model using the combined data. This approach tends to yield very powerful models since the trainer has access to all the raw data (more data usually means better accuracy). However, it comes with significant downsides: privacy concerns (uploading potentially sensitive data like in-cabin camera feeds or GPS tracks raises GDPR issues), bandwidth costs (a fleet of cars can generate terabytes of data per day; transmitting that constantly is expensive and sometimes infeasible), and latency (new learnings aren't real time). Centralized training can also suffer from data silos—if, say, two manufacturers could benefit from each other's data, they legally cannot simply pool it due to competition and privacy. Despite these issues, centralized cloud training is still widely used for initial model development and major updates. Automakers use techniques like data reduction (only uploading interesting events rather than continuous feeds) to manage bandwidth. For instance, Tesla's fleet learning famously does this: the car's software decides when an event is worth uploading (e.g., when the car's prediction was uncertain or when autopilot disengaged suddenly)—this acts as a form of semantic compression so that only valuable training data is centralized. Nonetheless, the industry has recognized the need for alternatives because simply streaming all raw data to the cloud is neither privacy-first nor cost-effective.

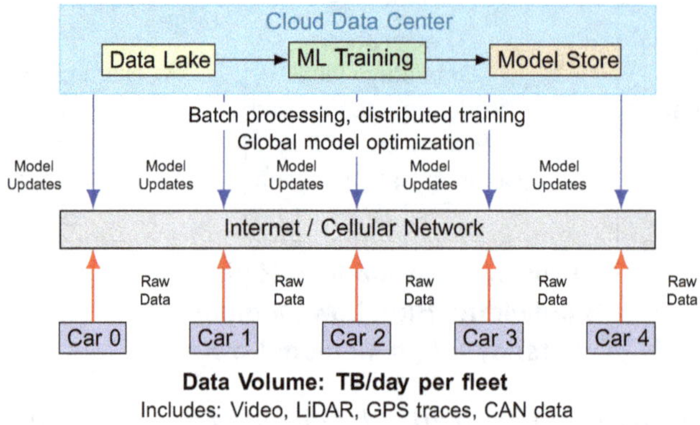

Figure 8-12. *Centralized learning architecture for automotive AI*

8.5.2 Federated Learning (FL)

Federated learning is a decentralized training approach specifically designed to address privacy and bandwidth issues. The core idea is "bring the model to the data, instead of data to the model." In a federated learning setup, each vehicle (or local device) keeps its raw data locally. The vehicle periodically downloads the current global model from the cloud, trains it on its local data, and then uploads only the model updates (learned parameter changes, gradients, etc.) back to the cloud. A central server (or a distributed protocol) then aggregates these updates (e.g., by averaging the gradient or weights—known as federated averaging) to form an improved global model, which is sent back to vehicles. Crucially, no raw sensor data leaves the car—only numerical weight updates, which by themselves reveal far less personal information. This approach is touted as "privacy-friendly AI" because it reduces the attack surface for data leaks. For instance, if a car has video of a pedestrian, in FL the car might adjust the model's weights to better detect pedestrians and send those weight tweaks to cloud; an eavesdropper cannot reconstruct the pedestrian's image from just those weight tweaks easily (especially if techniques like differential privacy are added).

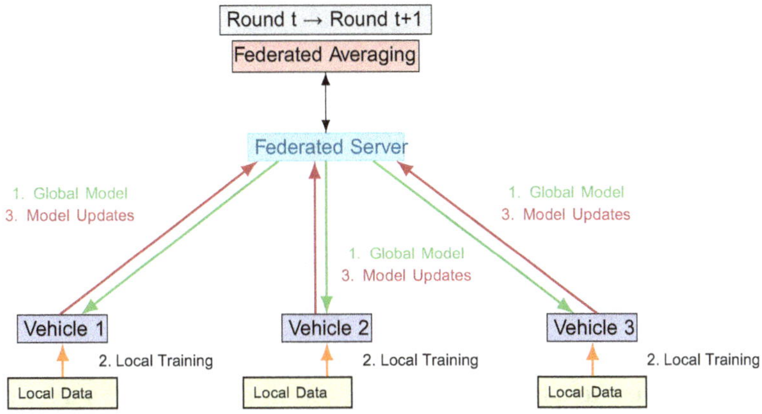

Figure 8-13. *Federated learning workflow in automotive networks*

Federated learning can thus comply more easily with regulations like GDPR, which prefer data to remain local or anonymized. Google famously pioneered FL for keyboard apps [243] (learning your typing patterns without uploading your texts), and in automotive, we see it used for things like learning vehicle energy management or predictive maintenance models across a fleet without sharing proprietary datasets among competitors. A concrete example: BMW or Toyota could have each of their cars train a model to predict battery range more accurately based on that car's data; the fleet's models are then aggregated to a master model that benefits from varied usage patterns—all without exchanging raw driving logs. Technical challenges remain: ensuring all those model updates don't conflict (e.g., if data distributions differ greatly), handling straggler devices or unreliable connections, and preventing certain attacks where model updates could potentially leak info (there is research on encrypting updates and using secure aggregation to mitigate this). Despite these challenges, federated learning is moving from lab prototypes into early automotive and IoT pilots, but it is not yet a mainstream production pattern for ADAS or ADS. It allows collaboration: multiple stakeholders (OEMs, suppliers, fleets) can jointly train a model without exposing their raw data to each other. Industry voices emphasize that FL enables collaboration across stakeholders—combining model improvements from diverse data sources—without centralizing raw personal data. In sum, FL offers a path to fleet-wide intelligence that is privacy-preserving, which is extremely attractive as vehicles become data hubs.

8.5.3 Edge Learning

Edge learning in this context refers to utilizing edge computing infrastructure—intermediate servers closer to the vehicles (e.g., cellular base stations, roadside units, or regional data centers)—to assist with training or adaptation of models. The idea is a hierarchy: the vehicle does some learning locally, the edge servers (perhaps one per city or highway region) aggregate and refine models for their locality, and then perhaps a cloud master model integrates those. Edge computing can significantly reduce latency and bandwidth usage. For instance, instead of every car sending updates to a central cloud, cars might connect to a multi-access edge computing (MEC) server run by a telecom at the 5G tower. That MEC node could quickly aggregate model updates from, say, all cars in Berlin to produce a "Berlin-specialized vision model" that accounts for local quirks (like different traffic light designs or predominant weather). That specialized model could be sent back to Berlin vehicles for improved performance in that region, while a global cloud model still exists for general knowledge. Edge nodes can also preprocess data: e.g., raw video might be heavy to send far, but an edge server could receive somewhat processed feature data from cars, do a heavier computation there (since it has more power than the car itself), and only transmit summarized insights to the cloud.

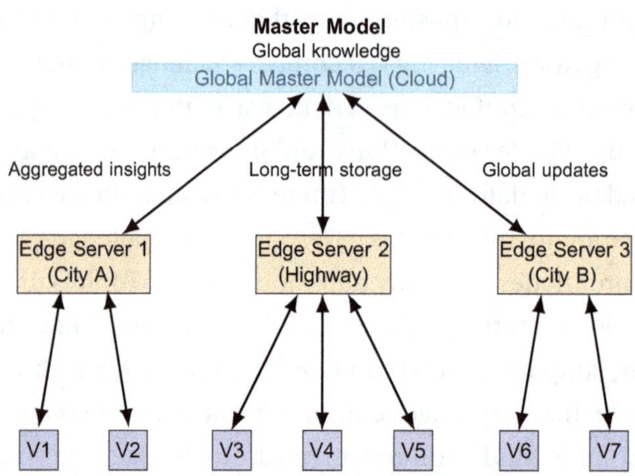

Figure 8-14. *Hierarchical edge learning architecture for automotive AI*

Essentially, edge learning distributes the training workload across a hierarchy of car ➤ roadside/edge ➤ central cloud. This aligns with initiatives like the Automotive Edge Computing Consortium (AECC), which posits that distributed edge processing is vital for connected car services. They demonstrated a proof of concept (PoC) where hierarchical edge computing combined with federated learning provided accurate battery range predictions while using up to nearly 10× less network and compute than a centralized baseline in that specific proof-of-concept setup [244]. Edge learning can be seen as a complement to federated learning—often, FL requires some coordinating server (which could be an edge server) to aggregate updates. By placing that aggregator at the network edge, OEMs reduce round-trip time and can even enable regional models when appropriate (e.g., a model for driving on snowy roads could be fine-tuned by edge servers in Nordic regions where data of snow is abundant and then shared to cars in those regions before winter storms).

To illustrate, consider data ownership and privacy: a big question in connected vehicles is who owns the driving data—the OEM, the driver, or others like the fleet operator or even the telecom providing connectivity? This ownership determines who has the right to monetize it and who bears regulatory risk like GDPR compliance. Federated learning is often pitched as a solution that is "privacy-first" since personal data stays on the device. But even if raw data isn't directly collected, OEMs can still derive aggregated insights from the federated process and potentially monetize those (e.g., knowing that "X% of drivers at location Y have to brake hard" could be valuable for a mapping or infrastructure company): the monetization doesn't disappear—it just operates one layer removed.

Business Note Data ownership: Who owns the driving data? OEM, driver, or telecom operator? The answer determines monetization rights, GDPR exposure, and ecosystem leverage. For instance, if the driver legally owns the data, the OEM must seek consent to use it for AI training, potentially even share revenue from features that benefit from it. Federated learning is marketed as "privacy-first" since raw data never leaves the vehicle, mitigating some GDPR concerns, but OEMs still monetize the aggregated insights. In other words, FL changes the technical process but the business goal remains: extract value from data, just without touching the raw personally identifiable information. Clarity in data ownership agreements is crucial—a telco might claim rights over data passing through its edge cloud, or an insurance partner might want a slice of driving behavior data. Moving forward, we expect new models of data licensing and privacy-preserving analytics (like FL and even blockchain-based data marketplaces) to reconcile these conflicts. The key is balancing value creation with transparency and consent.

In practice, you should think of centralized, federated, and edge learning as points in a design space rather than a strict evolution. Many current SDV programs still start with centralized training on a heavily filtered cloud data lake, then experiment with federated updates for specific models where privacy or bandwidth is tight, and use edge servers mainly for low-latency aggregation or regional specialization. A realistic near-term pattern is initial model development in the cloud, continuous improvement via centrally uploaded triggered events, and, in some regions, experimental federated updates coordinated by MEC or regional data centers. The long-term vision is a fleet where every mile contributes to learning, without violating data protection laws or collapsing the OEM's network budget—but getting there requires not only algorithms like FL, but also robust MLOps, OTA integration, and clear data governance contracts between OEMs, suppliers, fleets, and drivers.

8.6 AI Safety and Explainability

AI safety in SDVs can be understood as a simple flow. First, engineers define the operational context and identify what can go wrong. Second, they derive safety requirements and fallback behaviors for the AI-enabled function. Third, they train and validate the model using governed datasets and scenario coverage criteria. Fourth, they verify the complete system through simulation, test tracks, shadow mode, and controlled on-road evaluation. Finally, they monitor performance after deployment and restrict updates to controlled release processes. Standards and regulations are important because they formalize these expectations, but the engineering logic comes first: define the hazard, constrain the model, validate the behavior, and preserve a safe fallback.

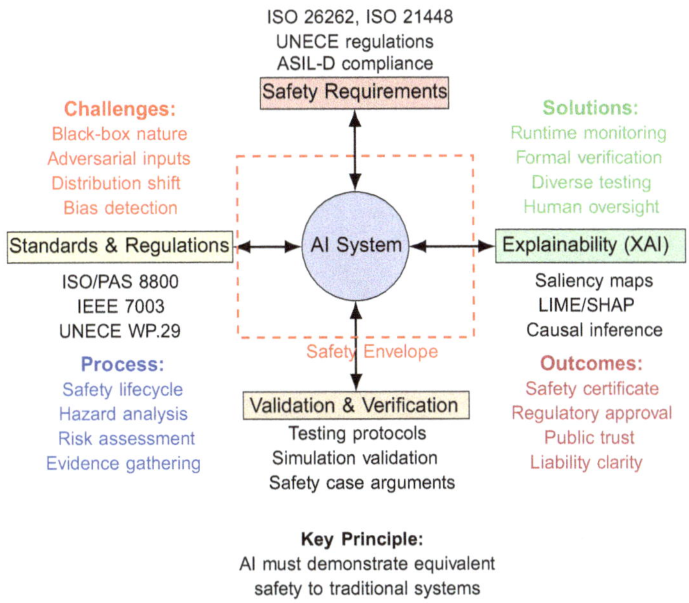

Figure 8-15. *AI safety and explainability framework for automotive applications*

This engineering flow is increasingly being reinforced by external standards and regulation.

Regulatory landscape: One key regulatory anchor is UNECE WP.29's modern vehicle regulations: UN R155 [69] (cybersecurity) and UN R156 [72] (software updates), in force since 2021 and phased into EU type approval from July 2022 (new types) and July 2024 (all new registrations). For automated driving, WP.29's GRVA coordinates the FRAV and VMAD groups, which develop the New Assessment/Test Method (NATM) framework—scenario catalogues and a multi-pillar approach spanning simulation, track, on-road testing, and audits. There is not yet a UN "R" regulation specific to AI itself; rather, these activities inform type approval for ADS functions. In the EU, the horizontal AI Act (2024/2025) introduces binding obligations for high-risk AI systems—including those in vehicles—covering risk management, data governance, and documentation. Practically, if an OEM includes ML components in safety-related control (e.g., braking/steering), the type approval safety case is expected to address AI-specific hazards (e.g., misclassification, adversarial robustness, and ODD limits) and fallback strategies, consistent with ISO 26262/21448-style evidence.

Regulatory approaches also diverge across regions. In the United States, e.g., the National Highway Traffic Safety Administration (NHTSA) has so far focused more on guidance, investigations, and post hoc enforcement than on detailed type approval rules for AI, while in China ministries such as the Ministry of Industry and Information Technology (MIIT) and local authorities are developing their own frameworks for intelligent and connected vehicles. For a global OEM, this means safety arguments and documentation must be robust enough to satisfy multiple, evolving regulatory regimes, not just the UNECE/EU stack.

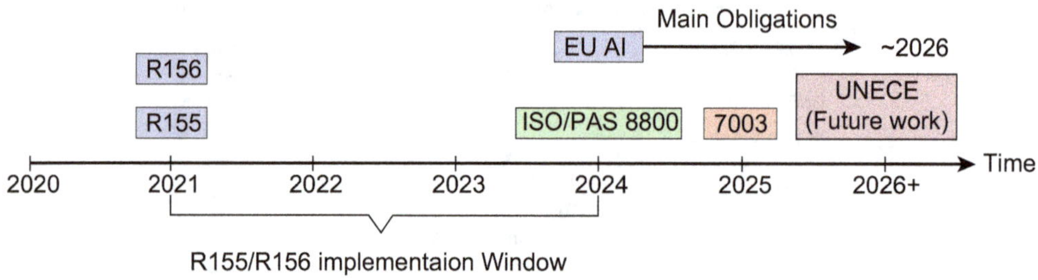

Figure 8-16. *Regulatory landscape for AI in automotive systems*

Industry safety standards: Industry safety standards are also evolving: ISO/PAS 8800:2024 [245] (Road vehicles—Safety and AI) provides an AI-specific safety framework that complements ISO 26262 (functional safety) and ISO 21448:2022 (SOTIF). It defines an AI safety lifecycle, guidance on data governance and representativeness (to mitigate distribution shift), and verification/validation methods for ML components. The PAS emphasizes deriving AI-specific safety requirements traceable to safety goals and building a structured safety argument (including considerations such as bias and, where applicable, online learning). Although ISO/PAS 8800 is not yet a full international standard, it is already being used as guidance by early adopters and is likely to influence future automotive AI assurance practice.

Another important standard is IEEE Std 7003-2024 [246] (Algorithmic Bias Considerations), published on January 24, 2025. It provides processes and methodologies to identify, assess, and mitigate bias in AI systems. In automotive contexts this is directly relevant to driver monitoring and perception systems (e.g., demographic performance disparities). IEEE 7003 is technology-agnostic: it does not prescribe specific models, but it requires documentation of bias risks, measurement, and mitigations. It forms part of the IEEE 7000 series of trustworthy AI standards that many automakers reference for user-facing applications.

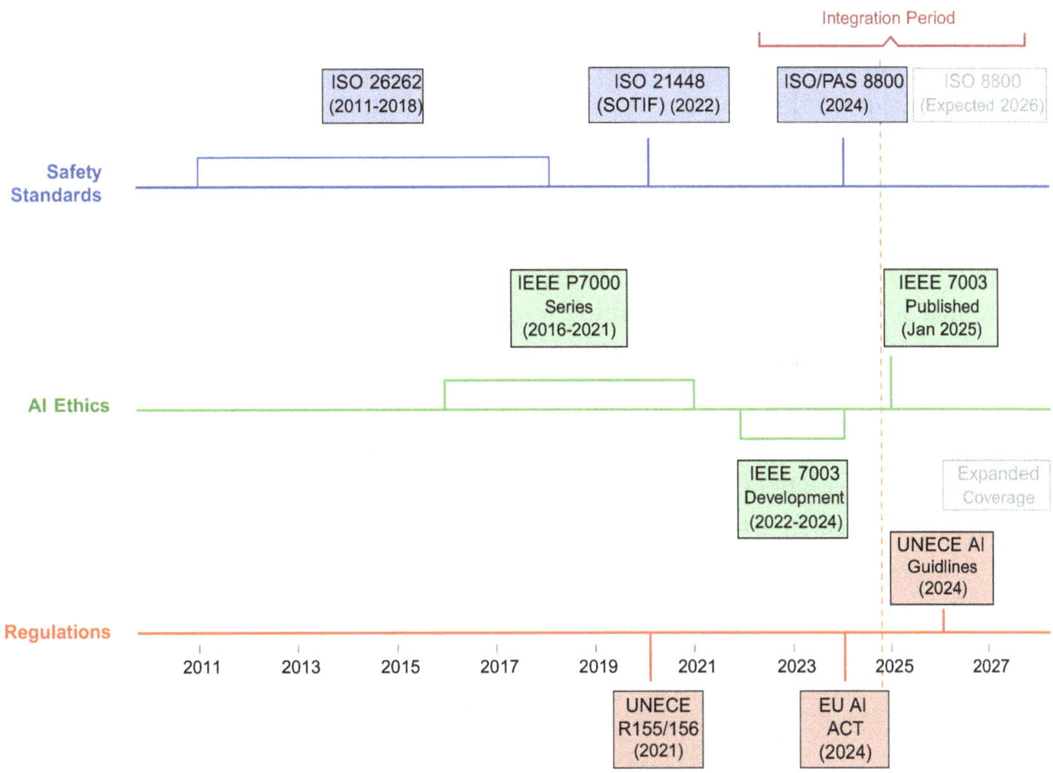

Figure 8-17. *Timeline of AI safety and ethics standards in automotive*

Explainable AI (XAI) techniques: Technical explainable AI (XAI) techniques are another crucial piece in building trust and meeting regulatory demands. Explainable AI refers to methods that make the decision-making of AI models more interpretable to humans. In the context of SDVs, an example XAI technique is saliency maps for vision networks: these highlight which parts of an image the neural network focused on when making a decision. For instance, if the car's perception AI decides "pedestrian ahead," a saliency map can show that the network indeed concentrated on the pedestrian's outline (and not, say, a shadow or a sign). This helps engineers verify that the AI is reacting to the right features. Saliency or heat maps have already been used to debug why an autonomous car's network failed to detect an obstacle—maybe the map shows it paid attention to irrelevant background, suggesting a dataset gap. Another approach is causal inference and scenario-based explanations. Rather than just highlighting pixels, one might use causal models to ask counterfactual questions: "If that truck were not occluding the view, would the AI have detected the pedestrian earlier?" If removing an occlusion changes the detection outcome, that's a causal explanation pointing to occlusion as a factor. Researchers are also exploring simplified surrogate models—e.g., train a decision tree to mimic the neural network's decisions in specific scenarios, because a decision tree is easier to interpret (this is related to methods like LIME or SHAP, which provide approximate explanations for complex models). The overarching goal is to create traceability: If the car makes a mistake, can we trace why (was it glare on camera, a weird object shape, or a flaw in the training)? And if it makes a decision, can we explain it to a user or an investigator? In safety-critical domains like automotive, some level of explainability is not just nice-to-have; it might be mandated. For example, an insurer or a court might ask: "Why did the autonomous car not brake for that obstacle?" And the company needs to provide a credible answer, potentially with evidence from XAI tools (e.g., "the object wasn't recognized because it was unlike any training data; here's a heat map showing the network's focus, and indeed it misclassified the object as a plastic bag instead of a tire due to the shape").

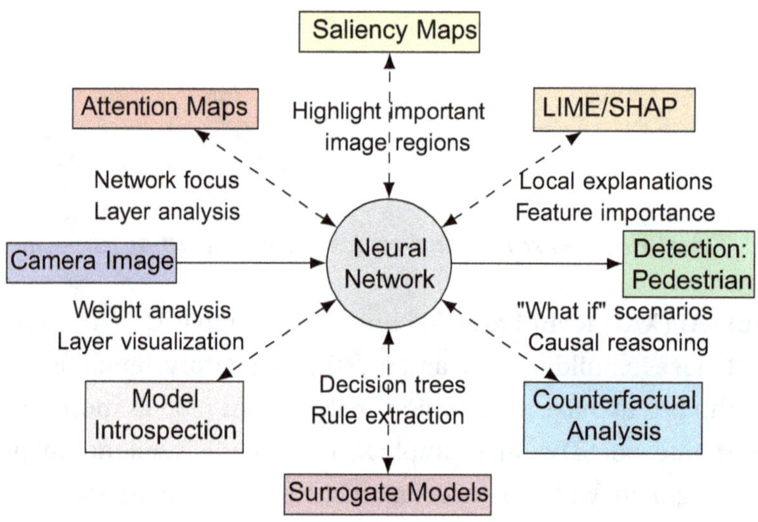

***Figure 8-18.** Explainable AI techniques for automotive applications*

Black-box AI in ASIL-D domains: One of the hardest issues remains: black-box AI in ASIL-D domains. ASIL-D (Automotive Safety Integrity Level D) is the highest criticality in ISO 26262, typically for systems where a failure could lead to life-threatening situations (think braking or steering). Traditionally, ASIL-D systems use very deterministic, well-verified components (redundant sensors, proven controllers). Introducing a deep neural network, which is by nature a black-box function approximator, into an ASIL-D context (like identifying obstacles for an emergency braking system) is viewed with skepticism. Without explainability and extensive validation, it's unacceptable to rely purely on a black box in such a scenario. The automotive safety community is actively researching how to build safety cases for deep learning—essentially to argue that even if we can't 100% explain every internal computation of the network, we have enough evidence of its reliability and mitigations for its failures. Methods include monitoring the AI output with a rule-based checker (if the AI output seems odd, the system can fall back or at least flag a need for driver takeover), runtime constraints (like imposing that the AI's detection range is limited to scenarios it was trained on and otherwise issuing a warning or graceful degradation), and formal verification of neural networks (an area of research where you try to mathematically prove that within certain bounds, the network's outputs won't violate safety requirements). There's also work on making neural nets more inherently interpretable (like by using architectures that align with physical concepts or training them to produce human-understandable rationales).

In practice, many OEMs also use so-called "shadow mode" deployments: new perception or planning models run on the vehicle in parallel with the production system but do not control the car. Their outputs are logged and compared against the live stack and ground truth, providing a bridge between simulation and full deployment. Only after a model has performed acceptably in shadow mode across large fleets and diverse conditions will it be considered for active control in safety-relevant functions.

Continuous or online learning after deployment introduces additional safety concerns: if a model can change its parameters in the field, the safety case must address how those changes are constrained, tested, and rolled back. Most current production systems avoid fully online learning for safety-critical functions and instead update models only via controlled, validated OTA releases.

Critic's Note **Industry-wide open problem:** How to build safety cases for deep neural nets that resist adversarial inputs and distribution drift? In simpler terms, how can we assure that an AI driving system remains safe when conditions change (lighting, weather, new object types) or when someone tries to fool it (like placing stickers on a stop sign to confuse vision)? Adversarial vulnerabilities and model drift are well-known in AI research—a slight tweak in input might cause a big mistake in output. For an automotive AI, this is a grave concern. Regulators and academics are brainstorming solutions: one idea is requiring an "AI safety buffer"—e.g., even if the neural net confidence is high, the car might still not accelerate to full speed unless a secondary sensor confirms the path is clear (so even an adversarial illusion won't directly lead to catastrophe). Another is continuous online learning under supervision, so the model gradually adapts to new conditions (though online learning itself raises safety issues if not carefully managed). There's also the concept of a safety envelope: ensure the AI never operates outside the domain it was trained for—if it finds itself outside (say, heavy snow when it was trained only on clear weather), it hands control back to the human or moves to a minimal risk condition. These are active research questions because the flexibility that makes AI powerful also makes it unpredictable in corner cases, and that unpredictability is not tolerated in safety-critical applications. Hence, solving this is a top priority for enabling full autonomy.

In summary, AI safety and explainability in SDVs is a multi-faceted domain involving compliance with new standards (UNECE, ISO 8800, IEEE 7003), technical XAI methods (saliency maps, causal reasoning, simplified models), and fundamentally new validation strategies. The automotive industry is, by necessity, more conservative than consumer tech—a glitchy smartphone app might frustrate, but a glitchy car AI can kill. Therefore, expect to see the phrase "AI safety case" in automotive: it means an evidence-backed argument that the AI will not introduce undue risk. Explainability is both a tool to build that case and a requirement in itself—especially if we want public acceptance. After all, riders in a driverless car might feel better if the car can explain its odd behavior ("I slowed down because my sensors picked up something unusual on the road ahead"). As AI in vehicles becomes more prevalent, being able to trust and understand these systems will be as important as their raw performance.

8.7 Data Pipelines

Data is the fuel for AI in SDVs, and managing that data—from the vehicle sensors all the way to cloud analytics—requires a well-designed data pipeline. This pipeline covers how data is generated, collected, filtered, transmitted, stored, and utilized (for learning or simulation). Without an efficient pipeline, even the best AI algorithms would starve or choke on data. Let's break down the typical pipeline stages.

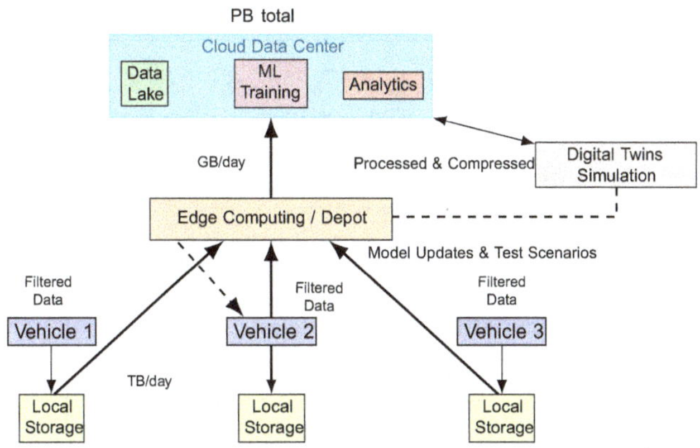

Figure 8-19. *Complete data pipeline architecture for SDVs*

8.7.1 On-Vehicle Data Buffering

Modern vehicles are rolling data centers. A single autonomous test vehicle can produce several terabytes of data per hour [24, 247] from cameras, LiDAR, radar, etc. Obviously, not all of this can be uploaded in real time. So, initially, data is buffered and logged locally on the vehicle. High-bandwidth sensors feed into onboard storage (SSDs) that can write data at tens of gigabits per second. At this stage, the vehicle may do some preprocessing: tagging data with metadata such as GPS location, timestamp, weather conditions, and even in-cabin events (e.g., "driver took over at this moment") to add context to the logs. Engineers in test vehicles often mark interesting moments in the data via a dashboard interface while it's fresh ("near-miss here" or "perception glitch at 12:05 PM"). This helps later during analysis. Essentially, the car acts as the first repository of data. Buffering is important because connectivity may not handle a constant raw stream; instead, the car can store and later transmit in bursts when connected (say, at a depot or over a strong 5G link). Additionally, the car's ECU network itself might filter some data—e.g., not every CAN bus message or every raw camera frame is needed; the vehicle might downsample or compress certain logs on the fly.

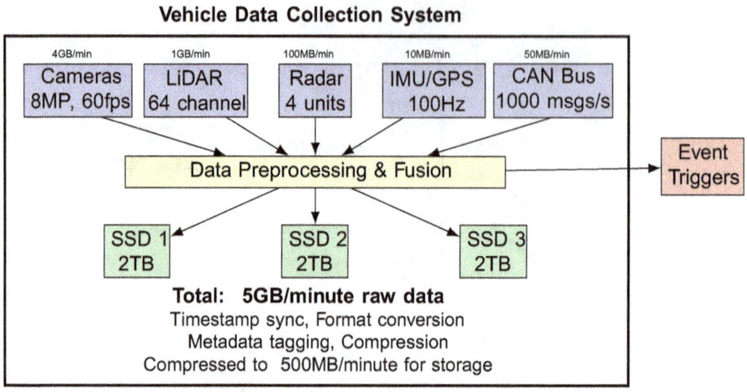

Figure 8-20. *On-board data collection and buffering system*

8.7.2 Edge/Depot Offloading and Filtering

After data are buffered on the vehicle, they must be offloaded selectively rather than indiscriminately. In consumer vehicles this may happen over Wi-Fi or cellular links; in test fleets it may occur at depots through high-bandwidth upload or physical storage transfer. Before upload, automated checks verify file integrity, timestamp consistency, and metadata completeness.

Edge or depot infrastructure often performs a second stage of filtering. Instead of transmitting continuous raw streams, the system prioritizes triggered events, rare scenarios, or uncertainty cases identified by the vehicle itself. This process, often called semantic compression, reduces bandwidth by sending only the most informative segments or summaries. The architectural goal is simple: preserve learning value while minimizing upload cost and unnecessary data retention.

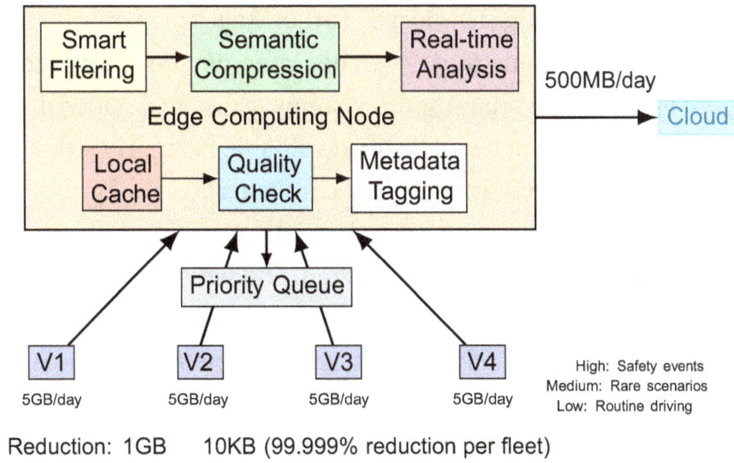

Figure 8-21. *Edge computing and data filtering architecture*

8.7.3 Cloud Storage and Processing

Once data has passed through the edge and been filtered/compressed, it lands in centralized cloud storage. Here, we might have a massive data lake with petabytes of driving data. At fleet scale, this storage and management is nontrivial: one estimate is that a fleet can generate 100+ Tb of data per day. Storing and managing that long-term is costly. Cloud providers charge not just for storage but also for data transfer (egress) and computation on it. This forces OEMs to be smart about what to keep and for how long. Often, there are retention policies: raw high-res data might be kept only for a short window unless flagged as interesting, while processed, reduced data is stored long-term. Techniques like deduplication are used—e.g., if 500 cars all saw the same landmark or same traffic jam, the back-end might only keep one representative log from those and discard redundant ones. Versioning is important too: as the AI models improve, they might want to go back and relabel or reanalyze old data; having an organized versioned dataset helps ensure comparisons are valid. Another strategy is "cold storage": move older data to cheaper, slower storage (like archive tapes or glacier storage), which can be retrieved if needed but isn't costing much in the interim. The cloud stage is where heavy computational analysis happens: building new training datasets and running analytics to find patterns (e.g., "how often do drivers trigger forward collision warnings and under what conditions?"). There's also a need to index data: so one can query "give me all instances of bicycles cutting in front of a car in rainy weather at night"—which requires rich metadata tagging of each log. This is why earlier stages tag context (location, weather, scenario tags)—to enable these searches later. We see AI applied here too, not just for driving but for managing data: some systems use AI to decide which clips are worth keeping by predicting which will be most valuable for training (active learning approach: keep those that current models find confusing).

Regulators are also increasingly interested in data provenance: being able to show where training data came from, how it was filtered, and whether it is representative of the intended operational design domain (ODD). This pushes OEMs to implement data lineage tracking—logging which vehicles, regions, and time periods contributed to each training dataset—and to audit datasets for bias (e.g., checking whether certain weather, lighting, or demographic groups are under-represented). These provenance and representativeness records later feed into the AI safety case and EU AI Act documentation, which require OEMs to explain not just what a model does, but what data shaped it.

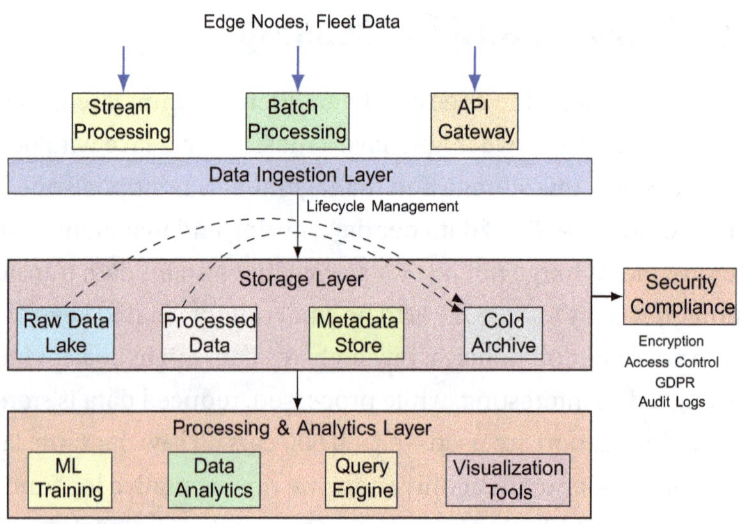

Figure 8-22. *Cloud data storage and processing architecture*

8.7.4 Digital Twins and Simulation

A distinctive aspect of SDVs is the use of collected data not just to improve the ML models directly, but also to feed simulation and digital twin systems. A digital twin in automotive is a virtual replica of either the vehicle or the environment (or both) that runs in simulation. Fleet data plays a key role here: rare or dangerous scenarios that were captured from the real world can be replayed in simulation to test new software updates or to train systems under variations of those scenarios. For example, if one car in the fleet encountered an unusual construction zone layout, the data pipeline can send that scenario to a cloud-based simulation where it's turned into a reproducible test case for all new AI versions. The pipeline might take sensor data and, via mapping and processing, reconstruct a 3D scenario in the simulator (or at least the key elements of it). Engineers can then simulate countless variations: What if the pedestrian was faster? What if two pedestrians? What if it was raining? All on that base scenario, thanks to the digital twin. An increasingly important trend is synthetic data generation: using simulation and procedural content tools to create artificial training examples that would be rare or unsafe to collect in reality. For example, an OEM might generate thousands of variations of a construction zone or a near-miss pedestrian event by perturbing positions, speeds, lighting, and weather in a digital twin. These synthetic clips can then be mixed with real data to enrich the training set, especially for long-tail edge cases. The challenge is ensuring that synthetic data is realistic enough and does not introduce artifacts that mislead the model.

Similarly, vehicle digital twins use real data to calibrate models of vehicle components (like tire models, battery models) to reflect actual wear and tear or production variations, and those models improve predictions of vehicle behavior. Companies like Volvo [248], for instance, build detailed environment twins of test sites and then simulate their autonomous trucks on those twins to validate safety on edge cases that are hard to test physically. Data pipelines thus increasingly loop back not just into model training but into simulation/validation. Figure 8-24 conceptually shows this loop: vehicle data goes to edge/cloud, is stored and possibly processed, and then feeds into a digital twin or simulation environment, which in turn helps design better algorithms for the vehicle. It's a virtuous cycle: collect ➤ learn ➤ simulate ➤ improve ➤ deploy and then repeat.

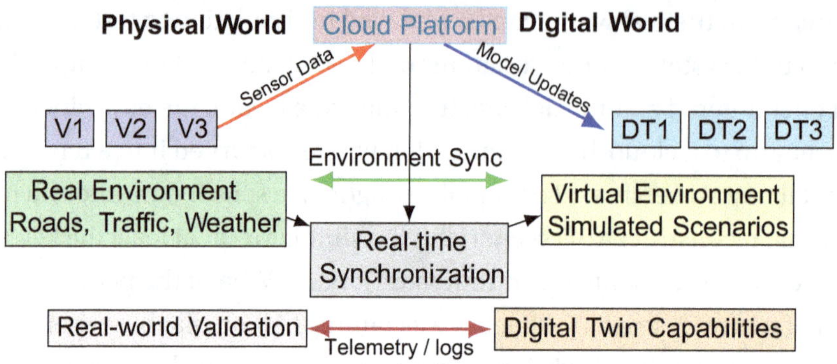

Figure 8-23. *Digital twin and simulation integration in the data pipeline*

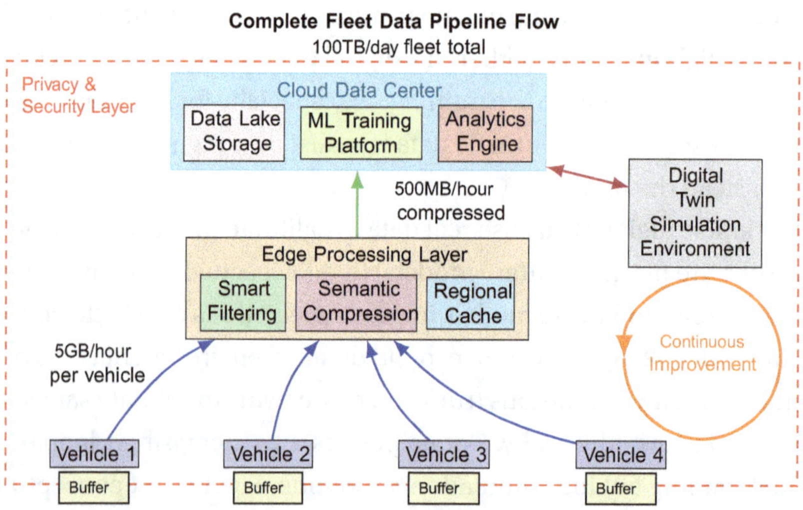

Figure 8-24. *Continuous improvement loop for SDV AI, linking vehicle data capture, edge filtering, cloud analytics, simulation, training, and deployment*

In practice, setting up such a pipeline requires addressing many practical issues: bandwidth limits (using techniques like semantic compression as mentioned; sending events, not raw video, to cut bandwidth by orders of magnitude), data privacy (e.g., anonymization of faces and license plates in recorded data to comply with privacy laws—often part of the pipeline is automatic blurring of personally identifiable info before data is analyzed), and synchronization (ensuring logs from different sensors line up in time for fusion, which is why preprocessing includes timestamp syncing with GPS/IMU). Security is also critical: these data are valuable (for model training and also potentially sensitive if leaked), so pipelines enforce encryption and access control. For example, an automaker will isolate data by region to comply with regulations (Europe's data stays in Europe and so on).

A well-oiled data pipeline is a strategic asset for any SDV program. It directly impacts how fast an OEM can iterate on their AI. Tesla's competitive edge, many argue, is not just their neural net architecture but their data engine—they can collect specific examples from millions of miles, label them overnight, and push a new model OTA within weeks. Waymo, similarly, has years of curated driving data and an advanced simulation (Carcraft) to test updates on billions of simulated miles using that data. Newer entrants, like startups, often struggle not with designing an AI, but with obtaining and handling the sheer quantity of data needed to refine it. Thus, understanding data pipelines isn't just an IT concern; it's core to making safe and intelligent SDVs.

In summary, data pipelines in SDVs start on the vehicle (with local logging and smart event capture), move through connectivity and edge processing (filtering and compressing data), land in centralized storage (with big data analytics and training processes), and then loop into development tools like simulation and digital twins (to maximize the value of each real-world datum by reproducing it virtually). The pipeline needs to be robust (no data loss), secure (protect privacy and IP), and efficient (keep only what's needed). The phrase often used is "from sensor to server to simulator." Mastering that flow enables faster learning cycles, which ultimately leads to better AI in the vehicle.

8.8 Monetization of AI and Data

One of the promises of software-defined vehicles is unlocking new revenue streams beyond the traditional car sale. AI and data play a pivotal role in these emerging monetization models. Essentially, once you have a car that's connected and intelligent, you can leverage its capabilities and the data it generates to offer new services or business models. Here are key monetization avenues built on vehicle and user data, along with examples. All of these models are bounded by a hard constraint: customer trust and regulatory consent—monetization that undermines either will not be sustainable.

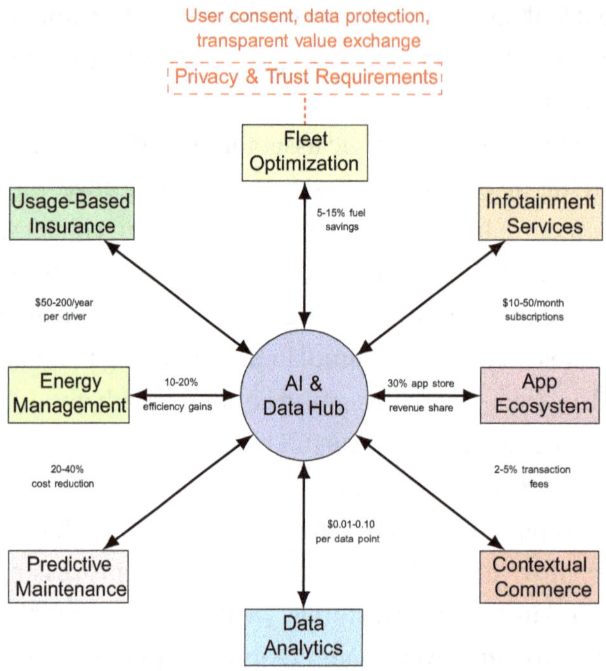

Figure 8-25. *AI and data monetization ecosystem in SDVs*

8.8.1 Usage-Based Insurance (UBI) and Safety Scores

Insurance is a multi-trillion-dollar industry ripe for disruption by granular driving data. Traditionally, insurers set premiums based on proxies like age, years of driving, or simple driving history. But now, with connected cars, insurers can use telematics data—how exactly you drive—to set personalized premiums. This is called usage-based or pay-how-you-drive insurance. For example, if the AI in the car or a smartphone app records that a driver regularly speeds, corners hard, and has close-following incidents, the insurer may deem them higher risk and charge a higher rate. Conversely, a very smooth, cautious driver might get discounts. Many insurers already offer such programs (like Progressive's Snapshot or those in partnership with automakers such as Tesla Insurance). Tesla uses driving behavior signals to compute a Safety Score [249, 250] for insurance pricing—based on evolving metrics (historically including items like hard braking, aggressive turning, unsafe following, and others; definitions have changed over time). This means safer drivers literally pay less, which proponents argue is fairer and also incentivizes safer driving. From a monetization perspective, driving data is increasingly used to power risk scoring and pricing services for insurers or to enable automakers to act as captive insurers themselves, rather than simply selling raw trip data. There's value in the predictive power of data: one study showed that incorporating telematics can improve risk prediction significantly, which in turn allows insurers to price policies more accurately (they might attract good drivers with cheaper rates and charge risky drivers more, improving profitability). Drivers benefit with potentially lower costs if they drive safely—it's almost like an "AI driving coach" could help lower your premium by warning you to drive gentler. However, this model only works if privacy is addressed (drivers must consent to share driving behavior data) and if the scoring algorithms avoid bias. Regulators also watch this space—e.g., in some regions insurers can't use certain data (like exact location data at certain granularity) due to privacy. But overall, monetizing driving data through insurance is one of the most immediate and quantifiable ways data translates to dollars. Automotive companies can either partner with insurance firms to provide analytics and risk scoring services or become providers themselves (Tesla did the latter to capture the full margin, effectively monetizing insights from its own cars' data exhaust rather than selling raw trip logs).

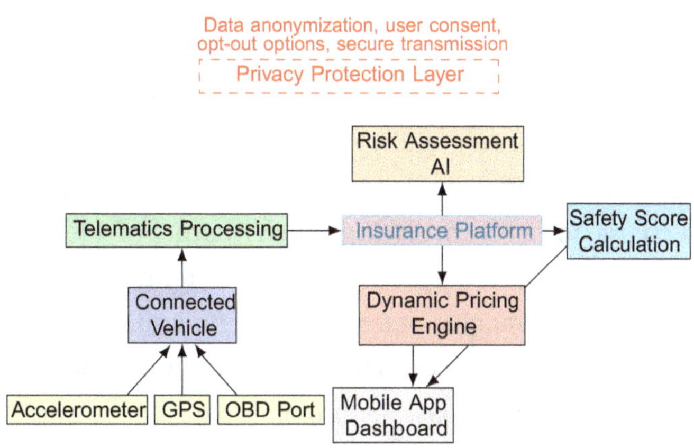

Figure 8-26. *Usage-based insurance system architecture*

8.8.2 Fleet Optimization and Fuel Efficiency

For commercial fleets (trucking, ride-hailing, delivery vehicles), data-driven AI can greatly improve operational efficiency, which equates to cost savings = profit. One prominent example is platooning for trucks. Platooning means a convoy of trucks driving close together to reduce aerodynamic drag, thereby saving fuel (the lead truck cuts the air resistance for the following truck). AI can coordinate platooning—adjusting vehicle gaps in real time, keeping safety distances with sensors, etc. Multiple controlled studies report ~3–10% combined fuel savings for two-truck platoons [251, 252] (varying with gap, speed, terrain, and wind), with higher values in favorable conditions. That's huge given fuel is a top cost for trucking. Monetization here is indirect: the AI or data solution itself might be sold as a service or add-on to fleets (e.g., a subscription to a "platooning coordinator" cloud service), or it might be an OEM feature that attracts fleet buyers (sell more trucks because your trucks save fuel). Even beyond platooning, AI can optimize routing for fuel efficiency—combining live traffic data, terrain, etc. or optimizing maintenance scheduling (avoid breakdown costs). Fleet management platforms often monetize by charging per vehicle per month for providing analytics dashboards, predictive maintenance (using data to predict part failures), and driver performance coaching. All of that is powered by vehicle data and AI algorithms. Another angle was platoon-as-a-service: companies like Peloton Technology (now defunct, ceased operations in 2021) envisioned matching trucks from different companies on highways to platoon together (splitting fuel savings), but Peloton's shutdown serves as a cautionary example of the gap that can exist between technical feasibility and long-term commercial and regulatory viability for such services. While regulatory and liability issues make mixed-fleet platooning tricky, the concept shows data's value: if you have the connectivity and trust, you can literally make money by having trucks cooperate via AI. For passenger vehicles, fuel efficiency can be monetized indirectly as well: some automakers might charge for an "eco-driving coach" feature or use eco-score gamification to encourage efficient driving, which reduces fuel (or battery usage) and could tie into incentives (imagine getting points convertible to rewards for efficient driving—those points could be sponsored by say an energy company, effectively monetizing efficiency data through partnerships).

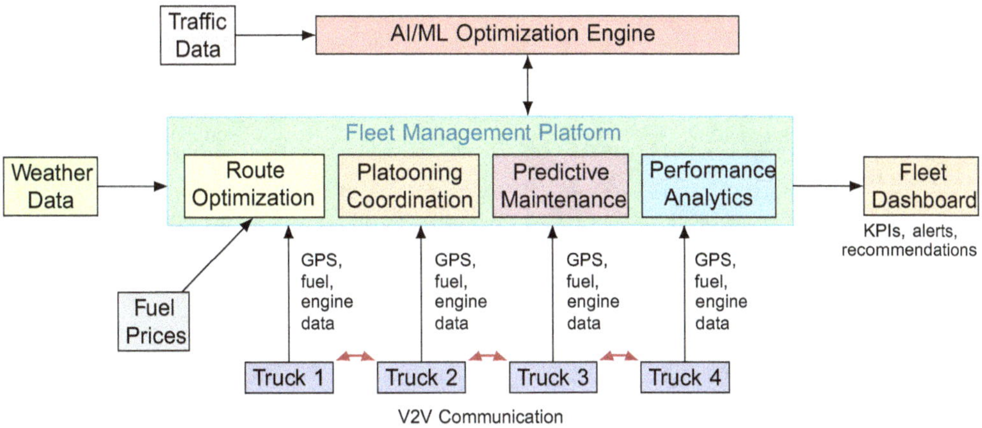

Figure 8-27. *AI-powered fleet optimization and platooning system*

8.8.3 In-Cabin Personalization and Infotainment Revenue

As vehicles become more software-defined, personalization creates several monetization paths. Some are direct, such as premium subscriptions for advanced assistants, adaptive comfort features, or enhanced infotainment services. Others are transaction-based, such as navigation-linked charging, parking, reservations, or contextual commerce. In all of these cases, AI increases value only if it improves relevance and convenience rather than creating distraction or distrust.

The commercial opportunity is real, but so is the risk of backlash. Personalization depends on user data, and monetization depends on customer willingness to exchange that data for visible value. Features that feel helpful and clearly optional may succeed; features that feel intrusive, manipulative, or double-charged are more likely to damage trust than generate durable revenue.

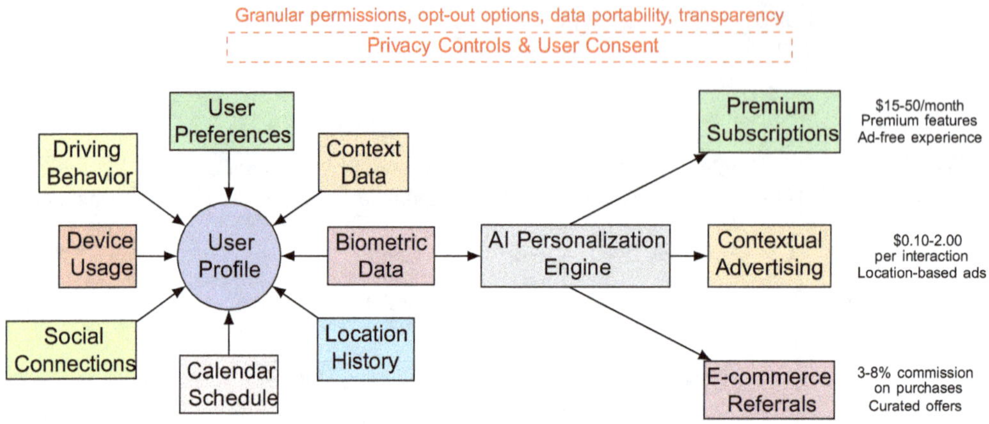

Figure 8-28. *In-cabin personalization and revenue generation model*

8.8.4 Third-Party Developer Ecosystems

Similar to how smartphones exploded in functionality via third-party apps, SDVs are heading toward an app ecosystem model. Automakers are building platforms (with SDKs and APIs) for external developers to create in-car apps or services. These apps could range from entertainment, navigation, and productivity to novel vehicle-specific uses. For example, a fitness company might create a "smart seat workout" app that uses the car's seat sensors and your schedule to prompt stretches on long drives. Or an AI-driven language tutor app might use the audio system to give you lessons during commutes. To enable this, OEMs are exposing certain vehicle data (with permissions) and functions through APIs. As Mark Gerban noted, open APIs can lead to richer experiences and revenue, but there's the challenge of scale (the car user base is smaller than phones). Monetization here can follow the app store model: the OEM might take a percentage of app sales/subscriptions, charge developers for data usage beyond a free tier, etc. Additionally, data-sharing partnerships fall under this category: automakers can monetize vehicle data by providing it (with user consent, aggregated or anonymized) to third parties for training their own AI models. For instance, a city might pay for access to real-time traffic sensor data from cars to improve urban planning AI; a mapping company might subscribe to the car's road sign recognition feed to keep maps updated (Tesla does this internally—their fleet notices new stop signs or speed limits and updates their maps—but one could sell that info externally too). Another example is usage data for designers of in-car digital services: if a startup is building a new voice assistant, an automaker might give them sandboxed access to some voice command data or car sensor data to train it—possibly for a fee or in exchange for integration rights. The key is that the car becomes a platform, and platforms thrive by attracting developers with innovative ideas. The OEM can monetize by acting as the platform provider (taking a cut, selling API access, or even selling certified datasets). Some OEMs have already launched developer programs (e.g., Ford's AppLink, BMW, and Mercedes have had APIs for integrating apps like Spotify and others). Moving forward, as vehicles standardize on something like Android Automotive OS or similar, we may see a more unified app ecosystem. The monetization in such cases often mirrors smartphones: revenue share from app sales and possibly advertising revenue shared if the platform supports it. One caution: safety—any third-party app that can influence the driving experience must be sandboxed so it cannot compromise safety or distract the driver inappropriately. So, unlike phones where devs had relatively free reign initially, car platforms will likely have curation and vetting, which means the platform owner (OEM) will tightly control what apps/data are allowed, potentially making their cut larger but the ecosystem more closed than mobile.

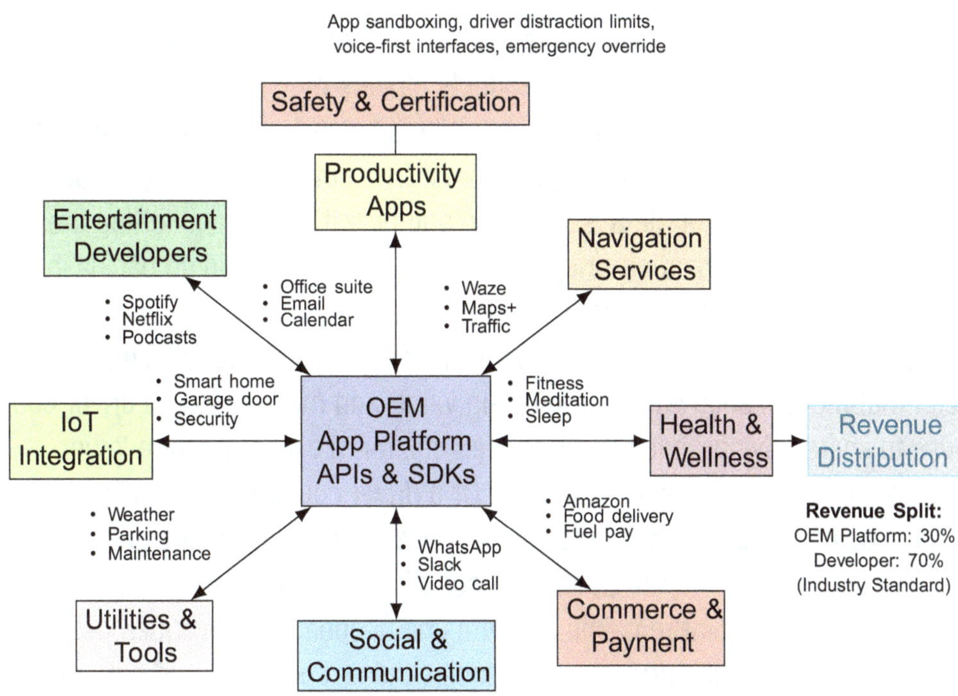

Figure 8-29. *Third-party developer ecosystem and revenue sharing model*

Finally, it's worth noting monetization vs. customer trust: Car buyers had historically paid for a product up front, and that was it. Moving to a world of ongoing monetization (subscriptions, data usage) changes the relationship. If done poorly—like charging for things that feel like double-dipping (e.g., a feature that the car physically has but is paywalled by software)—customers will rebel, as BMW learned with heated seats. If done transparently and with value, it can succeed—for instance, many people pay for Premium Connectivity in Tesla to get live traffic and streaming, because they see value.

Critic's Note "Flagship customer experience (CX)" depends on AI-driven personalization. But intrusive monetization risks backlash: transparency is critical. In plainer terms, the best, most delightful features in an SDV (the ones automakers market as their flagship experiences) often come from AI personalization—the car that knows you, preempts your needs, and entertains you. That's great for loyalty and could justify premium pricing or subscriptions. However, if customers feel the car is nickel-and-diming them or exploiting their data without clear consent, it can damage the brand. We saw a near-universal negative reaction to the idea of monthly fees for inherent capabilities. Similarly, if an AI voice assistant starts randomly recommending sponsored products, drivers may find it distracting or manipulative. Therefore, companies must strike a balance: monetize by enhancing the user's experience, not by detracting from it. The note implies that transparency (being up front about what data is collected and how it's used and letting the user opt in/out of monetization-oriented features) is key to avoiding backlash. In Europe, this is also legally mandated (GDPR would require, e.g., explicit consent for data being shared with third parties for monetization). Some industry analysts predict that monetization will shift to opt-in value-add models: e.g., a driver could choose to share driving-style data with their insurer in exchange for a lower premium—that's a clear value exchange. Or a driver could opt into an in-car marketplace because they want the convenience, and in return they get maybe some free services (like a free Spotify subscription sponsored by allowing some ads). The underlying point remains: the data and AI open new revenue possibilities, but customer trust is the currency that enables those. Lose that, and monetization schemes fail.

In conclusion, AI and data in SDVs enable monetization through new services (insurance tailored to you, apps in your car, personalized content), cost savings (fleet efficiency, predictive maintenance), and partnership ecosystems (sharing data or platform with others for mutual profit). Many estimate the automotive data monetization market will grow to tens of billions of dollars in coming years. Each car is not just a vehicle but also a node in a data network and a potential storefront or service platform. Automakers are racing to transition from one-time hardware sellers to providers of ongoing mobility services, and AI is at the heart of that transformation—making the car smart enough to deliver those services and churn out the valuable data that powers them. The winners will be those who can monetize while keeping customers delighted and confident that the AI is working for them, not just squeezing them.

8.9 Case Study: Tesla vs. Waymo

To ground the chapter's concepts, it is useful to compare two broad approaches to autonomous vehicle AI that are often associated with Tesla and Waymo. The purpose of this comparison is not to reproduce proprietary implementation detail, but to contrast two strategic philosophies: a fleet learning, consumer-deployed, vision-centric approach vs. a tightly validated, sensor-rich, geofenced deployment model. These examples are illustrative of broader industry design choices rather than exhaustive descriptions of internal company architectures.

8.9.1 Tesla's Approach

Tesla has pursued a vision of autonomy that is incremental and fleet data-driven. They deploy Autopilot and Full Self-Driving (FSD) (Supervised) features on customer vehicles (under driver supervision) and treat the problem as largely one of neural network learning at scale. Formally, Tesla's "Full Self-Driving (Supervised)" remains an SAE Level 2 driver assistance feature: the human driver is responsible at all times, and regulators do not consider it an autonomous driving system. Tesla's philosophy is often summarized as "binary search on data"—if the car makes a mistake, gather 1,000 more examples of that case, retrain, deploy an update, and repeat. They rely on end-to-end deep learning to a great extent. For instance, much of their perception and even some planning is handled by giant neural networks that take raw camera inputs and output things like lane trajectories, object kinematics, and driving path proposals. Tesla has notably chosen not to deploy LiDAR on its production vehicles and to rely primarily on cameras (vision), arguing that vision (plus radar in some generations) is sufficient if you have enough data and good neural nets—akin to how humans drive with eyes. They leverage their huge customer fleet (~millions of cars) as data collectors—building a powerful fleet learning loop. The cars constantly upload snippets of data where the Autopilot struggled, the driver took over, etc. Those get added to training sets. Tesla pushes OTA updates as often as every few weeks to incrementally improve the system. This OTA-first development means Tesla's "beta testers" are actually regular customers, giving Tesla an unprecedented rapid iteration advantage. In terms of decision-making, Tesla tends to favor a more monolithic AI approach: there is still a separation of perception and planning to some extent in implementation, but Elon Musk has expressed interest in end-to-end models (one big network that directly outputs steering/braking given camera input). The result of Tesla's approach is a system that improves quickly ("velocity") but often attracts criticism for potentially using public roads as test beds. Indeed, Tesla's FSD Beta, while very advanced in capability, has had a number of documented failures and near-misses, and some argue it is not as safe as it should be for wide deployment. Tesla counters by pointing to billions of miles driven on Autopilot and statistics (though the methodology of those stats is debated). A Bloomberg analysis even claimed Tesla's approach might be more cost-efficient and eventually safer due to scale, while others strongly disagree.

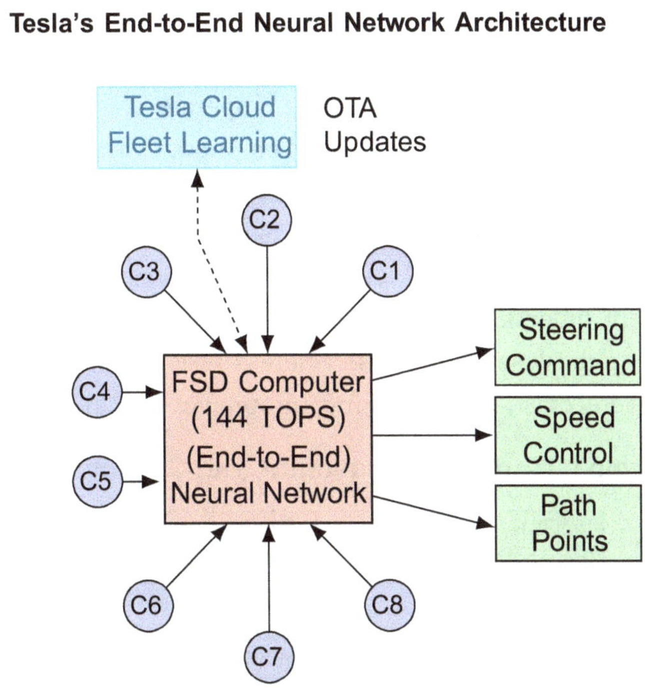

Figure 8-30. *Tesla's end-to-end neural network architecture*

8.9.2 Waymo's Approach

Waymo, on the other hand, emerged from the DARPA Grand Challenge legacy and has taken a "safety-first, no shortcuts" approach. Waymo's current services are SAE Level 4: within a geofenced ODD the automated driving system performs the entire dynamic driving task with no human driver on board, but outside that ODD the system will not engage. They use an array of high-end sensors: LiDAR, radar, and cameras—embracing sensor fusion to have rich redundancy. Their software architecture is modular: distinct subsystems for perception, prediction, planning, etc., often with more rule-based or hybrid AI logic. For instance, Waymo perception involves object detection and tracking using ML, prediction of other agents' behavior using probabilistic models, and planning using a mix of rules and optimization. They validate each module extensively. A hallmark of Waymo's strategy is extensive simulation and testing before deployment. They drive large volumes in simulation for every real mile, resimulating real-world events with variations (heavy use of their "Carcraft" platform). As of mid-2025, Waymo reports ~96 million rider-only miles and 20+ billion simulation miles [254, 255]; safety drivers are removed only after extensive validation within a defined ODD. They geofence service to well-mapped domains (Phoenix, San Francisco, Los Angeles, with additional availability via partners in other cities), whereas Tesla aims to operate wherever customers drive under supervision. In short, Waymo's approach emphasizes assurance—heavy upfront validation, formal safety cases, redundancy in hardware, and cautious deployment. This means slower rollout (they didn't offer a public "beta" broadly; instead, they run limited trials and then a commercial robotaxi service in defined areas), but arguably a more proven level of safety. Indeed, to date Waymo has a strong safety record with only minor incidents (and they publish safety reports), whereas Tesla's approach has been linked (fairly or not) to several crashes of cars using Autopilot or FSD inappropriately.

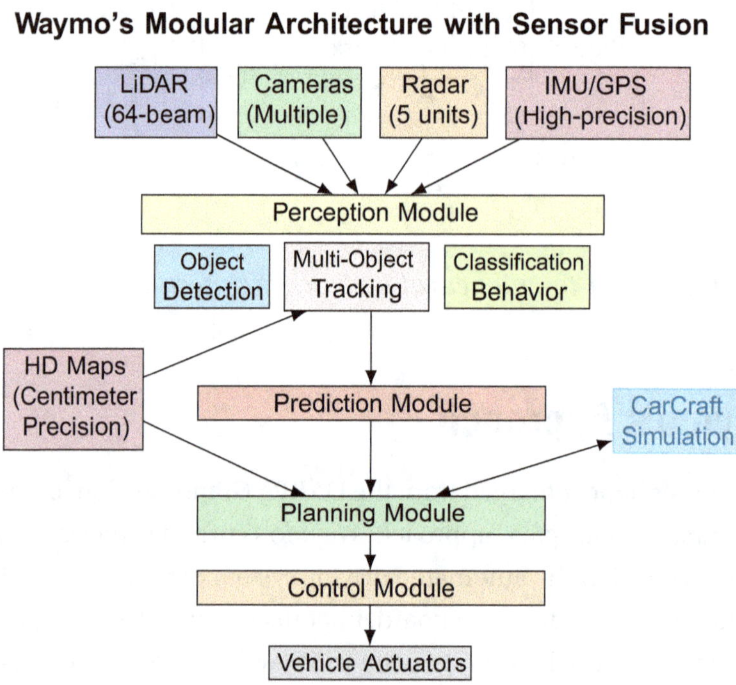

Figure 8-31. *Waymo's modular architecture with sensor fusion*

8.9.3 Comparing the Approaches

The contrast is often framed as "velocity vs. safety assurance." Tesla iterates fast and chases a general solution, willing to accept some risk by having beta features in customer hands; Waymo iterates methodically and only deploys when they're very sure, even if that means geofencing and slower expansion. There's also a cultural difference: Tesla markets its system directly to consumers (with notable bravado, using terms like "Full Self-Driving," which some find misleading), whereas Waymo doesn't sell cars or kits to individuals—it operates a taxi service and partners with OEMs for future integration. So Tesla's data mainly comes from private owners using the system on all kinds of roads; Waymo's data is from its dedicated test fleet and limited rider program, but highly curated.

In terms of AI specifics, Tesla's big bet is on neural networks figuring out almost everything, including developing "end-to-end" planning (they recently have networks that given videos of the surroundings output a planned path directly, essentially learning a driving policy from human data combined with some automated curriculum). Waymo uses neural nets too (for perception, some for behavior prediction) but likely with more human-engineered rules as backup. For example, Waymo might have explicit safety rules like "if object uncertain, slow down," whereas Tesla's might be implicitly learned by the network (and sometimes that fails in weird ways). On computing, Tesla tries to do as much as possible on-car (their FSD computer is very powerful), whereas Waymo's vehicles also have powerful compute, but they lean on cloud for big data crunching offline (not so much real-time driving, because communications latency is too high for that, but for mapping and learning). Waymo's reliance on HD maps (pre-mapped detailed environment) is another differentiator; Tesla tries to do more on the fly with minimal prior maps (a harder problem, but if solved, more scalable).

Table 8-1. *Tesla vs. Waymo Autonomous Driving Comparison*

Aspect	Tesla	Waymo
Sensors	Cameras + radar; vision-centric	LiDAR + cameras; sensor fusion
Architecture	End-to-end; neural networks	Modular pipeline; rule-based + ML
Data	Customer fleet; 1M+ vehicles	Dedicated fleet; 20M+ test miles
Deployment	Global, Level 2; beta testing	Geofenced, Level 4; commercial service
Safety	Statistical claims; some incidents	Rigorous testing; strong safety record
Business	Consumer sales; $12k FSD option	Robotaxi service; B2B partnerships
Timeline	2016–present; rapid iteration	2009–present; methodical approach

From a business perspective, Tesla's approach has already put semi-autonomy in hundreds of thousands of hands, creating arguably the most extensive real-world driving dataset, and a loyal fanbase that "beta tests" for them. This yields rapid improvement and a perception (no pun intended) of Tesla being ahead in applied self-driving for consumers. Waymo, while slower to reach the average person, has arguably a more mature Level 4 system (since they operate fully driverless in Phoenix). Many experts indeed consider Waymo the gold standard in autonomy safety, with Tesla's tech seen as not directly comparable since Tesla's is still Level 2 (driver responsible). Elon Musk's counter is that the data volume and real-world complexity Tesla faces will ultimately make their AI smarter and able to handle general roads, whereas Waymo might be stuck in geofenced areas for a long time (the classic scalability argument).

As of 2025, we've sort of seen these philosophies play out: Waymo has run limited robotaxi services in a few cities with impressive safety but high cost, while Tesla offers an unfinished self-driving option to consumers broadly, generating both enthusiasm and incidents. Cruise, another company pursuing a broadly similar Level 4 robotaxi approach, had operated services in several US cities but paused operations in late 2023 following incidents and regulatory scrutiny, underscoring how fragile public trust and approval can be in this space. It remains to be seen which approach "wins" or if the industry converges on a middle path. Some companies mix elements of both: e.g., Mobileye's strategy uses cameras heavily like Tesla but also pre-maps routes and focuses on safety models like Waymo.

For the purposes of this chapter's learnings: Tesla vs. Waymo illustrates why AI strategy matters. Tesla's strategy yields fast development and leveraging fleet network effects—they treat their entire customer fleet as part of the AI lab, which is unprecedented. Waymo's yields confidence and clarity—every behavior can be traced in their modular system, and they accumulate trust from regulators by being careful. The trade-off is sometimes characterized as "move fast and break things" (Tesla-ish) vs. "prove safety and then scale" (Waymo-ish). In reality, neither wants to break things (given lives are at stake), but it's about risk tolerance and methodology.

So, if asked who is ahead, one could say: Waymo leads in demonstrated autonomous capability (fully driverless operation in limited areas), and Tesla leads in volume of data and AI learning–driven approach (semi-autonomous features on a wide scale). Each is learning from the other too; Tesla is adding more redundancy (newer hardware includes high-resolution radar in some models, and an in-cabin radar was activated for occupancy sensing; the production driving stack remains primarily vision-centric), and Waymo has started to come out of its shell to deploy in more cities a bit faster than before. Ultimately, both could succeed in different segments (private cars vs. robotaxi). But this case study serves to highlight how different design choices in AI (sensor suite, reliance on maps, end-to-end learning vs. modular, validation philosophy) lead to different development trajectories.

In short, Tesla vs. Waymo is velocity vs. assurance and scale of data vs. safety rigor, and we can watch in real time how these trade-offs play out on the road. For a student of AI and SDVs, it's a fascinating real-world experiment: two "labs" deploying their theories on actual streets, one effectively crowdsourced, the other tightly controlled. The lessons from both will no doubt inform the next generation of autonomous vehicle programs.

8.10 Key Takeaways

- **AI in SDVs spans multiple domains:** Perception, planning, control, and in-cabin personalization—essentially covering everything from how the car senses the world to how it interacts with the occupants. A successful SDV integrates AI at all these levels for a seamless experience.
- **Machine learning types:** Supervised learning remains the workhorse (especially for perception), but is data-hungry because it needs large, well-curated labeled datasets (often assembled from multi-sensor driving scenes). Unsupervised and self-supervised learning are an emerging frontier, helping leverage unlabeled data—they are increasingly used to learn representations or detect anomalies without explicit labels. Reinforcement learning holds promise for decision-making but is simulation-heavy due to safety (you can't trial-and-error on public roads). In practice, a combination is used: e.g., supervised for vision, unsupervised for anomaly detection, and RL in research and pilot deployments for some motion planning and coordination problems in controlled settings.
- **Federated learning** is introduced as a privacy-aware approach to fleet intelligence. Instead of sending raw data, cars collaboratively learn a shared model with their data staying on the vehicle. This way, sensitive personal data (faces, locations) isn't constantly transmitted,

reducing privacy risks while still benefiting from "learning from the fleet." It's especially relevant under strict data protection laws (making it a likely correct answer for the GDPR-friendly training mode question).

- **AI safety evidence and explainability** are still largely industry-wide open challenges. While some standards (ISO 8800, IEEE 7003) are emerging, the industry has not fully solved how to formally assure safety for a deep neural network driving component. Explainable AI tools (like saliency maps) and extensive validation are the stopgap solutions. Future engineers might literally do PhDs on proving that an autonomous car's AI will never fail in a certain way. Ensuring an AI can handle adversarial conditions or that we can certify an ML model to the same confidence as, say, an aircraft control software is an ongoing challenge.
- **Monetization models** depend heavily on who controls the AI and the data. Data is being called the "new oil" of automotive. If the OEM owns/controls the data, they can create revenue streams from it (insurance, app ecosystems, partnerships). If the user has more control, monetization might be more opt-in and limited. We saw examples: usage-based insurance driven by data, AI-driven infotainment or ads, etc. The takeaway is that the business of SDVs is entwined with AI capabilities—e.g., personalized AI services can be sold as subscriptions, or aggregated vehicle data can be sold to third parties (with user consent). However, pushing monetization too far can backfire (as in BMW's subscription missteps), so it must be balanced with customer value and transparency.

CHAPTER 9

Safety and Security in Software-Defined Vehicles

9.1 Chapter Goals

After this chapter, you will be able to

- Explain functional safety (ISO 26262) and its adaptation to SDVs.
- Understand SOTIF (ISO 21448) for AI-based perception and other functional insufficiencies.
- Describe cybersecurity standards (ISO/SAE 21434, UNECE WP.29).
- Analyze intrusion detection, secure boot, and HSM roles in SDVs.
- Evaluate convergence of safety and security in system design.

Critic's Note In SDVs, safety and security are inseparable. An insecure SDV is unsafe, and an unsafe SDV is untrustworthy. The 2015 Jeep Cherokee hack, discussed later in this chapter, demonstrated this link brutally in practice.

S. Agarwal, *Software-Defined Vehicles*, https://doi.org/10.1007/979-8-8688-2718-1_9

9.2 Introduction

Software-defined vehicles fundamentally transform how safety and security must be approached. Traditional automotive safety engineering assumed relatively static systems—once validated, ECU software rarely changed. SDVs break this assumption with continuous OTA updates, AI-based perception systems whose behavior emerges from training data, and pervasive connectivity that exposes vehicles to cyber threats. This chapter examines how established safety and security frameworks are adapting to these challenges.

We begin with ISO 26262 functional safety, covering ASIL classification, hardware safety mechanisms, and the challenges of maintaining safety cases across continuous software updates. The chapter then addresses SOTIF (ISO 21448), which tackles hazards arising from functional insufficiencies—particularly relevant for AI-based perception systems that may fail without any component malfunction.

The cybersecurity landscape receives detailed treatment: ISO/SAE 21434 provides the engineering framework, while UNECE WP.29 regulations (R155, R156) make cybersecurity management and secure software updates legally mandatory in many markets. We examine key security mechanisms—secure boot, HSMs, intrusion detection, and secure OTA—and show how they form layered defenses.

The chapter concludes with safety-security convergence, demonstrating why these disciplines can no longer be treated separately. The 2015 Jeep Cherokee hack serves as a case study illustrating how cybersecurity failures directly become safety hazards and why integrated approaches are essential for trustworthy SDVs.

9.3 Functional Safety: ISO 26262

ISO 26262 is the international standard for functional safety of electrical and electronic systems in road vehicles. It provides a structured automotive safety lifecycle covering concept, development, production, operation, and decommissioning. Figure 9-1 illustrates the key phases of this lifecycle.

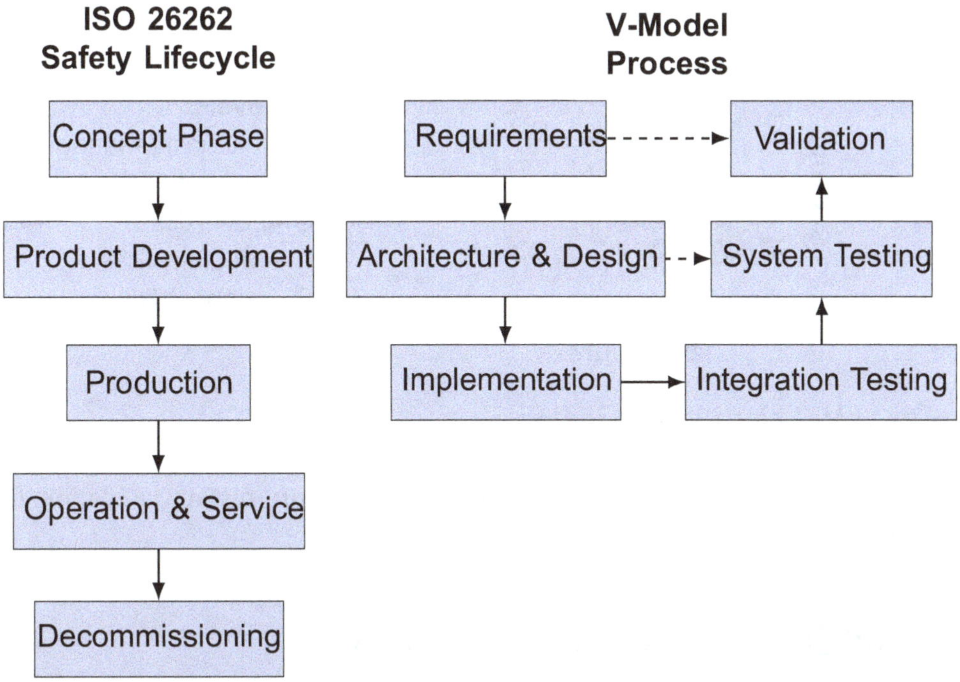

Figure 9-1. *ISO 26262 automotive safety lifecycle*

A key part of ISO 26262 is classifying hazards by Automotive Safety Integrity Level (ASIL) from A (lowest) to D (highest). The ASIL for a given hazard is determined by analyzing the potential Severity of harm, how often the scenario is encountered (Exposure), and the Controllability by a typical driver [59]. ASIL-D represents the most dangerous hazards (possible fatal injuries) and thus demands the most rigorous safety measures, whereas ASIL-A is lower risk. If a hazard is below ASIL-A (classified as QM (Quality-Managed)), it requires only standard quality management processes [59]. This risk-based classification is shown in Figure 9-2.

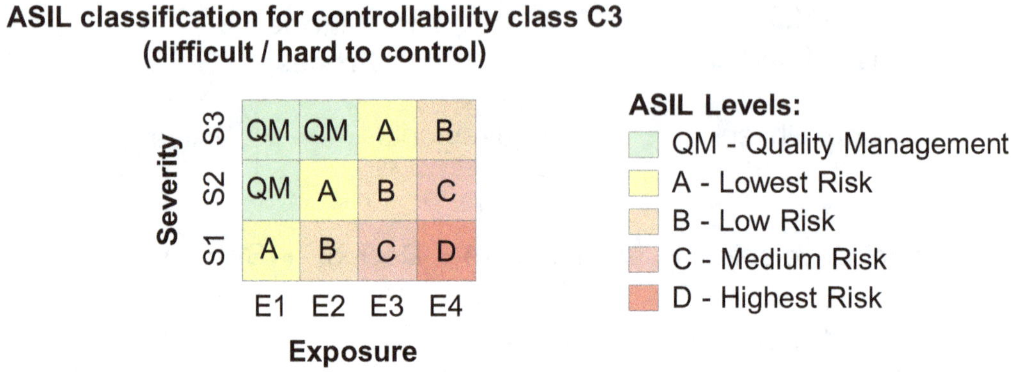

Figure 9-2. *ASIL classification matrix*

This risk-based approach ensures that development effort (testing, validation, fault tolerance) is commensurate with the hazard's risk level.

9.3.1 Hardware Safety Mechanisms

To achieve the high fault coverage required especially for ASIL-D systems (e.g., high single-point fault metric (SPFM) targets for ASIL-D) [59, 256], automotive electronics employ various hardware safety mechanisms [257]. For example, dual-core lockstep processors run duplicate computations in parallel and compare results cycle by cycle—if a mismatch is detected, it signals a fault, thereby catching CPU errors. In practice, adding dual-core lockstep can significantly improve diagnostic coverage and help an architecture move from ASIL-B-level random hardware metrics toward ASIL-D targets, provided the rest of the safety concept (peripherals, memories, monitors) is engineered accordingly [103].

Error-correcting code (ECC) on memory buses is another crucial mechanism: memory controllers calculate a syndrome for each memory word so that single-bit errors can be automatically corrected and multi-bit errors detected [258], preventing hidden corruption of critical data. Watchdog timers are used to detect software hang-ups or sequence violations; a windowed watchdog expects periodic "kick" signals from the software and will reset or put the system in a safe state if the software fails to respond correctly in time [80]. These hardware features (along with others like built-in self-test, clock and voltage monitoring, etc.) form a defensive safety net to detect or mitigate random hardware failures before they lead to unsafe behavior. Figure 9-3 summarizes these key mechanisms.

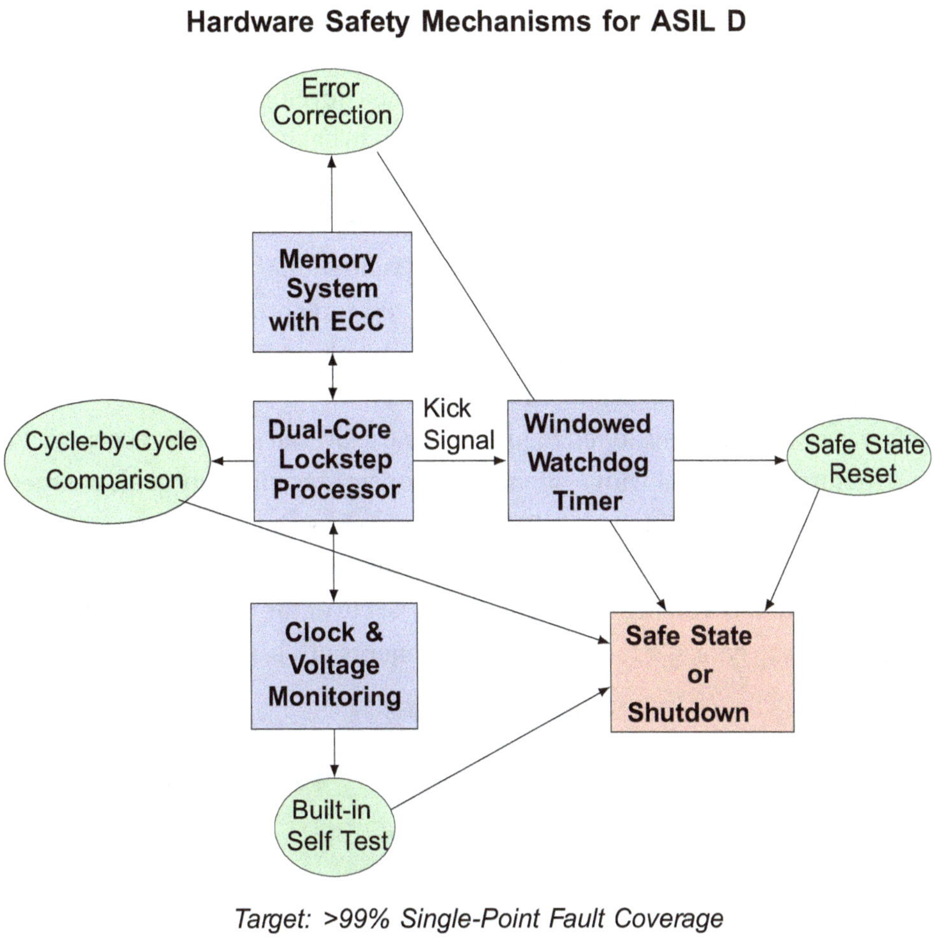

Figure 9-3. *Hardware safety mechanisms in ASIL-D systems*

Key Point Key hardware metrics include single-point fault metric (SPFM) requiring ≥99% for ASIL-D, latent fault metric (LFM) requiring ≥90% for ASIL-D, and probabilistic metric for random hardware failures (PMHF) typically constrained to ≤10^{-8}/hour for ASIL-D safety goals.

9.3.2 Software Processes and Safety Cases

On the software side, ISO 26262 prescribes a rigorous development process often aligned with the V-model (verification and validation linked to each development stage) [59]. There is an emphasis on requirements traceability, thorough unit/integration testing, and verification that the system "built" meets the safety requirements (verification) and that the right safety requirements were specified (validation) [259]. Tool qualification is required if software tools (like code generators or test tools) could potentially introduce errors; developers must either use trusted, certified tools or qualify them for use at the needed ASIL (demonstrating the tool's reliability).

A safety case must be developed to justify that the overall system is acceptably safe—this is a structured argument with evidence, demonstrating all safety goals are met and all hazardous scenarios mitigated [59, 259]. The safety case includes the hazard analysis (HARA) results, ASIL assignments, verification results, and validation tests. It's not a one-time document but an evolving argument that must cover the entire product lifecycle. Figure 9-4 shows the typical structure and components of a safety case.

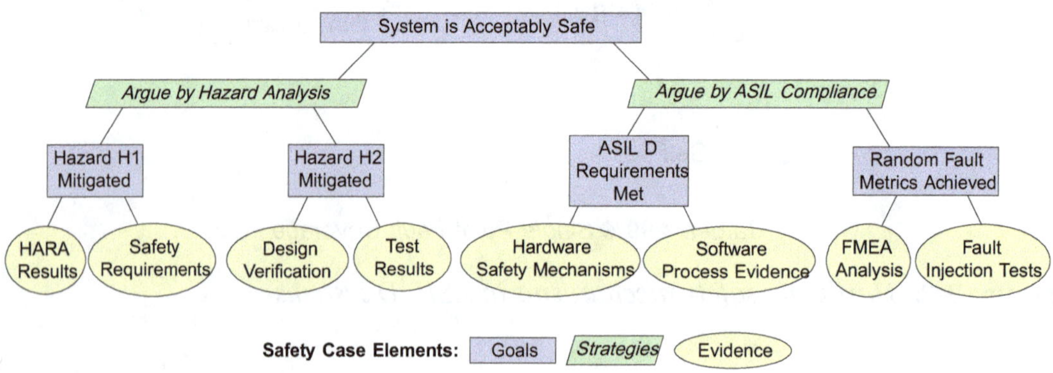

***Figure 9-4.** Safety case structure and components*

9.3.3 The SDV Twist: Continuous Updates

A major challenge for functional safety in software-defined vehicles (SDVs) is managing over-the-air (OTA) software updates. ISO 26262 was originally written against the backdrop of relatively static E/E systems: once an ECU's software was validated and released, it changed rarely. SDVs break this assumption. Features, calibrations, and even platform components may be updated multiple times during the vehicle lifetime, driven by bug fixes, new functions, and regulatory expectations for timely security patches, as reflected, e.g., in UNECE R156 on software updates [72, 73].

From a safety perspective, every safety-relevant change potentially invalidates part of the existing safety argument. The safety case therefore cannot be a one-off artifact; it must be incrementally extended and rejustified as the software evolves. In practice, this means OEMs and Tier-1s must

- Classify changes by safety impact.
- Rerun targeted regression test suites and simulations.
- Update hazard analyses where functionality or the operational design domain (ODD) has changed.
- Continuously collect post-deployment evidence from the fleet.

ISO 26262 provides the fundamental concepts (ASIL, safety goals, safety mechanisms, confirmation measures), while complementary standards like ISO 24089 and regulations like UNECE R156 frame update and monitoring processes [72, 73]. SDV manufacturers are therefore building continuous safety pipelines, as illustrated in Figure 9-5, where reusable Safety Elements out of Context (SEooCs), automated test environments, and in-field monitoring allow them to maintain compliance under repeated software releases rather than a single SOP freeze.

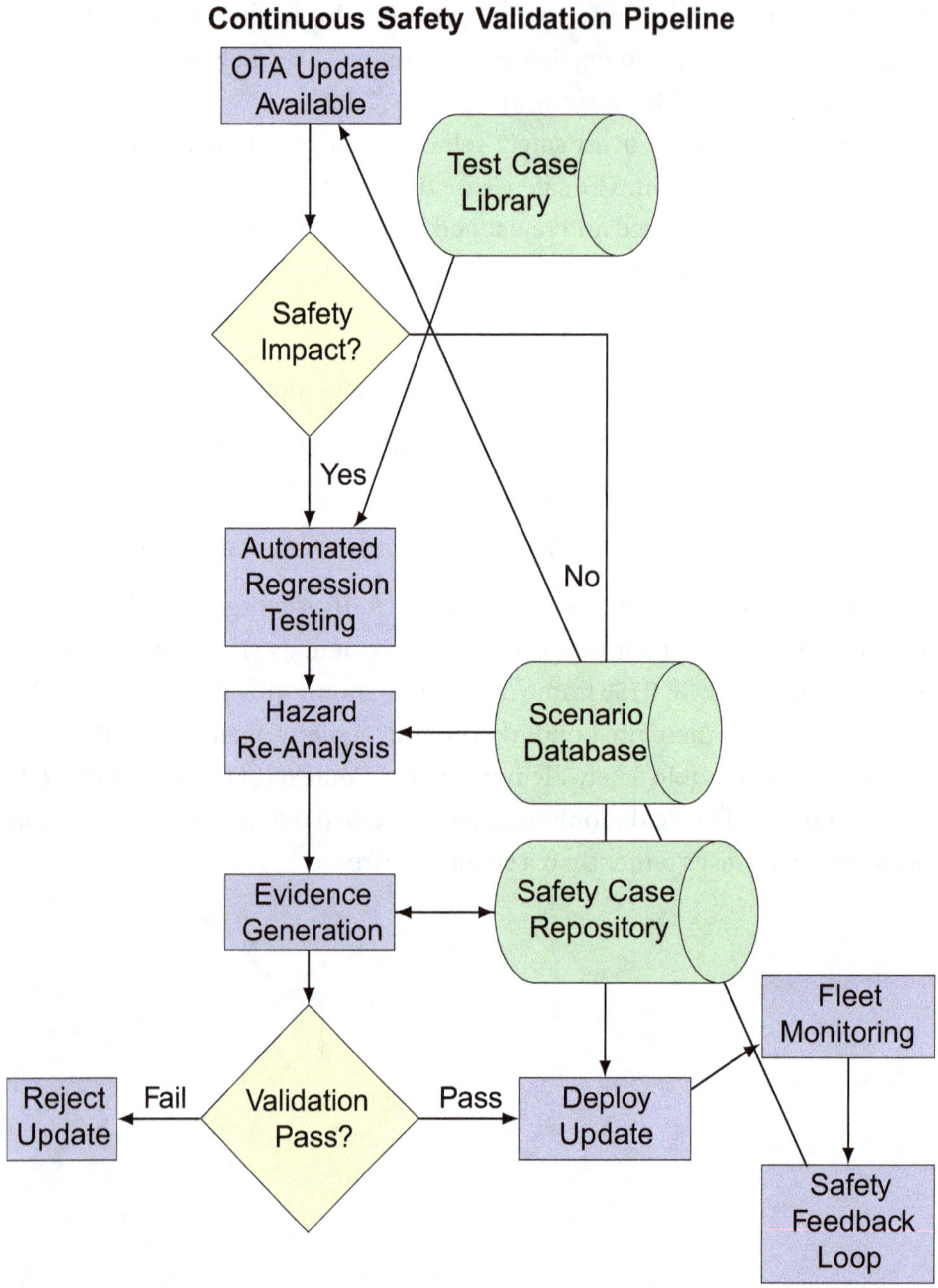

Figure 9-5. *Continuous safety validation pipeline for SDV OTA updates*

Critic's Note ISO 26262 was written for static ECUs. Continuous updates break assumptions. The SDV era demands evidence regeneration for every safety-relevant OTA.

9.4 SOTIF (Safety of the Intended Functionality)

Beyond component failures, autonomous and ADAS functions introduce a new category of safety risk: what if the system works as designed, but the design itself is insufficient for safe operation? This is the domain of ISO 21448, known as Safety of the Intended Functionality (SOTIF), which covers hazards arising from functional insufficiencies and performance limitations (with or without AI) rather than from random hardware failures [260]. Figure 9-6 contrasts the SOTIF approach with traditional ISO 26262 functional safety.

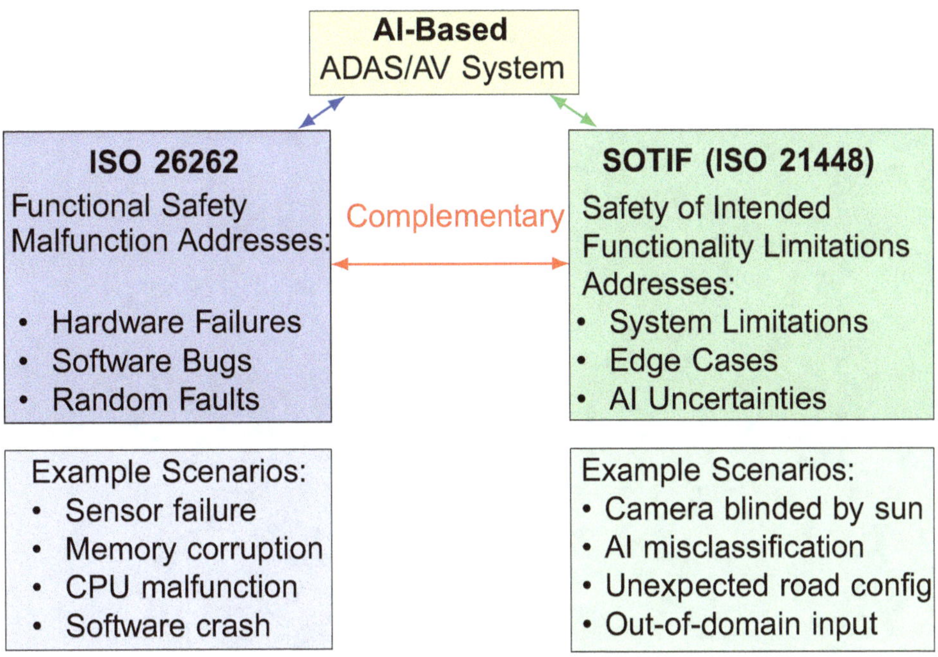

Figure 9-6. *SOTIF vs. ISO 26262: different approaches to safety*

9.4.1 Beyond Failure: When Correct Behavior Is Unsafe

ISO 26262 addresses random hardware failures and systematic software errors. But AI-based perception in autonomous vehicles can misinterpret scenes even when functioning correctly [261]. A camera-based pedestrian detector might work perfectly in clear weather but fail to recognize a person in heavy fog—not because of a component failure, but due to inherent limitations in the sensor and algorithm [260].

SOTIF categorizes scenarios into four areas: known safe (Area 1), known unsafe (Area 2), unknown unsafe (Area 3), and unknown safe (Area 4). The validation goal is to shrink Areas 2 and 3 through testing, analysis, and improvement [262]. Figure 9-7 visualizes these four areas: the horizontal axis represents our knowledge (known vs. unknown), the vertical axis represents safety (safe vs. unsafe), and each quadrant corresponds to one SOTIF area. This picture is useful when reasoning about where test and analysis effort should be focused. Area 2 scenarios are those we know are problematic (e.g., strong backlighting confusing cameras), while Area 3 represents the "unknown unknowns"—dangerous scenarios we haven't yet discovered [263].

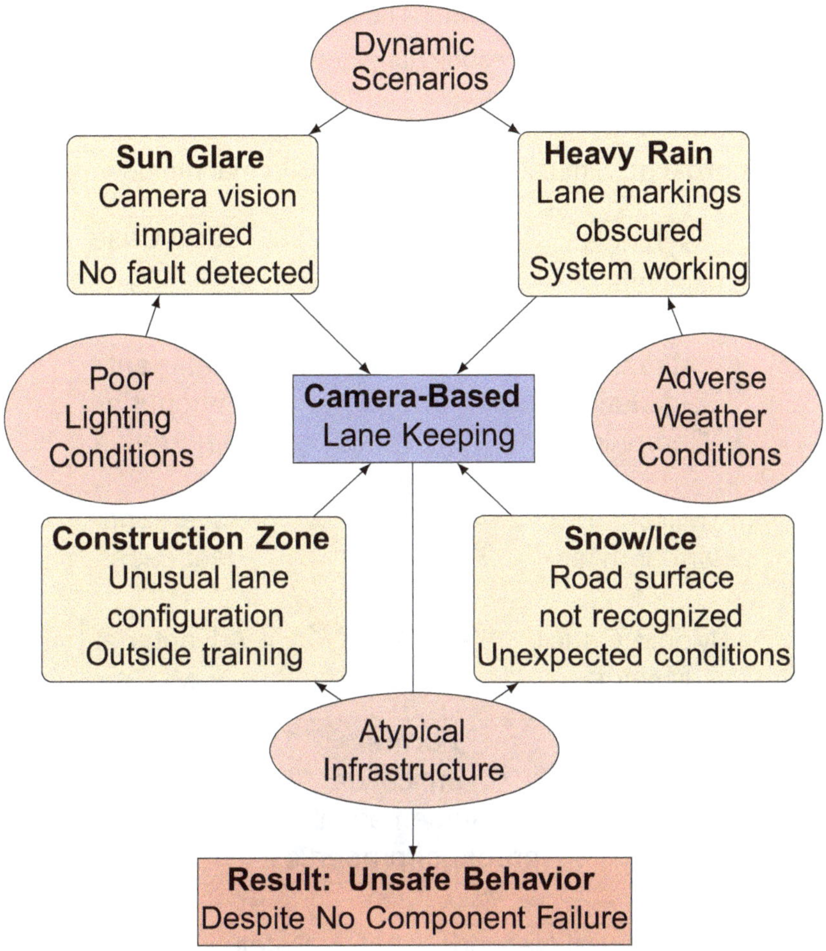

Figure 9-7. *SOTIF problem scenarios in autonomous driving*

9.4.2 AI Perception Challenges

Neural networks powering perception systems are particularly challenging for SOTIF validation, as highlighted in emerging pre-standard work such as ISO/PAS 8800 [245]. Their behavior is learned from data rather than explicitly programmed, making it difficult to predict all failure modes. Adversarial examples—inputs specifically crafted to fool AI—demonstrate that perception systems can fail in unexpected ways [264]. Validation approaches include massive scenario testing in simulation, real-world data collection campaigns, and formal verification techniques where feasible [265].

Explainable AI techniques like saliency maps help engineers understand what features the network relies on, potentially revealing dangerous dependencies [266]. Figure 9-8 summarizes these validation approaches.

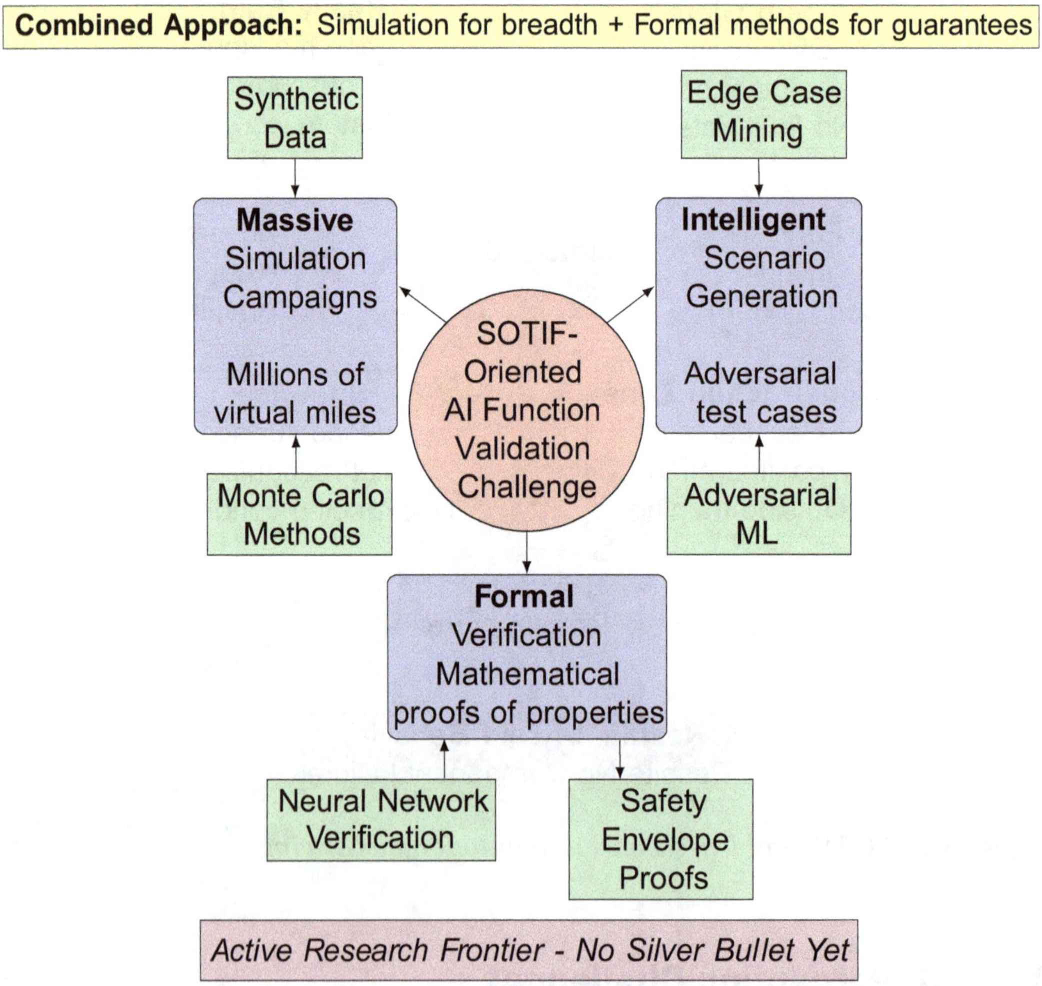

Figure 9-8. *AI safety validation approaches for SOTIF compliance*

Technical Detail While ISO 21448 defines SOTIF concepts at the function level, it is largely technology-agnostic. ISO/PAS 8800 goes deeper on machine learning–based perception systems, describing lifecycle activities such as dataset curation, training and validation strategies, performance monitoring, and change management for AI components. For SDVs that rely heavily on neural networks, a practical SOTIF strategy typically combines the high-level SOTIF framework from ISO 21448 with the AI-specific guidance from ISO/PAS 8800, plus OEM- or Tier-1-specific internal guidelines for data management and model deployment.

The SOTIF validation process typically involves (1) defining the operational design domain (ODD) where the function should operate safely, (2) identifying triggering conditions that could lead to hazards, (3) extensive testing including edge cases and corner cases, and (4) verification that residual risk is acceptable.

Triggering conditions and ODD drift: In practice, SOTIF triggering conditions go far beyond simple examples like fog or backlighting. For camera-based ADAS alone, typical triggers include lens contamination (mud, salt spray), degraded visibility (heavy rain, snow, tunnel exits), unusual object configurations (partially occluded pedestrians, trailers carrying irregular loads), and complex lighting (LED flicker, oncoming high beams, wet road reflections). Radar and LiDAR have their own SOTIF triggers, such as multi-path reflections, low-RCS objects, or interference from other sensors.

For SDVs, the operational design domain is not necessarily static. OTA feature rollouts can expand the ODD (e.g., extending a highway pilot function to include urban ring roads). Each such expansion must be reflected in both the SOTIF analysis and the associated test catalog; edge cases that were out of scope become in-scope and therefore SOTIF-relevant. This is particularly challenging for Area 3 (unknown unsafe) scenarios: OEMs rely on large-scale scenario generation, simulation-based fuzzing, and field data mining from the fleet to gradually discover and then systematize these "unknown unknowns" into explicit triggering conditions and regression tests.

For SDVs with OTA-updated AI models, SOTIF validation becomes continuous—each model update requires targeted revalidation over a representative scenario set and regression of known edge cases [267].

Critic's Note A camera sees a stop sign perfectly. But add a small sticker, and the AI reads "Speed Limit 45." SOTIF asks: how do we validate against infinite perturbations?

9.5 Cybersecurity Standards

As vehicles become connected and software-defined, cybersecurity transitions from optional to mandatory. The regulatory landscape now enforces comprehensive cybersecurity engineering through multiple standards and regulations. Figure 9-9 provides an overview of this evolving landscape.

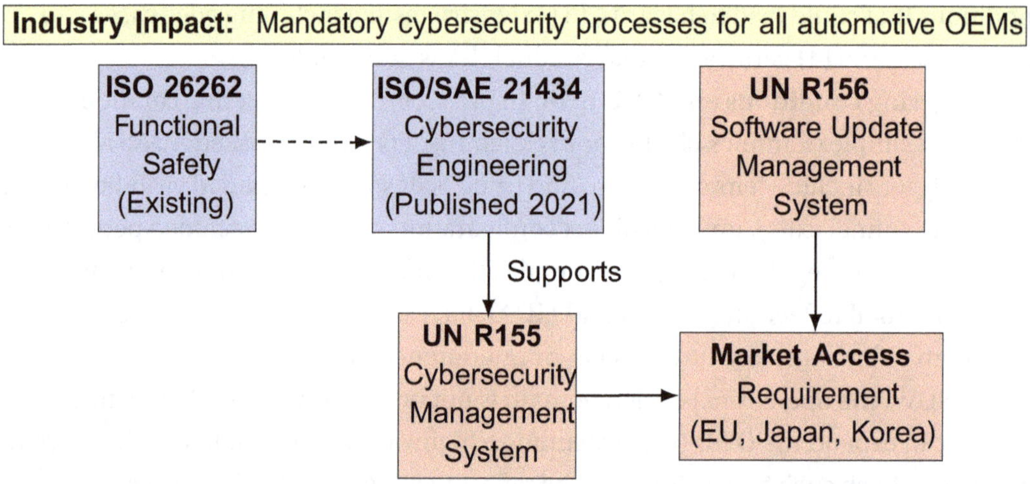

Figure 9-9. *Automotive cybersecurity standards and regulations*

9.5.1 ISO/SAE 21434

ISO/SAE 21434 provides the framework for cybersecurity engineering throughout the vehicle lifecycle [68]. Like ISO 26262 for safety, it defines processes from concept to decommissioning. Key elements include Threat Analysis and Risk Assessment (TARA), cybersecurity goals and requirements, secure design and implementation, verification and validation, and incident response [268]. The standard introduces Cybersecurity Assurance Levels (CALs), which grade the required rigor of cybersecurity activities based on evaluated risk (including threat severity and attack feasibility). CALs serve a role similar in spirit to ASIL in that they scale assurance effort, but they are defined differently and are not directly comparable or mappable one to one [269]. Figure 9-10 illustrates the cybersecurity engineering lifecycle defined by the standard.

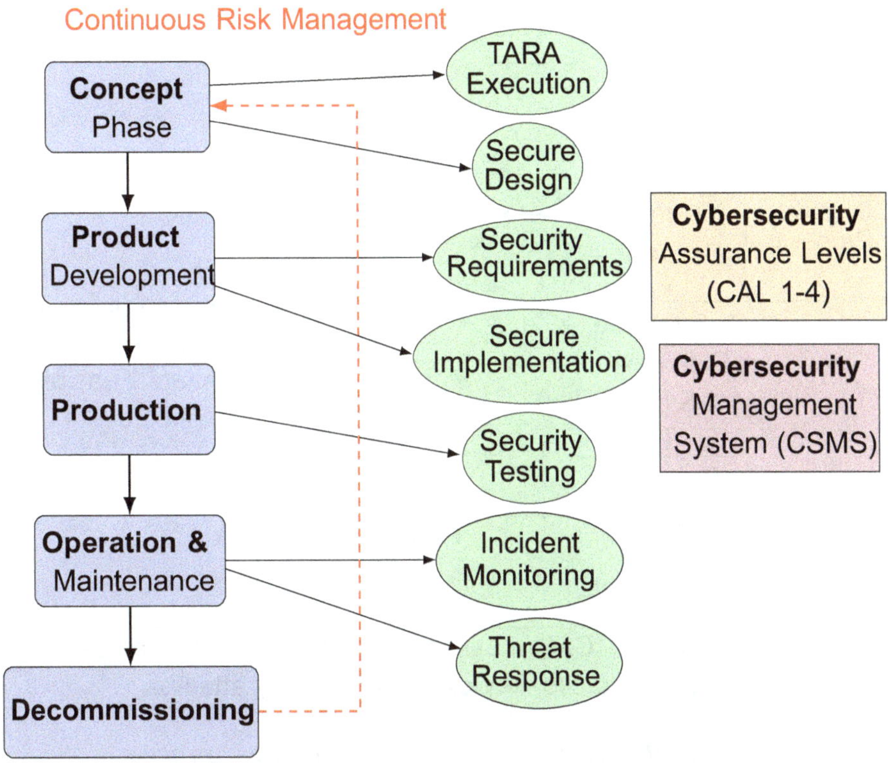

Figure 9-10. *ISO/SAE 21434 cybersecurity engineering lifecycle*

A critical element of ISO/SAE 21434 is the Threat Analysis and Risk Assessment (TARA) process, which systematically identifies threats, evaluates their likelihood and impact, and determines appropriate countermeasures. Figure 9-11 shows the key steps in this process.

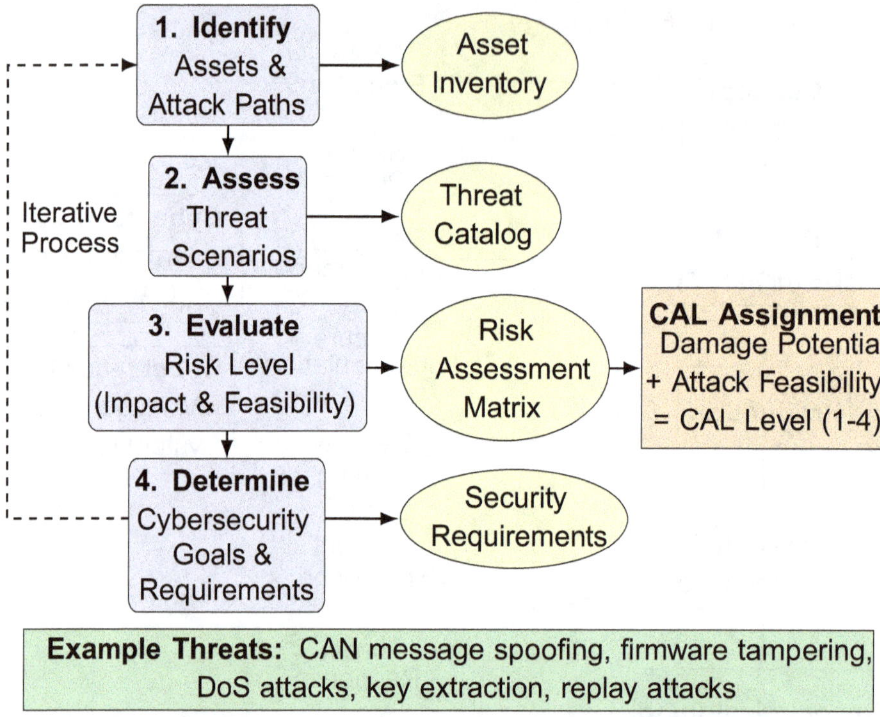

Figure 9-11. *Threat Analysis and Risk Assessment (TARA) process*

9.5.2 UNECE WP.29 R155 and R156

While ISO/SAE 21434 provides the "how," UNECE regulations provide the "must." R155 mandates a Cybersecurity Management System (CSMS) for vehicle manufacturers [69]. R156 requires a Software Update Management System (SUMS) ensuring secure OTA updates [72]. These became mandatory for new vehicle types in July 2022 and all new vehicles from July 2024 in contracting parties (EU, Japan, Korea, etc.) [31]. Non-compliance means vehicles cannot be type-approved for sale [270]. Figure 9-12 summarizes the key requirements of these regulations.

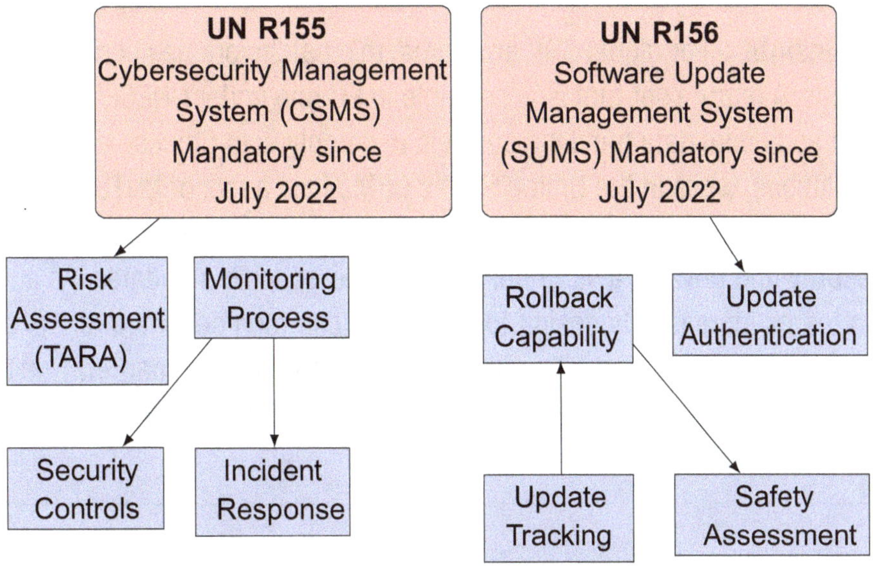

Figure 9-12. *UNECE WP.29 regulations R155 and R156 overview*

The regulations require manufacturers to demonstrate risk assessment for vehicle types, monitoring and response to incidents, secure software update capability, and protection throughout vehicle lifetime. Auditors verify compliance through documentation review and technical assessments.

9.5.3 Global Variations

While UNECE regulations apply in Europe and several Asian markets, other regions have different approaches. The United States relies on voluntary frameworks and NHTSA guidance rather than mandatory standards [271]. China has implemented its own automotive data security regulations focusing on data collection and cross-border transfer [228]. This patchwork creates challenges for global OEMs who must meet varying requirements across markets.

Industry insight For global SDV programs, this patchwork has concrete implications. A feature set that is acceptable in Europe under UNECE R155/R156 may need additional data handling controls to comply with Chinese automotive data regulations, while in the United States OEMs face a mix of NHTSA guidance, industry best practices (e.g., Auto-ISAC recommendations), and general cybersecurity and privacy laws rather than vehicle-specific mandates. As a result, platform teams increasingly design to a "highest common denominator" of security and data protection and then configure or restrict features per market. This has to be planned from the architecture phase onward; retrofitting regional compliance late in the program is both expensive and risky.

9.6 Security Mechanisms

Modern SDVs implement multiple layers of security controls, from hardware-based protection to network monitoring. These mechanisms work together to create defense in depth against cyber threats. Figure 9-13 provides an architectural view of how these mechanisms integrate within an SDV.

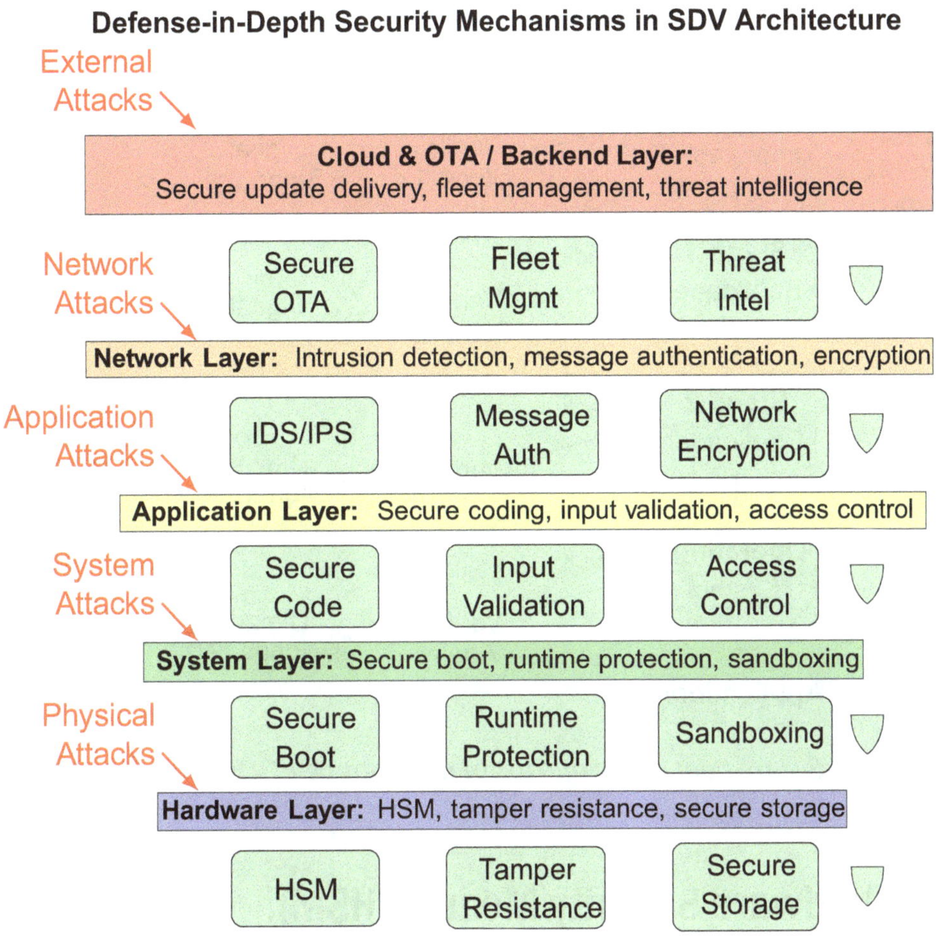

Figure 9-13. *Security mechanisms in SDV architecture*

9.6.1 Secure Boot

Secure boot establishes a chain of trust from power-on to application execution [272]. The process starts with immutable boot ROM containing a root of trust, typically implemented as a hard-coded public key or key hash used to verify the next boot stage. Each boot stage verifies digital signatures of the next stage before execution [22]. Figure 9-14 illustrates this chain of trust.

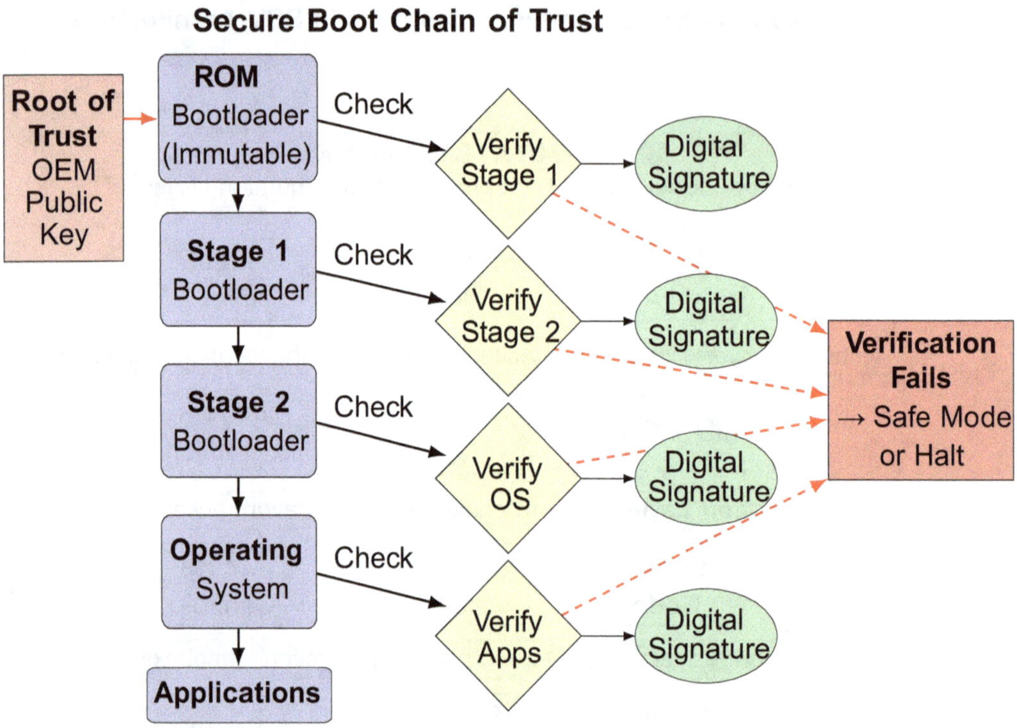

Figure 9-14. Secure boot chain of trust in automotive ECUs

9.6.2 Hardware Security Module (HSM)

HSMs provide hardened cryptographic services [273]. These dedicated security processors handle key generation and storage, cryptographic operations (encryption, signing, verification), secure boot support, and random number generation. Modern automotive processors like AURIX TC4x integrate HSMs meeting EVITA Full requirements [111]. HSMs enable secure communication between ECUs and help protect against certain classes of physical attacks, such as straightforward key extraction from external memories. Figure 9-15 shows the typical architecture of an automotive HSM.

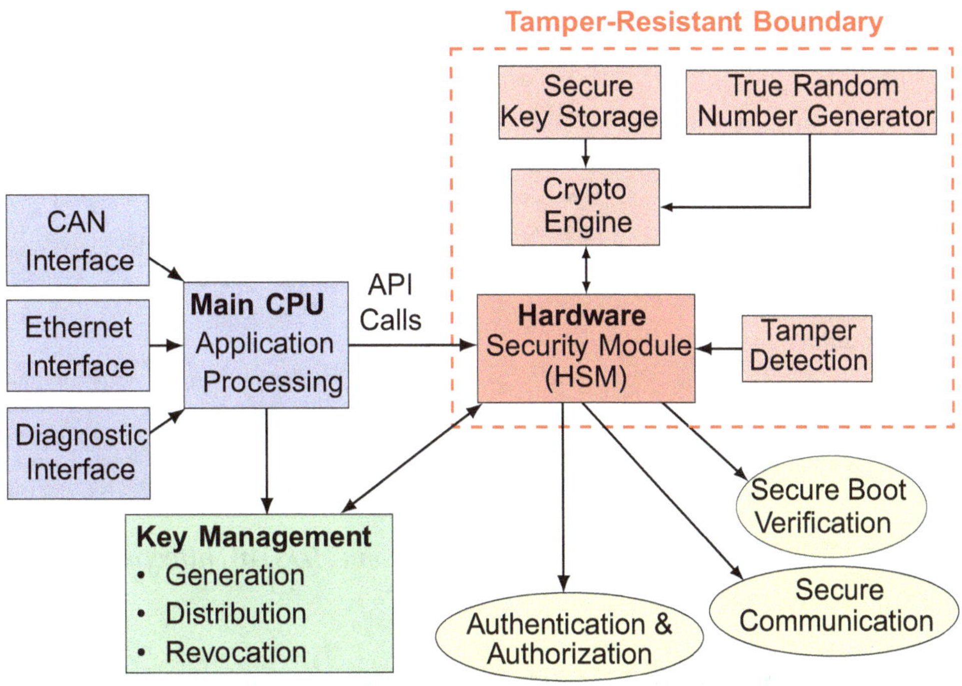

***Figure 9-15.** Hardware security module (HSM) architecture in automotive systems*

9.6.3 Intrusion Detection Systems

An automotive IDS monitors network traffic for anomalies and attacks [274]. Detection methods include signature-based (known attack patterns), anomaly-based (deviations from normal behavior), and specification-based (protocol violations). AUTOSAR IDSM provides standardized interfaces for IDS integration [67]. Machine learning enhances detection of zero-day attacks but requires careful training to avoid false positives. Figure 9-16 shows how an IDS integrates into the vehicle network architecture.

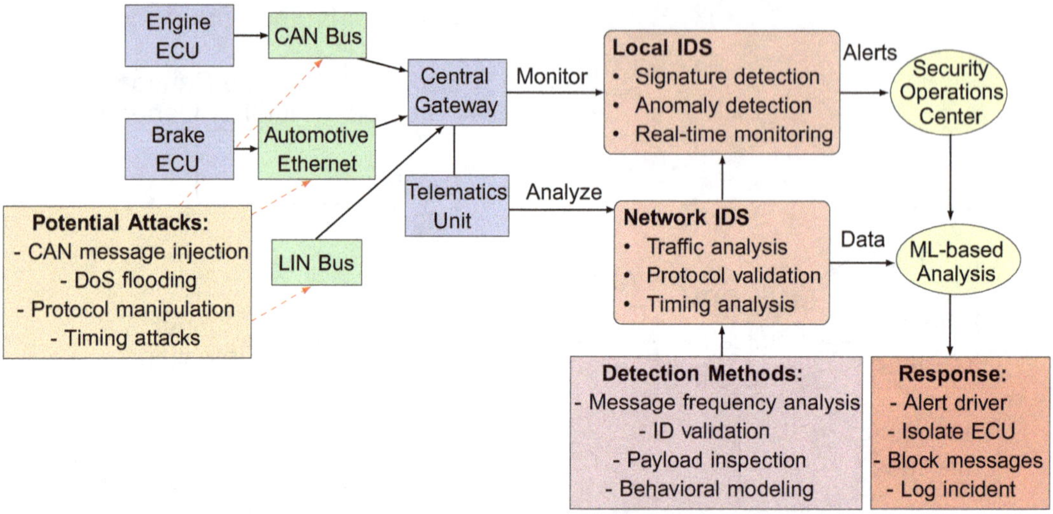

Figure 9-16. *Automotive intrusion detection system (IDS) architecture*

9.6.4 Network Segmentation and Message Authentication

Defense in depth requires isolating critical domains. Zonal architectures encourage segmentation by aggregating local I/O in zone ECUs and routing traffic via central backbones. However, true isolation still depends on intentional logical segmentation and gateway policies; a zonal topology alone does not guarantee physical separation of safety-critical and noncritical domains [64]. Central gateways filter and validate messages between zones. Message authentication codes (MACs) help prevent spoofing and replay attacks on CAN/CAN FD networks, within the limits of available bandwidth, latency, and key management [65]. Automotive Ethernet enables logical segmentation via VLANs and can leverage link- or network-layer encryption and authentication (e.g., MACsec, IPsec, or TLS) for additional isolation and protection against eavesdropping and tampering.

9.6.5 Secure OTA Updates

OTA updates require end-to-end security to prevent malicious firmware [70]. The Uptane framework, increasingly adopted and widely referenced in automotive, provides compromise- resilient design with multiple signing keys, metadata protecting against rollback and freeze attacks, selective updates for different ECU types, and bandwidth-efficient delta updates [134]. Uptane primarily ensures authenticity and integrity of updates via signed metadata; in robust deployments, update traffic is also encrypted in transit (e.g., via TLS) and always verified before installation. Figure 9-17 illustrates this framework.

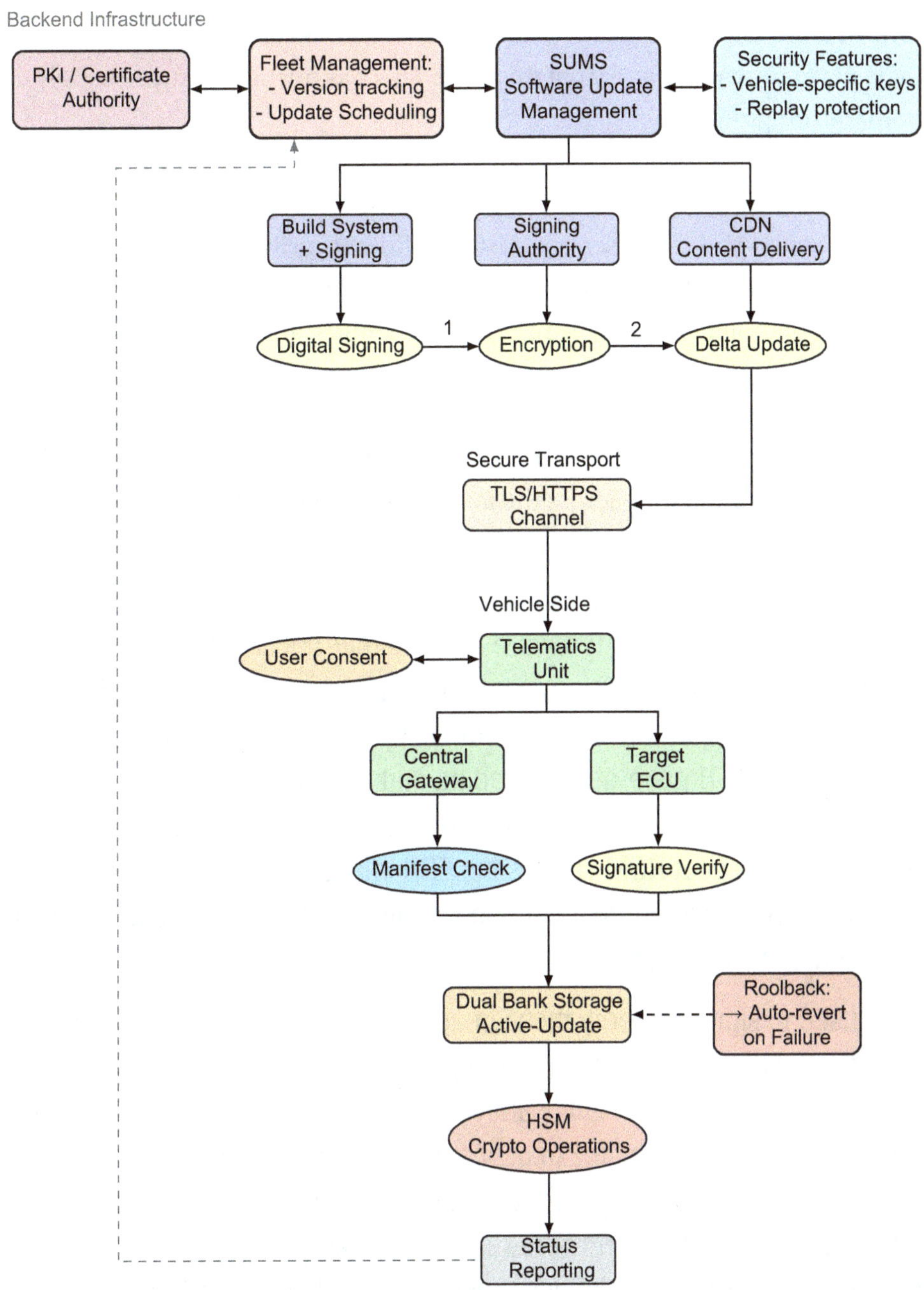

Figure 9-17. *Secure over-the-air (OTA) update framework*

9.6.6 Software Supply Chain and SBOM

Modern SDVs depend heavily on third-party software: open source operating systems and libraries, vendor SDKs, middleware stacks, and cloud components. A vulnerability in any one of these dependencies can become a vehicle-level cybersecurity issue, even if the OEM never touched that part of the code. This has pushed software supply chain security to the foreground.

Two practices are becoming essential. First, OEMs and Tier-1s are adopting software bills of materials (SBOMs) that enumerate the software components and versions present in each ECU and cloud service. SBOMs allow security teams to rapidly assess exposure when a new CVE is published in a widely used library. Second, build pipelines are being hardened: signed artifacts, reproducible builds, and strict segregation of development, integration, and production environments reduce the risk of tampered toolchains or injected dependencies. For SDVs, supply chain security links directly into both the CSMS (for managing third-party risk and vulnerability handling) and the OTA process (for deploying patches across the fleet once supply chain issues are discovered).

Example To see how these mechanisms work together, consider an attacker attempting to inject malicious firmware into a safety-critical ECU. The first line of defense is secure OTA distribution: update packages are signed (and often delivered over TLS), so an attacker cannot easily substitute their own image without breaking the Uptane-style metadata and signature checks. If the attacker somehow manages to get a modified image onto the ECU's flash, secure boot is the next barrier: the boot ROM verifies the ECU image against a root of trust (public key or hash) anchored in hardware. If the signature check fails, the ECU will not boot the compromised image.

The keys used to sign and verify these images are protected by the HSM, which isolates private keys and performs cryptographic operations on demand, making key theft via software attack significantly harder. Even if the attacker manages to abuse a legitimate signing key (e.g., via a compromised back-end), an in-vehicle IDS on the central gateway can still observe anomalous behavior on the network once the malicious firmware runs—unexpected diagnostic traffic, unusual message rates, or protocol violations—and raise alerts into the OEM's security monitoring back-end. In other words, secure OTA, secure boot, HSMs, and IDSs are not independent features: they form a layered defense, each reducing the attacker's options at different points in the firmware lifecycle.

Critic's Note Every connected interface is an attack surface. Every update is a potential vulnerability. Security isn't a feature—it's a continuous battle.

9.7 Safety and Security Convergence

Safety and security were traditionally separate disciplines, but in SDVs they're inseparable. A cyberattack causing unintended acceleration is both a security breach and a safety hazard. This convergence requires new approaches to system design and validation.

9.7.1 Unified Risk Assessment

Organizations increasingly combine HARA (safety) and TARA (security) into unified risk assessments [275]. This identifies scenarios where security vulnerabilities create safety hazards, safety mechanisms that could be exploited for attacks, and conflicts between safety and security requirements. For example, a fail-safe mode that stops the vehicle (safety) could be triggered maliciously for kidnapping (security) [276]. Figure 9-18 shows how these disciplines are converging in modern SDV development.

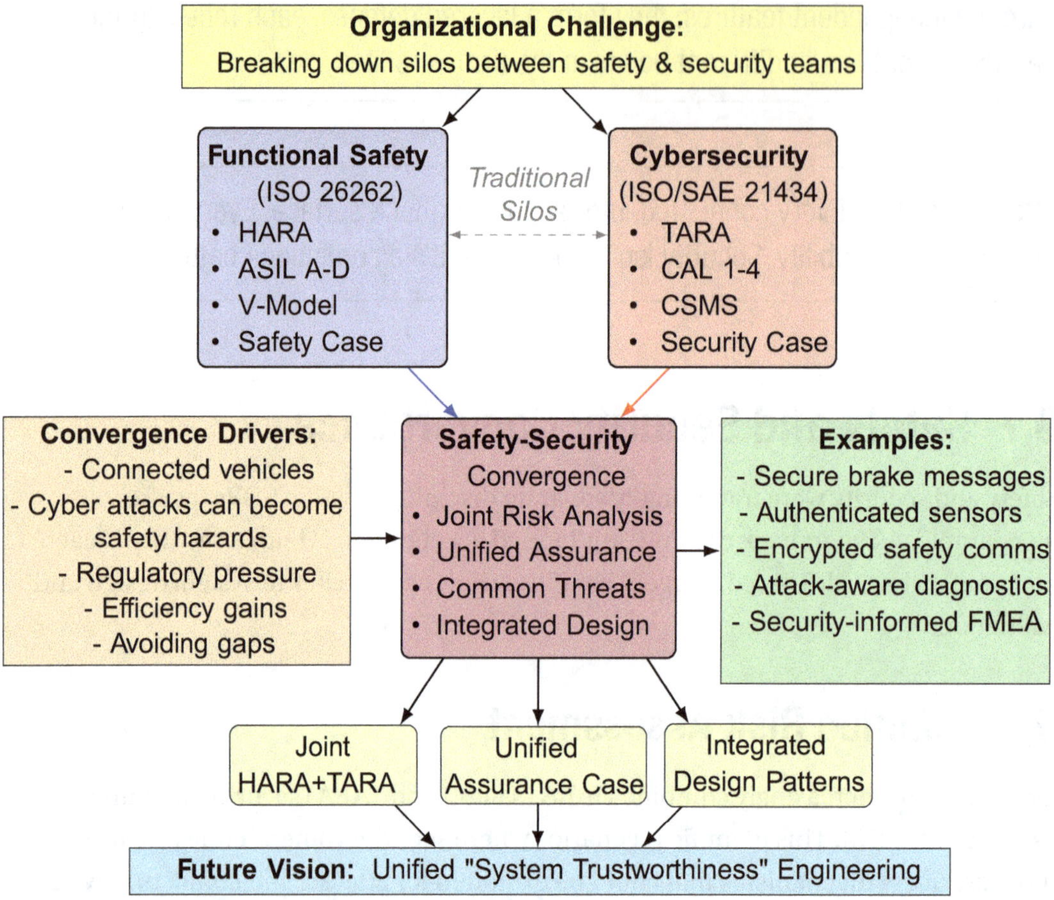

Figure 9-18. *Safety-security convergence in SDV development*

The practical implementation of unified risk assessment combines the HARA process from ISO 26262 with the TARA process from ISO/SAE 21434, as shown in Figure 9-19.

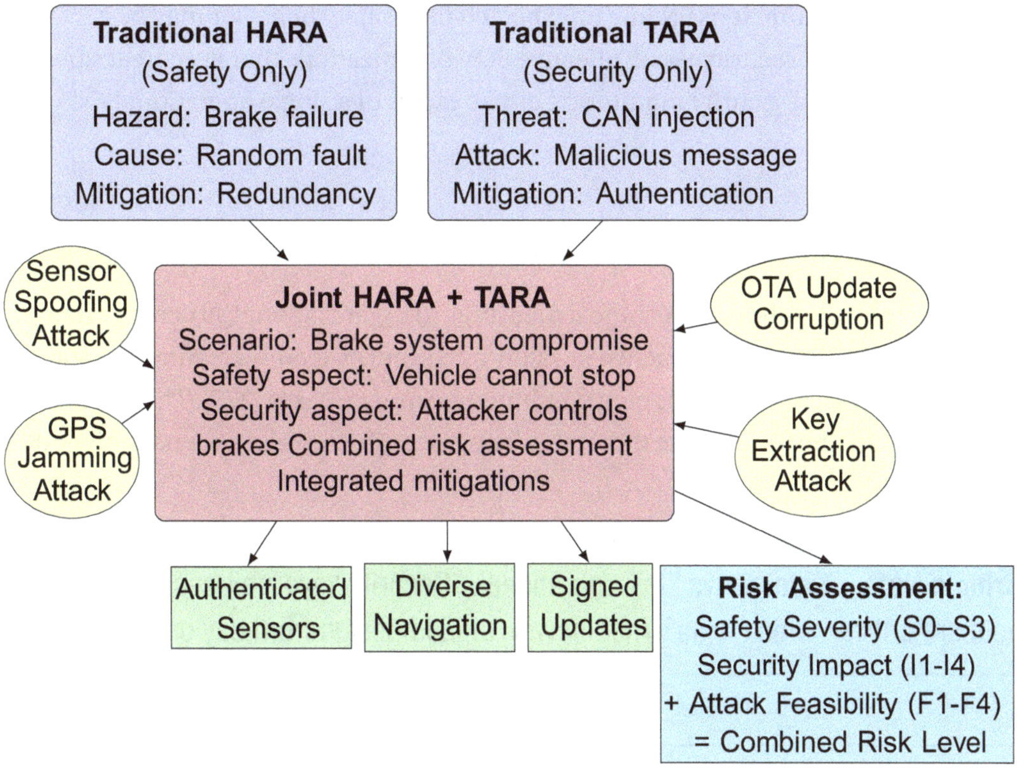

Figure 9-19. *Joint safety-security risk analysis (HARA + TARA)*

9.7.2 Operational Monitoring: VSOC and Field Feedback

Convergence of safety and security is most visible after SOP. ISO 26262 Part 7 already requires safety field monitoring and incident analysis, while ISO/SAE 21434 and UNECE R155 push OEMs toward continuous cybersecurity monitoring. In practice, many OEMs are building Vehicle Security Operations Centers (VSOCs) that ingest alerts from in-vehicle IDSs, telematics back-ends, and cloud infrastructure. These VSOCs triage events, correlate incidents across the fleet, and trigger containment and response actions such as disabling specific remote services or accelerating corrective updates.

From a safety perspective, the same telemetry can inform post-deployment safety monitoring: anomaly patterns, near-miss events, and performance degradations in perception or control functions feed back into the safety case and into SOTIF analyses. The operational reality for SDVs is that safety and security incident response cannot be fully separated: a cybersecurity incident may require safety measures (e.g., limiting automated driving functions), while unexpected field safety behavior may be a symptom of a latent security issue. Effective SDV organizations therefore treat safety field monitoring and security monitoring as two facets of a single operational risk management loop.

9.7.3 Organizational Integration

Convergence extends beyond technical measures to organizational structure. Leading OEMs are breaking down silos between safety and security teams, creating integrated validation processes, and developing combined assurance cases [277]. This requires new skills—safety engineers learning threat modeling, security experts understanding ASIL requirements.

Critic's Note Safety says "fail-operational." Security says "fail-secure." When both are critical, which wins? The answer: unified design from day one.

Example Consider unintended acceleration as a case study. From a pure safety perspective, a HARA might identify scenarios such as unintended torque increase at highway speed or in urban traffic, with high severity (S3), high exposure (E4), and poor controllability (C3), leading to an ASIL-D safety goal: "The vehicle shall not generate unintended positive torque beyond driver intent." Safety requirements then drive design measures such as plausibility checks between pedal position and requested torque, independent monitoring of torque commands, and fail-safe strategies that cut torque on detected inconsistencies.

From a security perspective, a TARA might identify threats where an attacker injects malicious torque commands over an internal network, manipulates calibration parameters, or exploits a vulnerability in a gateway or powertrain ECU. These threats could violate the same safety goal, but the controls look different: authenticated and integrity-protected messages, hardened diagnostic and flashing interfaces, secure boot and HSM-protected keys, and IDS rules to detect anomalous torque-related traffic.

The convergence challenge is to ensure that safety and security measures reinforce rather than undermine each other. For example, a safety fail-safe that cuts torque on inconsistencies must not be trivially triggerable from outside the vehicle, or it becomes a denial-of-service vector for attackers. Conversely, strict security isolation must not prevent a safety monitor from accessing the data it needs to detect dangerous conditions. A unified safety–security concept for unintended acceleration explicitly allocates responsibilities: what is handled by safety mechanisms, what is handled by security controls, and how the combined behavior is argued in the assurance case.

In summary, safety-security convergence in SDVs means that from concept to decommissioning, accidental failures and malicious acts must be analyzed, controlled, and argued side by side. The industry is still in transition: most OEMs today maintain separate safety and security processes, but the direction of travel is toward linked or unified assurance, where safety goals explicitly depend on security controls and security measures are constrained by safety goals. The practical objective is not a buzzword, but a credible, auditable claim of overall system trustworthiness: the safest vehicle is also secure, and a secure vehicle must also be demonstrably safe [62, 93].

Business Note Common safety–security pitfalls in SDVs include the following: (1) assuming zonal architecture equals isolation—simply moving to a zonal topology does not guarantee separation of safety-critical and noncritical domains without explicit gateway policies, VLANs, and filtering; (2) over-relying on ASIL decomposition—decomposing a safety goal into lower ASIL elements does not remove the need for a clear, system-level safety argument and independence justification; (3) separating safety and security incident response—treating these as independent processes leads to blind spots; and (4) treating security as a one-time SOP milestone—SDVs with OTA capabilities require ongoing threat monitoring, vulnerability management, and patching.

9.8 Case Study: Jeep Cherokee Hack (2015)

To understand why all this matters, let's look at a watershed moment in automotive cybersecurity: the Jeep Cherokee hack of 2015. This incident was a wake-up call for the auto industry and directly influenced regulators to act on vehicle cybersecurity. Figure 9-20 provides a timeline of the key events and their impact.

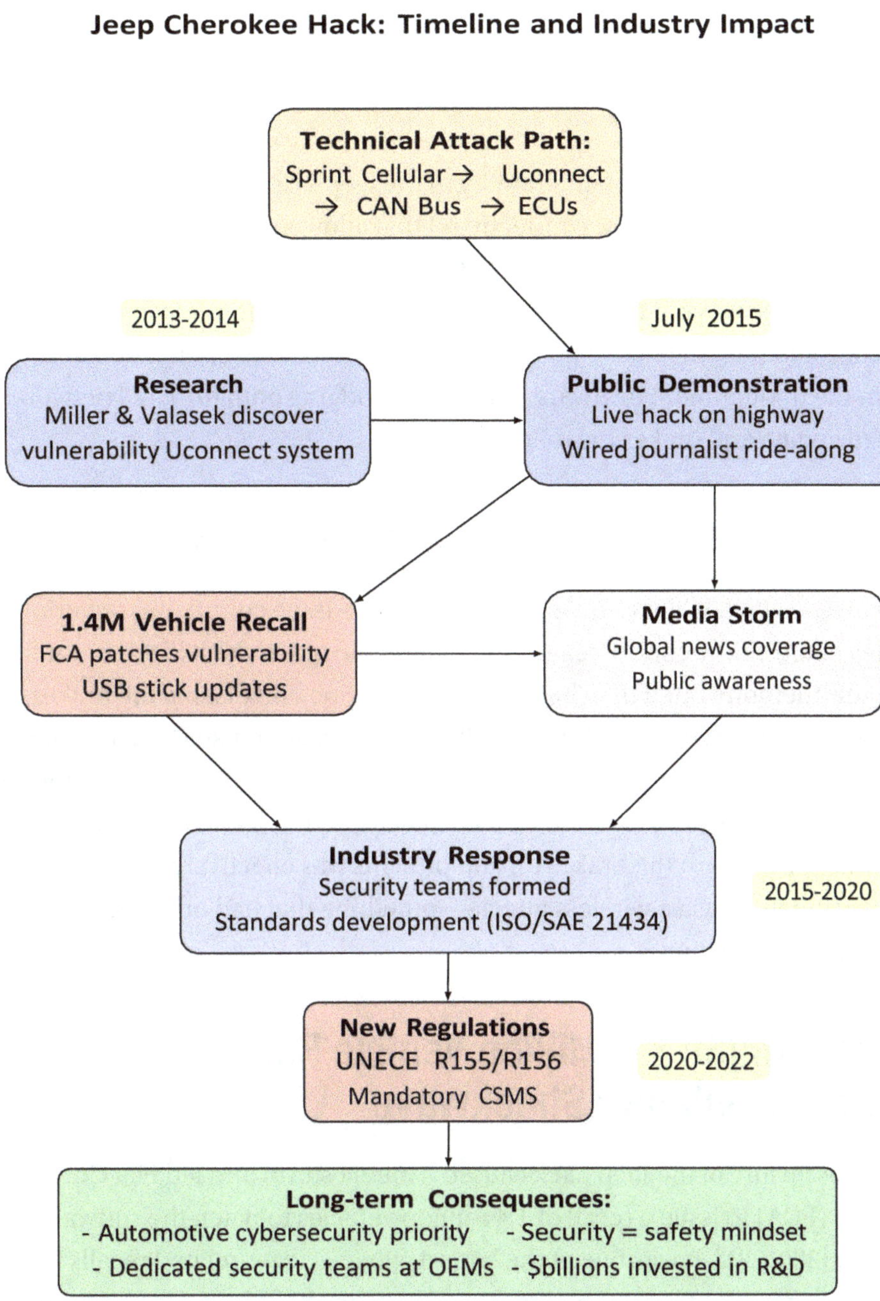

Figure 9-20. *Jeep Cherokee hack (2015)—timeline and impact*

9.8.1 Remote Exploit via Infotainment

In 2015, cybersecurity researchers Charlie Miller and Chris Valasek demonstrated a remote hack of a Jeep Cherokee SUV, which they famously showcased to a journalist from *Wired*. They discovered a vulnerability in the Jeep's Uconnect infotainment system (a head unit with cellular connectivity) that allowed them to send commands to the vehicle's CAN bus over the internet [278]. In technical terms, the Jeep's cellular telematics interface was inadequately isolated from critical internal networks. The researchers could penetrate through the vehicle's cellular data connection and reprogram the infotainment firmware, ultimately bridging onto the CAN network, which connects to engine and brake controllers.

9.8.2 Attackers Disabled the Engine and More

Once on the CAN bus, Miller and Valasek were able to issue commands to various ECUs. They could subtly control features like the radio or windshield wipers at first, but critically, they demonstrated the ability to kill the engine and disable the brakes of the Jeep remotely under certain conditions [279]. In the live demonstration, they cut the transmission while the journalist was driving on the highway, causing the vehicle to slow to a crawl. They also showed they could affect steering (in reverse, due to power steering control) and turn the brakes on and off. This was effectively a full takeover of the vehicle's key functions via a wireless attack—something that had only been theorized in academic papers until then.

9.8.3 Aftermath: 1.4 Million Vehicle Recall and Regulatory Shockwave

The public disclosure of the Jeep hack caused a media storm and led Fiat Chrysler Automobiles (FCA) to issue a recall of 1.4 million vehicles to patch the software vulnerability [280, 281]. It was one of the largest cybersecurity-related recalls in automotive history. The vehicles had to get software updates (some via USB stick, mailed to owners) that closed the loophole in the telematics system [281]. Beyond the recall, this event deeply rattled regulators and industry executives. It became a canonical example in discussions around WP.29 R155 [271], illustrating how a single exposed connectivity interface could undermine safety-critical functions. In Europe and Asia, regulators realized such cyber incidents were a global threat to safety, which undoubtedly hastened the adoption of mandatory rules. In short, the Jeep Cherokee hack was a pivotal factor that proved cars could be remotely attacked and that safety-critical functions were at risk. It moved automotive cybersecurity from a theoretical to an immediate practical concern.

Figure 9-21 provides technical details of the attack path, showing how the researchers moved from the external cellular interface through the infotainment system and onto the safety-critical CAN bus.

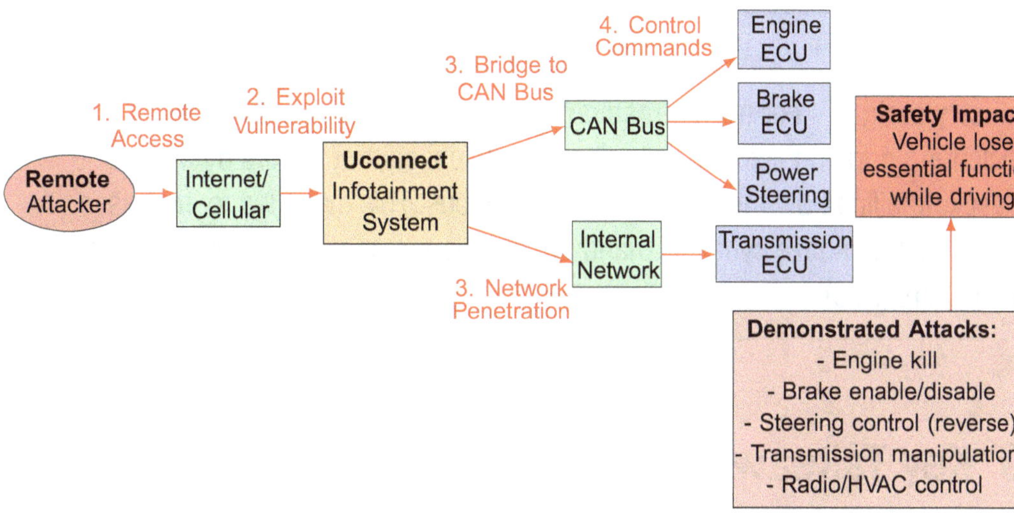

Figure 9-21. *Technical details of the Jeep Cherokee hack—attack path*

This case study underscores why SDVs need strong security. A single vulnerable entry point (an open port in an infotainment unit) allowed a catastrophic safety issue (engine/brake control by attackers). The response—massive recall and new regulations—also shows that the industry and governments now treat cybersecurity with the same gravity as product safety defects. For students and engineers, the Jeep hack serves as a lesson: connectivity must be accompanied by robust security design, and safety analysis must encompass malicious misuse, not just component failures.

Takeaway Key lessons for SDV architectures include strong network segmentation between external connectivity (telematics, infotainment) and safety-critical domains (powertrain, braking, steering); strict isolation and filtering at central gateways so that no single connected ECU can directly inject arbitrary CAN frames to safety ECUs; secure OTA and patch management processes that can rapidly deploy fixes without requiring physical recalls; and proactive red-teaming and penetration testing of connected interfaces before SOP, not only after incidents.

Industry insight For further reading, see Andy Greenberg's 2015 *Wired* article for a gripping account of the hack and subsequent papers by Miller and Valasek detailing how they infiltrated the CAN bus. This event led to increased funding in automotive cyber R&D and the creation of specialized teams at most automakers [278].

9.9 Key Takeaways

- **ISO 26262 and continuous safety**: ISO 26262 defines the functional safety process and ASIL levels A–D for risk classification, but in an SDV with OTA updates, safety assurance isn't one-and-done—continuous updates require incremental safety cases and revalidation [73, 145]. The V-model must adapt to iterative software releases.
- **SOTIF for intended functionality**: SOTIF (ISO 21448) addresses safety of the intended functionality, covering hazards from system limitations (especially in AI/ADAS) rather than hardware/software faults. It deals with things like sensor blinding or AI misinterpretation (e.g., sun glare causing a vision system failure) where no component failed but the behavior is unsafe [260].
- **Mandatory cybersecurity standards**: ISO/SAE 21434 and UNECE WP.29 (R155/R156) mandate a comprehensive cybersecurity lifecycle for vehicles. ISO 21434 provides the framework for threat

analysis, risk assessment, and implementing security by design, while UNECE R155 and R156 make having a certified Cybersecurity Management System and Software Update Management System a legal requirement for new vehicles (Europe 2022+ onward) [31, 68].

- **Layered security mechanisms**: Security mechanisms like secure boot and HSMs are increasingly standard in new SDV platforms—especially central compute SoCs and high- integration controllers—and in-vehicle IDS capabilities are increasingly deployed on central gateways and connected ECUs. Secure boot ensures only signed, untampered code runs on ECUs [272]. HSMs safeguard cryptographic keys and enable encrypted/authenticated communications [273]. Intrusion detection systems monitor in-vehicle networks for attacks [274]. Together with secure OTA update capability [70], these measures create a layered defense against cyber threats.
- **Safety–security convergence**: Safety and security convergence is essential: a cyberattack is effectively a new kind of hazard. Thus, automakers are moving toward unified safety–security risk assessments and assurance cases. Organizational silos between safety and security engineering are breaking down because secure vehicles must also be safe and vice versa [275]. The Jeep Cherokee hack vividly demonstrated that a lack of security can directly undermine safety, reinforcing the need for integrated approaches.
- **Practical implications**: For practitioners, the practical implication is that SDV safety and security cannot be bolted on to existing processes. They require integrated governance (CSMS plus safety management), lifecycle tooling for continuous updates, and organizational structures where safety, security, and operations teams share telemetry, scenarios, and assurance evidence rather than working in parallel silos.

Looking ahead, the field is moving toward tighter integration of these strands: formal co-analysis methods that treat safety and security risks in a unified way, stronger tool support for continuous assurance across OTA-driven lifecycles, and gradual harmonization of regional regulations so that global SDV platforms can be engineered and certified against a more consistent set of expectations.

CHAPTER 10

Ecosystem and Monetization

10.1 Chapter Goals

After this chapter, you will be able to

- Explain the shift from one-time vehicle sales to recurring SDV revenue streams.
- Identify ecosystem actors: OEMs, Tier-1s, infrastructure partners (cloud and connectivity), and regulators.
- Compare monetization models: subscriptions, data marketplaces, functions-on-demand (FoD), and fleet telematics.
- Evaluate app store models in SDVs and their strategic consequences.
- Discuss customer experience as the driver of long-term value.

Critic's Note Monetization is not a feature you bolt on after SOP. If the architecture, data rights, and customer trust are not designed in from day one, no subscription model will save a failed SDV strategy. The graveyard of "heated seats subscriptions" should be warning enough.

S. Agarwal, *Software-Defined Vehicles*, https://doi.org/10.1007/979-8-8688-2718-1_10

10.2 Introduction

Modern vehicles are increasingly being developed as long-lived, software-enabled platforms rather than as purely hardware-defined products. Revenue remains concentrated at the point of sale, but over-the-air (OTA) architectures allow some OEMs to extend value capture after delivery through connected services, optional software features, and data-enabled offerings. The extent of this shift varies by segment, market, regulation, and customer willingness to pay (see Figure 10-1).

Industry studies consistently point to meaningful economic upside from software-enabled services, even if the exact size of the opportunity differs by scope and methodology. A 2023 BCG/World Economic Forum report estimates that software-defined vehicles could create more than $650 billion in additional value by 2030, corresponding to roughly 15–20% of total automotive value creation [282]. Other analyses, including McKinsey's work on the automotive software market, project substantial growth in software-related revenues through the decade [283]. The precise numbers vary, but the directional conclusion is clear: software and services can materially expand the automotive value pool beyond traditional hardware sales.

Several OEMs already offer post-sale connectivity packages, software-enabled options, and OTA-delivered feature updates. This shift shares some platform economics characteristics with consumer electronics in that software, services, and data can extend value capture beyond the initial hardware sale. The comparison should be used cautiously, however. Vehicles have longer service lives, stricter safety and regulatory constraints, and different ownership economics than phones. Sustainable SDV monetization therefore depends not on replicating a smartphone model, but on delivering durable, trustworthy, and clearly differentiated digital experiences over the vehicle lifecycle [284].

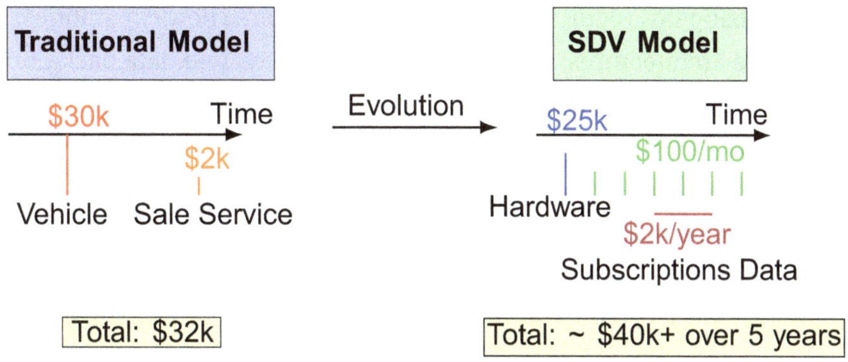

Figure 10-1. *Traditional one-time sales compared with SDV recurring revenue model. Left: conventional dealership transaction with revenue concentrated at point of sale. Right: ongoing software and service revenue streams distributed across vehicle lifetime*

10.3 From Hardware Sales to Recurring Revenue

Traditionally, auto OEMs relied on one-time sales: a customer bought the vehicle with any desired options, and the manufacturer's revenue ended there (plus service/parts later). In the SDV era, the core hardware (sensors, processors, connectivity) is paid for up front, but software-defined capabilities and digital services are sold over time. This means features like advanced driver assistance, heated seats, or additional battery range can be activated later—where legally permitted and technically validated—via subscription or one-time software unlock. The vehicle becomes, in effect, a service platform built atop the physical product: customers own the hardware but license capabilities over time. For example, Tesla offers its Full Self-Driving (Supervised) software—which, despite the name, requires continuous driver attention and does not provide full autonomy—as either a one-time purchase or a monthly subscription, allowing owners to activate the capability after taking delivery [285].

Market research across the last decade consistently points to substantial upside from software- and data-enabled services [286]. OEM business plans now routinely assume that, over a vehicle's lifetime, a meaningful share of gross margin will come from software licenses, subscriptions, and data products rather than from hardware alone. In short, OEMs are betting that, over time, the incremental value of software and data can rival or even exceed the margin on the underlying vehicle for at least some segments.

However, realizing this recurring revenue model requires new capabilities: centralized vehicle architectures, secure OTA infrastructure, and data back-ends (Figure 10-2). It also hinges on delivering a compelling customer experience. Analysts emphasize that digital services in SDVs must feel essential and valuable, not like opportunistic upsells [287]. In practice, OEMs strive to make over-the-air updates and personalization so seamless that drivers feel continually delighted. As one industry observer put it, revenue in an SDV is tied to how well the car "anticipates and delights the driver, not just how it drives" [284]—making the driver experience the real engine of profit.

Early evidence suggests these projections should be treated with caution. Publicly available data on subscription attach rates—the percentage of eligible vehicles whose owners actually subscribe—remains limited, but industry analysts report that initial FoD attach rates often fall below 10–15% for optional features and churn within the first year can exceed 50% [288]. Several OEMs, including GM and Ford, have publicly revised down earlier per-vehicle software revenue targets, acknowledging that customer willingness to pay has not matched initial assumptions. The recurring revenue opportunity is real, but capturing it requires more than simply putting price tags on software-locked features.

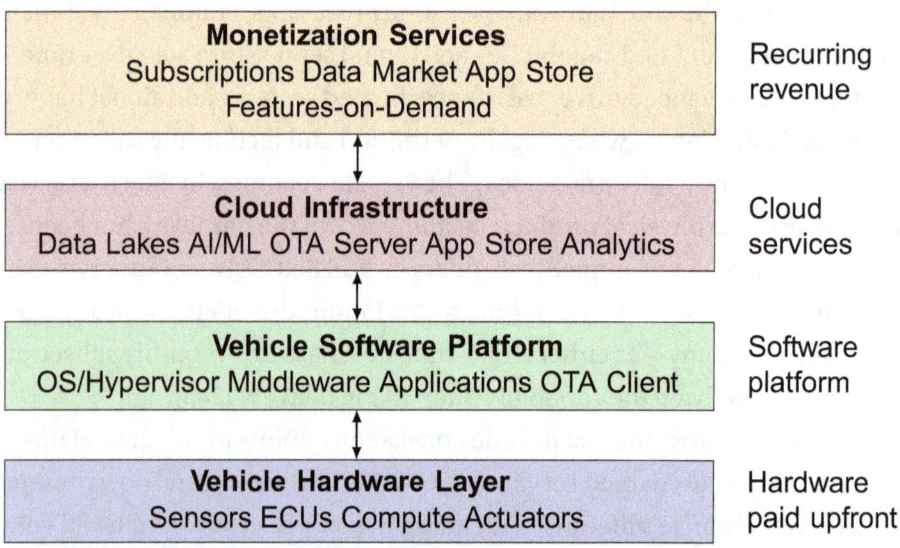

Figure 10-2. *SDV architecture supporting recurring revenue streams. Centralized compute, secure OTA infrastructure, and cloud back-ends enable continuous feature delivery and data monetization.*

10.4 Ecosystem Actors

The SDV business model extends beyond the OEM. A successful ecosystem involves multiple players: OEMs, Tier-1 suppliers, infrastructure partners (cloud providers and telcos), and regulators, as well as chip and platform vendors (e.g., automotive SoC providers), dealers and importers, fleet and leasing companies, and insurers. This chapter focuses on the first group of core actors (Figure 10-3) while acknowledging that the latter group strongly shapes how SDV services are priced, distributed, and regulated in practice.

10.4.1 OEMs (Automakers)

OEMs seek to capture customer data and create ongoing revenue streams. In the new model, OEMs often provide the software platform and customer interface, and they set subscription prices. For example, Tesla exemplifies a vertically integrated OEM: it controls the in-car software, OTA updates, and app ecosystem. Tesla sells Full Self-Driving (Supervised) as an add-on (one-time purchase or subscription) and even charges for Premium Connectivity (Wi-Fi, streaming) in its cars.

Likewise, BMW and other legacy OEMs are experimenting with software-as-service: BMW introduced subscription-based real-time traffic and early heated seats subscriptions (later rescinded) [34], and Volvo offers OTA-enabled software options. By owning the software layer, OEMs can build strong brand loyalty and higher profit margins.

10.4.2 Tier-1 Suppliers

Traditionally, Tier-1s (Bosch, Continental, Aptiv, etc.) sold components and electronics. In the SDV world, many are moving up the stack. They now provide integrated software platforms, middleware, AI stacks, and devtools for SDV development. For instance, Bosch has promoted the concept of a software-defined cockpit and provides unified vehicle computing architectures that support OTA updates. Many suppliers also offer "as-a-service" middleware and DevOps pipelines to help OEMs manage large software projects. These new offerings aim to capture value in the software domain, even as hardware becomes more standardized.

10.4.3 Infrastructure Partners: Cloud Providers and Connectivity

The SDV ecosystem depends on external infrastructure provided by two overlapping categories of partners: hyperscale cloud providers and telecommunications operators.

Hyperscale cloud providers—Amazon (AWS), Google (GCP), and Microsoft (Azure)—supply the compute backbone for SDVs: data lakes for vehicle telemetry, GPU clusters for AI training, and global content delivery networks for OTA updates. Volkswagen's CARIAD unit, e.g., uses Microsoft Azure for its connected car services, while BMW and GM rely on AWS for analytics and mapping. These partnerships accelerate development but raise strategic concerns: heavy dependence on a single cloud vendor can blur brand identity and shift data control away from the OEM [289].

Telecommunications operators provide the cellular connectivity (4G/5G) and, increasingly, edge compute nodes that enable real-time vehicle-to-cloud communication. Telcos are investing in multi-access edge computing (MEC) infrastructure to support ultra-low-latency V2X services; however, most MEC-based automotive use cases remain in pilot stages rather than mass-market deployment. Today, the primary telco revenue from SDVs still comes from connectivity bundles and eSIM partnerships with OEMs. The longer-term question—whether telcos can capture value beyond raw connectivity—remains open.

10.4.4 Regulators

Governments and standards bodies have a strong influence on SDVs. For safety and cybersecurity, under UNECE vehicle regulations—specifically UN R155 (Cybersecurity Management System) and UN R156 (Software Update Management System)—OEMs seeking type approval in adopting markets must demonstrate that they operate type-approved CSMS and SUMS for new vehicle types, and, in many contracting-party markets, this requirement subsequently extends to all new vehicle registrations according to defined phase-in timelines [69, 72, 270]. This means cars must be designed for secure OTA updates and continuous vulnerability management, following frameworks like ISO/SAE 21434 for cybersecurity engineering [68].

In addition, data protection laws (EU GDPR, California CCPA, China's PIPL, etc.) dictate how vehicle and user data can be collected, stored, or monetized. Regulators require explicit user consent for data use and strict anonymization and give individuals rights over their vehicle data. Compliance is non-negotiable: OEMs must build their monetization strategies around these rules or face fines, sales restrictions, and consumer distrust. For example, any data marketplace must guarantee privacy by design. Global privacy and cybersecurity rules thus form the guardrails of the SDV ecosystem.

10.4.5 Regional Variation: China's Distinct Ecosystem

The preceding discussion has implicitly centered on Western markets (North America, Europe). China's SDV ecosystem differs in several important respects and merits separate consideration.

First, domestic technology giants—Baidu, Alibaba, Tencent, and Huawei—play a far more central role than their Western counterparts. Baidu's Apollo platform provides autonomous driving software to multiple OEMs; Alibaba's AliOS (via the Banma joint venture with SAIC) powers in-vehicle operating systems; Huawei supplies HarmonyOS-based cockpits and full-stack ADAS solutions. These firms offer integrated platform capabilities that blur the traditional OEM–supplier boundary [290].

Second, data sovereignty rules differ. China's Personal Information Protection Law (PIPL) and Cybersecurity Law impose strict localization requirements: vehicle data collected in China is subject to stringent domestic storage and security assessment rules, and cross-border transfers typically require explicit regulatory review. This regulatory posture encourages reliance on domestic cloud providers (Alibaba Cloud, Tencent Cloud, Huawei Cloud) rather than AWS or Azure.

Third, consumer expectations around software-first vehicles are arguably more advanced. Chinese buyers, particularly in the EV segment, evaluate smart cockpit features, voice assistants, and OTA update cadence as primary purchase criteria. OEMs such as NIO, XPeng, and Li Auto compete intensely on software experience, creating a market dynamic where SDV capabilities are table-stakes rather than premium differentiators.

Business Note For global OEMs, China's distinct ecosystem implies that a single SDV strategy cannot simply be exported worldwide. Platform choices, data architectures, and monetization models must be tailored to local regulatory and competitive conditions.

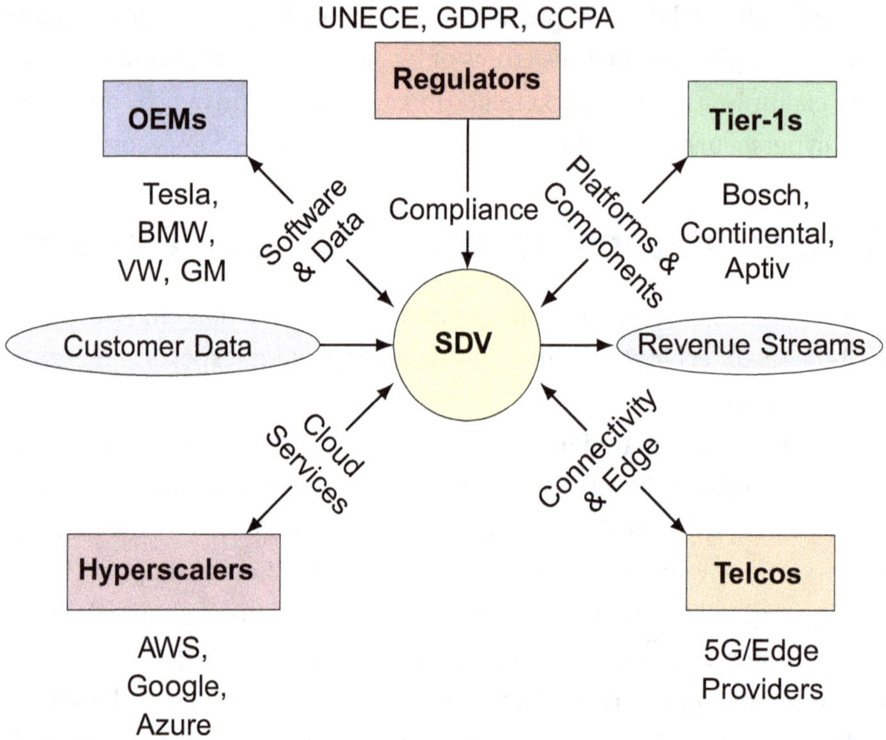

Figure 10-3. *SDV ecosystem actors and their interactions. OEMs sit at the center, interfacing with Tier-1 suppliers, cloud and connectivity partners, regulators, and end customers.*

10.5 Monetization Models

SDV platforms enable several monetization strategies beyond the initial vehicle sale. These strategies fall into two broad categories:

Business-to-Consumer (B2C):

Revenue collected directly from vehicle owners or drivers, such as feature subscriptions, premium connectivity packages, and app purchases.

Business-to-Business (B2B):

Revenue from enterprises, fleets, insurers, and public authorities, including telematics services, aggregated data licensing, and fleet management platforms.

In practice, most OEMs operate a mix of both, as illustrated in Figure 10-4. The subsections below examine each model in turn, noting where B2B and B2C dynamics differ.

10.5.1 Subscriptions and Functions-on-Demand (B2C)

Many vehicle functions can be packaged as ongoing services, commonly termed *functions-on-demand* (FoD). This includes comfort features (heated/cooled seats, adaptive suspension), advanced driver aids (e.g., hands-free parking, highway autopilot), and even performance upgrades (battery range boosts, engine tuning). For example, a customer might pay a monthly fee to enable heated seats that were physically installed but locked out by software. Tesla sells its Full Self-Driving software either up front or as a subscription.

These on-demand features can significantly boost revenue, but they are controversial. Customers often balk at "paying twice" for hardware they already own. The most prominent example—BMW's heated seats subscription, discussed in detail in the section "BMW Heated Seats Subscription"—illustrates how quickly customer goodwill can erode when FoD is perceived as extractive rather than additive.

Multiple consumer surveys indicate that subscription fatigue is real—drivers will resist a myriad of small monthly fees [291]. To succeed, OEMs must clearly communicate value and avoid an accumulation of small charges that customers perceive as excessive. Industry experts advise bundling services meaningfully and offering tiered packages [291]. In short, subscription features must feel like genuine enhancements (e.g., added safety or luxury) rather than hidden tolls.

10.5.2 Data Marketplaces (Primarily B2B)

A prominent B2B-oriented revenue source is monetizing vehicle data. In practice, many OEMs currently use data primarily to improve products and operations rather than as a standalone revenue line; external data monetization remains emerging and varies significantly by region. Modern cars collect massive telemetry (GPS, cameras, radars, diagnostics, etc.). Aggregated and anonymized, this data can be very valuable: e.g., traffic authorities will pay for live road condition feeds, insurers will pay for driving behavior data, and mapping companies will pay for real-time traffic patterns.

OEMs and data platforms are building marketplaces to trade such data. One example is the HERE Marketplace: connected car firms like RoadCloud sell high-fidelity road condition data (friction, weather, pavement quality) to OEMs and governments via HERE's platform [292]. Toyota's connected services include a "Mobility Services Platform" where anonymized vehicle data can be licensed to third parties (e.g., for AI training). In Europe, initiatives like Catena-X and Caruso are creating standardized automotive data ecosystems for cross-company data exchange.

Data marketplaces open new profit channels, but also raise privacy challenges. Any data monetization must comply with privacy laws and consumer trust. Automakers must ensure all data sharing complies with GDPR and CCPA regulations, with a focus on anonymizing personal information and securing consumer consent [293]. In practice, that means using federated analytics or clean-room techniques so individual drivers cannot be identified. The value of data can only be unlocked if customers trust their privacy is respected. Thus, successful data marketplaces balance monetization with strict data governance and clear consumer opt-in.

10.5.3 Third-Party App Stores (B2C with B2B Elements)

SDV infotainment platforms can host app ecosystems much like phones. There is a strategic split between closed and open models. Tesla represents the closed approach: it runs a proprietary operating system with its own curated app environment (no Apple CarPlay or Android Auto), and Tesla vets any apps or games for its cars.

By contrast, many OEMs have adopted Android Automotive OS (AAOS). AAOS is a full operating system that integrates Google's services, including the Google Play Store. Cars running AAOS (e.g., many Volvo, Polestar, Ford vehicles) allow drivers to install a curated set of third-party apps (navigation, streaming, selected services) that are vetted for in-vehicle use. This provides a relatively rich ecosystem out of the box compared with fully proprietary stacks.

The tension is control vs. scale. Using Google's platform accelerates app availability, but cedes some control to a tech giant. Analysts warn that if automakers fully "relinquish UI control to Apple or Google, they risk becoming mere hardware suppliers while software and service revenues flow to tech companies" [289]. In other words, Apple/Google might collect most user data and own the customer relationship.

We see this in the CarPlay/Android Auto debate: OEMs like GM began dropping CarPlay and Android Auto precisely to keep driver data for themselves [294]. Some OEMs mitigate this by using the open source AAOS without Google's proprietary services (e.g., VW and Volvo's approach), wrapping their own branding and app catalogs around it. In summary, offering a third-party app store can enhance the car's digital appeal, but it also involves strategic trade-offs about who really controls the in-cabin experience and monetization. The section "Android Automotive (Open Infotainment)" examines how specific OEMs have navigated this tension.

10.5.4 Fleet Telematics and B2B Services

While consumer subscriptions attract headlines, Business-to-Business (B2B) fleet services represent a more mature and, in many cases, larger revenue opportunity. The global commercial vehicle telematics market was valued at approximately $61 billion in 2024 and is projected to exceed $130 billion by 2030, growing at a compound annual rate of nearly 14% [295].

Fleet operators—logistics companies, rental agencies, delivery services, and municipal transit authorities—pay for

- **Real-time tracking and route optimization:** GPS-based fleet visibility reduces fuel costs and improves delivery windows.
- **Predictive maintenance:** Sensor data enables condition-based servicing, reducing unplanned downtime.
- **Driver behavior monitoring:** Telematics-derived safety scores support training programs and insurance pricing.
- **Usage-based leasing:** Pay-per-mile or pay-per-hour models align fleet costs with actual utilization.

Usage-based insurance (UBI): A particularly significant B2B application is usage-based insurance, in which insurers price policies based on actual driving behavior rather than demographic proxies. Telematics data—mileage, speed, braking patterns, and time of day—enables insurers to offer discounts to safe drivers while more accurately pricing risk. Programs like Progressive's Snapshot and Allstate's Drivewise have enrolled millions of customers, and OEM–insurer partnerships are expanding: Tesla offers its own insurance product using vehicle data, and GM's OnStar Insurance leverages in-car telematics directly. For OEMs, UBI partnerships offer a recurring data licensing revenue stream; for customers, the value proposition is tangible (lower premiums for safe driving). However, privacy concerns are acute—drivers may resist sharing granular location and behavior data with insurers—and regulatory frameworks for telematics-based insurance vary by jurisdiction. OEMs pursuing this revenue stream must balance monetization against the risk of customer backlash over surveillance.

Unlike consumer subscriptions, B2B telematics revenue is driven by demonstrable return on investment—fuel savings, reduced accidents, and lower insurance premiums—rather than perceived luxury or convenience. This makes fleet services less susceptible to subscription fatigue and provides OEMs with a stable, recurring revenue base that can offset volatility in consumer markets.

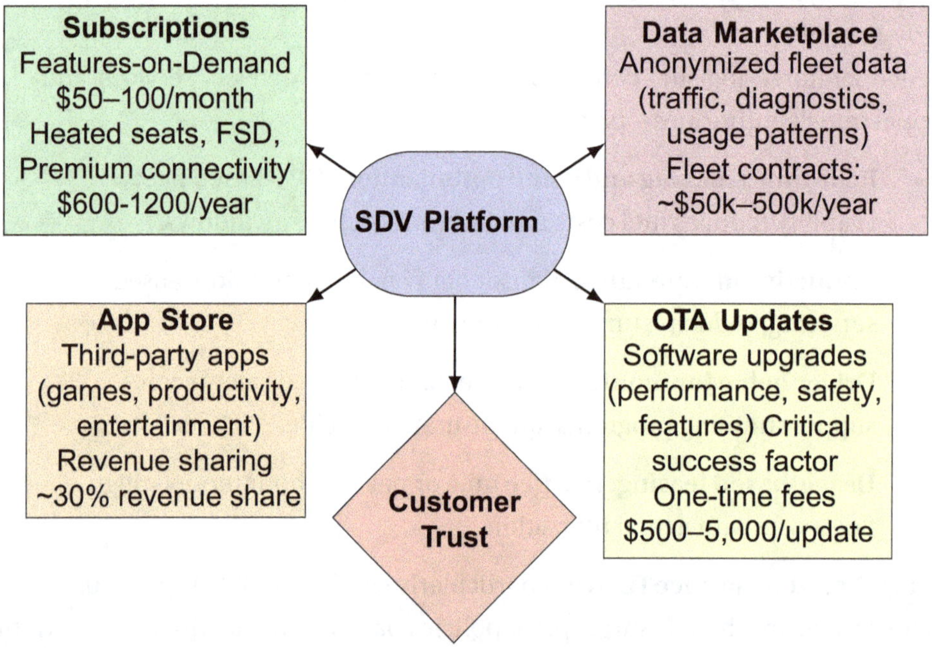

Figure 10-4. *SDV monetization models and revenue streams. B2C channels (left) include subscriptions and app stores; B2B channels (right) include fleet telematics and data marketplaces.*

10.6 Customer Experience and Trust

All monetization models ultimately hinge on customer experience and trust. In consumer surveys, drivers consistently report that while they like the idea of continuous improvement via software, they are increasingly skeptical of endless new fees. This so-called *subscription fatigue* is a visible barrier: many customers feel they are already paying for enough digital services outside the vehicle (video, music, cloud storage) and have a limited budget and attention span for in-car subscriptions as well [291].

In practice, customers differentiate sharply between *essential* and *optional* services. They are more willing to pay for offerings that provide clear safety or convenience benefits, such as connected emergency calls, real-time traffic and hazard information, or telematics-based insurance. By contrast, they tend to resist paying extra for features they perceive as basic entitlements of the vehicle, such as seat heating or fundamental connectivity. When customers feel they are being charged twice for the same hardware, brand goodwill erodes quickly.

In some regions, particularly in markets with strong dealer franchise laws, OEMs face material constraints on direct-to-consumer monetization. In the United States, state franchise laws in most jurisdictions prohibit manufacturers from selling directly to consumers, and dealer agreements often include provisions granting dealers a share of aftermarket service revenue. When OEMs attempt to sell subscriptions directly—bypassing the dealer—they risk legal challenges and channel conflict. Some OEMs have responded by routing subscription sales through dealers (who receive a commission), while others have structured offerings as "connected services" that fall outside traditional franchise definitions. Tesla, which operates its own retail network, avoids this friction entirely, but legacy OEMs with established dealer networks must navigate these constraints carefully. The result is that subscription pricing, marketing, and revenue recognition can vary significantly by market and by brand, adding operational complexity to an already challenging business model.

From a product management perspective, three design principles follow:

Perceived fairness: Customers must feel that they are paying for additional, ongoing value (new content, improved functionality, reduced risk or cost), not for the removal of arbitrary software locks.

Simplicity and transparency: Complex, opaque pricing structures and numerous small line items create suspicion and cognitive load. Bundling services into a few meaningful tiers with clear descriptions reduces the perception of "nickel-and-diming."

Continuity of value: Ongoing fees must be justified by visible and continuous improvements—e.g., regular map and ADAS updates, new content, or measurable insurance discounts—rather than static features.

Retention benchmarks: Subscription businesses typically track churn rate—the percentage of subscribers who cancel within a given period—as a key health indicator. Industry benchmarks suggest that a monthly churn rate below 5% is healthy for subscription services, with best-in-class operators achieving rates below 3% [296]. In the automotive subscription space, excluding natural churn (customers who intended a fixed-term arrangement from the outset), operators report average monthly churn rates of approximately 4% [297].

For SDV feature subscriptions specifically, public data remains scarce, but the same principle applies: sustainable monetization requires not just acquiring subscribers but retaining them over multi-year vehicle lifetimes. OEMs should therefore track cohort retention curves, identify drivers of regrettable churn (poor experience, unclear value), and invest in continuous feature improvement to justify ongoing fees.

From a business model perspective, churn is only one part of the equation. The economics of SDV subscriptions are driven by three levers: the attach rate (what percentage of eligible vehicles subscribe at all), the average revenue per user (ARPU), and the churn rate over time. Many OEMs have discovered that even optimistic ARPU assumptions cannot compensate for low attach rates or rapid churn, which is one reason several automakers have recently revised down earlier projections for per-vehicle SDV revenue.

Critic's Note A further constraint on monetization, particularly for driver assistance and safety-relevant functions, is that regulatory and safety obligations do not change when a feature is sold as a subscription. ISO 26262 [59], ISO/PAS 21448 (SOTIF), and UN R155/R156 [69, 72] still require rigorous change management, impact analysis, and verification for each software release, regardless of how the feature is priced. From the viewpoint of a safety assessor or type approval authority, a pay-per-use lane-keeping function is indistinguishable from a permanently enabled one: both must satisfy the same ASIL targets, safety case arguments, and homologation constraints over the vehicle's lifetime. Any incremental revenue from functions-on-demand therefore has to be weighed against the ongoing cost and risk of maintaining safety-compliant OTA pipelines for 10–15 years.

Trust also depends heavily on data protection and cybersecurity. As vehicles become more software-intensive, drivers worry about both hacking and misuse of personal data. A meaningful share of customers now treat a brand's data privacy stance as a deciding factor in purchase decisions [287] (see Figure 10-5). This aligns with the legal environment: frameworks such as the EU General Data Protection Regulation (GDPR), the California Consumer Privacy Act (CCPA), and China's Personal Information Protection Law (PIPL) require explicit consent, minimization of personal data, and robust technical and organizational controls. UNECE regulations R155 and R156, together with ISO/SAE 21434 [68, 69, 72], impose additional obligations to manage cybersecurity risks and software updates systematically.

For OEMs, the implication is clear. Sustainable SDV monetization is not simply a matter of putting prices on features; it is a long-term commitment to delivering reliable, safety-compliant software, honoring privacy expectations, and communicating pricing and value transparently. Vehicles that consistently deliver on promised benefits and visibly protect user data are more likely to retain subscribers and achieve low churn. Those that use software primarily as a mechanism for extracting short-term revenue at the expense of perceived fairness or trust will find customers quickly turning off subscriptions—or choosing another brand.

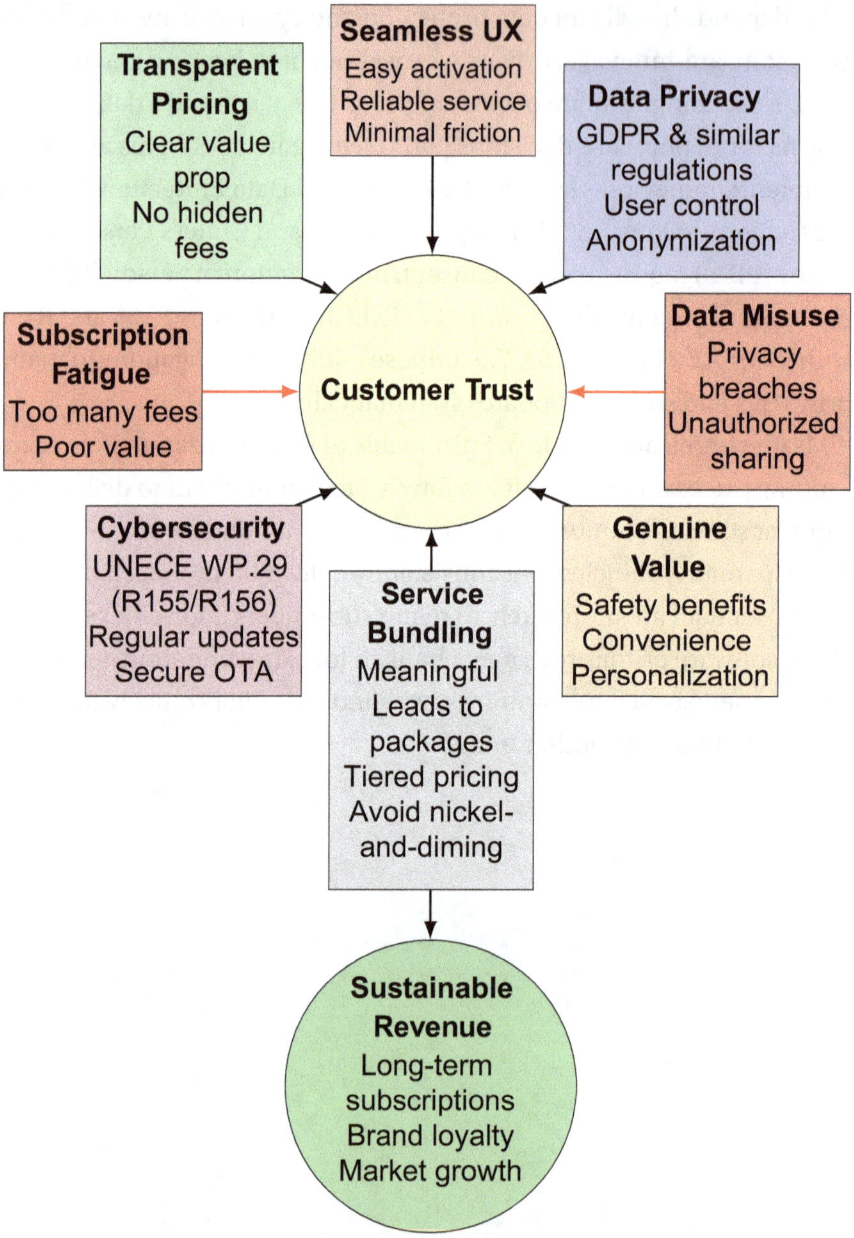

Figure 10-5. *Factors influencing customer trust in SDV monetization. Data privacy, transparent pricing, and continuous value delivery form the foundation of sustainable subscription relationships.*

10.7 Case Studies

The preceding sections outlined monetization models and ecosystem dynamics in conceptual terms. The following cases ground these principles in specific company experiences, illustrating both successful strategies and cautionary lessons. Where earlier sections referenced these examples briefly, the discussion here provides fuller context.

10.7.1 Tesla

Tesla's model is archetypically vertical. It develops most of its own software and maintains exclusive control over the vehicle's electronics. Tesla regularly pushes OTA updates each year, including several major feature releases and multiple minor improvements, enhancing cars long after sale. Its infotainment system is proprietary (no CarPlay/Android Auto), and Tesla dictates which apps run in-car.

Tesla monetizes software aggressively: the Full Self-Driving (Supervised) suite is priced in the high four-figure range for outright purchase and is also offered as a monthly subscription (with exact pricing varying over time and by market) [285], and "Premium Connectivity" (Wi-Fi streaming and maps) is a separate subscription. This vertical integration gives Tesla high margins and tight brand loyalty; owners feel continually engaged as the car improves.

However, it also draws scrutiny. In the United States, the National Highway Traffic Safety Administration (NHTSA) has opened multiple investigations into Tesla's Autopilot and FSD systems following crashes and has required recalls (implemented via OTA updates) to address safety concerns. Class-action lawsuits in several US states allege that Tesla misled customers about FSD capabilities and timelines [298]. In Europe, regulators have fined Tesla for deploying software updates without adequate disclosure, and Germany's Kraftfahrt-Bundesamt (KBA) has required modifications to Autopilot functionality. As of early 2025, most investigations remain ongoing, and Tesla disputes many of the allegations. Nonetheless, the pattern illustrates a broader risk: aggressive software monetization, particularly for safety-relevant features, invites regulatory and legal exposure that can offset revenue gains. Additionally, by limiting third-party apps to Tesla's ecosystem, the company trades off potential developer-driven innovation for tighter control over safety, UX, and monetization. In short, Tesla reaps high software revenue and control, but faces greater regulatory and consumer backlash risk.

10.7.2 BMW Heated Seats Subscription

In 2021, BMW attempted to sell heated seats as a software subscription, offering to activate factory-installed seat heaters for a monthly fee. Customer reaction was overwhelmingly negative: many buyers perceived this as "paying twice" for the same hardware [34]. BMW dropped the offer and subsequently acknowledged that customers "feel that they paid double," even though the base vehicle price was adjusted accordingly [34]. The episode made one lesson painfully clear: functions-on-demand are only acceptable when customers perceive them as additional value, not as retroactive tolls on capabilities they believe should be standard. BMW has since pivoted toward offering more obviously software-centric FoD options—such as parking assistance and driver assistance packages—where customers are more willing to accept ongoing fees.

Key Point The heated seats fiasco became a cautionary tale: without clear justification, customers won't accept recurring fees, and mishandling can damage trust. As one analyst put it, automakers "will continue to use subscription services as a way to extract revenue," but consumers will "vote with their wallets" against bad ideas [34].

10.7.3 Android Automotive (Open Infotainment)

Android Automotive OS represents a contrasting case. OEMs like Volvo, Polestar, Volkswagen, and GM have embraced it as the infotainment backbone. This open approach includes full Google integration: built-in Google Maps, Assistant, and, crucially, the Google Play Store. Drivers can install a curated set of Android apps on the car's display (music, podcasts, navigation, and other services) that are vetted for in-vehicle use, giving the vehicle a relatively rich app ecosystem.

From the OEM's perspective, this adds value and speeds up development. For example, GM recently moved its EV line to Android Automotive, highlighting Google Play support as a way to enable additional native in-vehicle experiences beyond what simple phone projection can offer. On the downside, this strategy dilutes OEM control. Google (and Apple with CarPlay) gathers significant user data through the infotainment system, often without the OEM's full visibility [294]. Critics argue this hands the smartest part of the car's ecosystem to tech giants. To manage this, some brands use Android

Automotive without Google's proprietary services. For instance, Volkswagen's CARIAD team is rolling out AAOS with its own app store (no Google Automotive Services), and Rivian does similarly, to preserve data ownership.

These real-world examples highlight the strategic tension: open app stores give customers variety and scale, but OEMs must carefully balance the benefit of third-party ecosystems against the risk of ceding their own customer interface and data to Google/Apple.

Table 10-1. *Comparison of Tesla, BMW, and Android Automotive OS Approaches to SDV Monetization and Ecosystem Strategy*

Dimension	Tesla	BMW	Android Automotive OS
Strategy	Full vertical control	Hybrid approach	Open platform
Approach	Proprietary OS; no third-party projection; high margins	Hardware-based FoD; pivot after customer backlash	Google Play integration; faster development; familiar UX
Benefits	Brand loyalty; data ownership; revenue control	Learned value perception is critical; refocused on software	Instant app library; lower dev cost; user satisfaction
Risks	Regulatory scrutiny; limited ecosystem; high dev cost	Trust erosion; brand damage; subscription fatigue	Google data control; brand dilution; revenue sharing

10.8 Key Takeaways

- **Recurring services:** SDVs shift OEMs from one-off product sales to ongoing service revenues [284]. Successful vehicles become digital platforms that earn throughout the lifecycle.
- **Ecosystem players:** The SDV ecosystem spans OEMs (software and data owners), Tier-1 suppliers (software platforms), infrastructure partners (cloud and connectivity), and regulators (cybersecurity

and privacy rules). Regional ecosystems differ markedly—China's domestic tech giants (Baidu, Alibaba, Huawei) and data localization rules create distinct competitive dynamics that global OEMs must navigate.

- **Monetization models:** Revenue can come from consumer feature subscriptions (functions- on-demand), B2B data marketplaces, fleet telematics services, and app store ecosystems (proprietary OEM stores or Android/Apple platforms). B2B fleet services are often more mature and less susceptible to subscription fatigue than consumer offerings. Each model involves trade-offs in control, scalability, and customer appeal.
- **Customer trust:** Transparency and UX drive value. Hidden fees or unclear terms can alienate buyers (as BMW's heated seats example shows) [34]. Bundling services into meaningful packages and highlighting genuine benefits (safety, convenience) helps. Ultimately, trust—through clear value, strong privacy/safety assurances, and reliable UX—is the "premium feature" that sustains subscriptions [287].

CHAPTER 11

Global Regulations and Compliance

11.1 Chapter Goals

After this chapter you will be able to

- Identify the global regulatory landscape shaping software-defined vehicles (SDVs).
- Explain the UNECE WP.29 cybersecurity and software update mandates.
- Compare GDPR, CCPA, and China's PIPL for data governance in connected vehicles.
- Understand how compliance requirements drive SDV architecture (e.g. SUMS/CSMS integration).
- Evaluate regional challenges faced by multinational OEMs in meeting divergent regulations.

Critic's Note Compliance is not just paperwork. In SDVs, compliance is design—architectures, development pipelines, and even business models must align with regulations from day one, not as an afterthought.

S. Agarwal, *Software-Defined Vehicles*, https://doi.org/10.1007/979-8-8688-2718-1_11

11.2 Introduction

Software-defined vehicles operate at the intersection of multiple regulatory domains: vehicle safety, cybersecurity, software updates, data protection, and, increasingly, artificial intelligence governance. Unlike traditional vehicles where regulatory compliance was largely a one-time certification event, SDVs face continuous compliance obligations throughout their operational lifetime—every OTA update, every data collection practice, and every AI-based feature must satisfy an evolving web of regional and international requirements.

This chapter examines the global regulatory landscape shaping SDV development and deployment. We begin with UNECE WP.29 regulations (R155 and R156), which establish mandatory cybersecurity and software update management requirements for vehicles sold in Europe, Japan, Korea, and other contracting parties. The chapter then surveys data governance frameworks—GDPR in Europe, CCPA and emerging state laws in the United States, and China's PIPL and associated regulations—that constrain how vehicle data can be collected, processed, and transferred across borders.

We examine the international standards (ISO/SAE 21434, ISO 24089, ISO/PAS 8800) that operationalize regulatory requirements into engineering practices and explore how compliance obligations drive architectural decisions from day one. The chapter concludes with a case study comparing OTA update regulations across regions, illustrating the practical challenges multinational OEMs face in navigating divergent regulatory regimes while maintaining efficient global platforms.

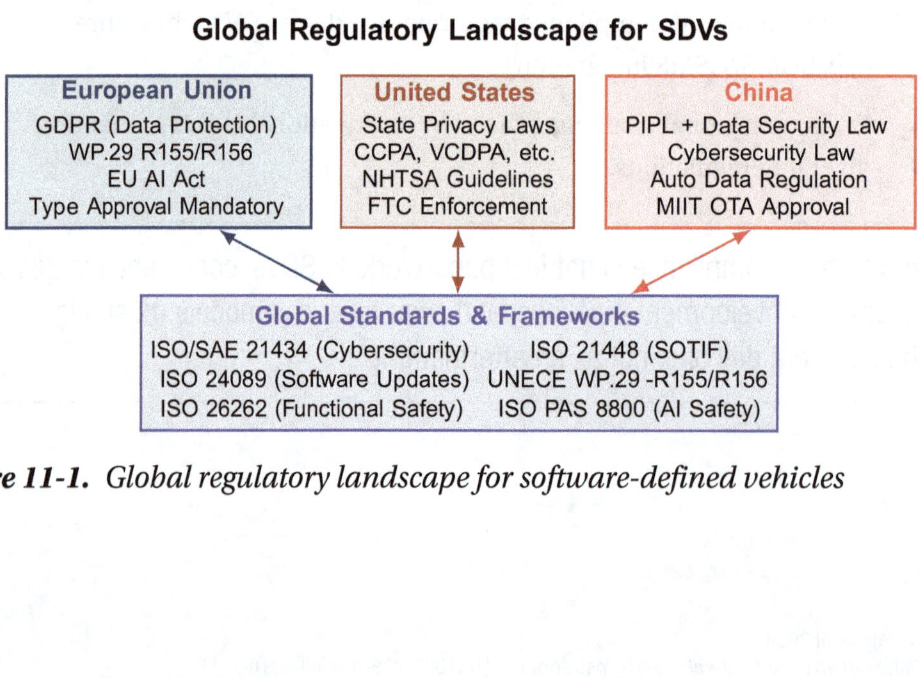

Figure 11-1. *Global regulatory landscape for software-defined vehicles*

11.3 UNECE WP.29: Global Vehicle Regulations

The United Nations Economic Commission for Europe (UNECE) World Forum for Harmonization of Vehicle Regulations (WP.29) has introduced landmark rules addressing automotive cybersecurity and software updates. In 2020, WP.29 adopted two regulations to tackle emerging cyber risks in connected vehicles [299, 300].

11.3.1 UN R155: Cybersecurity Management Systems (CSMSs)

R155 mandates that automakers implement an organization-wide Cyber Security Management System covering the vehicle's entire lifecycle [68, 299]. This includes conducting thorough threat and risk assessments for vehicular systems, integrating "security by design" in development, monitoring for incidents, and having response plans [68, 301].

A central pillar of R155 is a documented Threat Analysis and Risk Assessment (TARA) addressing potential attack vectors (e.g., wireless interfaces, supply chain vulnerabilities) and mitigation measures [68, 302]. However, the regulation goes beyond TARA to require an organization-wide Cybersecurity Management System that embeds these analyses into governance, development, and operations. Automakers must demonstrate to regulators that they have processes to manage cyber risks continuously—from design through production into post-production (updates and maintenance) [299, 303].

In practice, a manufacturer's CSMS will be audited for evidence like documented threat models, security test results, incident response procedures, and organizational roles (e.g., a dedicated cybersecurity manager). Without a certified CSMS, type approval for new vehicle models can be denied—no CSMS, no approval [304, 305].

Figure 11-2 should be read from top to bottom. At the governance level, the CSMS begins with management responsibility, including cybersecurity leadership, policies, and organizational training. These governance elements support the core security processes shown in the middle of the figure: Threat Analysis and Risk Assessment, security-by-design activities, security testing and validation, and incident monitoring and response. These processes operate across the full vehicle lifecycle—from concept and development through production, operation, and decommissioning. As the CSMS is executed, it generates the compliance artifacts shown at the bottom of the figure, such as threat models, test results, incident response logs, and version control records. Finally, the external interfaces on the right emphasize that the CSMS extends beyond the OEM's internal engineering teams to regulators, suppliers, and customer-facing communication.

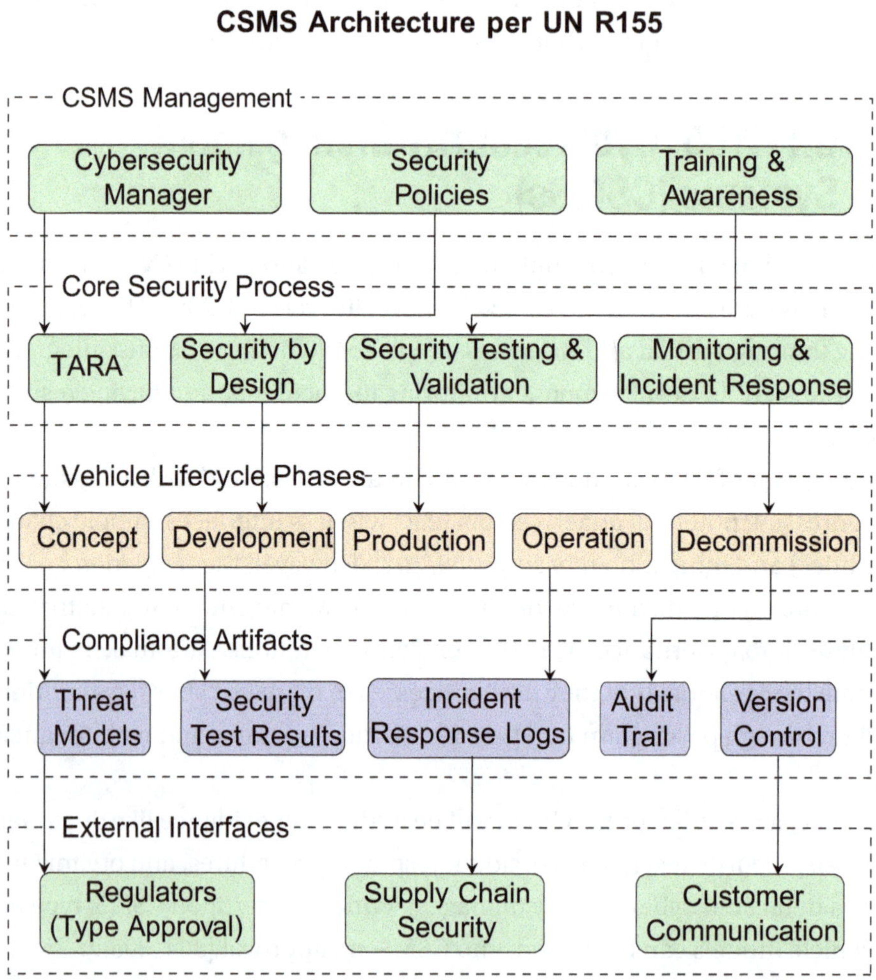

Figure 11-2. *Cybersecurity Management System (CSMS) architecture per UN R155*

Supply Chain Implications

A critical but often underestimated aspect of R155 compliance is its supply chain reach. The regulation requires OEMs to manage cybersecurity risks across their entire supply network [68, 299]. In practice, this means

- **Supplier cybersecurity requirements**: OEMs must contractually obligate Tier-1 suppliers to follow cybersecurity processes compatible with the OEM's CSMS. This typically involves requiring suppliers to demonstrate ISO/SAE 21434 alignment or equivalent practices.
- **Cybersecurity interface agreements (CIAs)**: Formal agreements between OEMs and suppliers that define cybersecurity responsibilities, information exchange requirements, and incident notification obligations [68].
- **Evidence propagation**: Suppliers must provide cybersecurity work products (threat analyses, test reports, vulnerability assessments) that the OEM can incorporate into their own compliance dossier. An OEM cannot claim CSMS compliance if critical ECU software from a Tier-1 lacks documented security analysis.
- **Cascading to lower tiers**: Tier-1 suppliers must similarly flow down requirements to Tier-2 and beyond. A vulnerability in a Tier-3 component (e.g., a communication chip) can compromise the entire vehicle's cybersecurity posture.

This supply chain dimension significantly expands the compliance burden. OEMs with hundreds of suppliers must establish assessment programs, audit capabilities, and contractual frameworks to ensure consistent cybersecurity practices across their network. Some OEMs have created supplier cybersecurity portals where partners upload evidence and certifications, enabling centralized tracking of supply chain compliance status.

11.3.2 UN R156: Software Update Management Systems (SUMSs)

R156 requires manufacturers to establish a robust Software Update Management System to ensure safe and secure over-the-air (OTA) updates [300, 306]. The regulation establishes the conditions under which OTA updates are acceptable for type-approved vehicles, provided that stringent processes are in place.

OEMs must

- Verify and validate all software updates before deployment (to prevent buggy or malicious code) [73, 306].
- Use security measures (like encryption and code signing) to protect update integrity [306, 307].
- Design update mechanisms with fail-safes—updates should only install when the vehicle is in a safe state (parked, sufficient battery) and should never compromise functional safety [300, 308].

R156 also requires that updates be managed so that, if something goes wrong, the vehicle can revert to a safe state [306, 309]—typically via rollback or an equivalent recovery mechanism. In other words, vehicles must not be bricked by a failed OTA; an automatic rollback or recovery procedure is required so that a failed update does not impair safety [73, 300]. Additionally, owners should be notified of update details and results (success or failure) [308]. The SUMS processes and records—including software version histories, cryptographic signatures, installation logs, and rollback tests—serve as evidence of compliance.

Figure 11-3 summarizes the logic of a compliant software update process under UN R156. The flow can be understood in five stages: prepare the update, verify its integrity and compatibility, confirm that vehicle conditions are safe for installation, perform the installation with backup or recovery support, and record the outcome for compliance evidence. The detailed decision points shown in the figure all serve this basic purpose: prevent unsafe installation, preserve the ability to recover from failure, and generate auditable records for regulators.

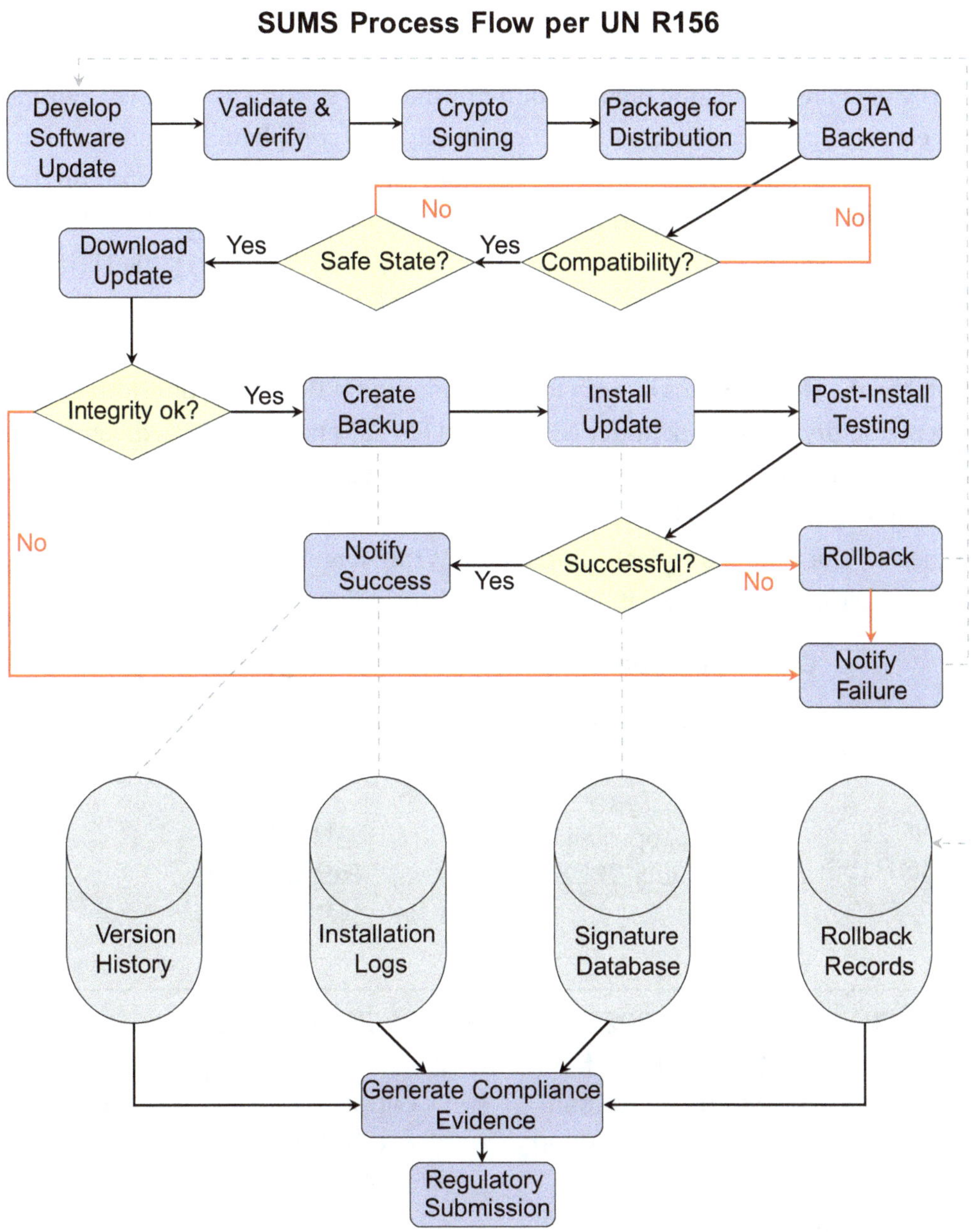

Figure 11-3. *Software Update Management System (SUMS) process flow*

11.3.3 Geographical Scope

These UN regulations became binding for many markets starting in 2022. The European Union, e.g., via its General Safety Regulation, made R155 compliance mandatory for all new vehicle type approvals from July 2022 (and for all new vehicle registrations by July 2024) [304, 310]. Japan and South Korea similarly adopted R155 and R156 for new models (Japan even required it earlier for Level 3 automated vehicles) [301, 311]. Many other countries that are contracting parties to the 1958 Agreement (the UN vehicle regulations framework) are following suit.

Notably, the United States has not formally adopted WP.29 regulations due to its distinct regulatory framework under NHTSA and FMVSS standards. This divergence persists regardless of year, as it reflects structural differences in how vehicle regulations are developed and enforced between the United States and UNECE contracting parties. Nevertheless, global OEMs typically implement WP.29-aligned processes universally to maintain consistent development practices and access European and Asian markets.

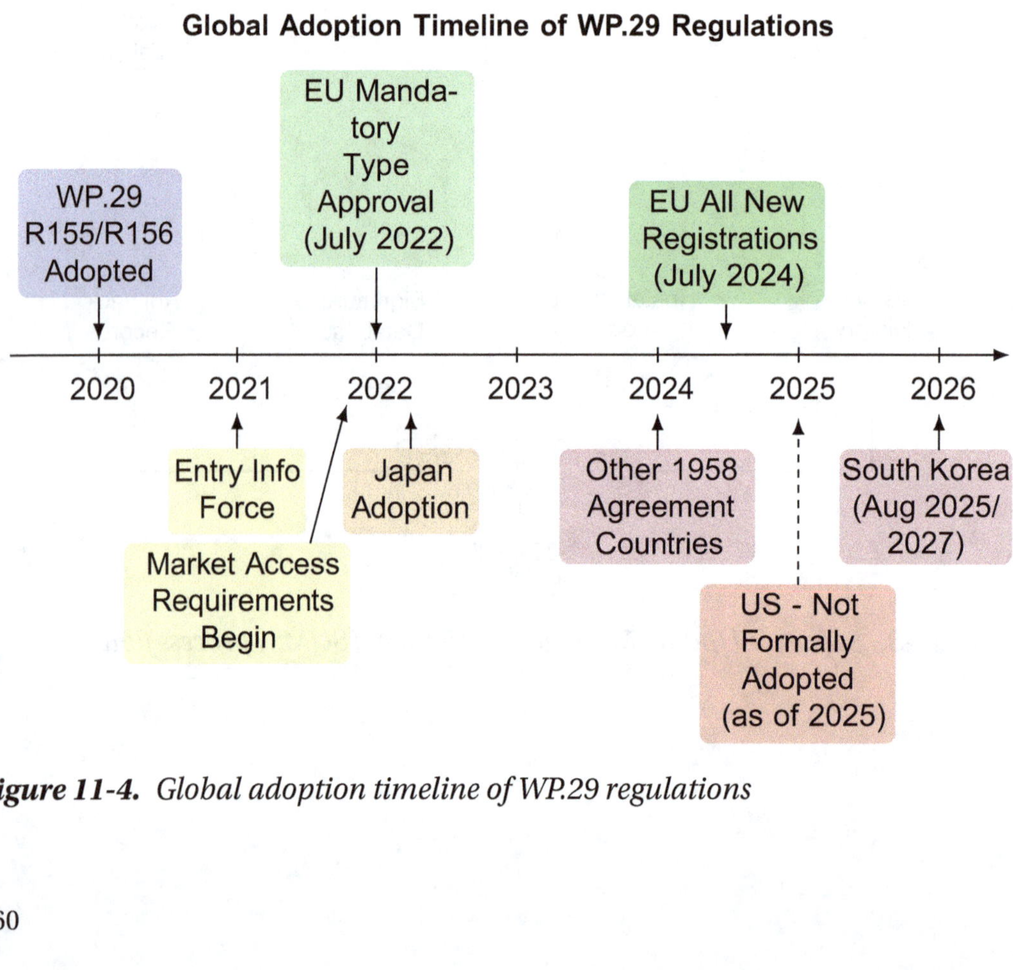

Figure 11-4. *Global adoption timeline of WP.29 regulations*

Regulators now demand concrete evidence of cybersecurity and update management. This means during type approval, manufacturers must present documentation and test results showing they have performed thorough threat analyses, implemented appropriate protections, and validated their update processes (including successful rollback trials). For instance, an automaker seeking EU type approval might need to show the examiners a complete cybersecurity risk assessment report and logs from simulated OTA update sessions proving that update packages are authenticated and can be safely reversed if issues arise [302, 304].

The bottom line is that failing to comply with UN R155/R156 is non-negotiable—an OEM that cannot demonstrate an adequate CSMS or SUMS will be denied type approval and cannot legally sell vehicles in adopting markets [304, 310]. Enforcement mechanisms include market exclusion (denial of type approval), withdrawal of existing approvals following post-market audits, mandatory recalls for cybersecurity vulnerabilities discovered in-field, and potential financial penalties under national implementations. Documented cases already demonstrate regulatory teeth: multiple OEMs have delayed European model launches by three to six months due to incomplete CSMS documentation.

Table 11-1. *Summary of WP.29 Adoption by Region*

Region	R155 (CSMS)	R156 (SUMS)	Notes
European Union	Mandatory (July 2022 new types; July 2024 all vehicles)	Mandatory (same timeline)	Enforced via General Safety Regulation
Japan	Mandatory (2022; earlier for L3 ADS)	Mandatory	Aligned with EU timeline
South Korea	Mandatory (2022)	Mandatory	Follows UNECE framework
United Kingdom	Mandatory (post- Brexit adoption)	Mandatory	Maintains EU alignment
United States	Not adopted	Not adopted	NHTSA voluntary guidelines only; no 1958 Agreement membership
China	National standards (GB/T)	National standards with MIIT approval requirements	More restrictive than WP.29 for ADS-related updates

Critic's Note OEMs failing WP.29 compliance lose market access—it's truly non-negotiable. These regulations have teeth: without a compliant Cybersecurity Management System, a new vehicle cannot be sold in the EU, Japan, and other adopting regions [303, 305]. In short, compliance is now a gateway to entry.

11.3.4 Type Approval Process and Technical Services

Understanding *how* WP.29 compliance is verified is essential for planning certification timelines. The type approval process involves several actors:

- **Type approval authority**: The governmental body that grants approval (e.g., Germany's KBA, France's UTAC-OTC, United Kingdom's VCA). They issue the formal certificate permitting sale.

- **Technical service**: An accredited organization that conducts the actual assessment on behalf of the authority. For R155/R156, technical services audit the manufacturer's CSMS and SUMS documentation, review evidence of threat analyses, inspect security test results, and may witness update deployment tests.
- **Manufacturer**: Must prepare and submit a comprehensive dossier including CSMS/SUMS process descriptions, organizational charts showing cybersecurity responsibilities, TARA reports, penetration test summaries, and evidence of rollback testing.

The audit typically proceeds in phases: an initial documentation review, followed by onsite assessment of processes and tools, and finally evaluation of vehicle-level evidence (e.g., demonstrating that an ECU rejects unsigned firmware). Technical services may issue findings requiring remediation before approval is granted.

Failure Consequences

If a manufacturer cannot demonstrate adequate CSMS/SUMS, the technical service will not recommend approval, and the type approval authority will refuse certification. The vehicle cannot legally be sold in that market. There is no "provisional" or "conditional" approval pathway for cybersecurity deficiencies—compliance is binary.

Audit cycles for CSMS certification typically require 6–12 months of preparation, and certificates must be maintained through periodic surveillance audits (typically every three years or when significant process changes occur) [312].

11.4 ISO/SAE 21434 and ISO 24089: Operationalizing Security and Updates

While WP.29 sets out what manufacturers must achieve in cybersecurity and update management, international standards provide the detailed how. Two key standards work hand in hand with R155 and R156.

11.4.1 ISO/SAE 21434: Road Vehicles Cybersecurity Engineering

Published in 2021, ISO 21434 is a comprehensive framework for implementing automotive cybersecurity from concept to decommissioning. It is essentially the automotive equivalent of a quality standard, but for security. It details processes for

- Threat Analysis and Risk Assessment
- Requirements elicitation for cybersecurity
- Secure design principles
- Verification and validation for security
- Incident response during operations

R155 explicitly references ISO 21434 as a guideline for manufacturers to follow [68, 299, 302]. By following ISO 21434, an OEM can structure its Cybersecurity Management System: e.g., performing regular risk assessments (as outlined by ISO 21434's Annexes), defining cybersecurity goals, and ensuring traceability of security requirements through development. Where used, Cybersecurity Assurance Levels (CALs) serve as informative (non-normative) indicators that express the required assurance rigor for specific functions. While conceptually analogous to ISO 26262's ASILs, CALs are guidance rather than mandatory classifications, and their use remains at the organization's discretion.

Rather than reading Figure 11-5 as a detailed process map, it is more useful to view it as a lifecycle model. ISO/SAE 21434 starts in the concept phase with item definition, cybersecurity planning, and risk analysis; continues through development with requirements, architecture, design, and verification activities; extends into production and operation through monitoring and incident response; and remains relevant until decommissioning. The central message is that cybersecurity is not a one-time engineering task but a continuous lifecycle discipline that accompanies the product from concept to end of service [68, 301].

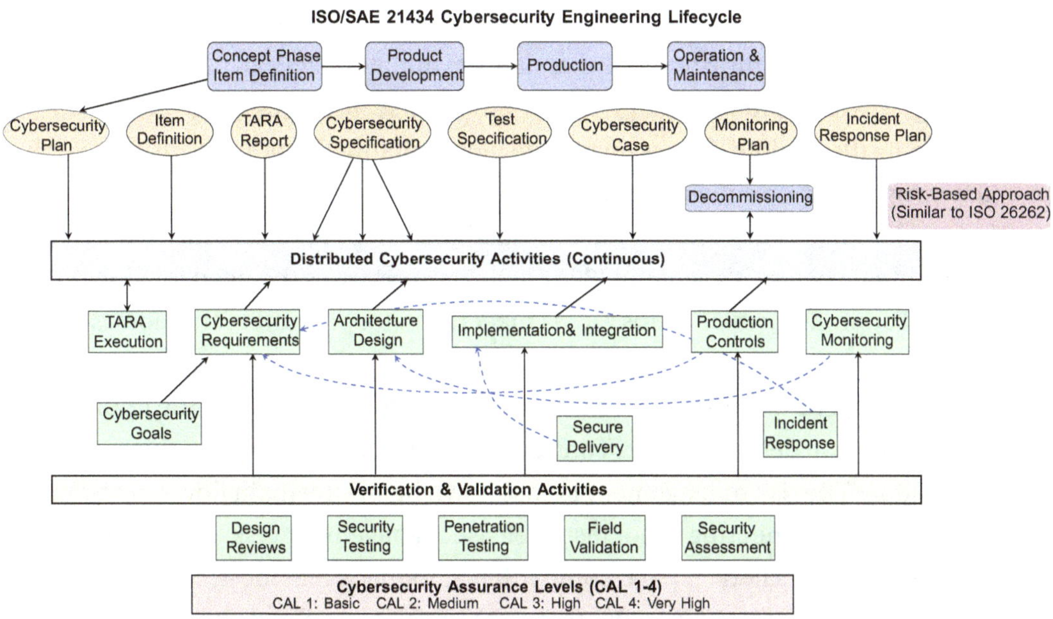

Figure 11-5. *ISO/SAE 21434 cybersecurity engineering lifecycle*

11.4.2 ISO 24089: Road Vehicles Software Update Engineering

Introduced in early 2023, ISO 24089 is a new standard focused on the entire software update lifecycle in vehicles [306]. It was developed to support and harmonize with UN R156 (and indeed is aligned with it) [73, 308]. ISO 24089 outlines best practices and requirements for software update management including

- How to package updates
- How to validate and verify update files
- How to secure the update delivery (encryption, authentication)
- Processes for safe deployment (e.g., only update in safe conditions)
- Post-update confirmation and auditing [73, 306]

It covers requirements not only for the vehicle and its electronic control units (ECUs) but also for back-end IT infrastructure that delivers updates [306, 307]. One key aspect is managing risks associated with updates—both cybersecurity risks (e.g., protecting against man-in-the-middle attacks on update files) and functional safety risks (ensuring an update won't inadvertently disable a safety feature).

The standard mandates verification and validation steps to ensure the update is reliable and safe before it's sent out [306, 309]. It also stresses the need for global uniformity in approach, which helps OEMs meet regulatory requirements across countries [308].

Figure 11-6 can be understood as a simplified update lifecycle: plan the update, develop it, validate it, deploy it under controlled conditions, and monitor the outcome after installation. The risk management items shown below the main flow remind the reader that update engineering is not just a release management task; it must also address cybersecurity, safety impact, compatibility, rollback readiness, and post-update verification. In other words, ISO 24089 treats updates as engineered products, not just software packages.

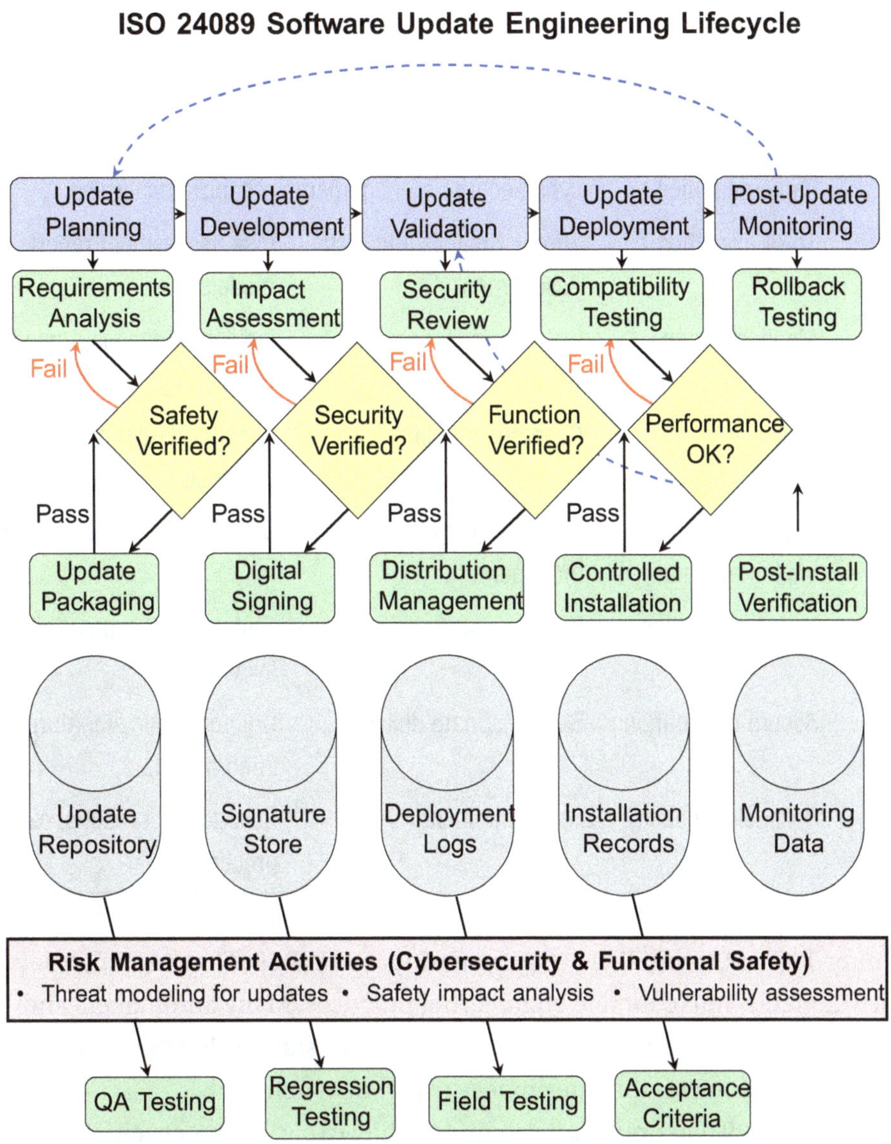

Figure 11-6. *ISO 24089 software update engineering lifecycle*

Compliance with ISO 24089 provides structured evidence that an automaker's OTA update process meets widely accepted industry best practices and aligns with R156 expectations. In fact, adhering to ISO 24089 is one way to prove fulfillment of UN R156 requirements, since the two are harmonized [73, 308]. For instance, if an OEM follows ISO 24089, they will typically implement controls such as anti-rollback [309] or equivalent downgrade-risk mitigation, integrity checks, and customer notification, all of which support R156 requirements.

Table 11-2. *UN R155/R156 Alignment with ISO/SAE 21434 and ISO 24089*

Regulation	WP.29 Requirement	ISO Standard Guidance	Key Work Products
UN R155 (CSMS)	CSMS implementation	ISO/SAE 21434: cybersecurity management	Cybersecurity policy; organizational roles
	TARA execution	Threat Analysis and Risk Assessment	Risk assessment reports; threat models
	Monitoring and response	Incident management	Incident response procedures; monitoring logs
	Lifecycle management	Cybersecurity lifecycle	Security requirements; V&V evidence
UN R156 (SUMS)	SUMS implementation	ISO 24089: update management	Update process documentation
	Update validation	Validation and verification	Test reports; compatibility evidence
	Secure distribution	Secure update delivery	Cryptographic signatures; integrity logs
	Rollback capability	Failure handling	Rollback test results; recovery procedures

Together, ISO 21434 and ISO 24089 operationalize WP.29. They turn high-level regulatory demands into concrete engineering practices. Many automakers and suppliers are getting certified or assessed against these standards as a way to reassure regulators (and customers) that they meet the global benchmark.

In essence, WP.29 tells you *what* you must achieve (e.g., "protect vehicles from cyberattacks and ensure safe updates"), while ISO 21434 and 24089 tell you *how* to build your processes and systems to achieve it (e.g., "perform threat analysis using method X; use coding standard Y; test updates in manner Z"). By implementing these standards, companies create the compliance artifacts—risk assessment reports, test records, and organizational policies—that they can then map directly to the regulatory requirements during an audit or type approval process [68, 301, 306].

Key Point For technical implementation of CSMS, threat analysis (TARA), and cybersecurity architecture patterns per ISO/SAE 21434, see **Chapter 9**.

11.5 Data Governance Laws and Privacy Regulations

Beyond safety and cybersecurity, SDVs must navigate a maze of data protection and privacy laws across different jurisdictions. Modern vehicles collect extensive data:

- Location and GPS logs
- Driver behavior and biometrics (camera feeds for driver monitoring, voice commands)
- Telematics on vehicle performance
- Personal settings or infotainment usage

All this falls under personal data in many regions, invoking strict privacy regulations. We examine three major pillars of data governance affecting SDVs: Europe's GDPR, the United States' evolving state privacy laws (exemplified by CCPA), and China's PIPL and related cybersecurity laws.

Table 11-3. *Major Privacy Regulations Affecting Connected Vehicles*

Aspect	GDPR (EU)	CCPA/CPRA (California)	PIPL (China)
Scope	Personal data of EU residents	Personal info of CA consumers	Personal info processed in China
Consent model	Opt-in required	Opt-out for sale/sharing	Separate consent per purpose
Data localization	Adequacy decisions for transfers	No requirement	Sensitive data must stay in China
Enforcement	DPAs; fines up to 4% revenue	CA AG + private right of action	CAC; fines + personal liability
Vehicle-specific	No (general regulation)	No (general regulation)	Yes (automotive data rules)
Location data	Consent + purpose limitation	Sensitive PI category	Local processing only
Biometric data	Explicit consent required	Opt-out for targeting	Safety purpose only
OTA updates	User notification required	Transparency in policies	Pre-approval needed
Architecture	Privacy-preserving design patterns	Flexible data deletion	Separate isolated systems

11.5.1 Europe: GDPR and Automotive Data

The General Data Protection Regulation (GDPR) is the EU's far-reaching privacy law that applies to any processing of personal data of individuals in Europe. Automotive data clearly falls under its scope when it can be linked to an individual (VIN tied to an owner, geolocation routes of a driver, in-cabin camera or microphone recordings, etc.). GDPR is often cited as the world's most rigorous privacy law [313].

Key GDPR principles and requirements relevant to connected cars include

Consent and lawful basis: Automakers or service providers must obtain explicit, informed consent from users for collecting and processing personal data from the vehicle, unless another legal basis applies [313, 314]. For instance, a car's infotainment system might ask the driver to agree to data collection for telematics or usage-based insurance programs. Simply collecting detailed telemetry by default could violate GDPR if not clearly disclosed and agreed to.

Data minimization and purpose limitation: Only data that is necessary for a specified purpose should be collected and used [313]. In practice, this means an SDV platform should avoid hoovering up all data "just in case"; it should collect what is needed for the stated function (e.g., location data for navigation services, but perhaps not retaining that location data indefinitely once the service is provided).

Transparency and rights: Under GDPR, individuals have the right to know what data is collected about them and to access that data, correct inaccuracies, and even request deletion (the "right to be forgotten") [313, 314]. For a connected car, this could mean the manufacturer must provide a user with a report of what personal data the vehicle has recorded (and perhaps transmitted back to the cloud) about them.

Privacy by design and default: GDPR requires that systems be designed with privacy in mind from the start, and default settings should be privacy-friendly [313, 315]. Applied to SDVs, "privacy by design" might involve designing the in-car networks such that personal data is isolated and protected or ensuring that any data sent off the car is encrypted and pseudonymized.

Data localization/transfers: While GDPR does not flat-out prohibit transferring EU personal data abroad, it imposes restrictions—data can only be exported outside the EU if certain safeguards or adequacy agreements are in place. Some European regulators (like France's CNIL) have been vocal that connected vehicle data should ideally be stored and processed in Europe or in a GDPR-compliant manner [315, 316], to avoid risks of foreign government access.

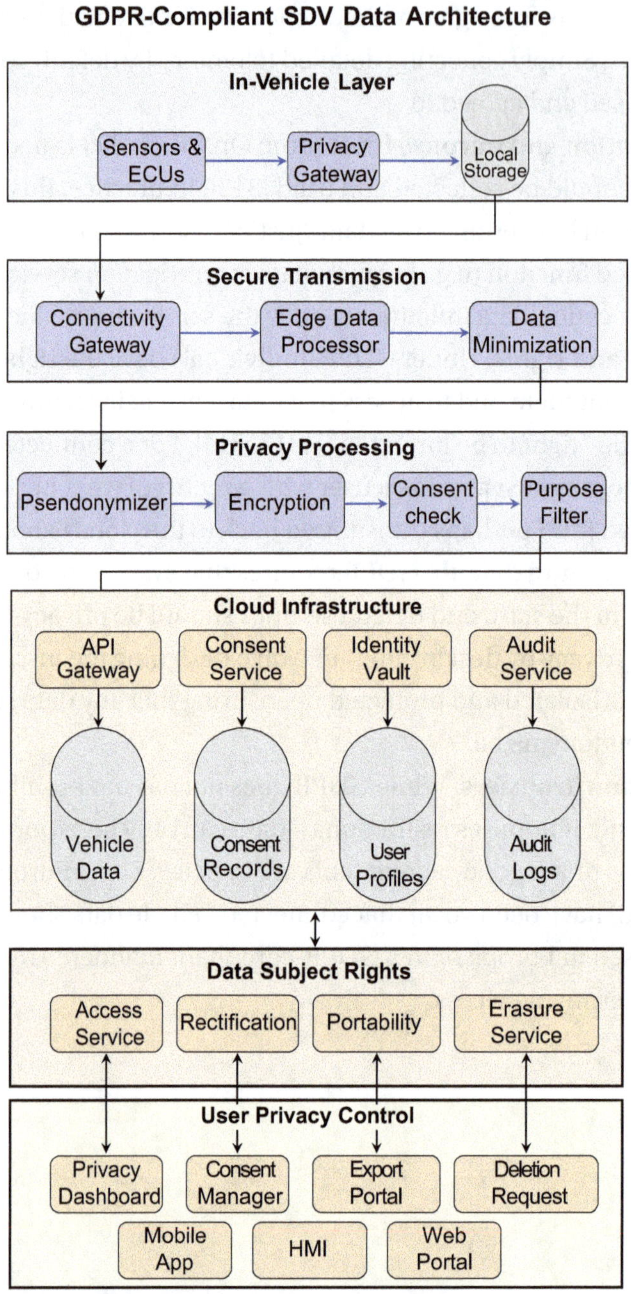

Figure 11-7. *GDPR-compliant SDV data architecture*

European data authorities have started focusing specifically on connected cars. For example, France's CNIL issued guidelines for car data, emphasizing that location data and telematics require clear user consent and that drivers should have control via in-car privacy settings [315, 317]. In 2023, the new European Data Governance Act and proposals in the EU's Data Act also suggest frameworks for sharing certain vehicle data (for aftermarket services and others) under privacy-preserving conditions [318, 319].

Automakers in Europe thus must navigate not only GDPR's general provisions but also sector-specific expectations. Non-compliance can result in heavy fines (up to 4% of global revenue), so the incentive is high to incorporate GDPR considerations into every data feature of an SDV.

11.5.2 United States: CCPA and an Emerging Patchwork

The United States does not yet have a single federal privacy law at the level of GDPR. Instead, a patchwork of state laws and federal sectoral regulations govern data. The most influential of these for consumer data is the California Consumer Privacy Act (CCPA) (amended by the CPRA). California's law, effective since 2020 (with enhancements in 2023), grants residents several key rights over their personal information [320, 321]:

- The right to know what personal information a business collects about them and how it's used.
- The right to delete personal information collected (with some exceptions).
- The right to opt out of the "sale" or sharing of their personal information to third parties. Notably, CCPA/CPRA defines "sale" broadly to include sharing data for cross-context behavioral advertising—a definition highly relevant to connected vehicles with ad-supported infotainment systems or data-sharing partnerships with insurance providers.
- The right to non-discrimination for exercising privacy rights.

For connected car manufacturers, CCPA means they need to disclose in their privacy policies all the categories of data a vehicle or related app collects (location, driver habits, media usage, etc.) and honor requests from California consumers to access or delete that data [320, 322].

Notably, precise geolocation data and biometric data are considered sensitive personal information under California law (CPRA), which triggers an opt-out requirement for use of such data for targeted purposes. This is very relevant to SDVs because location and biometrics (driver's face or fingerprint for vehicle entry) are exactly what cars now collect—manufacturers have to provide special notices and opt-outs for these sensitive data uses under California law [321, 323].

Beyond California, as of 2025, around a dozen or more US states have passed their own privacy laws (e.g., Virginia, Colorado, Connecticut, Utah, Iowa among others), each with slightly different scopes and requirements [324, 325]. This patchwork is challenging—an automaker effectively must comply with the highest common denominator or implement state-by-state compliance toggles.

The result is that multinational OEMs in the United States must treat privacy compliance as an evolving mosaic—closely monitoring each new state law and adjusting their data collection and retention accordingly [326, 327].

Federal Regulatory Landscape

While the United States lacks a comprehensive federal privacy law, the National Highway Traffic Safety Administration (NHTSA) has issued voluntary cybersecurity best practices for the automotive industry [271]. These guidelines, while non-binding, signal regulatory intent and are increasingly referenced in litigation and insurance assessments. NHTSA has also indicated it may pursue formal rulemaking on vehicle cybersecurity, particularly as ADAS and ADS deployments accelerate.

The Federal Trade Commission (FTC) represents another enforcement vector. Under its Section 5 authority to prevent "unfair or deceptive practices," the FTC has pursued actions against companies for inadequate data security and misleading privacy representations. Connected vehicle manufacturers making claims about data protection in their marketing materials face potential FTC scrutiny if those claims prove unfounded [328].

Notably, because the United States is not a contracting party to the 1958 Agreement, WP.29 regulations (R155/R156) have no legal force domestically. This creates a bifurcation: vehicles destined solely for the US market face no CSMS/SUMS certification requirement, while export-oriented models must comply. In practice, most global OEMs apply WP.29-aligned processes universally to avoid maintaining parallel development tracks, but smaller manufacturers or US-only startups may operate under less rigorous regimes.

Regulatory Scrutiny Ramping Up

Crucially, regulatory scrutiny in the United States is ramping up. In mid-2023, California's Privacy Protection Agency (the enforcer of CCPA) announced it was investigating connected vehicle manufacturers' data practices [323]. The agency highlighted that modern cars are "computers on wheels" collecting vast data (locations, recordings inside and outside the car) and that it would review how carmakers are complying with California law [323, 329].

This indicates that regulators are no longer overlooking the automotive sector—companies like Tesla, GM, Ford, etc. are under the privacy microscope. The likely outcome is more enforcement actions (indeed, in 2025 Honda agreed to a CCPA enforcement settlement with California's CPPA over privacy and connected vehicle data handling practices) and possibly the push for a federal auto data regulation.

11.5.3 China: PIPL and Cybersecurity/Data Laws

China has rapidly developed a stringent legal regime for data, which directly impacts connected vehicles. The Personal Information Protection Law (PIPL) of 2021 is China's analog to GDPR, setting rules for personal data handling—requiring consent for most data collection, limiting use to specified purposes, and granting individuals rights over their data. However, PIPL is just one piece; China's Cybersecurity Law (2017) and Data Security Law (2021), along with sector-specific regulations, impose additional obligations, particularly around data localization and government access.

For global OEMs, China's regulations mean data residency is mandatory for most vehicle data. Personal and important data generated by vehicles in China must be stored on servers within China [330, 331]. If a company wants to transfer any of this data abroad (e.g., sending back crash telemetry to a global R&D center in Europe), they must undergo a government security assessment and get approval from the Cyberspace Administration of China (CAC) [330, 332].

"Important data" is defined broadly in the automotive context—it can include

- Detailed location tracks
- Images or video collected by the car (especially if they capture sensitive locations or faces/license plates)
- Any dataset involving over 100,000 individuals [330, 333]

In practice, this pushes connected cars in China into a semi-silo: the primary cloud systems and data lakes that serve Chinese vehicles must be physically in China and are largely separated from global systems, with only tightly controlled and often aggregated exports. Tesla, for instance, announced in 2021 it had established local data centers in China to house all data from its Chinese cars [334], in response to these requirements and government pressure.

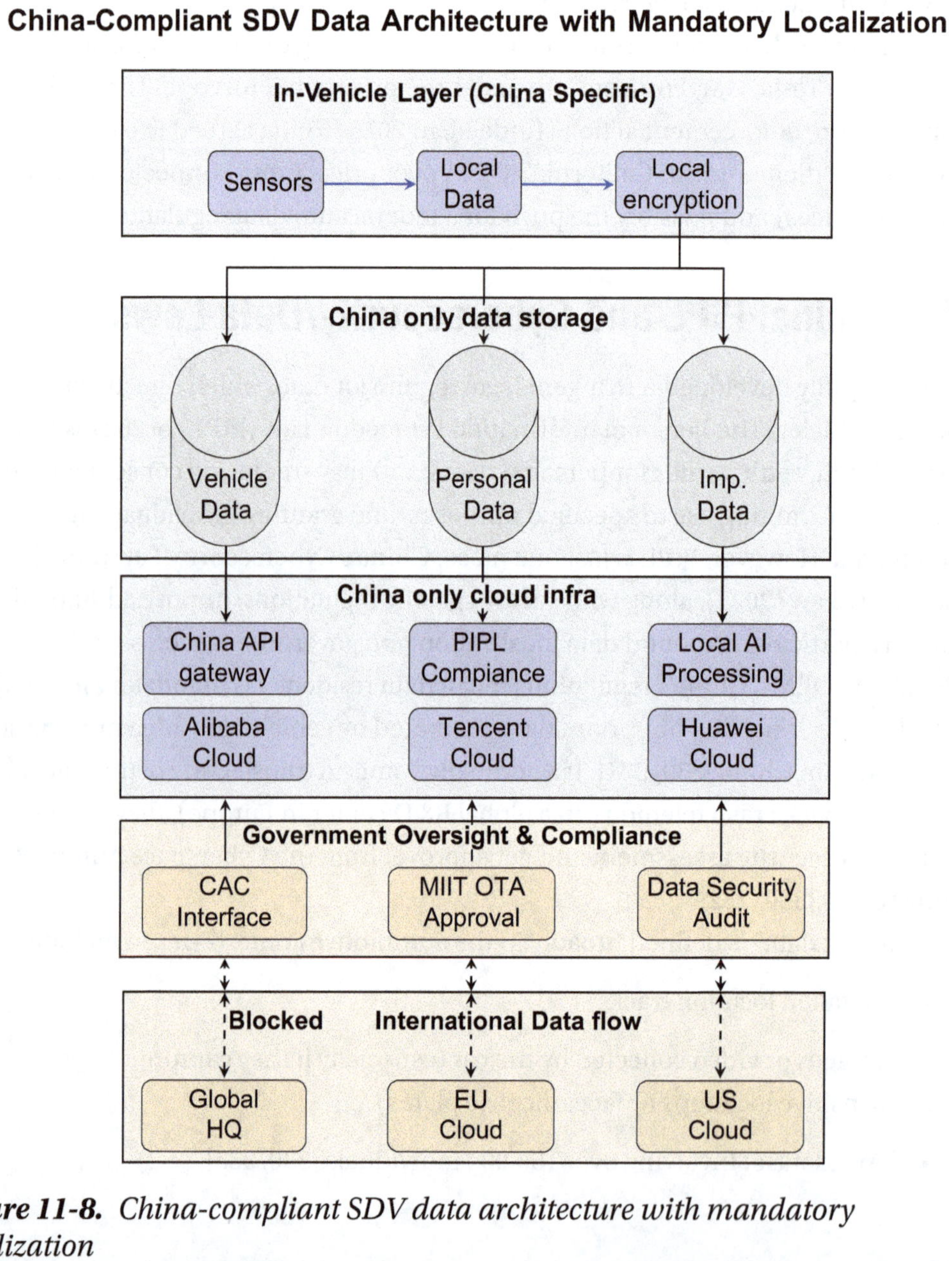

Figure 11-8. *China-compliant SDV data architecture with mandatory localization*

Moreover, China's Automobile Data Security Regulation (2021) introduced the concept of "in-car data processing" by default—meaning data should be processed locally in the vehicle and not leave the car unless absolutely necessary [330, 331]. Also, by default, vehicles should not collect personal data unless the driver opts in each time (no collection by default on each ignition) [330, 332]. This is essentially legislating privacy by default for vehicles.

OTA and Autonomous Features Regulation

Another critical aspect: China heavily regulates OTA updates and autonomous features. China's Ministry of Industry and Information Technology (MIIT) has progressively tightened OTA oversight, with regulations requiring that any OTA upgrade related to autonomous driving or critical functions receive prior regulatory approval [335]. This regulatory posture reflects China's broader approach of maintaining state oversight over vehicle software capabilities and is unlikely to relax. China doesn't want automakers using software updates to enable self-driving capabilities or fix defects without oversight. They treat OTA updates that fix safety issues as recalls—meaning the manufacturer must report them and possibly halt production of affected models until the "recall" (update) is approved [298, 335].

For a multinational OEM, accommodating China's PIPL and data laws often means maintaining a completely separate Chinese cloud infrastructure and software stack. This insular approach raises costs significantly—essentially duplicating development and operations for one country—but it is unavoidable for market access in China [336, 337].

Business Note **Regulatory fragmentation**: Global OEMs face a patchwork of regulations: EU's GDPR vs. US state privacy laws vs. China's PIPL and beyond. The result is often region-specific architectures. For example, an automaker may use a dedicated Chinese data cloud to satisfy China's localization laws [330, 334], a Europe-specific data platform (possibly aligned with initiatives like Gaia-X for EU sovereignty) [338, 339], and a separate system hosted on US hyperscalers for North America.

Each must be tailored to local rules—Chinese cars might have certain features disabled or modified, European users might experience stricter consent prompts due to GDPR, etc. This fragmentation undeniably increases complexity and cost—maintaining parallel engineering teams and infrastructure—yet it's unavoidable. Companies that try a "one- size-fits-all" approach risk legal non-compliance in one region or another. Thus, regulatory requirements directly shape not just software, but organizational structure and cloud strategy. The competitive upside is that those OEMs who manage to efficiently juggle these divergent compliance demands gain a strategic advantage in global deployment.

11.6 Other Standards and Initiatives

In addition to cybersecurity and data privacy regulations, several other safety and data ecosystem standards shape how SDVs are engineered and approved.

11.6.1 ISO 26262 (Functional Safety)

This standard defines how E/E systems must behave in the presence of random hardware faults and systematic design defects, with ASILs A–D guiding the required rigor. For SDVs, anything that can directly influence braking, steering, propulsion, or restraint systems is typically developed in accordance with ISO 26262, which has become the de facto state-of-the-art framework used to argue functional safety toward type approval, insurers, and courts.

11.6.2 ISO 21448 (Safety of the Intended Functionality (SOTIF))

ISO 21448:2022 (SOTIF) addresses a new dimension of safety for advanced driver assistance and autonomous features [260]. Unlike ISO 26262 (which focuses on failures and bugs), ISO 21448 deals with ensuring the intended function is safe even if there are no component failures. In other words, it looks at performance limitations or misuse—e.g., an AI vision system that struggles in heavy rain or a driver assist feature that could be used outside its design domain. SOTIF guides manufacturers to identify such potential unsafe scenarios and mitigate them through design or user warnings. As SDVs rely heavily on sensors and AI, SOTIF is becoming essential to achieve safety.

Since ISO 21448 became a full standard, assessors and NCAP-style programs increasingly expect OEMs to demonstrate SOTIF activities for ADAS and ADS functions, even where not yet mandated in law.

11.6.3 ISO/SAE 21434:2021 (Cybersecurity)

It is the lifecycle cybersecurity standard that underpins a manufacturer's CSMS. It defines risk analysis, cybersecurity goals, and assurance levels, and its work products are exactly what technical services expect to see when they audit compliance with UN R155.

11.6.4 ISO 24089:2023 (+Amd 1:2024)

Software update engineering is the software update counterpart to 21434. It defines how organizations plan, engineer, validate, and operate OTA and workshop updates in a way that supports UN R156. It doesn't just cover the in-vehicle update agent; it also covers back-end infrastructure, configuration tracking, deployment policies, and post-update audits.

11.6.5 ISO/PAS 8800: Safety and Artificial Intelligence

The automotive industry has published a dedicated Publicly Available Specification for AI in safety-related vehicle systems: ISO/PAS 8800:2024, *Road vehicles—Safety and artificial intelligence* [340]. This standard addresses a critical gap: ISO 26262 and ISO 21448 largely assume deterministic software behavior, but machine learning models are inherently probabilistic and may fail in ways that traditional hazard analysis does not anticipate.

Scope and Relationship to Other Standards

ISO/PAS 8800 targets safety-related E/E systems that incorporate AI technology, covering

- Output insufficiencies (e.g., misclassification, missed detections)
- Systematic errors in trained models
- Random hardware faults affecting AI computation
- Interactions with external AI services (cloud-based inference)

The standard does not replace ISO 26262 or ISO 21448 but extends them. In practice, a perception system using deep learning would be developed under all three frameworks simultaneously:

- **ISO 26262**: Addresses hardware random faults (e.g., bit flips in GPU memory) and systematic software errors in non-AI components
- **ISO 21448 (SOTIF)**: Addresses functional insufficiencies and foreseeable misuse at the system level
- **ISO/PAS 8800**: Addresses AI-specific risks including training data quality, model robustness, and operational domain coverage

Key Activities and Work Products

ISO/PAS 8800 introduces an AI-specific safety lifecycle with activities such as

- **AI safety requirements**: Defining safety-related properties that the AI element must exhibit (e.g., "the pedestrian detector shall achieve ≥99.5% recall under specified lighting conditions")
- **Data quality management**: Establishing requirements for training, validation, and test datasets—including coverage of operational design domain, labeling accuracy, and bias assessment
- **AI hazard analysis**: Systematically identifying how AI insufficiencies could lead to vehicle-level hazards (extending traditional HARA with AI-specific failure modes)
- **Verification and validation**: Defining test strategies appropriate for ML components, including robustness testing (adversarial inputs, edge cases), out-of-distribution detection validation, and statistical confidence arguments
- **Runtime monitoring**: Implementing mechanisms to detect when the AI is operating outside its competence envelope and trigger appropriate fallback behavior

Practical Implications for SDV Development

For SDV architects, ISO/PAS 8800 has several concrete implications:

1. **Data pipeline as safety-critical**: The processes that collect, curate, label, and version training data become subject to safety management. Dataset provenance, annotation quality assurance, and change control must be documented and auditable.

2. **Model lifecycle management**: Unlike traditional software where a version is "done" after testing, ML models may require periodic retraining as operational data reveals gaps. ISO/PAS 8800 requires processes for safe model updates, including regression testing and performance monitoring.

3. **Explainability and interpretability**: While not mandating specific techniques, the standard expects manufacturers to provide rationale for why an AI system is considered safe. This may involve interpretability tools, sensitivity analyses, or formal coverage arguments.

4. **Continuous validation**: Post-deployment monitoring to detect performance degradation (e.g., due to sensor aging, environmental drift, or adversarial manipulation) becomes a safety requirement, not merely a quality improvement activity.

As ISO/PAS 8800 matures toward full international standard status, expect regulators and technical services to increasingly reference it when assessing ADAS/ADS type approval applications (see section "Type Approval Process and Technical Services" for the approval process). OEMs that proactively align their AI development processes with 8800 will be better positioned for certification as requirements solidify [260, 340].

11.6.6 Catena-X and Automotive Data Spaces (Gaia-X)

Catena-X is a European automotive industry initiative aimed to standardize how automotive data is shared across OEMs, suppliers, and service providers in a way that respects European data sovereignty and competition requirements [318, 341]. For an SDV architect, this means designing data models and APIs that can plug into these federated data spaces without violating GDPR or giving away strategic control of data.

Taken together, these standards and initiatives are not optional extras. They are increasingly what regulators, NCAP bodies, and large fleet customers expect to see in your safety case and your architecture decisions. An SDV platform that ignores SOTIF, AI safety, or emerging data space expectations may be technically impressive, but in mainstream AD/ADAS segments in Europe, China, and increasingly US states with aggressive privacy enforcement, it will be commercially unviable.

In summary, these standards and initiatives (functional safety, SOTIF, AI safety, data spaces) are all pieces of the puzzle to ensure that SDVs are not only innovative but also safe, secure, and compliant with both technical and ethical expectations. Automakers must keep an eye on all of them—it's not enough to meet today's regulations; one must anticipate the next wave (like AI safety requirements) and proactively participate in shaping standards (many OEMs send experts to ISO working groups for this reason).

11.7 Compliance-Driven Architecture and Processes

A central theme of this chapter is that compliance is a design constraint, not a documentation exercise. For SDVs, WP.29 (section "UNECE WP.29: Global Vehicle Regulations"), privacy laws (section "Data Governance Laws and Privacy Regulations"), and functional safety standards (section "Other Standards and Initiatives") shape the architecture as much as CPU performance or memory bandwidth. An OEM cannot "bolt on" a CSMS, SUMS, or GDPR compliance dossier in the final project phase. Instead, the vehicle architecture and the development process must be structured from day one to generate the evidence that regulators, technical services, and data protection authorities will later demand. In practice, this means building compliance hooks into the software development lifecycle (SDLC) and DevOps toolchain so that threat assessments, safety analyses, test reports, logging, and traceability artifacts are created continuously, not reconstructed in a panic before SOP.

11.7.1 Integrating Compliance into the SDLC

The software development lifecycle for vehicle software should incorporate steps to address compliance at each phase. In practice, this could mean the following:

Requirements engineering: The team explicitly lists relevant regulations (WP.29, GDPR, etc.) and derives requirements like "The system shall log all access to safety-critical ECUs (per R155 monitoring requirement)" or "User personal data shall be pseudonymized at rest (per GDPR)."

Design phase: Architects ensure there are modules for security (e.g., an intrusion detection system in the vehicle network as required for CSMS monitoring) and for data protection (e.g., an identity vault that manages user consent tokens).

Implementation and testing: The organization must include compliance checks—for instance, static code analysis not just for bugs but also for compliance (some static analysis tools can check for MISRA safety compliance or even certain security vulnerabilities that tie into standards) [68, 306].

Deployment: By the time of deployment, the product should have generated all necessary artifacts to prove compliance.

Figure 11-9 illustrates the idea that compliance should be embedded into each stage of the software lifecycle rather than handled as a final certification exercise. Requirements must already reflect regulatory obligations; architecture and implementation must incorporate security, privacy, and traceability mechanisms; testing must generate auditable evidence; and deployment and maintenance must preserve logs, approvals, and monitoring data. The figure therefore shows compliance as a series of gates and artifacts distributed across the lifecycle, not as a separate activity performed after engineering is complete.

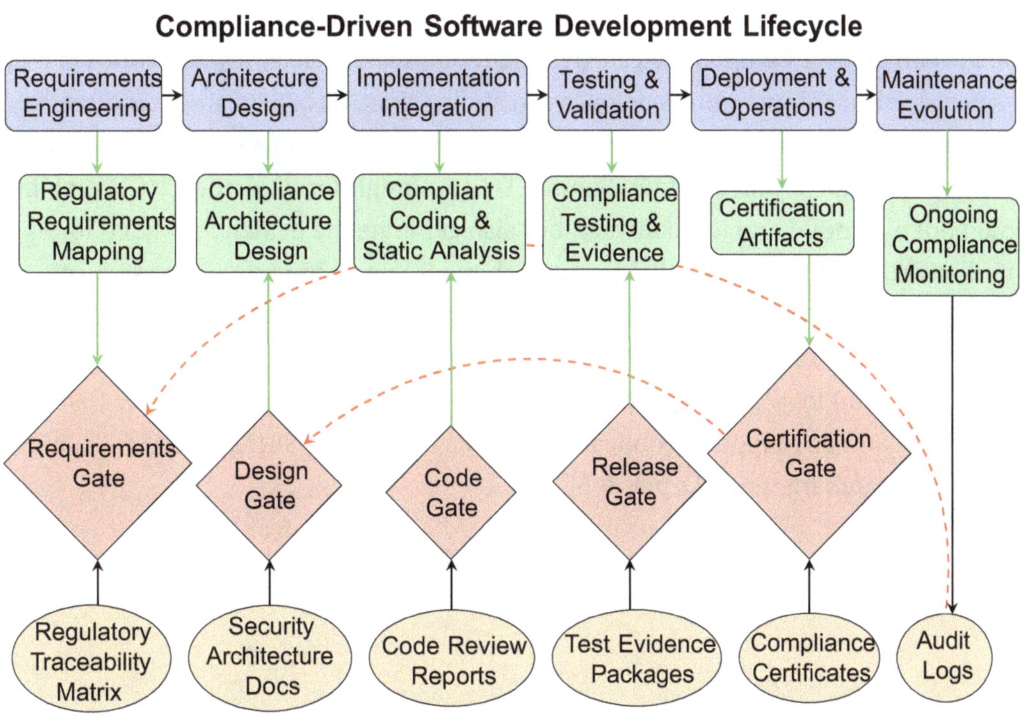

Figure 11-9. *Compliance-driven software development lifecycle*

11.7.2 CI/CD Pipelines Producing Evidence

Modern software development uses continuous integration/continuous deployment pipelines. By extending these pipelines, automakers can automatically generate compliance evidence as part of every build or release. For example, when a new software update (OTA package) is built, the pipeline can automatically produce a "regulatory compliance report" including

- The list of cybersecurity tests passed (penetration testing results, fuzz testing logs)
- The software bill of materials (for open source license compliance and to check no known vulnerable components)
- The update package's cryptographic signature and hash (proving integrity) [301, 307]

This report can be stored and later presented to authorities or auditors. Likewise, the pipeline can enforce compliance gates: it might block a release if, say, the code coverage for safety-critical components is below a threshold (since ISO 26262 might indirectly demand thorough testing) or if static analysis finds a violation of a security coding rule.

In practice, the key idea behind Figure 11-10 is straightforward: the CI/CD pipeline should not only build and test software, but also generate the evidence needed for compliance. A mature pipeline links source changes to requirements, runs security and quality checks, packages and signs release candidates, records test outcomes, and preserves artifacts such as traceability matrices, software bills of materials, vulnerability reports, and audit logs. The regulatory references shown in the figure indicate that these outputs can later be mapped to obligations under WP.29, ISO/SAE 21434, ISO 24089, ISO 26262, and related frameworks [68, 306].

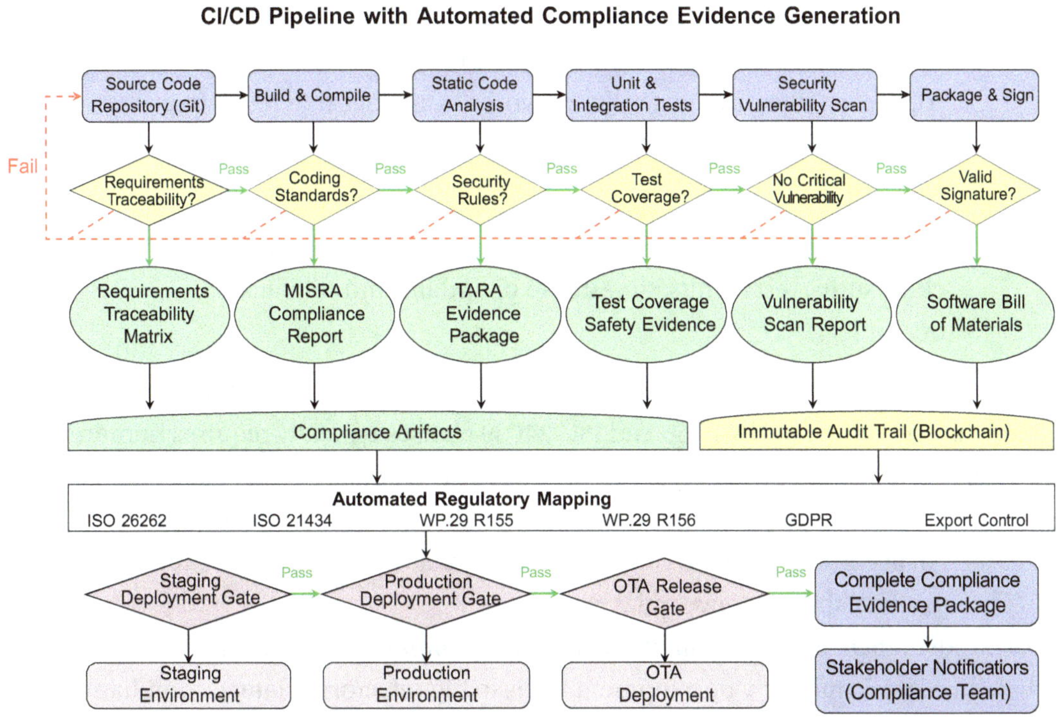

***Figure 11-10.** CI/CD pipeline with automated compliance evidence generation*

11.7.3 Example: OTA Update Pipeline

Imagine an OEM preparing a software update for a fleet of electric cars. A compliance-driven pipeline would automatically run through steps:

1. Run all unit and integration tests to ensure functionality (basic QA).

2. Run security scans on the new code (to ensure no new vulnerabilities, satisfying R155's need for vulnerability management).

3. Package the update and sign it with the company's private key (satisfying R156's requirement for secure update delivery).

4. Simulate an update installation on a virtual ECU or digital twin of the vehicle. During this simulation, the system intentionally triggers a failure to see if rollback works—and logs that result (e.g., "Update failed CRC check, system reverted to previous version successfully") [73, 306].

5. The pipeline then compiles a compliance log: version numbers, checksums, test results, timestamp of update, and rollback outcome.

In a mature setup, tooling can tag artifacts with relevant regulation references, though final mapping to UN R156 and ISO 24089 clauses typically requires human review by compliance specialists [308]. By the time the update is ready to be deployed to customer cars, the company has a full set of evidence that this update was developed and tested in accordance with WP.29 rules. If a regulator or an external auditor asks, the OEM can produce this evidence quickly.

The advantage of such automation is avoiding *compliance debt*. Similar to technical debt (when quick and dirty development leads to big refactoring later), compliance debt accumulates when teams postpone the work of meeting regulatory requirements. For instance, if an OEM doesn't integrate logging and traceability from the start, by the end of the development cycle, they might have to comb through thousands of documents and lines of code to pull together evidence for R155/R156—potentially delaying launch by months.

Critic's Note Compliance debt is as dangerous as technical debt—and often harder to pay down, because you cannot "refactor" your way out of missing safety or regulatory evidence at SOP. If you don't automate the production of logs, documentation, and evidence as you go, you'll face a mountain of work (or impossible gaps) when it's time for certification. In an SDV context, failing to address these needs early can bottleneck your entire release—you might have a great product ready to ship, but the regulators won't let it on the road because you can't readily prove it meets the rules.

11.8 Case Study: Over-the-Air Updates—Europe vs. China

Over-the-air software updates are a defining feature of SDVs, enabling new features and bug fixes to be delivered to vehicles remotely. However, regulatory approaches to OTA differ markedly between regions, and those differences directly drive how OEMs design their OTA back-ends, safety arguments, and release cadences.

11.8.1 European Union (and Similar Markets)

In Europe, OTA updates are permitted within a regulated framework centered on UN R156 and the manufacturer's approved Software Update Management System (SUMS) [300, 310]. The practical implication is that OEMs do not need separate approval for every minor update, provided their update process has already been validated and the update does not compromise safety, integrity, or type approval compliance. If an update affects homologation-relevant functions, additional notification or review may still be required. The European model therefore supports OTA innovation, but within a process-controlled and auditable compliance framework.

11.8.2 United States

The United States takes a more permissive regulatory approach to OTA updates than UNECE-aligned markets. There is no direct equivalent to WP.29 R156 requiring pre-approved update management certification, and manufacturers can generally deploy software updates without prior regulatory authorization for routine changes. However, if an OTA update remedies a safety defect, it falls into the recall framework and must be handled accordingly under NHTSA rules [271].

This model gives OEMs greater flexibility and faster release cadence, but it also creates ambiguity at the boundary between ordinary software improvement and safety-relevant remediation. In practice, the US framework places more responsibility on manufacturers to judge when an update has regulatory significance, which can enable rapid iteration but also increase legal and reputational risk if the judgment is challenged later.

11.8.3 China

China's approach to OTA updates is more heavy-handed. While Chinese vehicles are expected to support OTA, a 2025 regulation by MIIT explicitly requires prior regulatory approval for *autonomous driving-related* OTA upgrades and software updates that act as a remedy for safety defects (i.e., recall-like fixes) [335].

Under these rules, if an OTA is intended to correct a defect with safety implications, the automaker must first treat it as a recall measure: halt deployment of new vehicles with the defect, file the remediation plan, and obtain approval for the software fix before rolling it out fleet-wide [298, 335].

Similarly, manufacturers in China cannot use OTA to secretly enhance a car's autonomous capabilities beyond what's been approved—e.g., upgrading a Level 2 driver assist to a Level 3 autonomy via software would likely require new testing and approval. Furthermore, China's rules tie into data security: any OTA package distributed in China must abide by data localization (the update files, if they contain maps or data collected from users, might need to be stored and processed in China).

Another nuance is that Chinese standards (like GB/T on OTA) demand robust fail-safe mechanisms: vehicles must have a strategy if an update fails (so China, like WP.29, insists on rollback or "limp mode" in case of update issues) [333].

***Table 11-4.** Comprehensive Comparison of Regional OTA Regulatory Frameworks*

Aspect	European Union (WP.29 R156)	China (MIIT)
Regulatory Framework		
Approval Model	Self-certification; pre-approved SUMS	Government pre-approval required
Philosophy	Innovation-friendly; trust OEM compliance	Safety-first; government control
Rollback	Mandatory; customer notification	Mandatory; official documentation
Data Localization	Not required; single global OTA possible	Mandatory; separate China stack
Update Type Treatment		
Infotainment	Self-regulated; no notification needed	Generally allowed; minimal oversight
Powertrain	Notify authorities; SUMS validation	Pre-approval; extensive documentation
Safety Systems	Type approval check; SUMS required	Treated as recall; full government review
Autonomous Driving	SUMS validation; notify for major changes	Strict pre-approval; features may be restricted
Business Impact		
Infrastructure	Single global OTA stack possible	Separate China OTA stack required
Compliance Cost	Lower overhead; streamlined process	Higher overhead; dual processes
Time-to-Market	Faster; self-certification enables agility	Longer approval cycles

Dual Infrastructure Requirements

The net effect is that global OEMs often maintain dual (or multiple) OTA infrastructures: one for China and one for the rest of the world. The China OTA system will interface with government systems for filings and approvals, perhaps automatically generating the dossiers needed for MIIT before an update can be deployed. It will also use Chinese cloud servers and might have slightly different encryption as per local cryptography regulations.

The global OTA system (covering the EU, United States, etc.) operates under the more self-regulated paradigm of WP.29 and industry best practices, without needing to ask governments for permission each time. This split increases complexity. Companies must synchronize software versions across two pipelines without violating rules.

From a cost perspective, maintaining dual OTA stacks is costly and complex—you essentially duplicate effort in development, testing, cloud maintenance, and legal review. But for any OEM doing business in China and globally, there's little choice. As a result, some automakers have begun designing their software platforms to be modular by region: the core vehicle OS remains the same, but region-specific compliance "wrappers" handle the differences in update delivery and data handling.

Nonetheless, the case of OTA updates clearly illustrates how divergent regulations force engineering trade-offs. An optimist might hope over time regulators will converge (e.g., if China sees Europe's successful OTA safety record, it might ease up; or if Europe sees a need for more oversight, it could tighten up). Until then, OEMs essentially have to play by the strictest rules in each locale to avoid legal trouble.

11.9 Key Takeaways

- **UNECE WP.29 R155 and R156 are now mandatory** in many regions for vehicle type approval, addressing cybersecurity (CSMS) and software updates (SUMS), respectively. An OEM must implement organizational processes and technical measures to meet these or lose access to those markets [299, 300, 304, 310]. These regulations essentially force automakers to treat cyber and software update capability as critical as brakes or airbags in the homologation process.
- **ISO/SAE 21434 and ISO 24089 operationalize WP.29 requirements.** ISO 21434 provides the detailed engineering processes for cybersecurity risk management (aligning with R155) [68], and ISO 24089 does the same for software update management (aligning with R156) [306]. Adopting these standards helps manufacturers systematically achieve compliance, by following industry best practices for secure development and update delivery.
- **Data governance laws (GDPR, CCPA, PIPL) impose region-specific rules** on how SDVs handle personal data. GDPR in Europe mandates strict consent, user rights, and privacy by design [313, 315]; the United States has a patchwork of state laws like CCPA that require transparency and opt-outs [320, 321]; China's PIPL and related laws

demand data localization and government oversight for vehicle data [330, 331]. OEMs must tailor their data architectures to each region's requirements, which increases complexity but is necessary to avoid legal violations.

- **"Compliance debt" is a serious risk in SDV projects**. Just as technical debt accumulates when code is rushed without refactoring, compliance debt accumulates when processes ignore regulatory requirements until late. Managing this via automation and integration into CI/CD is essential—e.g., automatically generating logs, test reports, and documents that will be needed for audits [68, 301, 306]. Investing in tools and practices to continuously produce compliance evidence prevents costly delays at the time of certification or launch.
- **Emerging regulations will expand compliance scope**. The EU AI Act (effective 2025–2027) classifies certain automotive AI applications as high-risk, imposing additional conformity assessment and documentation requirements that will layer atop existing automotive standards [342]. India's Digital Personal Data Protection Act (2023) introduces consent and localization requirements that will affect OEMs operating in that growing market. A potential US federal privacy law, if enacted, could harmonize the current state patchwork but may also introduce new automotive-specific provisions. Forward-looking OEMs should monitor these developments and engage in standards-setting processes to shape requirements before they crystallize into law.

CHAPTER 12

Careers and Future Outlook

12.1 Chapter Goals

After this chapter, you will be able to

- Map SDV knowledge to real-world career paths (engineering, research, business).
- Understand skill expectations for MS vs. PhD graduates in SDVs.
- Recognize how technical marketing and product management roles emerge in SDVs.
- Relate SDV expertise to MBA/management education.
- Identify future industry and academic trends in SDVs.

Critic's Note *"An SDV career is not only about coding. It is about orchestrating ecosystems, regulations, and business models around software-defined mobility."*

S. Agarwal, *Software-Defined Vehicles*, https://doi.org/10.1007/979-8-8688-2718-1_12

12.2 Introduction

The software-defined vehicle represents a convergence of automotive engineering, software development, cybersecurity, data science, and business strategy. This convergence creates unprecedented career opportunities—and demands new combinations of skills that traditional automotive or software curricula rarely addressed. Whether you are an engineering student, a mid-career professional transitioning from adjacent fields, or an executive seeking to understand the talent landscape, navigating SDV careers requires understanding both the technical domains and the organizational contexts in which they operate.

This chapter maps the SDV landscape to concrete career pathways. We examine three broad categories: engineering roles (building and securing the technology), research roles (advancing the state of the art in academic or industrial R&D settings), and business roles (strategizing, productizing, and monetizing SDV capabilities). For each pathway, we outline skill expectations, typical employers, and career progression patterns.

The chapter then presents a skill roadmap differentiating expectations for master's-level engineers, PhD-level researchers, and those combining SDV domain expertise with MBA or management backgrounds. We address transitions from adjacent fields—general software engineering, IT security, cloud/DevOps, and data science—identifying the shortest bridges into SDV roles.

Finally, we survey the future outlook: technical trends reshaping vehicle architectures and AI applications, business trends transforming revenue models and ecosystem dynamics, and academic trends formalizing SDV education. The goal is to equip readers not just with knowledge of today's opportunities, but with frameworks for anticipating where the field is heading and positioning themselves accordingly.

12.3 Career Pathways

The ecosystem of software-defined vehicles (SDVs) offers a spectrum of career pathways. Broadly, these can be categorized into engineering roles (building and securing the technology), research roles (advancing the state of the art, often in academic or R&D settings), and business roles (strategizing and monetizing SDV technologies). Each pathway requires a distinct skill set and focus, with significant opportunities for cross-functional movement as careers progress.

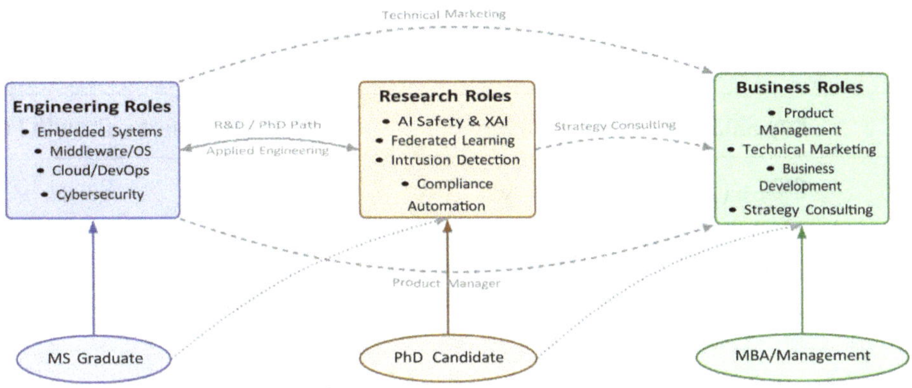

Figure 12-1. *Overview of SDV career pathways and their interconnections*

12.3.1 Engineering Roles

Engineering roles form the technical backbone of the SDV industry. These positions range from low-level firmware development to cloud infrastructure management, each requiring specialized skills while sharing a common foundation in automotive software principles.

Embedded systems developers: These professionals work at the hardware–software boundary, writing low-level firmware for microcontrollers and SoC devices. They implement real-time control algorithms under strict resource and safety constraints, following MISRA C guidelines. The demand for these engineers is surging as modern vehicles integrate dozens of networked computing platforms [6, 343].

Middleware/OS engineers: These engineers design and maintain the software platform between vehicle hardware and applications—operating systems like Automotive Grade Linux or QNX and middleware frameworks such as AUTOSAR Adaptive. They ensure support for OTA updates, secure boot, and safety isolation between critical and noncritical software [136, 137].

***Table 12-1.** Engineering Roles Matrix: Skills, Tools, Employers, and Career Progression*

Role	Key Skills	Tools	Typical Employers	Growth Path
Embedded systems developer	C/C++ (MISRA); RTOS; hardware interfaces; functional safety	IAR, Keil; JTAG debuggers; CAN analyzers; MATLAB/Simulink	OEMs; Tier-1s (Bosch, Continental); chip vendors (NXP, Infineon)	Senior → staff → architect
Middleware/OS engineer	Linux kernel; AUTOSAR Adaptive; hypervisors; IPC mechanisms	Yocto; QNX; Docker; AUTOSAR tools; Git/CI pipelines	OEMs (VW, BMW); platform companies (BlackBerry QNX, Elektrobit)	Platform lead → system architect
Cloud/DevOps engineer	CI/CD pipelines; container orchestration; OTA systems; data pipelines	AWS/Azure/GCP; Kubernetes; Terraform; Jenkins; Grafana	OEMs; mobility startups; cloud providers; telematics firms	DevOps lead → infrastructure architect
Cybersecurity engineer	Threat modeling; crypto/PKI; IDS/IPS; secure boot	Wireshark; CANoe; HSM tools; static analyzers; pen-test frameworks	OEMs; security firms (Argus, Upstream); Tier-1s	Security lead → CISO/security architect

Cloud/DevOps engineers: These professionals build the CI/CD pipelines and cloud infrastructure supporting millions of vehicles. With regulations like UNECE WP.29 mandating robust Software Update Management Systems (SUMSs), these engineers must ensure every update is authenticated, tested, and delivered fail-safe [72, 145, 147].

Cybersecurity engineers: These specialists protect vehicle networks and software from intrusion. They design IDSs for in-vehicle networks, implement secure communication protocols, and ensure compliance with ISO 21434 and WP.29 R155 [69, 344, 345].

12.3.2 Research Roles (MS/PhD)

Research roles push the boundaries of what's technically possible, developing new methods, algorithms, and frameworks that eventually find their way into production vehicles. These positions typically require advanced degrees and involve publication, collaboration with academia, and long-term thinking about technology evolution.

Table 12-2. *SDV Research Career Landscape: Topics, Sponsors, and Outcomes*

Research Area	Key Topics	Typical Sponsors	Career Outcomes
AI safety and explainability	XAI for ASIL-D systems; runtime monitors; fail-operational architectures	OEMs (BMW, Mercedes); Tier-1s (Bosch); government grants (EU Horizon)	ADAS algorithm lead; safety engineer; standards contributor
Federated learning	Privacy-preserving ML; fleet-scale training; heterogeneous data	OEMs; cloud providers; consortia (AECC)	ML platform engineer; data science lead; privacy specialist
Intrusion detection (IDS)	Automotive Ethernet/ TSN security; anomaly detection; V2X security	Cybersecurity firms; government (defense); Tier-1s	Automotive security researcher; security architect; compliance lead
Compliance automation	CI/CD for safety; automated traceability; regulatory tooling	Tool vendors (vector, dSPACE); OEMs; consulting firms	DevOps/compliance engineer; process architect; certification specialist

AI safety and explainability: Researchers in this area ensure AI components in critical vehicle functions are safe, reliable, and transparent. When AI contributes to ASIL-D functions, its behavior must be understood and controlled. Work typically aligns with ISO 26262, ISO/PAS 21448 (SOTIF), and UL 4600 [260, 346].

Federated learning: Researchers in this domain develop algorithms allowing vehicles to jointly train AI models without centralizing raw data. The Automotive Edge Computing Consortium has demonstrated that FL can improve battery range predictions while protecting privacy [243, 347].

Intrusion detection: Researchers develop IDSs suitable for automotive Ethernet and TSN, using deep learning to classify cyberattacks with high accuracy [344, 345]. Their work feeds into tools and practices OEMs adopt to meet UN R155 requirements.

Compliance automation: Researchers in this space explore DevOps tools that automatically verify compliance as code is written, creating continuous compliance pipelines that reconcile agile practices with regulatory obligations [147].

Critic's Note Many PhD positions in SDV-related topics are industry-funded, offering access to proprietary data and real vehicle platforms, higher stipends, and clearer paths to industry employment. The tradeoff is typically reduced freedom in choosing research directions and potential publication restrictions. Candidates should weigh whether the applied focus outweighs constraints on academic independence.

Table 12-3. *Academic vs. Industrial PhD: A Decision Framework*

Dimension	Academic PhD	Industrial PhD
Research freedom	High: choose topics aligned with advisor and funding; publish freely	Constrained: agenda set by company roadmap; publication may require approval
Data and resources	Limited: relies on public datasets, simulations, or small-scale experiments	Rich: access to proprietary vehicle data, real platforms, production-scale systems
Funding and stipend	Variable: depends on grants; typically lower stipends	Higher: industry-competitive salary; stable funding throughout
Career path	Academia, national labs, or industry R&D; broader optionality	Strong pipeline to sponsoring company; may have employment obligations
Intellectual property	Typically retained by university; patents possible but less common	Often assigned to company; invention disclosures expected
Networking	Academic conferences; cross-university collaborations	Industry contacts; internal mobility; supplier/partner exposure

12.3.3 Business Roles

Business roles translate technical capabilities into market value, bridging engineering teams with customers, partners, and strategic decision-makers.

***Table 12-4.** SDV Business Roles: Responsibilities, Stakeholders, and Backgrounds*

Role	Responsibilities	Key Stakeholders	Required Background
Product manager (SDV platform)	Define roadmap; prioritize features; drive monetization strategy; coordinate launches	Engineering; design; marketing; legal; customers	Technical degree + MBA or product experience; understanding of automotive software
Technical marketing	Craft product narratives; create demos/white papers; present at conferences; support sales	Product; sales; engineering; customers; media	Engineering background; strong communication; domain expertise
Business development	Build OEM/Tier-1/telco partnerships; negotiate deals; identify M&A targets	Executives; legal; partners; finance	MBA or deal experience; industry network; technical literacy
Strategy consulting	Advise on digital transformation; market analysis; build business cases; guide investments	C-suite; board; investors; government bodies	Top MBA or consulting background; automotive domain knowledge; analytical rigor

Product managers: Product managers define and drive the roadmap of vehicle software platforms. They focus on monetizing software through features-on-demand and subscriptions [34], coordinating across engineering, design, marketing, and legal teams.

Technical marketing: Technical marketing professionals bridge engineering teams and customers for highly technical products. They craft narratives explaining why an automotive AI chip or OTA platform is superior, often through B2B marketing at conferences and standards bodies.

Business development: Business development professionals build partnerships across the increasingly interconnected automotive, telecom, and tech sectors. They negotiate data-sharing agreements, platform partnerships, and licensing deals [10].

Strategy consultants: Strategy consultants advise clients on navigating the SDV shift—formulating software strategies, analyzing emerging revenue streams, and guiding investment decisions. Given that SDVs could unlock $600 billion in new value pools by 2030, the stakes are high [7, 348].

Business Note Strategy consulting roles are demanding: 60–70-hour weeks during active engagements, intensive travel, and high-pressure client work. The trade-off includes accelerated learning, strong exit opportunities, and competitive compensation. Candidates should honestly assess whether they thrive under such conditions.

12.4 Skill Roadmap

What skills do you need to thrive in an SDV career? It depends on the pathway. Here we outline typical skill sets for master's-level engineers, PhD-level researchers, and those combining SDV with MBA/management backgrounds.

Table 12-5. *Skills Matrix Comparison: MS, PhD, and MBA Profiles*

Skill Area	MS Expectation	PhD Expectation	MBA Expectation
Technical depth	Broad foundations; able to implement and integrate across the stack	World-class expertise in one sub-domain; publishes novel methods	Understands technology well enough to evaluate and communicate trade-offs
Systems thinking	Integrates components into working prototypes; debugs across layers	Designs new architectures; foresees second-order effects	Maps technical capabilities to market needs and business models
Research and analysis	Reads and applies existing literature; conducts structured testing	Generates new knowledge; peer-reviewed publications; rigorous evaluation	Market analysis; competitive benchmarking; financial modeling

(continued)

Table 12-5. (*continued*)

Skill Area	MS Expectation	PhD Expectation	MBA Expectation
Communication	Documents work clearly; presents to engineering teams	Writes papers; influences standards bodies; advises on future directions	Builds business cases; presents to executives; negotiates with partners
Leadership	Contributes effectively in teams; mentors junior members	Leads research initiatives; shapes technical strategy	Manages cross-functional programs; builds and scales teams

12.4.1 MS Graduate (Entry-Level SDV Engineer)

A master's graduate entering an SDV engineering role is expected to be well-versed in fundamentals: automotive-grade electronics, operating systems and middleware, networking (CAN/Ethernet and wireless), and functional safety and cybersecurity basics. Breadth is valued—you should be comfortable reading a microcontroller datasheet, working with Linux-based systems, and understanding why safety-critical software must fail safe.

MS graduates should be able to take components (software libraries, ECUs, cloud APIs) and integrate them into working systems. They should know tools like MATLAB/Simulink, automotive IDEs, and testing frameworks and be "device fluent"—comfortable flashing ECUs, interpreting CAN logs, and setting up Docker containers for simulation.

With these skills, MS grads are employable as system integrators, junior software developers, or junior architects. The key is versatility: strong foundations enable working across different parts of the SDV stack and communicating effectively with specialists.

12.4.2 PhD Candidate (Deep Specialist and Innovator)

A PhD in SDV signifies world-class expertise in a particular sub-domain—AI safety, formal verification, or vehicular communication protocols. This depth makes PhDs valuable for roles requiring solving new problems or evaluating cutting-edge approaches.

Being capable of publishing novel methods is a hallmark of a PhD. This experience implies strong analytical thinking, familiarity with scientific methods, and programming skills in research-oriented frameworks. PhDs can produce high-quality technical documentation and influence industry standards.

PhD-level experts can shape future industry directions, representing companies in standardization committees or consortia. For example, a cybersecurity PhD might advise that quantum computing could threaten current vehicle cryptography and push for quantum-safe algorithms—aligned with the 2030–2035 planning horizon for post-quantum cryptography transition [349].

12.4.3 MBA/Management (Techno-commercial Leaders)

Individuals with MBA plus SDV domain knowledge become invaluable in product strategy and general management. Their strength lies in relating technical aspects to market needs, customer experiences, and business models.

They drive the shift from one-time vehicle sales to recurring revenue streams, asking: How do we convince consumers to subscribe? What's customer lifetime value? How to mitigate churn? They craft business cases for data marketplaces and mobility services, using market segmentation, financial modeling, and pricing strategy.

SDV initiatives span multiple departments. A management-oriented SDV expert frequently ends up in program management roles coordinating software engineering, IT, quality, marketing, and legal. They are bilingual—fluent in engineering and business—enabling them to orchestrate the complex ecosystem around software-defined mobility.

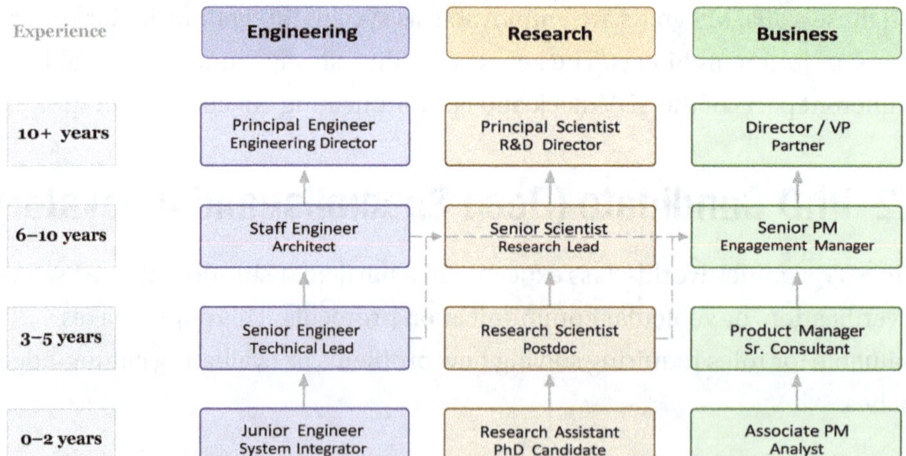

Figure 12-2. *Career progression ladder by tracks*

12.4.4 Transitioning from Adjacent Fields

Not everyone entering SDV careers comes from an automotive background. The field actively recruits from adjacent domains.

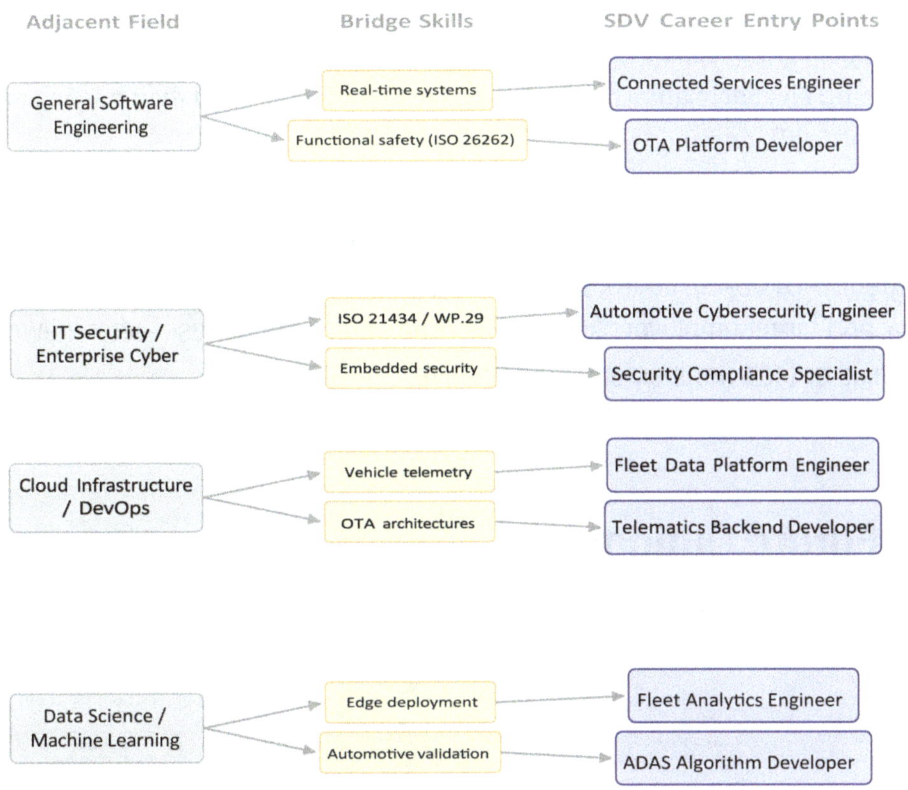

Figure 12-3. *Career transition map from adjacent fields to SDV roles*

From general software engineering: Key gaps to address are real-time systems thinking, functional safety awareness, and automotive-specific protocols (CAN, LIN, automotive Ethernet). Entry path: Cloud/back-end roles at OEMs—connected services engineer or OTA platform developer.

From IT security: Automotive cybersecurity shares foundational concepts but applies them under different constraints—limited compute, 15+-year lifecycles, and safety implications. Entry points: Security assessment roles at suppliers, positions at automotive security firms, or compliance roles at OEMs.

From cloud/DevOps: Skills in container orchestration and infrastructure-as-code transfer well. Learning curve: Automotive data types, regulatory requirements around vehicle data, and deploying updates to millions of edge devices with intermittent connectivity.

From data science/ML: Transition requires understanding automotive validation rigor, edge deployment constraints, and domain-specific data challenges. Practical starting point: Fleet data analytics for predictive maintenance and then moving toward vehicle-centric ML roles.

Business Note For all transitions: Complete automotive-specific certifications (ISO 26262, AUTOSAR), contribute to open source projects (Autoware, CARLA, Apollo), and target employers known for hiring across industries—often newer EV companies or tech firms entering automotive.

12.5 Future Outlook

SDVs are at the center of multiple converging trends. This section highlights key developments that will shape careers and opportunities in the coming years.

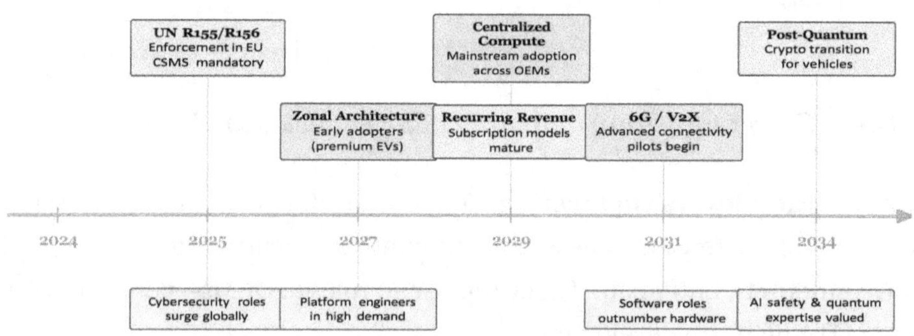

Figure 12-4. *SDV future trends timeline with career implications (2024–2035)*

12.5.1 Technical Trends

Centralized Compute and Zonal Architectures

Automotive E/E architecture is undergoing wholesale redesign. Future cars are moving to centralized computing with a few powerful domain controllers connected to simpler zonal modules by high-speed networks [11, 36]. This greatly reduces wiring complexity, enables easier updates, and decouples hardware from software.

For engineers, this means developing skills in high-performance computing (automotive SoCs with GPUs/NPUs), network design (Ethernet TSN), and virtualization/containerization. Careers will shift from single-ECU software to platform software spanning the whole vehicle.

AI Beyond Perception

AI is expanding from perception (object detection, lane keeping) to personalization and fleet optimization. Modern cars use AI to adapt cabin experience to learned preferences and monitor driver attention [350]. Fleet optimization covers predictive maintenance, route optimization, and swarm learning [351].

Expect job roles centered on UX research with AI, data analytics for connected services, and AI model training at scale.

Cybersecurity and Compliance by Design

With UN WP.29 in force across major markets, cybersecurity and data privacy are core design drivers [69, 72]. Future architectures will include embedded firewalls, anomaly detectors, encryption, and secure hardware enclaves as standard.

The concept extends to data privacy under GDPR, China's PIPL, and California's CCPA [352, 353]. Companies implement on-device processing, explicit consent flows, and robust anonymization.

This trend elevates automotive cybersecurity engineers, privacy officers, and regulatory specialists. Security and compliance experts will have a seat at the table from day one.

Quantum Computing and 6G Connectivity

Quantum computers pose long-term threats to current cryptography. Vehicles remain in service 10–20 years, so platforms launched in the late 2020s may need to withstand attacks in the 2030s. Architects should evaluate quantum-resistant algorithms for OTA signing and V2X stacks [349].

Research roadmaps for 6G envision higher data rates, tighter latency, and integrated terrestrial-satellite coverage [354]. The pragmatic stance for SDV professionals is awareness and architectural preparedness rather than betting near-term programs on speculative timelines.

12.5.2 Business Trends

Recurring Revenue Models

The automotive business model is shifting toward subscriptions and feature upgrades [7]. However, early experiments exposed risks—BMW's subscription for heated seats generated backlash. Features requiring ongoing operational costs (cloud navigation, AI assistants) are easier to justify as subscriptions than static capabilities.

Winners will align technical architecture (OTA delivery, secure activation), legal frameworks (regional compliance), and customer psychology (perceived value exceeding cost).

OEM-Telco-Hyperscaler Dynamics

A complex power struggle unfolds between OEMs, telcos, and hyperscalers. OEMs need connectivity (telcos) and cloud infrastructure (hyperscalers), creating interdependence that breeds both cooperation and tension [10].

For professionals, this means working on cross-industry collaboration projects and understanding adjacent industries. Those forming win-win partnerships will thrive.

Regulatory Patchwork

Different regions enact distinct rules on autonomous driving, data use, and digital services. Table 12-6 summarizes key differences.

Note *India's SDV regulatory framework is developing, with draft rules expected in 2025–2026.*

This patchwork drives demand for specialists in regional homologation, regulatory affairs, and software configuration management.

12.5.3 Academic Trends

Academia is responding to industry demand with formal SDV programs. Germany's TH Deggendorf offers a master's in Automotive Software Engineering[1]; BITS Pilani's WILP highlights SDV topics [3]. South Korea's KAIST, China's Tsinghua and Tongji, and Singapore's NUS/NTU are also expanding programs.

Table 12-6. *Regulatory Comparison Across Major SDV Markets*

Dimension	United States	European Union	China
AV testing	State by state; 30+ states with varying rules [355]	Harmonized via UN ECE; L3 permitted in some states	City-level permits; designated testing zones
Cybersecurity	Voluntary guidelines (NHTSA)	UN R155 (CSMS) mandatory	GB/T standards under development
Data privacy	CCPA (California); no federal law	GDPR; strict consent requirements	PIPL; data localization mandated [356]
OTA updates	Largely self-certified	UN R156 (SUMS) mandatory	Security review requirements emerging

Progressive programs incorporate interdisciplinary courses—automotive software curricula include functional safety standards and business models; MBA programs include software product management and Mobility-as-a-Service.

Industry-academia collaboration is rising through testbeds and consortia. Europe's Catena-X and Gaia-X involve dozens of companies and research institutions [357]. Government-funded testbeds (Michigan's Mcity, European test corridors) enable co-development under real-world conditions.

12.6 Key Takeaways

- **Diverse career paths**: SDV careers span engineering, research, and business domains—and often involve collaboration across them. Opportunities exist in cloud computing, AI research, cybersecurity, and technical business roles.

- **Education levels**: MS graduates are strong integrators and developers. PhD experts become deep specialists contributing novel solutions and guiding standards. MBA professionals serve as strategists translating technical capabilities into marketable products.
- **Future trends**: Technical shifts include centralized computing, AI expansion beyond perception, and compliance by design. Business shifts include recurring revenue models and OEM–telco–hyperscaler dynamics. Academically, SDV topics are becoming formalized through interdisciplinary approaches.
- **Taking action**:
    - **Students**: Seek internships with automotive OEMs or Tier-1s. Contribute to open source projects (Autoware, CARLA, Apollo).
    - **Professionals transitioning in**: Identify the shortest bridge from current skills and pursue targeted certifications (ISO 26262, AUTOSAR).
    - **Those in automotive**: Expand horizontally—mechanical engineers should learn embedded systems; software engineers should learn functional safety.
    - **All**: Follow industry consortia (Eclipse SDV, COVESA, AUTOSAR), attend conferences, and monitor regulatory developments. Staying current is itself a competitive advantage.

References

[1] TH Deggendorf. *M.Eng. Automotive Software Engineering.* 2024. URL: https://th-deg.de/ase-m-en (visited on November 6, 2025).

[2] Accenture. *Accenture LearnVantage and IIT Madras's CAAR collaborate to skill talent for Software-Defined Vehicles.* SDV skilling collaboration (press release). 2025. URL: https://newsroom.accenture.com/news/2025/accenture-learnvantage-and-iit-madras-s-caar-collaborate-to-skill-talent-for-software-defined-vehicles (visited on November 6, 2025).

[3] BITS Pilani WILP. *M.Tech. in Automotive Engineering.* Program page. 2024. URL: https://bits-pilani-wilp.ac.in/m-tech/automotive-engineering.php (visited on November 6, 2025).

[4] IBM. *What is a Software Defined Vehicle?* 2025. URL: https://www.ibm.com/think/topics/software-defined-vehicle (visited on November 6, 2025).

[5] Sonatus. *The Definitive Guide to Software Defined Vehicles.* 2024. URL: https://www.sonatus.com/blog/what-is-a-software-defined-vehicle/ (visited on November 6, 2025).

[6] IEEE Spectrum. *How Software Is Eating the Car.* Harness can exceed 5 km and 68 kg in modern vehicles; motivation for zonal. 2024. URL: https://spectrum.ieee.org/software-eating-car (visited on November 6, 2025).

[7] Omdia. *Connected Car Report 2024.* Tech. rep. Global parc from 356.7 M (2023) to 1.261 B (2035). 2024. URL: https://omdia.tech.informa.com/om122929/connected-car-report-2024 (visited on November 6, 2025).

S. Agarwal, *Software-Defined Vehicles,* https://doi.org/10.1007/979-8-8688-2718-1

[8] EE Times Europe. *True SDVs Are Out of Reach in Automotive's Legacy Model.* 2024. URL: https://www.eetimes.eu/true-sdvs-are-out-of-reach-in-automotive-legacy-model/ (visited on November 6, 2025).

[9] Quest Global. *How Software-Defined Vehicles Are Revolutionizing the Automotive Ecosystem.* 2024. URL: https://www.questglobal.com/insights/thought-leadership/from-hardware-to-software-evolution-in-the-automotive-ecosystem (visited on November 6, 2025).

[10] McKinsey & Company. *Getting Ready for Next-Generation E/E Architecture.* 2024. URL: https://www.mckinsey.com/industries/semiconductors/our-insights/getting-ready-for-next-generation-ee-architecture-with-zonal-compute (visited on November 6, 2025).

[11] Molex. *Zonal Architecture vs. Domain Architecture.* 2024. URL: https://www.molex.com/en-us/blog/zonal-architecture-vs-domain-architecture-modular-automotive-infrastructure-face-off (visited on November 6, 2025).

[12] Semiconductor Engineering. *Auto Ecosystem Begins Shift To Software-First.* 2024. URL: https://semiengineering.com/auto-ecosystem-begins-shift-to-software-first-transition/ (visited on November 6, 2025).

[13] Eclipse Foundation. *Eclipse Software Defined Vehicle.* Definition used by the Eclipse SDV Working Group. 2024. URL: https://projects.eclipse.org/working-group/eclipse-software-defined-vehicle?utm_source=chatgpt.com (visited on November 6, 2025).

[14] Synopsys. *Accelerating Development of Software Defined Vehicles with Virtual ECUs.* Tech. rep. 2024. URL: https://www.synopsys.com/content/dam/synopsys/verification/white-papers/virtual-ecu-wp.pdf (visited on November 6, 2025).

[15] Microsoft. *SDV DevOps toolchain / reference architecture content.* 2024. URL: https://learn.microsoft.com/en-us/industry/mobility/architecture/software-defined-vehicle-reference-architecture-content (visited on November 6, 2025).

[16] Microsoft. *Overview of the reference architecture for software defined vehicles.* 2024. URL: https://learn.microsoft.com/en-us/industry/mobility/architecture/ra-mobility-sdv (visited on November 6, 2025).

[17] Applied Intuition. *Impact Analysis for AV Validation.* 2024. URL: https://www.appliedintuition.com/blog/continuous-validation-and-versioning-of-complex-systems (visited on November 6, 2025).

[18] NVIDIA. *NVIDIA DRIVE AGX Thor.* Recent adoptions in Level 4 programs (production track signal). 2025. URL: https://nvidianews.nvidia.com/news/nvidia-uber-robotaxi (visited on November 6, 2025).

[19] Qualcomm. *Snapdragon Ride Flex.* 2023. URL: https://www.qualcomm.com/news/releases/2023/01/qualcomm-unveils-snapdragon-ride-flex---the-automotive-industry- (visited on November 6, 2025).

[20] Renesas. *R-Car S4.* Gateway/Zonal Controller positioning. 2024. URL: https://www.renesas.com/en/products/r-car-s4 (visited on November 6, 2025).

[21] BlackBerry QNX. *QNX OS for Safety 8.0.* Current certification details. 2024. URL: https://blackberry.qnx.com/en/products/safety-certified/qnx-os-for-safety (visited on November 6, 2025).

[22] BlackBerry QNX. *QNX Hypervisor for Safety.* Pre-certified ISO 26262 ASIL D / IEC 61508 SIL3. 2024. URL: https://blackberry.qnx.com/en/products/safety-certified/qnx-hypervisor-for-safety (visited on November 6, 2025).

[23] Sibros Technologies. *UNECE WP.29 for R155 & R156: Cybersecurity in Depth and by Design.* Whitepaper and compliance overview for WP.29 R155/R156 (CSMS and SUMS). 2021. URL: https://www.sibros.tech/compliances/unece-wp-29 (visited on November 17, 2025).

[24] NVIDIA Developer Blog. *Getting to Know Autonomous Vehicles.* Test fleet ≈1.6 PB/day for 50 cars (≈32 TB/day/car) when logging raw sensors. 2024. URL: https://developer.nvidia.com/blog/getting-to-know-autonomous-vehicles/ (visited on November 6, 2025).

[25] Amazon Web Services. *AWS IoT FleetWise documentation overview.* Vehicle models, VSS based signal catalogs, selective collection. 2024. URL: https://aws.amazon.com/documentation-overview/iot-fleetwise/ (visited on November 6, 2025).

[26] Amazon Web Services. *AWS IoT FleetWise Developer Guide.* Comprehensive developer documentation. 2024. URL: https://docs.aws.amazon.com/pdfs/iot-fleetwise/latest/developerguide/iot-fleetwise-guide.pdf (visited on November 11, 2025).

[27] FCC. *Second Report & Order.* Tech. rep. Codifies C-V2X technical rules in 5.9 GHz. 2024. URL: https://docs.fcc.gov/public/attachments/FCC-24-123A1.pdf (visited on November 6, 2025).

[28] FCC. *FCC Adopts "C-V2X" Auto Safety Spectrum Rules.* Plain English summary. 2024. URL: https://www.fcc.gov/document/fcc-adopts-c-v2x-auto-safety-spectrum-rules (visited on November 6, 2025).

[29] 5GAA. *Updated Roadmap for C-V2X.* 5G V2X Direct mass deployment 2026–2029 (Europe first). 2025. URL: https://5gaa.org/5gaa-publishes-updated-roadmap-for-c-v2x/ (visited on November 6, 2025).

[30] 5GAA. *Visionary Roadmap III.* Tech. rep. White paper. 2025. URL: https://5gaa.org/content/uploads/2025/01/5gaa-wi-cv2xrm-iii-roadmap-white-paper.pdf (visited on November 6, 2025).

[31] UNECE. *Three landmark UN vehicle regulations enter into force.* Makes clear that R155/R156 apply to all new vehicles produced from July 2024 in contracting markets. 2024. URL: https://unece.org/sustainable-development/press/three-landmark-un-vehicle-regulations-enter-force (visited on November 6, 2025).

[32] European Commission. *Data Act explained.* Confirms applicability 12 Sept 2025. 2025. URL: https://digital-strategy.ec.europa.eu/en/factpages/data-act-explained (visited on November 6, 2025).

[33] Latham & Watkins. *EU Data Act—What businesses need to know.* Lays out 12 Sept 2026 access by design obligations for connected products/services. 2025. URL: https://www.lw.com/en/insights/eu-data-act-what-businesses-need-to-know (visited on November 6, 2025).

[34] *BMW Scraps Heated Seat Subscription, Shifts Focus to Software Services.* 2023. URL: https://www.forbes.com/sites/alistaircharlton/2023/09/07/bmw-drops-controversial-heated-seats-subscription-to-refocus-on-software-services/

[35] The Verge. *BMW drops plan to charge monthly fee for heated seats.* Corroboration. 2023. URL: https://www.theverge.com/2023/9/7/23863258/bmw-cancel-heated-seat-subscription-microtransaction (visited on November 6, 2025).

[36] EE Times. *Automotive Architectures: Domain, Zonal and the Rise of Central.* 2024. URL: https://www.eetimes.com/automotive-architectures-domain-zonal-and-the-rise-of-central/ (visited on November 6, 2025).

[37] ET Auto. *Vehicle Electronic/Electrical (EE) Systems: Automakers Shift to Zonal Architecture for Efficiencies.* 2024. URL: https://auto.economictimes.indiatimes.com/news/auto-technology/automakers-shift-to-zonal-architecture-for-efficiencies/118844882 (visited on November 6, 2025).

[38] Texas Instruments. *How a Zone Architecture Paves the Way to a Fully Software-Defined Vehicle.* Tech. rep. SPRY345 Rev. C. Texas Instruments, 2024. URL: https://www.ti.com/lit/spry345 (visited on November 6, 2025).

[39] Semiconductor Engineering. *Zonal Architectures Play Key Role in-vehicle Security.* 2024. URL: https://semiengineering.com/zonal-architectures-play-key-role-in-vehicle-security/ (visited on November 6, 2025).

[40] "Optimizing Electric Vehicle Power Nets: A Data-Driven Approach to Zonal LV Architecture." In: *Proceedings of EVS38.* 2024. URL: https://evs38-program.org/images/Proceedings/G%20Power%20Electronics/44_Optimizing%20Electric%20Vehicle%20Power%20Nets%20A%20Data-Driven%20Approach%20to%20Zonal%20LV%20Architecture.pdf (visited on November 6, 2025).

[41] InsideEVs. *Zonal Architecture: Software-Define Electric Car.* 2024. URL: https://insideevs.com/features/724945/zonal-architecture-software-define-electric-car/ (visited on November 6, 2025).

[42] Rivian Newsroom. *Meet the New R1: Redesigned Electrical Architecture.* 2024. URL: https://stories.rivian.com/meet-the-new-r1 (visited on November 6, 2025).

[43] Charged EVs. *At Rivian's Electrical Hardware Lab, Sandy Munro Checks Out the New Gen2 Architecture.* 7 ECUs, −1.6 mi wire, −44 lb. 2024. URL: https://chargedevs.com/newswire/at-rivians-electrical-hardware-lab-sandy-munro-checks-out-the-new-gen2-architecture/ (visited on November 6, 2025).

[44] BMW Group. *The Neue Klasse: Wiring Harness Reduction and Digitalization.* 2025. URL: https://www.bmwgroup.com/en/company/neue-klasse.html (visited on November 6, 2025).

[45] "Handling System Complexity in Zonal E/E Architectures." In: *Journal of Automotive Software Engineering* (2024). URL: https://www.sciencedirect.com/science/article/pii/S2666691X23000350 (visited on November 6, 2025).

[46] *High-performance computers from Continental as the central nervous system.* 2025. URL: https://www.continental.com/en-us/products-innovation/innovation/electric-mobility/eight-things-you-might-not-know/high-performance-computers/ (visited on November 6, 2025).

[47] InsideEVs. *Rivian Zonal Architecture Development.* 2024. URL: https://insideevs.com/news/761865/rivian-zonal-architecture-development/ (visited on November 6, 2025).

[48] Mobility Engineering Technology (SAE). *48V Is Coming, and Not Just for EVs.* SAE MA-07610. 2024. URL: https://www.mobilityengineeringtech.com/component/content/article/53339-sae-ma-07610 (visited on November 6, 2025).

[49] Robert Bosch GmbH. *Gear Up Vehicle Powernets for Future Mobility: 48V.* Tech. rep. Bosch Mobility, 2024. URL: https://www.bosch-mobility.com/media/global/mobility-topics/powernets/240611-bosch-xc-whitepaper-powernets-en.pdf (visited on November 6, 2025).

[50] Texas Instruments. *Automotive Applications—48V Ecosystems and Topologies.* Tech. rep. Texas Instruments, 2024. URL: https://www.ti.com/applications/automotive/48v-in-automotive/overview.html (visited on November 6, 2025).

[51] In Compliance Magazine. *The Rise of Time-Sensitive Networking (TSN) in Automobiles, Industrial Automation and Aviation.* 2024. URL: https://incompliancemag.com/the-rise-of-time-sensitive-networking-tsn-in-automobiles-industrial-automation-and-aviation/ (visited on November 6, 2025).

[52] "A Survey on Time-Sensitive Networking Standards and Applications for Intelligent Driving." In: *Processes* 11.7 (2023), p. 2211. URL: https://www.mdpi.com/2227-9717/11/7/2211 (visited on November 6, 2025).

[53] AUTOSAR. *SOME/IP Protocol Specification*. Tech. rep. FO R22-11. AUTOSAR, 2022. URL: https://www.autosar.org/fileadmin/standards/R22-11/FO/AUTOSAR_PRS_SOMEIPProtocol.pdf (visited on November 6, 2025).

[54] AUTOSAR. *SOME/IP Service Discovery Protocol Specification*. Tech. rep. FO R24-11. AUTOSAR, 2024. URL: https://www.autosar.org/fileadmin/standards/R24-11/FO/AUTOSAR_FO_PRS_SOMEIPServiceDiscoveryProtocol.pdf (visited on November 6, 2025).

[55] Object Management Group (OMG). *Data Distribution Service (DDS), Version 1.4*. 2015. URL: https://www.omg.org/spec/DDS/1.4/PDF (visited on November 6, 2025).

[56] AUTOSAR. *Requirements on Data Distribution Service (DDS)*. Tech. rep. FO R24-11. AUTOSAR, 2024. URL: https://www.autosar.org/fileadmin/standards/R24-11/FO/AUTOSAR_FO_RS_DataDistributionService.pdf (visited on November 6, 2025).

[57] RTI. *AUTOSAR and DDS: A Fresh Approach to Enabling Flexible Vehicle Architectures*. 2024. URL: https://www.rti.com/blog/fresh-approach-to-enabling-flexible-vehicle-architectures (visited on November 6, 2025).

[58] *Automotive Middleware Performance: Comparison of FastDDS, Zenoh and vSomeIP*. arXiv preprint 2505.02734v1. AUTOtechagil project (FKZ 01IS22088x). 2025. URL: https://arxiv.org/html/2505.02734v1 (visited on November 6, 2025).

[59] *ISO 26262: Road Vehicles—Functional Safety*. Standard. 2018. URL: https://www.iso.org/standard/68383.html

[60] TASKING. *Freedom from Interference*. Tech. rep. TASKING, 2021. URL: https://resources.tasking.com/sites/default/files/2021-02/TASKING-Whitepaper-Freedom-from-Interference-Pt-1_WEB.pdf (visited on November 6, 2025).

[61] Volvo Autonomous Solutions. *Doubling Down on Safety: Understanding Our Approach to Redundancy in Autonomous Vehicles*. 2024. URL: https://www.volvoautonomoussolutions.com/en-en/news-and-insights/insights/articles/2024/jul/doubling-down-on-safety.html (visited on November 6, 2025).

[62] Automotive World. *Key Steps to Securing Real-Time Systems in Connected Cars*. 2024. URL: https://www.automotiveworld.com/articles/key-steps-to-securing-real-time-systems-in-connected-cars/ (visited on November 6, 2025).

[63] NHTSA. *Cybersecurity of Firmware Updates*. Tech. rep. National Highway Traffic Safety Administration, 2020. URL: https://www.nhtsa.gov/sites/nhtsa.gov/files/documents/cybersecurity_of_firmware_updates_oct2020.pdf (visited on November 6, 2025).

[64] Broadcom. *Securing Software-Defined Vehicles with Zonal E/E Architectures*. 2024. URL: https://www.broadcom.com/blog/securing-software-defined-vehicles-with-zonal-e-e-architectures (visited on November 6, 2025).

[65] AUTOSAR. *AUTOSAR Secure Onboard Communication (SecOC)*. Protocol Specification R24-11. AUTOSAR, 2024. URL: https://www.autosar.org/fileadmin/standards/R24-11/FO/AUTOSAR_FO_PRS_SecOcProtocol.pdf (visited on November 6, 2025).

[66] Object Management Group (OMG). *DDS Security, Version 1.2*. 2022. URL: https://www.omg.org/spec/DDS-SECURITY/1.2 (visited on November 6, 2025).

[67] AUTOSAR. *AUTOSAR Intrusion Detection System (IdsM)*. Protocol Specification R24-11. AUTOSAR, 2024. URL: https://www.autosar.org/fileadmin/standards/R24-11/FO/AUTOSAR_FO_PRS_IntrusionDetectionSystem.pdf (visited on November 6, 2025).

[68] *ISO/SAE 21434:2021: Road Vehicles—Cybersecurity Engineering*. Standard. 2021. URL: https://www.iso.org/standard/70918.html

[69] *UN Regulation No. 155: Cybersecurity and Cybersecurity Management System (CSMS)*. Regulation. 2021. URL: https://unece.org/transport/documents/2021/03/standards/un-regulation-no-155-cyber-security-and-cyber-security

[70] Uptane Project. *Uptane Standard for Design and Implementation, Version 2.1.0*. 2023. URL: https://uptane.org/docs/2.1.0/standard/uptane-standard (visited on November 27, 2025).

[71] Monolithic Power Systems. *Primer: Cold Crank to Load Dump*. Tech. rep. Version Ver 1.3. Monolithic Power Systems, 2024. URL: https://media.monolithicpower.com/mps_cms_document/c/o/cold_crank_to_load_dump-primer_ver1.3.pdf (visited on November 6, 2025).

[72] UNECE Working Party 29. *UN Regulation No. 156—Software Update and Software Update Management System*. Tech. rep. 2021. URL: https://unece.org/transport/documents/2021/03/standards/un-regulation-no-156-software-update-and-software-update (visited on November 20, 2025).

[73] ISO. *ISO 24089: Road vehicles—Software update engineering*. 2024. URL: https://www.iso.org/standard/77796.html (visited on November 9, 2025).

[74] Wikipedia. *100BASE-T1 (IEEE 802.3bw)*. 2024. URL: https://en.wikipedia.org/wiki/100BASE-T1 (visited on November 6, 2025).

[75] Texas Instruments. *DP83TG720S-Q1—1000BASE-T1 (IEEE 802.3bp)*. 2024. URL: https://www.ti.com/product/DP83TG720S-Q1 (visited on November 6, 2025).

[76] Analog Devices. *Why 10BASE-T1S Is the Missing Ethernet Link (IEEE 802.3cg)*. 2024. URL: https://www.analog.com/en/signals/thought-leadership/why-10base-t1s-is-the-missing-ethernet-link.html (visited on November 6, 2025).

[77] Microchip. *10BASE-T1S Single Pair Ethernet*. 2024. URL: https://www.microchip.com/en-us/products/high-speed-networking-and-video/ethernet/single-pair-ethernet/10base-t1s (visited on November 6, 2025).

[78] ISO. *ISO 14229-5: Unified Diagnostic Services (UDS) on Internet Protocol (UDSonIP)*. 2022. URL: https://cdn.standards.iteh.ai/samples/76882/25837ab5f8654d06b09db83904928df5/ISO-14229-5-2022.pdf (visited on November 6, 2025).

[79] ISO. *ISO 13400-2: Road Vehicles—Diagnostic Communication over Internet Protocol (DoIP)*. 2020. URL: https://www.iso.org/standard/13400-2 (visited on November 6, 2025).

[80] Renesas. *RH850/U2A—Zone/Domain Microcontroller Series*. 2024. URL: https://www.renesas.com/en/products/rh850-u2a (visited on November 6, 2025).

[81] Renesas. *RH850/U2B—Zone/Domain/Vehicle Motion Microcontroller Series*. 2024. URL: https://www.renesas.com/en/products/rh850-u2b (visited on November 6, 2025).

[82] Renesas. *RH850/U2B Group Gbit Ethernet Application Note*. Tech. rep. R01AN7074EJ0100. Renesas, 2024. URL: https://www.renesas.com/en/document/apn/rh850u2b-group-gbit-ethernet-application-note-r01an7074ej0100 (visited on November 6, 2025).

[83] Infineon. *AURIX™ TC4x—32-bit TriCore Microcontroller*. CAN XL/TSN capable. 2024. URL: https://www.infineon.com/products/microcontroller/32-bit-tricore/aurix-tc4x (visited on November 6, 2025).

[84] NXP. *S32Z2 Real-Time Processors*. 2024. URL: https://www.nxp.com/products/S32Z2 (visited on November 6, 2025).

[85] NXP. *S32G2 Vehicle Network Processors*. 2024. URL: https://www.mouser.com/pdfDocs/NXP_S32G2_DS.pdf (visited on November 6, 2025).

[86] Texas Instruments. *Wide-VIN Front-End with Cold-Crank*. Design Guide TIDUB49. Texas Instruments, 2024. URL: https://www.ti.com/lit/ug/tidub49/tidub49.pdf (visited on November 6, 2025).

[87] ARM Community. *Automotive Real-Time Virtualization: An Embedded Hypervisor*. 2024. URL: https://community.arm.com/arm-community-blogs/b/automotive-blog/posts/automotive-virtualization-embedded-hypervisor (visited on November 6, 2025).

[88] IEEE. *IEEE Std 802.1DG-2025: TSN Profile for Automotive In-Vehicle Ethernet Communications*. 2025. URL: https://standards.ieee.org/ieee/802.1DG/7480/

[89] IEEE 802.1. *Time-Sensitive Networking (TSN) Task Group*. 2025. URL: https://1.ieee802.org/tsn/ (visited on November 17, 2025).

[90] AUTOSAR. *AUTOSAR Diagnostic over IP*. Software Specification R20-11. AUTOSAR, 2020. URL: https://www.autosar.org/fileadmin/standards/R20-11/CP/AUTOSAR_SWS_DiagnosticOverIP.pdf (visited on November 6, 2025).

[91] S. Rodrigues et al. *Synchronization in Time-Sensitive Networking: An Introduction to IEEE Std 802.1AS*. 2023. URL: https://ieeemagnetics.org/files/ieeemagnetics/2023-06/Synchronization_in_Time-Sensitive_Networking_An_Introduction_to_IEEE_Std_8021AS.pdf (visited on November 27, 2025).

[92] *Experimental Evaluation of a Hybrid 5G and TSN System with IEEE.* arXiv preprint. 2024. URL: https://arxiv.org/html/2407.05989v1 (visited on November 6, 2025).

[93] Siemens PLM Software. *Methodologies for Achieving Functional Safety Using AUTOSAR in E/E Architecture.* Tech. rep. Siemens, 2024. URL: https://www.plm.automation.siemens.com/media/global/ja/Siemens%20SW%20Methodologies%20for%20obtaining%20functional%20safety%20using%20AUTOSAR%20White%20Paper_tcm57-109038.pdf (visited on November 6, 2025).

[94] "HyFAR: A Hypervisor-Based Fault Tolerance Approach." In: *Journal of Systems Architecture.* 2024. URL: https://www.sciencedirect.com/science/article/pii/S1383762124002005 (visited on November 6, 2025).

[95] Electronic Design. *Real-Time Processors Accelerate Software-Defined Vehicle Apps.* 2024. URL: https://www.electronicdesign.com/auto-electronics/video/21244977/electronic-design-real-time-processors-accelerate-software-defined-vehicle-apps (visited on November 9, 2025).

[96] Electronic Design. *Hardening the Automotive Processor Architecture.* 2024. URL: https://www.electronicdesign.com/markets/automotive/article/21143315/electronic-design-hardening-the-automotive-processor-architecture (visited on November 9, 2025).

[97] NVIDIA Corporation. *DRIVE AGX Orin Platform for Developers—Product Brief.* Tech. rep. NVIDIA Corporation, 2024. URL: https://developer.nvidia.com/downloads/drive/docs/nvidia-drive-agx-orin-platform-for-developers.pdf (visited on November 9, 2025).

[98] Qualcomm Technologies. *Snapdragon Ride SDK.* 2024. URL: https://www.qualcomm.com/developer/software/snapdragon-ride-sdk (visited on November 9, 2025).

[99] Arm Limited. *TrustZone for Cortex-M.* 2024. URL: https://www.arm.com/technologies/trustzone-for-cortex-m (visited on November 9, 2025).

[100] NXP Semiconductors. *TrustZone with ARMv8-M and the NXP LPC55S69-EVK.* 2024. URL: https://community.nxp.com/t5/NXP-Tech-Blog/TrustZone-with-ARMv8-M-and-the-NXP-LPC55S69-EVK/ba-p/1130956 (visited on November 9, 2025).

[101] Arm Limited. *Arm Cortex-R52+ Enhances Time-Critical Automotive Designs.* 2024. URL: https://newsroom.arm.com/blog/automotive-cortex-r (visited on November 9, 2025).

[102] Infineon Technologies. *32-bit TriCore™ AURIX™—TC4x.* 2024. URL: https://www.infineon.com/products/microcontroller/32-bit-tricore/aurix-tc4x (visited on November 9, 2025).

[103] Infineon Technologies. *AURIX™ TC4xx Documentation—Feature list.* 2024. URL: https://documentation.infineon.com/aurixtc4xx/docs/lie1539949338389 (visited on November 9, 2025).

[104] Infineon Technologies. *AURIX™ TC4xx Documentation—Functional overview.* 2024. URL: https://documentation.infineon.com/aurixtc4xx/docs/grb1539949338838 (visited on November 9, 2025).

[105] NVIDIA Corporation. *Jetson AGX Orin Series—Technical Brief.* Tech. rep. NVIDIA Corporation, 2023. URL: https://www.nvidia.com/content/dam/en-zz/Solutions/gtcf21/jetson-orin/nvidia-jetson-agx-orin-technical-brief.pdf (visited on November 9, 2025).

[106] NVIDIA Corporation. *IGX Orin Developer Kit—Specifications (Product Brief).* Tech. rep. NVIDIA Corporation, 2024. URL: https://docs.nvidia.com/igx-orin/developer-kit-product-brief/latest/specifications.html (visited on November 9, 2025).

[107] Arm Limited. *Arm's Automotive Enhanced IP Portfolio*. 2024. URL: https://newsroom.arm.com/blog/automotive-enhanced-ip-portfolio (visited on November 9, 2025).

[108] Arm Limited. *Cortex-A78AE—Product Page*. 2024. URL: https://www.arm.com/products/silicon-ip-cpu/cortex-a/cortex-a78ae (visited on November 9, 2025).

[109] S&P Global AutoTechInsight. *CES 2025: Arm and Nvidia advance automotive AI with NVIDIA DRIVE AGX Thor*. 2025. URL: https://autotechinsight.spglobal.com/news/5279879/ces-2025-arm-and-nvidia-advance-automotive-ai-with-nvidia-drive-agx-thor (visited on November 9, 2025).

[110] TechInsights. *Qualcomm Integrates Cockpit, ADAS*. 2024. URL: https://www.techinsights.com/blog/qualcomm-integrates-cockpit-adas (visited on November 9, 2025).

[111] Infineon Technologies. *AURIX™ TC4x—Innovative Cybersecurity Architecture*. 2024. URL: https://www.infineon.com/product-information/safety-security-and-connectivity (visited on November 9, 2025).

[112] Signal Integrity Journal. *NXP Extends the S32G Family of Network Processors to Accelerate Higher Performance Software-Defined Vehicle Applications*. 2024. URL: https://www.signalintegrityjournal.com/articles/2360-nxp-extends-the-s32g-family-of-network-processors-to-accelerate-higher-performance-software-defined-vehicle-applications (visited on November 9, 2025).

[113] NXP Semiconductors. *S32 Safety Software Framework (SAF) and Safety Peripheral Drivers (SPD)*. 2024. URL: https://www.nxp.com/design/design-center/software/functional-safety-software/s32-safety-software-framework-saf-and-safety-peripheral-drivers-spd:SAF (visited on November 9, 2025).

[114] WardsAuto. *Qualcomm "Elite" Computing Platform Moves Industry Closer to SDVs.* 2024. URL: https://www.wardsauto.com/suppliers/qualcomm-elite-computing-platform-moves-industry-closer-to-sdvs (visited on November 9, 2025).

[115] General Motors. *GM Brings Powerful New Compute Architecture to Ultra Cruise.* 2024. URL: https://investor.gm.com/news-releases/news-release-details/gm-brings-powerful-new-compute-architecture-ultra-cruise-help (visited on November 9, 2025).

[116] The Verge. *GM is getting rid of "Ultra Cruise" branding as it reevaluates its ADAS program.* 2024. URL: https://www.theverge.com/2024/1/22/24046928/gm-ultra-cruise-merge-super-cruise-adas (visited on November 9, 2025).

[117] NVIDIA Corporation. *In-Vehicle Computing for Autonomous Vehicles.* 2024. URL: https://www.nvidia.com/en-us/solutions/autonomous-vehicles/in-vehicle-computing/ (visited on November 9, 2025).

[118] Magna International. *Magna and NVIDIA Team Up to Advance Next-Gen Automotive Technologies.* 2025. URL: https://www.magna.com/stories/news-press-release/2025/magna-and-nvidia-team-up-to-advance-next-gen-automotive-technologies (visited on November 9, 2025).

[119] Renesas Electronics. *R-Car V4H — Best-in-Class Deep Learning at Very Low Power.* 2024. URL: https://www.renesas.com/en/products/r-car-v4h (visited on November 9, 2025).

[120] Renesas Electronics. *AI Accelerator: DRP-AI.* 2024. URL: https://www.renesas.com/en/software-tool/ai-accelerator-drp-ai (visited on November 9, 2025).

[121] Renesas Electronics. *Renesas Unveils Industry's First Automotive Multi-Domain SoC Built with 3-nm Process Technology*. 2024. URL: https://www.renesas.com/en/about/newsroom/renesas-unveils-industry-s-first-automotive-multi-domain-soc-built-3-nm-process-technology?srsltid=AfmBOoqRhr6Fv1lZV5_TOKmQC8YXtVitNykzyrBElodTITejxt5o8nZQ (visited on November 9, 2025).

[122] Electronic Design. *Chiplets Extend Automotive SoC AI and GPU Capability*. 2024. URL: https://www.electronicdesign.com/technologies/embedded/digital-ics/processors/microprocessors/video/55252079/electronic-design-renesas-r-car-x5h-provides-scalable-automotive-compute (visited on November 9, 2025).

[123] Quintauris. *The first RISC-V Real-Time Platform for Automotive*. URL: https://www.quintauris.com/rt-europa/ (visited on November 9, 2025).

[124] Qualcomm Technologies. *Leading Semiconductor Industry Players Join Forces to Accelerate RISC-V*. URL: https://investor.qualcomm.com/news-events/press-releases/news-details/2023/Leading-Semiconductor-Industry-Players-Join-Forces-to-Accelerate-RISC-V-08-04-2023/default.aspx (visited on November 9, 2025).

[125] SiFive. *Automotive E6-A Cores*. 2024. URL: https://www.sifive.com/cores/automotive-e6-a (visited on November 9, 2025).

[126] SiFive. *SiFive rolls out powerful new RISC-V portfolio to address automotive*. 2024. URL: https://www.sifive.com/press/sifive-rolls-out-powerful-new-risc-v-portfolio-to-address (visited on November 9, 2025).

[127] eeNews Europe. *Renesas launches 64-bit RISC-V microprocessors with Arm compatibility*. 2024. URL: https://www.eenewseurope.com/en/renesas-launches-64bit-risc-v-microprocessors-with-arm-compatibility/ (visited on November 9, 2025).

[128] RISC-V International. *Renesas introduces industry's first general-purpose 32-bit RISC-V MCUs.* 2024. URL: https://riscv.org/blog/renesas-introduces-industrys-first-general-purpose-32-bit-risc-v-mcus-with-internally-developed-cpu-core/ (visited on November 9, 2025).

[129] SiFive. *ASIL-B-ready certification for SiFive Automotive solutions.* 2024. URL: https://www.sifive.com/blog/asil-b-ready-certification-for-sifive-automotive-solutions (visited on November 9, 2025).

[130] SiFive. *SiFive + Arkmicro accelerate RISC-V automotive electronics adoption.* 2025. URL: https://www.sifive.com/press/sifive-arkmicro-accelerate-risc-v-automotive-electronics-adoption (visited on November 9, 2025).

[131] *Codasip. Codasip announces RISC-V processors now certified up to ASIL-D.* 2025. URL: https://codasip.com/press-release/2025/10/01/codasip-processors-certified-asil-d/ (visited on November 9, 2025).

[132] RISC-V International. *IAR Systems functional-safety certified development tools for RISC-V.* 2024. URL: https://riscv.org/blog/iar-systems-functional-safety-certified-development-tools-for-risc-v-support-latest-sifive-automotive-solutions-iar-systems/ (visited on November 9, 2025).

[133] IEEE. *Compute Solution for Tesla's Full Self-Driving Computer.* URL: https://www.computer.org/csdl/magazine/mi/2020/02/09007413/1hJKngjLkdi (visited on November 29, 2025).

[134] Mender. *OTA Update Best Practices for Industrial IoT & Embedded Devices.* 2024. URL: https://mender.io/resources/reports-and-guides/ota-updates-best-practices (visited on November 9, 2025).

[135] Aptiv. *What Is Middleware in Automotive?* 2024. URL: https://www.aptiv.com/en/insights/article/what-is-middleware-in-automotive (visited on November 9, 2025).

[136] eSOL. *The Difference Between AUTOSAR Adaptive and Classic Platforms.* 2024. URL: https://blog.esol.com/autosar_ap_cp_difference (visited on November 9, 2025).

[137] *BlackBerry QNX. Foundational Software Solutions for the Modern Vehicle.* URL: https://armkeil.blob.core.windows.net/developer/Files/pdf/ai-ecosystem-catalogue/BlackBerry-QNX-Automotive-Brochure---Digital-Version.pdf (visited on November 9, 2025).

[138] Aptiv. *The Next Step in Mixed-Criticality Processing.* 2024. URL: https://www.aptiv.com/en/insights/article/the-next-step-in-mixed-criticality-processing (visited on November 9, 2025).

[139] Promwad. *QNX vs Zephyr vs Embedded Linux in Safety-Critical Projects.* 2024. URL: https://promwad.com/news/qnx-vs-zephyr-vs-embedded-linux-safety-critical (visited on November 9, 2025).

[140] AUTOSAR. *Specification of SOME/IP Transformer.* Classic Platform Specification R21-11. AUTOSAR, 2021. URL: https://www.autosar.org/fileadmin/standards/R21-11/CP/AUTOSAR_SWS_SOMEIPTransformer.pdf (visited on November 9, 2025).

[141] AUTOSAR. *Specification of Operating System Interface (SWS OSI).* Adaptive Platform Specification R19-03. AUTOSAR, 2019. URL: https://www.autosar.org/fileadmin/standards/R19-03/AP/AUTOSAR_SWS_OperatingSystemInterface.pdf (visited on November 9, 2025).

[142] AUTOSAR. *Requirements on Operating System Interface (RS OSI).* Adaptive Platform Requirements R22-11. AUTOSAR, 2022. URL: https://www.autosar.org/fileadmin/standards/R22-11/AP/AUTOSAR_RS_OperatingSystemInterface.pdf (visited on November 9, 2025).

[143] AUTOSAR. *Specification of Update & Configuration Management (UCM).* Adaptive Platform Specification R24-11. AUTOSAR, 2024. URL: https://www.autosar.org/fileadmin/standards/R24-11/AP/AUTOSAR_AP_SWS_UpdateAndConfigurationManagement.pdf (visited on November 9, 2025).

[144] BlackBerry QNX. *QNX Hypervisor for Safety (Product Brief).* Tech. rep. 2019. URL: https://qnx.software/content/dam/qnx-xwalk/pdf/product-briefs/qnx-hypervisor-for-safety-8-product-brief.pdf (visited on November 9, 2025).

[145] TÜV SÜD. *UN Regulation 156 Assessments—Automotive Software Updates.* 2024. URL: https://www.tuvsud.com/en-us/industries/mobility-and-automotive/automotive-and-oem/autonomous-driving/assessment-of-automotive-software-updates (visited on November 9, 2025).

[146] EDN. *Accelerating Time-to-Market as Cars Become Software Defined.* EDN. June 30, 2025. URL: https://www.edn.com/accelerating-time-to-market-as-cars-become-software-defined/ (visited on November 20, 2025).

[147] *An Open-Source CI/CD Pipeline for Variant-Rich Software-Defined Vehicles.* arXiv preprint. 2025. URL: https://arxiv.org/html/2507.19446v1 (visited on November 9, 2025).

[148] BlackBerry. *A BlackBerry Milestone and the Road Ahead.* URL: https://www.blackberry.com/en/secure-communications/insights/blog/blackberry-milestone-road-ahead (visited on November 9, 2025).

[149] Automotive World. *BlackBerry: QNX embedded technology powers 255 million vehicles on the road today.* 2024. URL: https://www.automotiveworld.com/news-releases/blackberry-qnx-embedded-technology-powers-255-million-vehicles-on-the-road-today/ (visited on November 9, 2025).

[150] Texas Instruments. *GHS-3P-INTEGRITY-RTOS | Green Hills Software.* 2024. URL: https://www.ti.com/tool/GHS-3P-INTEGRITY-RTOS (visited on November 9, 2025).

[151] BlackBerry QNX. *QNX Containers (OCI/Kubernetes-compliant on QNX SDP 8.0)*. 2024. URL: `https://blackberry.qnx.com/en/products/foundation-software/qnx-containers` (visited on November 9, 2025).

[152] BlackBerry QNX. *QNX Software Development Platform 8.0 (product page)*. 2024. URL: `https://blackberry.qnx.com/en/products/foundation-software/qnx-software-development-platform` (visited on November 9, 2025).

[153] Zephyr Project. *First Functional Safety Certification Submission for an Open Source RTOS*. 2024. URL: `https://www.zephyrproject.org/zephyr-project-rtos-first-functional-safety-certification-submission-for-an-open-source-real-time-operating-system/` (visited on November 9, 2025).

[154] Linux Foundation. *Enabling Linux in Safety Applications (ELISA)*. ELISA Project. URL: `https://elisa.tech` (visited on November 20, 2025).

[155] Linux Foundation. *PREEMPT_RT Overview*. Linux Foundation. URL: `https://wiki.linuxfoundation.org/realtime/start` (visited on November 20, 2025).

[156] Linux Foundation. *Automotive Grade Linux Platform Debuts on the 2018 Toyota Camry*. 2018. URL: `https://www.linuxfoundation.org/press/press-release/automotive-grade-linux-platform-debuts-on-the-2018-toyota-camry` (visited on November 9, 2025).

[157] The Verge. *Volvo will be the first to install Google's Gemini in its cars (AAOS context)*. 2024. URL: `https://www.theverge.com/news/670954/volvo-google-gemini-ai-cars-android-automotive` (visited on November 9, 2025).

[158] Reuters. *Google, Volvo deepen partnership to develop Android automotive software (faster OS upgrades)*. 2025. URL: `https://www.reuters.com/business/autos-transportation/google-volvo-cars-deepen-partnership-develop-android-software-vehicles-2025-05-21/` (visited on November 9, 2025).

[159] Nissan. *Renault–Nissan–Mitsubishi and Google Join Forces on Next-Generation Infotainment.* 2024. URL: https://usa.nissannews.com/en-US/releases/renault-nissan-mitsubishi-and-google-join-forces-on-next-generation-infotainment (visited on November 9, 2025).

[160] Android Open Source Project. *Vehicle HAL (VHAL) Overview.* 2024. URL: https://source.android.com/docs/automotive/vhal (visited on November 9, 2025).

[161] Android Open Source Project. *Vehicle System Isolation (AAOS Security Guidance).* 2024. URL: https://source.android.com/docs/automotive/security/vehicle_system_isolation (visited on November 9, 2025).

[162] Excelfore. *Excelfore Partners with AWS to Streamline SDV Development.* 2024. URL: https://excelfore.com/blog/excelfore-and-aws-accelerate-development-of-software-defined-vehicles-sdvs-by-over-the-air-distribution-of-containerized-software-to-digital-twin-work-bench-1732195794269 (visited on November 9, 2025).

[163] OpenSynergy. *COQOS Hypervisor SDK for Automotive.* URL: https://wiki.automotivelinux.org/_media/pana_opsy_virtio_status.pdf (visited on November 20, 2025).

[164] BlackBerry QNX. *Advanced Virtualization Frameworks (QAVF) for Android/Linux/QNX Guests.* 2024. URL: https://qnx.com/developers/docs/7.1/com.qnx.doc.qavf.overview/topic/overview.html (visited on November 9, 2025).

[165] Semiconductor Engineering. *Automotive Ethernet, Time Sensitive Networking (TSN).* Knowledge Center. 2024. URL: https://semiengineering.com/knowledge_centers/automotive/automotive-networking/automotive-ethernet-time-sensitive-networking-tsn/

[166] IEEE 802.1. *Time-Sensitive Networking (TSN) Task Group.* Primary standards hub. IEEE. URL: https://1.ieee802.org/tsn/

[167] CAN in Automation. *CAN XL—CAN in Automation (CiA).* Primary CAN XL reference. 2024. URL: https://www2.can-cia.org/canxl

[168] Ettifos. *DSRC vs. C-V2X: Understanding the Two Technologies.* 2024. URL: https://www.ettifos.com/post/dsrc-vs-cv2x

[169] F. de Ponte Müller et al. *ITS-G5 and C-V2X Link Level Performance Measurements.* Tech. rep. German Aerospace Center (DLR), 2021. URL: https://elib.dlr.de/142341/1/ITS-G5_and_C-V2X_Link_Level_Performance_Measurements_dePonteMueller_v4.0.pdf

[170] Drivetech Partners. *Global C-V2X Status: Regulatory Progress and OEM Adoption.* 2024. URL: https://drivetech.partners/360/global-c-v2x-expansion-regulatory-progress-oem-adoption

[171] H. Bagheri et al. "5G NR-V2X: Towards Connected and Cooperative Autonomous Driving." In: *IEEE Communications Standards Magazine* 5.1 (2021). arXiv preprint, pp. 48–54. URL: https://arxiv.org/pdf/2009.03638

[172] US Department of Transportation. *Vehicle-to-Everything (V2X) Deployer Resource.* Tech. rep. FHWA-JPO-24-149. Federal Highway Administration, 2024. URL: https://rosap.ntl.bts.gov/view/dot/79215/dot_79215_DS1.pdf

[173] VicOne. *In Search of Automotive Ethernet TSN Solutions: Results From Our Hands-On Lab.* 2024. URL: https://vicone.com/blog/in-search-of-automotive-ethernet-tsn-solutions-results-from-our-hands-on-lab (visited in 2024).

[174] Various. "On-line Alternation of Modulation Techniques Using a Dynamic Switch." In: (2021). URL: https://www.academia.edu/87762247/On_line_Alternation_of_Modulation_Techniques_using_a_Dynamic_Switch

[175] OnStar. *The History and Evolution of OnStar.* 2024. URL: https://www.onstar.com/why-onstar/evolution-of-onstar-innovations

[176] Compass IoT. *Connected Vehicles Guide | Part 1: Background on Connected Vehicles and Connected Vehicle Data.* 2024. URL: https://www.compassiotglobal.com/ultimate-guide-to-connected-vehicles/part-1-background-on-connected--vehicles-and-connected-vehicle-data

[177] Toyota Connected. *MSPF (Mobility Service Platform)—TOYOTA Connected.* 2024. URL: https://toyotaconnected.co.jp/en/service/connectedplatform.html

[178] Toyota Motor Corporation. *Toyota Expands Partnership with Connected Analytic Services.* 2024. URL: https://pressroom.toyota.com/toyota-expands-partnership-with-connected-analytic-services/

[179] The Drive. *How the 3G Shutdown in 2022 Could Screw Your Car.* 2022. URL: https://www.thedrive.com/tech/43187/how-the-3g-shutdown-in-2022-could-screw-your-car

[180] 5G Americas. *Vehicular Connectivity: C-V2X and 5G.* Tech. rep. 5G Americas, 2021. URL: https://www.5gamericas.org/wp-content/uploads/2021/09/Vehicular-Connectivity-C-V2X-and-5G-InDesign-1.pdf

[181] Tesla. *Connectivity | Tesla Support.* 2024. URL: https://www.tesla.com/support/connectivity

[182] Globe Newswire. *The Global Automotive Telematics Market is Anticipated to Grow with a 13.41% CAGR During 2023–2032.* 2023. URL: https://www.globenewswire.com/news-release/2023/07/27/2712409/0/en/The-global-automotive-telematics-market-is-anticipated-to-grow-with-a-13-41-CAGR-during-the-assessment-period-2023-2032.html

[183] Various. "On Business Models for Vehicle-to-Everything Systems Based on Cellular Networks." In: *Proceedings of the 2020 International Conference on Networking and Services (ICNS).* 2020. URL: http://www.thinkmind.org/articles/icns_2020_1_60_10043.pdf

[184] Logistics Manager. *European Truck Platooning Challenge Reaches Climax.* 2016. URL: `https://www.logisticsmanager.com/european-truck-platooning-challenge-approaches-climax/`

[185] Fleet Owner. *Two-truck Platooning Could Deliver 4% Average Fuel Savings.* 2024. URL: `https://www.fleetowner.com/technology/article/21694524/two-truck-platooning-could-deliver-4-average-fuel-savings`

[186] IEEE Spectrum. "Truck Platooning: The Near Future of Freight." In: *IEEE Spectrum.* 2024. URL: `https://spectrum.ieee.org/truck-platooning-ohio-indiana`

[187] eSOL. *Central Computing in Modern Vehicle E/E Architectures.* 2024. URL: `https://www.esol.com/embedded/solutions/central_computing.html` (visited on November 29, 2025).

[188] *SAE. "Zonal" for the win.* URL: `https://www.sae.org/periodicals/zonal-win-sae-ma-07273` (visited on November 29, 2025).

[189] Peter Bannon. *Tesla Autonomy Day: Full Self-Driving Computer Presentation.* Technical presentation on Tesla FSD computer architecture by chip designer. Tesla. 2019. URL: `https://old.hotchips.org/hc31/HC31_2.3_Tesla_Hotchips_ppt_Final_0817.pdf` (visited on November 29, 2025).

[190] Mender. *Lowering Costs in the Software-Defined Vehicle.* Guide on cost reduction strategies in SDV architectures. Alias for mender_sdv_costs. 2024. URL: `https://mender.io/resources/reports-and-guides/lowering-costs-software-defined-vehicle` (visited on November 29, 2025).

[191] Rajesh Singh. *Tesla's Software-Defined Vehicle Architecture Evolution.* Analysis of Tesla's centralized compute approach. EE Times. 2024. URL: `https://www.eetimes.com/tesla-sdv-architecture/` (visited on November 29, 2025).

[192] STMicroelectronics. *STMicroelectronics and Volkswagen Collaborate on Next- Generation Vehicle Architecture.* Partnership announcement for VW zonal architecture components. 2022. URL: https://newsroom.st.com/media-center/press-item.html/t4470.html (visited on November 29, 2025).

[193] Analog Devices. *Automotive Ethernet Connectivity Technology.* 2024. URL: https://www.analog.com/en/solutions/automotive/automotive-ethernet-connectivity.html (visited on November 29, 2025).

[194] Verge. *Tesla's new self-driving chip is here and this is your best look at it yet.* Coverage of Tesla Autonomy Day and FSD chip reveal. Electrek. 2019. URL: https://www.theverge.com/2019/4/22/18511594/tesla-new-self-driving-chip-is-here-and-this-is-your-best-look-yet (visited on November 29, 2025).

[195] *Why VW Fails with Cariad: Analysis and Learnings.* 2024. URL: https://www.adt.media/software-defined-vehicles/why-vw-fails-with-cariad-analysis-and-learnings/644658 (visited on November 29, 2025).

[196] Darren Shelcusky. *A Comprehensive Guide to UNECE R155/R156 Compliance.* Automotive IQ. 2024. URL: https://www.automotive-iq.com/cybersecurity/interviews/a-comprehensive-guide-to-unece-r155r156-compliance (visited on November 29, 2025).

[197] *Toyota Connected Uses AWS to Respond in Seconds to Driver Emergencies.* Amazon Web Services. 2023. URL: https://aws.amazon.com/solutions/case-studies/toyota-connected-generative-ai/ (visited on November 29, 2025).

[198] *Azure Digital Twins Documentation—Overview.* Microsoft. 2025. URL: https://learn.microsoft.com/en-us/azure/digital-twins/overview (visited on November 29, 2025).

[199] AUTOSAR. *AUTOSAR CP R22-11—Explanation of Firmware Over-The-Air.* 2022. URL: https://www.autosar.org/fileadmin/standards/R22-11/CP/AUTOSAR_EXP_FirmwareOverTheAir.pdf

[200] Microsoft. *CARIAD Creates a Service Platform for Volkswagen Group Vehicles Using Microsoft Azure.* 2022. URL: https://www.microsoft.com/en/customers/story/1703517312786819888-cariad-volkswagen-group-azure-kubernetes-service-germany (visited on November 29, 2025).

[201] McKinsey & Company. *The future of automotive computing: Cloud and edge.* URL: https://www.mckinsey.com/industries/semiconductors/our-insights/the-future-of-automotive-computing-cloud-and-edge

[202] Gaia-X AISBL. *Gaia-X: A Federated Data Infrastructure for Europe.* 2024. URL: https://gaia-x.eu/ (visited on November 29, 2025).

[203] Gaia-X AISBL. *Gaia-X Trust Framework and Compliance Standards.* 2024. URL: https://gaia-x.eu/gaia-x-framework/ (visited on November 29, 2025).

[204] Catena-X Automotive Network e.V. *Catena-X: The Automotive Data Ecosystem.* 2025. URL: https://catena-x.net/ (visited on November 29, 2025).

[205] Catena-X Automotive Network e.V. *Understanding the Catena-X Data Space.* 2024. URL: https://catenax-ev.github.io/docs/operating-model/why-understanding-the-catena-x-data-space (visited on November 29, 2025).

[206] Forrester. *Where Did Gaia-X Go Wrong?* 2023. URL: https://www.forrester.com/what-it-means/ep289-future-of-gaiax/ (visited on November 29, 2025).

[207] *Automotive Data Sovereignty.* 2023. URL: https://www.netapp.com/media/158175-sb-4484-automotive-data-sovereignty.pdf (visited on November 29, 2025).

[208] Ingenics Consulting. Catena-X. 2022. URL: https://www.ingenics.com/en/catena-x/

[209] W. Anwar et al. "Evaluation Platform for 5G Vehicular Communications." In: *Vehicular Communications.* 2022. URL: https://www.sciencedirect.com/science/article/pii/S2214209622000845

[210] "5G Vehicular Communications: Architecture and Latency Analysis." In: *Vehicular Communications.* 2022. URL: https://www.sciencedirect.com/journal/vehicular-communications

[211] *Advancing Connected Vehicle Technology.* Tech. rep. Automotive Edge Computing Consortium, 2022. URL: https://aecc.org/wp-content/uploads/2022/10/white-paper-advancing-connected-vehicle-technology.pdf

[212] *Wholesale Billing in the 5G Era.* Tech. rep. GSCBP1761_11. GSC Group/Subex, 2025. URL: https://gscgroup.org/wp-content/uploads/2025/06/GSCBP1761_11_Subex_Wholesale_Billing_in_5G_Era.pdf

[213] "On Business Models for Vehicle-to-Everything Systems Based on Cellular Networks." In: *Proceedings of ICNS 2020.* 2020. URL: http://www.thinkmind.org/articles/icns_2020_1_60_10043.pdf

[214] 5GAA. *C-V2X Trials in Blacksburg: Real-World Testing of Cellular V2X.* 2021. URL: https://5gaa.org/c-v2x-in-action/ (visited on November 29, 2025).

[215] Stellantis. *Stellantis 5G Connected Vehicle Testing.* 5G V2X trial collaboration with telecom partners. 2022. URL: https://www.stellantis.com/en/news/press-releases/2022/april/stellantis-participates-in-u-s-test-of-5g-connected-vehicle-technologies-for-real-time-safety-notifications

[216] Android Open Source Project. *A/B (seamless) system updates.* 2024. URL: https://source.android.com/docs/core/ota/ab (visited on November 11, 2025).

[217] Mender. *Robust OTA updates with A/B Partitions for Linux devices.* 2024. URL: https://mender.io/blog/robust-ota-updates-with-partitions-for-linux-devices (visited on November 11, 2025).

[218] *Opportunistic Data Transfer and Edge Processing Concepts.* Supplementary material to AECC white paper. 2022. URL: https://aecc.org/proof-of-concepts/entry/751/

[219] *IoT Device Management for Connected Vehicles.* Standard cloud IoT practice for vehicle fleet management. URL: https://www.researchgate.net/publication/376640898_Comprehensive_IoT-driven_Fleet_Management_System_for_Industrial_Vehicles

[220] *Formal Methods and Validation Techniques for Ensuring Automotive Systems Security.* 2023. URL: https://www.researchgate.net/publication/376639366_Formal_Methods_and_Validation_Techniques_for_Ensuring_Automotive_Systems_Security

[221] *Optimizing Data Pipelines in Advanced Cloud Computing: Innovative Approaches to Large-Scale Data Processing, Analytics, and Real-Time Optimization.* 2023. URL: https://www.researchgate.net/publication/387881378_Optimizing_Data_Pipelines_in_Advanced_Cloud_Computing_Innovative_Approaches_to_Large-Scale_Data_Processing_Analytics_and_Real-Time_Optimization

[222] Various. "Recent Advances in Vibration Analysis for Predictive Maintenance of Modern Automotive Powertrains." 2025. URL: https://www.researchgate.net/publication/397229826_Recent_Advances_in_Vibration_Analysis_for_Predictive_Maintenance_of_Modern_Automotive_Powertrains

[223] Mireo. *Tesla Rolls Out Usage-Based Insurance. Why Should You Care?* 2021. URL: https://blog.mireo.com/tesla-usage-based-insurance

[224] Tesla. *Tesla Insurance Safety Score*. 2024. URL: https://www.tesla.com/support/insurance/safety-score (visited on November 29, 2025).

[225] *Understanding Car Data Monetization: A Taxonomy of Data-Driven Business Models in the Connected Car Domain*. 2023. URL: https://www.researchgate.net/publication/358248592_Understanding_Car_Data_Monetization_A_Taxonomy_of_Data-Driven_Business_Models_in_the_Connected_Car_Domain

[226] *Guidelines 01/2020 on Processing Personal Data in the Context of Connected Vehicles and Mobility Related Applications*. 2021. URL: https://www.edpb.europa.eu/system/files/2021-03/edpb_guidelines_202001_connected_vehicles_v2.0_adopted_en.pdf

[227] Bird & Bird. *China Tightens Data Protection in Automotive Industry*. 2021. URL: https://www.twobirds.com/en/insights/2021/china/china-tightens-data-protection-in-automotive-industry

[228] Future of Privacy Forum. *China's Car Privacy and Security Regulation Is Effective on October 1, 2021*. 2021. URL: https://fpf.org/blog/update-chinas-car-privacy-and-security-regulation-is-effective-on-october-1-2021/

[229] California Privacy Protection Agency. *CPPA to Review Privacy Practices of Connected Vehicles and Connected Vehicle Apps*. 2023. URL: https://cppa.ca.gov/announcements/2023/20230731.html

[230] S&P Global Market Intelligence. *Connected Vehicle Data Market Faces Setbacks as Two of Its Largest Players Exit*. 2023. URL: https://www.spglobal.com/market-intelligence/en/news-insights/research/connected-vehicle-data-market-faces-setbacks-as-two-of-its-largest-players-exit

[231] CarThrottle. *Mercedes Is Introducing an Acceleration Subscription Fee—No, This Isn't Satire*. 2022. URL: https://www.carthrottle.com/news/mercedes-introducing-acceleration-subscription-fee-no-isnt-satire

[232] GM Authority. *"We're Not Selling Monitors": GM Doubles Down on Anti-CarPlay Move.* 2024. URL: https://gmauthority.com/blog/2024/11/were-not-selling-monitors-gm-doubles-down-on-anti-carplay-move/

[233] J.D. Power. *What Is GM Ultifi?* 2023. URL: https://www.jdpower.com/cars/shopping-guides/what-is-gm-ultifi

[234] General Motors. *GM Ultifi Built on Linux Foundation.* GM partnership with Red Hat for Linux-based Ultifi platform. 2022. URL: https://investor.gm.com/news-releases/news-release-details/general-motors-and-red-hat-collaborate-trailblaze-future

[235] General Motors. *General Motors and Red Hat Collaborate to Trailblaze the Future of Software-Defined Vehicles.* 2022. URL: https://investor.gm.com/news-releases/news-release-details/general-motors-and-red-hat-collaborate-trailblaze-future

[236] Sam Abuelsamid. *General Motors Open Sources Interfaces for New Software Platform.* Forbes. 2023. URL: https://www.forbes.com/sites/samabuelsamid/2023/10/12/general-motors-open-sources-interfaces-for-new-software-platform/.

[237] MacRumors. *GM Again Attempts to Explain Its Decision to Drop CarPlay in New EVs.* 2024. URL: https://www.macrumors.com/2024/11/05/gm-further-explains-phasing-out-carplay/

[238] General Motors. *GM Vehicle Intelligence Platform (VIP) Architecture.* GM's advanced electrical architecture enabling Ultifi. 2021. URL: https://news.gm.ca/en/home.detail.html/Pages/news/ca/en/2021/Sep/0929-ultifi.html#:~:text=Ultifi's%20functionality%20builds%20upon%20the,and%20lightning%20fast%20processing%20power

[239] *CARLA: An Open Urban Driving Simulator.* 2017. URL: https://carla.org/

[240] *LGSVL Simulator: A High Fidelity Simulator for Autonomous Driving*. 2020. URL: https://www.researchgate.net/publication/341284150_LGSVL_Simulator_A_High_Fidelity_Simulator_for_Autonomous_Driving

[241] Nuro Team. *CIMRL: Combining Imitation and Reinforcement Learning for Safe Autonomous Driving*. Nuro. 2024. URL: https://medium.com/nuro/cimrl-combining-imitation-and-reinforcement-learning-for-safe-autonomous-driving-13148ac99527 (visited on November 29, 2025)

[242] Joseph Booher et al. "CIMRL: Combining Imitation and Reinforcement Learning for Safe Autonomous Driving." arXiv preprint https://arxiv.org/abs/2406.08878. Primary paper. 2024. URL: https://arxiv.org/abs/2406.08878

[243] H. Brendan McMahan et al. *Communication-Efficient Learning of Deep Networks from Decentralized Data*. 2017. URL: https://arxiv.org/abs/1602.05629

[244] Automotive Edge Computing Consortium. *Distributed Battery Electric Vehicle (BEV) Range Estimation via Personalized Federated Learning*. AECC, 2024. URL: https://aecc.org/proof-of-concepts/entry/995/ (visited on November 29, 2025).

[245] *ISO/PAS 8800:2024: Road vehicles—Safety and artificial intelligence*. 2024. URL: https://www.iso.org/standard/83303.html

[246] *IEEE Std 7003-2024: Standard for Algorithmic Bias Considerations*. 2024. URL: https://standards.ieee.org/ieee/7003/11357/

[247] WardsAuto. *Archive Wards Storage Almost Full: Driverless Cars Create Data Crunch*. Autonomous test cars 30 TB/day (industry benchmark; shows order of magnitude, not production upload). 2024. URL: https://www.wardsauto.com/news/archive-wards-storage-almost-full-driverless-cars-create-data-crunch/791673/ (visited on November 6, 2025).

[248] Volvo Autonomous Solutions. *Digital Twins: The Ultimate Virtual Proving Ground.* 2025. URL: https://www.volvoautonomoussolutions.com/en-en/news-and-insights/insights/articles/2025/jun/digital-twins--the-ultimate-virtual-proving-ground.html (visited on November 29, 2025).

[249] *Tesla Safety Score.* 2024. URL: https://www.tesla.com/support/safety-score

[250] Tesla. *Tesla Insurance.* 2024. URL: https://www.tesla.com/insurance (visited on November 29, 2025).

[251] "Organization of Autonomous Truck Platoon Considering Energy Consumption and Traffic Flow." In: *Transportation Research Part C: Emerging Technologies.* 2020. URL: https://www.sciencedirect.com/science/article/abs/pii/S136192092030852X

[252] ITS Knowledge Resources. *Illinois Study Found Automated Truck Platooning Powered by an AI-Based System Improved Fuel Economy.* US Department of Transportation. 2024. URL: http://www.itskrs.its.dot.gov/2024-b01819 (visited on November 29, 2025).

[253] Device Chronicle. *Service Monetization in the Software-Defined Vehicle and OTA.* Interview with Mark Gerban on automotive data monetization. 2023. URL: https://www.devicechronicle.com/service-monetization-in-the-software-defined-vehicle-and-ota (visited on November 29, 2025).

[254] *Waymo Safety.* 2025. URL: https://waymo.com/safety/

[255] Reuters. *Waymo Expands Robotaxi Services.* 2025. URL: https://www.reuters.com/technology/waymo-expand-robotaxi-service-las-vegas-san-diego-detroit-next-year-2025-11-03/ (visited on November 29, 2025).

[256] Tessolve. *Hardware Safety Metrics for ISO 26262 Compliance.* URL: https://www.tessolve.com/dvclub-europe-november-2018-hardware-safety-metrics-for-iso-26262-compliance/ (visited on November 29, 2025).

[257] SemiWiki. *Functional Safety for Automotive IP*. Covers hardware safety mechanisms including dual-core lockstep, ECC, watchdogs. 2022. URL: https://semiwiki.com/eda/321844-functional-safety-for-automotive-ip/ (visited on November 29, 2025).

[258] NXP Semiconductors. *S32G Vehicle Network Processors — Product Family*. 2024. URL: https://www.nxp.com/products/processors-and-microcontrollers/arm-processors/s32-automotive-platform/s32g-vehicle-network-processors (visited on November 9, 2025).

[259] Edge Case Research. *What ISO 26262 Expects from Your AV Safety Case*. 2025. URL: https://www.ecr.ai/resource/what-iso-26262-expects-from-your-av-safety-case (visited on November 29, 2025).

[260] *ISO 21448:2022: Road Vehicles—Safety of the Intended Functionality*. Standard. 2022. URL: https://www.iso.org/standard/77490.html

[261] Leadvent Group. *Functional Safety vs. SOTIF: Understanding the Key Differences*. 2024. URL: https://www.leadventgrp.com/blog/functional-safety-vs-sotif-understanding-the-key-differences-and-their-role-in-automotive-safety (visited on November 29, 2025).

[262] LHP Engineering Solutions. *What is SOTIF? Safety of the Intended Functionality*. Explanation of SOTIF four-area model. 2025. URL: https://www.lhpes.com/blog/what-is-sotif-safety-of-the-intended-functionality/iso-21448 (visited on November 29, 2025).

[263] ASAM Standards Organization. *ISO 21448 SOTIF*. Technical details on SOTIF validation approaches. 2021. URL: https://report.asam.net/iso-21448-sotif (visited on November 29, 2025).

[264] Jin Zhang et al. "Testing and verification of neural-network-based safety-critical control software: A systematic literature review." In: *Journal of Systems and Software*. 2019. URL: https://www.researchgate.net/publication/336577178_Testing_and_verification_of_neural-network-based_safety-critical_control_software_A_systematic_literature_review

[265] dSPACE. *Scenario Generation for Autonomous Driving Validation*. 2024. URL: https://www.dspace.com/en/inc/home/applicationfields/foo/scenario_generation.cfm (visited on November 29, 2025).

[266] Shahin Atakishiyev et al. *Explainable Artificial Intelligence for Autonomous Driving: A Comprehensive Overview and Field Guide for Future Research Directions*. 2024. URL: https://www.researchgate.net/publication/382403041_Explainable_Artificial_Intelligence_for_Autonomous_Driving_A_Comprehensive_Overview_and_Field_Guide_for_Future_Research_Directions

[267] UNECE WP.29. *Considerations on Artificial Intelligence in the context of road vehicles*. 2024. URL: https://unece.org/sites/default/files/2024-06/WP.29-193-20e.pdf

[268] Synopsys. *ISO/SAE 21434's Role in Automotive Cybersecurity*. 2023. URL: https://www.synopsys.com/articles/iso-sae-21434-automotive-cybersecurity.html (visited on November 29, 2025).

[269] Code Intelligence. *The Role of Cybersecurity Assurance Levels (CALs) in ISO 21434*. 2024. URL: https://www.code-intelligence.com/blog/iso21434-cybersecurity-assurance-levels (visited on November 29, 2025).

[270] Applus+ Laboratories. *UNECE WP.29 R155/R156: New cybersecurity regulations for vehicles*. Overview of UNECE regulations timeline and requirements. 2022. URL: https://www.appluslaboratories.com/global/en/news/publications/new-cybersecurity-regulations-vehicles-unece-wp29 (visited on November 29, 2025).

[271] *Cybersecurity Best Practices for the Safety of Modern Vehicles (2022 Update)*. Technical Report. 2022. URL: https://www.nhtsa.gov/sites/nhtsa.gov/files/2022-09/cybersecurity-best-practices-safety-modern-vehicles-2022-pre-final-tag_0_0.pdf

[272] Renesas Electronics. *Achieving a Root of Trust with Secure Boot in Automotive RH850 and R-Car Devices*. 3-part blog series on secure boot implementation. 2023. URL: https://www.renesas.com/en/blogs/introduction-about-secure-boot-automotive-mcu-rh850-and-soc-r-car-achieve-root-trust-1 (visited on November 29, 2025).

[273] AUTOCRYPT. *In-Vehicle Cybersecurity: A Closer Look at HSM and TEE*. 2023. URL: https://autocrypt.io/hsm-tee-closer-look-at-vehicle-cybersecurity/ (visited on November 29, 2025).

[274] AUTOCRYPT. *Securing Vehicles with Automotive Intrusion Detection Systems (IDS)*. 2023. URL: https://autocrypt.io/securing-vehicles-with-automotive-ids/ (visited on November 29, 2025).

[275] Various. "Research on Safety and Security Co-Analysis Methods." In: *ACM Digital Library*. Joint HARA-TARA approaches. 2024. URL: https://dl.acm.org/doi/10.1145/3729706.3729716

[276] Various. "Combined automotive safety and security pattern engineering approach." In: *Reliability Engineering & System Safety*. 2020. URL: https://www.sciencedirect.com/science/article/abs/pii/S095183201830499X

[277] Cybellum. *Merging Security and Safety in-vehicles: ISO 26262 and ISO/SAE 21434*. 2024. URL: https://cybellum.com/blog/iso-26262-and-iso-sae-21434-automotive-cybersecurity-must-go-hand-in-hand-with-functional-safety (visited on November 29, 2025).

[278] Charlie Miller and Chris Valasek. *Remote Exploitation of an Unaltered Passenger Vehicle*. Whitepaper. Primary technical source; CAN injection, exploit path. IOActive, 2015. URL: https://www.ioactive.com/wp-content/uploads/pdfs/IOActive_Remote_Car_Hacking.pdf

[279] Andy Greenberg. *Hackers Remotely Kill a Jeep on the Highway—With Me in It*. Online Article. Journalistic account, public demo. 2015. URL: https://www.wired.com/2015/07/hackers-remotely-kill-jeep-highway/

[280] The Guardian. *Fiat Chrysler recalls 1.4m vehicles in wake of Jeep hacking revelation*. Major media coverage of Jeep Cherokee recall. 2015. URL: https://www.theguardian.com/business/2015/jul/24/fiat-chrysler-recall-jeep-hacking (visited on November 29, 2025).

[281] NHTSA. *Recall 23V-085*. Tech. rep. FSD Beta remedy via OTA. Feb. 2023. URL: https://static.nhtsa.gov/odi/rcl/2023/RCLRPT-23V085-3451.PDF (visited on November 6, 2025).

[282] Boston Consulting Group. *Rewriting the Rules of Software-Defined Vehicles*. In collaboration with World Economic Forum. 2023. URL: https://www.bcg.com/publications/2023/rewriting-rules-of-software-defined-vehicles

[283] McKinsey & Company. *Automotive software and electronics 2030*. 2023. URL: https://www.mckinsey.com/~/media/mckinsey/industries/automotive%20and%20assembly/our%20insights/mapping%20the%20automotive%20software%20and%20electronics%20landscape%20through%202030/outlook%20on%20the%20automotive%20software%20and%20electronics%20market%20through%202030/automotive-software-and-electronics-2030-full-report.pdf

[284] TechArena. *How Software-Defined Vehicles are Reshaping the Auto Industry*. 2024. URL: https://www.techarena.ai/content/how-software-defined-vehicles-are-reshaping-the-auto-industry (visited on January 15, 2025).

[285] Andrei Luca. *Tesla Drops Full Self-Driving Price From $12,000 To $8,000.* April 2024. URL: https://insideevs.com/news/716963/tesla-fsd-price-drop/

[286] McKinsey & Company. *Automotive revolution—perspective towards 2030.* 2016. URL: https://www.mckinsey.com/industries/automotive-and-assembly/our-insights/disruptive-trends-that-will-transform-the-auto-industry (visited on December 1, 2025).

[287] Cubic*. *Digital Services and Safety: The New Pillars of Automotive Trust.* Research based on survey of 8,000 consumers across US, UK, Germany, and Japan, plus 60 global OEM executives. May 2025. URL: https://www.cubic3.com/blog/digital-services-and-safety-the-new-pillars-of-automotive-trust/ (visited on December 1, 2025).

[288] S&P Global Mobility. *2025 Connected Car Study: Inside consumer priorities.* 2025. URL: https://www.spglobal.com/automotive-insights/en/blogs/2025/07/connected-car-study-consumer-priorities-on-connected-services (visited on January 15, 2025).

[289] Endava. *A New In-Car Experience: How Automakers Are Responding to a Changing Market.* Originally published on autogazette.de in German. April 2025. URL: https://www.endava.com/insights/articles/a-new-in-car-experience-how-automakers-are-responding-to-a-changing-market (visited on December 1, 2025).

[290] Rest of World. *China's AI-powered self-driving car market is ahead of the U.S.* 2025. URL: https://restofworld.org/2025/china-ai-powered-self-driving-cars/

[291] Steve Finlay. *Do Your Customers Suffer From "Subscription Fatigue"?* WardsAuto. November 2024. URL: https://www.wardsauto.com/finance-insurance/do-your-customers-suffer-from-subscription-fatigue- (visited on November 29, 2025).

[292] Traffic Technology Today. *RoadCloud to offer premium road condition and weather data on the HERE Marketplace.* September 2020. URL: https://www.automotiveworld.com/news-releases/roadcloud-to-offer-premium-road-data-on-the-here-marketplace/ (visited on December 1, 2025).

[293] Credera. *A new era of mobility part two: Monetizing connected vehicle data.* October 2024. URL: https://www.credera.com/insights/a-new-era-of-mobility-part-two-monetizing-connected-vehicle-data (visited on November 29, 2025).

[294] Doug Newcomb. *The Real Reason Automakers Are Ditching Apple CarPlay and Android Auto.* MotorTrend. May 2025. URL: https://www.motortrend.com/features/apple-carplay-android-auto-automakers-ditching-them-for-data (visited on November 29, 2025).

[295] Grand View Research. *Commercial Vehicle Telematics Market Size Report, 2030.* 2024. URL: https://www.grandviewresearch.com/industry-analysis/commercial-vehicle-telematics-market-report

[296] CustomerGauge. *What's the Average Churn Rate by Industry?* 2025. URL: https://customergauge.com/blog/average-churn-rate-by-industry

[297] Loopit Academy. *Churn Rate—Performance Metrics.* 2023. URL: https://academy.loopit.co/article/churn-rate

[298] Reuters. *Tesla drivers can pursue class action over self-driving claims, judge rules.* August 2025. URL: https://www.reuters.com/sustainability/boards-policy-regulation/tesla-drivers-can-pursue-class-action-over-self-driving-claims-judge-rules-2025-08-19/ (visited on November 29, 2025).

[299] UNECE Working Party 29. *UN Regulation No. 155—Cyber Security and Cyber Security Management System.* 2021. URL: https://unece.org/transport/documents/2021/03/standards/un-regulation-no-155-cyber-security-and-cyber-security (visited on December 1, 2025).

[300] UNECE Working Party 29. *UN Regulation No. 156—Software Update and Software Update Management System*. 2021. URL: https://unece.org/transport/documents/2021/03/standards/un-regulation-no-156-software-update-and-software-update (visited on December 1, 2025).

[301] Mender. *How to Comply with ISO/SAE 21434 & UNECE R155/R156 for Robust Automotive Cybersecurity*. 2023. URL: https://mender.io/blog/how-to-comply-with-iso-sae-21434-and-unece-r155-r156-for-robust-automotive-cybersecurity (visited on December 1, 2025).

[302] UNECE. *UN Regulations on Cybersecurity and Software Updates Pave the Way for Mass Roll Out of Connected Vehicles*. 2020. URL: https://unece.org/sustainable-development/press/un-regulations-cybersecurity-and-software-updates-pave-way-mass-roll (visited on December 1, 2025).

[303] Perforce Software. *Cybersecurity Update: What Do the Latest WP.29 UNECE Regulations Cover?* 2021. URL: https://www.perforce.com/blog/sca/wp29-unece-cybersecurity (visited on December 1, 2025).

[304] European Commission. *Commission Implementing Regulation (EU) 2021/535—Type- Approval Requirements for Cyber Security*. 2021. URL: https://eur-lex.europa.eu/eli/reg_impl/2021/535/oj (visited on December 1, 2025).

[305] Bosch Engineering. *Cyber Security UN R155 and R156*. 2024. URL: https://www.bosch-engineering.com/stories/cybersecurity/ (visited on December 1, 2025).

[306] International Organization for Standardization. *ISO 24089:2023: Road Vehicles—Software Update Engineering*. 2023. URL: https://www.iso.org/standard/77796.html (visited on December 1, 2025).

[307] wolfSSL. *Meeting Secure Boot Compliance Requirements*. 2023. URL: https://www.wolfssl.com/meeting-secure-boot-compliance-requirements/ (visited on December 1, 2025).

[308] SAE International, OICA, and CLEPA. *Proposal to UN R156 Interpretation Document re. ISO 24089-2023.* 2023. URL: https://wiki.unece.org/download/attachments/228622774/TFCS-29-04%20%28SAE-I%2C%20OICA%2C%20CLEPA%29%20Proposal%20to%20UN%20R156%20interpretation%20doc.%20re.%20ISO%2024089-2023%20-%20v3.0.docx (visited on December 1, 2025).

[309] International Organization for Standardization. *ISO 24089:2023/Amd 1:2024: Road Vehicles—Software Update Engineering—Amendment 1.* 2024. URL: https://www.iso.org/standard/87522.html (visited on December 1, 2025).

[310] European Commission. *Commission Implementing Regulation (EU) 2021/535—Type- Approval Requirements for Software Updates.* 2021. URL: https://eur-lex.europa.eu/eli/reg_impl/2021/535/oj (visited on December 1, 2025).

[311] Kai-Frederik Zastrow. *UN Regulation 156—Software Update & SUMS.* Tech. rep. Stellantis/ITU FG-VM, 2021. URL: https://fnc.itu.int/wp-content/uploads/2021/03/Kai-Frederik-ZASTROW-STELLANTIS-V2.pdf

[312] TÜV SÜD. *ISO 24089: Vehicle Software Update Engineering Standard.* 2023. URL: https://www.tuvsud.com/en-us/industries/mobility-and-automotive/automotive-and-oem/autonomous-driving/iso-24089-standard-for-automotive-software-update-engineering (visited on December 1, 2025).

[313] European Parliament and Council of the European Union. *Regulation (EU) 2016/679—General Data Protection Regulation (GDPR).* 2016. URL: https://eur-lex.europa.eu/eli/reg/2016/679/oj (visited on December 1, 2025).

[314] European Commission. *Data Protection in the EU.* 2024. URL: https://commission.europa.eu/law/law-topic/data-protection/data-protection-eu_en (visited on December 1, 2025).

[315] Commission Nationale de l'Informatique et des Libertés (CNIL). *Connected Vehicles: A Compliance Package for a responsible Use of Data.* 2018. URL: https://www.cnil.fr/en/connected-vehicles-compliance-package-responsible-use-data (visited on December 1, 2025).

[316] Gaia-X AISBL. *Data for Good: How Gaia-X Is Changing the European Data Landscape.* 2023. URL: https://gaia-x.eu/data-for-good-how-gaia-x-is-changing-the-european-data-landscape/ (visited on December 1, 2025).

[317] Commission Nationale de l'Informatique et des Libertés (CNIL). *CNIL Guidelines on Connected Vehicle Data Processing.* Draft guidelines for connected vehicle data. 2025. URL: https://www.cnil.fr/sites/cnil/files/atoms/files/cnil_pack_vehicules_connectes_gb.pdf (visited on December 1, 2025).

[318] Catena-X Automotive Network e.V. *About Catena-X: The Automotive Data Ecosystem.* 2024. URL: https://catena-x.net/en/about-us (visited on December 1, 2025).

[319] Catena-X Automotive Network e.V. *Why Catena-X? Benefits of the Automotive Data Space.* 2024. URL: https://catenax-ev.github.io/docs/operating-model/why-understanding-the-catena-x-data-space (visited on December 1, 2025).

[320] State of California. *California Consumer Privacy Act (CCPA).* 2018. URL: https://oag.ca.gov/privacy/ccpa (visited on December 1, 2025).

[321] California Legislative Information. *California Consumer Privacy Act of 2018—Civil Code Section 1798.100-1798.199.100.* 2023. URL: https://leginfo.legislature.ca.gov/faces/codes_displayText.xhtml?division=3.&part=4.&lawCode=CIV&title=1.81.5 (visited on December 1, 2025).

[322] Alliance for Automotive Innovation. *Consumer Privacy Protection Principles for Vehicle Technologies and Services.* 2019. URL: https://www.autosinnovate.org/innovation/Automotive%20Privacy/Consumer_Privacy_Principlesfor_VehicleTechnologies_Services-03-21-19.pdf (visited on December 1, 2025).

[323] California Privacy Protection Agency. *CPPA to Review Privacy Practices of Connected Vehicles and Related Technologies.* 2023. URL: https://cppa.ca.gov/announcements/2023/20230731.html (visited on December 1, 2025).

[324] International Association of Privacy Professionals. *US State Privacy Legislation Tracker.* 2025. URL: https://iapp.org/resources/article/us-state-privacy-legislation-tracker/ (visited on December 1, 2025).

[325] Bloomberg Law. *Which States Have Consumer Data Privacy Laws?* 2025. URL: https://pro.bloomberglaw.com/insights/privacy/state-privacy-legislation-tracker/ (visited on December 1, 2025).

[326] National Law Review. *Navigating the Data Privacy Landscape for Autonomous and Connected Vehicles: Best Practices.* 2024. URL: https://natlawreview.com/article/navigating-data-privacy-landscape-autonomous-and-connected-vehicles-best-practices (visited on December 1, 2025).

[327] US Government Accountability Office. *Vehicle Data Privacy: Industry and Federal Efforts Under Way, but NHTSA Needs to Define Its Role.* 2017. URL: https://www.gao.gov/products/gao-17-656 (visited on December 1, 2025).

[328] Federal Trade Commission. *Privacy and Data Security Update: 2023.* 2023. URL: https://www.ftc.gov/system/files/ftc_gov/pdf/2024.03.21-PrivacyandDataSecurityUpdate-508.pdf (visited on December 1, 2025).

[329] California Privacy Protection Agency. *California Privacy Protection Agency Enforcement Action—Honda*. CCPA enforcement settlement with Honda over connected vehicle data practices. 2025. URL: https://cppa.ca.gov/ (visited on December 1, 2025).

[330] Cyberspace Administration of China. *Several Provisions on the Management of Automobile Data Security (Trial)*. 2021. URL: http://www.cac.gov.cn/2021-08/20/c_1631049984897667.htm (visited on December 1, 2025).

[331] Pillsbury Law. *China Publishes Regulation on Management of Automobile Data Security*. 2021. URL: https://www.pillsburylaw.com/en/news-and-insights/china-regulation-on-automobile-data-security.html (visited on December 1, 2025).

[332] Future of Privacy Forum. *China's Car Privacy and Security Regulation Is Effective on October 1, 2021*. 2021. URL: https://fpf.org/blog/update-chinas-car-privacy-and-security-regulation-is-effective-on-october-1-2021/ (visited on December 1, 2025).

[333] dissecto GmbH. *China's GB Standards (44495–44497) Revisited*. 2024. URL: https://dissec.to/regulations/chinas-gb-standards-revisited/ (visited on December 1, 2025).

[334] Fortune. *Tesla Changes Its China Data Policy After Government Scrutiny*. 2021. URL: https://fortune.com/2021/05/26/tesla-china-data-policy-storage-sharing/ (visited on December 1, 2025).

[335] Reuters. *China Mandates Regulatory Approvals for Autonomous Driving Software Upgrades*. 2025. URL: https://www.reuters.com/business/autos-transportation/china-mandates-regulatory-approvals-autonomous-driving-software-upgrades-2025-02-28/ (visited on December 1, 2025).

[336] Tech Policy Press. *China's Connected Vehicle Data Regulation Framework*. URL: https://www.trade.gov/market-intelligence/china-data-regulations-connected-vehicles (visited on December 1, 2025).

[337] Tsaaro. *Real-Time Risk: The Privacy Implications of Connected Vehicle Data*. 2024. URL: https://tsaaro-consulting.medium.com/real-time-risk-the-privacy-implications-of-connected-vehicle-data-7cf7ab7d3e6d (visited on December 1, 2025).

[338] Gaia-X AISBL. *What Is Gaia-X?* 2024. URL: https://gaia-x.eu/what-is-gaia-x/ (visited on December 1, 2025).

[339] Gaia-X AISBL. *Gaia-X 4 Future Mobility*. 2024. URL: https://www.gaia-x4futuremobility.de/en/home (visited on December 1, 2025).

[340] International Organization for Standardization. *ISO/PAS 8800:2024: Road Vehicles—Safety and Artificial Intelligence*. 2024. URL: https://www.iso.org/standard/83303.html (visited on December 1, 2025).

[341] Catena-X Automotive Network e.V. *Catena-X Organizational Structure and Governance*. 2024. URL: https://catena-x.net/association/structure-and-role/ (visited on December 1, 2025).

[342] *Regulation (EU) 2024/1689—Artificial Intelligence Act*. 2024. URL: https://eur-lex.europa.eu/eli/reg/2024/1689/oj

[343] UST. *How to Overcome Talent Shortages in Embedded Systems*. 2025. URL: https://www.ust.com/en/insights/overcoming-talent-shortages-in-embedded-systems (visited on December 1, 2025).

[344] Various Authors. "Multi-stage Deep Learning-Based Intrusion Detection System for Automotive Ethernet." In: *Ad Hoc Networks* 156 (2024). URL: https://www.sciencedirect.com/science/article/abs/pii/S1570870524001598

[345] Various Authors. "Machine Learning-Based Intrusion Detection System for Automotive Ethernet: Detecting Cyber-Attacks with a Low-Cost Platform." In: *ResearchGate*. 2022. URL: https://www.researchgate.net/publication/362626565

[346] Johann Schumann et al. "A Review on AI Safety in Highly Automated Driving." In: *Frontiers in Robotics and AI* 9 (2022). Open-access review of explainability, verification, validation, and safety assurance for AD/ADAS AI systems. URL: https://pmc.ncbi.nlm.nih.gov/articles/PMC9574258/

[347] Automotive Edge Computing Consortium. *Proofs of Concept: Distributed Battery Electric Vehicle (BEV) Range Estimation via Personalized Federated Learning*. 2023. URL: https://aecc.org/proof-of-concepts/entry/995/ (visited on December 1, 2025).

[348] *Reframe Your Strategy: The Great Automotive Value Shift*. Strategic analysis of emerging automotive value pools including SDVs, electrification, connectivity and software services. Ernst & Young (EY), 2024. URL: https://www.ey.com/en_gl/insights/advanced-manufacturing/reframe-your-strategy-the-great--automotive-value-shift

[349] The White House. *National Security Memorandum on Promoting United States Leadership in Quantum Computing While Mitigating Risks to Vulnerable Cryptographic Systems*. NSM-10. 2022. URL: https://www.whitehouse.gov/wp-content/uploads/2022/11/M-23-02-M-Memo-on-Migrating-to-Post-Quantum-Cryptography.pdf

[350] DDN. *How AI is Reshaping the Automotive World*. 2024. URL: https://www.ddn.com/blog/how-ai-is-reshaping-the-automotive-world/ (visited on December 1, 2025).

[351] Geotab. *AI in Fleet Management: How to Improve Efficiency and Reduce Costs*. 2024. URL: https://www.geotab.com/blog/ai-fleet-management/ (visited on December 1, 2025).

[352] Wards Auto. *Connected Vehicles Covered By Data Protection Laws.* 2024. URL: https://www.wardsauto.com/regulatory/connected-vehicles-covered-by-data-protection-laws (visited on December 1, 2025).

[353] European Data Protection Board. *Guidelines 01/2020 on Processing Personal Data in Connected Vehicles and Mobility Related Applications.* Primary GDPR guidance for connected vehicles, telematics and mobility services. 2020. URL: https://www.edpb.europa.eu/our-work-tools/our-documents/guidelines/guidelines-012020-processing-personal-data-context_en

[354] Horizon Connect. *An Overview of 6G-V2X Communications.* 2024. URL: https://horizonconnect.de/overview-of-6g-v2x-communications/ (visited on December 1, 2025).

[355] Automotive World. *Regulatory Patchwork Threatens Autonomous Freight Progress.* 2024. URL: https://www.automotiveworld.com/articles/regulatory-patchwork-threatens-autonomous-freight-progress/ (visited on December 1, 2025).

[356] Morgan Lewis. *China's Data Laws and Impact on the Automotive Industry.* 2022. URL: https://www.morganlewis.com/pubs/2022/03/chinas-data-laws-and-impact-on-the-automotive-industry (visited on December 1, 2025).

[357] Continental AG. *Continental and Hewlett Packard Enterprise Launch Blockchain-Based Data Monetization Platform.* URL: https://www.continental.com/en/press/press-releases/2019-02-26-cooperation-hpe/

Glossary of Terms

Notation	Description
1000BASE-T1	Single-pair Ethernet 1 Gbps
100BASE-T1	Single-pair Ethernet 100 Mbps
10BASE-T1S	Single-pair Ethernet 10 Mbps
2G	Second-Generation mobile network (GSM/CDMA)
3G	Third-Generation mobile network (UMTS/CDMA2000)
3GPP	3rd Generation Partnership Project
4G	Fourth-Generation mobile network (LTE/LTE-Advanced)
5G	Fifth-Generation mobile network (NR)
5GAA	5G Automotive Association
6G	Sixth-Generation mobile network
802.1Qbu	IEEE Frame Preemption for TSN
802.1Qbv	IEEE Time-Aware Shaper for TSN
802.1Qcc	IEEE Stream Reservation Protocol Enhancements for TSN
802.1Qch	IEEE Cyclic Queuing and Forwarding for TSN
802.1Qci	IEEE Per-Stream Filtering and Policing for TSN
802.3br	IEEE Interspersing Express Traffic (Ethernet frame preemption)
A/B (partitions)	Dual-partition scheme for robust OTA updates (active/in-active slots)
AAOS	Android Automotive OS
ABS	Anti-lock Braking System
AD	Autonomous Driving
ADAS	Advanced Driver Assistance Systems
ADC	Analog-to-Digital Converter

S. Agarwal, *Software-Defined Vehicles*, https://doi.org/10.1007/979-8-8688-2718-1

Notation	Description
ADS	Automated Driving System
AE	Automotive Enhanced (Arm core variant)
AEB	Automatic Emergency Braking
AECC	Automotive Edge Computing Consortium
AES	Advanced Encryption Standard
AGL	Automotive Grade Linux
AI	Artificial Intelligence
AMC	Adaptive Modulation and Coding
ANC	Active Noise Cancellation
API	Application Programming Interface
APN	Access Point Name (cellular network)
AR	Augmented Reality
ara::com	AUTOSAR Adaptive Communication Management API
ARAI	Automotive Research Association of India
ARINC	Aeronautical Radio, Inc. (partitioning standards)
ARPU	Average Revenue Per User
ARXML	AUTOSAR XML (configuration/description file format)
AS (802.1AS)	Timing and Synchronization for TSN (gPTP)
AS6802	SAE Time-Triggered Ethernet (TTEthernet) standard
ASIL	Automotive Safety Integrity Level (ISO 26262)
ASPICE	Automotive SPICE (Software Process Improvement and Capability dEtermination)
Auto-ISAC	Automotive Information Sharing and Analysis Center
AUTOSAR	AUTomotive Open System ARchitecture
AUTOSAR AP	AUTOSAR Adaptive Platform
AUTOSAR CP	AUTOSAR Classic Platform
AV	Autonomous Vehicle
AVB	Audio Video Bridging (IEEE 802.1)

Notation	Description
AVnu	AVnu Alliance (Time-Sensitive Networking certification consortium)
AWS	Amazon Web Services
Azure	Microsoft Azure cloud platform
B2B	Business-to-Business
B2C	Business-to-Consumer
BCG	Boston Consulting Group
BCM	Body Control Module
BEV	Battery Electric Vehicle
BMS	Battery Management System
BMU	Battery Management Unit
BOM	Bill of Materials
BPSK	Binary Phase Shift Keying
C-V2X	Cellular Vehicle-to-Everything
C66x	Texas Instruments C66x Digital Signal Processor
C7x	Texas Instruments C7x Digital Signal Processor
CAC	Cyberspace Administration of China
CAL	Cybersecurity Assurance Level (ISO/SAE 21434)
CAN	Controller Area Network
CAN FD	CAN with Flexible Data Rate
CAN XL	Third-Generation CAN (extended payload/rate)
CAPEX	Capital Expenditure
CARIAD	Volkswagen Group software company
Catena-X	Automotive data ecosystem under Gaia-X
CCAM	Cooperative, Connected and Automated Mobility (EU initiative)
CCPA	California Consumer Privacy Act
CDMA	Code Division Multiple Access
CDN	Content Delivery Network

Notation	Description
CI/CD	Continuous Integration/Continuous Delivery
CNIL	Commission Nationale de l'Informatique et des Libertés (French data protection authority)
CNN	Convolutional Neural Network
COVESA	Connected Vehicle Systems Alliance (formerly GENIVI)
CPPA	California Privacy Protection Agency
CPRA	California Privacy Rights Act
CPU	Central Processing Unit
CRC	Cyclic Redundancy Check
CSI	Camera Serial Interface
CSMS	Cybersecurity Management System (UNECE R155)
CUDA	Compute Unified Device Architecture (NVIDIA)
CVE	Common Vulnerabilities and Exposures
CX	Customer Experience
DBC	Database CAN (vector format)
DC	Diagnostic Coverage
DC/DC	DC-to-DC Converter (voltage conversion)
DDS	Data Distribution Service (OMG)
DevOps	Development and Operations (culture/tooling)
DevSecOps	Development, Security, and Operations (integrated security in DevOps)
DLA	Deep Learning Accelerator
DNN	Deep Neural Network
DoIP	Diagnostics over Internet Protocol (ISO 13400)
DoS	Denial of Service
DOT	Department of Transportation (United States)
DP	Differential Privacy
DRAM	Dynamic Random Access Memory

Notation	Description
DRP-AI	Dynamically Reconfigurable Processor for AI (Renesas)
DSP	Digital Signal Processor
DSRC	Dedicated Short-Range Communications
DSU	DynamIQ Shared Unit (Arm CPU cluster fabric)
DTLS	Datagram Transport Layer Security
E/E	Electrical/Electronic (architecture)
ECC	Error-Correcting Code (memory); Elliptic Curve Cryptography (crypto)
ECU	Electronic Control Unit
ELISA	Enabling Linux In Safety Applications (Linux Foundation project)
eMBB	Enhanced Mobile Broadband (5G)
EMC	Electromagnetic Compatibility
EPI	European Processor Initiative
EPS	Electric Power Steering
ESC	Electronic Stability Control
eSIM	Embedded SIM (Subscriber Identity Module)
ESP	Electronic Stability Program
ETA	Estimated Time of Arrival (scheduling/logs)
ETSI	European Telecommunications Standards Institute
EU	European Union
EU AI Act	European Union Artificial Intelligence Act (Regulation 2024/1689)
EV	Electric Vehicle
EVITA	E-safety Vehicle Intrusion Protected Applications
FCA	Fiat Chrysler Automobiles (now part of Stellantis)
FCC	Federal Communications Commission (United States)
FEC	Forward Error Correction
FET	Field-Effect Transistor

Notation	Description
FFI	Freedom From Interference (ISO 26262)
FFT	Fast Fourier Transform
FL	Federated Learning
FlexRay	Deterministic automotive network protocol
FMEA	Failure Modes and Effects Analysis
FMEDA	Failure Modes, Effects, and Diagnostics Analysis
FMVSS	Federal Motor Vehicle Safety Standards (United States)
FO	Fail-Operational
FoD	Functions-on-Demand (subscription-based feature activation)
FOTA	Firmware Over-The-Air
Franca	Franca Interface Definition Language
FRAV	Functional Requirements for Automated Vehicles (UNECE informal group)
FSD	Full Self-Driving (Tesla autonomous driving system)
FTA	Fault Tree Analysis
FTC	Federal Trade Commission (United States)
Gaia-X	European federated data infrastructure initiative
GB/T	Guobiao Tuijian (Chinese Recommended National Standard)
GCC	GNU Compiler Collection
GCP	Google Cloud Platform
GDPR	General Data Protection Regulation (EU)
GENIVI	GENIVI Alliance (now COVESA)
GM	General Motors
GNSS	Global Navigation Satellite System
GPIO	General-Purpose Input/Output
GPS	Global Positioning System
gPTP	Generalized Precision Time Protocol (IEEE 802.1AS)
GPU	Graphics Processing Unit

Notation	Description
gRPC	gRPC Remote Procedure Calls
GRVA	Working Party on Automated/Autonomous and Connected Vehicles (UNECE)
GSM	Global System for Mobile Communications
GSN	Goal Structuring Notation (safety case)
HARA	Hazard Analysis and Risk Assessment
HARQ	Hybrid Automatic Repeat Request
HD	High Definition (e.g., HD maps)
HEV	Hybrid Electric Vehicle
HIL	Hardware-in-the-Loop
HLOS	High-Level Operating System (e.g., Linux or Android)
HPC	High-Performance Computer (central compute)
HSM	Hardware Security Module
HTTP	Hypertext Transfer Protocol
HTTPS	Hypertext Transfer Protocol Secure
HVAC	Heating, Ventilation, and Air Conditioning
ICAS	In-Car Application Server (VW domain controller)
ICE	Internal Combustion Engine
ICS	In-Car Services (sometimes: Instrument Cluster System)
IDPS	Intrusion Detection and Prevention System
IDS	Intrusion Detection System
IDSM	Intrusion Detection System Manager (AUTOSAR)
IEC 61508	Functional Safety of Electrical/Electronic/Programmable Electronic Safety-related Systems
IEEE	Institute of Electrical and Electronics Engineers
IEEE 7003	Standard for Algorithmic Bias Considerations
IID	Independent and Identically Distributed (statistics)
IIM	Indian Institute of Management

Notation	Description
IMU	Inertial Measurement Unit
INT8	8-bit Integer (quantization precision)
IoT	Internet of Things
IP	Internet Protocol
IPC	Inter-Process Communication
IPsec	Internet Protocol Security
ISA	Instruction Set Architecture
ISB	Indian School of Business
ISO	International Organization for Standardization
ISO 21434	Road Vehicles—Cybersecurity Engineering
ISO 24089	Road Vehicles—Software Update Engineering
ISO 26262	Road Vehicles—Functional Safety
ISO/PAS 8800	Road Vehicles—Safety and Artificial Intelligence
ISO/TR 4804	Road Vehicles—Safety and Cybersecurity for Automated Driving Systems
ISP	Image Signal Processor
IT	Information Technology
ITS	Intelligent Transportation Systems
ITS-G5	European profile of IEEE 802.11p for ITS
IVI	In-Vehicle Infotainment
JTAG	Joint Test Action Group (debug interface)
K8s	Kubernetes
KBA	Kraftfahrt-Bundesamt (German Federal Motor Transport Authority)
KPI	Key Performance Indicator
KVM	Kernel-based Virtual Machine (Linux virtualization)
LFM	Latent Fault Metric (ISO 26262)
LiDAR	Light Detection and Ranging
LIME	Local Interpretable Model-agnostic Explanations

Notation	Description
LIN	Local Interconnect Network
LLVM	Low-Level Virtual Machine (compiler infrastructure)
LPDDR	Low-Power DDR (memory)
LSTM	Long Short-Term Memory (recurrent NN)
LTE	Long-Term Evolution (4G)
LTV	Customer Lifetime Value
MaaS	Mobility-as-a-Service
MAC	Message Authentication Code (cryptography)
MAC (networking)	Media Access Control (OSI Layer 2 sublayer)
MACsec	Media Access Control Security (IEEE 802.1AE)
MBA	Master of Business Administration
MCAL	Microcontroller Abstraction Layer (AUTOSAR)
MCU	Microcontroller Unit
MEB	Modularer E-Antriebs-Baukasten (VW Modular Electric Drive Matrix)
MEC	Multi-access Edge Computing
MIC	Message Integrity Code
MIIT	Ministry of Industry and Information Technology (China)
MiL	Model-in-the-Loop
MIPS	Million Instructions Per Second (CPU performance metric)
MISRA	Motor Industry Software Reliability Association
ML	Machine Learning
MLOps	Machine Learning Operations
mMTC	Massive Machine Type Communications (5G)
MMU	Memory Management Unit
mmWave	Millimeter Wave (radio frequencies 30–300 GHz)
MNO	Mobile Network Operator

Notation	Description
MOBI	Mobility Open Blockchain Initiative
MoRTH	Ministry of Road Transport and Highways (India)
MOSFET	Metal-Oxide-Semiconductor Field-Effect Transistor
MOST	Media Oriented Systems Transport
MPU	Memory Protection Unit
MQTT	Message Queuing Telemetry Transport
MTE	Memory Tagging Extension (Armv8.5/Armv9 security feature)
NATM	New Assessment/Test Method (UNECE framework for ADS validation)
NCAP	New Car Assessment Programme
Neoverse	Arm Neoverse high-performance CPU family
NHTSA	National Highway Traffic Safety Administration (United States)
NN	Neural Network
NPS	Net Promoter Score
NPU	Neural Processing Unit
NR-V2X	New Radio Vehicle-to-Everything (5G-based)
NTP	Network Time Protocol
NVDLA	NVIDIA Deep Learning Accelerator
OBD-II	On-Board Diagnostics (second generation)
OCI	Open Container Initiative (container runtime and image standards)
ODD	Operational Design Domain
OEM	Original Equipment Manufacturer
OFDM	Orthogonal Frequency-Division Multiplexing
OMG	Object Management Group (DDS standards body)
ONNX	Open Neural Network Exchange
OpenCL	Open Computing Language
OPEX	Operational Expenditure
OS	Operating System

Notation	Description
OSEK	Offene Systeme und deren Schnittstellen für die Elektronik im Kraftfahrzeug (Open Systems and Interfaces for Electronics in Motor Vehicles)
OTA	Over-the-Air (software updates)
PAC	Pointer Authentication Code (Armv8.3 security feature)
PB	Petabyte
PC5	PC5 sidelink interface (3GPP direct V2X communication)
PCIe	Peripheral Component Interconnect Express
PFE	Packet Forwarding Engine (NXP S32G)
PHEV	Plug-in Hybrid Electric Vehicle
PHY	Physical Layer (network)
PIPL	Personal Information Protection Law (China)
PKI	Public Key Infrastructure
PLC	Power Line Communication
PMHF	Probabilistic Metric for random Hardware Failures (ISO 26262)
PMU	Power Management Unit
PoC	Proof of Concept
POSIX	Portable Operating System Interface (IEEE 1003)
PPU	Parallel Processing Unit
PQC	Post-Quantum Cryptography
PREEMPT_RT	Real-time preemption patch set for the Linux kernel
PSE51	POSIX System Environment 51 (minimal real-time profile)
PSI5	Peripheral Sensor Interface 5
PTP	Precision Time Protocol (IEEE 1588)
PVA	Programmable Vision Accelerator (NVIDIA)
PWM	Pulse Width Modulation
QA	Quality Assurance
QAM	Quadrature Amplitude Modulation

Notation	Description
QEMU	Quick Emulator (machine emulator and virtualizer)
QM	Quality Management
QNX	QNX Neutrino RTOS/QNX Hypervisor
QoS	Quality of Service
QPSK	Quadrature Phase Shift Keying
QUIC	Quick UDP Internet Connections (IETF transport protocol)
R155	UNECE Regulation No. 155—Cybersecurity
R156	UNECE Regulation No. 156—Software Update and SUMS
R&D	Research and Development
R&R	Risk & Residual risk (cybersecurity assessments)
RAM	Random Access Memory
RCS	Radar Cross-Section
REST	Representational State Transfer (API architecture)
RISC	Reduced Instruction Set Computer
RISC-V	RISC-V Open Instruction Set Architecture
RL	Reinforcement Learning
RNN	Recurrent Neural Network
ROM	Read-Only Memory
ROP	Return-Oriented Programming (security attack)
ROS	Robot Operating System
RPC	Remote Procedure Calls
RSA	Rivest-Shamir-Adleman (cryptographic algorithm)
RTOS	Real-Time Operating System
RTPS	Real-Time Publish–Subscribe (DDS wire protocol)
SAE	Society of Automotive Engineers (now SAE International)
SAE Level 0	No Driving Automation
SAE Level 1	Driver Assistance

Notation	Description
SAE Level 2	Partial Driving Automation
SAE Level 3	Conditional Driving Automation
SAE Level 4	High Driving Automation
SAE Level 5	Full Driving Automation
SAIC	Shanghai Automotive Industry Corporation
SBOM	Software Bill of Materials
SDK	Software Development Kit
SDLC	Software Development Lifecycle
SDV	Software-Defined Vehicle
SEC-DED	Single Error Correction, Double Error Detection
SecOC	Secure Onboard Communication (AUTOSAR)
SELinux	Security-Enhanced Linux
SEooC	Safety Element out of Context (ISO 26262 reusable component)
SerDes	Serializer/Deserializer
SHA	Secure Hash Algorithm
SHAP	SHapley Additive exPlanations
SHE	Secure Hardware Extension (automotive crypto standard)
SIL	Safety Integrity Level (IEC 61508); Software-in-the-Loop (testing)
SIM	Subscriber Identity Module
SIMD	Single Instruction, Multiple Data
SMP	Symmetric Multi-Processing
SMU	Safety Management Unit
SNR	Signal-to-Noise Ratio
SOA	Service-Oriented Architecture
SOAFEE	Scalable Open Architecture for Embedded Edge
SoC	System-on-Chip

Notation	Description
SOME/IP	Scalable service-Oriented MiddlewarE over IP
SOME/IP-SD	SOME/IP Service Discovery
SOP	Start of Production
SOTA	Software Over-The-Air
SOTIF	Safety of the Intended Functionality (ISO/PAS 21448)
SPFM	Single-Point Fault Metric (ISO 26262)
SPI	Serial Peripheral Interface
SRAM	Static Random Access Memory
SRE	Site Reliability Engineering
SSD	Solid State Drive
SSL	Secure Sockets Layer (deprecated; use TLS)
SSL (learning)	Self-Supervised Learning
STPA	System-Theoretic Process Analysis
SUMS	Software Update Management System
SWaP	Size, Weight, and Power
SWOT	Strengths, Weaknesses, Opportunities, Threats (strategic analysis framework)
TARA	Threat Analysis and Risk Assessment (ISO/SAE 21434)
TB	Terabyte
TCO	Total Cost of Ownership
TCP	Transmission Control Protocol
TCU	Telematics Control Unit
TEE	Trusted Execution Environment
TLS	Transport Layer Security
TLS 1.3	Transport Layer Security version 1.3
TOPS	Tera Operations Per Second (AI compute metric)
TPM	Trusted Platform Module
TSMC	Taiwan Semiconductor Manufacturing Company

Notation	Description
TSN	Time-Sensitive Networking (IEEE 802.1)
TSN Qav	Credit-Based Shaper (802.1Qav)
TSN Qbu	Frame Preemption (802.1Qbu)
TSN Qbv	Time-Aware Scheduler (802.1Qbv)
TSN Qcc	Stream Reservation/Configuration (802.1Qcc)
TSN Qch	Cyclic Queuing and Forwarding (802.1Qch)
TSN Qci	Per-Stream Filtering and Policing (802.1Qci)
TTEthernet	Time-Triggered Ethernet (AS6802)
TÜV	Technischer Überwachungsverein (German technical inspection association)
UBI	Usage-Based Insurance
UCM	Update and Configuration Management (AUTOSAR Adaptive service)
UDP	User Datagram Protocol
UDS	Unified Diagnostic Services (ISO 14229)
UE	User Equipment (cellular)
UFS	Universal Flash Storage
UL 4600	Standard for Safety for the Evaluation of Autonomous Products
Ultifi	GM's end-to-end vehicle software platform
UN R155	UNECE Regulation No. 155—Cybersecurity and CSMS
UN R156	UNECE Regulation No. 156—Software Update and SUMS
UNECE	United Nations Economic Commission for Europe
Uptane	Automotive OTA software update security framework
URLLC	Ultra-Reliable Low-Latency Communications (5G)
USB	Universal Serial Bus
Uu	Uu interface (3GPP cellular air interface between UE and base station)
UX	User Experience
vECU	Virtual Electronic Control Unit
V2I	Vehicle-to-Infrastructure

Notation	Description
V2N	Vehicle-to-Network
V2P	Vehicle-to-Pedestrian
V2V	Vehicle-to-Vehicle
V2X	Vehicle-to-Everything
VCA	Vehicle Certification Agency (UK type approval authority)
VDX	Vehicle Distributed eXecutive
VHAL	Vehicle Hardware Abstraction Layer (Android Automotive OS)
VIL	Vehicle-in-the-Loop
VIN	Vehicle Identification Number
VIP	Vehicle Integration Platform (e.g., NXP S32G VIP)
VLAN	Virtual Local Area Network
VLM	Vision–Language Model
VM	Virtual Machine
VMAD	Validation Method for Automated Driving (UNECE informal group)
VMM	Virtual Machine Monitor (hypervisor)
VPN	Virtual Private Network
VR	Virtual Reality
VSOC	Vehicle Security Operations Center
WCET	Worst-Case Execution Time
Wi-Fi	Wireless Fidelity (IEEE 802.11 wireless networking)
WILP	Work Integrated Learning Programme
WP.29	World Forum for Harmonization of Vehicle Regulations (UNECE)
WPA3	Wi-Fi Protected Access 3
WSS (DevOps)	Workload Safety Signals (safety/DevOps telemetry)
XAI	Explainable Artificial Intelligence
ZCU	Zone Control Unit (Zonal Controller)

Index

A

S. Agarwal, *Software-Defined Vehicles*, https://doi.org/10.1007/979-8-8688-2718-1

D

E

F

J

K

L

M

N

O

P

Q

R

S

T

U

V

W, X, Y

Z

www.ingramcontent.com/pod-product-compliance
Lightning Source LLC
LaVergne TN
LVHW082011200926
848481LV00010B/2837
* 9 7 9 8 8 6 8 8 2 7 1 7 4 *